Between Conflict and Conformity

FREEMASONRY DURING THE WEIMAR REPUBLIC AND THE "THIRD REICH"

RALF MELZER

TRANSLATED BY
GLENYS A. WALDMAN

WESTPHALIA PRESS
An imprint of Policy Studies Organization

Also from Westphalia Press

westphaliapress.org

Between Conflict and Conformity

FREEMASONRY DURING THE WEIMAR REPUBLIC AND THE "THIRD REICH"

RALF MELZER

BETWEEN CONFLICT AND CONFORMITY:
FREEMASONRY DURING THE WEIMAR REPUBLIC AND THE "THIRD REICH"

ORIGINALLY PUBLISHED IN GERMAN AS: *KONFLIKT UND ANPASSUNG: FREIMAUREREI IN DER WEIMARER REPUBLIK UND IM "DRITTEN REICH,"* HERAUSGEGEBEN VON ANTON PELINKA UND HELMUT REINALTER, *VERGLEICHENDE GESELLSCHAFTS-GESCHICHTE UND POLITISCHE IDEENGESCHICHTET DER NEUZEIT BAND 13,* WIEN (WILHELM BRAUMÜLLER) 1999.

TRANSLATION BASED ON THE UNPUBLISHED, REVISED AND EXPANDED GERMAN EDITION, 2002-2007.

Westphalia Press
An imprint of Policy Studies Organization
1527 New Hampshire Ave., NW
Washington, D.C. 20036
info@ipsonet.org

ISBN-13: 978-1-63391-760-6
ISBN-10: 1633917606
Cover and Interior design by Taillefer Long at Illuminated Stories:
www.illuminatedstories.com

Daniel Gutierrez-Sandoval, Executive Director
PSO and Westphalia Press

Cheryl Walker, Development and Programs Associate
PSO and Westphalia Press

Updated material and comments on this edition
can be found at the Westphalia Press website:
www.westphaliapress.org

*For my parents
and Jaron*

Contents

CHAPTER 5 - THE GERMAN LODGES BETWEEN CONFLICT AND CONFORMITY 1933-1935

CHAPTER 6 - CASE STUDY I: GROSSE LANDESLOGE DER FREIMAURER VON DEUTSCHLAND (GRAND LODGE OF FREEMASONS OF GERMANY OR GLL)

CHAPTER 7 - CASE STUDY II: SYMBOLISCHE GROSSLOGE VON DEUTSCHLAND (SYMBOLIC GRAND LODGE OF GERMANY OR SGL)

CHAPTER 8 - NAZI STATE AND FREEMASONRY

Author's Preface

This study is the result of many years of research on Freemasonry. Presented here is the revised and expanded English-language version of my book *Konflikt und Anpassung: Freimaurerei in der Weimarer Republik und im Dritten Reich*, which appeared in Vienna in 1999 as the publication of my dissertation accepted during the winter semester of 1997-1998 by the Department of History of the Freie Universität Berlin, Germany. My master's thesis, *Völkische Freimaurerei 1922-1935 (Völkisch Freemasonry 1922 - 1935)*, completed in 1994, is the foundation of this research. Since then the questions and the sources used have been continually broadened.

I would like to express my gratitude to the Große Landesloge der Freimaurer von Deutschland which, ever since the beginning of my research, granted me, a non-Mason, free access to their archives and later facilitated access to the Secret State Archives of Prussian Cultural Possessions. The Grand Lodge of the Ancient Free and Accepted Masons of Germany kindly honored my request, and without hesitation, granted the required access rights to the State Archives of the Symbolische Großloge von Deutschland residing at the Secret State Archives of Prussian Cultural Possessions.

I would like to extend my gratitude to the employees of the archives and libraries in Berlin, Magdeburg, Bayreuth, Moscow, and Washington D.C., where I have conducted my research. Among others I would like to particularly thank Alain Bernheim (Montreux, Switzerland), Thomas Richert (Berlin, Germany), Henning Wolter, (Delmenhorst, Germany), Nathan Fischer (†), and Werner Ansorge (†) (both Israel). All of them have supported, or in varied ways contributed to the genesis of this book by means of personal conversations, and in some cases, written correspondence often lasting for years. They gave suggestions, valuable ideas and critique, opened their private archives, or put literature and other source material at my disposal. However, it goes without saying that any possible gaps or shortcomings are my sole responsibility.

Special thanks go to Professor Dr. Helmut Reinalter (Innsbruck, Austria), the editor of my original German book, for his sponsorship and his promotion and to family members, friends, and acquaintances for their generous support and their part in proof-reading. In addition, I owe the deepest debt of gratitude to Dr. Glenys A. Waldman (Philadelphia), who provided the translation of the original German text into English, with indefatigable willingness, great competence, and enthusiasm as well as to the Rev. Willard W. Wetzel (†) (Philadelphia) for his support during the process of translation.

Last but not least, I would like to thank the Friedrich Ebert Stiftung, which awarded my dissertation project a three-year doctoral stipend, and the United States Holocaust Memorial Museum (USHMM), which granted me a fellowship in 2001 that enabled me, as a scholar-in-residence at the Center for Advanced Holocaust Studies, to deepen my research. Because of this sojourn in Washington, D.C., I was able to engage in supplemental studies using the extensive source material in the archives of the USHMM as well as in the archives and library of the Supreme Council of the Ancient and Accepted Scottish Rite, Southern Jurisdiction (AASR, S.J.). The very productive interaction with my colleagues at the Center for Advanced Holocaust Studies and the Supreme Council AASR, S.J. was for me personally very enriching and gave important new stimulation to my work. Finally, I do not want to miss including my gratitude to Professor Dr. Wolfgang Wippermann (Berlin, Germany), who encouraged me to continue with my research after the completion of my master's thesis, and looked after the scholarly aspects of my doctoral dissertation with a great sense of commitment.

Above all I would like to thank my parents, who have always thoroughly supported me. Without their love, advice, and support, this book would have been inconceivable. To them, and to my son Jaron, who was born in 2000, I dedicate this book.

Berlin, May 2014

Ralf Melzer

Translator's Preface

Many thanks are due the author, Dr. Ralf Melzer, with whom I worked very closely, especially for his clarification of historical concepts. Thanks are due to the publisher, *new academic press* (Vienna, Austria) who, in 2012, took over the academic branch of Wilhelm Braumüller (publisher of the original dissertation), for their permission to publish this translation of which the author's original had been published by Wilhelm in 1999. Thanks also to the young Westphalia Press for their willingness to take on this project.

I also owe deep debts of gratitude to Paul M. Bessel who put author and translator together, to my husband, the Rev. Willard W. Wetzel (†), for the copyediting in which he delighted until he could no longer work, and to the Rev. Dr. Robert E. Koenig (†) for his tireless copyediting, taking up where my husband was forced to stop. My heartfelt thanks go also to Robert L. Dluge, Jr., Esq., Grand Master of Masons of Pennsylvania 2000-2001, and to many other colleagues and friends for their encouragement of this project. Translating such as work as this, with so many unique names and terms, provides ample challenge. In an effort to make the text clear, abbreviations were used as little as possible and clarifications were inserted in the text – even at the risk of awkwardness.

Three terms, however, need further elaboration:

Völkisch is to be understood as a very specific philosophical concept of the Nazi era, referring to people in total conformity with the Nazi Party's idea of what the German people were supposed to be.

Freimaurer Orden, specifically the Große Landesloge der Freimaurer von Deutschland – a unified overarching Grand Lodge for all of Germany much like the United Grand Lodge of England. This does not exist in the United States.

Gestapa-Gestapo: there is an important distinction to be made. *Gestapa* is the shortened form of "*Geheimes Staatspolizeiamt*" ("Office of the Secret State Police") – the agency, or its location. *Gestapo* is the abbreviation for "*Geheime Staatspolizei*" ("Secret State Police") – the men, the officers. *Gestapo* also refers to the whole institution of secret state police in Nazi Germany.

This translation is dedicated to the memory of the Rev. Willard W. Wetzel.

Philadelphia, Pennsylvania, May 2014

Glenys A. Waldman

Introduction

A t the beginning of the twenty-first century, almost three hundred years after Freemasonry came into being, prejudice and ignorance clouded the understanding of the history of the fraternity and what is that lodges actually do. Indeed, Freemasons were generally thought of as victims of persecution by the National Socialist dictatorship. Meanwhile, historians were content with the brief statement that Freemasons were persecuted during the "Third Reich"; members of lodges therefore became an "object of attention for the Nazi Party and the Gestapo"[1] or were fought against and classified to be an "enemy of the state"[2] by those in power. Is that really all there was? Were the German Freemasons really solely the victims as were the Jews, Sinti and Roma, and political opponents, who were persecuted on grounds of racism or ideological views?

Is it true that they were "one of the first victims of the reigning power" in 1933 and walked into "a time of bondage and persecution," as phrased by the Spiritus Rector of the German post-war Masons, Theodor Vogel?[3] No later than the end of World War I, the Freemasons, supposedly directed by the so-called "international Jewry," developed into a preferred target for the *völkisch* anti-Semitic propaganda war in Germany. The phrase "by the Jews and the Freemasons" established itself as much as a stereotype as an effective slogan, and Hitler announced in *Mein Kampf* that "the Jew" possesses in "Freemasonry, which is completely under his spell, a superb instrument."[4] Two-and-a-half years after National Socialists came to power, the German lodges were indeed destroyed. Masonic societies were either forced to self-liquidate or were forbidden, the lodge buildings were used for other purposes, and the lodge archives were confiscated. This, however, is only one side of the actually more complicated scenario.

The status of research on the history of Freemasonry in the twentieth century is still unsatisfactory. Several studies specifically related to the role of the history of ideas of Freemasonry have been published, but most of them portray Freemasonry in the eighteenth century, and primarily cover the exchange among Freemasonry, the Enlightenment, and the French Revolution.[5] What part German Freemasonry played in the developmental history of the twentieth century, and what specific political and social attitudes the lodges held toward the Weimar Republic and the "Third Reich" have been neglected in Masonic and scholarly research. This circumstance is particularly surprising in the light of the fact that Freemasonry played a prominent role in public discourse. In their prime during the mid-1920s, the lodges had more than 82,000 members, and in many ways, Freemasons provided an interesting subject for the German social history.

The National Socialist (NS) historiography research especially should have recognized the importance of this field earlier on. The assumption is not far-fetched that by the application of the conspiracy hypothesis during National Socialism, stemming from the political premise of the "question of the Freemasons," and not least by the specific police and secret service treatment of (former) lodge members, one can derive fundamental statements about the operation of the apparatus of terror, with regard to the structural components and the constitutive tenets of the "Third Reich." In spite of this, Freemasons have only been very superficially covered in general studies on National Socialism, if at all. In other words, the complex interrelation between Freemasonry and the *völkisch* or National Socialist movement has not been previously considered. This phenomenon "fell through the cracks" of the different research approaches taken because the perspectives focused alternately on "the big picture of history," "history from the bottom-up", or tried to prove the "intentionalistic" concepts or the competing concept of polycracy and anarchy of competence. In fundamental monographs on the Weimar Republic, Freemasonry appears at its best marginally.

Likewise, in studies about the history of Freemasonry, the National Socialist era was frequently omitted or transformed. The commonly held opinion that German Freemasons as a whole had been adversaries of National Socialism rests mainly on a "leveled-off" self-portrait of Freemasonry, which, however, does not stand examination. This is true especially for the three Old Prussian jurisdictions: Große Landesloge der Freimaurer von Deutschland (Grand Lodge of Freemasons ––hereafter Grosse Landesloge), Große Nationalmutterloge Zu den drei Weltkugeln (Grand National Mother Lodge of the Three World Globes—hereafter Three World Globes), and the Große Loge von Preussen, genannt (Royal York) Zur Freundschaft (Grand Lodge of Prussia called [Royal York] of Friendship—hereafter Grand Lodge Friendship).[6]

Meanwhile, the histories of anti-Masonry and of the conspiracy hypothesis are relatively well researched. Fundamental studies by Norman Cohn, Jacob Katz, and Johannes Rogalla von Bieberstein about the genesis and purpose of the world conspiracy hypothesis aimed at Jews and Freemasons have been published.[7] The latest work of Armin Pfahl-Traughber[8] does not contain any essential new discoveries, but summarizes the current results of research.

For a long time, the only fundamental work to be presented that covered the relationship between Freemasonry and National Socialism was produced by Helmut Neuberger in 1977.[9] Neuberger first deals with the national propaganda war and with German Freemasonry up to 1933. Afterwards, he covers the anti-Masonic politics of the NS regime until the complete destruction of Masonic structures in Germany, as well as the expansion of the National Socialist politics against Freemasonry in the conquered territories. Neuberger also turns his attention to the National Socialistic influence outside the German borders and compares persecution of Masons qualitatively with other European countries in the twentieth century. The national tendencies within the German lodges obviously have not gone unmentioned in Neuberger's investigation, which was altogether commendable but hardly noticed in the scholarly world. The author, however, does not see *völkisch* Freemasonry as an independent movement. Therefore, and in particular, the question of a possibly shared responsibility of parts of German Freemasonry is given short shrift. Neuberger places the origin of the suppression of Freemasonry "less in the extermination mania of National Socialism" than in "the opposition of Freemasonry towards totalitarianism in general."[10] Owing to his emphasis on the antagonism between Freemasonry as a whole and "Totalitarianism," which did not exist as such, Neuberger does not arrive at the necessary and fundamental re-evaluation of the Masonic history of ideas and institutions in the twentieth century–an example, incidentally, that shows the unsuitability of the concept of totalitarianism, and with it the implied equation of the National Socialist and Bolshevik power structures.

After all, even Neuberger agrees that the persecution of Freemasons by the National Socialists occupies a special position and cannot be explained by purely pragmatic motives. The ideological connection between Judaism and Freemasonry is supposedly specific. Opposition to and suppression of Freemasonry in Germany has seemingly been "ideologized, mystified, and had imaginative legends woven around it"[11] in greater proportion than in other right extremist dictatorial regimes of Europe or in the Soviet Union. To be sure, Neuberger named the *völkisch* forces within the German lodges. But he discusses in detail the broad nationalistic efforts of the Masonic establishment as "an attempt to conform to the political right,"[12] without sufficient differentiation of this complex phenomenon, nor does he assess it sufficiently in its constitutive character.

Disregarding a few exceptions,[13] the research on Freemasonry in the Weimar Republic and "Third Reich" has, even after the publication of Neuberger's work, received little attention. Some of the few contributions in this regard are Helmut Reinalter's investigations about Freemasonry and National Socialism following Alfred Rosenberg's example and the article by Werner Freudenschuß about the Wetzlar Ring in which he ascertained "*völkisch* tendencies in the German Freemasonry after World War I." (The phase after the "Rise to Power" is not covered.) Another work is the brief essay by Wolfgang Fenner and Joachim Schmitt-Sasse about Freemasons as "national power" before 1933. In this, however, raising the question about the roots of this phenomenon is, unfortunately, almost completely neglected.[14] A work by Jörg Rudolph also deserves mentioning. Oriented to the archival history of Office VII of the Reichssicherheitshauptamt (Main Office of the Reich Security), it contains new discoveries with regard to the intelligence service and the treatment of Freemasonry in the Sicherheitsdienst Hauptamt (Main Office of the Security Service [SD]) and in the Reichssicherheitshauptamt (Reich's Main Office of Security).[15]

The book presented here is intended as a contribution to the study of political history in the Weimar Republic and the Third Reich on the basis of a section of the population that in many aspects was typical and at the same time atypical. This approach includes the position of Freemasonry as a part of the European history of ideas, which is to be reflected as a whole. Moreover, as a critical study of ideology within the frame of reference of idea and institutional history, this particular approach has to include, at the same time, questions about the social actions of Freemasons, in relation to their closeness to political milieus and their social background. However, neither an all-encompassing analysis of social stratification nor systematic inquiries of social economic conditions of lodges or its members can be expected.

The perspective of the inquiry of the following research is mainly focused on the Masonic "umbrella corporations," which represented the subsidiary lodges of a system in the entire Reich. This is justified because the leading participants operated at the functionary level of the grand lodges and because decisions were made in their governing bodies about defense measures, relationships with the state departments and other institutions, as well as about the course of action of the grand lodge as a whole. In short, it was here that the decisions were made. This work deals with their intentions, root causes, and consequences. This study also includes the subsidiary lodges, especially where differences in opinion concerning political dealings of the grand lodges could be ascertained. On the other hand, an approach depending primarily on the local history did not seem to be promising for methodical or factual reasons. It was inevitable that concentration would be on the main emphasis and not only because of the extraordinarily extensive source materials. It did not seem practical to treat all grand lodges in an equally detailed way, but to bring out the two main streams of German Freemasonry and within these, to carry out case studies.

In contrast to the previous research approaches, briefly outlined, which talk quite cautiously about "attempts at conformity," "national tendencies," or Freemasons as "national force," this work takes the heterogeneous structure of German Freemasonry as the point of departure, and puts the two extreme wings–the *völkisch* and left liberal movements within the German jurisdictions–into the center of the study.

The following are the leading questions guiding this study:

1. Which ideological currents were reflected in Freemasonry and influenced its development?

2. What part did the German lodges play in the social spheres of influence during the first half of the twentieth century? What was their position with respect to the Weimar Constitution and the political problems of the Republic, and how did they finally react when the National Socialists took over power?

3. What was the relationship of other social institutions with the lodges? To which political and social milieus did German Freemasons belong, and what societal connections were present aside from affiliation with the lodge?

4. Which organizations and what meanings were behind the collective term Freemasonry? Did an independent concept of Christian-Aryan Freemasonry develop?

5. Which conditions caused the lodges to be treated with hostility and finally to be persecuted by the National Socialist state, while at the same time in some lodges, *völkisch* and an anti-Semitic body of thought manifested itself?

6. Which status did anti-Masonry have within the National Socialistic ideology, and how did it fit into the context of anti-Semitism?

7. What impression did the officials in the "Third Reich" have of the lodges and their members, and what impression did the Freemasons have of themselves?

8. How was the combination and competition shaped between departments that dealt with Freemasonry such as offices of the Nazi Party, SS, Gestapo, and state bureaucracy?

9. Were Freemasons in the "Third Reich" only persecuted or did they perhaps share blame and responsibility?

10. Were the transformations of grand lodges into German Christian orders in 1933 a result of ideological convictions or expression of superficial adaptation and deceit?

11. Was the exclusion of the few brothers of Jewish heritage as a consequence of the introduction of "Aryan paragraphs" solely a result of the pressure of the circumstances, which one believed could not be dealt with otherwise?

12. Is it legitimate to interpret the national–socialistic testimonies as "camouflage" that served the purpose of survival as an institution?

13. Was it only intended to save what could be saved, as one theory proposes, and which is still and persistently kept alive?[16]

Answering these questions is made possible by the now-improved situation with respect to sources. The previously existing hesitation of research on National Socialism to deal with Freemasonry can be partially traced back to the decades-long difficult circumstances of the sources. The situation has changed with German reunification and with the political changes in Eastern Europe and the former Soviet Union. Material believed to be missing has reappeared in the so-called "Special Archives," the former Central State Archives (now the Osobyi Archives in Moscow), which had been under the control of the Soviet Department of the Interior.[17]

The restricted access to archives in the German Democratic Republic, which was in effect until 1989, presented a major problem. Masonic documents were stored at the department of the former Central State Archives at Merseburg. Moreover, the disclosure of these documents at Merseburg was deferred in favor of documents of state provenance, and therefore their disclosure could only be completed in the early 1980s. After the dissolution of the department at Merseburg, the documents were moved to Berlin where they now reside in the Geheimes Staatsarchiv Preußischer Kulturbesitz (Secret State Archive of the Prussian Cultural Possessions), and where nowadays regulated access is possible. The use of the archives still requires a permit from the Grand Lodges. In the meantime, a comprehensive overview of the contents has been completed and published under auspices of the commission of the Research Society of Freemasonry in Austria and Germany.[18]

The files brought from Merseburg to Berlin are mostly records containing Masonic materials confiscated between 1933 and 1935. Even though it can be assumed that many of the captured records have been destroyed, among them complete records of individual subordinate lodges,[19] most of the records had been collected in a central location and analyzed by the SD in Berlin and later deposited in the Archive of the Reich Security Headquarters (Department VII C 1). The comprehensive (often confidential) documents are mostly made up of correspondence of the grand lodges, among them communication with subordinate lodges and other Masonic organizations. Next to political affairs and relations to social institutions, there are a great many communications concerned with defense measures against anti-Masonic agitation. In the wake of the growing National Socialism, the ambivalent relations with the Nazi Party became prominent, so did the correspondence with ministries and other state departments after the "seizure of power."

Toward the end of the war, the confiscated documents had been moved from Berlin to the castles Fürstenstein, Wölfelsdorf and Schlesiersee in Silesia because of the bombing raids. They were discovered there by the Red Army in 1945 and brought to Moscow. Owing to a contract with the USSR, many documents were brought to the GDR in 1957.[20] A few scattered documents from Warsaw were added. Only in 1968 was it decided to collect the Masonic material in the Central State Archives in Merseburg. Since then, Masonica have been bought or taken over from other archives. The Secret State Archives materials of the Grosse Landesloge and the Symbolische Grossloge brought from Merseburg were systematically analyzed for this research. Many of the documents secured by the Red Army in 1945 were, however, not given to the GDR. Those records stayed in the Soviet Union, among them lodge documents from the Gestapa (Secret State Police Office) and the SD Headquarters.[21] It was possible to analyze these documents as well as sources of Masonic provenance of the former "Special Archive" (Osobyi Archives) in Moscow. Moreover, the former "Special Archives" also contain NS documents about Freemasonry abroad, which however could not, for the most part, be taken into consideration.

Concerning the question and the relevant time period, there are not many government documents of Merseburg origin in the Berlin Secret State Archives. One exception--however only in a quite limited sense--is the Repository 84a (Ministry of Justice, former 2.5.1.). On the other hand, parts of the old West Berlin Secret State Archives collection of Repository 90 P are of importance. The sources used were reports of the Berlin state police, as well as others, mainly from the Gestapa and SD headquarters. Of special interest were those files that were expected to shed light on the activities of the sometimes competing departments of the NS bureaucracy dealing with lodges. In addition, the files from the Federal Archive and the Bremen State Archives were used. On one hand, the Archives contain reports and communications on lodge issues issued by the Gestapa and the SD Headquarters; on the other hand, there are bureaucratic issues of different NS departments, as well as instruction and propaganda material. Files concerning the relationship between the Evangelical Church and Freemasonry were located at the Evangelical Central Archives in Berlin and have been studied on site.

Other printed and nonprinted materials available in the German Masonic Museum in Bayreuth were consulted, among them documents concerning the history of the Symbolische Grossloge.[22] In addition, files compiled after World War II by Bernhard Beyer, a former director of the Museum, were used. The latter records show the orientation of the Old Prussian Grand Lodges in the Weimar Republic and "Third Reich."[23] The archives collection as part of the Museum is the most extensive library in Germany containing relevant periodicals and works about all aspects of Freemasonry.[24] The use of the library materials located at the University of Poznan, however, was omitted because after examination of the microfiche available in Bayreuth, there was no additional information to be anticipated from them.

Another fundamental source was the house archives of the Grosse Landesloge in Berlin. These files were analyzed, for the first time, in a scholarly manner in my master's thesis "'Völkisch Freemasonry' 1922–1935," which has been completely subsumed in this work. So far, the material had been looked at only internally and had been collected in chronological order. It is not otherwise organized and is not cataloged; therefore, more precise statements than those furnished as footnotes are not possible. The collection contains mostly internal communications, memos, and correspondence with party and government departments, as well as protocols and white papers about strategies. It is a supplement to the material located at the Geheimes Staatsarchiv but also contains several duplicates. The largest part by far of today's Grand Lodge House Archives——among them are the files used here–+is compiled from the formerly scattered archives. Many sources were in private possession of

Freemasons or their families for decades before they could be brought together in the Lodge House of Berlin.[25] Personal records obtained by the former Berlin Document Center (BDC) and now integrated into the Bundesarchiv (Federal Archives) in Berlin–Licherfelde have been added, as well as archival material brought together from several private collections or studied on site. The picture is rounded out by documents in the archives of the Supreme Council of the Ancient and Accepted Scottish Rite, Southern Masonic Jurisdiction (Washington, D.C.) and by the rich sources that are to be found in the form of microfilms in the United States Holocaust Memorial Museum (Washington, D.C.), the originals of which are from archives in Russia and Eastern Europe.

There is so much for the formulation of questions and the status of sources. The following central hypotheses are the foundation of this research:

1. Under the influence of different and sometimes opposite intellectual trends, Masonic systems have diverged to such a degree that to speak of a common intellectual philosophy during the first half of the twentieth century is out of the question. Even though some of the common principles are shared among lodges, such a broad spectrum had been established, especially in Germany, that actually it should be referred to as Freemasonr*ies* rather than Freemasonr*y*.

2. *Völkisch* Freemasonry presented an essential power within this spectrum. Accordingly, the formation of the Old Prussian orders in 1933 did not constitute a camouflage, but constituted an expression of a growing attitude of political and instructional categories. The political and ideological tensions between lodges and their opponents were lastingly marked by the frequent difference between Freemasonry's self-perception and outsiders' perceptions of it.

3. Although a unified political line of the National Socialists toward Freemasons did not exist, there was a common ideological consensus. The decisive factor was that anti-Masonry had existed long before the "seizure of power" and was part of a firmly rooted

anti-Semitic pattern in attitudes. The widely held premise of Free-masonry being a "tool" of the Jews continued to have the effect of being a central tenet during the Third Reich, and last but not least, had an integrating function far beyond the Nazi Party.

The methodology is derived from these goals, which are not only close to the sources, but also consciously dispensed with a strict chronological portrayal in favor of a thematic focus and necessary digressions. The chapters are structured as follows:

The two introductory chapters deal with the history of Freemasonry and anti-Masonry. First, important developmental tendencies of Freemasonry are described in general. One cannot dispense with an examination of the different Masonic teachings, higher degrees, and systematic idiosyncrasies, but that is limited to what is necessary for the subject being discussed. The focal point is the history of the German Grand Lodge for which the year 1922 was a particular decisive point. Fifty years after its creation, the Deutscher Großlogenbund (Federation of German Grand Lodges) broke apart. On May 27, 1922, the three Old Prussian Grand Lodges, as the national wing, declared their resignation from the umbrella organization, which continued to exist in much weakened and diminished form.[26]

In the second chapter, the history of anti-Masonry is discussed. Anti-Semitic and anti-Masonic traditions are analyzed, especially with regard to their culmination in the theory of a Jewish–Masonic conspiracy: in other words, the genesis and function of the "world conspiracy myth."

The third chapter is dedicated to Freemasonry in the sphere of influence or "force-field" of the Weimar Republic. First, the course of the right wing of the German lodges, which was defined by tradition as well as by its willingness to adapt, is researched. Afterwards, a short sub-chapter deals with the relation between Freemasonry and the Protestant church. Special attention is paid to the defense mechanism and its associated isolation of the left-wing minority of German Freemasons.

Chapter 4 deals with the reception of *völkisch* and national–socialist ideology in German Lodges. The focal point is the establishment of *völkisch* Freemasonry in the 1920s. Separately viewed is the change of tradition of the national lodges in conjunction with the formation of German–Christian orders as a consequence of the "seizure of power."

The fifth chapter deals with the German lodges during the time between 1933 and 1935. Developments in the humanitarian wing are shown first, followed by the futile struggle for the continued existence of the Old Prussian lodges and for state recognition, up to the forced self-dissolutions and the subsequent liquidations.

The two following chapters each show a case study, one dealing with the Große Landesloge and the other with the Symbolische Großloge. The decision to do so was influenced by the study of content and methods. This made it possible to discuss aspects in detail that otherwise would have been forgone. Moreover, the case studies give grounds to put the two opposite poles of the German Freemasonry into the forefront.

Since the "Freemasonry question" was not at all concluded with the ban of the Lodges, the eighth chapter emphasizes the NS state and Freemasonry as a central theme after the year 1935. The portrayal includes the Lodges in the politics and propaganda of the Third Reich as well as the behavior of the Freemasons themselves. In particular, it deals with the activities of the Gestapo and SD departments, with the enforcement of the state policy on Freemasonry domestically, and with its spreading and its propagandistic function during the war, and, last but not least, with the connection between the resistance and the Masonic milieu.

Finally, in the form of a brief vignette, or overview, the epilogue outlines the new beginning of the lodges in the Federal Republic of Germany and points out the mostly missing critical reflection of their role in the Weimar Republic and in the Third Reich. It is an exemplary "coping with the past" for German post-war history, including structural and personal continuities.

Chapter 1

ORIGIN AND DEVELOPMENT
OF FREEMASONRY

"Arcana publicata vilescunt: et gratiam prophanata amitunt.
Ergo: ne margaritas objice porcis, seu asino substerne rosas."

- Johann Valentin Andreae
Die Chymische Hochzeit Christiani Rosencreutz (1616)

1.1 THE GERMAN GRAND LODGES AND
THE HISTORY OF FREEMASONRY

The nature of Freemasonry is, according to [Gotthold Ephraim] Lessing, "nothing willful, nothing disposable, but something necessary, which is grounded in the beings (essence) of people and bourgeois society."[1] Freemasonry represents the expression of the human search for knowledge. Masonic "work" during ritual meetings therefore means, above all, the ritual itself and the striving for self-knowledge, self-mastery, and self-improvement.[2]

In every kind of Freemasonry, there are three grades or degrees of knowledge of the so-called "blue" or "St. John's" Freemasonry: Entered Apprentice, Fellow Craft, and Master Mason, for which the organization into lodges provides cohesiveness. Lodges see themselves as "places of Masonic work, fraternal meeting, and friendly fellowship."[3] Seven regular

Master Masons are needed to found a new lodge [the number varies by jurisdiction—trans. note]. The new lodge is activated by the ceremony of "Bringing in the Light" which is performed by an extant regular Masonic institution. Three or four lodges can unite, in turn, to form a grand lodge, the umbrella organization of the system at the national level. In addition, some grand lodges have district or provincial lodges [in the United States of America, each state (including the District of Columbia) has its own jurisdiction with its own grand lodge; there is no national grand lodge—trans. note]. There is a chain of command (authority) between the grand and subordinate lodges, which has the special task of concerning itself with the far-flung blue (St. John's) lodges of a given system, and assist the grand lodge in its work.[4] Lodges that are not chartered by a grand lodge are considered irregular and are usually called "clandestine."

The members of Masonic lodges call each other "Brother" within the lodge. In the German Grosse Landesloge, they are called "Ordens-brüder" ("Brothers of the Order"). The name of the office of the elected chairman of a lodge is "Worshipful Master" or—in the case of the Grosse Landesloge—"Lodge Master"; the corresponding officer on the grand lodge level is "Grand Master" or "Land (Provincial) Grand Master." The "Deputy (Grand) Master" functions as (the Grand Master's) representative. To join a lodge, the "Petitioner" must be sponsored by a member of the lodge who will vouch for the new Brother. Resigning from a lodge is called, in Masonic parlance, "demitting."

Ritual and metaphor in the Entered Apprentice degree, the level of self-knowledge, reflect symbolic work on the imperfect person—the Rough Ashlar. The Fellow Craft degree follows, in which the now Smooth Ashlar allows itself to be fitted into an harmonious part of the whole in the symbolic building of Solomon's Temple, which finally culminates in the Master Mason Degree, the level of self-ennoblement, symbolized by the Masonic tools, the Square and Compasses. The Brother is supposed to be stimulated by this spiritual building to ask and to answer, on his own, the questions of the meaning and design of life, whereby Solomon's

Temple stands as the symbol for an ideal spiritual construction, erected in the sense of building humanity.

The goal is not the end of the journey, but the journey itself,[5] the process of seeking, and the attempt at understanding. Freemasonry understands itself to be a communal experience, and as such, "one of several possible ways a person can go in his striving for humanity, in his struggle for freedom."[6] That is supposed to make Freemasonry something universal: not bound to an epoch, and independent of nationality, societal form, or religious belief.

It is generally agreed that Freemasonry as it is now practiced began formally on June 24, 1717, when four lodges in London and Westminster united to form a Grand Lodge of London, and together celebrated the Feast of St. John in honor of John the Baptist, patron saint of stone masonry. In Masonic lore, as well as in specialized scholarly research, this is the birthing hour of organized Freemasonry.

The members of these four lodges were no longer operative masons. Since the seventeenth century in England and Scotland, "non-operative (speculative) workers" had been accepted into the guilds of stone masons as patron members—"accepted Masons." For centuries, building was the domain of the Church. Only at the end of the Middle Ages, did the "Bauhütten" (English "lodges"; French "loges") turn into secular master builders' workshop associations and meeting places secluded from the public, as well as places of specialized knowledge about architecture, stationary engineering (statics), and geometry.[7] The lodges developed with the accepted members of other groups in society into the first associations to overcome the barriers of classes of society.

In 1723, six years after its founding, the London Grand Lodge received its constitution. The English Grand Master, the Duke of Montagu, assigned the Reverend James Anderson to put together a book of constitutions, the so-called "Ancient Obligations" ("Old Charges"). With the appearance of the "Ancient Obligations"—still today the basic law of most Masonic lodges—the transformation of the working or operative

Masonry of the workshops into spiritual-symbolic Freemasonry was completed.[8] The symbols from the stone-masons' tradition remained, and found entrance into the ritual of speculative Freemasonry, establishing their metaphorical usages. Since norms of custom, as a rule, are subject to constant change, Freemasonry forgoes the setting of ethical ground rules. Its spiritual bases are reflected in the ritual work, applied in a new way and made possible to experience by pictures and symbols.[9]

Anderson's *Constitutions* assert: "Freemasonry is an association of people for the dissemination of tolerant and humanitarian fundamental principles, in which the Jew or Turk can have as much part as the Christian in the work of the Order."[10] Neither one's rank in society, nor income, nor religious adherence should decide membership, but one must be only "a free man of good reputation" to become a Freemason. In 1738 in the second edition of the *Constitutions*, Anderson qualified his general concept of a religion "in which all men agree" in favor of a clearly Christian-oriented Freemasonry, "but the Grand Lodge of England did indeed return to the first position of bridging all religious views."[11]

Freemasonry has its roots in the early modern "field of tension" between scholasticism and tolerance, in the disputes between medieval, Christian-monastic virtues and the new bourgeois concept of virtue drawn from natural law. Since the time of Plato, reason had played a central role in the thinking of natural law. The secularized concept of nature and the doctrine of reason freed from theology resulted in the change from natural law to the law of reason, in which the principles of knowledge and justice were equally expressed. In the eighteenth century, natural law was finally taken out of the context of Hobbes' "Contract of Society." Whatever wounds or damages a community of reasoning people was understood as unjust by the natural law of the Enlightenment. Early Freemasonry understood its affirmation of reason not as opposition to belief, but as opposition to lack of reason. The Masonic ideal of humanity meant, therefore, not a rejection of "Deity" but of that sort of inhumanity that had characterized the seventeenth century in Europe in the forms of persecution of heretics, witch trials, and religious wars. Freemasonry always attempted to overcome the chasm between realistic and idealistic thinking, and to grasp human existence rationally and emotionally in equal measure.[12]

Anderson's "Ancient Obligations" were influenced by the ideas of Deism about tolerance.[13] The ideas of the Enlightenment acquired their early form in the lodges from the precepts of Locke and Hume, and from the discussion of rationalism and empiricism, which also determined the discussions in the political-literary salons and circles of the time, and became the summons to revolution in 1789. That people came together in the lodges and engaged in conversation on an equal level in a way that they could not, in their "profane" (non-Masonic) life, played an important role.

Freemasonry offered the possibility of a free-ranging space within the feudal-authoritarian power structure, and thus developed a model of operation for forms of organization and discourse in middle-class society.[14] In this way, Freemasonry formed one of those mediums "by which ideas of the philosophers such as liberty, equality, tolerance, and respect for the human being spread among intellectuals" in pre-revolutionary France.[15] The question as to how large a part early Freemasonry played as an intellectual current in the French Revolution is, however, much debated in research. At this juncture, it is helpful to distinguish between Freemasonry and so-called "Masonic-like organizations," such as, for example, the Jewish association B'nai B'rith, or the Odd Fellows, or the Druids. While there are many parallels and similarities in the organizational structures and goals, there are also considerable differences. In other words, Freemasons and "Masonic-like organizations" should not be, as they often are, lumped together. The complexity of the subject would indicate the advisability of "untangling" the latter groups.

A further distinction must be made between the strictly Masonic lodges and the many secret political groups and mystical-esoteric, occult, and Gnostic-theosophical associations in the eighteenth century. Thus, for example, the thought-world and activities of the mystery group, the Rosicrucians, with its alchemical-cabalistic character, are related to Freemasonry only on a very limited basis, and otherwise to be categorized as being in the anti-Enlightenment camp. As heir to the throne, the then king, Friedrich Wilhelm II of Prussia, who repealed many of the domestic political reforms of his predecessor with his religion and censorship edict of 1788, was rather strongly under the Rosicrucian influence of his advisors, Johann Christoph von Woellner and General Johann Rudolf von Bischoffwerder. Bischoffwerder as prime minister and Woellner as justice minister (as of 1788), who both dedicated themselves to Rosicruciansim "in its most fantastic form,"[16] determined the monarch's policies to a great extent. The Illuminati, on the other hand, were a radical- Enlightenment and anti-Catholic group founded by the law professor Adam Weishaupt of Ingolstadt in 1776. It established itself primarily in Bavaria, and had as its goal the spreading of rationalistic, fundamental principles. In 1784, the Illuminati were outlawed, and had to cease their activities, because of the decree of the Elector of Bavaria, Karl Theodor, who was pressured by Catholic-Jesuit and Rosicrucian groups. The accusations ranged from treason to secret plans to take over the world to poisonings. Weishaupt fled to the Free City of Regensburg. Efforts of the Elector of Bavaria to extradite Weishaup failed when Duke Ernst II of Saxony-Gotha and Altenburg placed Weishaupt under his protection by calling him to his embassy in Regensburg. Later, Weishaupt returned to Gotha, and continued his activity against his opponents in a series of political writings. During the French Revolution, rumors arose, stating that the Illuminati had come to life again. This resulted in a new Electoral edict forbidding them. At the beginning of the twentieth century, a so-called Order of Illuminati again appeared, but with no connections whatsoever to regular Freemasonry.[17]

Although Masonic elements were found in the internal and external forms of the original Order of Illuminati—and Weishaupt called his association "real" Freemasonry for a time—he had nothing to do with Freemasonry as far as organizational forms were concerned. The widespread thesis that the Illuminati of the eighteenth century were the revolutionary wing of Masonic lodges is misleading: it suggests that there was a kind of division of labor network, which is just not so. Nevertheless, even today, there still creep into publications about the Illuminati, as well as B'nai B'rith, ridiculous statements about a Jewish-Masonic world conspiracy guided by a "secret leader."[18]

Various studies—mostly with a social–historical orientation—which have appeared in the last few years, concern themselves with the influence of Freemasonry on the beginning and course of the French Revolution. They show that the conspiracy theory—whose main idea is always the alleged Masonic authorship of the French Revolution—is what it always was: a reactionary invention.[19] Undoubtedly, eighteenth-century Freemasonry had a spiritual influence on the French Revolution. Also, the significance of Masonic lodges on the struggles for emancipation of middle-class citizens and Jews in the 18th and 19th centuries[20] is not to be underestimated. Indeed, lodge life in general was of lasting historical effect. The reception of Masonic body of thought and its inclusion in the other institutions of society were widespread. But with all the significance that attaches to Freemasonry as a medium of the Enlightenment, one must also not overestimate its role in the shaping of the events of the French Revolution. Individual Freemasons, such as Danton, had leading roles in the Revolution, but many Freemasons were ordinary people.[21] All together, the lodge membership did not have a "radical enlightenment," philosophy even in France, and much less so in the small German states.[22] French Freemasons were overwhelmingly royalist, and worked for reform along constitutional lines.[23] Lodges as organizations were not known as "expressly in favor of a forcible overthrow of the societal order,"[24] nor did they secretly seek one. Corresponding arguments as they have been maintained by devotees of the conspiracy theory from the days of the French Revolution into the present are products of counter-revolutionary agitation, in whose effects many sorts of factors—psychological, social and political—overlap.[25]

Only a few decades after the founding of the London Grand Lodge, Freemasonry was carried into the English colonies; and from there, it soon spread over almost the whole world. The founding of lodges or grand lodges followed, for example, in Madrid (1728), Gibraltar (1729), Calcutta [and Philadelphia—trans. note] (1730), Boston (1733), Jamaica (1739), St. Petersburg (1740), Manila (1756), Cuba (1762), British Honduras (1763), and Canton (1767).

Even before its spread into Germany, Freemasonry had gained a foothold in France by way of the Stuarts who had fled England. The first lodge in Paris originated about 1725. The first lodge on German soil was founded in 1737 in Hamburg,[26] which maintained traditionally close trade ties with England. The founders were already members of English lodges, and at first the Hamburg lodge was subordinate to the Grand Lodge of England. The Prussian Crown Prince Friedrich was accepted into Freemasonry in 1738. In 1740, the year he ascended the throne, two lodges founded by Friedrich were working in Berlin (or at the Rheinsberg Castle): the "Königliche Loge" ("Royal Lodge") and the Lodge "Au Trois Globes" ("Three World Globes"). The latter became the seed of the later Old Prussian grand lodges. With the permission of the King, it rose to the rank of a "Grand Royal Mother Lodge."[27]

In other places, also, the large number of new lodges led to the development of overarching organizations (provincial and grand lodges). Meanwhile, in addition to Hamburg, Berlin had quickly established itself as a second Masonic center. From these two places, lodges in Vienna, Bayreuth, Leipzig, Breslau, Braunschweig, and Hannover were founded by 1748.[28] Already in 1740 and 1741, there were provincial grand lodges founded under the constitution of the Grand Lodge of England in Hamburg, Lower Saxony, and the lodge "L'Union" ("Union") in Frankfurt/Main. In Dresden, the lodge "Aux Trois Aigles Blancs" ("Three White Eagles") worked for a time as "the Grand Lodge of Saxony."[29]

In this early phase, German Freemasonry was still dominated by the nobility in social composition and mentality. That it could find acceptance by the lower nobility as well as the upper was due in no small part to the fact that it "indeed arched over the classes [of society], but was not socially open in all respects."[30] Only in the 1780s did the rising middle class win decisive influence. The lodges, as "middle-class-aristocratic mixed society,"[31] became not only meeting places of the political–service elite, but "in their social composition reflected mostly the social structure of the upper classes of the cities in question."[32]

By the middle of the century, Freemasonry began to develop more haphazardly because of the advent of the systems of higher degrees. The so-called "red" or Scottish Rite Freemasonry had its origin in France, and carries Masonic work in symbolic Knights' degrees beyond the three "blue" or St. John's lodge degrees into ever deeper and more abstract forms. The Scottish Rite forms the basis of all further higher-degree systems, which work in differing numbers of degrees. The term "Scottish Lodges" or "Scottish Rite" for higher-degree Freemasonry does not necessarily have anything directly to do with Scotland itself. The origin of the Masonic knights' degrees goes back to the Scots Chevalier Andreas Michael Ramsay. He worked in France as tutor to the son of the Stuart King James III, who had fled England. As such, Ramsay was also suspected of being a "Jacobite," a follower of the Catholic direction of Freemasonry. As Grand Orator of the Grand Lodge of France, Ramsay advocated the revival of old Masonic fundamental principles, and was inspired by the tradition of the Crusades. Whether the later spread of the higher degrees was what he meant them to be is doubtful. In any case, the term "Scottish" for the part of Freemasonry that goes beyond the third degree can be explained by its supposed origin in Scotland and the Stuarts who had fled to France.[33]

Baron von Hund founded the higher-degree system of the Strict Observance in 1751.[34] The foundation of this type of Masonic esotericism was the connection to Templar tradition. In the framework of the debate about the Strict Observance, of which the Three World Globes Grand Lodge had meanwhile seized possession, Johann Wilhelm Kellner von Zinnendorf founded the Grosse Landesloge der Freimaurer von Deutschland [Provincial Grand Lodge of the Freemasons of Germany or Freemasons Order—hereafter: Grosse Landesloge], which subscribed to the Swedish System in 1770. This established an eleven-degree, Protestant-Christian system in Germany.

The Swedish System had received its inspiration from the legend of the Templars' secretly continuing to survive. It is still the basis of the Grosse Landesloge. Meanwhile, the Strict Observance collapsed in 1782 at the Conference of Wilhelmsbad, despite the fact that this convention was called together by Duke Ferdinand of Braunschweig, the Grand Master of all Scottish lodges, in order to forestall that collapse. At the same time, the end of the Strict Observance marked a turning point in the history of Freemasonry: "the feudal concept of knighthood had played itself out; the thoughts of the citizens' revolution made themselves known."[35]

The time of the turbulent period of the Strict Observance was marked by the attempt to return to Masonic roots more deeply: to St. John's ("blue") lodge Masonry. In addition, the structure of the individual, independent grand lodges began to develop. First, the "Grand Lodge 'Royal York,' called 'Friendship,'" was founded as the third Old Prussian jurisdiction. Its history also begins during the tensions called forth by the Strict Observance. In opposition to their "Three World Globes" mother grand lodge when it moved to the Strict Observance, two lodges had split off, one of which was the Loge De l'Amitié ("Friendship"), which after the entrance of the Duke of York, brother of the English king (in 1765), called itself "Royal York de l'Amitié" in his honor. At first, the lodge sought a direct connection to the Grand Lodge of England, but it also sought to be recognized as an independent mother lodge. When this did not suc-ceed, after a short affiliation with the Grosse Landesloge, seven lodges constituted themselves "by their own complete power, a legitimate and perfect grand lodge" in 1798.[36]

In 1811, the Grand Lodge of Hamburg declared its independence; in the same year, the Grand Lodge of Saxony founded itself. In 1823, the "Eclectic Association of Freemasons" established itself as a mother lodge in Frankfurt. Because of the splitting off of several subordinate lodges from the "Eclectic Association of Freemasons," which in contrast to the liberal mother lodge, were expressly of Christian orientation,[37] the Grand Lodge (in the Freemasons Association) "Zur Eintracht" ("Harmony" constituted itself in Darmstadt in 1846. Together with the Grand Lodge "Zur Sonne" ("Sun") in Bayreuth, which had been founded in 1741, there were no fewer than eight grand lodges which "called themselves 'regular' insofar as they recognized one another as Freemasons, and were also recognized as such by the Grand Lodge of England."[38] Indeed, the criteria necessary for recognition were not uniformly regulated, which again and again led to the fact that "completely regular grand lodges denied each other recognition because of fundamental differences in their comprehension of Freemasonry."[39]

Since 1929, the eight points of the so-called "basic principles" represent the foundation for the practice of recognition by the English. They are the Landmarks laid down by the United Grand Lodge of England that overarch Masonic systems. To these belong, among others, the profession of a general divine principle in the form of the "Great Architect of the Universe," the regularity of descent (i.e. in order for a grand lodge to be legitimate, it must "be founded lawfully by another recognized grand lodge, or by three or more regularly constituted lodges"),[40] and the forbidding of discussions about religion and politics in the lodge.[41] In a double manner, the "basic principles" illustrate the claim of the United Grand Lodge of England: first as the cradle of Freemasonry, and second as playing the pivotal role in the practice of recognition all over the world.

In 1872, one year after the founding of the Reich, despite all their unresolved conflicts, the eight German grand lodges came together and founded the German Association of Grand Lodges. The new association replaced the previous "more or less regularly-held 'conventions of grand masters,'" which did contribute to a certain "reconciliation of standpoints"[42] among the systems. The idea of an association of grand lodges was anything but new. What actually brought the project to fruition is that there was more a general mood of national euphoria than a really cooperative Masonic mentality. Effective work of a more substantial or even organizational kind was made more difficult by the rule that there had to be unanimity in all decisions. The association proved to be more of an advisory than a governing body.[43] The Grosse Landesloge claimed that the Grand Lodge Association had been created in 1872, by dint of hard work by their Order [Grand] Master, Prince Friedrich Wilhelm.[44] This is surprising in view of the fact that the Grosse Landesloge usually kept itself clearly separate from the other German grand lodges.

Unimpressed by the creation of the common umbrella association, the Old Prussians—in contrast to the humanitarian grand lodges—hung on to their claim of being the only Masonic representatives in Prussia, even after the founding of the [Third] Reich. In their efforts to thwart the founding lodges in Prussia by other systems, they harked back to a special privileged position, granted by the Prussian kings, who were extremely effective, not only in tolerating Freemasonry, but also encouraging it, yet controlling it by limiting it to a few organizations.

Friedrich II provided the Grosse Landesloge with "confirmation patents" and patronage in 1774, and later did the same for the Three World Globes Mother Lodge. Immediately after its founding, the "Royal York" Grand Lodge also received patronage, which it promptly and rightly considered equal to those of the two other mother lodges. The three Old Prussian grand lodges and their subordinate lodges then assumed "a special place vis-à-vis all other associations in the Prussian State."[45]

On October 20, 1798, King Friedrich Wilhelm III, who was not a Member of the Craft, issued an edict "for the prevention and punishment of secret societies, that could be detrimental to the general security."[46] In this edict, the activity of every kind of secret society was strictly forbidden. The only exception was the three Old Prussian grand lodges. At the same, however, they were told to adhere strictly to their constitutions which were recognized as non-threatening to the state. This special position "in form and content a general 'Landes' law",[47] stemming from the edict gave the three Old Prussian mother lodges a Masonic right of monopoly in the Prussian states. While later representatives of the non-Prussian grand lodges supported the view that the privilege had been lifted by the decree on the right of freedom of assembly and association, of April 6, 1848,[48] the

Old Prussians hung onto their old claims. In 1892, it came to the so-called "Settegast-Fight," when Professor Heinrich Settegast, former Rector of the Technical High School of Economics in Berlin, after leaving the Royal York Grand Lodge, founded a new humanitarian "Grand Masonic Lodge of Prussia called Kaiser Friedrich zur Bundestreue" ("Emperor Friedrich of Loyalty to the Federation"). The legal struggle with the Old Prussians was carried all the way to the royal chief administrative court, which as the highest entity, upheld the legality of the founding, and thereby declared the edict of 1798 invalid. Now the Grand Lodges of Hamburg and Frankfurt opened subordinate lodges in Berlin. The Settegast Grand Lodge, in the form of the Provincial Grand Lodge of Hamburg in Berlin, merged into the Grand Lodge of Hamburg.[49]

The development of the function model for the rising middle-class society was favored (encouraged) by the form of organization of the lodges, which formed islands within the class society. However, as the ideals and goals of the Enlightenment were achieved and the middle class established itself as the new political elite in the nineteenth century, Freemasonry lost its reforming-progressive character. The result was a reorientation of extended portions of world Freemasonry under the leadership of the grand Lodge of England. The large majority of German Freemasons followed it: there was a process of introversion and reduction to esoteric concerns.[50]

Especially in France and the Iberian Peninsula, some grand lodges were concerned not with self-limitation but with openness. They concerned themselves, for example, with contributing to the emancipation of the developing proletariat. In Germany, not only the Old Prussians went the way of presumably "a-political" contemplation; "The former avant-garde of progress increasingly became ordinary lodges and keepers of frozen traditions."[51] Even more important, such a development could not remain without influencing the sociopolitical position of the lodges. With the shift "from active necessity to lovingly maintained tradition, the great mass of Freemasonry" also completed the swing from the progressive to the conservative camp.[52] This resulted in, among other things, that Freemasonry in Germany—aside from some scattered "workers lodges" that belonged to the fringes of Freemasonry, and without societal relevance—played no role in the history of the workers' movement.

There is more: In the 19th and early 20th centuries, there arose overlappings and connections between "fatherland" associations and Christian-national Freemasonry. Thus, for example, a great many members of Masonic lodges in Leipzig belonged to the "German Union of Patriots for the Erection of a Monument to the Battle of Leipzig" [1815—trans. note], which had been founded in 1894. As such, they figured prominently in the erection of the memorial, which was dedicated in 1913.[53] This was an early example of the mixing of politics and Freemasonry, or of *völkisch* thinking and Masonic thought tradition. It was a mixture that was mirrored in the choice of words in the consecration speech by the Freemason and chairman of the "German Union of Patriots," Clemens Thieme: "The battleground all around Leipzig has become a consecrated place, a shrine of the whole German people, sanctified by the sacrifice of property and life…sanctified, because here our heroic fathers ground the oppressive chains of the conqueror into the earth, to become a people of brothers once again."[54] With this Leipzig monument project, so strongly influenced by Freemasons, the clear beginnings of a visionary *völkisch* Freemasonry characterized by solemn nationalism can already be seen. Because of the outcome of the war in 1918, this tendency would harden.

Völkisch Freemasonry had been developing in the context of the *völkisch*ly defined German national consciousness since the time of the Wars of Liberation and their formation into myths by means of a sacral nationalism, as demonstrated by the Battle of Leipzig Monument, which was dedicated solely to the German victims. The following is an examination of the special direction of German Masonic history, including idiosyncrasies determined by the type of teaching, especially with regard to the aspect of the development of the phenomenon of *völkisch* Freemasonry.[55]

The German Masonic lodges blossomed during the period of industrialization, and membership grew by leaps and bounds. The reasons for this can be found in the growth of the cities and the establishment of the middle and upper classes. The milieu of the large city had always favored the development of Masonic organizations. Thus, the membership of the German grand lodges grew to more than 47,000 until the turn of the century.[56] The social composition of the lodges in all [Masonic] systems at the same time showed a preponderance of merchants with a percentage for every grand lodge that varied between 15% (Grand Lodge of Saxony) and 41% (Eklektischer Freimaurerbund—Eclectic Association of Freemasons). By the same token, the groups of manufacturers and directors were the second largest[57] in all the grand lodges. This shows a rather uniform picture: the humanitarian and Old Prussian lodges scarcely differed in their social divisions at this time. Worth noting is the very low percentage of clergy in the lodges; even the Grosse Landesloge was no exception.[58] Since, for example, no exact conclusions about heritage, possessions, or actual social standing of the social group of merchants could be made, the numbers evidence basically only a dominant position of the middle and upper classes. For specific declarations, the social structure of the lodges would have to be examined more closely. Without question, this is a very desirable subject for research. Detailed studies of the social composition of Masonic lodges in the eighteenth century have recently been offered.[59]

The left-liberal wing of German Freemasonry in the form of the "Freimaurerbund zur Aufgehenden Sonne" ("Masonic Association of the Rising Sun" or "Rising Sun") was formed, in 1907, by an independent, reform-minded grand lodge with monistic overtones. Two years before, the merchant, Heinrich Loeberich, who published the monistic journal *Freie Glocken* (*Free Bells*), initiated the formation of a "German Free-thinkers' lodge," which formed the basis of a "General Association of Freemasons" obligated to Monism [a belief that there is only one ultimate substance—trans. note] as Loeberich understood it.[60] At the general meeting on July 27, 1907, in Frankfurt/Main, the name was changed to "Freimaurerbund zur Aufgehenden Sonne."[61] The "Rising Sun" brought out its own journal, at first under the name of *Sonnenstrahlen [Sunbeams]*, then as of 1927 *Das Neue Freimaurertum [The New Freemasonry]*. Its lodges worked according to a new ritual without a Grand Architect of the Universe (GAOTU) and without a book of Sacred Law.

The specific relationship between Old Prussian Freemasonry and the House of Hohenzollern meanwhile assured the existence of the lodges and their special status as sanctioned by the state. Under the conditions of protection, a revolutionary tradition of thought could develop only with difficulty, because members of the ruling family sometimes held top lodge offices. The fact that there were protectorates by princes not only in Prussia but also in England and Sweden—a member of the royal family is traditionally grand master (in England, the Grand Lodge has a "reigning grand master" for administrative purposes) —alters nothing in the special character of Old Prussian Freemasonry. The "close, voluntary connection to the Hohenzollern monarchy" went beyond the personal to mental–structural interweavings, which also "successively changed the catalogue of virtues that the Prussian lodges wanted to pass on to their members."[62] The Old Prussian lodges, therefore, developed into a kind of state Freemasonry, whose characteristics will be discussed in detail, and in whose self-image the connection to the Freemason Friedrich II was of great significance.

In the 18th and 19th centuries, neither the nobility nor the majority of the middle class stood in opposition to the Prussian state. This fact played an important role in the development of Old Prussian Freemasonry. That was very true for "those members of both social groups, who were in the service of the state, from which the Freemasons recruited their members." These men "made an important contribution to the development of the new elite, as they served to form a framework for dialogue and political–ideological—partially also social—amalgamation of the two classes into a central corpus for the stability of Prussia, which supported the state."[63]

It is impossible even to sketch roughly all the currents of European Freemasonry. With respect to the subject of this examination, however, it appears to be necessary to make an excursus into French Freemasonry, because Romance Freemasonry in general—and that of the Grand Orient of France in particular—stand for the principle of the much-debated "international Freemasonry."

As in most countries, more than one grand lodge was established in France. The Grand Lodge of France was founded between the end of 1728 and the spring of 1729.[63a] In 1773, the Grand Orient split off, but rejoined the Grand Lodge of France in 1799. With the spread of the system of higher degrees of the Ancient and Accepted Scottish Rite (AASR),[64] a new Masonic umbrella organization originated, namely the Supreme Council of France. Toward the end of the nineteenth century, resistance grew against the hegemony of the Higher Degrees. The Symbolic Scottish Grand Lodge was founded, which recognized only the three St. John's or Blue Lodge Degrees. It was in competition with the Supreme Council, which attempted to maintain its influence over the first three degrees, but finally had to give in. At the beginning of 1895, it transferred its right over the Blue Lodge Degrees to a new Grand Lodge of France, which joined the Symbolic Scottish Grand Lodge in 1896. By decree of the Supreme Council, the separation of the responsibilities of the Supreme Council ("workshops," i.e. Degrees 4-33) and the Grand Lodge (Degrees 1-3), meaning the separation of "Blue" and "Red" Freemasonry, followed in 1904. In contrast, in the case of the Grand Orient, the Higher Degrees together with the "Grand College of Rites," which governed them, remained an integral part of the Grand Lodge.[65]

There was a break between the Grand Orient and England in 1877, after the French, in the same year, dispensed with the principle (Landmark) of the existence of God and the immortality of the soul in their constitution. In contrast, the oft-repeated statement that the Grand Orient had dispensed with the formulation "Almighty Architect of all Worlds" is incorrect.[66] Rather, the Grand Orient's understanding of itself was as a federation of rites, with the subordinate lodges [having] the right of freedom of ritual. That means, it was, and is, up to the judgment of each individual lodge under the Grand Orient as to whether it uses the Bible or instead a neutral

"White Book" in the ritualistic work, and whether it holds onto the symbol of the "Almighty Architect of all Worlds" or not. All the same, the Anglo-Saxon grand lodges broke off connections with the Grand Orient because it gave up these Landmarks. In French Freemasonry, strictly rational and atheistic, pronounced anticlerical positions were always represented, completely different from Germany. Justifiably, the English saw tendencies in the Grand Orient that ran afoul of the questionable postulate of political abstinence. Indeed, it appeared to be basic to Romance Freemasonry "that where it believed itself responsible for its ideals, it gladly lifted its voice."[67] French Freemasonry understood itself always as a factor in the socio-political power play and behaved accordingly. To this day, only the third French grand lodge, the Grande Loge National de France, is recognized by the Grand Lodge of England and the German United Grand Lodges [and, to our knowledge, all the Grand Lodges in the United States and Canada—trans. note]. Of course, there were, and are, French lodges in Germany with German members. Thus, two lodges ("Roue d'Or" ["Golden Wheel"] and "Etoile hanséatique" ["Hanseatic Star"]) were working at least temporarily in the nineteenth century in Osnabrück under the Grand Orient. "George-Jacques-Danton" Lodge, founded in 1922 in Saarbrücken, and "Mont-Tonnerre" ("Mount Thunder") chartered in 1924 in Baden-Baden, by the Grand Orient, are still working today.[68]

Since its beginning, one thing in common has remained among the different forms of Freemasonry: the reference to the idea of a spiritual brotherhood, which—depending on the system—stems either from the English–humanitarian, Enlightenment-influenced brotherhoods of stone-masons, or from the Christian–Templar tradition. In spite of all changes and in spite of sometimes unbridgeable philosophical opposition, it is discretion—the ability to keep silent—that contributed to the retention of certain characteristics of a Masonic identity. The secretiveness or mysteriousness (as perceived from the outside), the social-class mixing, and the (really lessening) social exclusivity of the lodges have always been explained as an expression of social arrogance and political radicalism, and formed the stuff of misguided accusations.

Initiation is a structural element of Freemasonry. To be sure, initiation rites are widespread. They are found, for example, in primitive civilizations, who "still clearly view the onset of sexual maturity as an important transition in the life of a person."[69] In the same way, initiations are found in German-*völkisch* and occult groups, who often for their part, harked back to the medieval Temple orders and harbored a racist spirit in their orders. Therefore, it is necessary to consider intra-Masonic differences as well as the distinction between Freemasonry and Non-Masonry. This distinction immediately leads to the determination of clearly existing differences.

The Masonic initiation—that is, acceptance and entrance into a community of like-minded people connected with the experience of new phases and levels of knowledge–would hardly function without being secluded. The widespread inclination to reproach Freemasonry per se because of its seclusion, together with the judgment of being "out of step with the times," is thus not justified. It must be firmly kept in mind, however, that with the establishment of middle-class societies and the formation of modern governments, there occurred a change in the function of the Masonic obligation to silence: in the eighteenth century, silence and secretiveness were necessary as a protection from persecution. For the twentieth century, that does not hold so true, although Brethren in some Catholic areas are still obliged to keep their lodge membership to themselves, because of well-founded concerns for professional disadvantages and social exclusion. The names of Freemasons and the addresses of lodge buildings, however, are often known and publicly accessible. Freemasonry has not been a secret society in the narrower sense, for a long time; and the seclusion connected with initiation serves mostly to preserve Masonic self-comprehension as well as to protect the symbolism and ritual from "profanation." This claim, justified as it is, does not, of course, say anything about the respective esoteric arrangements in the lodges themselves. It will be shown that the questionable idea of an elitist, spiritual chivalric order had a complex history of effectiveness, no matter what sort of Masonic instruction and higher-degree system was used. To this day, each system has different characteristics.

1.2 MASONIC HIGHER DEGREES, INSTRUCTION SYSTEMS, AND THE SPECIAL CASE OF THE THREE OLD PRUSSIAN GRAND LODGES

For the purpose of distinction among the various currents and camps of (German) Freemasonry, there are different models, which all function best when they are applied not alternately but complementarily. The easiest scheme to understand is the separation of the humanitarian and the Old Prussian lodges. According to this scheme, the five jurisdictions (obediences) represented in the Association of Grand Lodges, as well as the Grand Lodge "Deutsche Bruderkette" [German Chain of Brothers], a union of the five independent lodges in Saxony formed in 1924, stood in contrast to the three Old Prussian grand lodges.

This scheme becomes problematic when one also considers the two other German grand lodges: the "Rising Sun," founded in 1907, and the Symbolische Grossloge ([Großloge] "Symbolic Grand Lodge"), founded in 1930. The members of both associations thought of themselves as humanitarian Freemasons in the broader sense. The "Rising Sun" was held to be irregular, and the regularity of the Symbolische Grossloge was disputed. Even a general distinction between regular and irregular Freemasonry cannot encompass the actual relationships, completely aside from the fact that regularity has no really firm, clearly defined norms as its basis, and that the practice of recognition always gave rise to disputes among the grand lodges.

In addition, any categorization is made more difficult by the fact that—as we shall see—not only instruction systems and "intramasonic" recognition criteria but also political categories play a role. It appears sensible therefore to introduce an additional, complementary differentiation scheme—namely the separation of established and non-established German Freemasonry. The Grand Lodge "Rising Sun" and the Symbolische Grossloge fall into the latter category; all the other grand lodges fall into the former.

Humanitarian Freemasonry means, in the narrower sense, English Freemasonry. It has as its point of departure the "perfection of the three St. John's [Blue Lodge] degrees," and therefore rejects any kind of higher degrees.[70] This, of course, does not hinder innumerable humanitarian lodge members from working through the higher degrees. English Freemasonry sees itself as being in the tradition of the stone-masons' brotherhoods: its foundation is the "Old Charges." From these are derived, among other things, the requirement of political abstinence, tolerance, and the profession of the GAOTU as a supra-religious (overarching) Divine Principle. The consciousness of God without religious or denominational constraints opened lodges all over the world to non-Christians and allowed them to take root quickly all over the British Empire. During Masonic work, the Old or New Testament, the Koran, the Torah,[71] or, as an expression of an overarching consciousness of God, the so-called "White Book" may lie open on the altar. For example, the "White Book" was used between 1872 and 1930 in the so-called "Freiburg Ritual" of the Grand Lodge "Sun," in order to take all forms of religious dogmatic character away from Lodge Work.[72]

Another possible differentiation is that between Christian and humanitarian Freemasonry. According to this model, the Grand Lodge "Zur Freundschaft" [Friendship], the least dogmatic of the three Old Prussian ones, with its three "Fessler"[73] St. John's degrees, would belong to the humanitarian groups because they do not define the St. John's degrees as expressly Christian. In 1924, however, it closed its St. John's degrees, which had been open to Jews since 1872. Of course, this exclusion of members of a religious community contradicts the "Old Charges" in the sense of the humanitarian-Masonic tradition. The attitude had begun to gain a foothold in the Friendship Grand Lodge that the concept of religion formulated in the "Old Charges" was to be understood as Christian. The question of a relevant explanation of the "Old Charges" represents a fundamental conflict within Freemasonry. While in the opinion of the Christian lodges Anderson could only have meant the various Christian denominations, the postulate of religious tolerance according to the humanitarian principle extends to all faiths. The Bible, in this context, stands for a general divine world order.

The change in the way of thinking of the Friendship Grand Lodge—in the middle of the 1920s, of all times—can safely be seen as a concession to the anti-Jewish *Zeitgeist*. Already in 1915, the addition "Royal York" had been struck,[74] because this would have led to the conclusion that there was a connection with the wartime enemy England. In the giddiness of enthusiasm for the war and national exuberance, one did not want to expose oneself at all—and certainly not by a name—to any reproach of untrustworthiness vis-à-vis the Fatherland. In the same year, the Association of Grand Lodges broke off relations with the grand lodges of the Entente-Powers. The Grosse Landesloge, meanwhile, had always denied membership to Jews and thus expressed its concept of itself as a Christian order of Freemasons.[75] Thus, logically, it had never recognized the "Old Charges." On the question as to whether the National Mother Lodge was Christian in the narrower sense, there is a difference of opinion.[76] At least its instruction system is not so explicitly Christian as the Swedish System, according to which the Grosse Landesloge works. It handled the acceptance of non-Christian Brothers as inconclusively as did the Friendship Grand Lodge. Very probably under pressure from Crown Prince Friedrich Wilhelm and the Grand Lodge of England, Jews had been allowed the right of visitation since 1868.[77] Later, they were clearly even temporarily allowed membership in the first three degrees.

In the humanitarian grand lodges, there was no fundamental rejection of Jews. The lack of statutory exclusion did not mean at all that "Seekers" of the Jewish faith were accepted without reservation. On the contrary, not only religiously but also racially anti-Semitic views, which had spread increasingly in a great portion of the German population since the nineteenth century, could become effective in the individual lodge, belonging to any system, by the rejection of any individual candidate.

Acceptance of a new Brother into a Masonic lodge is decided by balloting, meaning that lodge members vote with a white or black ball.

White means acceptance, black rejection. The manifestation of anti-Semitic currents was now the "often systematic black-balling of Jewish candidates."[78] The "Settegast-Fight" stemmed directly from this context. Settegast, as "Royal York" Grand Master, made an effort to reform the constitution of his Grand Lodge such that from then on, black balls had to be justified. Religious preference was not to be accepted as grounds for rejection. When he was defeated in this effort, Settegast resigned his office and his lodge membership. With the constitution of the humanitarian "Große Freimaurerloge von Preußen, genannt Kaiser Friedrich zur Bundestreue" ("The Masonic Grand Lodge of Prussia, called 'Emperor Friedrich of Loyalty to the Association'"), he abolished the Old Prussians' sole reservation to the "right to sprinkle holy water" (i.e. consecrate, constitute) lodges within Prussia.[79] A final possibility for distinction is the separation of Higher-Degree and St. John's (Blue Lodge) Masonry. Actually, there was never any unified Higher-Degree Masonry. In the middle of the eighteenth century, two Higher-Degree Masonic systems arose with roots in France: the Strict Observance and the Swedish System, which would influence the development of Freemasonry in Germany in no small way. The tumults in which the National Mother Lodge became involved because of the Strict Observance system have already been mentioned. Even though the Wilhelmsbad Convention of 1782 brought an end to the Strict Observance, elements of it remain in the Higher Degrees of the Grosse Landesloge and the Three World Globes Grand Lodge. The Swedish System spread in Scandinavia and gained a foothold in Germany through Zinnendorf. This is a Christian instruction system that rejects the principle of tolerance, but which perhaps may have been recognized by the English mainly because of its Protestant character.

Thus, among the German grand lodges, two paths were established: the humanitarian English tradition without Higher Degrees, and the Old Prussian tradition with them. While the Old Prussians followed their own integrated instructional building methods, other Masonic higher degree systems, in which a somewhat scurrilous nature cannot be denied, developed the world over were based upon St. John's (Blue Lodge) Masonry. For instance, the Rite of Misraim which appeared in Italy in 1805, and spread especially in France (90 degrees, among them some hermetic–cabalistic) or its competition, the Rite of Memphis (at first 92, then 97, then 95 Degrees). In North America, including Mexico, the York Rite established itself. The number of systems, orders, lodges, chapters, and symbolic chivalric degrees, that were active all over, especially in France, makes the assessment and categorization of Scottish [Rite] Masonry, as well as its fringe groups, almost impossible. One thing is sure: since its development in the eighteenth century into the Masonic Higher Degrees, traditions of alchemical and cabalistic instruction systems and a scarcely hidden occultism have flowed in.

The AASR with its 33 Degrees, became the most effective and widespread system, with the establishment of the Supreme Council in 1801 in Charleston, South Carolina. The AASR has a national "Supreme Council" in each country: for example, in France (as of 1804), in Brazil (1826 or 1832), in England (1845), or in Austria (1925).[80] In the United States, there is a supreme council for each of the Northern and Southern Jurisdictions. In 2000, there were just about 300,000 members in the Northern Jurisdiction, and 280,000 in the Southern.[80a] The local units of the Scottish Rite are called "ateliers." This is the term for the "workshops" in each of which several degrees are worked [in the United States, they are called "valleys" or "orients," and these names change between the Northern and Southern Jurisdictions!—trans. note]. Degrees 4-14 are Lodges of Perfection, 15-18 Chapter, 19-30 "Areopag," and 31-32 are Consistory [in the United States, 4-14 are Lodges of Perfection, 15-16 Council, 17-18 Chapter, and 19-32 are Consistory – trans. note]. The 33rd Degree is ritual as well as administrative [in the United States, it is an honorary Degree called Sovereign Grand Inspector]. Different from the United States, in Europe, the 33rd Degree is bestowed almost exclusively for administrative purposes. Those who possess it, and who are designated "actives," form the actual Supreme Council, the "law-giving" leadership body of the AASR for a country or jurisdiction.[81] The name of the highest office, whose occupant is elected from the Supreme Council, is Grand Commander (U.S. Sovereign Grand Commander); his deputy is the Lieutenant Grand Commander.

For quite a long time in Germany, the introduction of the AASR failed to take hold because of resistance by the established grand lodges. Thus, the Second World Conference in Washington, DC in 1912 concluded that such an undertaking was hopeless, although Frederick II is considered the creator of the "Revised Constitutions" of 1786, according to which the Supreme Councils all over the world still work. The growth of the AASR in Germany meanwhile, was aided greatly by Emil Adrianyi-Pontet, a Masonic researcher, who was mainly occupied with questions of ritual. At first, his efforts to spread the ritual failed, thanks to a great extent to the Grosse Landeslodge, to which Adrianyi-Pontet belonged.[82] Bernhard Beyer, the Chief at the Bayreuth Masonic Museum and associate Grand Master of the Grand Lodge "Sun" followed the activities of the Supreme Council with suspicion, which in his words were "essentially under Roman influence" in other countries, and thus would represent "the political direction of Freemasonry."[83] In light of this background, the Masonic establishment—united in this instance for once—managed successfully to prevent an institutionalization of the AASR Higher Degree system in Germany for a long time. It is surprising that Bernhard Beyer, although he was not a member of an AASR body, held the 33rd Degree, granted him by Adrianyi-Pontet. It seems that Beyer's reservations were not directed at the work of the Higher Degrees (although he tried to hide the fact of his membership in the Scottish Rite), but at the Supreme Councils (i.e. the circle to which he himself belonged), meaning also the principle of internationalistic and politically offensive Freemasonry. Later it seems that Beyer changed his mind. After World War II, he even temporarily held the office of Lieutenant Grand Commander, and actively worked in the Supreme Council.[84] The constitution of a Supreme Council for Germany was finally accomplished in 1930.[85]

Because of their legal status, their position, and function in society, but mostly because of their Masonic understanding of themselves, the Old Prussians were a special case compared to the rest of the world.[86] As the only lodges not forbidden in Prussia, but even protected, they demanded to keep their privilege vis-à-vis other Masonic organizations, in defiance of the altered societal relationships by trying in vain to hinder not only humanitarian jurisdictions wanting to found lodges but also the Jewish organization B'nai B'rith wanting to establish branches in Prussia.

Because of their public-legal status given by the Edict of 1798, the Prussian lodges that had been founded before 1900 were not associations, but corporations of public law, and registered as such in the offices of the prescribed Prussian or Reichs interior authorities. The grand lodges informed the king—or later, the appropriate authorities—about changes in personnel in their administration as well as about new establishments, dissolutions, changes of location, or reactivation of subordinate lodges. In addition, permission for charter and name changes had to be obtained,[87] which in 1933, made the transformation into "German-Christian Orders" carried out by the Old Prussians difficult, because the National Socialistic government offices did not permit the name changes.[88]

The change in purpose—in the sense of a more pronounced drawing inward and depoliticization that took place in the second half of the nineteenth century in almost all of German Freemasonry—affected especially the privileged, national[istic]-conservatively oriented lodges in Prussia. The Old Prussians, following in the wake of the Grand Lodge of England, subscribed to the concept of "a-political." This had far-reaching consequences: turned inward on themselves, monarchistic, nationalistic, also anti-Semitic, the "a-political" had a political, restorative function.[89] It is a thoroughly accurate judgment that the German Lodges—at least at this time—were "rather more like middle-class, monarchistic associations than places to cultivate the Masonic mind,"[90] at least from the perspective of the liberal tradition of humanitarian Freemasonry.

The structures of the Grosse Landeslodge, meanwhile, were so encrusted that thinking was to some extent retrograde. The protector of the Old Prussians, Crown Prince Friedrich Wilhelm (later Emperor Friedrich III), resigned from his position of Order [Grand] Master in 1874, and went back to his Grand Lodge, keeping a clearly critical distance.[91] The immediate cause for this step of Friedrich Wilhelm—who was also an honorary member of the two other Old Prussian grand lodges—was internal differences about the alleged ancient origin of the Swedish System. Because this claim could not be proven, the Crown Prince turned from his efforts at renewal. In his resignation speech as Grand Master,[92] he bemoaned the lack of preparedness for unconditional historical research within the Order. He demanded that the lodge be confirmed as an institution of historical research, with due regard for tradition, "by all the means that today's scholarship offers," even if the "ruling tradition and belief in authority go head to head with critical research."[93] Friedrich Wilhelm proclaimed himself loyal to the enlightenment principle of discourse as he also stood up for an "exchange of views."[94] His modern speech—remarkable every respect—is one long plea for openness and readiness for reform, which he obviously had found lacking in the ranks of his Brethren: "The plain, stubborn holding fast to that which has been handed down is not sufficient,"[95] Friedrich Wilhelm summarized. He also unsuccessfully stood up for the acceptance of Jews into the subordinate lodges of the Grosse Landesloge.[96] It says something that Heinrich Settegast, after he resigned from Old Prussian Freemasonry, named his humanitarian grand lodge "Kaiser Friedrich zur Bundestreue" ("Emperor Friedrich of Loyalty to the Association") in honor of the Emperor and former Grand Master of the Grosse Landesloge in 1892—four years after the Emperor's death.

The Swedish System in Scandinavia mentioned earlier, as in Prussia, contributed to the development of a "state Freemasonry," in which its position became ever firmer, the greater its isolation became.[97] The inherent spiritual connection of Christian Freemasonry to the Temple Orders made it advisable to return to the Strict Observance and the circumstances under which the Swedish System was introduced into Germany.[98] This is an intersection of the lines of development of the new Templarism and Freemasonry. The basis of the Strict Observance, founded by Karl Gotthelf, Reichsherr von Hund, was the legend of the Templars. They saw themselves as the rightful heirs of the medieval Knights Templar. The Order of the Templars, so it is maintained, survived in secret after the Paris *autodafé* (burning at the stake, book-burning) of 1314, and the execution of Grand Master Jacques DeMolay. The Templars' story was, of course, neither new nor especially original. Theories about the Templar Fraternity's alleged going underground and their continued existence had been around before and after the Strict Observance. These theories are connected, as a rule, with diverse speculations about secret world plans of the Templars and of the ominous final secrets that would be the key to incredible power and strength.

What happened up until the events of 1314 are historically sub-stantiated. The Order of the Temple ("The Poor Brothers of Christ of the Temple in Jerusalem"), founded by Hugo de Payens in Jerusalem in 1118—since 1139 directly under the Pope, and thus freed from episcopal supervision—had become too rich and powerful for Pope Clement V and King Phillip, the Fair of France. The accusations raised officially by the Pope and the King against the members of the order included heretical crimes such as pederasty, idolization of Baphomet, and desecration of the Cross. In addition, there were reproaches, according to which the Templars allegedly sought to strike a balance with Islam. Indeed, some elements of Templar-influenced architecture, church designs, and art do point to a kind of symbiotic Christian and Islamic form of design. Jacques DeMolay, together with all the knights of the Order in France who could be found, was arrested in 1307 [on Friday, October 13—trans. note]. Under torture by the Inquisition, confessions were extracted. The Order was dissolved in 1312, and DeMolay was burned alive in 1314, after he swore to the innocence of the Order, and cursed the Pope and the King. The Templars were also persecuted in other countries.

There is speculation that some Brethren managed to evade arrest, and fled Paris hidden in a hay wagon. Finally, so the unproven story goes, they found refuge in Scotland under Robert the Bruce. They entered his service and helped to win the Battle of Bannockburn. As a reward, the king supposedly made them the nucleus of a new Order of "Knights of St. Andrew of Scotland." The Temple Order thus continued to exist covertly. After Neo-Templarism, under Ramsay, had gained a foothold in Freemasonry by way of France by 1737,[99] it found a new intellectual form in the Strict Observance. The Neo-Templar concept of the Order as spiritual chivalry was revived in the same way.[100] The Strict Observance further copied the system practiced by the Templars of dividing the earth into seemingly arbitrary provinces.

Elements of knighthood in the Strict Observance, as well as of the Higher Degrees going back to the Templar legends, are found to this day in different systems. Thus, for instance, the 7th Degree of the Grosse Landesloge (in its older form) is the symbolic acceptance into the secretly continued Temple Orders. The 30th Degree, "Knight Kadosh" (Hebrew: holy, sacred, initiated), of the AASR is also connected to Jacques DeMolay and the Temple Orders. The ritualistic, symbolic "revenge" for the innocent victim of King and Pope is not a repayment of like with like; rather the candidate being put forward swears to stand up against temporal and spiritual dictatorships. In other words, the Freemason is obligated to fight dogmatism and intolerance as well as to respect every religious belief.

The Higher-Degree confusion in the second half of the eighteenth century was the reason that the system and teaching of the National Mother Lodge were in "chaotic condition."[101] While the Three World Globes Mother Lodge was in the process of adopting the Strict Observance system, Johann Wilhelm Kellner von Zinnendorf entered the scene. He was a Grand Master of the Three World Globes Mother Lodge and in the context of the Strict Observance, Prefect of Templin (Berlin), and thus chief of that system in the Prussian States. In connection with rumors, according to which the "real" Freemasonry had appeared in Sweden, Zinnendorf stumbled upon the so-called "Eckleff Documents" in 1766. He believed that he recognized the only true Freemasonry in these Swedish ritual documents. At first he saw absolutely no contradiction to the Strict Observance, because the Swedish model was also based on the secret teachings of the Templar Order. Zinnendorf tried an amalgamation with the Strict Observance, which failed, because von Hund rejected the acceptance of the "Eckleff Documents" into his system. At that, Zinnendorf turned away from the Strict Observance and his mother lodge, and founded the "Grand Lodge of Freemasons of Germany" [the Grosse Landesloge][102] on St. John the Evangelist's Day, December 27, 1770. However, it took until far into the nineteenth century for the Order to be developed into its present form.

While the Three World Globes follow a seven-Degree system, the Grosse Landesloge uses eleven, of which ten are worked ritually. The St. Andrew's lodges are made up of St. John's Masters [Master Masons], who work in the fourth through sixth Degrees. The seventh through tenth form the Capitular Degrees.[103] The eleventh, which is not understood as a Degree in the narrower sense, is the "Highest Chapter Order," which consists of all "Temple Masters." Their officers' council ("Order Council") is also called the "Highest Department of the Order."

The St. Andrew's Degrees, or the name "St. Andrew's Freemasonry" for Scottish or Higher Degree Freemasonry, is not only used in the system of the Grosse Landesloge, It is also the name of the patron saint of Scotland, St. Andrew,[104] and goes back to the legend of the Templars as Knights of St. Andrew in Scotland. The Grosse Landesloge, according to Lennhoff and Posner, had the "character of a Christian order of knights, formed to honor God, for its own ennoblement and the ennoblement of the Brethren."[105] Christian Freemasonry emphasizes the exemplar character of Jesus Christ, who is called "Supreme Master" in the Grosse Landesloge. The goal of the Brothers is to lead the kind of life for which Jesus Christ is the Exemplar.[106]

The Grosse Landesloge also rejected the "Old Charges" because its Swedish System claims to be older. The Templars, according to the claim, had survived as members of the stone-masons' guilds disguised behind the Masonic Apron, and thus passed on the lore of the order.[107] This thesis cannot be proven. It is considered much more certain that the Strict Observance and the Swedish System go back to the same roots as all other Higher Degrees, namely Ramsay and the Scottish Rite. Proving an earlier origin for the Swedish System was impossible, even for the Grosse Landesloge. Connections to the old Temple Orders are alive in the Grosse Landesloge. The Festival of the Order of the Seventh Degree and Higher on the last Saturday in March is dedicated to the memory of Jacques DeMolay.[108] The same is shown by the dress of the Council of the Order for this festival (white coat and red Templar Cross), the spirit of the Order, and the identification with the tradition of the Crusades: the red Cross of the Order on a white field is considered the victory sign of Christianity. The self-concept as an "Order of Freemasons" upheld by the Grosse Landesloge is thus to be understood as programmatic.

The ritual and symbolism of Freemasonry can be treated in the framework of this examination only to the extent that the statement of the problem demands it. The Temple of Solomon as a building and as a symbolic "temple of humanity" is of central significance. The connection with the ancient construction derives from the representations and customs of the stone-masons' lodges. Concerning its reception by Christianity, it was less a question of the actual earlier existence of the Jewish icon than of the meaning of the Temple as an "image of God's celestial dwelling."[109] It became "clearly the pre-figuration of the church, in the practical, building-structural respect as a model for measure and proportion as well as also...in the figurative sense a purely spiritual, metaphorically ideal adaptation."[110] In addition, the real, ancient, twice-destroyed Temple overlapped with the different variations on the "temple in Jerusalem" in Christian tradition. The picture of Solomon's Temple was confused with the images of the Christian Church of the Holy Sepulchre in Jerusalem, which was also called a "Temple of the Lord (Jesus Christ)." The same is true for the Islamic Dome of the Rock, built in the seventh century on the grounds of the earlier Jewish Temple. The Crusaders turned it into a church, and also called it "Temple of the Lord." In contemporary depictions, it was often called the "Temple of Solomon."[111]

Despite this Christian tradition, the harking back to the tradition of Solomon's Temple was not spared when it came to the strong efforts to get rid of all Jewish or Old Testament overtones during the establishment of a *völkisch* Freemasonry even before the Nazis' seizure of power.

1.3 THE SPLITTING OF GERMAN
FREEMASONRY IN 1922

The outbreak of World War I threw the modest beginnings of international Masonic cooperation into a deep crisis. The lodges in Germany and Italy to a great extent retreated to a national political position and noisily joined the nationalistic chorus of war enthusiasts. It is no coincidence that Freemasonry dropped any political hesitancy in precisely these two countries. Germany and Italy both experienced their national unifications only in the second half of the nineteenth century, and found themselves in the midst of a "phase of national-state consolidation."[112]

During the war, German lodges made themselves noticeable not only verbally but also by offering their lodge buildings as military hospitals, thus making sure that their solidarity with the Fatherland was emphasized.[113] The grand lodges of the warring powers had meanwhile opened the theatre of a Masonic secondary war: after the Italian declaration of war in 1915, the German Freemasons broke off all connections with Italian (and French) lodges. The national administrations of European Freemasonry were of the opinion that they had to wage war among Freemasons. It came to journalistic fisticuffs. One accused the other of breach of international law and of the horrors of war or, on the other side, "treason against the German Reich" and direct conspiracy against Germany. In short, "national and Masonic interests were amalgamated into an inseparable unit," and the first voices arose, which as a consequence, resulted in "demands for a pure German 'Germanic, Teutonic' Freemasonry."[114] On one hand, the reproach was raised and promulgated by a member of the Grosse Landesloge (who later placed himself in Ludendorff's service) that German Freemasons had done serious damage to the Fatherland by having contacts with foreign Brothers in the so-called military lodges. On the other hand, the really overwhelming chauvinism in the military lodges promoted, to no small extent, the development of the idea of a *völkisch* Freemasonry, which in no way was as contradictory as Neuberger maintains.[115]

The emphasis on the "national" by German Freemasonry, however, did not result in the Lodges' getting out of the line of fire of their nationalistic and Catholic opponents. On the contrary, the attacks from the *völkisch* side became ever sharper. Italy's entrance into the war against the Central Powers and the fact that Italian Freemasonry had advocated this step[116] had the effect of a starting gun. Thus, the anti-Semitic journal *Auf Vorposten (At the Advance Post)*—the organ of the "Association Against the Arrogance of Judaism"—saw allegedly anti-German machinations at work in the grand lodges of France and Italy.[117]

In 1919—after the defeat in war and the appearance of the book *World Freemasonry, World Revolution, World Republic* by Friedrich Wichtl—the aggressive struggle of clerical and anti-Semitic nationalism against German Freemasonry reached a new height.[118] The more there were furious attacks, the more the organizations of German Freemasonry made nationalistic positions their own.

The opposing position was represented by a small group that, encroaching on the system, had come together to re-establish relations with foreign grand lodges interrupted by the war, and to contribute to the furtherance of the idea of a federation of peoples. Eight German Freemasons, some of them prominent, belonged to this group, among them Ludwig Müffelmann, his son Leo Müffelmann, as well as the later Reichs Bank President and Economic Minister Hjalmar Schacht, who was a member of Friendship Grand Lodge. The declaration published in the National Mother Lodge's *Bundesblatt* of December 1919 said that the signatories had united themselves into a "Blüntschli-Ausschuss" ("Blüntschli Committee")[119]; its task was "to represent and spread the idea of a federation of peoples, which is so much a part of Freemasonry."[120] As was to be expected, the challenge got hardly any support. The views promulgated by the "Blüntschli-Ausschuss" remained isolated and opposed, and not only in the Old Prussian camp, in which it was shown how much in opposition the political positions in one and the same grand lodge could be.

Only three years later, the allegedly internationalistic position of the humanitarian lodges and the "Jewish Question" were the catalysts used by the Old Prussians to bring about an open division in German Freemasonry. Much later, in 1934, in confidential announcements of the Secret State Police, the completely logical conclusion was drawn that the reasons for this split had been of a political nature, and that especially the "Jewish Question" had played a "not insignificant role."[121] Beyer laid the responsibility for the breakup of the Federation of Grand Lodges primarily on the Grosse Landesloge, where he established correctly that in addition to a "sharply Protestant mysticism" there existed a "scarcely veiled anti-Semitism."[122] Anti-Jewish polemics had sharply increased in the German public opinion, especially since 1910. The more strongly racially determined anti-Semitism took hold, the more Jews were perceived as the antithesis to "Germanness." [123] With that, the question of acceptance or continuing membership of Jewish Brothers became more explosive. Although the *modus vivendi* was possible so long as the "Jewish Question" was limited to the religious aspect for Freemasons,[124] now, increasingly, the discussion of race was dragged into internal and external decision-making levels of lodges and grand lodges.

Politically, the membership in the Old Prussian grand lodges subscribed to the German national milieu, with definite tendencies toward the anti-democratic right.[125] Therefore, it is not surprising that the Old Prussians, in well-thought-out distinction from the humanitarian grand lodges, emphasized that they stood "with all of their members on a pure national standpoint."[126] The group in humanitarian Freemasonry was not at all unified with respect to politics. The Grand Lodge of Saxony, with its headquarters in Dresden and the Grand Lodge "Deutsche Bruderkette" ("Chain of Brothers"), formed in 1924 by five independent lodges in Leipzig constituted the right wing within humanitarian Freemasonry. They thus stood between the Old Prussians and the moderate wing of established Freemasonry, which is politically best characterized as national-liberal. The grand lodges of Bayreuth, Darmstadt, and the Eclectic Association in Frankfurt belonged to this group. The Grand Lodge of Hamburg was traditionally labeled conservative. With all attempts to determine a political orientation of the German lodges, it must be taken into consideration that during the Weimar years, there was a more or less strong rapprochement to nationalistic and *völkisch* standpoints in the established humanitarian grand lodges. Left-liberal, internationalistic, and pacifistic views were held, in contrast, only by the membership of the numerically small part of non-established German Freemasonry, consisting of the Symbolische Großloge (Symbolic Grand Lodge) and the Grand Lodge "Rising Sun," which were not recognized by the other German grand lodges.

Immediately before the collapse of the Association of Grand Lodges, the group was characterized by disputes about the Verein Deutscher Freimaurer (Association of German Freemasons).[127] The purpose of the Association of German Freemasons, founded in Berlin in 1861, was historical, scholarly, archival research work. The Association operated independently of grand lodges and systems. Nearly a third of German Freemasons, from all the different systems, were members of the Association, which developed into "the real spiritual center of German Freemasonry...the only place seriously considered to be where the Masonic spirit was nurtured in Germany."[128]Regarded especially by Old Prussian grand lodge functionaries with suspicion and negativity, the Association came under fire from the right wing of the German jurisdictions because of its comparatively liberal attitude. It was maintained that the Association obstructed or frustrated the "Spirit of Fatherland" line, supported by the meeting of grand lodges, because of its publicity work.[129] The leadership of the Große Landesloge (the only one to do so) even went so far as to forbid its members to work in the Association—an extraordinary affront—because all the members of the Association's board at the time, except for Chairman Diedrich Bischoff (Bayreuth), were members of Old Prussian subordinate lodges.[130] At the same time, it was shown that there could be considerable differences between the activity of individual Old Prussian Freemasons and the official grand lodge policy.

Meanwhile, on the side of the *völkisch*-anti-Semitic groupings, the Große Landesloge was urged to explain its "Position on Germanness." "Even belonging to the Große Landesloge" was enough to engender mistrust.[131] The still-extant remnant of the relationships with other (humanitarian) grand lodges and with the so-called "international Freemasonry" was thrown as a reproach at the Große Landesloge. *Völkisch* circles, which according to Beyer's opinion, had instinctively sensed their worst enemy [which it really was not—author's note] began "to attack the fortress at its weakest spot—which the Große Landesloge had always been."[132] In other words, the external disturbances to which Masonic structures were exposed strengthened the centrifugal forces within.

In 1922, Grand Master of the Grosse Landesloge Müllendorff finally wrote to Hagedorn, the Grand Master in Hamburg, who was the sitting business administrator of the Association of Grand Lodges, that the Association of Grand Lodges really was supposed to work "internally for the good of Freemasonry" and "assume a unified position externally." In Müllendorff's opinion, it "really did not fulfill either of these purposes"; rather it was only an "artificial form," and it had the effect of being "more of a hindrance than a help for us" [the Old Prussians—author's note].[133] The contrasts appeared no longer bridgeable to the Old Prussians. Aside from that, they were not at all interested in a rapprochement of views. All attempts by Hagedorn at negotiations for preventing the breakup of the German Association of Grand Lodges were doomed to failure. The Old Prussians blamed the "pacifistic and cosmopolitan" views in the other lodges for the conflict. In addition, they felt attacked by the "Humanitarians" because of their attitude of rejection vis-à-vis the Jews, and saw themselves limited by the Association of Grand Lodges in their task of contributing to the "re-establishment of the German people by means of education to love of the Fatherland, to national feeling, and to a common way of thinking as well as the furthering of religiosity in the people."[134]

The sensitivities that swirled around in such reasoning stood diametrically opposed to the actual relationship of forces within the German lodge landscape. A look at membership development shows that, already in the middle of the nineteenth century, more than half of the then 22,000 German Freemasons belonged to an Old Prussian lodge. At the beginning of the twentieth century, the Old Prussians had a clear two-third majority. At the time of their resignation, the three Old Prussian grand lodges had almost 47,000 Brothers and thus were about 70% of the 67,000 members of established (recognized) lodges in Germany.[135]

As of May 27, 1922, the Old Prussian grand masters officially announced their resignation from the German Association of Grand Lodges. This step marked the transition from a more or less uneasy coexistence to a time of open splitting, in which the increasing politicization of the lodges was reflected. The fact that the Old Prussians remained part of the common charitable organizations could not conceal that fact. The intra-Masonic dispute was continued from that point on, under the rubric of their worldviews, whereby—also in connection with questions of ritual—national and racist ideological points of view came into the forefront. Not least, the resignation strengthened the isolationism of the Old Prussians from liberal foreign grand lodges (e.g. the Grand Lodge of Vienna and the Swiss Grand Lodge Alpina, with whom no fraternal relationship was maintained.

The Grand Lodge of Saxony followed the example of the Old Prussians in 1924, and left the Association of Grand Lodges. The Grand Lodge Chain of Brothers, constituted the same year, did not even make any overtures concerning joining the umbrella organization[136]; both of these facts were expressions of the continuing fragmentation of the Masonic scene in Germany. Before the German Association of Grand Lodges finally dissolved itself, essentially under the pressure of the "seizure of power," only the Grand Lodges of Bayreuth, Frankfurt (the Eclectic Federation), and Hamburg belonged to it.[137]

Chapter 2

THE THESIS OF THE JEWISH-MASONIC WORLD CONSPIRACY: THE HISTORY OF ANTI-MASONRY

2.1 ORIGIN AND DEVELOPMENT OF THE CONSPIRACY MYTH

The idea that the world has been guided by a conspiracy of hidden powers is a phenomenon known since the Middle Ages. From the beginning, Freemasonry has been the subject of conspiracy scenarios. Until the end of the nineteenth century, Jews and Freemasons were, independently from one another, accused of making secret plans to conquer the world, or as the case might be, of conspiracy against throne and altar. The genesis of the delusion of a Jewish-Masonic conspiracy came later, mainly in France. In Germany during World War I, or just after, the chimera of a Jewish-Masonic conspiracy spread significantly. But since the time of the French Revolution, various allusions to "Jews as 'useful tools' of the Illuminati and Jacobins"[1] were handed down. This paradigm, exactly reversed, would become widespread in the context of Jewish-Masonic integration theory. But first, it is necessary to examine, separately and briefly, the traditions of both world conspiracy myths, before looking at the combined conspiracy.

The history of anti-Masonry is as old as Freemasonry itself. "Secret societies of elitist character ... by nature, are targets of accusations and hostility of every kind."[2] In addition, Freemasonry, as a forum of citizens' emancipation, became a societal factor, so that nobles and clergy, the foundations of the *Ancien Régime*, felt challenged. The rejection of Free-masonry during the eighteenth century took different forms from those of the twentieth century: "the main structure of this rejection" was generally seen as "[having] remained essentially the same for the whole period."[3] The confrontation of Freemasonry by its opponents—the conflict between the principle of tolerance and that of exclusivity—has been reflected in pluralism and dogmatism.[4] This view does not consider, as we shall see, that great portions of German Freemasonry in the Weimar Republic subscribed neither to the principle of tolerance nor to political pluralism. Obviously, this explanation only touches on the interpretation of complex relationships among the various manifestations of Freemasonry and its enemies. It is necessary to make at least a differentiation among them.

From the beginning, the Holy See has been one of the sharpest oppo-nents of Freemasonry. The attacks by the Catholic Church, especially the Jesuits, have been a constant factor in anti-Masonic history. Pope Clement XII handed down the first sentence on April 28, 1738 when he promulgated the papal bull, "In Eminenti," against lodges.[5] Many papal encyclicals and bulls against Freemasonry followed.[6] In 1739, the Inquisition took action against Freemasonry in Florence. There were Masonic persecutions all over Europe, primarily in countries controlled by Catholic monarchs: for exam-ple, in 1743, Maria Theresia sent the military to close the Vienna Lodge.

A bizarre and notorious chapter in the long history of excessive Catholic polemics against Freemasonry is the so-called "Taxil Swindle."[7] In 1885 in France at the climax of an anti-Semitic and anti-Masonic wave, "Leo Taxil" put himself at the disposal of Catholic Church as a star witness against Freemasonry. He was a bookseller, publicist, and former Freemason; his real name was Gabriel Jogand-Pagès. He used the popular accusation that Freemasons were a Satanic cult which practiced ritual murder. He told about lodges as places of wild heretical and sexual transgressions. Official Rome was full of enthusiasm for this new ally. It rewarded the author of these fantastic "revelations" with a personal audience with the Pope. Correspondingly great was the horror, when, twelve years later, Taxil exploded his deception, and revealed that he had led the Pope and his entourage around by the nose. The sensation was enormous, as was the humiliation of the Catholic Church. After that, "the reputation of ridiculousness" was attached to its fight against Freemasonry.[8] But even the uncovering of "Taxil's deception" could not cause the Church to desist.

The idea of Masonic conspiracy arose in 1789 in France as the *Ancien Régime* was brought down by the revolutionary demand for "Liberty, Equality and Fraternity." In August 1790, a secretary of Vienna's Government wrote in a memo addressed to Emperor Leopold II that "the wheels of the current disputes and revolutions in Europe were driven by the brotherhood of Freemasons."[9] The French Revolution became decisive for the further development of anti-Masonry in all of Europe.[10] The picture of classless humankind held by the lodges and the form of equality and brotherhood practiced here—or in any case strongly postulated—clearly expressed an antagonism to traditional power claims made by nobles and clergy. The conspiracy thesis was the reaction of the feudal mindset to the ideal of equality. It was used by representatives of the *Ancien Régime*, as well as by supporters of the later antiliberal, laic right-radicalism.[11]

Into the theory of the Masonic world conspiracy slipped the legend of the supposedly secret continuation of the Knights Templar ("Temple Order"), in the form of a constantly overused story about "Unknown Superiors," who supposedly had an ominous plan for world conquest. After the death of [Jacques] De Molay, the Templars, now a secret society, were thought to be working to abolish the power of kings and the Pope, and to build a world republic. Thus, the Templars supposedly took possession of Freemasonry, along with other groups.

The blossoming of the Scottish lodges during the eighteenth century with their degrees of Knighthood and the tradition of the Templars gave additional ammunition to their opponents, who created arguments to support their statements on the subversive activity by Freemasonry. This was approximately the situation of the Neo-Templars' system of "Strict Observance," which explained itself as being led by "Secret Superiors."[12] Freemasonry itself also helped to keep alive the rumors that it was the guardian of the "Templars' secrets."

The conspiracy theory made its first appearance in book form, *Memoirs to Be Useful to the History of Jacobinism (Memoire pour servir à l'histoire du Jacobinisme)*, published in 1797/1798 by the former Jesuit Abbé, Augustine Barruel. The crux of the book was that the French Revolution was the result of a centuries-old conspiracy of secret societies. Barruel theorized that the origin of Freemasonry had to be sought in—besides the Knights Templar—the Albigensian and Manichean heresies.[13] With this voluminous work, the author, living in exile in England, tried "to please at the same time his exiled lord's house, the English government and the papacy."[14] Barruel was first to coin powerful concepts such as "world conspiracy" or "struggle against throne and altar." These expressions still belong to the propaganda vocabulary of conspiracy theoreticians.

Some decades would pass before the intellectual connection for a common Jewish–Masonic conspiracy would be made. It came out during the second half of the nineteenth century, first in France, where unlike in denominationally closed Germany, only "the front of belligerent Catholicism stood against the enlightened citizenry characteristically influenced by Jews and Freemasons."[15]

Some charges such as ritual death, desecration of the Host, or usury, are found in "classical"—primarily Christian-motivated—hatred for Jews as well as in modern racial anti-Semitism. In the same way, religious anti-Judaism already knew the thesis that the Jew was a conspirator against government.[16] The idea of the existence of a Jewish world conspiracy is present in a whole series of anti-Jewish myths, which became a solid component of Western culture, and which still recur today in the form of certain stereotyped pictures: "Jew as murderer of God, Jew as demoralizer, Jew as intellectual, Jew as usurer, or Jew as capitalist and Bolshevik" are only some of these images.[17] A decisive role in the development of these images was played by the position of Jews in the Middle Ages and the early modern economic and social order. Forcing Jews to live in ghettos, and the obligatory limitation on certain less-respected occupations, as well as many other forms of discrimination, along with the granting of privileges to a few Jews, had as a consequence the long-standing hostility toward Jews—motivated by religion—by the Christian majority. This was superimposed onto social and economic enmities.

The assertion of concrete Jewish plans to conquer the world, just like the alleged conspiracy of the Freemasons, is a product of the profound political and social process of transformation brought about by the French Revolution. The disintegration of the traditional structures of society found its expression in this transformation in the same way as the fears of the consequences of modernization did in the course of incipient industrialization. In the eyes of anti-liberal and anti-emancipatory reactionary circles, Jews appeared as representatives (exponents) and beneficiaries of this hated development. Political anti-Semitism arose in addition to Christian anti-Semitism and to social and economic hatred of Jews. The process of emancipatory-revolutionary development resulted in attacks against Jews.

In 1806, the alleged Jewish world conspiracy acquired clearer outlines. In a letter addressed to [Abbé Augustin] Barruel [1741-1820], a captain from Florence, by the name of Giovanbattista Simonini, told about the extraordinary power possessed by the Jewish community: to reach their goal—to rule the world in less than a hundred years—Jews had already infiltrated the Catholic Church; their next objective was to concentrate on the Bourbon dynasty.[18]

A further contribution to the genesis of the Jewish conspiracy legend, in no small way, was the so-called "Cemetery Episode" in the novel "Biarritz" published in 1868. The author was Hermann Goedsche, a former Prussian post office employee, who called himself Sir John Retcliffe. The book tells about a nighttime meeting in which representatives of 12 tribes of Israel had come on the Jewish Feast of Tabernacles. The subject of the meeting, which took place in a cemetery, was the question of how Jews could subjugate all other people.[19] The story of the "Cemetery Episode" appeared in 1876 in a Russian anti-Semitic inflammatory pamphlet. Five years later, it appeared in a French newspaper, "Le Contemporain," reported as though it had really happened. Generations of later anti-Semitic authors based their work on this "source," as a basis for their assertion of a conspiracy. At the end of the nineteenth century, suspicion of a Jewish conspiracy was so solid as to "take on the characteristics of an obsession."[20]

The susceptibility to anti-Jewish propaganda as a whole, and specifically to the conspiracy concept, can be traced to the processes of economic dispossession caused by industrialization, the loss of traditional commitments and value systems, and a diffuse cultural pessimism, in other words, to the consequences of modernization. Under this premise, the function of "scapegoat" found a new application—toward Jews who were considered representatives of phenomena perceived as negative by a middle-class, capitalistic social and economic order.

The concept of "anti-Semitism" was born around the end of the 1870s as an expression of the "modern" —from then on prevailing—kind of völkisch hatred of Jews.[21] The background of this concept was formed by the socio-economic crisis, the so-called Gründerkrachs [financial collapse] of 1873. Shortly thereafter, there was an intensification of anti-Jewish polemics from the Catholic camp. Because of the previously mentioned hatred for Jews—motivated for overlapping religious and völkisch reasons, a clear conceptual delineation between anti-Judaism and anti-Semitism could not be fixed in scholarly literature. Racial categories were also not new. The beginning of this völkisch concept of nation-states harks back to the time when, in the course of French occupation and wars of liberation, a specifically German national feeling developed. The concept of a people's state based on [ethnic] origin, as defined by the model of a Western state as based on the French Revolution, excluded "foreign people" who "were not of German blood." Ernst Moritz Amdt and Johann Gottlieb Fichte defined "nation" from a racial point of view, as a "*völkisch* community of fate."[22] In his "Speeches to the German Nation" (published in 1807-1808), Fichte waxed passionate about the "pure" and "uncontaminated" Germanic peoples of yore. He inveighed against "excessive foreign elements" from the West, spread the opinion that Germans had a special mission to fulfill in comparison with all other people, and ended by defining a concept of "the people" [*Volk*], according to which the individual had to take a place secondary to that of the people.[23]

It is worth noting that Fichte was a Freemason. In his oft-quoted declaration that love of one's country is the deed of the Freemason and a sense of world citizenship is his thought, Fichte attempted a synthesis of both.[24] That, however, did not hinder him from developing the concept of an exclusive German state—very much oriented against Jews—or creating the mental foundations for the conception of the higher value of German culture. At the same time, there was a characteristic shift of the great majority of German lodges from the 'enlightenment category' of humankind in general to the "call to nation and folk [people] to be the places of finding identity."[25] The dissolution of the strained relationship between cosmopolitanism and patriotism was interpreted by the circles of right-oriented lodges during the Weimar Republic years thus that Fichte had concluded that "cosmopolitanism could not really exist, therefore in reality cosmopolitanism must necessarily become patriotism."[26]

The development of racial ideology in Germany was encouraged by the reception of Gobineau's work "An Inquiry into the Inequality of Human Races."[27] The history of Gobineau's effect is chiefly connected with the figure of Richard Wagner, his Bayreuth "retinue," and particularly with his son-in-law Houston Stewart Chamberlain. Wagner himself promulgated a sharp anti-Semitism describing "the Jew" as the "most astonishing example of race-consistency that the history of world has ever delivered."[28] Chamberlain, for his part, not only reinforced strong trends to "Teutonicize" Christianity, but in 1899 he also drafted his two-volume "magnum opus," *The Foundation of the 19th Century*, in which he took over and developed Gobineau's racism into a *völkisch*-mystical ideology of an Aryan *Weltanschauung*.[29]

Social and cultural criticism directed against Jews had been entrenched in literature since the middle of the 1870s. Adolph Stoecker, the court and cathedral canon in Berlin, began his "military campaign" of hate against Jews in 1878. Stoecker was the leader of the so-called "Berlin Movement," and founder of the Christian-Social Workers' Party. He was a long-time member of the Reichstag. In 1879, the publicist Wilhelm Marr founded the "Anti-Semitic League" in Berlin, whose "aim was to rescue the German fatherland from succumbing to Jewish influence."[30] He coined the concept "anti-Semitism." In the same year, the historian Heinrich von Treitscke sparked the "Anti-Semitism-Struggle of Berlin" with a series of essays inimical to Jews. Treitscke also contributed greatly to the fact that anti-Semitism found wide diffusion and acceptance in the German middle-class educational establishment.

In the spirit of those times, which was influenced by an enthusiasm for science, the pseudo-scientific-biological theories of social Darwinism thrived. In this context, anti-Semitism became a "*Weltanschauung*."[31] It developed into a "cultural code,"[32] meaning a characteristic central element of a cluster of nationalistic, racist, antiliberal, and antidemocratic attitudes. In this kind of situation, new forms of political organizations developed qualitatively: anti-Semitic parties such as Stoecker's Christian-Social, whose only program was anti-Semitism. Moreover, anti-Semitism remained in the German empire—different from France after the Dreyfus Affair—and with it the conspiracy theory. Anti-Semitism became a method of political integration and a powerful symbol—or a code word—"accepted by the cultural, political, and social elite."[33] Just as the aim of Jewish emancipation—legal and social equality combined with social integration—was the result of enlightenment and a liberal world-view, so the crisis of liberalism in Kaiser Wilhelm's Germany furthered the spreading of anti-emancipatory ideas.

The first time the concept of a joint Jewish–Masonic world conspiracy directed against Christianity appeared was in 1869 in a book by Gougenot de Mousseaux, *Le Juif, le Judaism, et la judaisation des peubles chrétiens (The Jew, Judaism, the Hebraicization of the Christian Populace).* A little later, a grotesque accusation developed from this—that of a satanic Jewish-Masonic conspiracy, whose aim was to help the Antichrist and the Jew prepare the way to domination of the world.[34] The temporary highpoint of this artificially manufactured combination was supposedly reached with the notorious "Protocols of the Wise Men of Zion." These protocols enjoyed worldwide dissemination in millions of copies. They made a decisive contribution to the creation of the legend of a Jewish-Masonic conspiracy and its continued effect up to the present. Of fundamental significance for the lasting effect of the theory of conspiracy—excessively raised to a "system of a philosophy of history" —was that "it was summoned up by political sectarians as well as by socially and politically relevant groups, as an instrument of ideological–political struggle and propaganda."[35]

2.2 CONNECTION WITH THE JEWISH-MASONIC CONSPIRACY THEORY: GENESIS AND FUNCTION OF THE MOTTO "JEWS AND FREEMASONS"

The demagogic motto "Jews and Freemasons" was born on November 11, 1918, when the armistice took effect between the Central Powers and the Entente, and a wave of anti-Semitic and anti-Masonic publicity began its massive spread. Representatives of the monarchy had to present their traumatized people with scapegoats if they wanted to survive politically. The assertion of Masonic authorship of the assassination at Sarajevo fits this purpose perfectly, as did the myth of a Jewish-Masonic conspiracy against throne and altar, to which the Empire connected the idea of the [itself as a sacrifice] to "forces/powers superior to all nations."[6]

In this way, the defeat in war and the [economic] collapse were construed as being the result of the Jewish-Masonic conspiracy, whose "marionetteers" now would be one step farther in their aspiration to topple all monarchies and build a "world republic." Germany's path to the "Disgrace of Versailles" began with the "Masonic murder in Sarajevo" and finished with "treachery against the German army, which had not been defeated on the battlefield."

Against the background of the political and economical crises of the young republic, which began immediately, this kind of explanation was eagerly accepted, because it presented scapegoats and because it reflected the embitterment over the conditions of peace and the temporarily failed German aspirations to be a world power. In the eyes of the supporters of German nationalism and militarism, such a fictitious image presented a thoroughly effective instrument of manipulation. In other words, the unbroken claim on power of the old political and social elite found expression in the connection between "dagger-stab-legends" and the conspiracy myth, whereby the "dagger-stab-legends" functioned as "an element lending wings to the conspiracy myth."[37] Once more, periods of societal change revealed themselves as fertile fields for conspiracy theories.

One of the first, and most important, exponents of the anti-Semitic, anti-Masonic conspiracy theory was Dr. Friedrich Wichtl, the Austrian parliamentary representative, whose book *World Freemasonry—World Revolution—World Republic*[38] was published in 1919. Chronicled in it is the "politics of encirclement" of "Revolutionary Freemasonry," which had already taken over power in most countries, and flinched at nothing in its struggle against still existing monarchies. Thus, Francis Ferdinand, heir to the Austrian throne, was condemned to death by international Freemasonry, and executed by Serbian lodge brothers in Sarajevo, a statement that has remained fixed in the public consciousness into the present. Falsified court transcripts, published in 1918 under the title "The Trial of the Assassins of Sarajevo, presented as authentic by Prof. Pharos," served Wichtl as documentation. The Jesuit Father Puntigam hid behind the pseudonym "Professor Pharos."[39] The "Pharos Documents" were finally declared false in 1930, when Albert Mousset published the actual stenographic transcripts of the trial.[40] There are no reference points for any Masonic involvement in the assassination. Nevertheless, the assertion was obstinately kept alive, chiefly by the *völkisch* and nationalistic press in National Socialist propaganda. Very popular was the interpretation that "the marionetteer of the conspiracy was the Grand Orient of France." It is noteworthy that even the Grand Archivist of the Grosse Landesloge, Felix Witt-Hoë, considered Wichtl's statement an exaggeration, but declared in the same breath that "Entente-Freemasonry and, in any case, the Grand Orient of France was an accomplice—at the outbreak of the war—to the encirclement of Germany and especially to the campaign of lies against Germany during and after the war."[41]

In the meantime, the supposed "role of the Jews" in Freemasonry assumed a large significance to Wichtl. The core assertion was that the Jews "within Freemasonry would aspire to dominate in all countries"; "they had already seized power unto themselves," and now aimed to take advantage of it for the benefit of their race."[42] Wichtl's work "World Freemasonry" reached the fifth printing during the year of its first publication, and decisively influenced future relevant publications of the *völkisch*-National Socialist spectrum. The leading representatives of the "all Germany Association" discovered through Wichtl's work, the "Freemasons question," and integrated it into their nationalistic–anti-Semitic propaganda.[43] Furthermore, its influence on the young Heinrich Himmler is unmistakable. Himmler noted that it was "a book that elucidates everything and tells against whom we must fight."[44]

After Wichtl's death in 1921, his political comrades saw two more editions. Above all, Ernst Berg took on this task in 1923. Finally, in 1938, Robert Schneider prepared an enlarged and "updated" edition—that is, a modified version of Wichtl's work. In his preparation of the work, Schneider added more or less imaginative inventions about the sexual content of Masonic symbolism and ritualism and took into account the current political context: he accused the lodges of starting the Spanish Civil War.[45] Schneider was an attorney-at-law from Karlsruhe, and a former Freemason. In 1923, he was accepted in his father's lodge—at the time belonging to "Bayreuth System" —and later moved to the National Grand Lodge "Friendship." In 1929, Schneider turned his back on Freemasonry, apparently because of the refusal of the Grand Lodge journal to publish one of his speeches. As a follower of Ludendorff, he developed into a furious Mason-hater. He became a leading ideologue of the "Tannenbergbund." In association with it, he worked as an itinerant speaker. He plotted legal proceedings against Freemasonry and prepared relevant papers.[46]

Without a doubt, neither Wichtl's original publication nor one of its later editions, but rather a forgery that became known under the title "Protocols of the Sages of Zion" had the greatest effect. The so-called "Protocols" appeared first in Russia, and in all probability originated with Pjotr Ivanovich Ratschkovski. He belonged to the anti-Semitic group, the "Black Hundred," and worked in Paris as a foreign representative of the czarist secret police. Ratschkovski derives "Protocols" from a satire on Maurice Joly versus Napoleon III published in 1864 in Brussels, called "Dialogue in Hell between Machiavelli and Montesquieu." He wrote it presumably at the time of the Dreyfus Affair, thus in about 1894. One can assume that its main purpose was to deliver a document that not only proved a connection between Dreyfus and a Jewish conspiracy, but also helped to justify Russia's anti-Semitic policies.[47] Between 1903 and 1905, various editions of the "Protocols" were published; that of Sergei Nilus, who was also an agent of the Czar, had the most influence.

The supposed protocols of a supposed conspiratorial meeting disclosed the scenario of Jewish plans to conquer the world with the help of Masonic lodges that were under the influence of Jews. In order to do this, the Jews had infiltrated European states, encouraged revolutions according to the plan, and initiated socialism, liberalism, and communism. After a modest response at the beginning, the "Protocols" developed into the "classic work" on the theory of Jewish–Masonic integration—at least by the time it was absorbed into the Nazi propaganda in 1923. Not by chance has it been suggested that the origin of the "Protocols" was the Zionist congress of Basle in 1897. The goal was to nurture the concept in such a manner that political Zionism would be a "visible peak of a secret global conspiracy."[48]

At the turn of the year, 1919 to 1920, the "Secrets of the Sages of Zion" was also published in a German edition, by "Auf Vorposten" Publishers. It was edited by Ludwig Müller von Hausen, the leader of the "Society Against the Super Elevation of Judaism." A personal friend of Ludendorff's, his name was really merely Ludwig Müller; he used the name Gottfried zur Beek only as editor.[49] In a very effective way, the structure of the "Protocols" consisted of setting up, placard-like—using titles and headlines—suggestive assertions, such as the "invincibility of Jewish Masonic domination." These were not to appear in the actual translation of the supposed "Documents." Especially in the voluminous introduction and commentary, there is much written about Jewish-Masonic crimes, although in the original Russian text, Freemasons had hardly been mentioned. Müller not only kept that quiet, but also he expanded the German edition in the tradition of Wichtl's propaganda, with the component on Freemasonry,[50] and thus undertook a falsification of the falsification!

Divided into 24 chapters, the so-called "Protocols" were introduced and distributed in the form of a speech by an anonymous Jewish conspirator. The speaker reports on the current situation and progress of the conquest of the world by the "Sages." Through Freemasonry, it was possible to have access to politics, as they already had control over political parties [and thus ultimately, it is suggested, the whole parliamentary system—author's note]. Basically, they had begun undermining Christian states; now it was a question of fomenting unrest and damaging the economic system, as well as encouraging alcoholism and prostitution.[51] The grotesque story of underground galleries, tunnels, and subways with which the "Sages" would penetrate the Earth became quite famous: "Soon all important cities of the world will be honeycombed by subways. From these galleries, in case of danger to us, we shall blow up every capital with all their installations and documents."[52]

Jacob Katz rightly emphasizes that the "Protocols" were used by monarchists and nationalists in Germany to attack the republican constitution—and beyond that, the democratic–pluralistic principle as a whole—by means of exaggerating anti-Semitism [also antiliberalism—author's note].[53] The procedure consisted of solidifying widespread prejudices, fomenting a diffuse unrest with respect to complex political relations, painting the spectre of a threatening Jewish dictatorship, and finally recommending to the reader the "resurrection" of the German state on *völkisch* principles as the only way out. "What kind of national constitution can one give to a society in which corruption dominates everywhere, where one can become rich only by clever tricks and fraudulent racketeering, where lack of discipline reigns, where morality can be upheld only by punishment and strict laws (…), where love of the Fatherland and belief in God are smothered by cosmopolitan convictions? The constitution of such a resurrected society can be based only on a totalitarian government. We shall regulate all branches of the public life of our underlings by new laws, like the working of a machine."[54]

In 1923, Alfred Rosenberg seized the "Protocols" again, and disseminated his draft of a Jewish–Masonic conspiracy under the title "The Protocols of Zion's Sages and Jewish World Politics." One year later, Theodor Fritsch published a new version of the material.[55] Fritsch managed the "Hammer Press" in Leipzig, in which, among other aggressive anti-Semitic publications, a magazine with the same name appeared. His credo was "the elimination of Judaism from the life of the people." According to Fritsch, there had been an "old and honorable" kind of Freemasonry, "which took its moral goals seriously." Later came a "new falsified kind, which aimed for the stultification, corruption, subjugation, and exploitation of honest men."[56] The old Freemasonry was "Aryan" and Christian; the new one, in contrast, was Jewish. Therefore, he saw as "his first duty," the imparting of this view to "the millions of unsuspecting

Brothers." The "Freemasonry question" Fritsch went on to ask, stood in the forefront of all problems of the time.[57] Thus, the ideological field was delineated, and Freemasonry was functionally bound to the anti-Semitic concept. Although the difference determined by Fritsch was obviously completely absurd, it had as a consequence that, among *völkisch* journalists, it assumed a comparatively moderate position with respect to lodges, which consequently led to a dispute with Ludendorff.In the meantime, few other publications enjoyed such a lasting and vigorous history as did the "Protocols of the Sages of Zion." An early example of the effect and application is the anti-Semitic agitation against Walter Rathenau that led to his murder in 1922 by members of the extreme right-wing, secret society "Consul Organization." The Foreign Minister of the Reich, so it was said, was counted as one of the "three hundred Sages of Zion." It was explicitly confirmed in court by participants in the murder conspiracy that the spiritual authorship of the assassination, and the previously unprecedented hate campaign against Emil and Walter Rathenau was to be found in the "Protocols."[58]

In 1934-1935 in Bern, upon the initiative of the local Jewish community and the Federation of Swiss Jewish Communities, a trial was held that was followed all over the world. Five members of the fascist "National Front" or "Alliance of National Socialist Confederates (*Eidgenossen*)," who had also distributed copies of Theodore Fritsch's "The Protocols" during a demonstration, were charged with criminal violation of a law that forbade the printing and dissemination of "trashy literary works." In this manner, the accusers saw a chance to find the "Protocols" to be an invention and to invalidate them legally. A similar trial took place in Grahamstown (South Africa) in 1934. In both cases, it was found that the "Protocols" (in the South African trial, there were comparable "documents") were falsifications.[59]

The origin of an extraordinary anti-Masonic publication entitled "The Temple of the Freemasons" can be ascribed to the trial at Bern, which will be discussed in detail later.[60] Hiding under the pseudonym Konrad Lerich was the writer and journalist Dr. Kurt Reichl, a well-known personality in Austrian Freemasonry. He became the prime witness for the National Socialists. Apparently, Reichl let himself be involved in the Bern trials by retired Lieutenant Colonel Ulrich Fleischauer, who led the so-called "World Service." This group published an anti-Semitic magazine, with editions in many languages, which was, in turn, part of a network of the same name that operated a kind of "anti-Semitic international office." After the National Socialists took power, it was supported by the State. Fleischauer, who belonged to Theodore Fritsch's group, came onto the scene in Bern through the NSDAP (German National Socialist Workers' Party), as an expert for the accused.[61] In addition to his position as expert, Fleischhauer hoped to be permitted, with Reichl, to testify in court as a witness. For this purpose, they both went to Bern, but the court refused to listen to them.[62] Nevertheless, the contact with Reichl had as a consequence that he, Fleischhauer, received the assignment task from "World Service" "to write a short description of Freemasonry,"[63] the purpose of which was to support the developing Swiss popular sentiment against Freemasonry with propaganda.[64] It is noteworthy that to give the appearance of seriousness, the place of publication was given as Bern, not Erfurt, where the "World Service" had an office, as did "U. Bodung Publishing," founded by Fleischhauer in 1919, which had published Reichl's work. From this, it is evident that the Swiss "Frontists," in the context of the initiatives they introduced to forbid Freemasonry, tried to keep their connections with Italian Fascists and German National Socialists secret, and especially to hide their inherent dependence as much as possible.

Kurt Reichl, born in 1899, had become well known internationally for his correspondence with the Jesuit Father Gruber in 1926; he contributed to cautious rudiments of an objectivization in the relationship between Catholicism and Freemasonry. Gruber, who had the reputation as the most decisive Jesuit-Catholic enemy of Freemasonry, showed himself ready, in order to safeguard contrasts, to give up slandering polemics. Nevertheless, the famous "Aachen Conference" of 1928, in which all contacts merged and in which, in addition to Gruber and Reichl, Eugen Lenhoff and the

New York Mason Ossian Lang also participated, led to no concrete results, because they did not succeed in establishing a lasting dialog.[65]

With reference to the "Protocols" and in the spirit of the theory of integration, Kaiser Wilhelm II, who had never left a doubt about his anti Semitic position, considered "Jewish Masonic lodges" responsible for his loss of the throne, and accused them of having incited war against Germany.[66] Wilhelm's hostile position toward Freemasonry, which had already existed during his reign and included the Old Prussian lodges, was a break in the old tradition of the House of Hohenzollern. In contrast to his father and his grandfather, William II never belonged to a lodge. In all probability, he wished this fact to be understood as an expression of his strong differences with Frederic III, and the latter's liberal-constitutional views. For him, neither the heterogeneity of Freemasonry nor the estrangement that had occurred between his father and the National Grand Lodge played a role.[67] Instead of the last German Kaiser, Prince Friedrich Leopold, a great-nephew of Friederich Wilhelm IV and Wilhelm I, fulfilled the duty of being a patron of the Ancient Prussian Grand Lodges until 1918. He connected this with the office of "Master of the Order" of the National Grand Lodge, after the example of the then Crown Prince Friedrich Wilhelm.

Bismarck's anti-Masonic feeling was less strongly pronounced than that of Wilhelm II. This is apparent from his autobiography.[68] Bismarck, however, was used by the former Freemason, Robert Ebeling, for his National Socialist antilodge propaganda.[69]

The leaders of the National Socialist Party strongly supported the Jewish-Masonic conspiracy concept in general, and the "Protocols of Zion's Sages" in particular. Hitler wrote about this clearly in his book *Mein Kampf*. It is significant that he writes: "The 'Protocols of Zion's Sages' discloses with absolutely gruesome reliability the essence and activity of the Jewish population and set forth their internal relations as well as their final objectives."[70] If one can believe Hermann Rauschning, Hitler expressed on many occasions his aversion to Freemasonry, but at the same time a certain admiration for it as well as his determination to abolish lodges.[71] In *Mein Kampf*, Hitler resolutely affirmed that "the Jew" sought "to demolish racial barriers and those of civil citizenry that constantly restrict him, in order to reinforce his political position." To this end he [the Jew] fights with all his characteristic tenacity for religious tolerance" and has "an excellent instrument in Freemasonry, which has completely fallen under his control."[72] In the same way, we find in Hitler's so-called "Second Book," dictated during the early summer of 1928, that "the Jew" supported his domination "through spiritual deprivation of the people with the help of Freemasonry, as well as by the work of the press, which had become dependent on it." [73] It can be shown that previous to *Mein Kampf*, anti-Masonry had become a firm element of Hitler's anti-Semitic concept of conspiracy. Between 1920 and 1923, the stock theme of Freemasonry appeared in a number of speeches at meetings of the NSDAP, and always with the common meaning of a tool of the Jews or as "disintegration-causing" power. Freemasonry would protect Judaism "spiritually"; it was a "beater" and a "special organization" of the "Israelite alliance," a "disintegration machine" for the "clerical echelons," "a Jewish superpower," the "best," or "most potent weapon" of Judaism. For Hitler, even the hammer in the communist state symbol of the Soviet Union represented "the sign of Freemasonry."[74] Hitler's attacks against the lodges were always closely connected with the supposed conspiratorial machinations of Jews, capitalists, and Bolsheviks.

In the context of this phenomenon of historical ideology, Johannes Rogalla von Bieberstein finally took great pains to analyze the number of public officials, including those of Jewish origin in the Bolshevik Revolution, the KPD (German Communist Party), the Munich Soviet Republic, or the Komintern apparatus, in order to arrive at the so-called "real basis" of the conspiracy theory.[75] Both the fundamental stance and the value of such a methodology are extraordinarily debatable. That Jews were among those who played a leading role in the events of the revolution and that this circumstance accelerated the concept of a Jewish world conspiracy are indisputable, indeed almost banal. Which part of this had the greater importance and historical effect for National Socialist politics with respect to Jews is not clear, nor is it significant. In any case, the anti-Semites' concept of a conspiracy is insane and even older than the Russian Revolution. One must seriously doubt, therefore, that "empirical examinations of cross-connections among Masonic lodges, socialist groups, and assimilated Jews," really represent "an important desideratum" of research.[76]

In 1927, the "Ludendorff House" began its fight against so-called "international powers." Thereafter, it produced the "Ludendorff Movement," a large collection of slanderous writings and "revelations," of which this is not the place for a detailed discussion.[77] Ludendorff and his second wife, Matilda, made excessive accusations against Freemasonry, including that of high treason. They "disclosed" that lodges were places of degrading, criminal actions and were accomplices "in the more than one-thousand-year racial struggle that the Jew has waged against all people on earth."[78]

Ludendorff's obvious decline into madness did not escape even his völkisch and National Socialist contemporaries. Alfred Rosenberg, "no less an enemy of Freemasonry than the General," perceived a "psychosis"[79] in Ludendorff, who had become entangled in his own mystical numerology that cycled around Yahweh. Before his marriage to neurologist Dr. Matilde von Kemmitz in 1926, Ludendorff showed himself to be impressed by her discourses on the "German recognition of God." Under the determining influence of Matilde, "House Ludendorff" developed the theory of a conspiracy of "international powers." According to it, besides the Jewish-Masonic conspiracy, there was that of the "Church of Rome," and finally that of Tibetan monks led by the Dalai Lama.[80]

The early mistakes and "derailments" of Ludendorff and his followers had, at times, a certain comic aspect. Notwithstanding the break between the Tannenbergbund and the NSDAP, the former had a definite influence on the future policies of the National Socialist Party with respect to Freemasonry. Besides this, the general personified like no one else the connection between "the dagger stab" and "the conspiracy legend."[81]

In spite of its clearly psychopathic character, his campaign represented a new element in the history of anti-Masonry. It introduced a racial category into "the Masonic question." In 1927, Ludendorff's work, "The Destruction of Freemasonry through Disclosure of Its Secrets,"—surely one of the most repulsive of anti-Masonic publications—was published. Until the end of World War II, its sales doubled those of Wichtl's work— about 182,000 copies.[82] By adulterating and falsifying rituals used by the National Grand Lodge, Ludendorff expressed himself about the "training" of the Freemason, by making him into an artificial Jew. According to Ludendorff, within the lodges, a "transformation of race of the Aryan took place." "The Secret of Freemasonry" was "the Jew everywhere"; thus, Freemasonry was the instrument of world Judaism.[83] As false as these statements were, they were not without effect. The Ludendorff campaign reinforced one tendency within German national and *völkisch* circles: to put Old Prussian Freemasonry under pressure, because of its remaining contacts with lodges of other countries.[84] All those officials of German national and *völkisch* alliances who refused to break completely with Old Prussian lodges were also subject to attacks from within their own ranks.[85]

While Ludendorff and his group continued the debate on Freemasonry from the viewpoint of the "transformation of the race" using allegedly symbolic circumcision rituals, the slogan "Jews and Freemasons" increasingly established itself as a political weapon against the rapprochement policies of Reich Foreign Minister Gustav Stresemann. The idea of a League of Nations and "politics of fulfillment" were defamed by the nationalistic powers in Germany. In connection with this, Stresemann was stigmatized as a "lodges' politician." In 1926, the extreme right preferred to polemicize against Stresemann's supposed use of Masonic secret signs during his speech in Geneva on the acceptance of Germany into League of Nations. The occasion was given by Stresemann's clearly extensive use of Masonic vocabulary, such as the appellation in the following:

> "The Divine Master Builder of earth did not create mankind as one homogeneous whole. He gave the people different bloodstreams (sic!); He gave them their mother tongues as sanctuary

for their souls. He gave them, as native lands, countries with various characteristics. But it cannot be the concept of a divine world order, that men use their highest national achievements against each other and thus set back general cultural development again and again."[86]

On January 23, 1927, Stresemann turned to his Grand Master, Karl Habicht, and asked about his personal opinion as to whether he could respond "without reservation" to a congratulatory letter from the Swiss Grand Lodge "Alpina." Stresemann wrote that he "had to be a little careful in these matters...because they could be too easily used against me and against the whole lodge movement."[86a] Alpina had previously thanked the Nobel Prize winner in a new year's greeting "for the great peace effort" that he "had begun together with Brother Briand on Swiss soil."[86b] Habicht's opinion was clear: Alpina had "not yet found it necessary...to make up for the injustice done to German Freemasonry during the war." Stresemann should lay aside the letter "unanswered *ad acta*," because "If you answer, Grand Lodge Alpina will certainly take advantage of it, by publishing your response, and that will only give water to the mills of our opponents."[86c] In addition to Stresemann and Rathenau, other leading politicians of the Weimar Republic, such as Reich Defense Minister William Groener or Finance Minister Rudolf Hilferding, were accused by German-*völkisch* anti-Semites of participation in efforts by Jews and Freemasons supposedly destructive of the state or of high treason and treason against the homeland in connection with the fall of the Kaiser.[87] To the SS organization, "Heir of ancestors," the "Church, liberalism, Freemasonry, Judaism" were "the ideological brake-block of the past."[88] As is still to be shown, Freemasons of the right-oriented lodges not only played "their role in almost all varieties of national socialism, from the moderate to the extreme,"[89] but there were also farther-reaching intentions to put the ritual of Freemasonry on a *völkisch* basis. In Germany, the individual Masonic currents had developed separately from one another, such that even a common intellectual–political orientation of lodges was out of the question. On the other hand, a corresponding differentiation—albeit half-hearted—was made by opponents of Freemasonry, some because of ignorance and some intentionally. This goes indeed also for the National Socialists. In the ideological debate with lodges led by the SD (Security Service) starting around 1937, an impartial line prevailed that included a certain differentiation among the various trends of German Freemasonry.[90]

Given all the consistency with which lodges were rejected and fought, both because of ideological stubbornness and tactical-propagandistic calculation, National Socialist policies toward Freemasonry were largely determined by pragmatism. It is difficult to establish concretely to what extent leading National Socialist politicians were themselves influenced by the idea that Freemasonry constituted a threat. Thus, statements attributed to Heydrich in which Freemasonry would be "a guard troop of Judaism" and an "instrument of Jewish revenge"[91] worked in the framework of the then current argumentation, and show once more that Freemasonry was an element of the anti-Semitic "inventory." Himmler, above all, seemed fully convinced that "Freemasonry" was `controlled by "Judaism."Hitler, using so-called "table talks," delivered some opinions that had little thought behind them. The subjects of these talks were the "arch-Mason Roosevelt" and Schacht's "Freemasons' methods." In his opinion, also, hunting is a passion in which hunters "like a modern Freemasonry" bond with one another.[92] Hitler's further (half)-private statements, which suggest how he really thought about Freemasonry, are based on Rauschning, an unreliable source. A statement confirmed by Rauschning says: "Either us, or Freemasonry, or the Church."[93] If one follows Rauschning's depiction, Hitler went on to say, in the same context, that National Socialism borrowed certain methods and forms from Freemasonry. Among these were the "hierarchical organization and training by symbols and rites through the magical influence of cultic symbols."[94] Completely aside from [the issue of] Rauschning's credibility, it would be hardly debatable that this was true. Therefore, it is also plausible that Hitler did not think for one minute of tolerating lodges in the Third Reich. On the other hand—still according to Rauschning—Hitler explained that he "did not really believe that there was a chasm-like depth of depravity and perniciousness in this now philistine association for mutual benefit, which had always been harmless in Germany."[95] Again, we can only speculate about the value of this tradition. A few things seem to support the statement in principle; others make it appear as though it is invented. It is true, that after January 30, 1933, no priority was given to the exclusion of lodges. Also, the "Freemasonry question" received a lot of attention up to the end, and restrictions imposed against former lodge members remained in effect. Besides this, National Socialist propaganda was smart enough to take advantage of the already-established legend about a Jewish-Masonic conspiracy.

Of the leading figures of the National Socialist party, Alfred Rosenberg was more or less intensively occupied with Freemasonry on the theoretical level. His opinions and publications are unsystematic, ideologically prejudiced, and marked by a pseudoscientific style like that of most of the *völkisch*-National Socialist authors.[96] Though the position and actual positive influence of the so-called "theoretician" should not be overrated, he does stand for the inclusion of the anti-Masonic tradition with its planned continuation by the National Socialists. For example, Ludendorff's statement of the purely Jewish origin of Freemasonry was not preserved by the NSDAP. Rosenberg, however, wrote in detail on both Wichtl and the "Protocols of Zion's Sages." According to him, the "Protocols" demonstrate the role of Freemasonry as the political instrument of Judaism. Rosenberg maintained that Jewish B'nai B'rith lodges were the nerve center of the world conspiracy.[97] He and his *Völkisch Observer*, in their primitive and scruple-less propaganda, managed to list the names of members of B'nai B'rith lodges continuously through several editions,[98] as a public exposé, and an attack on the personal integrity of the victims.B'nai B'rith (Hebrew for "Sons of the Covenant") was established in 1843 in New York by a group of émigré German Jews led by Henry Jones (Heinrich Jonas). The association, with its worldwide membership, and its organizational principles, which are similar to those of Freemasonry, has been and continues to be used by anti-Semitic authors to spread conspiracy scenarios. Since B'nai B'rith founder Jones had been a member of a Masonic lodge in Germany, it is not surprising that many elements of Freemasonry flowed into B'nai B'rith's body of thought.[99] The growing anti-Semitic mood in the context of the "Berlin anti-Semitic struggle" contributed to the spread of B'nai B'rith lodges in Germany, which did not stop even in the face of the humanitarian systems of Masonic lodges. During this period, numerous disappointed Jewish Brothers turned away from Freemasonry and joined B'nai B'rith lodges. Reaction was not long in coming. On May 29, 1887, the Congress of German Grand Lodges promulgated a resolution in which B'nai B'rith was described as "a clandestine association, in which no member of the German associated lodges is allowed to join."[100] As of 1924, Dr. Leo Baeck served as President of B'nai B'rith in Germany; later he became chairman of "the representation of German Jews in the Reich." In April 1937, German lodges of B'nai B'rith were destroyed at the instruction of Himmler and their patrimony confiscated.[101]

Rosenberg, like Ludendorff, became obsessed by the Jesuits—along with Jews and Masons—who were "back in the wings of world politics." This obsession promptly precipitated itself into print. According to his anti-Catholic polemics, Jesuits were sent by "Roman trickery" to the "northern heretical lands."[102] At the beginning of Rosenberg's development of the conspiracy theme, his proximity to Wichtl['s thinking] was especially clear. Rosenberg saw Judaism as a determining element of Freemasonry and vice versa, Freemasonry had paved the way for Judaism.

Rosenberg's *magnum opus, The Myth of the 20th Century*, was published in 1930.[103] It was the attempt—overvalued primarily by the author himself—to put the *Weltanschauung* of the NSDAP, which was becoming a party of the masses, into "an all-embracing basis of racial and historical theory."[104] In the *Myth*, the alleged connection between Freemasonry and Marxism moved into the foreground. Consequently, it presented the democratic-pluralistic principle represented by Freemasonry as the precursor to the Marxist movement.[105] On the other hand, with respect to "the theory of racial conflict" favoring ideological contrasts, which had been developed in the *Myth*, the legend of the Jewish-Masonic conspiracy moved into the background. Christianity and Freemasonry were attacked as these powers that stood in the way of the "racial conflict." Both had stretched the "organic" thought of mankind, which was limited to folk and race, "by means of the principle of equality of all men before God—or the rights of man—to an 'inorganic, unlimited universalism,' which finally led to a political system of parliamentary democracy that was 'destructive of race.'"[106] In pathetic and grandiloquent language, Rosenberg challenged that "the myth of blood… alone, completely alone and without compromise, had to permeate all life."[107]

Despite a huge printing, the importance of the *Myth* was rather marginal compared with that of other popular works. Even members of the inside group of National Socialist leaders did not read their "theoretician's" book, let alone take it seriously. Hitler and his retinue were not interested in Rosenberg's efforts to cobble together a theoretical basis for National Socialism. The NSDAP counted on the appeal of the stereotypical formula "Jews and Freemasons" and thus on the continuation of the Jewish-Masonic conspiracy legend. The slogan "Jews and Freemasons," as Katz opined, "became one of the most powerful weapons of the National Socialists' propaganda campaign during the 'seizing of power' phase."[108]

In almost all sectors of the Third Reich, public and private, an undifferentiated paradigm of enmity toward Freemasonry consolidated itself— —a hatred that as a rule, followed the same thought and argumentation pattern, and that, directly or indirectly, was based on the established conspiracy theory. Its components were: Jewish origin—or as the case might be, the character of lodge ritual used by lodges; Freemasonry as an instrument of international Judaism; the humanitarian ideal, and Freemasonry's postulate of equality, as well as the international connections and the "overarching of all people" principle of the lodges.

Despite conflicts about competencies in lodge matters, a differing strength of interest in Freemasonry on the part of National Socialists leaders, and somewhat diverging conceptions, anti-Masonry was a consensual component of National Socialist ideology, whose development was well-known to be over before "the seizure of power." At the latest, before the end of World War I, anti-Masonry had integrated itself into the ideological history of anti-Semitism in Germany. An attitude directed against lodges became an element of "Common Sense" in the national milieu. In other words, it was a "cultural code" with respect to enmity toward Jews, as defined by Shulamit Volkov. The fact that many Freemasons belonged to that national milieu added fuel and a special character to the conflict. Anti-Semitism and anti-Masonry cannot be compared qualitatively. They were linked to each other to the extent that the opposition toward lodges, as a rule, was part of the ideological inventory of anti-Semitism, even where it was not transformed into a clearly defined subject. Neither during the Weimar Republic nor at the beginning of "Third Reich" did German lodges represent an element of political power. By all appearances, National Socialism nevertheless actually feared, on an ideological plane, the influence of Freemasonry. Otherwise, it would not be possible to explain the restrictions, kept to the very end, that applied to former lodge members in both the State and the Party.

As will be shown, already during the Weimar Republic, a great many German Freemasons reacted to the *völkisch*-National Socialist attacks with a mixture of tactless familiarity and emphasis on their own patriotic traditions. The idea, for instance, of opening lodge archives to the opponent was met with opposition and skepticism from the Fraternity—indeed, mainly as to the effectiveness of doing so. For example, a representative of Grand Lodge of Freemasons in Germany stated in the *Niedersächisch Logenblatt* of 1928/1929, "The wicked enemy will not believe even complete candor."[109] Voices like these had to be considered valid, since a serious examination of "the Freemasonry question" was a matter of complete indifference to the National Socialists. Otherwise, with respect to harmless and loyal lodges, it would have been difficult to maintain such an extremely strong legend of a Jewish-Masonic conspiracy.

2.3 CONNECTION BETWEEN VÖLKISCH ANTI-SEMITISM AND ANTI-ENLIGHTENMENT ANTI-MASONRY

The conspiracy theory, as already explained, has its "nourishing foundation" in "times of fundamental ideological and political-economic uncertainty."[110] It offers a simple, demonizing explanation for complex social processes that the recipient perceives as existentialist. It is not an instrument of knowledge but, directed by an interest group, it becomes a propaganda weapon with dangerous orientation, manipulation, and repressive functions.[111] In this manner, it served in historical phases of revolution and restoration, during the cultural struggle or after the collapse of the Wilhelminian Empire. As such, its propagandists—completely indifferent to anything cognitive—withdrew from any kind of rational discussion.

Anti-Enlightenment, counter-revolution, and anti-modernism are essential for the conspiracy myth. Much research has already shown the fundamental attitude of Hitler and other National Socialist leaders against the Age of Enlightenment and Intellectualism.[112] Hitler was of the opinion that within the citizenry, the "wrong part" had taken command, precisely those who lacked "heroic" and "epic" qualities. The intellectuals were that layer of citizenry particularly close to the Jews. The emancipation of women was an invention of "Jewish intellectualism."[113] What Freemasonry had introduced "into circles of the so-called intelligentsia concerning a general pacifist paralysis of the instinct of national self-preservation," was publicized by the "Jewish press."[114]

Reactionary, *völkisch*, and National Socialist powers had a well-defined view of the enemy, consolidated with a whole group of national, anti-emancipatory, and anti-intellectual categories. These were the prime examples in a pamphlet published in 1929 entitled "Murder of the Future." It states that the "intellectual class," which had existed since the time of Voltaire, was the "procreator of all thinking and spiritual powers; it had undermined and was continuing to destroy "that which is biologically healthy and right." Optimistic belief in progress, social democracy, the women's movement, reconciliation among peoples, free commerce, freedom of thought, … equality of humankind, … the story of the genesis of all this sham belief would lead, sooner or later, back to intellectualism." The intellectual, it was concluded, would be the "real world citizen, above nations and peoples."[115]

Artur Moeller van den Bruck, who had already coined the concept "Third Reich,"[116] called the republican form of state a "rule by parties." This was considered the antithesis to the concept of the "Third Reich," in which he saw the "German nation of the future," or "realm of the great German union," and the "realm of intra-societal pacification in the thought of the common nation."[117] Reason, which determined the essence of modernity, was rejected as destructive and divisive in favor of categories that corresponded to the "laws of life." A sharp anti-intellectualism paralleled this bio-logistic super-elevation of life, which Moeller expressed by placing the category of judgment in opposition to intellect, which he associated with the political left.[118] Besides a clearly defined anti-liberalism and rather common resentment of the concept of Republic and its constitutional organs, anti-intellectualism here appears as a constitutive ideological element of *völkisch* nationalism and the "conservative revolution." It is significant that the anti-intellectual model of integration seized the *völkisch* portion of Freemasonry. Kurt Schmidt, chairman of a group of right-oriented Masonic lodges associated with the so-called "Wetzlar Ring,"[119] set "national feeling" and "the thinking of the world citizen" as antipodes in the debate on the concept of the world citizen. National feeling, according to Schmidt's words, derives from "immediate experience." On the other hand, cosmopolitan thought comes "only from mediated experience—that is, filtered through the medium of the intellect." Also, "the 'intellectuals' of all classes of life," who have become accustomed to giving priority to this "mediated experience," and thereby put intelligence higher than feeling, would be advised "to have no illusions about the real relationship of power[s]."[120]

Meanwhile, Moeller van den Bruck, like most politically right-oriented authors of his time, concerned himself with the "Freemasonry question" in the area of journalism. In his case, the implicit anti-Masonic idea shows a peculiarity that deserves our attention. For Moeller, the rejection of Freemasonry at first stood in the context of antiliberalism. He hawked the conspiracy scenarios with little originality. In contrast to the popular patterns of argumentation, however, he explained that "it had not always been a policy of enlightenment to which Freemasonry had dedicated itself," that "secret associations" sometimes would have had "the most opposite purposes," and that Freemasonry itself was "indeed, even the most changeable." Moeller espoused the rhetorical question as to whether this "changeability" did not contain a reference to the "peculiarity of its mental status," in order to make lodges, as a specific manifestation, fit his concept of anti-liberalism: the history of Freemasonry proceeds with a "loosening of principles, which presupposes a certain specific [kind of] person," meaning the "liberal person."[121] While he denounced the so-called "changeability" as a liberal lack of principles, and simultaneously clung to the idea that something like "Freemasonry" [as an institution] existed, he refrained from any serious debate with politically right-oriented German lodges.

In its political, social, and racist character, modern anti-Semitism was the expression of a societal power for which abolishing the legal equality of Jews and—as the case may be—revising of the idea of emancipation *in toto* was important. There is much evidence that the basis of this opposition movement had already been planted. In contrast to France, where, at the National Assembly of 1791, the immediate and total equality of Jews was instituted, emancipation was half-hearted in the German component states; it proceeded in stages, and moreover, was fraught with exceptions and backslidings. In the individual states, emancipation laws [for Jews—trans. note] were passed at different times. They were educational (in the sense of Christian Wilhelm Dohm) or motivated by economics and more like exemplary achievements than rights to which Jews had a claim. In the German territories occupied by Napoleon, the granting of equality resulted in emancipation edicts remaining connected with national[istic] anti-French resentment and were revoked. The Prussian emancipation edict of 1812, on the other hand, was the work of Hardenburg's liberal politics of reform, not the result of a large public change of consciousness. Taken together, the kind and duration of the emancipation process was not seen as irreversible. While the model of national integration in France rested "on the foundation of universal principles" since the French Revolution, the German model had been marked "by the idea of the Nation as a closed ethnic-cultural community" since the "Romanticism revolution."[121a] As a result, the equality of Jews was again brought into a serious question, right after it had been made legally secure in the 1871 imperial constitution, and without having become a social reality.[122]

National Socialist politics took up the anti-Semitic programs of the late nineteenth century, refined them, and implemented them. Directly tied to the phenomenon called "elimination" of Jews, the objective was to nullify the Revolution of 1789, "whose achievements dictated rules of life for western humanity for more than a century," as Engelbert Huber explained in his book published in 1934, *Freemasonry: The World Power behind the Scenes.*[123] Huber supported in detail the thesis in which Judaism and Freemasonry, since the French Revolution, were "indissolubly" tied with each other. He characterized Jews as conspirators and "beneficiaries" of the revolutionary development.[124] The race theory and its basic ideas of different values, "racial constraints," and national character as a determining element turned itself against the enlightenment concept of human rights, individual freedom, and equality. Dr. Alfred Franz Six, previously the national leader of the SD, became in 1939, director of Office II ("Worldview Exploitation") in the Main Security Office of the [Third] Reich, and after the reorganization, he became director of Office VII ("Worldview Research and Exploitation"). He was thus responsible for the theoretical-propagandistic "fight against the enemy." He had expressed his point of view on this subject in various publications, and thus underscored the hostility of the Third Reich to Western democracies. National Socialism "in all its postulates" represented "an antithesis to the West, a world in contrast to the leveling tendency of the interpretation of humanity of democratic parliamentary nihilism, the rule of the majority and the inferior."[125] In the same vein, Rudolf von Sebottendorf, founder of the "Thule Association," expressed similar opinions. In 1918, he wrote: "We repudiate the teaching of Freemasonry that conditions, circumstances, and relationships shape people. This is a teaching that Marxism has espoused… We do not recognize a Universal Brotherhood, but only *völkisch* interests, we do not recognize a brotherhood of men but only blood brotherhood … We hate the motto of equality … We are not democrats … Democracy is Jewish."[126]

In this connection, it is noteworthy that after liberation from National Socialism, the breakdown in civilization committed by the Germans through right and new-right ideologues, even up to the present, is still being reinterpreted. In the course of self-exoneration, the mass crimes which, despite "modern" execution, were a project of counter-Enlightenment, were reversed into their conceptual opposite and presented as a product of a radicalized, emancipatory modernism.

Jews and Freemasons were attacked by a conspiracy thesis directed against them equally by monarchists, clerics, and right-radical circles, as exponents of the republican-democratic system and the ideal of equality. The conspiracy thesis therefore constituted an "anti-modern picture of the enemy who … unified conservatives and National Socialists into a common combat position."[127] The principle of the internationality of Freemasonry—even if it was not, by a long shot, practiced in all lodges—nonetheless offered the opportunity to stigmatize the lodges as anti-German.[128]

After the collapse of the Prussian and Hapsburg monarchy, Prince Otto von Salm-Horstmar, a key figure of the Pan-Germany movement, who had promoted the publication of the *Protocols of the Sages of Zion*, protested against the struggle of opposing world views: the Jewish-democratic principle was fighting the Jewish-aristocratic principle.[129] Looking at the legend of the Jewish-Masonic conspiracy from the point of view of its creators—indeed, therefore, from the point of view of expediency—it is hard to be surprised by the fact that Jews and Freemasons became an ever stronger conceptual unit and, in this connection, Freemasons were quickly declared "disguised Jews." The elite of the *Ancien Régime* had represented the Revolution of 1789 as being the result of the transferring of Masonic organizational principles onto the level of the political system. The concept that Freemasonry overarches class and religion was thought of as subversive, a power destructive of legitimate societal values. Accordingly, the old order was undermined by ideas immediately associated with Freemasonry. In the nineteenth and twentieth centuries, these paradigms were the basis of a transformation process, in the course of which the "historical-theological elements retreated more and more to the background in favor of worldly, political actions."[130] It was a development that was continued and sharpened in National Socialism. The idea of a Masonic conspiracy directed against throne and altar was also "stripped of its Christian-religious image,"[131] as a clerical-counterrevolutionary theorem of a supposed Jewish conspiracy. The two threads of conspiracy, which before had been united into one, were developed in the mass propaganda of National Socialism as needed, congruent with the theory of race, and were made into a supposed conspiracy of international Jewry with the aid of Masonic lodges against Germany.

At about the same time that Alfred Franz Six assumed command of the Central Department II/1 of the SD Main Office, a report from the subordinate section responsible for lodges concluded that Freemasonry would be able "even at the present to enforce its influence in most nations." Further, "with its ideological basic concept, it prepared [the way for] the emancipation of Jews, in order to determine the development of the last two centuries and be the trailblazer for internationalism, pacifism, League of Nations."[132] Six himself espoused the view that "without the preparatory work of Freemasonry, the destruction of European private and public life would have been unthinkable ...."[133] In a voluminous inflammatory pamphlet of 1937 entitled "Judas' Struggle and Defeat in Germany," it states: "the Jew used the French Revolution "to slip secretly under the ringing tones of liberty, equality, and fraternity inside the body and whole life of nations."[134] The author, Ernst Earl von Reventlow, had already made himself known both as a publicist and NSDAP Reichstag delegate during the Weimar Republic in the propaganda war against Freemasonry. According to another National Socialist work, it refers both to "the fragmenting front of racist-*völkisch*-class traditions," and to an "international, anti-popular, anti-racist world front," which has one "all-world mischmasch of people in mind."[135] Also in Rosenberg's *Myth*, it was stated that from the "teaching of humanity … the 'religion' of the Freemasons … the political motto of the last 150 years was coined: 'liberty, equality, fraternity,' and the chaotic destroyer of people, 'humane' democracy, was born."[136] Traditional anti-Masonry, sharply defined by the anti-Enlightenment spirit and the racist ideology of the "Third Reich," converged in their rejection of the principle of equality and in their effort to unhinge it. The sense in which the National Socialists wanted to classify historically even the Nuremberg laws on race[137] is immediately clear in the commentaries written by Wilhelm Stuckart and Hans Globke on German race legislation. They clearly stated that the National Socialist thinking on race means "an estrangement from liberalistic principles of equality of all men";[138] whence, at the same time, the *Führer* principle was derived. The (pre)supposition that the national character is based on "one or more races that are essentially equal in nature" was still denied from time to time because it was "out of the old liberal thought that all men are equal by nature."[139] On the other hand, "blood and race" in the end would form the National Socialists' world- and historical vision: The "Germanic conceptual world" would be set in opposition to "Romance thought," and likewise the "people's [*Volks*] community" in opposition to the principle of the individual.[140]

According to a work published by the NSDAP, whose title was "the Eternal Jew," the "Humboldt-Hardenberg law of March 11, 1812 (the edict of emancipation—author's note) and Adolph Hitler's law for the protection of German blood and German honor of 15th of September 15, 1935 …, were "the beginning and the end of the absolute domain of Judaism in Germany."[141] The pamphlet "Why the Aryan Paragraph?" by the Racial

Policy Office of the NSDAP expressed in the same vein the idea that "with the Enlightenment and the French Revolution, the barriers between Jews and Germans had fallen."[142] There are corresponding comments in von Reventlow's publication—already cited—that leave no doubt about the political aims of racial laws and their historical implications. According to them, Hitler "took the Jew ... out of German life, after he [the Jew], having constantly pushed at the crack in the door opened by the French Revolution of 1789, was finally able to push himself completely through it."[143]

If the state system of the *Ancien Régime* was still sacredly legitimized, the glorification of the 'Aryan race,' 'Folk,' and 'Fatherland' in the nineteenth and twentieth centuries in Germany increasingly took on ever sacred characteristics. Ludendorff's idea of a religion "appropriate to race and nature" represented a tumor on this development, which reached its zenith in deification of race in the Third Reich. Hitler had already said in *Mein Kampf* that he believed he acted "in the same vein as the Omnipotent Creator," in that he warded off the Jew, as he announced, "I fight for the work of God."[144]

The National Socialists did not want to go back to a class society of the old sort. The tradition-bound part of its ideological concept, however, agreed with the program of the restorative, German-nationalistic, and religious circles and thus also with the ideas of Old Prussian Freemasonry. Certainly, it should be seen as an illusion that conservative national forces would be able to stop National Socialists in their criminal radicalism. This expectation was widespread, however, among the members of the national Grand Lodges. Also, people worked to convince the new government of the seriousness of its own political mobilization. Goebbels clearly showed how little promise this held, at a time (in 1934) when Grand Lodges, which had transformed themselves into German-Christian orders, still survived. It was in the "execution of affairs" that "Fascism, from its anti-liberal and anti-pacifistic position, had to declare a fight to the death on Freemasonry, because even it [Freemasonry] was identical with the spiritual centre of Marxism."[145]

Freemasonry, in the eyes of the National Socialistic *Weltanschauung*, was not simply the representative of liberalism, individualism, and Enlightenment. The organizational structure of the lodges also stood fundamentally in contrast to the concept of the uniformly, hierarchically divided, and racially composed "popular community." The separation espoused by the Old Prussians between national-Christian and humanitarian Freemasonry was condemned to failure—indeed in a double way—because of the requirement of complete organizational inclusion, it was unimportant to which essential principles the current Fraternity subscribed. A distinction of essence between grand lodges would have had, in turn, as a consequence, that the concept expressed and introduced by the Freemasons would have lost propagandistic attraction.

Chapter 3

FREEMASONRY IN THE "FORCE-FIELD" OF THE WEIMAR REPUBLIC

3.1 THE OLD PRUSSIANS EN ROUTE TOWARD VÖLKISMUS: TRADITION AND CONFORMITY

The lost war, its sociopolitical results, and the fall of the monarchy were felt as deeply humiliating by large segments of the German people. Making it worse, before the cease-fire, the public, for the most part, had been left uninformed or deceived about the real military situation. The nobility, the nationalistically minded citizenry, the Reichs Army, and the moderate to extreme right-wing mourned the loss by the German Reich of its role as a world power. As a result, people were not ready to accept the postwar scheme of things as a political foundation. The elite functionaries succeeded in shoving off the responsibility for the defeat and peace terms onto the opponents of the war, the democratic politicians in Germany, and especially the so-called "November criminals" [those who surrendered on November 11, 1918—trans. note]

The German Freemasons were affected by the fall of the monarchy and the national trauma caused by the "legend of the dagger-thrust" in two ways: by far, most of them were at a loss, finding themselves under fire from society because of the aggressive propagandizing of the "Jewish-Masonic Conspiracy." In addition, the worsening of the economic situation as a result of war and inflation did not spare the lodges and their members. The German Freemasons were thus limited in their spheres of action by financial considerations. The assets of the grand lodges and Masonic foundations were merged. At the same time, as a direct consequence of war, the financial arrangements of the lodges for widows and orphans were especially taxed.[1] In light of this, a defense fund was set up by the Große Landesloge, which supported the subordinate lodges, sometimes also the *Abwehrredner* ["defense speakers": lodge members who walked the tightrope of hewing to the party line, yet influencing the local populace in favor of Freemasonry....—trans. note], and covered legal costs as well.[2]

The erection of a memorial by the Große Landesloge to the Brethren who had fallen in the First World War affords an insight into the economic situation of Freemasonry: the process took from 1920 right up to the dedication in 1926. When the Grand Master announced the project in May 1920 and asked for contributions from the membership, he found internal support. Money was also collected in some subordinate lodges. For example, the lodge in Saarbrücken collected five Reichsmarks per member; the lodge in Bremen gave 1000 Reichsmarks; the one in Stettin 580, as did Lübeck; and others participated with comparable contributions. Considering the general economic situation and the estimated cost of 70,000 Reichsmarks, the Master of the subordinate Lodge "Nordstern" (North Star) in Rendsburg said, "with a bleeding heart," that "temporarily we can give nothing." It was suggested that the erection of the monument "be postponed until a better time."[3] A memorial plaque was finally laid inside the lodge hall in Eisenach Street, the erection of which was considerably less expensive than the originally planned one of limestone.

At its solemn dedication on October 31, 1926, for which Reichs President von Hindenburg sent a congratulatory message,[4] Grand Master Müllendorf opined that "history would tell of the enemy's falsehood and deceit, Germany's victory and humiliation, hopes and disappointments, desperate grappling and struggling for a threatened existence." Müllendorf said he was dedicating the memorial with three hammer blows "under the flag that the Brothers followed, and for which they fought, as a lasting reminder of the three duties of German men: Trust in God! Love the Fatherland! Courage to Sacrifice … At its foot I lay this laurel wreath, decorated with the black, white, and red colors for which our Brothers died."[5]

The German grand lodges, on average, lost about one percent of their members during the war. That is clearly under the more than three percent that the German Reich chalked up to losses of its whole population. From this, however, no one can deduce a "lack of patriotic readiness to participate actively" on the part of Freemasons, because the average age of the lodge members was over 50.[6] In the eyes of the dyed-in-the-wool Freemason-haters, though, that meant as little as the fact that many lodge buildings were put at the disposal of the authorities for use as temporary military hospitals. Equally vain were the efforts of the "Reichsbund jüdischer Frontsoldaten" (Reichs Federation of Jewish Soldiers on the Front, founded in 1919 and later numbering 50,000 members) and the Old Prussian Masons to use their statistics as a defense against the völkisch polemics aimed at them. The names of the lodge members killed or wounded were compiled and published.[7] Extreme right-wing groups— like the "Thule Gesellschaft" (Thule Society), the "Deutsche Turnerbund" (German Gymnastics Association), reactionary student associations, or other "patriotic" organizations—were completely unimpressed. They continued their attacks, which were effective in a mass-psychological way—indeed, usually without differentiating among the different lodge systems. Ludendorff's "Tannenbergbund" (Evergreen Mountain Association) carried on the harassment most vehemently, using "all methods of demagoguery."[8] In the "Alldeutschen Verband" (Pan-German Union) there were also anti-Masonic efforts, though indeed the "Freemason Question" was emphasized differently, and greater distinctions were made between Romance and German[ic] Freemasonry. The mood inimical to the lodges had quickly shifted to such right-oriented organizations as the "Nationalverband Deutscher Offiziere" (National Union of German Officers) or the "Stahlhelm," to which many Old Prussian Freemasons belonged. For this reason, the debate was focused on the question as to what extent the Old Prussians and the Humanitarians had to be differentiated. Those efforts, which rejected every form of Freemasonry in this regard, resulted in altercations with the pro-Old Prussian faction, lasting for years, among the leading opinion makers.[9]

The majority of members of established German lodges were unprepared and irritated as they reacted to the new situation: they were patriotic and loyal to the Emperor in their basic sociopolitical attitudes. Loyalty to the fatherland and Emperor had been instilled especially in the Old Prussians from birth.[10] Like large segments of German citizenry, they had approved of the Weimar Constitution "only hesitantly or not at all."[11] They belonged to the opponents of the system: they shared this role not only with individuals of the power elite, but also with large segments of the educated citizenry who opposed democracy from the beginning.[12] In addition, the old and new middle classes, as well as some of the workers— of course for other reasons—distanced themselves from, or even rejected, the parliamentarian State of Weimar. The "republic without republicans" belonged "to the heaviest burdens of the first German democracy."[13] For the Old Prussians, who were formerly granted privileges by the ruling house, the new state of affairs represented a loss of status.

While *völkisch* forces attacked the lodges as "jewed," liberal, and pacifistic, the enmity against the bourgeois institution Freemasonry was formulated in different ways and in sharp words from the opposite perspective including that of communist theoreticians. Lodges were never tolerated in the Soviet Union. Similarly, Freemasonry was forbidden in the Communist states of Eastern Europe after 1945, and indeed in all Communist countries except Cuba. On the ideological level, Trotsky's position in *Izvestia*, in 1923, can be seen as an example. According to it, especially French Freemasonry was a "plague-boil of Communism," a reactionary influence against it. "[French Freemasonry] is the capitalistic enemy of Communism; it is as backward as the Church, as Catholicism. It dulls the sharpness of the class struggle with mysticism, sentimentality, and moralistic formulas." It "and its adherents" had to be "rooted out with glowing irons, because it weakens the teaching of Communism, with its bourgeois (middle class) journalists... Better a communistic society of only 50,000 able-bodied men, than one Freemason among 100,000 of them."[14] Already in 1922, the Fourth World Congress of the Communist International, which overwhelmingly stood under the sign of the unit[ed]-front policy (Einheitsfront Politik), had concerned itself with Freemasonry. It was declared to be "an unconditional necessity" that the leading organs of the Party "break down all bridges, that lead to the middle class, and for this reason also to make a radical break with Freemasonry." The chasm that separated the proletariat from the middle class had to be made completely clear to the members of the Communist Party. A fraction of the leading elements of the Party had wanted to try "to build disguised bridges across this chasm, and use the Masonic lodges [for their own purposes]." Freemasonry was the most "dishonest and infamous swindle of the Proletariat on the part of the radical-leaning middle class. We see ourselves forced to fight against it to the extreme."[15]

The widespread notion that one could derive from the anti-Masonic attitudes of Bolshevism and National Socialism an equally persistent philosophical contrast to the Soviet system and National Socialism—that is an antagonism between Freemasonry and so-called "totalitarianism"— does not stand up to critical testing; the manifestations of Freemasonry in Germany were too diverse. Furthermore, such an interpretation aimed at a totalitarian model leaves the self-image of the national-Christian lodges completely out of consideration. Those lodges experienced the conflict between their own basic political outlook and the enmity of the *völkisch* circles. This conflict, in many respects, is comparable to the sociopolitical situation of the group of "over-assimilated" German-nationalistically thinking Jews in the face of the ever-increasing anti-Semitism after the

First World War. Because of the heterogeneity of German Freemasonry, there existed equally diverse outlooks with respect to Communism. While the majority of lodges, in their idealistic view of society, separated themselves more or less brusquely from historical materialism, there was within the Grand Lodge "Aufgehende Sonne" (Rising Sun) and Symbolische Großloge (Symbolic Grand Lodge) the emphasis that at least the original teaching of Karl Marx did not stand in fundamental opposition to Freemasonry.

The poles of the political sphere of influence met in the opposition to Freemasonry, but there was a serious qualitative difference. In the eyes of the Communists, the lodges represented a specific manifestation of the middle-class society, and as such, they were opposed. For the *völkisch*-National Socialistic camp, Freemasonry had, *ex negativo*, a quasi-constitutive function: it was a synonym for the liberalistic, Western, democratic-pluralistic—"Jewish-Masonic" principle—of which the *völkisch*-National Socialistic camp defined itself as the antithesis. In Bolshevik propaganda, the lodges did not have nearly the value they did for the political right-wing, and the effect of the [right-wing] propaganda was lasting. The main characteristic of public discussion was an ideologically bound confirmation of existing patterns of judgment and opinions, not a consciousness-building based upon reflection. At the same time in the 1920s, the intellectual Right developed the worldview framework of the *völkisch* State—ideologically loaded and characterized by esprit de corps: "a combination of Radicalism, world-view impulse, and a specific form of cleverness—an ideological internal rationality, on one hand, and an efficient and rational *modus operandi* combined with a fundamental assumption of 'objectivity' on the other hand."[16] The intellectual historical as well as the biographical continuities that stretched from Weimar through the "Third Reich" into the Federal Republic are strikingly manifest in the person of Dr. Werner Best, the future Chief in the Main Office of the Security Police and the Reichs Main Security Office.[17] Best, in his news service or secret police work, as well as in his personal life,[18] came into contact with the "Freemason question." He was the one, who, before the "seizure of power" in the intellectual context of a "fight for the sake of fighting," coined the concept of "heroic realism" harking back to Ernst Jünger. For Best, National Socialism represented an inner attitude that "affirmed the truth of the peace-less world, filled with struggle and tension."[19] As will be shown, such mindsets found resonance with some of the German lodges. Usually, however, they functioned as contrary ideas to the Masonic principle of humanity.

In the meantime, after the breakup of the federation of German grand lodges, the "Jewish question" figured prominently in intra-Masonic discussions. As already mentioned in the previous chapter, after the Dreyfus affair, anti-Semitism remained effective in Germany—unlike in France—as a means of political integration and was accepted among society's elite.[20] This was manifested, for example, as renewed anti-Jewish dogma in 1924 in the Grand Lodge "Zur Freundschaft." Its members, so the rule now read, had to qualify as men, "who were rooted in the German folk and stood on the ground of the Christian outlook."[21] The Große Landesloge, especially, never let an opportunity pass to emphasize to opponents of Freemasonry that Jews had never been accepted in its ranks.[22]

At the end of 1930, the Große Landesloge emphasized its separate direction by adding the name "German-Christian Order,"[23] which would become its sole name in 1933. That was attributed to the considerable increase in votes for the Nazi Party at the time of the Reichstag elections in September [1930]. *The Hamburger Logenblatt (Hamburg Lodge Paper)*, on the other hand, commented on that step with the prediction that the next step would probably be the splitting up of Freemasonry.[24] After the "seizure of power," the relinquishing of Masonic identity externally did occur, not only by the Große Landesloge. Continuing this development, the former Große Landesloge Grand Master Friedrich Bolle still insisted—even in 1940—on the differentiation between specifically national-*völkisch* Freemasonry and world Freemasonry.[25] As a result of Bolle's early pronouncements, already in 1925, the administrative council of the Große Landesloge, considered putting aside the Masonic forms of the order.

Since about 1926, there had been distinctly noticeable efforts within the Nationalmutterloge (National Mother Lodge Three World Globes) and the Große Landesloge to free the whole usage from Jewish or Old Testament traditions, and to "root out" Jewish influences by changing the ritual to Germanic-"Aryan" usage.[26] Ideas of this kind were not unusual, especially as discourse about race was gaining significance within Masonry. Indeed, they were in the context of an ideological change in orientation, a change that was driven by the leadership of the Order as well as having been brought to the Grand Lodge by the Brethren. In the case of the demand for abolishing Jewish symbolism, religious motives may have been uppermost. However, the demand cannot be reduced to just these motives. Anti-Semitism had long ago become a structural part of society in the national scene. In contrast to Neuberger,[27] it must be emphasized that the relative reticence with regard to the "Race Question" of the Old Prussian Grand Lodge functionaries—practiced in public, but given up after the "seizure of power"— can by no means be interpreted as a token of fundamental differences with National Socialism.

Significant for the widespread passive anti-Semitism in Old Prussian Freemasonry was the reaction to the demand of the chairman of the "National Association of German Officers" and former military educator, Count Waldersee. On February 28, 1925, he called upon the Old Prussians to take part in the struggle against Judaism. The three Old Prussian grand masters refused. In order not to anger the National Association, but to weaken objections, people reacted very cautiously and emphasized in the reply that they had given enough proof of nationalistic and Christian convictions.[28]

Felix Witt-Hoë, a retired major and military attaché, who held the office of Grand Archivist and later that of first Deputy Grand Master within the Große Landesloge, wrote a detailed 51-page rebuttal of the attacks of the National Association put forth in the letter of February 28 and at other times. In it, Witt-Hoë, who was also the sitting Master of the Berlin Grand Lodge subordinate lodge, "Minerva," communicated, among other things, that neither the "Ancient Obligations" nor the "cosmopolitical goals of the humanitarian lodges, nor the efforts of the Union of German Freemasons (…) had anything in the least to do with the aims and modus operandi of the Große Landesloge."[29] The letter also says, regarding the insistence of the National Association of German Officers that Old Prussians had "pacifistic fundamentals": "in none of the levels of the Große Landesloge is the struggle, whether spiritual, moral, naturo-philosophical, or for upholding of honor, disputed as being necessary."[30] This opinion came from an authority: Witt-Hoë, as a prominent Freemason in Berlin and a Grand Lodge functionary, played a key role in the politics of resistance coordinated by him, and in the worldview alignment of the Große Landesloge as codetermined by him. An officer of the second rank, he indelibly imprinted the outward character of the Große Landesloge.

Despite the widespread anti-Masonic agitation, and despite the economic need of many of the Brethren, there were at first, during the Weimar years, very few resignations from lodges for political or economic reasons:[31] an expression of the continuing high degree of capacity for integration in the lodges. Moreover, Freemasonry in Germany, which had survived the [First World] War relatively unscathed, recorded a constant growth in membership: many new lodges were founded. The peak of membership was reached in 1925 with more than 82,000 Brothers and 632 St. John's Lodges. In detail at this time: the National Mutterloge (Mother Lodge) had 22,896 members in 171 lodges, and the Große Landesloge had 23,039 members in 168 lodges, which temporarily meant the top position, which it lost the following year to the Drei Weltkugel (Three World Globes) Grand Lodge. The Grand Lodge Zur Freundschaft (Friendship) had up to 11,000 Brothers in 96 lodges. The Grand Lodge of Saxony was the largest among the humanitarian lodges with 7502 members in 40 lodges, followed by the Grand Lodge of Hamburg with 6000 in 61 lodges, the Grand Lodge Zur Sonne (Sun) with 4041 in 39 lodges, the Eclectic Federation with 3475 in 25 lodges, the Grand Lodge Deutsche Bruderkette (German Brother-Chain) with 1730 in 5 lodges, and finally the Darmstadt Grand Lodge Zur Eintracht (Harmony) with

876 Brothers in 10 lodges. In addition, the statistics show 1635 Brethren in 17 independent lodges.[32]

After 1925, the membership numbers began to fall, but not the number of lodges, however, except for those under the Grand Lodge of Hamburg. In 1932, the established grand lodges counted 71,285 Brethren in 658 St. John's Lodges. Except for the Grand Lodge Deutsche Bruderkette and the Darmstadt Grand Lodge, all systems had lost membership. Individually, the grand lodges showed the following numbers: the Drei Weltkugel Grand Lodge had 21,000 members in 183 lodges; the Große Landesloge had 20,400 members in 180 lodges; the Grand Lodge Zur Freundschaft had 9370 members in 108 lodges; the Grand Lodge of Saxony had 6920 members in 47 lodges; the Grand Lodge of Hamburg had 5000 members in 54 lodges; the Grand Lodge Zur Sonne had 33,335 members in 41 lodges; the Eclectic Federation had 2570 members in 25 lodges; the Grand Lodge Deutsche Bruderkette had 1800 members in 10 lodges; and finally the Darmstadt Grand Lodge Zur Eintracht had 890 Brothers in 10 lodges.[33]

The lodges in general enjoyed great popularity as "places of meeting for like-minded people, away from political differences and economic misery,"[34] until the middle of the 1920s and beyond. Since 1920, more and more individual subordinate humanitarian lodges left their jurisdictions and transferred to the Old Prussians. The system change for "Amalia" Lodge in Weimar, which left the Grand Lodge of Hamburg and went to the National Mother Lodge, is one example of this trend. The conflict surrounding "Amalia" Lodge began when the Lodge "Zur Vaterlandsliebe" ("Patriotism" or "Love of Native Land") in Wismar had proposed the motion "to remove the former Settegast Lodges from allegiance to the Grand Lodge of Hamburg" in the previous year. The Settegast Lodges, allied with "Romance" Freemasonry, had adopted very little of an appropriate mindset vis-à-vis the German national feeling.[35] Altogether, 13 lodges, among them "Amalia", supported this demand. As attempts at negotiation on the part of the administration of the Grand Lodge [of Hamburg] failed, the right-leaning lodges withdrew.

These "transfers" illustrate the "political radicalization and polarization"[36] of German Freemasonry, which became more bitter the harder
the Old Prussians and some of the Humanitarians tried to adapt to the
extreme right. These adaptation attempts increased as the *völkisch* and
National Socialistic forces gained political influence. In fundamental
orientation, German majority Freemasonry was reflected in the old and
new middle class: it supported neither the communistic-socialistic nor
the pluralistic-capitalistic, but the authoritarian-*völkisch*-Nazi concept.

In the meantime, the intra-Masonic conflict, which "increasingly
took on the characteristic of massive enmity,"[37] was carried on primarily
at the grand lodge functionary level, to which one might add that contradiction was hardly articulated at the local level. The Große Landesloge
maneuvered itself methodically into an "ultra-right position"[38] under its
longtime Grand Master Eugen Müllendorff, an engineer and Ph.D., who
can be considered a key figure in Christian Freemasonry in the Germany
of the Weimar years. Müllendorff, according to the contemporary judgment of Lennhoff and Posner, was the "exponent of that stiffly dogmatic
attitude of Old Prussian Freemasonry" that "contributed so much to the
splitting of German Freemasonry."[39] Of course, the philosophical world-
view of the Große Landesloge was in no way primarily the work of one of
its grand masters. Rather, such a political position lay in the continuity
of the historical development of the institution of the Große Landesloge,
and was carried on in the same way by the rest of the administration.

The Worshipful Master of the Munich Lodge "Empor" ("On High,
Upward"—under the Nationalmutterloge (National Mother Lodge Three
World Globes) included himself with those who felt called to place Old
Prussian Masonry on a "racist base." He was a privy councilor, by the
name of Sanna, who considered it a capital idea to invite the Freemason-
hater Erich Ludendorff to an "enlightenment soirée." Clearly, it was his
purpose to convince the General of the *völkisch* philosophy of his lodge,
as well as to exploit his name for his own goals. Astonishingly, Ludendorff
actually showed up for the visit on May 2, 1923. Alleged opinions that

he must have revised his opinion of Freemasonry were later disputed by him. The General, entrapped in his mad imaginings, was not to be moved to a change of opinion on Freemasonry. His entry in the guest book of the Lodge revealed nothing new: The Fatherland required that national German Freemasonry "form hard characters and raise movers and shakers," wrote Ludendorff.[40]

Wilhelm II proved to be equally unteachable: From his Dutch exile, he continued to hold the Freemasons responsible for the loss of his throne. On a postcard dated Doorn, August 23, 1928, he noted: "How can officers take part in such work [Freemasonry—author's note]?!"[41] The background for this outburst is probably a report passed to him by Admiral Friedrich Eschenberg, according to which German Freemasonry had caused the collapse of the monarchy, and had conspired with the "entente lodges." Among other things in this group of alleged "secret documents," it said that Judaism achieves "its purpose of totally destroying Christ and Christianity through Freemasonry. World Freemasonry serves Judaism as an instrument for setting up of a Jewish political and religious world dominion, in order to make people into impoverished slaves of the will and law of Judah."[42]

The realization that Masonic propaganda was effective in national-conservative circles must have engendered great insecurity on the part of the Old Prussians. A publishing house director named Adolf Groche put forth especially great effort on behalf of the Große Landesloge in combatting the hostility. He also belonged to the "Stahlhelm." First in Hildesheim, then in Chemnitz, he worked as a "Stahlhelm" regional group leader. Contrary to Bundesführer Franz Seldte, the founder of the "Stahlhelm" and later Reichs Minister of Labor in Hitler's cabinet, Seldte tried to dissipate the reservations against the German lodges. He could not, however, repress an ordinance of the Bundes administration which was issued at the turn of the year 1927-1928 against the members of humanitarian lodges—according to which they would be required to leave the "Federation of Soldiers on the Front."[43]

Already in May 1927, according to the directives of the "German Association of Nobility," it had been decided that "a member of the 'Stahlhelm' could not be a member of an humanitarian lodge." It was made an obligation for the members of Old Prussian lodges "to work in the spirit of the principles of the 'Stalhelm.'"[44] After the members of the Old Prussian lodges were threatened with exclusion from the "Stahlhelm" because of the above-mentioned ordinance of the Bundes administration, protests began, especially in Saxony. But in a session of the Bundesvorstand (Federal executive board) on March 11, 1928, the decision was weakened. Now it stated that after additional testing, it was found that there was "no reason to doubt the 'national trustworthiness' of the Freemasons in the 'Stahlhelm.'"[45] In the end, those Freemasons who had struggled for their position in the "Stahlhelm" had to be content with this formulation.

As previously with the "German Association of Nobility," and the National Union of German Officers, it was decided by the "Stahlhelm" administration in 1926 to set up a testing commission, whose purpose was to explain its position vis-à-vis Freemasonry. In the announcement in the *Führer-Nachrichten-Blatt (Führer's Newsletter)*, it was carefully pointed out that neither the Bundesführer (Federal Führer) nor the two vice-chancellors were lodge brothers.[46] In fact, only one of the members of the "Stahlhelm-" Bundesvorstand belonged to a Masonic lodge. Among the many Old Prussian brothers, who worked with the "Stahlhelm" all over the Reich, there had been unrest for a long time because—and quite rightly so—it was feared that there would be conflicts like those that had already occurred in the ranks of the National Union of German Officers.[47]

In contrast to the administration of the Große Landesloge, Adolf Groche was trying to confront the federal administration of the "Stahlhelm" with a certain uniformity among the German grand lodges. There were probably two main reasons for this: first, he perceived among the members of the Grand Lodge of Saxony who were threatened with exclusion "a considerable number of comrades, tested in war and peace, who were dedicated to loyalty to country and the 'Stahlhelm.'"[48] Second, he may have predicted that the hostilities, for better or worse, would spread to the Old Prussians. Clearly, in addition, Groche was earnestly convinced that, in case of a change of the disposition of the exclusion, legions of Old Prussian Freemasons would leave the Union, in which he saw a weakening of the "Stahlhelm." Groche complained that "one could have permitted him careful treatment of this question and consultation with expert associates. If that had happened, the order of the Federal administration would not have been able to be issued."[49] The administration of the Große Landesloge, however, in keeping with the guidelines of their resistance, insisted first on upholding the sharp distinction vis-à-vis the humanitarian lodges, and second, on emphasizing that "We, in contrast to all other grand lodges in Germany, are a Christian order."[50]

Meanwhile, the Testing Committee of the "Stahlhelm" established itself in the Fall of 1928 and met, changing its composition as it did so, perhaps five times altogether. The main point was the connection between the German lodges and foreign Freemasonry, in which Ludendorff's attacks blaming the "Stahlhelm" for the floundering fight against the "supra-state power" played an important part. The Große Landesloge did not content itself with just influencing the anti-Masonic committee members. Parallel to that, individual Brothers, who also belonged to the "Stahlhelm," informed on local events and tendencies that seemed counter to the opinion of the "Stahlhelm" leadership concerning (Old Prussian) Freemasonry. Then the federal administration would intervene directly. Felix Witt-Hoë, in a letter to the Grand Master of the Grand Lodge Zur Freundschaft, Oscar Feistkorn, recommended in no uncertain terms that this procedure be followed.[51]

On May 14, 1929, the last known meeting of the "Stahlhelm" Committee took place in the Große Landesloge building, at which the leaders of the Große Landesloge (Eugen Müllendorff, Felix Witt-Hoë, and Kurt von Heeringen) were heard. To all appearances—at least at the administrative level of the "Stahlhelm"—this contributed to a certain easing of attitudes vis-à-vis Old Prussian Freemasonry, whereas in places like

Chemnitz or in the area of Westhavelland it resulted in verbal attacks against the lodges in the area by members of the "Stahlhelm."[52] Prince August Wilhelm, who, it seems, belonged to the Große Landesloge, was temporarily pressed into service in the efforts to get the federal leadership onto the side of the Old Prussians. The Prince expressed himself vis-à-vis the lawyer Martin Korsch, who—as the representative of the Große Landesloge—sat on the Testing Committee, saying that there was no reason for fear.[53] In December 1930, Korsch was told by Colonel von Luck, Chairman of the Board, that he had let the work of the commission "fall asleep," and would not profit from a continuation of the negotiations. He was "completely clear" [in a positive sense—author's note] about the Große Landesloge. As to the other German grand lodges, he could get no further because the grand lodges did not want to give any explanation.[54]

In a circular dated December 5, 1931, addressed to the Landes federations, the opinion of the "Stahlhelm's" Federal Office was once again summarized to the effect that the members of Masonic lodges in Germany were "for the most part good, solid German men of the same world philosophy as the 'Stahlhelm.'" Further, it said, "In many lodges the partyless *völkisch* thought process is becoming more and more standard. The earlier international outlook to which the lodges generally adhered, is losing more and more ground." Many lodges were now purely *völkisch*, and would consciously emphasize, "we are now, God be praised, free of Jews." (*Judenrein*). If the "Stahlhelm" closed its membership to Freemasons, this happy development for the Fatherland would be hindered, "because the 'Stahlhelmers' certainly were among the most eager proponents and trailblazers of a national outlook for the German lodges in contrast to an international one."[55] Except that never, in the case of the Old Prussians, could there be a discussion of an "international outlook"; this analysis is completely valid.

The leadership of the Pan-German Union had already reached the same conclusion, in which an action committee to deal with the "Freemason-Question" had been formed. In February 1928, the results of the world-philosophical (*weltanschaulichen*) debate with Freemasonry were published in full in the *Alldeutschen Blätter* (Pan-German Newsletter), which exercised its influence on political opinion far beyond its own membership. In the report, written with a sharp anti-Semitic undertone, a difference was made between the humanitarian and the Old Prussian lodges. The humanitarian lodges "had very many members of the Jewish race," and "would maintain many international connections."

Also, a "very strong international spirit reigns" among their ranks.[56]

In the case of the Old Prussians, however, "besides the nationally-minded thought process… the *völkisch* one…had forced its way in." In addition, there were in their ranks, "men of the best *völkisch* turn of mind, whose work strives to have the *völkisch* way of thinking take hold through the lodges." Subordinate lodges also existed, "which in composition and attitude could indeed really be called '*völkisch*'."[57] Declared false were the popular opinions of "secret superiors," of "plots in favor of a Jewish domination," or of "un-Fatherland-favorable desires."[58]

The action committee and [Pan-German] Union leadership thus took a moderate stand on the "Freemason question" by *völkisch* standards, which was reflected in the lively and friendly correspondence between the Union leadership and the Große Landesloge, but which was hardly undisputed within the Pan-German Union. At the same time, the report left no doubt that the development of Old Prussian Freemasonry in the *völkisch* sense was in no way completed. Jewish/Old Testament practices had to be abolished; lodge membership could consist only of members of the German race; and Old Prussian Freemasonry had to undertake a complete separation from the humanitarian lodges.[59] Implementation of these demands would be repeatedly urged.

In the case of the "German Association of Nobility," the Große Landesloge could score a success. Its purposeful strategy of limitation had contributed to the fact that the "German Association of Nobility" exempted only the Große Landesloge from a ruling on incompatibility. The so-called "Adels-Kapitel" (nobility chapter) unanimously followed a proposition of the main office of statute changes, according to which members of the Grand Lodge Zur Freundschaft, the National Mother Lodge Three World Globes, and the humanitarian grand lodges could not become members of the "German Association of Nobility."[60]

Also among students, and even more so among the Burschenschaften (university fraternities), there were similar discussions on the "Freemason question," which, in turn, mobilized the many Old Prussian Freemasons who simultaneously belonged to fraternities. Thus, in the case of the Große Landesloge, as far as possible on the grand lodge level, the names of those Brothers who belonged to academic students' associations such as the "Alte Herren" (Old Gentlemen) were listed. On January 4, 1927, the leadership of the Große Landesloge announced in a circular letter that the attacks from nationalistically minded circles that the Old Prussian lodges had experienced would force timely and effective resistance: "It turns out, that a successful resistance can only be accomplished in this way: that the grand lodges make use of the cooperation of those Brothers who are members of the association that is attacking us."[61] Because of the reports from their subordinate lodges, the Große Landesloge drew up a list of the members of fraternities belonging to its system. Altogether, 193 members from 66 lodges from all parts of the Reich and two subordinate lodges in Vienna were listed by name.[62]

On July 13, 1928, Felix Witt-Hoë, putting a good spin on it, said that indeed the "student question" was up in the air, even though the St. John's Order, the "German Association of Nobility," the Pan-German Union, "Stahlhelm," the Protestant Union, and other organizations "have convinced themselves of our Christian and nationalistic view and our character as the only Christian order. In contrast to the other grand lodges in Germany, they are not continuing their struggle against us."[63] The fight about membership of Freemasons in student associations—or the question as to what extent the Old Prussians were to be treated differently —peaked after the "Seizure of Power" and lasted until most of the associations and fraternities had dissolved between 1934 and 1935, or metamorphosed into the so-called "Comrade Brigades" in the "National Socialistic German Student Association." After the associations introduced the "Aryan Paragraphs" and, by means of questionnaires, had been pressed into ridding their ranks of all Freemasons, the primary question still remained, whether the members of the Old Prussians—which had become (Christian) Orders—were justified in denying that they were lodge members on these questionnaires. For example, in 1933, the ADW (Allgemeiner Deutscher Waffenring—General German Weapons Group), the umbrella organization of the existing student associations, circulated notices saying that members of the metamorphosed former Old Prussian Lodges could not be considered Freemasons.[64]

Under Groche, the Freemason from Chemnitz and "Stahlhelm" functionary, the characteristic combination of Old Prussian Freemasonry and German-nationalistic social environment was brought about in a characteristic way. In 1929, Groche was involved in the preparations for the plebiscite directed against the Young Plan, to which Hugenberg and Hitler had allied themselves. At the same time, he registered the attacks carried out by the National Socialists against the lodges and the efforts of the National Socialistic Workers' Party to win away members of the "Stahlhelm" with special aggressiveness. He doubted that the National Socialists would be willing to distinguish between Old Prussian and humanitarian Freemasons, and at the same time warned his grand lodge of the danger that threatened it from the National Socialistic Workers' (Nazi) Party, in case that [distinction] did not succeed. The Große Landesloge in Berlin came to another conclusion: Felix Witt-Hoë, who was also responsible for the magazine of the Große Landesloge *Zur Aufklärung (Enlightenment)* wrote on May 9, 1930, "Your fear, that Fascism in Germany will come into domination in the foreseeable future, I do not share in any way."[65] In addition, Witt-Hoë opined, "The Red Peril and its vehement, merciless desire" was much more threatening.[66]

In the meantime, Groche advocated an offensive strategy of resistance, but affirmed the obvious hopelessness of convincing the Nazi Party of the

Old Prussians' nationalist views.[67] It was also Groche who in an internal analysis of the National Socialist movement clearly distanced himself from Nazi racism, which was "borrowed from cattle breeding" and was objectionable. In the same text he pointed, rightly, to the sanctification of the thought of racism by National Socialism, which set the "confession of blood" in the place of God. Contrary to his usual wont, Groche explained here that the Nazi Party presented, "first of all," no danger to Freemasonry because it would not come to power alone, and its "possible co-workers..." would "definitely not allow a closing of our grand lodges."[68]

That the participants in the Harzburg Front (Deutschnationale Volkspartei [German National People's Party], "Stahlhelm," Vereinigte Vaterländische Verbände [United Fatherland Associations], Nazi Party) could not agree on one common candidate for the 1932 election for Reichs President was above all an indication of the dramatic political balance shift in favor of the Nazis. A change of course on the part of the Old Prussians also had no effect. Instead, one looked to a balance with the National Socialistic movement. Although there was hardly any reason for this, the responsible functionaries of Old Prussian Freemasonry gave the impression that an agreement with the Nazis would be possible. Meanwhile, the "aggressive growth of National Socialism among academic youth" gave the leadership of the Große Landesloge cause for concern, because it was "the same thing as the academics' turning away from our Order."[69] This revealed a widespread opinion in Old-Prussian Freemasonry: it was not the Nazi programs that were seen as the root of the problem but the fact that the National Socialists did not make any distinction between the humanitarian and Old Prussian lodges in their anti-Masonic views.

That national movements and Freemasonry could form connections is seen by a look at developments in Italy; there, Freemasonry and the tradition of the national liberty movement were tightly bound together. Leading representatives of the *Risorgimento* were Freemasons, which, of course, later had another meaning as the later, quite nationalistic tones were heard emanating from Italian lodges—and not only during the First

World War. Italian Freemasons expected that their grand lodges would participate actively in discussions of questions of national interest and political decision-making, which they did, and indeed always in the sense of national and anticlerical liberalism.[70]

Italian Freemasonry was hardly thanked for its generally patriotic attitude, although at first Freemasons were well represented among the ranks of the Fascist movement. On February 13, 1923, the "Grand Fascist Council" announced in a "Declaration of Ununitability" that Fascists, who were also Freemasons, had to choose between belonging to the party or to lodges. The call was worded thus: "In consideration of the fact that…Freemasonry follows programs and applies methods, that stand in contradiction to those which inspire all activity of Fascism, the Council, 'invites' the Fascists who are Freemasons to choose between belonging to the national Fascist party or to Freemasonry. Because, for Fascists there is only a single discipline, that of Fascism; only one hierarchy, that of Fascism; and only a single obedience, the absolute, submissive, and total obedience vis-à-vis Il Duce and the other leaders of Fascism."[71]

It would not remain just words: Already in the same year, there were severe actions against lodge buildings in several cities. In 1925, an anti-Masonic law was enacted.[72] The Grand Orient declared that Italian Freemasonry would not allow terrorism to keep it from raising its voice against the illegal dictatorship. By the end of the year, (Italian) Freemasonry was already beaten down: the lodges under the Grand Orient were dissolved by Grand Master Domizio Torrigiani, who was then arrested and exiled without trial for five years. The Grand Orient established an office-in-exile in London; from there it took a position against the Fascist government and kept the grand lodge offices occupied.[73]

Despite the differing situations in the two countries, the fate of their Italian Brethren should really have been a clear warning to German Freemasons: It had just been shown that Italian Fascism would not allow Freemasonry to continue. However, even the decisiveness with which Mussolini fought the lodges could not distract the right-conservative

Brethren in Germany from their striving to adapt themselves to the German-*völkisch* people and the Nazis. On the contrary, in order to disarm the reproach of internationalism, they continued offensively to distance themselves from "Roman Masonry" and played, perhaps not accidentally, into the hands of the Italian Fascists. In June 1930, for example, the "Circular letter" of the Große Landesloge let its readers know that within Freemasonry, "the contrasts of the people's characteristics 'Germanic or Romance,' the purposes 'with or without politics,' the fundamentals 'of the Fatherland or without Fatherland (stateless)' were struggling," for which reason an international Freemasonry was a "monstrosity," a "contradiction in itself," and a "destroying freak of the thoughts of Freemasonry."[74] The breaking off of relations with the liberal Grand Lodge of Vienna in 1931—of which more will be said later—was a consequence of the Old Prussians' campaign against internationally oriented Freemasonry. Just as resolutely fought was the very cautiously developed rapprochement with England and France within the established humanitarian camp, an understanding for which the humanitarians had to pay with a loss of members.[75] In the Spring of 1932, the Old Prussians—and with them the Grand Lodge "Zur Eintracht"—broke off "fraternal relations" with the Grand Lodges of Hamburg, Bayreuth, and Frankfurt. These had previously resumed relations with the English Mother Lodge. One did not "want to build a chain either in thought or reality" with the English, announced a statement of the Grand Lodge "Zur Freundschaft." France and England bore the main responsibility for the "Versailles Humiliation": "We resist with all decisiveness (most vehemently) against fraternizing with England."[76] Noteworthy in such declarations is not only the use of concepts like "damage to the culture because of the lie about responsibility for the war." Bernhard Beyer recognized in it a readiness to carry out the much-besought "liberation (deliverance) and re-elevation" by means of a new war, since the statement more or less said that "an important position in legal matters and power would belong to the German *Volk* because of their industriousness and numbers."[77]

In the same manner, in 1932, the Große Landesloge announced in a flyer, "St. John's Greetings," quoting from previous years, that "in any case we...completely reject...any kind of humanitarian stupor such as internationalism, pacifism." In the same flyer under point three, it said, "Our German Order is *völkisch*." The text explained further that "the community of the Creator" did not set aside the differences of races, peoples, and individuals. The "humanity-enthusiasm" had led to a "mixture and degeneration of all cultures, art forms, races, and peoples, to a flood that threatened to drown everything that was ennobled and highly valued in pure cultures. Our Order, which has always made an effort to reach the highest ennoblement of its constituent parts [meaning the membership!—author's note] by the most careful choices and maintenance of purity, seeks to build a dam against these slimy, murky waters."[78] With the evidence of such pronouncements, it can be proven that social and ethno-racist thought had gained a foothold in the Große Landesloge in the form of cultivation and separation concepts, which, as Beyer says, had "very clearly been based on the Nazi Party line." From this point on, a "veritable contest" on the part of the Old Prussians for the favor of the National Socialists had begun, "into which the Grand Lodges of Saxony and the 'German Brother-Chain' were drawn."[79]

On the other hand, there is not a single declared affirmation of the Weimar Republic in any publications of the Old Prussians. Wolfgang Fenner and Joachim Schmitt-Sasse had come to this conclusion in their paper on German Freemasonry as "national power" before 1933.[80] They supported their findings mainly on the evaluation of articles in the two magazines *Am rauhen Stein (Rough Ashlar)* (Grand Lodge "Zur Freundschaft") and *Bundesblatt (Union Paper)* (Nationalmutterloge [National Mother Lodge]), which were merged in September 1934.[81] Common to all the essays was "the turning away from basic positions of humanism, from thoughts of a 'supranational' brotherhood and peace, the rejection of the Enlightenment postulate of equality and the ideal of a social state."[82] The authors sketch briefly the wavering of the grand lodge functionaries between fear and fascination vis-à-vis the National Socialist movement. They refer, and rightly so, to the dangerous myth of Fatherland as opposed to the political reality of Weimar by some of the German lodges; a "mythicizing" from which, for example, the postulate of "*völkisch* self-conciousness"[83] in *Am rauhen Stein* was derived.

German-national lodge circles shared some thought patterns with the representatives of the so-called "conservative revolution": the concept of the "restoration" of the German Fatherland, anti-intellectualism, or the conviction that pluralism in Germany had to be replaced by a *völkisch* System. However, the tenor of the Christian-national lodges was on the whole neither conservative-revolutionary nor committed to a return to the monarchy, although people doubtless lamented the empire and revered Hindenburg as a kind of "substitute emperor."[84] Some sort of authoritarian state model—not further elaborated—was favored. It is therefore doubtful whether, as Fenner and Schmitt-Sasse proposed, that the world-view consensus of national Freemasonry could be seen unequivocally as part of the "conservative revolution."[85] This defined itself as an active counter movement to the political-societal reality of Weimar. It did not fulfill itself in "peace and order, power and strength, throne and altar, but forced a new kind of humanity, an organic concept of state, the making of a community (a communion) of the whole people," meaning a "totality of the state and the person"[86] and attached concepts that futurism in Italy had developed. Artur Moeller van den Bruck chose the new—"modern" —revolutionary conservatism as the "eternal human outlook," and postulated a new epoch with new values, people, political forms, and institutions. Moeller and his followers were not concerned with "restoration," but "re-connection"[87] Edgar Jung, another exponent of the "conservative revolution," formulated it thus: Laws and values, without which man would lose the connection with God and nature, had to be reestablished. In place of equality [would be], "the inner value"; in place of social sentiment, "the proper building into the stratified society"; in place of political choices, "the organic leadership succession"; and in place of so-called happiness of the masses, the "right of the community of the people." Jung called for the creation of a "new order of people" and a "new western unity under German leadership."[88] In contrast to this new quality of nationalism, the German-nationals and with them the Old Prussians were concerned with the restoration of "German honor," which, of course, did not necessarily have to mean the same thing as a less militant position. Open ideological disputes were to be avoided if they permitted anti-Masonic attacks.

Nevertheless, the alleged abstinence from politics of the lodges did bring about their nationalization. If one considers that, in Masonic publications, a new armed conflict was indicated as the appropriate means to put an end to the results of the First World War,[89] the absurdity of the supposed understanding of themselves as "unpolitical" becomes obvious. Leading "Old Prussians," such as the publicist and cultural philosopher Dr. August Horneffer, put the "true German community of people" in opposition to the Weimar Republic, which they saw as "negative democracy."[90] Horneffer transferred from a humanitarian lodge to the system of the Grand Lodge "Zur Freundschaft," where he took over the office of Grand Secretary and edited the magazine *Am rauhen Stein (Rough Ashlar)*.

Frank Neumann arrived at parallel conclusions to those of Fenner and Schmitt-Sasse in his analysis of *Am rauhen Stein*: Significant portions of the Weimar constitution, such as treating of the right to vote or the parliamentary system, were rejected just like the European postwar system.[91] A distinctly un-conciliatory tone was raised against the former opponents of the war. In that spirit, unfriendly essays appeared with titles like "The Rhine Is Ours!" or "Versailles!"[92] In 1932, August Horneffer became exceedingly friendly with National Socialism and described Hitler as "the captain [Führer!] of a ship in distress at sea."[93] In other words, the *völkisch modus operandi* was being tightened up and the advances vis-à-vis the National Socialists were increasing. In this way, the publicists' line, reinforced, could be maintained after the "Seizure of Power."

The psychological pressure on German Freemasons had risen, especially since the considerable increase in votes for the Nazi Party in the Reichstag election of September 1930. In many parts of the Reich, there were verbal and sometimes physical confrontations with the Nazis. In light of this, those responsible for resistance favored direct contact with Hitler and those around him. Two considerations played a role in all this: first, it had become clear, as shown in a variety of ways, that neutral debates in open gatherings, in view of the Nazis' defense strategy, were just about impossible, because, as a rule, lodge members would just be shouted down. Second was the conviction held by some lodge leaders that the Nazis' rabble rousings were not approved of by their leaders.[94]

Meanwhile, the party leadership was completely unimpressed by such "cozying up." For example, when the Grand Master in Hamburg, Richard Bröse, asked Hitler in a letter in August 1931 to have the Grand Lodge Archives inspected by a confidential agent of the Nazi Party administration, he never received an answer from their offices.[95] In the same year, the Worshipful Master of a Three World Globes subordinate lodge in Essen was gruffly turned away when he asked the Reichs administration for a clarification. The later chief of the *Oberstes Parteigericht* (Supreme Party Council), Walter Buch, let him know in his letter of response that he (the Worshipful Master) should give up "wasting his time on something that from the beginning is condemned to fail. The fundamental view of the Party toward any Freemasonry is immutable."[96]

In the meantime, the leadership of the Große Landesloge established contact with Hermann Göring through his half-brother, Friedrich Wilhelm Göring. He belonged to the [Große Landesloge subordinate] lodge in Wiesbaden called "Nassau-Oranien zu den bestandlichen Quellen (Nassau-Orange of the Enduring Springs)," held the office of secretary, and volunteered himself for this job.[97] A meeting took place in Hermann Göring's apartment in Berlin on November 19, with the new Grand Master of the Große Landesloge, Kurt von Heringen, as well as Felix Witt-Hoë, which these two representatives of the Große Landesloge found extremely encouraging. Witt-Hoë, "still under the influence of this meaningful preliminary talk" with Friedrich Wilhelm Goering, shared afterward that now a basis for further negotiations had been established.

"We left with the impression," Witt-Hoë continued, "that one had finally begun to recognize what the important thing about negotiations is, namely differentiation." One had to recognize finally "in the opposite camp that our Order, by its whole development and nature, is something foreign to the other system, even opposes it."[98]

On January 25, 1932, Friedrich Wilhelm Göring wrote to the Grand Lodge that he had once more begged of his brother "to use his influence in such a way that further discussions be resumed as soon as possible, so that clarity would finally be established."[99] At almost the same time, a letter from Heeringens, dated January 18, 1932, must have arrived at Hermann Göring's house. This letter, in an allusion to the conversation of November 19, emphasized the request for communicating the desire of the Große Landesloge to meet personally with Alfred Rosenberg for discussions.[100] Goering's secretary's office did indeed forward the request to Rosenberg.[101] It is certain that the meeting never took place any more than a meeting with Hitler happened.

Likewise, during 1933, the Große Landesloge tried to exert influence on Goebbels, by using familial connections. This short and equally unsuccessful episode began with a piece written by Paul Rosenthal for the administration of the Order to Robert Haasen, the Master of the Lodge in Krefeld, in which there was information regarding the alleged membership of Goebbels' father-in-law. It was confirmed that Oscar Ritschel, the father-in-law of the propaganda minister, had belonged to the Große Landesloge subordinate lodge "Eos" in Krefeld since May 17, 1930.[102] From this, there developed a correspondence among Haasen, Ritschel, and the Große Landesloge. The object was to make the political or contemplative view of the Order credible, with Ritschel's help. The attempt to arrange a personal conversation with Goebbels was specifically made, in which Rosenthal quite broadly encouraged that if possible, "Mr. Goebbels would be shown the lodge hall in Eisenach Street (up to the actual lodge rooms of the 9th Degree—author's note), and to explain thoroughly 'who we are and what we do.'"[103]

Ritschel declared that he was ready to help arrange such a meeting; most probably, it never happened. As far as can be determined on spotty evidence, the project was dropped in September 1933. It seems that Goebbels' wife had told her father that the relationship between Goering and her husband was very bad. Since Goering was looked upon as the most important person in lodge affairs, Ritschel and Haasen concluded that such an attempt at an arrangement by Goebbels would do more harm than good.[104]

About the same time that contact with Goering was established, Dr. Carl Happich, a physician in Darmstadt and member under the Große Landesloge, succeeded in making a connection with Werner Best. At the end of January 1932, there was a personal conversation, during which Best appeared astonished at the differences within German Freemasonry as made by the Große Landesloge. In addition, Best requested a clear avowal of the *völkisch* principle: the exclusion of baptized Jews.[105]

Despite all the adaptation by the Große Landesloge, the Nazi Party insisted on allowing no Freemasons in their ranks.[106] Nevertheless, many Brothers sympathized with the National Socialists and even voted for them. In the fall of 1932, a certain Wilhelm Golombek, who apparently at this time still belonged to a subordinate lodge of the Grosse Landesloge in Berlin, began an intense correspondence with the "Reichs Propaganda Administration" of the Nazi Party and offered his services. Golombek provided, among other lodge lists, private addresses of leading Freemasons. He also enlightened the Nazi Party about Hindenburg's alleged (but untrue) lodge membership by repeating a confidential conversation that he had had (clearly with Friedrich Bolle). In addition, Golombek gave his evaluation of the structure of Freemasonry in Germany, and presented proposals as to how one might best combat it.[106a] Carl Happich had already told Witt-Hoë, the archivist of the Grosse Landesloge, in November 1931, that according to his estimate, in the Hessian parliamentary election, half the members of his lodge would vote National Socialist.[107] Applications of individual lodge members were thus granted by the National Socialists, showing that the Party's opinion was directed not against individual Free-

masons, but against the "organization of the lodge."[108] Thus, Freemasons of whichever system, who wished to join the Party, had to either leave the lodge beforehand or keep quiet about their Freemasonry during the process of becoming party members. On the side of national-Christian Freemasonry, the inability of unity was completely unacceptable and decried as a one-sided prohibition. "Not the slightest hesitation" existed in the eyes of the Große Landesloge against the membership of Masonic Brothers in the National Socialist Party, according to Grand Master von Heeringen.[109] In other words, the positions already differed from the national trends, before the election results of the National Socialist Party in Prussia, Württemberg, Anhalt, Hamburg, and Bavaria, before Papen's Cabinet of "National Concentration," and before the National Socialist Party became the strongest party as of the parliamentary (Reichstag) elections of July 31, 1932. After the "Seizure of Power," sundry decrees regulated the association of former lodge members with respect to membership and participation in the National Socialist Party, which will be discussed in detail later.

3.2 RELATIONSHIP BETWEEN FREEMASONRY AND THE EVANGELICAL CHURCH

The Roman Catholic Church has always been steadfastly opposed to Freemasonry. Apart from a few attempts, there has never been a serious critical dialog. There have always been Catholic lodge members, but these brothers have constantly been threatened with excommunication, and have therefore concealed their membership from the Church if at all possible. It is quite different with the Evangelical (the Church of the Prussian Union; German: *Evangelische*) Church. In Scandinavia and Germany especially—and, above all, the Swedish System— where more or less strongly Christian-based teaching is anchored by tradition, one finds Protestant clergymen in leading positions. Freemasons are also often found among the lay officers of many congregations. The same is true for independent organizations within the Protestant Church. Thus, for example, the curriculum director, Dr. Wilhelm Fahrenhorst, who had been chairman of the Protestant Federation at the beginning of the 1930s, was a member of the Große Landesloge.[110] Protestant pastors were, and still are, represented in the ranks of humanitarian Freemasonry—which is not surprising, given the character of the work of the lodge: to make transcendence able to be experienced by the individual by means of ritual and symbolism.

The decentralized organizational structure of the Protestant Church in Germany contributed to the fact that the Church's relationship to Freemasonry was concentrated on the regional level. In addition, the highest-level boards and church authorities were very reserved with respect to the "Freemasonry question." A fundamental stance vis-à-vis Freemasonry was taken by neither the Protestant High Consistory nor the General Synod of the Evangelical Church of the Old Prussian Union, in which Lutheran and (German) Reformed were combined in Prussia.[111]

Meanwhile, in the *Landes* (provincial) churches within the *Deutsche Evangelische Kirchenbund* (German Association of Protestant Churches), opposing tendencies were apparent, since *völkisch* forces put all their efforts into involving Protestantism in the opposition to the lodges. So, for instance, the *Landes* Association of Greater Berlin of the German-*Völkisch* Officers' Association complained in a letter to the Protestant Church High Council in December 1927 that there had been no clear position from the Protestant Church vis-à-vis the "Freemasonry question": a Christian church in Luther's sense and Freemasonry were irreconcilable, and the membership of Protestant clergy in Freemasonry was a "monstrosity." It was demanded, therefore, that "all Protestant clergy of our *Landeskirchen*, who are Freemasons, and who have not sworn that they have resigned from their lodges by April 1, 1928, will be relieved of their offices."[112] Naturally, the Große Landesloge reacted aversely to such efforts. In an open letter to the Protestant church officials, Felix Witt-Hoë complained that, in some states of the German Reich, there was at present a movement afoot to cause the responsible church officials to forbid membership in Freemasonry to all their subordinate Protestant clergy under threat of losing their positions. There would be no distinction among the individual German grand lodges, despite their fundamentally different religious positions. The Große Landesloge was, of course, a "purely Christian order." It claimed to be "no schoolmaster on the subject of religious belief." that it left to the church. There was, however, a farther-reaching rumor, according to which the goal was to deny Freemasons the right to work in Protestant churches. "Such a decision would be of great consequence. Our Order has, true to its purpose of spreading Christianity… always considered it of value, that her members participate as much as possible in the practical work of the Church."[113]

The position in the Church was split. The critical-to-bitterly opposed voices expressed themselves more strongly in public, and in no way granted the Old Prussians any clemency. A few examples will suffice: national Grand Master Habicht told the General Superintendent of the Kurmark in a letter in October 1926 that most of the Freemasons he knew were "somewhat strange to ecclesiastical custom." He could, however, certainly not insist that "there was no sense of Christianity in German lodges." Much more prevalent was "perhaps an idealism colored by Christianity, an idealism that cannot deny its paternity in the Enlightenment." He further wrote: "You recognize that I cannot judge this spirit on the whole—individual exceptions are always admitted—to be the one in the Gospel of Christ as I understand it."[114] Witt-Hoë's recommendation of forming a "united fighting front with the help of the highest church leadership" was deemed inappropriate according to a letter of February 1929 from Andreas Paulsen, the chairman of the Association of Lodge Masters of Schleswig-Holstein. As far as he knew, the Bishop of Holstein was no friend of Freemasonry.[115] The 18th regular Provincial Synod in Pomerania even declared on October 25, 1929, that clergy lodge membership was undesirable "for the sake of the congregation."[116] The Provincial Synod in Brandenburg on October 1, 1929, also followed the example of the intra-church committee, and had decided to switch over to "the order of the day," by way of an existing resolution, which said that clergy membership in Freemasonry was undesirable.[117]

Although *völkisch* circles could not enforce the dichotomy between clergy and lodge membership, a distinct enmity on the part of individual functionaries within the Protestant Church toward Freemasonry was unmistakable. Thus, for example, Hermann Sasse, a minister from Berlin, maintained to his general superintendent, "that Masonic lodges have fundamentally corrupted the life of the church."[118] The attacks excited a considerable stir, and caused "Drei Weltkugel" Grand Lodge Grand Master Habicht to become involved in the affair.[119] The same is true of the clergyman, Probst from Frankfurt am Main, who was employed as association chaplain of the "Inner Mission." As a successor to Friedrich Naumann, he edited their magazine *Sonntagsgruß* (Sunday Greetings) and took a hostile stance vis-à-vis Freemasonry.[120] Or retired Pastor Eylau of Bad Doberan, who took Ludendorff's leaving the church as a reason to egg on the Protestant Church in the struggle against Judaism and Freemasonry.[121] All of this could not alter the fact that the Old Prussians, in their anti-democratic, anti-socialistic, nationalistic, and anti-Semitic positions, agreed with many branches of the Protestant churches, which had supported the Deutschnationale Volkspartei and at the end of the [Weimar] Republic likewise developed sympathies for the Nazis.[122]

In July 1932, Oberkirchenrat (president of the consistory) Dr. Bernhard Goesch informed the Große Landesloge that it had best transform itself into a Christian-nationalist direction. "I sincerely hope that the Lodge may recognize in time that it had best follow the example of the German Christian Luther, and break wide windows into the high but dark walls, through which the sweet light of Heaven can shine in complete clarity. If the two columns at the portal were not called Jachin and Boaz, but something like 'Armin and Martin,' and ornamented with the sword and Luther-Rose, after the two who liberated Germany with sword and cross, it would be hard to imagine what a new wave of spirituality would emanate from the new construction."[123] At any rate, Große Landesloge Provincial Grand Master Kiesow from Mecklenburg was the first to refuse Goesch's demand to expunge various parts of the ritual and symbolism stemming from Judaism, and instead to make the ritual "purely German and purely Christian." The refusal was supported by the Order's top officers. In addition, Witt-Höe emphasized that "the first measures against the current attacks, and clever, cautious tactics" had been necessary.[124]

Dr. Heinrich Behm, Landes Bishop of Mecklenburg-Schwerin, was especially opposed to Freemasonry. Like Goesch, he did not shy away from marching shoulder-to-shoulder with *völkisch* forces. In January 1928, at a program of the "Deutsch-Völkisch Offizierbund" (the German-*völkisch* Officers' Association) in Bad Doberan, Behm discussed the relationship between the Church and Freemasonry, not in the sense of an ecclesiastically regimented position, "because the 'Peoples' Church has to put up with some unique features within itself," but "as a scientific theologian and as spiritual caretaker characteristic of my office as bishop." To that extent, he had to judge that "Christianity and Freemasonry in principle were mutually exclusive. As in the early centuries of the church, Christianity and Gnosticism were contrary to each other, so—observed objectively—does the Freemasonry of the Christian Lodges—which is related to Gnosticism, fundamentally contradict Christianity." Behm also said, "in principle, there cannot exist two parallel paths to the same goal." To the question whether ecclesiastical office and Freemasonry could be united, he concluded, "If I knew that a pastor was a Freemason, I would, as a minister, tell him that the two…are incompatible."[125] That was different from the case of a Christian layman: he would encourage the clergyman "either to give up his office or resign from the lodge."[126] Ludendorff took up Behm's views in his own way: he congratulated the provincial bishop on his "clear position, in which he comported himself completely in the spirit of Luther, who had also forbidden secret societies in his Church."[127]

On June 8–9, 1928, there was a meeting of the German Protestant Church Committee, which concerned itself, among other things, with the position of the Protestant Church vis-à-vis Freemasonry. Several petitions regarding this question had come in to the committee, which caused the President of the Committee to ask the top Church officials for their opinions by means of a questionnaire. The results of this survey were summarized in a consultant's report to the session.[128] Particularly because of the letter from the "Deutsch-Völkisch Offizierbund" to the Supreme Church Council (which had forwarded the same to the committee) and because of a submission of the "Deutsch-Christlichen Arbeitsgemein-schaft" (German-Christian Union), in which the dangers of Freemasonry that allegedly threatened the Church were pointed out, and in which it was demanded that clergy be warned against entering lodges, questions were formulated that were aimed first at the fundamental relationship between the Church and Freemasonry; second, at the influence of the lodges in congregational life; and third, at the role of pastors who belonged to lodges. The tenor of the answers, as can be seen in the consultant's rather fragmented report, was reserved, partisan, but not at all inimical to Freemasonry. A fundamental conflict was denied by all high church officials. Some lodge members would stay away from services, but on the other hand, some congregants had been led back into the Church because of Freemasonry. Considering the lodge membership of Protestant clergy and their effect on community life, there was, as expected, no unified vote. A demand for the firing of such pastors was also not raised by any of the sides. A warning against a "position of opposition" to Freemasonry was also more or less harmoniously given.[129]

In the course of the Church Committee meeting, in which the consultant's report was considered, Landes-Bishop Behm expressed his conviction that there was a reform movement underway within Freemasonry, "in which the positive evangelical direction was striving for validity." It would be advisable to leave "Freemasonry to its own devices in this crisis." Behm did not recommend a declaration from the Protestant Church Committee that took a position vis-à-vis Freemasonry, because taking such a position "toward this or that side, with the Party situation the way it is at present, would be politically exploited and thus invalidated."[130]

In further discourses, it was emphasized, among other things, that distinctions had to be made between humanitarian and Christian lodges. It was also pointed out that although various other groupings wanted to influence the Church, "the diversion of pastors from their office," "the arising of Masonic undercurrents in community entities," as well as "the closed practice of Freemasonry in contrast to other open societies" would make the dangers of Freemasonry in the community appear "significant" and "an explanatory and warning word" should be spoken to the coming generation of pastors.[131]

At the time of the voting, a proposition lay on the table, according to which, out of the "tension that exists between the Protestant Church and Freemasonry," for "the professional servants of the Protestant Church 'collisions' could occur because of their membership in Freemasonry," but since there were no legal measures, it would be left to the provincial churches to take responsibility for a position. This watered-down anti-Masonic proposal did not get a majority. Instead, a proposal from the Church Committee to take no position with regard to content and to leave the whole "Freemason-question" to the provincial churches was adopted.[132]

3.3 FREEMASONRY ON THE DEFENSIVE: RESISTANCE AND ISOLATION OF LEFT-LIBERAL LODGES

The extensive anti-Masonic polemics that began after the war increased during the early Weimar years in proportion to the spread of radical national socialistic and anti-Semitic thought. The German lodges had to defend and justify themselves publicly, and indeed were more on the offensive than they had been earlier. The Association of German Freemasons, which overarched the jurisdictions, served as a political journalistic exchange, which was boycotted by the Große Landesloge. Besides that, it was up to each grand lodge whether and how to react to the usually nebulous and often infamous attacks. A united or even only outwardly-directed resistance was never agreed upon, which weakened the public position of Freemasonry, and reduced the chances of eliminating the widespread ignorance or reservations about it in general society, let alone changing anything in the hostile position of *völkisch* parties.

On the one hand, the defense of Freemasonry remained "too genteel to fight energetically against the continuing assumptions and slander," and too naïve to comprehend the baseness of its opponents."[133] On the other hand, in the case of the right wing of the lodges, it was less a question of naiveté than a question of will to understand the *völkisch* circles ideologically and politically as opponents. This was because the *völkisch*-nationalistic and antidemocratic part of German Freemasonry did not recognize such a distinction.

Here is where we must seek the reason for the terrifying "conformity of apologetic political journalism."[134] The authors of articles on justification were mostly those Brothers who "identified with the values of extreme nationalism,"[135] which was disputed by opponents of the lodges in propaganda against them. Representatives of the moderate wing, in light of the misguidedness of many accusations, often considered their opponents unworthy of serious discussion. The left-liberal wing of the German lodges articulated their opinions more clearly. In this connection, Neuberger was of the opinion that the relationship between the political Right and German Freemasonry could not be reduced to a "path of appeasement" of grand lodge functionaries. Rather, there appeared to be a numerically strong, but politically journalistically inactive group of Brethren "who were critical of the politics of adaptation manifested by the grand lodges."[136] For some of the humanitarian lodges, this may have been an accurate assessment, but empirical proof would be hard to establish. In the case of the Old Prussians, however, the concept "path of appeasement" does not apply to the actual relationships. Aside from that—at least in the case of the Große Landesloge, as correspondence between it and subordinate lodges clearly shows—one can find only a few indications that allow one to conclude that there were views among the Brothers differing from the course set by the Große Landesloge.[137] For other Old Prussians, one could draw an analogous conclusion.

In any case, the nationalistic-*völkisch* value system determined the publications of the grand lodges as well as the discourse on resistance,[138] which indeed culminated in the defenders being "completely on the defensive." The formerly liberal Association of German Freemasons under its chairman, Diedrich Bischoff, allowed the rules of the game to be forced on them by the *völkisch* discourse. Even in the late resistance papers published by the Association of German Freemasons, the differences with Romanic Freemasonry were set forth. Thus, Stephan Kékulé von Stradonitz, the national-conservative editor of the Drei Weltkugel-Bundesblatt (Three World Globes Association Paper) published his rebuttal to the Association of German Freemasons, "The Murder of Sarajevo: An Explanation." It was so closely reasoned that "it would be hard to extract a real subject from it for discussion."[140] In the same year, Diedrich Bischoff announced that Freemasonry was a "completely rich complement" to National Socialism.[141] In the face of such mental adaptability and politically mistaken assessment, even the judgment of Lennhoff and Posner, which as a rule was dependable, appeared questionable. Bischoff considered Lennhoff and Posner "according to his innermost conviction to be humanitarian Freemasons."[142] In any case, declarations such as this were indications of the great measure to which even leading representatives of established humanitarian grand lodges oriented themselves in the direction of National Socialism.

In the meantime, it had taken Ludendorff's extreme libel, "Annihilation of Freemasonry by Divulgence of Its Secrets," to bring all nine German regular grand lodges to a united position for once. The grand masters published their declaration on September 15, 1927, in which Ludendorff's condemnations that Freemasonry "assumed downright lunatic aims" such as inciting and hoodwinking the vast masses of people were categorically denied.[143] It would be the only united stand of the grand lodges against their *völkisch* opponents.

The Große Landesloge had reluctantly decided to participate in the meeting, during which the rebuttal of Ludendorff's accusations took place. Grand Master Wilhelm Augustin Balthasar-Wolfradt had asked people to bear in mind that "the Große Landesloge, in recent years, had fought with special vehemence against the image of a German Freemasonry's seeming to break apart externally, but remaining united within." It was feared that "the clarity of this position could be clouded again" by the meeting.[144] "An extraordinary tension had arisen among the subordinate lodges because of a complete isolation of our Order." In the words of Provincial Grand Master Müllendorf, he [Müllendorf] recommended participation. This discussion should be used to "make clear that the differences of opinion among the grand lodges should not necessarily have a negative effect on the mutual relationship of the subordinate lodges." This is "what our subordinate lodges really fear."[145]

In accordance with this, the Große Landesloge withdrew from further cooperation. In confidential guidelines "for resistance against *völkisch* attacks," it was announced that the three Old Prussian grand masters had decided in February 1929 that "each [grand lodge—author's note] should mount its own resistance, and eschew cooperative resistance measures." The subordinate lodges would be free—insofar as local conditions seem to indicate its desirability—to initiate cooperative resistance measures."[146] In December 1930, the Master of the Große Landesloge subordinate lodge in Königsberg was admonished to refrain [from cooperating in resistance— trans. note], after it resulted, under the impression of Nazi attacks, in a representative meeting of all lodges in East Prussia. It was announced that the Große Landesloge was to decide on the utility of such united actions, thus limiting the subordinate lodges' latitude of action. In addition, an organized union would not be considered by the Große Landesloge.[147] In the meantime, the Order's administration followed its understanding of resistance by compiling lists of earlier announcements, St. John's messages, speeches, and declarations. Such material was recommended to the Brothers in the subordinate lodges to convince opponents of the "German mindedness" of the Order (under the Große Landesloge).[148] In addition, in 1922, it had already been said in Old Prussian circles, "not the religious, but the *völkisch* is of prime importance."

The Old Prussians put up an emphatically stern public front vis-à-vis the Humanitarians. That further increased the isolation of those lodges that nurtured the liberal-Masonic spirit. "Spirit of the Order" was played off against "Spirit of the Lodges":[150] Members of humanitarian lodges were no longer greeted on the street by their Old Prussian Brothers. In other words, it was decided to bar the humanitarian lodges, in order to appear in a better light, and to blame the non-Old Prussian Brothers as well as the "so-called" Association of German Freemasons for the widespread reservations held by the public: "If they hadn't tried to push themselves on the public—completely misconstruing the signs of the times—this harassment of the Freemasons probably would not have happened."[151]

On March 1, 1929, the Große Landesloge's archivist Felix Witt-Hoë, whom the Große Landesloge had made responsible for the coordination of the work of enlightenment, sent a letter to his counterpart in Chemnitz, Adolf Groche, in which he asked, among other things, to be kept up to date on the "position in principle" of the national administration of the "Stahlhelm" vis-à-vis Freemasonry. In addition, the letter says about the strategy of resistance: "I emphasize specifically, that you should always feel compelled to speak only for the Große Landesloge of the Freemasons of Germany as the only one found in Germany that is a Christian Order completely free of Jews, and that the restrictions and obligations of both the other Old Prussian grand lodges, to the Association of German Freemasons, do not apply to us, and that we cannot be made responsible for them."[152] The verbal and physical demarcation on the part of the Old Prussians led to a certain retreat by the humanitarian grand lodges. There were even thoughts of coming together into a united grand lodge. A proposal to this effect was accepted by the constitution committee of the humanitarian grand lodges in Frankfurt am Main in February 1931, and forwarded for deliberation.[153] Such a unification, though, never came to pass: humanitarian Freemasonry was too disunited, and the representatives of smaller jurisdictions were afraid that they would be overshadowed so that they would lose their Masonic identity.

The lodges were not able to withstand the pressure under which they found themselves. In addition, something occurred that was predicted by a minority of German Freemasons: the German-*völkisch* circles and the Nazi Party (newly founded in 1925) were not indebted to the Old Prussians for either their accommodation policy or their demarcation strategy vis-à-vis other lodges. Rather the lodges assumed, whether rightly or wrongly in individual cases, that there were still contacts with the "bejewed" humanitarian lodges, and cheerfully continued their defamation of all of Freemasonry. Such attacks focused on a person close at hand—Gustav Stresemann. His membership in Freemasonry (and in a Three World Globes lodge!), as well as the open debate about it, was acknowledged by the right wing of the Old Prussians with annoyance. Felix Witt-Hoë represented the opinion within that Stresemann was "a great burden" for the three Old Prussian lodges, "because this man is always inflicted on us," and complained about the "clumsy prominence given" to Stresemann "by his grand master."[154] Most assuredly, Stresemann would have done not only Witt-Hoë a favor had he resigned from his lodge. There was only one problem: he did not do so.

It was easier for those politicians, whom the *völkisch* circles accused of being Freemasons, but were not, to distance themselves than it was for Stresemann to withdraw. Belonging to this group from the beginning, for example, was Prince Max von Baden, the last Reichs Chancellor called by Wilhelm II. He ended the U-Boat war in 1918, carried out the firing of Ludendorff, and without waiting for the formal declaration of Wilhelm II announced his abdication. Already in 1922, Große Landesloge Grand Master Müllendorff took the exemplary position in a letter to the "German Defensive and Offensive Association" on the oft-raised assertion that the former Reichs Chancellor was a Freemason and had acted politically as one. Müllendorff stated "that neither Prince Max von Baden...nor any of the other men, who consciously helped work on the breakdown of Germany...belonged or ever had belonged to the Große Landesloge of Freemasons of Germany. If they had belonged to it, their crime against our fatherland would have unequivocally had as its consequence their immediate expulsion. … From the material at our disposal, one cannot conclude that they ever belonged to any German Masonic lodge, and we may correctly conclude, because of the completeness of this material, that none of those men has ever been a German Freemason."[155]

In time, the six regular humanitarian grand lodges increasingly tried, under the pressure of the attacks against Freemasonry, to adapt to the *völkisch* and anti-Semitic *Zeitgeist*. In any case, there was no unity at all. For example, the Masonic brother Carl Happich reported to his grand lodge that the humanitarian lodge in Darmstadt was trying "very hard to get rid of the Jews": A Jewish member had been forced to resign, and no more new ones were accepted.[156]

In the "Großloge zur Sonne," there were violent arguments with consequences about the so-called "Heidelberg Theses." The points formulated at the beginning of May 1931 by the Brethren said: (1) All German Masonic lodges should make clear that they accept "religious belief and purpose as binding for them— (atheistic Freemasonry stops being Freemasonry)." (2) Only the nine established grand lodges should be recognized. (3) Any connection with other systems should be refused. (4) Freemasonry was first "service to one's own people." German Freemasonry could be healed "if it concerned itself primarily with the tasks that develop for it within the framework of the homeland, and stayed away from fruitless international fraternization fantasies."[157]

The Lodge "Beethoven zur ewigen Harmonie" ("Beethoven-Eternal Harmony") protested against the position thus expressed by sending out a "rebuttal circular." When, during the annual convocation of the Große Landesloge held in Braunschweig May 29-June 1, 1931, these "Heidelberg Theses" were accepted, it came to an open break: The pediatrician Paul Selter, because of his refusal to concur with the majority opinion, resigned from his board membership. In the letter explaining the reason for this step, Selter wrote that "National[istic] and religious orthodoxy" had "completely seized" the "Zur Sonne" Grand Lodge. He concluded that "the *völkisch* standpoint, and the *völkisch* sort of suppression and rejection of those who thought differently" had become significant.[158] As a consequence of these events, the Lodge "Beethoven zur ewigen Harmonie" left its mother lodge in Bayreuth and joined the Symbolische Großloge *en masse* on December 19, 1932. Selter, for his part, later leaned toward Nazism, and declared himself for Hitler, even to his war and race policies.[159]

Resignations and protests by individual members and whole subordinate lodges made it clear that there was indeed a liberal minority within the established grand lodges. The only problem was that internally (i.e. within their grand lodges) they could not hold out against the course of German nationalistic and *völkisch* forces, which had been determined by accommodation. Apart from a few exceptions, a sharp shift to the right took place in the German grand lodges. In this connection, people cut themselves off ever more decisively from the Jews, with whom they no longer wished to have any connection. Even so, that did not alter the fact that, for their part, even Old Prussian Freemasons had to suffer the loss of social acceptance in the German nationalistic milieu, and *völkisch* associations as a whole distanced themselves from Freemasonry.

In the "National Association of German Officers," for example, there were strenuous arguments in connection with the striving of the *Hauptvorstand* (High Commission) and the Landesvorstand (Provincial Commission) of Greater Berlin to force disunity between Freemasonry and the membership of the National Association. In 1924, it was decided by the Reichs House of Representatives to keep members of humanitarian lodges—in which Judaism was said to play "a dominant role—out of our association." On the other hand, reservations against the Old Prussians were erased, in the expectation "that the *völkisch* striving to cleanse would be carried out within these lodges."[160]

In the meantime, the grip of the *Hauptvorstand* and the Berlin functionaries on their position against the lodges was indeed controversial among the other provincial associations. It was rejected especially by the provincial association of northwest Germany. Among other things, these differences of opinion with respect to Old Prussian Freemasonry led the largest provincial association to split with the representatives of northwest Germany in 1926[161] and become the independent "National Association of German Officers of Northwest Germany" (NDON).

In March 1925, the Old Prussian grand masters reacted to renewed attacks with the remark that they had nothing to add to their repeated declarations of their [pro]-national (*vaterländischen*) and Christian position, and resisted attempts [by the National Association of German Officers—*trans.*] at involvement.[162] In August 1925, the *Hauptvorstand* announced that "the knowledge of the essence of Freemasonry—because of the necessity of our association to protect itself against the influence and infusion of views so contrary to ours—must be seriously broadened and deepened." This is about the "institution of Freemasonry…which we reject, not because of lack of trust in our individual members, who may still belong to lodges. We are justified in assuming that they have not yet recognized that being members of both lodges and of the National Association of German Officers will lead them to inevitable conflict."[163] A group of Association members, who were also Old Prussian lodge members, reacted with a letter to the *Hauptvorstand*. In it, they asked which members of the National Association of German Officers who belonged to lodges had tried "to permeate the National Association of German Officers with such conflicting views?" Further they declared that "membership in both of these institutions had brought none of us into inner conflict, and according to our firm conviction, never will. If that were the case, we would have long since resigned from one of the two institutions." If the Reichs House of Representatives session had decided in May 1925, that "by the time of the next Reichs House of Representatives session, no Freemasons were to be accepted as new members." Otherwise, it would be "bitterly avenged" on the National Association of German Officers, according to the undersigned, who would have demanded the immediate resignation or dissolution of the *Hauptvorstand*. "Tens of thousands of nationalistically-minded, educated comrades, who belonged in the National Association of German Officers because of their philosophical position…would indeed have taken care not to join an officers' association, which … expressed such a mistrust of them."[164]

Already in 1924, because of an attack by the National Association, the grand masters of the three Old Prussian grand lodges had passed a joint declaration, in which they strengthened their position that "there is no general ideal of humanity, but that as each personality stems from its roots [lit: is rooted in its stem!] only unconditional love and loyalty to this root can develop the personality."[165] Possibly it is this joint stance by the Old Prussians that brought about the free (voluntary) unification of the five lodges in Saxony that were still independent, and caused them to make known even more clearly their nationalistic direction, which unquestionably already existed. In conclusion, it was to be feared that the isolationist strategy of the Old Prussians could expand. With this backdrop, the five lodges declared, incorrectly, that there were no differences in essence within recognized German Freemasonry. The humanitarian lodges, united in the Association of Grand Lodges, it went on, would not let themselves "be talked out of their consciousness of a higher responsibility with respect to the German people, in any way by anyone. The furthering of a national structure and strengthening of the feeling of community of the people is a sacred German duty for us!"[166]

During, or as a result of, the Reichs representatives' convention of October 1925, there was a change in the Supreme Board of Directors of the National Association of German Officers. The new chairman was Captain von Struensee, who, however, was a professed opponent of Freemasonry. In the course of a conversation between the administrations of the Große Landesloge and the National Association of German Officers, a temporary relaxation of tension occurred. In December 1925, the Supreme Board of Directors decided to form a representative committee "for the purpose of enlightenment of our members about the Freemasonry question."[167] Habicht, the Grand Master of the Three World Globes, declared, in the meantime, that his grand lodge was no longer of a mind to let the National Association of German Officers tell it what to do.[168] Differing interpretations already existed concerning the status of the Masonic committee members. Instead of the originally-planned three association representatives, who also belonged to Old Prussian lodges (the Humanitarians were consistently not even invited), only two participated in the five meetings between January and March 1926. While the National Association of German Officers considered Hamburg lawyer and Große Landesloge Brother Alfred Jacobsen the official representative of the Old Prussians, the Old Prussian Grand Masters' Association, at their February 24, 1926 session, made it clear that this was completely incorrect. Rather, Brother Jacobsen took part in the deliberations only as an association member. Furthermore, the three Old Prussian grand lodges would refuse to engage in any further discussion with the National Association of German Officers.[169]

The committee obtained no concrete results. The advice in the closing report at the Reichs representatives convention on April 16, 1926, did lead finally to the decision that there would be no more new acceptances of members, whatever their grand lodge.[170] Those people, however, who already belonged to the Association and were Freemasons should not be forced to resign.[171]

In the meantime, other humanitarian grand lodges followed the example of the Hamburg lodges and offered the Nazi Party a look into the internal workings of the lodge. As the associated Grand Master Bernhard Beyer from Bayreuth reported, he himself had offered the Nazi area commander for Oberfranken, and later Bavarian Culture Minister, Hans Schemm, access to the archive and the ritual [of the Grand Lodge Zur Sonne—author's note], which otherwise was to be handled confidentially. Schemm was, "according to reliable information," to be entrusted with the examination of the Freemasonry question. Grand Master Beyer, however, never received an answer.[172]

Only two German Grand Lodges consistently placed themselves in opposition to the *völkisch* efforts: the Freimaurerbund zur aufgehenden Sonne (Masonic Association "Rising Sun") —to which the winner of the Nobel Prize in Chemistry Wilhelm Ostwald (for a time Grand Master) and later Kurt Tucholsky and Carl von Ossietzky belonged—and the Symbolische Großloge, which had been formed in 1930. Neither the irregular Freimaurerbund zur aufgehenden Sonne nor the Symbolische Großloge was recognized by the other German grand lodges.

The historical relationship of the ideas of the Freimaurerbund zur aufgehenden Sonne, which specifically accepted atheists, to monistic materialism, especially to the ideas of Ernst Haeckel[173] and the freethinking "German Monistic Association," founded by him and others in 1906 is worth a closer examination. The obligation to its principles was accurately described in a sharply anti-Catholic paper by the Freimaurerbund zur aufgehenden Sonne, which appeared ten years after the founding of the Reformgroßloge (Reform Grand Lodge). It said that all modern life strove to rid itself of "supernatural circles of imagination." The enlightened person sought to destroy "every theological trace in himself. The democrat emphasized the social characteristics of the new ethic..." To see that this scientific way of thinking spreads ever wider must be one of our main tasks."[174] More: "We are absolutely clear about this: that morality without the help of religious or transcendental imaginings is possible, because it has sufficiently strong roots in the feelings and intelligence of the individual. For this ethic—an inherent, not spiritual; social, not religious; stemming from history, not revealed; developing with mankind and culture, not completed and unalterable [and imposed—trans. note]— we are to secure an appropriate place in our lives once and for all."[175] In connection with the struggle of spirit, belief, and conscience, one was to intercede for the freedom of the two major aspects of culture: school and science. "We are fighting, so that schools will be freed from old-fashioned religious instruction, so that only science stands in the service of truth and free research."[176] However, since people are not only rational beings that satisfy themselves with the search for truth, most of mankind would have a yearning for satisfaction of their artistic and esthetic needs. The lodge work would have to try "to prepare a place for beauty and an experience with the perfect, sublime, the higher things in life."[177]

The profession of the Freimaurerbund zur aufgehenden Sonne of the scholarly method in the monistic sense implied—at least indirectly—a proximity to the radical Darwinian stance formulated in the initial phase of monistic circles. For example, a member of the board of directors of the German Monistic Association defined its policy as "the continuation of the general struggle for our being," and raised challenges for "the most possible reduction of the unfit, the most possible encouragement for the industrious, and elimination of all parasitism," as well as "the announcement of everyone's obligation to work."[178] Although this point of contact in the history of ideas seems surprising at first, it becomes clear that the Darwinian principles and the so-called "monistic religion of nature" could find support with those forces which revered a mystical understanding of nature or were looking for a substitute for Christianity. Thus, the influence of Darwinism on the racist madness of the "Arianosophers" provides an example not only of the manifold history of the influences of Darwinism but also for the syncretic genesis of "Volkism" (*völkisch* "philosophy"). One cannot deduce from this, however, that the Monistic Association as a whole or even the Freimaurerbund zur aufgehenden Sonne remained in social Darwinian waters for any great length of time. The above-mentioned chemist and Freimaurerbund zur aufgehenden Sonne Freemason Wilhelm Ostwald took over the chairmanship of the Monistic Association with the help of Haeckel at the turn of the year 1910-1911, and as such gave the free-spirited movement new impetus. In the discussion of political, cultural, and social questions, concepts that sought to apply Darwinism to human society retreated into the background.[179] Ernst Haeckel himself, who belonged to the Pan-German Federation, was ambivalent in his political positions.

During the Weimar Republic, the Freimaurerbund zur aufgehenden Sonne was pacifistic and social-democratic in orientation. In its circles, the *Völkerbund* (People's Association) was understood as an expression of Masonic thought, and was therefore bent on supporting the ideas of the Association as much as possible. Thus, a report of November 25, 1920, to the Grand Lodge of France said that one was enthusiastic "about the ideas of the *Völkerbund* and the peaceful exchange of peoples for which these ideas would smooth the way." The Association made it "an obligation for its members to work in this vein in the future—indeed inside their lodges as well as outside."[180] As the first—and at this point the only—German grand lodge of Freemasons, the Freimaurerbund zur aufgehenden Sonne, under the vigorous leadership of the author, Dr. Rudolf Penzig, who was in office from 1919 to 1926, sought contact with French Brothers of the Grand Orient and the Grande Loge de France. This rapprochement vis-à-vis the two French grand lodges led to mutual recognition in 1921, and developed into a close relationship, including the annual demonstration of common manifestations of peace. In its heyday at the beginning of the 1920s, the Freimaurerbund zur aufgehenden Sonne had about 3000 members.[181]

The beginning of connections with France was taken as a reason for a declaration from the German Association of Grand Lodges, which was adopted and promulgated by the plenary session on May 29, 1921. It emphasized that the German Association of Grand Lodges had no connection at all "to the so-called Freimaurerbund zur aufgehenden Sonne." For instance, the Grand Lodge "zur Sonne" in Bayreuth, which belonged to the German Association of Grand Lodges, was not to be confused with the aforementioned Freimaurerbund zur aufgehenden Sonne. "That the so-called Freimaurerbund zur aufgehenden Sonne would enter into a connection with French Freemasonry at a time of the deepest debasement of our German Fatherland, does not sit well (agree at all) with the nationalistic frame of mind of those German Freemasons united in the German Association of Grand Lodges. It is sharply repudiated by the Association as contrary to German national feeling."[182]

In the meantime, the Masonic organizations that worked internationally persistently tried to encourage understanding among peoples. The grand lodges which were members of the Association Maçonnique International (AMI—The International Masonic Association) met in conferences with international and pacifistic themes. The first conference of this kind took place in 1921, the year AMI was founded, in Geneva, upon the invitation of the Swiss Grand Lodge Alpina, followed by more conferences in 1923 (Geneva), 1924 (Brussels), 1926 (peace demonstration under the patronage of AMI in Belgrade), 1927 (Paris), and 1930 (Brussels). The headquarters of AMI was Geneva (later Basel).

The English, American, and regular grand lodges did not belong to this union, which naturally weakened the position of AMI. The Freimaurerbund zur aufgehenden Sonne had been represented at first, but then, at the second Geneva conference, after controversy-filled discussions of the question of [Masonic] Regularity, it withdrew—without, however, ending differences of opinion. During the next AMI convention in Brussels, the Freimaurerbund zur aufgehenden Sonne increased its demand to be recognized as a full member without renewed examination of its Regularity. It was supported in this by the Grand Orient de France. The problem was tabled, and could not be cleared up in a friendly manner either at this or at the following conventions. But a resolution was passed, in which the work of the *Völkerbund* was applauded, and expression was given to the hope that the fundamentals of the *Völkerbund* might become the common property of all nations. At the AMI conference held in Brussels in 1930, representatives of 26 grand lodges took part. In addition, representatives of eleven more grand lodges holding visitor status participated, among them die Symbolische Großloge von Deutschland.[183]

In contrast to the AMI, which was composed of member grand lodges, the Allgemeine Freimaurerliga (AFL—the General League of Freemasons) was an international association of individual members,[184] which had its roots in a circle of Esperanto-speaking Freemasons. The "Esperanto Framasona" Association constituted itself in Boulogne on the occasion of the first international convention of "Esperantists" in 1905. The natural close relationship between the ideas of a world language and a world-encircling Masonic brotherhood led to an extension of the constitution and to a change of name to "Universala Framasona Ligo" (Universal Masonic League) in 1913. The main thrust was no longer the spread of Esperanto but the effort to unify Freemasons no matter of which system the world over. For this reason, membership access was extended beyond the circle of Esperantists. Dr. Fritz Uhlmann, a Swiss physician and pharmacologist, had taken a leadership role in this change, by becoming the secretary of the League.[185] In 1926, Eugen Lennhoff spearheaded another reorganization and extension of the League. In addition, a central office was established in Vienna; regional groups were set up, and a newsletter was started. Fritz Uhlmann, chairman of the Universal Masonic League since 1923, was kept in office. Lennhoff took over the function of chief of the Vienna main office and was a key figure on the international Masonic scene. In addition to his work in the General Masonic League, he was, among other things, editor of the publication of the Grand Lodge of Vienna, the *Wiener Freimaurerzeitung (Vienna Masonic Newspaper)*, representative of this grand lodge to the AMI, and (in 1925-1930) the first Grand Commander of the Supreme Council of the A.A.S.R. for Austria.

Dr. Leo Müffelmann, the prominent Berlin Freemason, was elected first chairman of the German regional group of the League. When he stepped down from this office in 1928, because of stiff opposition from his Grand Lodge of Bayreuth, an engineer, Dr. Raoul Konor, another important figure on the international Masonic stage, succeeded him. Koner demitted from the Grand Lodge of Hamburg the same year and in 1929 joined the Vienna Lodge "Labor," which belonged to the liberal Grand Lodge of Vienna.

The work of the Universal Masonic League was strictly rejected, especially by the Old Prussians. The leadership of the Große Landesloge distanced itself most decisively. Even the usually very moderate Eclectic Association forced the resignation of those Brothers in its ranks who remained in the Universal Masonic League.[186] It seems that all of the established German grand lodges finally forbade their brethren to be members of the League. The Grand Lodge "Zur Freundschaft" gave an ultimatum to a Brother who had signed a proclamation from the Universal Masonic League: either resign from his lodge or withdraw his signature.[187] The proclamation stated that Freemasonry, among other things, was being attacked from many sides and slandered. Therefore, it was necessary that it "clearly and vividly, determine its goals and delineate its ideas sharply. The content and essence of Freemasonry is the idea of the unity of humankind, the idea of love of all people for each other, and of the brotherhood of all mankind. Freemasonry pushes for the ideal of humanity, and realization of universal human love and fraternization, beyond the borders of nations and lines of religions, beyond racial and religious differences. One is to safeguard national and cultural uniqueness vigorously and forcefully, but despite that to emphasize the thought of the unity of mankind."[188]

On the occasion of the next year's conference in Amsterdam, the *Vossische Zeitung* reported that the League meanwhile counted among its members regional groups in every European country, wherever lodges were not forbidden (as they were in Italy and Hungary). Fundamentally important, the report continued, is that The Grand Lodge of England had opened its membership. By way of criticism, it said that Masonic events were dismissed in public with "light horror" or with "quiet smiles": "Hardly a good testimony for the activity and the development of a formerly powerful, lively, aggressive *Zeitgeist* (spirit of the times) -forming movement, that it should come to this attitude." The author evaluated the Amsterdam Conference on the whole as positive and productive in light of the League's efforts: "to overcome the unfruitfulness of lodge life, the stagnation and deintellectualization, by setting forth the greater concerns of humanity."[189]

Within the Universal Masonic League, there was a "Group for an Active Peace Effort," which in 1932 drafted a petition, together with the Grand Lodge of Vienna, to the Disarmament Committee of the *Völkerbund*, in which the necessity of a comprehensive disarmament policy was emphasized, and possibilities for conversion were outlined. The resolution was carried by twenty jurisdictions worldwide, including the Symbolische Großloge.[190] Although the League, as an international organization with about 5000 members,[191] had only a relatively small numerical base and thus its practical political influence remained small, its significance as an active, country-and-lodge encompassing association should not be underestimated. Indeed, it formed an important platform—precisely because of the conditions in Germany—for many a liberal Freemason who was in the great minority in his grand lodge. The league took a clear stand vis-à-vis the European Fascisms. In its declarations and publications, Nazism, which was ever increasing in numbers, was recognized as a political danger and harshly condemned.[192]

In 1925, for the first time since the end of the [First World] War, an international convention under the rubric of "Masonic event" took place, in which, among others, the Universal Masonic League participated. By the revival of this tradition dedicated to world peace and brotherhood, the initiators wanted to declare that "a time of annihilating hate and brutal force" would be replaced by "an epoch of solidarity, truth, and justice."[193] A panel named the "International Masonic League"[194] invited people to the Basel conference, out of which a committee grew that was composed of French Freemasons and members of the Freimaurerbund zur aufgehenden Sonne. It organized Masonic peace initiatives from 1928 on. These events took place peripherally to, and probably often in competition with, the conferences of the Universal Masonic League.

Meanwhile, the liberal brethren in Germany saw themselves exposed to the hostility of a more or less solid front of the Masonic establishment. The discussions culminated in the person of Leo Müffelmann, the CEO of the Vereinigung der Leitenden Angestellten (Vela or the Association of Executive Employees). He grew into a key figure in the international-pacifistic wing of Freemasonry in the 1920s and early 1930s. First a member of subordinate lodges of the Hamburg system, and co-founder of the "Bluntschli-Committee,"[195] Müffelmann decided to switch to the Grand Lodge "Zur Sonne," because he was isolated with his internationalistic views and humanitarian principles from the Hamburg system. He belonged to the "Bluntschli zur reinen erkenntnis" (Bluntschli of pure perception) Lodge, in Berlin, subordinate to the Bayreuth Jurisdiction, of which lodge he became Worshipful Master.

While Müffelmann took part in the conference (September 11-15,

1926) for the peace demonstration of the International Masonic League (Association Maçonnique Internationale) in Belgrade, he exchanged fraternal kisses with the Grand Master of the Grand Orient de France, Arthur Groussier. This gesture, which was greeted with great approval by the delegates, released a firestorm of protest in Germany, and led to expressions of anger and indignation throughout the established grand lodges. Besides that, the fraternal kiss became a spectacular proof for the alleged justification of their anti-Masonic campaign by the *völkisch* opponents of Freemasonry.[196] In the meantime, Müffelmann coupled the rapprochement with France with an attempt to awaken an understanding for Germany's political demands. For example, he appealed to French Freemasons to end the occupation of the Rhineland.[197]

Meanwhile, as a reaction to the Belgrade "affair," the Old Prussians thought up a special way to exclude Müffelmann. In November 1926, they decided henceforth to ignore both lodges subordinate to Bayreuth: Müffelmann's Lodge "Bluntschli" and her sister lodge "Galilei," in their monthly Masonic calendar. This, of course, turned the brethren of "Galilei" against Müffelmann, and caused great internal consternation in the ranks of the Grand Lodge "Zur Sonne."[198] In addition, Müffelmann, who had participated in the peace demonstration—not in any official capacity, but as a private person—had to put up with severe attacks, not only because of Belgrade, but because of his activity in the Universal Masonic League, for which his grand lodge put him under pressure. At the beginning of June 1928, he was constrained to leave the Grand Lodge "Zur Sonne" and join the Viennese Lodge "Labor," even before Koner did.

In the summer of 1930, a concentrated effort of a group of Freemasons around Leo Müffelmann—a collection of internationalistic-pacifistic-minded German Brothers— resulted in the establishment of the Symbolische Großloge. A circle of German members of the Grand Lodge of Vienna, led by Müffelmann and Koner, as well as former Freimaurerbund zur aufgehenden Sonne Brethren, some of whom had belonged to additional subordinate lodges of the Grande Loge de France, formed the core. In addition, Freemasons came from other German systems, who did not agree with the standard national-conservative orientation. The founding fathers of the new jurisdiction were devoted to strict adherence to the forms of Masonic Regularity. They deemed it important that the former members of the Freimaurerbund zur aufgehenden Sonne in recognized lodges would be individually made regular if necessary before they participated in the establishment of new lodges. These new lodges, in turn, formed the Symbolische Großloge on July 27.[199] After its constitution, the Brothers who had been shut out of the Freimaurerbund zur aufgehenden Sonne could be made regular as they were accepted into a lodge subordinate to the Symbolische Großloge.[200]

Yet Müffelmann found—because of competition, and for political reasons—that no established Masonic body in Germany was prepared to provide a Warrant of Constitution for the new lodges. When even the Grand Lodge of Vienna refused, the Supreme Council A.A.S.R. of Germany, which had been in existence for only a few months, performed the official constitution, the "Bringing in the Light" for the eight founding lodges of the Symbolische Großloge. This was a problematic solution because it was debatable whether the Supreme Council had the right to constitute blue lodges. Thus, there was debate even in the ranks of the Universal Masonic League, in connection with the unresolved question of Regularity, whether members of the Symbolische Großloge should be accepted or not.[201] The Constituting by the Supreme Council, which was rejected anyway by the established German grand lodges, led to Müffelmann's isolation being made worse. When the Grand Lodge of Vienna, after some delay, found itself prepared to recognize the Symbolische Großloge, this step was seen by the German grand lodges as a reason to break off relations with the Austrians.[202] In 1931, one year after the founding of the Symbolische Großloge, Müffelmann, as its Grand Master, declared that now gradually "a parting of the minds would crystallize out: world Freemasonry, built on the foundation of the Ancient Obligations on one side, and Christian-nationalistic, German Freemasonry, with a more or less strong anti-Semitic infusion on the other."[203] One side included the group of established grand lodges, by which Müffelmann meant expressly the Old Prussians and Humanitarians; the other consisted only of the Symbolische Großloge, which "is the only one actively advocating world Freemasonry."[204] What happened to the political parties in the center would happen to this part of German Freemasonry, which represented the libertarian-humanitarian standpoint: "New, clear movements [would] wear them down."[205] Müffelmann wrote just before the "seizure of power" —the "takeover"—that above all, the attacks of the Nazis were to be taken seriously, as they remained "not without effect in several fraternal circles." Old Prussians as well as individual humanitarian grand lodges had "even tried to reach an understanding with the Nazis." These efforts, Müffelmann contended, had remained in vain: "Hitler has rejected every one of the connections for which we strove on principle."[206]

Chapter 4

THE RECEPTION OF THE *VÖLKISCH-*NATIONAL SOCIALISTIC IDEOLOGY IN GERMAN FREEMASONRY

4.1 ESTABLISHMENT OF A *VÖLKISCH* FREEMASONRY IN THE "RING MOVEMENTS" AND IN THE MASONIC ORDER

During the whole period of the Weimar Republic, the right-wing conservative majority of German Freemasonry (Freemasons) kept to their distant, occasionally hostile attitude vis-à-vis former enemies in war and their Masonic institutions.

The Grand Orient of Italy was especially accused of being partially responsible for the entrance of its country into the war. It is true that the Grand Orient officially greeted the entrance into the war as a long-expected event. It is also true that in the chauvinistic climate, all the more heated by the war, Masonic functionaries from the Entente countries had at times aimed sharp attacks at German Brothers. Since about 1920-21, there was at first no lack of cautious attempts by the grand lodges of some victor nations—especially attempts by the French—to normalize relations with the Germans, and to contribute to a step-by-step reconciliation.[1] In contrast to this, August Horneffer justified Mussolini's actions against the lodges, and demanded the prohibition of Italian Freemasonry in 1925.[2]

Many segments of German Freemasonry—as also of the German people—were neither inclined nor in a position to accept the turning point of 1918 as a chance for a new beginning in society. Instead, the question of a "lie about blame for the war" was made a central issue, especially by the Old Prussians, and without their seeing that they were in contradiction to their own questionable postulate of being "Unpolitical." As a rapprochement between the Eclectic Association and the Grand Lodge of Darmstadt on one side, and the Grand Orient as well as the Grand Lodge of France on the other became clearer in 1927, the Große Landesloge reacted promptly. Landes Grand Master Müllendorff judged the fact that the two German grand lodges sought to include representatives of other German jurisdictions (even the Old Prussians) to be a sign of little understanding of what the Große Landesloge considered "consistent with German honor."[3] Müllendorff saw himself constrained to note in a circular letter that the Große Landesloge rejected "most vehemently" any sort of negotiation toward reconciliation: "As long as a French soldier stands on German soil, no German Freemason may have any kind of connection with a Frenchman, aside from the fact that, we, as a Christian Grand Lodge could never have relations with an atheistic association."[4] National political interests and Masonic affairs were consciously mixed in this way. Thus, in 1932, the Grand Communication of the Große Landesloge complained that England was, "as always, reaping the benefits of the German colonies stolen from us"[5] and decided at the same time to break off relations with the humanitarian grand lodges, which had remained in the Association of Grand Lodges, after they had resumed connections with England at the beginning of the year.

The fact that established German Freemasonry as a whole, which was marked by a bourgeois–nationalistic consciousness, held to its introverted attitude insofar as it did not take part offensively in the political difference of opinion, must not deceive more than that it was political as a societal subject *per se*. Whether the individual Freemason, lodge, or grand lodge was more national–liberal or *völkisch* in outlook played no role. In contrast to the Old Prussians and the group of established humanitarian grand lodges, the Grand Lodge Zur aufgehenden Sonne and the Symbolische Großloge had a strong sociopolitical understanding of Freemasonry, and they agreed in this, not by chance, with the French Brethren. In this vein, the Grande Loge de France, which stood in close communication with the Symbolische Großloge, put out a declaration in 1932, with which it took a stand on the question of the obligation of Freemasonry, and implicitly expressed a harsh contrast to the Christian-national lodges in Germany. In it was said, fundamentally, that Freemasonry had the right and duty to concern itself with political, social, and economic problems. The role of Freemasonry was seen as being on the perimeter [avant-garde?] of the forming of political opinion: in France as well as in Germany, it was to foster trust on both sides, "without which no healing takes place."[6]

The fact that there had been a "need for the greater part of German Freemasonry to adapt to the more-or-less radical right"[7] was, meanwhile, not an expression of tactically determined (conditioned) compromises, but a consciously political manifestation. Neuberger perceived (saw) in the *völkisch* tendencies within German Freemasonry, completely correctly, a definitive cause for political radicalization and polarization of the lodges,[8] without drawing the logical conclusion that the *völkisch* factor was a structural element of German Freemasonry after the First World War. Aside from the fact that the right-wing conservative lodges, under the impression of a basic anti-Masonic mood in the national camp, saw themselves more and more cut off from their own political milieu, grand lodge politics was under the internal pressure of radical efforts whose aim was to have Freemasonry dissolve completely into the *völkisch* Weltanschauung.

Attempts to connect Freemasonry with the body of *völkisch* thought can be documented already from the time of the First World War. These attempts were the result of a spirit of nationalism and hereditary enmity, which conditioned almost the entire Masonic landscape at the time, including the so-called military lodges.[9] There had been military lodges since the eighteenth century and during the wars of independence. In them, Freemasons of different nationalities and training could meet.[10] It is also clear that in the First World War, at least on the German side, an irreconcilable fatherland spirit reigned in the mostly improvised soldiers' lodges. The course and end of the war no doubt strengthened the spirit. The development of the military lodge "Stern von Brabant" (Star of Brabant),[11] as well as the personal continuities, attests to the fact that one may see here a source from which the idea of a "purely Germanic" and anti-Semitic Freemasonry was fed. Thus, Felix Witt-Hoë, the later functionary of the Große Landesloge, in his capacity as designated (assigned) Master of the military lodge "Zum aufgehenden Licht an der Somme" ("Rising Light on the Somme"), wrote a manuscript entitled "Concerning the Spirit of the Military Lodges." In it, he called for "supreme accomplishments in the field and at home" from German-nationalistic Freemasonry, as well as "the expurgation of even the smallest notion of utopian pacifism...with its roots."[12]

In spite of that, the charge of a treasonous conspiracy was constantly raised against the military lodges.[13] Proofs of such treason were of course never brought forward. For the oft-repeated insistence and its broadly propagandistic exploitation, it was quite enough that during the war there had been mutual visitations by Freemasons from warring countries. In this connection, the Nazi publication "The Freemasons' Lodge Museum in Nürnberg" wrote in 1938 that even though "no actual overt treason" could be proven, it was in "the basic philosophy of Freemasonry."[14] In the same publication, there was a detailed discussion of the visit of the Freemason and Captain of the "Landsturm" (Land-storming) Battalion of Bayreuth to a Belgian lodge in Liège on August 30, 1914. It was emphasized as particularly shameful that the Belgian Brethren had signed their names on his military postcard to his lodge "Eleusis zur Verschwiegenheit" ("Eleusis of Silence") in Bayreuth. "There is, in spite of war, still noble humanity," said a part of the text on the card. "Belgian civilians sat in the officers' military lodges," the Nazi publication railed, "and had every opportunity to overhear military conversations and explanations, when we were surrounded everywhere by enemy spies!"[15]

The Hamburg merchant Robert F. Eskau made himself noticeable as the first self-appointed advocate for a *völkisch*-anti-Semitic Freemasonry in 1923. In Easter and Pentecost messages or in "Letters of Hermann" that he disseminated within the circle of Brethren of different Masonic systems, he professed nationalistic and anti-Semitic goals, and demanded that Freemasonry break with liberal concepts.[16] Eskau had allied himself with Theodor Fritsch, and espoused his analysis of the "power of Jews, which destroys states and incites peoples."[17] According to Eskau, Jews "had unquestionably a huge part in the fundamentally ruinous transformation of all relationships—even in Freemasonry." Because of the Jewish Brethren, a spirit had been carried into the lodges "that turned the essence of Freemasonry completely into its opposite."[18] Thus, concepts from the context of the Jewish–Masonic conspiracy theory gained entrance into internal Masonic discourse. Eskau accepted the attacks of *völkisch* anti-Masons in relationship to the humanitarian and romance lodges as partially applicable; in no way, of course, did he want them to be applied to himself, that is, the German Christian-national lodges. Eskau went so far as to promulgate his ideas in the "Stürmer" ("The Storm-Trooper"), the notoriously sexually oriented, anti-Semitic propaganda sheet by Julius Streicher. In 1924, Eskau's essay entitled "A Freemason above Freemasons" appeared. Streicher and Eskau shared the idea of a "German Christianity that was true-to-type,"[19] which – as was generally true of the *völkisch* effort—was concerned with constructing a specifically "German religion," whereby arrangements were made either to revive the so-called "Nordic" religion of the Germanic tribes or to interpret Christianity as a "German religion" by excising the Old Testament.[20]

Eskau was a member of the Hamburg lodge "Gudrun," which worked under the humanitarian system of the Grand Lodge of Hamburg. His lodge had expelled him in 1923; the expulsion, however, was revoked by the Grand Lodge six months later. Such an official reaction was inevitable.

Although the nationalistic views were not foreign to the Grand Lodge of Hamburg, Eskau had become intolerable because of his activities. The expulsion from the lodge was unable to restrain him from his advocacy of a *völkisch* Freemasonry. Instead, he continued his work with the help of the "*Werkbund deutscher Freimaurer* (Labor Association of German Freemasons."[21]

While Eskau's tracks were lost in the 1920s, the concept of *völkisch* Freemasonry found encouragement: its bastion was the lodge in Bad Pyrmont, "Friedrich zu den Drei Quellen" ("Frederick of the Three Sources"), which was reconstituted in 1928 and was affiliated with the Grand Lodge Zur Freundschaft. The driving force for the *völkisch* aspect was Oskar Zetzsche, a professed, practicing dowser who, as a member of the association for "Ancient Germanic Prehistory," belonged to the circle around Wilhelm Teudt, and held the office of orator in his lodge. Teudt is considered the founder of the theory according to which the so-called "Externsteine" (external stones) in the Teutoburg Forest were an early Germanic cult place of worship. Zetzsche specialized in the alleged connection between ancient Germanic customs and Masonic ritual. In May 1922, he published his findings in the official journal of the Grand Lodge "Am rauhen Stein" ("The Rough Ashlar").[22]

Already in 1924, the Munich lodge "Freundschaft im Hochland" ("Friendship in the Highlands"), also a subordinate lodge of the Grand Lodge Zur Freundschaft, put forth in its constitution a proposition that "only seekers will be accepted in our Grand Lodge, who are of German blood and profess the destiny and culture of the community."[23] In the further explanations, it continued, "Perfect Freemasonry is for us Germans not just identical with *völkisch* thinking, but it must be *völkisch* through and through its inner self."[24] The text complained about the danger of "foreign infiltration" and "decay" of the "blood community," and came to the conclusion that there was only one way to save Germany: "Preservation of the People's community and its most important constituting element: the "blood community." "Foreign blood among us is poison and explosive."[25]

The social Darwinist principles, taken from eugenics, of preservation of the species and natural selection were further mirrored in the challenge of reaching a "hygiene adequate for healthy German lodge life. We are not (…) satisfied with just assurance or even with signs of the German way of thinking, and specifically demand German blood, because daily experience shows that the German "species" is tied to German blood."[26]

The aim of the Munich proposition was to make the desired conditions of determination obligatory at the grand lodge level. That did not succeed; but nevertheless, in 1924, the Grand Lodge Zur Freundschaft rescinded the admission of members of the Jewish faith, which had existed for a few decades. Whether this happened directly because of the Munich initiative is unclear. Also, that the St. John's Lodge in Munich itself acted arbitrarily according to racist views in the case of new admissions can be assumed, but not stated unequivocally, because the sources are incomplete.

The "reconstituted" and reactivated Masonic military lodge "Star of Brabant" was the first to institute officially the "Arianism Paragraph," thus openly subscribing to *völkisch* anti-Semitism. Only German Brothers "of whose Germanic descent there was no provable doubt" (against which there were no reservations) would be accepted.[27] The dentist Dr. Otto Bordes, Worshipful Master of the lodge, had a decisive influence on the introduction of this regulation. He was a leading representative of the extreme right wing of the Three World Globes Grand Lodge. Since 1929, he had served as the assigned first Grand Warden. Bordes became Grand Master of the National Mother Lodge (Three World Globes) in 1933. His moderate predecessor, Karl Habicht, had refused the request to "work toward racial purity" in 1928.[28] From the minutes of a discussion among the three Old Prussian grand masters and the leadership of the Pan-German Association that had occurred on March 6, 1928, one learns that in contrast, the Grand Master of the Grand Lodge "Zur Freundschaft" ("Friendship"), Dr. Otto Zimmer, shared that he "would like very much to see" his membership (i.e. that of his Grand Lodge) make such a decision. The Grand Master of the Große Landesloge, Müllendorf, explained that the Große Landesloge had concerned itself with this question for a long time but had not yet come to a conclusion.[29]

The concept of a *völkisch* Freemasonry attained its fullest expression during the middle of the 1920s in the form of the Wetzlar and Bielefeld Rings. The so-called "Ring Movements" formed institutional platforms for *völkisch*-anti-Semitic Brothers (of different jurisdictions), who were striving to broaden their influence over all right-wing conservative Freemasonry. The two "gathering movements" originated in the joining together of lodges into the Three World Globes system. The Wetzlar Ring, the numerically larger association, constituted itself on July 4, 1925, for "the strengthening of the position of Old Prussian Freemasonry, especially in defense of and in the struggle for the breakthrough of German and Christian thought in Freemasonry." The main task was seen as "the filling of Masonic Mystery with Christian and German spirit."[30] Representatives of eleven lodges were at the founding meeting, among them delegates from the Munich lodge, "Empor" of "Ludendorff-episode" fame.[31] The Bielefeld Ring, also founded in 1925, soon found reinforcement through like-minded lodges of the other two Old Prussian [grand lodges].[32]

The Rings set themselves against the "Berlin Freemasonry scene," which was definitive in the eyes of all Old Prussians: It was too dominant and not *völkisch* enough for them.[33] No Masonic grand body had adopted the racial standpoint of the Ring lodges, but the concepts developed here were later used to legitimize ideologically the attempt to live on in the "Third Reich." In the formation of the Rings, there was a process that was observed with a certain concern by the leadership of the Grand Lodges, because such tendencies always weaken the authority of grand lodges. In the course of the deliberations of the association of the Old Prussian grand lodges, agreement was reached on March 1, 1928, "that Rings which stretch over different grand lodges were not possible and were not permitted."[34] In the same place, National Grand Master Habicht stated in 1932 that in case of conflict, the Association Directorate would go so far as to forbid the Rings.[35] However, the grand lodge level failed to have such a clear delineation of content. Instead, ideas from the Rings could be spread through the Association organs of the Old Prussians. Moreover, the efforts of the Bielefeld Ring were financially supported by the Große Landesloge. A receipt of February 22, 1926, indicates that a contribution of 1000 Reichs Marks from the Große Landesloge was placed at the Ring's disposal.[36]

Erich Awe, an engineer and Chairman of the Bielefeld Ring of the Old Prussian lodges, was Worshipful Master of the Bielefeld "Freiherr vom Stein" Lodge, a subordinate of the Three World Globes Grand Lodge. On May 1, 1933, Awe tried to join the Nazi Party. He was, however, refused membership in June 1934, in all probability, because of his lodge membership.[37] Like many other *völkisch* Freemasons, he continued his Masonic career in the Federal Republic after the end of National Socialism, and also played an active role in the German Supreme Council.[38] Awe had stayed connected with the Old Prussian grand masters in order to vote on their position vis-à-vis the National Association of German Officers, and with the German Society of Nobility with regard to their examination of the "Freemasonry Question."[39] In June 1926, the three Old Prussian grand masters granted financial support in the amount of 860 Reichs Marks, obviously in connection with an opposition paper published by the Bielefeld Ring. The dissension became public at the same time: the grand lodges accused Awe not only of using a challenging tone in his dealings but also of insufficient inclusion [of people]. Thus, the paper was not presented to them for examination; nor were they apprised in advance.[40]

The founder and Chairman of the Wetzlar Ring was the clergyman Jakob Heep. From 1921 to 1928, Heep was Worshipful Master of "Wilhelm zu den Drei Helmen" (William of the Three Helmets) Lodge in Wetzlar, a subordinate of the Three World Globes Grand Lodge. In 1934, he was called by Reich Bishop Müller to the unified "Reichskirchenkabinett" ("Reichs Church Cabinet").[41] At first, the Ring lodges had planned to resign en masse from the National Mother Lodge (Three World Globes Grand Lodge).[42] Later, they refrained. The country lodges united in the

Ring felt discriminated against by Berlin, and insufficiently represented. Their collective appearance at grand lodge communications, agreed upon in advance, was directed primarily against the relatively liberal Berlin faction of the National Mother Lodge under the leadership of Grand Master Dr. Karl Habicht, which took seven of the ten seats in the Federal Directorate.

According to Heep's concept, Freemasonry was "without doubt of German origin—the English ...having taken over from the German."[43] [!]. Racist thought and pompous pathos are reflected in a speech by Heeps at the anniversary of the founding of his lodge in 1925. In it he said, borrowing from concepts of "racial hygiene," "the *ur*-element in us: to be clean and racially pure down to our blood. The Brothers' motto: the same blood from mother's womb. Let us be careful that the Wetzlar remains a Grail fortress! Be exclusive! Loyalty to you, hail to you, 'Wilhelm zu den Drei Helmen' Lodge!'"[44] In his paper of 1926, "German Wrestling for the Soul of the Royal Art [Freemasonry]," Heep expressed the idea that for the German "blood community," it was necessary to feel "Volkstum" ["nationhood"]: "Foreign blood, foreign races can somehow live with us, and I can in some respects develop a commonality of interests with such fellow citizens...but he can never be a Brother to me... In addition, there is for us Germans the *ur*-element of Christianity...That for us Germans, in our blood, is our most elemental characteristic."[45]

In 1928, the philologist and professor, Dr. Kurt Schmidt of Gotha, succeeded Heeps. On the occasion of his anticipated election as chairman at the seventh convocation of the Wetzlar Ring in Detmold, Schmidt summarized the rationale and purpose of the association: "The Wetzlar Ring is no artificially created 'organization,' but a spiritual movement, completely carried by (based on) thoughts of *Der Führer*, arising out of concern for the future of German Freemasonry."[46]

In another place, Schmidt defined the concept "humanity" not as "brotherhood of humankind" or as "unspecific humanness," but as "national humanity" and "German noble humanness."[47] Schmidt had already expressed this opinion at the beginning of October 1927 during the first training session of the Bielefeld Ring of Old Prussian lodges. Another participant held the view that "Masonic intellectual exercises… could only be engaged in by Brethren of the Christian system, because neither tolerance or humanity, the main content of non-Christian teachings, are psychologically suited to be brought into the mentality necessary for such exercises."[48]

Just as some Nazis tried to prove the alleged "Aryan essence" of Jesus Christ or the "Aryan" nature of the Holy Grail, some *völkisch* Freemasons attempted to figure out congruences between their symbolism and "Aryan" light- and sun-mysticism. Hermann Wirth, a German-Dutch independent scholar, at times a protégé of Himmler, stumbled onto something surprising during his research into the "Aryan" origin of Christianity. His "cult-symbolic research" had shown that the tradition of Freemasonry was "an historical fact stemming from a connection between the tradition of the medieval operative lodges and the pre-Christian, pre-Wotanic and old Germanic *Weltanschauung*." This tradition had had "an oriental-Jewish-Kabbalistic essence superimposed" on it.[49] Wirth, who is considered to be one of the members of the "conservative revolution," had been since 1932 the Director of the "Research Institute for Spiritual Ancient History [Geistesurgeschichte]" in Bad Doberan. As of 1933, under the protection of Prussian Minister of Culture Bernhard Rust, he drew his salary as a full professor in Berlin. The certificate of appointment, signed by Hermann Göring, was, however, never delivered to him.[50] After Wirth attracted Himmler's attention in 1934, the developing connection culminated in 1935 in the founding of the SS society "Ahnenerbe" ("Ancestors' Patrimony, Heritage") together with the Minister of Agriculture and "Reichs-farmers'-leader" Richard Walther Darré. Wirth was its first chairman. Nevertheless, in 1937, because of differences with Himmler, he was "kicked upstairs" into the powerless position of Honorary President, and in the following year was shoved completely out of "Ahnenerbe."[51]

In the process of his studies of symbolism, which were part of his idea of the existence of an "ancient intellectual historical" cultural background, he stumbled perforce onto Freemasonry. It must be emphasized that his heathen-occult-influenced conjectures had nothing in common with the serious historiography of ancient history, and its methodology. Instead, his studies rested on "the compilation of debatable or speculative research topics from various cultural studies like ethnology, theology, anthropology, ancient history, and linguistics."[52] His rejection of "the culture-less, technical-materialistic civilization" he connected with the demand for an "Atlantic-Nordic" Ur-culture, which he ascribed to a so-called Nordic "Race-soul."[53] According to Wirth, Freemasonry was put before the "decision-question [which was whether or not], to go back to its ancient inner tradition…in case it were not excluded from German intellectual life."[54]

Ring Chairman Schmidt considered the question only too gladly, developing the theory of Nordic light cults as the origin of Freemasonry[55]: "The belief in light [worship of light]," said Schmidt, picking up on Wirth's theses, "was a priceless heritage from prehistoric times that now (be)comes alive again in us [Germans—the author]." Schmidt managed the turn (twist) toward Freemasonry by maintaining that "the belief in light was the original foundation of all Masonic symbolism."[56] Like the symbolisms of community and building, also, according to Schmidt, the symbolisms of Weltanschauung and light belong very close together. "Christianity and German-ness are the firm foundations of our 'German-Christian' Freemasonry. These two foundations of our people's soul find their deepest melting together in the belief in light [worship of light] of our Nordic forefathers nurtured and protected by Freemasonry."[57] In October 1932, Wirth appeared as the speaker at a convention of the Wetzlar Ring and "with many illustrations," spoke of "Origins and further life of the Ur-Nordic cult symbolism of death and becoming."[58] Even the Nazi historian Rudolf John-Gorsleben took on the task of interpreting Masonic ritual as "ancient" in the context of a pseudoscientific foundation of the Nazi cult of the Teutonic by using Tacitus's *Germania*. They had therefore "not grown up from foreign, racially Jewish ground, but *ur*-germanic, today partly 'judaicized.'"[59]

On April 2, 1933, Oskar Zetzsche's lodge in Bad Pyrmont staged a conference that concerned itself with "external stones." The affair was led by Christian Zetzsche. His brother, Oskar Zetzsche, had been Worshipful Master for a few months. During the conference, Schmidt and Christian Zetzsche repeated Hermann Wirth's already known opinions about the connection between Freemasonry and "*ur*-nordic cult symbolism" in a slightly different or expanded form. It examined the claim of *völkisch* Freemasonry that it was the bearer of Germanic custom. Christian Zetzsche's demands that his lodge brothers concern themselves in detail with the aforementioned "cult-symbolism research" followed from this: the Order should keep its "true religious nature (essence)" in mind, and its "true tradition" should be kept alive by the Brethren's pilgrimages to Germanic cult shrines of the "external stones."[60]

Wirth was originally supposed to take part in the conference. He declined, however, after the provincial government of Mecklenburg set up by Berlin gave him to understand that there would be consequences to suffer if he did, and after he saw that he was exposed to attacks by Nazi colleagues in his field because of his Masonic contacts. Instead of appearing personally, Wirth sent a written message to Bad Pyrmont, in which he confirmed his thesis of the connection between medieval lodges and the ancient Germanic *Weltanschauung*.[61] Oskar Zetzsche spoke on "What do the External Stones say to us Freemasons?"[62] In his lecture, he maintained first that Freemasons, in contrast to other researchers who concern themselves with the "external stones," had a great advantage, because the [other researchers] could not understand their results "in the complete depth of their cultic meaning,"[63] and therefore posited a connection between the alleged symbolism of the "external stones" and Masonic rituals. Zetzsche interpreted the meaning of the "external stones" as "the firm forms of an ancient Germanic cult," which in its "symbolic actions had to be similar to our Freemasonry."[64] One can find the same thing with Zetzsche's clear attempts to make (manufacture) a "uniquely appropriate" German Christianity – which are reminiscent of other attempts from the *völkish*-Nazi spectrum—by pulling religious elements from the pre-Christian era, making an amalgam of Christianity and deification of the Teutonic peoples. In this event, Oskar Zetzsche differed (separated himself) from the Roman Catholic Church, which, according to him, had undermined the Germanic belief in light [worship of light].[65] With reference to Wirth, Zetzsche differentiated between a "religion of God's sun" and "sun-god religions." The latter originated "as a final result of Nordic ruling peoples making their home in southern latitudes, and mixing with lower, dark-skinned ancient races." Spiritualization and abstraction of a "Nordic-cosmic God-experience" evolved into a "worship of nature-gods and demons, which forced its way up from the lower levels of the dark-skinned ancient native peoples in the mixing of races."[66]

Neuberger exhibits a more subtle methodology compared to Eskau's "Work Association of German Freemasons."[67] Whether it is justifiable to speak of a "less verbal radicalism"[68] is impossible to say (remains to be seen). Altogether, the two Ring movements were not bereft of success in their struggle for direction, even though the result of their directed exercise of influence is hard to show in detail. Thus, the breaking of connections with the Grand Lodge of Vienna by the Three World Globes Mother Lodge in 1931 was, in the end, probably not carried out by the Ring lodges.[69] In the same way, these circles, which in any case [had] few prospects of a reestablishment of fraternal contacts between the Old Prussians and English Freemasonry, were successful in staying in contact [with the Grand Lodge of Vienna]. Corresponding signals from London were refused for the last time by the Prussian side in 1932. The "Rump" Grand Lodge Association was cut off because of its connections with England. In the demand for "defense against anything non-German"[70] that came out of the Wetzlar Ring, the "change from an at first only religious anti-Semitism to a moral one," in the words of Fenner and Schmitt-Sasse, had taken place.[71] That is doubtless correct as far as it goes. Something actually happened that went much farther at least by this time: in the raising of "racial purity" to the "ideal for Freemasonry,"[72] an independent form of *völkisch* Freemasonry with a Christian–"Aryan" cast was created.

The Große Landesloge held fast to the notion that "our enemy sits in the English lodges."[73] In the same year, the Große Landesloge functionary, Oswald Bielig, declared, "the maintenance of our Christian, national, and *völkisch* Freemasonry, her victorious marching forward, depends upon our leadership. We must forge ahead, continuing to believe and resist."[74] With the decision of the Große Landesloge to add "of the German Christian Order" to its name in 1930, according to Freudenschuß, the "change of a Freemasons' lodge into a national order was introduced."[75] This assessment needs correction insofar as the process of change had already begun long before. When, exactly, is hard to pinpoint, since questions of the mode of education were overlaid with political problems. The end of the First World War, unquestionably, marks an important historical point, but already the arguments about the attempts at reform by the Order's Master Friedrich Wilhelm in 1874 pointed in this direction. In any case, the Große Landesloge's acceptance of the sobriquet "of the German-Christian Order" visibly expressed the connection to the tradition of orders in the sense of an increased turning toward that part of its self-image and naturally its separation from all other grand lodges. Felix Witt-Höe, one of the most influential men in the Große Landesloge, had earlier expressed his *völkisch* comprehension of Masonic symbolism: it was an error to believe, he wrote in 1927 to a Masonic brother, "that our ritual has taken over large portions from Jewish symbolism. Thus as certainly, as the Kabbalah is of a purely Aryan origin, and goes back to the Vedas of the Indic people and the sun worship of the Sumerians, so certainly are all symbols of the Old Testament, veiled symbols for the ancient wisdom of the Upanishads, that teaching, which is a thousand years older than the historically much younger writings of those parts of the Old Testament which refer to those symbols." The whole wisdom of the Old Testament was "Aryan heritage and veiled teaching about the Aryan sun-god."[76]

It goes without saying that the extremist positions espoused by the two Ring movements and leading individual Großloge functionaries were disputed within Old Prussian Freemasonry. In several subordinate lodges, a rejection of the *völkisch* character of Freemasonry prevailed. At the same time, it was possible, in the *Bundesblatt* (*Association News*) of the national Mother Lodge, sometimes to propagandize openly anti-Semitic thoughts under the rubric "Unofficial."[77] In exactly the same way, Herman Wirth's pseudoscientific works were printed in the *Bundesblatt*.

Meanwhile, Freemasonry presented itself as all for the Fatherland (*vaterländisch*), even in the humanitarian camp: work in the temple on the occasions of national commemorations—as Hindenburg's birthday, or the celebration of the founding of the Reich—was not uncommon.[78] The Grand Lodge of Bayreuth decided in 1924 to raise the battle flag of the Reich to the status of a Masonic symbol "for stronger emphasis on the Fatherland."[79] In the Grand Lodge of Hamburg in contrast to the liberal direction of the Brethren in Berlin—there was an aggressively anti-Semitic attitude on the part of the subordinate lodges in middle Germany, aimed at changing the Masonic system of teaching.[80] In the same vein, individual members or whole St. John's lodges sought affiliation with the Old Prussians, which, at least on the part of the Große Landesloge, was reluctantly accepted. Felix Witt-Höe, in his capacity as First District Deputy Grand Master, wrote in this connection on May 6, 1932: "It is indeed possible, that individual Brothers and perhaps even lodges en masse, resign from the Grand Lodge of Hamburg, because the direction that their Grand Lodge prefers to take with respect to matters of the Fatherland does not fit, or because too many elements foreign to the race are among the Brethren." One should, Witt-Höe continues, "be very cautious with regard to such an increase…and make clear, in long discussions, the deep difference between our understanding of Freemasonry and theirs."[81]

Old Prussian Freemasonry felt it necessary "[to justify] its national positions on Christianity."[82] In addition, Christian profession, national-ism, anti-Semitism, and Masonic esotericism were consolidated into a specific form of *völkisch* Freemasonry, in which one aspect did not have to be drawn in to justify the other. Of course, fundamental Christian principles such as reconciliation or love for mankind and neighbors were subordinated to the national standpoint without further thought, especially by the Große Landesloge, the one with the system constructed in the most Christian manner. The Große Landesloge, in its rejection, was very loosely connected with the humanitarian brothers. Again and again, responsible functionaries paraded their Christian- and *völkisch*-stamped understanding of Freemasonry into the field as an express opposition to internationalism and pacifism. According to the Große Landesloge, therefore, Freemasonry had "nothing to do with reconciliation among peoples, pacifism and international understanding...the efforts carried by the utopian belief in the reality of a worldwide chain of Brothers are irreconcilable with our views of Freemasonry, and thus dangerous for their effects on many of our people."[83] Felix Witt-Höe wrote in 1925, "Since the Order raises (educates) its members to be 'Masonic Knights,' the symbol of the struggle is especially highly valued. There is no official ceremony, no celebration, no earnest work, without thought for the need of our Fatherland against our oppressors and the encouragement of justice."[84] Here, the spirit of the Order manifested itself as ideology.

The essence of the Order needs a separate explanation at this point. The continuation of Templarism, or the historical orientation to the German Order, which had been founded at the end of the twelfth century on the pattern of the overwhelmingly Romance Templars, played a central role in the Große Landesloge. Calling upon the Strict Observance and the Swedish System, the changeover into the "German-Christian Order" was to be justified even in 1933 as a "return to the original [*ur-*] form,"[85] meaning a return to the original form of the Order. The Große Landesloge "rejected everything that had to do with Freemasonry, expunged anything having an echo of Judaism, and remained what it basically always was: a Christian order."[86]

In the Weimar Republic, many antidemocratic groups styled themselves "Order."[87] As with the specifically Masonic kind, they had in common what Klaus Hornung formulated in his monograph on the Young German Order: The term "Order," as a rule, had "*per se* a political agenda" as part of its makeup, indeed "the profession of [interest in] the Prussian spirit, German history and tradition."[88] In addition, with the principle of "Order," there was an ideological closeness to the *völkisch*. The intellectual and organizational historical connections between the *völkisch* movement in the Empire[89] and that of the Weimar Republic are unmistakable. The *völkisch* idea-conglomerate of the former as well as the latter can be traced largely to a fundamental model of racial ideology: from the economic–romantic, Christian–fundamentalist viewpoint and the search for a "racially tailored" substitute religion (including elements of anti-Semitism, anti-Slavism, blood and earth myths, an incipient anti-emancipatory women's movement, and a racial understanding of elitism) to radical Darwinism, bio-logistical concepts even reaching the point of commonality with the free-thinking, anti-clerical movement.[90] Clearly, an interpretation that narrows the cultural historical phenomenon of the *völkisch* down to the function of a "pool of ideas" of Nazism falls far short. By the same token, the whole ideological inventory existed, from which the Nazi Party took parts, loosely mixing them into their agenda and compressing the whole into the Nazi racial state.

Völkisch groupings were persistently marked by obscure "Order" ideas. Two examples will serve: In 1900, the former Cistercian monk Adolf Joseph Lanz, who styled himself Baron Jörg Lanz von Liebenfels, founded the Order of the New Temple (Ordo Novi Templi [ONT]), which considered itself to be in the tradition of the medieval Templar Order. Professors, scientists, other academics, and writers—among them August Strindberg—were adherents.[91] Lanz, with Guido (von) List, a leading proponent of the so-called "Ariosophy," stylized the "Aryan race" into a religion in the sense of a "cult of pure blood,"[92] and drafted a program (agenda) that cloaked Daim in the somewhat questionable concept "secret teaching of National Socialism."[93] In his specialized concept of race, Lanz had previously thought up the idea of genocide in the "Third Reich." He advocated a social Darwinist body of thought (social Darwinism): master race, breeding and elimination practices, deportation, and liquidation in order to protect the "European master race from downfall (destruc-

146

tion)."[94] The "Thule Society," founded in 1918 by Rudolf von Sebottendorff (really Rudolf Glauer) as an offshoot of the "Germanic Order" founded by Theodor Fritsch in 1912, tried out the mixture of occultism, Templarism, and racism. The "Thule Society," which was "built on the model of a Masonic lodge,"[95] but was extremely anti-Masonic, propagandized for Pan-Germanicism and the superiority of the "Aryan race." It enjoyed the best connections with the elite of Munich society. Hitler, Hess, Frank, and Rosenberg moved in its sphere. From time to time, it was the "center of almost all nationalistic and anti-Semitic power of Munich."[96] Presumably, the founding of the Deutsche Arbeiterpartei (German Workers Party) in 1919 had its roots in the "Thule Society."[97]

It is thus not surprising that even National Socialism adapted the ideology of the Order in a secularized variant. Above all, Himmler often referred to the SS as the "Order," or "new Order." The so-called "Fortress of the Order" Krössinsee was considered the elite establishment of the SS, and Himmler also called the Nazi Party an "Order" at its convention in 1936.[98] The Nazis happily went to great pains to use the history of the German Order for their purposes: "The new Reich had to go on the march on the path of the Knights of the Order of old," Hitler explained.[99] At the same time, however, Hitler distanced himself from Himmler's and Rosenberg's mysticism of the Order, and warned—a contradiction in itself—against "unclear mystical elements slipping into the movement."[100] According to Rauschning, Hitler had appropriated "the thought process of an order, with its inviolable oath of obedience and silence, and its secret teaching revealed stepwise with symbols" from Freemasonry.[101] Independent of the very dubious source, the meaning that was attributed to the cultish–ritualistic use of symbols in the "Third Reich" without question remains. In its characteristic of an order, the SS especially reminds one of Freemasonry: In addition to a ritualized echo accomplished by means of symbols, there are other external characteristics such as initiation, isolation, and hierarchical structures. Thus, unquestionably, the ideology of the order was most characteristic of Himmler's thought-world. He conceived of the "Order under the Skull [and Crossbones]" as an elite laboratory [experimental station] for the "racial renewal" of Germany, which could not succeed without conquering land in the east.[102] "Thus, we have set forth," Himmler elaborated at the Reich Farmers' Convention in Goslar in 1935, "and march as a National Socialistic, military Order of certain Nordic men, and as a sworn community of their kindred, according to immutable laws."[103] Himmler clarified his concept of an order in 1937 in a speech before SS group leaders: "We have…set ourselves the goal, not to found a men's association, which, like all men's or military associations, sooner or later falls apart, but we have set ourselves the goal, here actually to have an order that grows gradually…I hope that in ten years we are…not an order only of men, but of kinship communities. An order, to which women equally necessarily belong as do men…We want a select elite, chosen again and again over centuries——a new nobility for Germany."[104] In 1940, he declared to the officers' corps, "the bodyguard SS for Hitler," that the whole aim for him was to create "an order of good blood that can serve Germany."[105]

The SS, the kernel of the Nazi race-state, developed the thinking and actions of a commander-caste, committed to a common ideology, a common mental attitude, and a common lifestyle, in whose self-concept as an order its own crimes were transfigured, legitimized, and yet more: reassessed. The consciousness of belonging to an "exclusive commander-caste initiated into the secrets of power" began by keeping the spirit of the order and self-concept as elite troops of the "movement."[106] Only upon the "psychological ground of such an extension of existence could the execution of unimaginable mass crimes have been ideologically legitimized."[107] Furthermore, the idea of having the right and duty of executing the model of the race-state was derived from this basis of legitimization. In other words, this resulted in the "ideological revaluation of excessive crime as a selfless philosophical (world-view) deed,"[108] and—because it was incongruent with the "race-struggle"—the disempowerment of general human values.

Nazi propaganda depicted the medieval order-state as the precursor to Prussia in a line of tradition to Nazism, which had, in its content, been

148

practiced by historians since the nineteenth century,[109] and which Artur Moeller van den Bruck conceptually rewrote with regard to the "Third Reich" that he had postulated for the future. He saw a "new race" in Prussia, and a "new space" and to that extent an "omen" for just that "Third Reich."[110] Hitler surely veiled his primarily racial-ideologically motivated policy of *Lebensraum* ("room to live") with the assertion that he embodied the heritage of Prussia and of the order-state.[111] Himmler's demand that only "people of really German Teutonic blood"[112] could live in the East went far beyond the connection to the order-state and German eastern settlement promulgated by the *völkisch* historians. By the same token, however, it is possible that both sought an historical point of connection in the medieval order-state for the qualitative new eastern expansion of the SS-state, indeed in a mixture of functionality and ideological transformation, in their *Drang nach Osten* ("Push toward the East"). In any case, Hitler, Himmler, Rosenberg, and other Nazi leaders strengthened, at the same time, "the attraction of the Nazi regime for these circles, which had already oriented themselves to such hazy ideas of orders, during the time of the Weimar Republic," when they "harked back to the historic German orders in order to increase their personal positions of power."[113] In addition, an intellectual and geopolitical function as a model for Prussia was ascribed to the German Orders or order-state. The national grand lodges in turn harked back in just the same way to Prussian history. As they preferred to represent themselves in the tradition of Frederick II, so did they carefully distance themselves from the system of the Weimar Republic and its representatives, with whom they did not want to be connected.

Also in the form of a discourse on race, whose stature, as we have seen, increased in the lodges, the German-*völkisch* paradigm of an order superimposed itself with the Masonic spirit of order. Thus, the Große Landesloge-Order-Master Balthasar-Wolfradt admitted in 1928 in the context of contacts with the German Nobles (Nobility) Association that a way was being sought "to give racism a validity in the Order."[114] Further, Balthasar-Wolfradt opined that according to the advisors' protocol, "in connection with racism and [the execution of] keeping the Christian Order pure," one could "approach the thought" that in order to be accepted "the grandparents had to be born as Christians."[115]

After the "seizure of power" by the Nazis, recourse was increasingly taken to the interpretation pattern developed by the Ring lodges. In May 1933, the journal of the Große Landesloge, in connection with the philosophy of the Order, announced that it had been "indeed always the essence [of the Große Landesloge—author's note]. Our view is that there is an ancient transmission, bent into the Christian-Germanic in the days of early Christianity and in the Middle Ages, which was transplanted into the narrowest circles. One of the most important symbols of the Order was and is, light as a sign of the revelation of God." Further, the veneration of the Creator happens in the spirit of "the noble Nordic kind." The Große Landesloge showed itself to be convinced of "the purity of that, which we and our fathers did under the protection of the House of Hohenzollern."[116] Such a text expresses in an exemplary way the mental climate in which political, religious, and *völkisch* arrogance had been able to develop. The clinging to neo-Templar, the tradition of the self-conception of a privileged Old Prussian Freemasonry, and German-national identity as well as more or less strong racist influences led to the fact that the Große Landesloge retreated increasingly into a self-imposed isolation as of the 1920s.

In the case of *völkisch* Freemasonry, it was not about the phenomenon of a single grand lodge or about the ideas of a small sectarian circle, but a collective (whole) picture that included the activities of outsiders like Eskau as well as the pronouncements (discourse) of a Three World Globes grand officer, who, in the presence of a disgusted Reichs Secretary of State Stresemann, revealed anti-republican and *völkisch* ideas.[117] Because of the hostility from the Brotherhood, which was aimed primarily at his foreign policy, Stresemann considered, for awhile, leaving the national Mother Lodge. It did not come to that: Stresemann remained a Freemason, and kept his membership in his mother lodge; however, he withdrew from active participation in Freemasonry. It could not have escaped him that the notion of a "Nordic race" taken from anthropology and popularized had taken hold in a specifically Christian–Masonic form. The dedication of significant German Freemasons such as August Horneffer to Nazism, the tradition of military lodges, the interpretations advocated in the orbits of the Wetzlar and Bielefeld Rings, an increasingly crass anti-Semitism, as well as the Principle of Order of the Große Landesloge sketched above, mark a broad and many-faceted current within the German lodges, which justifies speaking of the establishment of a *völkisch* Freemasonry long before the seizure of power by the Nazis. For a judgment of the conduct of the national grand lodges between 1933 and 1935, this circumstance must necessarily be taken into consideration. In other words, *the* attempt at a mobilization must be placed into the context of the longer-term historical developments of ideas and institutions.

4.2 TRANSFORMATION AND CHANGE OF TRADITION OF THE NATIONAL GRAND LODGES

At first, Old Prussian Freemasonry reacted to the Nazi takeover and the beginning of the unification of State and Society with expressions of loyalty. From the beginning, those responsible were obliged to express their philosophically (world view—Weltanschauung) motivated claim to an appropriate position in the "Third Reich," and to succeed with it against the anti-Masonic basic position of the Nazi Party. On the occasion of the so-called "Day of Potsdam," March 21, 1933, which marked the end of the Weimar democracy for propaganda purposes, the Old Prussians sent Reichs Chancellor Hitler a telegram with the following message: "On the 'Day of Potsdam,' which is so significant for Germany, the three Old Prussian Grand Lodges present to the national government, in consideration of their close connection with the Prussian royal, and the German imperial, house, the assurance of their deepest devotion. As we have previously made every effort, true to our national and Christian tradition, to work for the good of the German people, so we shall continue unswervingly to be most loyally obedient to the national

government, and with all the powers at our disposal, aid in the rebuild-
ing of our beloved Fatherland."[118] In addition to the Grand Masters Kurt
von Heeringen (Große Landesloge) and Oskar Feistkorn (Grand Lodge
'Friendship'), Karl Habicht (for the National Mother Lodge) signed the
telegram. He (Habicht), however, could only have done this functioning
as a commissary, because, already on March 10, the moderate, national-
liberal wing of the Three World Globes Grand Lodge had capitulated, in
the face of hostility of forces of the extreme right in its own ranks. With
Grand Master Habicht, who left his lodge soon thereafter and turned his
back on all of Freemasonry,[119] the whole old Grand Lodge line (all the
Grand—National Mother—Lodge officers) withdrew. The dentist Dr.
Otto Bordes was designated his successor, against the voices (over the
objections) of the Berlin faction. Bordes was said to have belonged to the
circle of Hitler's personal acquaintances.[120]

The majority of German Freemasons, especially in the Old Prussian
lodges, had decided to ally (mobilize) themselves with Nazism. Consequently, they sought direct contact with the powers that were, and asked
for a renewal of state protection, in connection with the Wilhelmanic
Reich, by means of petitions. The Große Landesloge, meanwhile, felt
itself hindered by all of the other Masonic Bodies on the way to its goal
of convincing the Reichs Government and the Nazi Party of its own conviction, which conformed to the system. In an internal memo of March
30, 1933, the Grand Lodge leadership accused the other Old Prussians
of holding a "hardly clear position," which had an "unfavorable" effect.[121]

On April 7, 1933, the day on which the "Civil service law" and the
"Law unifying the Länder with the Reich" were issued, there was a meeting between the administration of the Große Landesloge Freemasons and
Hermann Göring, who at this point was still serving as Reichs Minister
without Portfolio and "Commissar Prussian Minister of the Interior."[122]
The conversation with Göring, in which Große Landesloge Grand Master
von Heeringen, Felix Witt-Höe participated, turned out to be a large
failure. The idea that representatives of the National Mother Lodge were

there can be disproven by the sources. While Peters[123] tells us that Bordes and three other Three World Globes functionaries had taken part in the discussion, a circular letter of April 11 from the Three World Globes Association Directorate allows the conclusion that some representatives were absent. It said, "On Monday, April 10, in the morning, the Landes Grand Master of the Große Landesloge of the Association of German Freemasons, von Heeringen, appeared in our Association House. He repeated the content of the conversation which he had had on Friday, April 7 with Minister Goering. The Minister had remarked, according to what von Heeringen said, that…in a national socialist state of fascistic bent, there is no room for Freemasons…It is exceedingly regrettable for us [?], that the Grand Master did not inform us of the content of his conversation with Minister Goering already on Saturday or Sunday, thus robbing us of the possibility of making decisions on this important question in our special annual meeting" [of the Grand Lodge on that weekend in Berlin—author's note].[124]

Shortly thereafter, Witt-Hoë expressed his disappointment about this conversation—which had clearly taken place in a very cool atmosphere—and had been only a few minutes long, in a letter to the friendly (allied) Grand Lodge of Sweden.[125] Moreover, the course of the meeting must have caused such an upset that the Grand Lodge sent out two circulars on the same day. The first one said that Goering, as Commisarial Prussian Interior Minister, had declared himself as not responsible for the "Freemason Question," and had indicated that "it was much more a concern of the national (Reichs) authorities."[126] The other one was concerned with the disposition of the Supreme Order Department on the revamping of the order. The announcement said, "After the experience of the discussions with the responsible positions, one may safely assume that the government of the National Socialists will not be in a position, for internal and external reasons, to allow associations to remain, which have the designation "Lodge, and whose members call themselves 'Freemasons'…Extraordinary times also require extraordinary measures from a leadership conscious of its responsibilities. In light of this situation, the leaders of the Order decree that which follows: 1. The Order returns to its original form. The designation as 'Große Landesloge der Freimaurer von Deutschland (Grand National Lodge of the freemasons of Germany),' assumed in the eighteenth century, ceases today. The Order will call itself, corresponding to its essence, from now on: Deutsch-Christlicher Orden (Gral [handwritten addition]) der Tempelritter (German Christian Order Grail of the Knights Templar)... 2. With this decision, the Order has ceased to be a Masonic body."[127]

The decision to change the name and, as the case may be, the transformation occurred without previous discussion with the other two Old Prussian grand lodges. When the step was announced to the National Mother Lodge three days later, on April 10, the Lodge made an analogous decision, and informed its subordinate lodges in the already-quoted circular letter of April 11.[128] The Grand Lodge "Friendship" did the same thing.

On April 15, an internal judicial decision within the Große Landesloge opted for the chosen way (blazed trail). According to the vote which supported the decree of the Master of the Order, it was recommended that the judicial person of the Order not be destroyed: "We consider the risk of termination of the old, but newly made judicial personality less than the risk that the State will not permit a new judicial personality."[129] Consequently, the leadership of the Order later confirmed that there could be no thought of a dissolution, and that the resultant new internal order was much more "within the framework of the legal determinations."[130]

With the decree of the Supreme Order Department of the Große Landesloge on April 7, there went out a summons to the Grand Lodge Committee for April 23. The decision-making about the new disposition introduced by the leadership of the Order was on the agenda. There were differences of opinion only in regard to the name. It was decided by a majority that the addition "of the Knights Templar," against which disfavor was expressed by the membership, as well as "of the Grail," favored by the Master of the Order, because it "indicated the deep Christian kernel of essence of the Order," would be dropped.[131] Otherwise, the grand

Lodge Committee agreed with the new structure. After the meeting of the sitting Masters of St. Andrew's and St. John's Lodges of the Große Landesloge agreed to the new structure, the last plenary session of the old Große Landesloge constituted itself, which similarly had been summoned because of the decree of April 7. After a short discussion, it agreed to the new structure under the name "German Christian Order." Directly following that, a meeting of the German Christian Order was held for the purpose of writing a constitution. The minutes were written, and were printed in the May 1933 issue of the Order's newsletter. The most important subject of the discussion was the presentation of a resolution about an enabling act. By the term "enabling act" they specifically made the connection with the national enabling act, which had been passed on March 23, 1933, and announced the next day. The leadership of the Order was concerned with enforcing the "authoritarian principle" and transferring "constitutive competences" of the plenary session to the Master of the Order and therefore onto the executive. The resolution, which was accepted without dissention, said, "The constitutional convention has firm faith in the Leader of the Order, Master of the Order Brother Balthasar-Wolfradt, that the new structure of the Order is in the best of hands with him. It empowers him, therefore, to carry out the internal and external building up of the Order according to his judgment on the basis of the guidelines announced today."[132]

In addition, a 19-paragraph constitution was passed. It said, among other things:

1. The German Christian Order is a corporation of free men of German blood based on the principle of fatherland ...

2. The aim and purpose of the order is...to make convinced champions of the Christian religion and protagonists (lit: professors!) of the German-*völkisch* world-view...

3. It follows from the German and Christian essence of the Order, that only Germans of Aryan descent, who are baptized Christian can be members."[133]

Already on April 12, the National Christian Order Frederick the Great had informed the Nazi Party leadership "that after the war [WW I—trans. note] our Order carried the designation 'Freemasons' Lodge' only as a traditional name. The connections with foreign lodges were completely broken off 'long ago,' and with German lodges that accept Jews and those of Jewish heritage, a year ago." Further, "It has been expressed in many public and private statements of the above-mentioned lodges, that since we have turned away from them, that we incorrectly kept the name 'Freemasons' Lodge.' Because of this, we, for our part, have drawn the necessary conclusions in a fundamental and complete manner."[134] On the same day, the Three World Globes Grand Master, Bordes, in a letter to Goebbels, asked "for the honor of a visit by you or a deputy commissar ordered by you to have unrestricted access to our archives, and all our facilities, and to participate in a solemn assembly of the order."[135] On April 8 and again on April 25, the Große Landesloge encouraged the Reichs—Prussian—Ministry of the Interior to nominate a Reichs commissar for the "Freemason Question."[136]

With respect to Party and government positions, the German Christian Orders valued the statement that they had freed themselves from their Masonic identity: "We are no longer Freemasons. That is to be said immediately to every outsider and every Brother of the order."[137] In keeping with these points, internal designations, officers' titles, forms of address, forms of greeting, as well as certain formalities were changed. The concept "Freemason" was replaced to some extent by the designation "Ordensjünger" (disciple of the order).[138] The (former) St. John's and St. Andrew's lodges of the Große Landesloge now called themselves "Konvente" (assemblies). The circular letters became the "Ordensblatt" (Newsletter of the Order; the organ of the Three World Globes had the same name); the binding, however, was decorated with the Cross of the Order instead of the six-pointed star as symbol of the Supreme Architect of the Universe. In short, the Masonic tradition was sloughed off as a solely superficial shell that was used for awhile—since the eighteenth century.

The transformations continued with various changes in the ritual and symbolism, which had long been discussed and encouraged to some extent in the circles of *völkisch*-leaning St. John's lodges. There was not one hint in the sources that would support the statement made later from the Masonic side, that the altered rituals were developed only for disguise or camouflage and not prepared anew. The Old Prussians indeed changed old challenges around[139]: They eliminated Hebrew concepts from the "work" and replaced Old Testament elements with those of the Germanic saga- and Grail-worlds. The Hiram legend was traded for the Baldur Saga (Baldur, the Germanic "beaming" god). The columns Jachin and Boaz from Solomon's Temple used in many Masonic illustrations were, without further ado, renamed "Light" and "Folk." The Trestleboard carpet in the Three World Globes system now decorated the Straßburg Minster (Cathedral) instead of Solomon's Temple.[140]

Even the swastika found a place in the symbolism of the German-Christian Order: in the case of a subordinate lodge of the Grand Lodge "Friendship" that occurred long before the Nazis' seizure of power, and clearly in direct connection with the Nazi Party symbol, which had been in use since 1920. It was a Regensburg lodge, the "Three Keys of True German Brotherhood," which came out of a "Circle of friends of national and *völkisch*-minded men" in September 1924, that used the swastika in their lodge logo, the so-called jewel. The membership of this lodge consisted mostly of former officers, who were active in patriotic-nationalistic (lit: "fatherland-minded") associations such as the "German-*Völkisch* Defense and Offense Association," the "Treasure of the Teutons," "Bavaria and the Reich," "Stahlhelm," or the "National Association of German Officers" after the end of the [First World] War.[141] The lodge decided in 1933 to dissolve itself for this reason: "The St. John's Lodge 'Three Keys of True German Brotherhood,' in Regensburg was founded in 1924 on a purely *völkisch* basis in order to unite patriotic, nationalistic, and *völkisch*-minded men; to further this way of thinking; and to carry this way of thinking out into the struggle for the seizure of power. After internal national freedom was won under the leadership of Adolf Hitler and through his national socialistic movement, the coming together of patriotic and *völkisch*-minded men in lodges is not necessary. It is much more appropriate for each and every German to become a part of the present great national event ('happening'). We have therefore unanimously decided to dissolve our lodge… and at the same time, each man for himself, to resign from Freemasonry."[142]

The swastika jewel (possibly the best known of its kind) of the Three World Globes subordinate lodge "The Golden Wheel on the Rhine" in Mainz originated in another historical context. It had been used since 1909, the year the lodge was founded. There is a description of the emblem in the documentation of the founding from March 1909, which says that it consisted of a "silver cross with enamel overlay in the arms." Further: "Between [the arms] is the Hessian lion. The middle shield bears the ancient [lit: archaeological] swastika (sign of good wishes) surrounded by a chain and the name of the lodge."[143] On October 30, 1928, the Conference of Masters decided to remove the swastika from lodge illustrations: "That no political leanings be pursuant to this sign" needed no further explanation, said the reasoning. "However, in recent years, when this sign was given a political meaning, we changed …our lodge emblem, seal, stamp and stationery, so that 'a golden wheel on a red ground' was placed there instead of the swastika."[144]

Despite the fact that the lodge in Mainz had distanced itself, at least politically, from the Nazis, the swastika jewel was brought up by the leadership of the National-Christian Order as an indication of ideological agreement with National Socialism. This conclusion occasioned a circular letter, signed by Bordes in January 1934, in which it said, "Must I remind you that our lodge in Mainz put the symbol of National Socialism, the swastika, the rune of spring into its jewel at the time of its founding in 1909?"[145]

After the "seizure of power," the representation of angled circles stylized into a swastika (with its arms facing left) was used as a general emblem of office of the worshipful master of the (former) National Mother Lodge and the Grand Lodge "Friendship."[146] Both grand lodges went one step farther:

They raised the swastika to a so-called official symbol on the "Reichs" level, as is seen in a circular letter of April 29, 1933, from Grand Master Oscar Feistkorn: "Herewith I decree in agreement with the National order of Frederick the Great, that the ancient, Aryan sign of the victorious spring sun, 'the swastika' is, from now on, the symbol of light of our German-Christian Order 'Friendship.' On festive occasions in Berlin, the Order will raise the swastika flag next to the black, white, and red flag."[147]

In the meantime, a party edict from the Nazi Reichs Administration of May 1933 stated that "dual membership of party members in lodges or orders, even those that maintain they stand for national or ethical matters of importance and the betterment of the German people…is to be rejected."[148] The Chief of the Examination and Arbitration Committee of the Nazi Reichs Administration, Walter Buch, who held an especially relentless attitude toward the "Freemason Question," had the decisive role in the realization of this party decree.

On June 27, the Grand Masters of the Order of the (former) National Mother Lodge and the Grand Lodge "Friendship" expressed in a letter to Hitler that they felt their "honor insulted" by the reproach that the "setting aside of the name Freemason and the transformation…was a… disguise." The Grand Masters continued: "Never in the Old Prussian grand lodges was the black, red, and gold flag unfolded." The "results" of Wirth's "research" and the preliminary work of the *völkisch* lodges in the Ring movements were now struck (stricken out): "The old Germanic treasure of well-being, dressed in Christian-medieval clothing" has been "rescued for us in our time" by the German-Christian Order. Both grand lodges subjugated themselves to "'Der Führer' unconditionally," and asked him "to give our Order a place in the national movement." At the same time they announced that they wanted to work "for the Fatherland as they had previously done outside the National Socialist Party."[149]

Besides the various petitions from the Order administrations, individual members of the Old Prussian organizations turned to party and government positions, partly to protest against the increased anti-

Masonic encroachments by SA-Strike Troops after the Reichstag elections of March 5, and partly to emphasize their *völkisch* views. So, for example, a member of the appropriately well-known Three World Globes subordinate lodge "Empor" in Munich in a government petition of June 4, 1933, wrote: "We, especially our former St. John's Lodge…have been, from the very beginning, strictly German, Aryan, and national, much earlier in fact, than the National Socialist Party existed."[150]

The resolution to enforce the racial principle was made clear by the Order's Große Landesloge on September 6, 1933. After people hesitated before the "seizure of power" and a decision to adopt racial anti-Semitism was not made, the ruling of April 23 was intensified by a decree from the grand master (Ordens-Meister). A notice to all branches of the Order said, "The meaning of the race question, so fateful for our people, which achieved general recognition with the victory of the national revolution," gave occasion for a decree "because of the enabling act of April 23, 1933." It said in detail:

1. Brethren of the Order who are not of Aryan descent, are dismissed honorably, effective immediately.

2. This determination does not apply to Brethren of the Order who entered the Order before 1914, or who have fought for the German Reich or its allies in the World War in the front lines, or whose sons and fathers have fallen in the World War.

3. For the purposes of this decree, people of Aryan descent are those whose parents and grandparents were Aryans.

4. For Brethren of the Order whose wives are Jewish, ruling no. 1 applies."[151]

To put this into effect, all members had to fill out a questionnaire. Among others, the following questions were to be answered:

"1. Were your parents and grandparents of Aryan descent? …

2c. Did you fight in the front lines in the World War, or did you take part in the battles in the Baltic States, in Upper Silesia, against 'Spartacists' and Separatists, or against enemies of the national uprising [i.e. 'Seizure of Power']?

Is your wife Jewish?"[152]

The same rules applied to new acceptances. In the acceptance process, the "Seeker" had to fill out a corresponding obligation certificate.

The other German-Christian orders introduced the "Aryan paragraph" on the pattern of the "permanent official law," and thereby forced all "non-German descent" Brothers to leave the organization. Thus, the (former) Grand Lodge "Friendship" gave notice that "only men of Aryan descent could be members: Jews and Marxists were excluded." There was more: "The order wishes to be a school for leaders, a nursery, green house of German-Christian public spirit, and to make the valuable old Germanic intellectual treasure useful for the building up of the new State."[153] In the same vein, 42 of the By-Laws of the National Christian Order Frederick the Great said that only he could be a member who was of "Aryan descent at least three generations back."[154]

The national-Christian grand lodges took over the rulings of the "permanent official law," up to the named exception rulings,[155] and applied them. In doing so, the lodges were no different from other non-state establishments, such as class organizations, student associations, or press and cultural businesses, which did the same thing, and indeed without having been forced to do so, up to this point. In other words, they hastened to do so in "advance" obedience. In addition, the sharper version of the "Aryan paragraph" that the Nazi Party used[156] was applied; the so-called "closely related to a Jew," i.e. those members married to Jews, was excluded. Implementation rulings of November 6, 1933, determined social contacts with such brothers. According to them, members married to women of the Jewish faith were to be "honorably discharged," whereas those "who were married to baptized Jews" were to be discharged, "in case the determinations of Point 2" did not apply.[157]

In October 1933, the Freemasons (Große Landesloge) took the resignation of the German Reich from the League of Nations and the Geneva Disarmament Conference as the occasion to renew its expressions of loyalty to Hitler. In a telegram signed by Grand Master Balthasar-Wolfradt, the Freemasons "thanks, most respectfully for the manly decision to free Germany from the League of Nations, and assures the most loyal adherence, come what may."[158]

The other two Old Prussian orders followed suit. In a telegram sent together to Hitler, they declared, "We greet the Reich government's decision, which reflects the honor and worthiness of the German people, with pride and joy, and we place ourselves in loyal adherence behind our Reichs Chancellor."[159]Meanwhile, the leadership of the Große Landesloge, in circular letters, continuously informed the Fraternity about the continuation of the efforts to gain state recognition. People were especially concerned with spreading confidence in this regard. Despite their assertions that there would soon be a "positive" decision by the responsible government offices on the continued existence of Freemasonry, the leadership of the Große Landesloge saw itself forced to announce a setback on August 7, 1933. In a circular, they made known for the first time that "the authority placed over us, the Prussian Interior Ministry, has not yet taken care of our petition concerning the change of our names, etc." This meant "that we are forced, very much against our will, to use our old designation in the public or legal sphere," which would not disturb "the internal transformation" of the Order.[160] A conversation held by Bolle and Witt Hoë, representing the Fraternity, with an official of the Prussian Interior Ministry (presumably Ministry Director Eickhoff), on September 12, 1933, resulted in the following: that in official affairs, as always, the designation "Große Landesloge of Freemasons of Germany, German Christian Order" was to be used.[161]

The expectation that the new formation as a German-Christian Order would forever be able to prevent the threatening danger of forced dissolution and prohibition had, up to then, not come to pass. These transformations had been made under the impression of actual distress. By the same token, it did not come to this suddenly. As has been shown, long before the Nazis seized power, the ideological orientation toward *völkisch* thinking within the national Christian had begun to assert itself. It was a process--less a break with tradition than a change of tradition. There is not a single indication in the sources that people acted only because they were forced to by political circumstances, and after a possible end of the Nazi domination would give up "Aryan paragraphs" and the Fraternal constitution. The change of tradition carried out by the Order's leadership under the motto "Back to the origins" was thus neither camouflage nor self-denial. Much more, people hoped, as always, that by adaptation of the external form, and by changing the ritual and symbols, they would succeed in convincing the new rulers of their German-*völkisch* persuasion.

The contact lay also in the consistency of this policy with the German Christians since, more than ever before, the question about those allied (i.e. who were members) arose. From the perspective of national-Christian Freemasonry, it was obviously [sensible] to join with the "German Christians" or especially the later Reichs bishop Ludwig Müller who stood close to this movement. The Königsberg (Kaliningrad) military district pastor Müller had at first served as an "authorized agent of the Reichs Chancellor for Affairs of the Evangelical Church." On August 4, 1933, Göring named him a Prussian privy councilor, which, to be sure, brought no political influence but indeed prestige with it. On the same day, the Prussian church senate named Müller as provincial bishop. In this capacity, he was responsible, with others, for the passage of an "Aryan paragraph" at the Prussian ("Brown") Synod in September, which in turn gave rise to the deciding reason for the establishment of the Pastors' Need Alliance. On September 27, 1933, at the National Synod in Wittenberg, Müller was elected Reichs Bishop.[162]

Shortly before it dissolved itself in 1935, the idea came to circles within the (former) National Mother Lodge of making the Reichs Bishop the Grand Master to save the Order.[163] It is possible that the Old Prussians offered even Goering the grand mastership of a presumably united Fraternity.[164] Joining the "German-Christians" had been already discussed within the Große Landesloge since May 1933.[165] As can be seen in the correspondence of the Landes Grand Master von Heeringen with a Brother in Königsberg, the Große Landesloge at first preferred consciously circumspect contact. There was mail and telephone contact between von Heeringen and Müller, while the two other Old Prussian Grand Masters, Bordes and Feistkorn, met with Müller for a face-to-face conversation in May 1933.[166] The leadership of the Große Landesloge reacted to the fact that the "German-Christians" expressly tolerated no Freemasons in their ranks and required a declaration to that effect. It said, in connection with the completed transformation, that Brethren could sign the form with a clear conscience because "we no longer belong to a Masonic lodge."[167] In all this, there was no distinction made between humanitarian and German-Christian lodges by the "German-Christians," in their anti-Masonic agitation during membership convocations. This prompted a Große Landesloge Brother to write a letter to Reichs Bishop Müller.[168] The response from Müller's authorities, the so-called "Reichs Church Government," was clear. It was stated that "the propagandistic work of the religious movement 'German-Christians,' was its own business," and "in no way—at least not directly—did it belong to the ecclesiastical area of authority." Thus, it was made clear that Freemasonry was rejected by the national socialistic state "for reasons surely known to them," and that this rejection also extended to the Große Landesloge. The "German-Christians" would share the rejection "of lodge work that grew out of the spirit of a humanitarian and liberal world citizenry," and "the Evangelical (i.e. Protestant, Lutheran) Church in the "Third Reich" did not see itself in a position, "to take a stand against the work coming from the national socialistic *Weltanschauung*."[169]

The top brass of the Große Landesloge was very interested in making direct personal contact with Müller, but by early summer 1933 it had already become more difficult to do so. In the fall, Müller declared himself ready for a meeting with Bishop Joachim Hossenfelder, the co-founder and first Reichs Leader of the "German-Christians." He got into this whole affair through his father, Kurt Hossenfelder, who was a Freemason—first in the National Mother Lodge, then in the Große Landesloge.[170] Another intermediary came into the circle of contacts—the already-mentioned merchant from Kiel and Brother Andreas Paulsen, who had a connection to the Fraternity's leadership as well as to Kurt Hossenfelder. Hossenfelder informed Paulsen about the correspondence with his son (i.e. Joachim Hossenfelder) and about the son's conversation with Müller, and Paulsen had told the Große Landesloge about the outcome. Only then did the latter turn in the person of the later Order (Grand) Master Friedrich Bolle directly to Joachim Hossenfelder on November 8, 1933.[171] In addition to a conversation with Müller, the Große Landesloge was concerned to test thoroughly the conditions of a possible integration of the Order into the new structure of the Protestant Church in the "Third Reich."[172] While Kurt Hossenfelder indicated that such a model (idea) would have a chance at success only together with Old Prussians, if at all,[173] the Fraternity's leadership had probably envisioned a solo try. It is not certain whether the planned conversation among the Fraternity's leadership, the Reichs Bishop, and Joachim Hossenfelder actually occurred, due to incomplete sources. In any case, the thought of continuing the desired existence with the help of the "German-Christians" or, as the case might be, Reichs Bishop Müller—even if this meant a loss of independence (self-sufficiency)—was dropped, in the case of the Große Landesloge, so it seems, during 1934—or, at least it was not pursued any farther. The possible reason was that, until then, no concrete agreement with Müller had been reached. The fact that the "Reichs Church Government" was not successful in establishing a "Church Peace," and the realization that Hitler would drop the "German-Christians" and the Reichs Bishop, could also have played a role.[174] Perhaps the Große Landesloge also recognized that a strictly centralized State Church, strictly obedient to the Nazis, did not guarantee the continued existence and recognition of a Christian-*völkisch* Order. In any case, one is not surprised that the temporary advances of the Old Prussians remained one-sided. Because the powers that be within the Protestant Church were aiming for elimination of opposition, they had no interest in cooperating with the Freemasons as a more-or-less independent creation, thus giving them some freedom.

The confidence of the Old Prussian functionaries that they could maintain themselves as far as possible within their institutions was, at the beginning, strengthened by the expectation that the German-nationalistic people in Hitler's cabinet would be in a position to exercise a moderating influence on Nazi politics in general and on the question of the German Christian Order in particular. However, even after these people were long gone, and even leading National Conservatives had been murdered in connection with the Röhm Affair, the responsible parties in the (former) national grand lodges persisted in their attempt to find a niche for *völkische* Freemasonry in the form of an order within the National Socialistic state.

In the meantime, the liberal-humanitarian "Blaubuch der Weltfrei-maurerei" ("Blue Book of World Freemasonry") noted that Freemasonry had ceased to exist in Germany: "because the former grand lodges, which had been eliminated" had "nothing to do, either externally or internally, with world Freemasonry—meaning that of the Ancient Obligations."[175] This was a correct conclusion in which the principles of tolerance of the Ancient Obligations were rejected—not for the first time. Completely untenable in contrast is the idea that these lodges, which had decided to hang on "for the monolithic National Socialistic state," became the more dangerous, the more they sought to put their reliability to the test.[176] The Freemasons who mobilized themselves were neither a political danger for the Nazis' keeping and consolidating power, nor did the wielding of sovereignty in the "Third Reich" manifest itself as monolithic. However, the ruling system was based on ideological consensus. A continuation of *völkisch* lodges in the framework of this basic consensus would have been possible from their own point of view, but not from the standpoint of the Nazi principle of totalitarianism and the ideology of the people's community, which directed themselves against the elite and the bourgeoisie.

Chapter 5

THE GERMAN LODGES BETWEEN CONFLICT AND CONFORMITY 1933-1935

5.1 THE HUMANITARIAN LODGES

For some time after January 30, 1933, real priority was not given to the "Freemasonry question." For this reason, the coercive action against lodges in the consolidation phase of the National Socialist (Nazi) regime was less centrally directed, but rather determined by the arbitrariness of local SA and SS units. Individual Freemasons were persecuted because of their opposition to National Socialism rather than their lodge affiliation, but these can hardly be separated from each other. Prominent examples of this are Carl von Ossietzky, Kurt Tucholsky, or a political person such as Leo Müffelmann. In his case, an added factor was that he had belonged to the SPD (German Social Democratic Party) for a while.[1] Strangely enough, and largely unknown, is that the Social Democrats William Leuschner and Julius Leber, who as prominent representatives of the resistance were executed, had likewise been Freemasons.[2]

After the "seizure of power," the repudiations within German Freemasonry continued as expected. Loyalty to National Socialism was occasionally justified by reference to the passage in the "Ancient Obligations" that treats of civil authority, according to which the lodge brother had to be "a peaceable subordinate to civil power."[3] The left liberal minority of the Masonic organizations, however, did not see any prospect for their continuation under the conditions of National Socialistic state terror. The Symbolische Großloge terminated its work in Germany and eventually moved its seat into exile in Palestine. The FzaS ("Freemasons' Association of the Rising Sun") and the German Regional Group of the General Masonic League were dissolved.[4] The Scottish Rite was "put to sleep" on March 31, 1933, by a resolution of the Supreme Council of Germany, which meant that it withdrew from Germany, but did not dissolve. The symbolic lodges had already passed a similar resolution three days earlier. The "inactivation" of the Scottish Rite and the Symbolische Großloge were purposeful measures, because with latent continuation, the organizational structures of the "grand bodies" were kept intact. The governing bodies continued to exist formally, thus ensuring that the possibility of future action was maintained.[5] In connection with the later activity of the Symbolische Großloge of Germany in exile, Müffelmann guaranteed that their members could be moved into the Scottish Rite. To this end, in his capacity as a "Grand Inspector Commander," he signed an authorization, on April 24, 1934, which also contained permission for the installation of AASR (Ancient Accepted Scottish Rite) "workshops" in Palestine. The deduction from this that he had created a "Supreme Council for Germany in Exile" (which he obviously would not have been at all authorized to do)—is still debated in Masonic research.[6]

The widespread statement that most of the established humanitarian grand lodges dissolved themselves after the takeover of the government by the Nazis is unfounded.[7] In truth, their action was more complicated and contradictory, as a look at the Bayreuth Grand Lodge of the Sun shows: its Grand Master, Hermann Koelblin, had not only resigned because of impaired health but had also retired from his business. A successor could not be found. Thus, the management lay with Associate Grand Master Bernhard Beyer.[8] On April 12, 1933, he delivered an opinion in a circular that lodges could remain in existence only by adding the "Aryan-

168

Paragraph" to their charters. Meanwhile, most Jewish members would not only have "drawn the consequences in the most selfless way," but also have voluntarily withdrawn, for which they were assured by Beyer that the lodges owed them "a great debt of gratitude." Furthermore, he asked all subordinate lodges to "continue their work despite the inevitable changes in principle." He recommended that those lodges which still had Jewish members "urge" voluntary withdrawal.[9] Only six days later, Beyer announced the resolution for the dissolution of the Grand Lodge, and made it clear to the subordinate lodges that they should follow his recommendation and join one of the numerically larger Christian orders. Otherwise, he called upon the subordinate lodges either to dissolve completely or change into a "profane association" in expectation of an imminent prohibition of Masonic organizations.[10] On April 30, the General Assembly, which was meeting in Würzburg, confirmed all of Beyer's decisions. At the same time, a successor institution was born—an association with the name "Society for Culture and Knowledge," which introduced the "Aryan Paragraph." With the assistance of this "Society," an attempt was made to save the lodge possessions and the Masonic museum collection. After the Gestapo learned of the intention to transfer the holdings into the Masonic archives of the friendly Netherlands Grand Lodge in The Hague, the collection was seized on September 16, 1933. On September 21, the lodge hall was plundered, and was used from then on by the National Socialist People's Welfare (NSV). Ritual objects, the archives, and the library were removed to the Sicherheitsdienst Headquarters in Berlin, and the administration of the lodge assets put under the Bavarian political police.[11] The establishment of a "Society for Culture and Knowledge" failed primarily because of the objection of the town councilor of Bayreuth.[12]

Without becoming friendly with the National Socialist government—although not without internal conflicts—the Eclectic Association dissolved on March 20, 1933. During the last meeting of the official Council on March 28, the resolution to dissolve was called a "declaration of a state of emergency," which had been made "for the sake of the integrity of the Masonic work." Grand Master Dr. Friedrich Ganser had come to the conclusion that the Frankfurt Grand Lodge "no longer held together internally." He did not want to subscribe to the demand for voluntary withdrawal of the Jewish members "because he was still convinced that the Jewish brothers were faithful German men." However, the Eclectic Association installed a successor arrangement,[13] with the name "Wolfstieg-Gesellschaft" [Wolfstieg Society],[14] which very probably happened in the same way as with the Grand Lodge of the Sun. The absence of concrete references, according to which the intention could have been carried out, that is, by exclusion of the brothers of Jewish origin to continue Freemasonry in the *völkisch* sense, points to the idea that, as in the case of Bayreuth, the primary motivation was to save real estate and lodge possessions from seizure.[15]

On the other hand, the Grand Lodge of Harmony in Darmstadt decided at first to continue by a *völkisch* transformation. Neuberger's assumption that the Darmstadt group, as a numerically small grand lodge, would be frightened back into a Christian-national order was not confirmed. Because of only meager resources at that time, Neuberger assumed that they had liquidated their Grand Lodge organization and had left it to the subordinate lodges to join one of the Old Prussian orders.[16] Instead, on April 1, 1933, at an extraordinary Grand Lodge Communication, amendments to the by-laws were decided upon according to the "national attitude," by which "Aryan" descent and Christian confession were now compulsory.[17] In a letter dated April 24, the association leadership of the (former) Darmstadt Grand Lodge informed readers of the fact that they had separated from Freemasonry and from now on would bear the name "Fraternal Association of Harmony."[18] This seems to indicate that a converted grand body continued the work at least for a short time, even though the dissolution resolution was announced on April 29, 1933.[19]

The external as well as internal transformation (the exclusion of Jewish members) was carried out and practiced with vigor by the Grand Lodge of Hamburg. On April 13, 1933, Grand Master Richard Bröse resigned his office and immediately afterward had himself (re)elected Grand Master at the meeting for the constitution of the "German Order Hamburg."[20] According to the charter of the new organization, it consisted "of German men of Aryan descent and Christian religion."[21] According to the report of a Brother from the Große Landesloge from the end of October 1933, the members from Hamburg had "removed" fifty percent of their members in the meantime, and would now flaunt the "German-Christian," as was noted with irritation.[22] It is unfounded, as one may conclude from Peters, that the Order had already stopped its activity on July 30, 1933.[23] Rather, Grand Master Bröse delivered his closing speech in the presence of Gestapo officers during the dissolution meeting on July 30, 1935. Therein he explained, among other things, that "our now-dissolved Order" had existed for too short a time to develop. "There is not much more to say about it than that it offered us the possibility to meet at old places that have become dear and to nurture that most spiritual friendship, which has connected us for so many years. However, it has gone otherwise with the organization, from which our Order came two and a half years ago. It signifies a great and beautiful past for us." In closing, "That for which we strove, what we did in the way of deeds for love of country, we put quietly and humbly into the hand of the sublime Creator."[24]

The Hamburg Grand Lodge maintained three foreign lodges in Chile: in Valparaíso, in Santiago, and in Concepción. These refused to carry out the transformation and dissolution resolutions of their mother institution. Their recognition as a "Committee of the Grand Lodge of Hamburg" by the Grand Lodge of Chile in 1942 suggested that a Grand Lodge of Hamburg in Chilean exile had existed. The question of whether it could be so can be debated even now.[25] In the literature, the predominate view is that there was no Exile Grand Lodge, strictly speaking, but that the German brothers in Chile were allowed by Hamburg to maintain their independence. Even after more recent research, this view should not be cast into doubt. However, sources from the Secret State Archives in Berlin permit the conclusion that in 1937 the 200th anniversary of the Hamburg Grand Lodge was celebrated in Valparaíso. At a meeting of the subordinate lodges "Lessing" and "Three Rings" in Santiago de Chile, a resolution was passed on April 30, 1933, which stated that the independence of Chilean Freemasonry was to be protected, and that the existence and further development of the Hamburg Grand Lodge was to be guaranteed as well.[26] It is very possible that the members who lived in Chile understood their Masonic existence as "exile." Beyond all formal questions that dominate the intramasonic discussion about this problem, one thing is certain: There was no decision on the part of the administration of the Hamburg Grand Lodge to withdraw from Germany due to political conditions, and to set up a Grand Lodge in Chile.

While introducing the "Aryan Paragraph," the two Saxon grand lodges took part in the contest for state sanctioning: The Große Landesloge of Saxony (Dresden) converted itself into the "German-Christian Order [of] Saxony" and, with words similar to the Old Prussians, paid homage to the so-called "spirit of Potsdam." It offered the new ruling power its "obligatory loyalty" because of the "act of state" on March 21, and greeted "the national elevation of the German people and native country at today's dedication."[27] The Großloge Deutsche Bruderkette (Grand Lodge [of the] German Fraternal Chain [Leipzig]) from now on called itself the "Christlicher Orden Deutscher Dom" ("Christian Order [of the] German Cathedral") and advocated the "promotion of German nationality and national consciousness on a Christian basis."[28] On June 15, 1933, Dresden Grand Master Fischer asked his colleagues in the Große Landesloge whether or not the recognition of the Masonic Order [i.e. GLL] had already taken place, and reported that, in the meantime, the General Ministry of Saxony had issued a decree against the Masonic lodges.[29] After the creation of the humanitarian orders, there arose in the spring of 1933 the beginnings of a union of several jurisdictions. At the beginning of May, envoys of the jurisdictions of Bayreuth, Dresden, and Leipzig actually met for appropriate consultations, in which a representative from Darmstadt was supposed to have participated.[30] The driving force at this time was apparently the Saxons. From their ranks, the suggestion was proposed to the Old Prussians to unite for strength

172

into a single German-Christian Order. As anticipated, the unexpected request was rejected brusquely by the Große Landesloge; their entire strategy was based on the concept of strict demarcation, in particular vis-à-vis the humanitarian grand lodges.[31] The idea clearly found just as little resonance with the functionaries of the two other Old-Prussian Orders. In any case, such a project never progressed to a more concrete planning phase. Except for the two Saxon organizations, which united in the late autumn of 1933 and continued in this form until June 1935,[32] there was no unification among the humanitarian lodges.

The fraternal circle of FzaS (Freemasons' Association of the Rising Sun) and the Symbolische Großloge, which had been formed by the established grand lodges, opposed Hitler's government unambiguously and drew clear conclusions from the Nazis' seizure of power. In particular, the Symbolische Großloge, the only Grand Lodge to do so, "guarded the light of the German Freemasonry in exile ...,"[33] so that German Freemasons today can look back on a 250-year continuity.[34] In a secret meeting in Frankfurt am Main in June 1933, Leo Müffelmann and his closest "traveling companions" decided to transfer the Grand Lodge to Jerusalem and thus reactivate it. The constitution of the Grand Lodge in Exile took place there on November 17. The choice of place was made easier because there were already two subordinate lodges in Jerusalem, namely the lodges "At the Well of Siloah" and "Ari," and the fact that Müffelmann had the apparently very concrete thought of emigrating to Palestine himself.

Meanwhile, Müffelmann had been arrested on September 5—just after he had returned from a stay abroad—and taken to prison in the Berlin police headquarters at the Alexanderplatz, after being booked in the Secret Office of the State Police. The hearing on the following day took place in the Gestapa. According to Müffelmann's own report,35 the hearing was limited to his Masonic activities, the Symbolische Großloge, and its writings,36 In the police prison, Müffelmann met the SPD politician and former Reichstag President Paul Loebe, who had likewise been taken into "protective custody." He used the opportunity for a rather long discussion. On October 6, Müffelmann was transferred to the Sonnenburg concentration camp near Küstrin. Carl von Ossietzky, whom he apparently did not meet, was also imprisoned there. Müffelmann, who had heart disease, was abused and forced to do hard physical labor. Also arrested was Fritz Bensch, a prominent functionary of the Supreme Council for Germany.37 He was brought together with Müffelmann to Sonnenburg, where the two shared a cell for awhile. Raoul Koner had been arrested even before Müffelmann and Bensch (August 28). The catalyst for all three arrests was presumably a denunciation by Koner's stepson. He had informed against his stepfather and had referred to allegedly forbidden writings in the latter's possession. Thereupon, the arrests38 as well as house searches took place at the homes of Koner and Müffelmann. In addition, the Grand Lodge archives fell into the hands of the Gestapo, although Koner had sought for a long time to prevent this. Müffelmann assumed that it had been intended, "to convict Freemasonry of high treason by means of an enormous sensational trial."39

What role Koner played after the arrest is still disputed. The suspicion of collaboration, which he most vehemently disputed, and which also was never proven, hangs on the possible statements and circumstances of his release. Nevertheless, his report "A Freemason's Life" was considered an essay of justification, whose value as a historical source statement is limited in many respects. Independent of that, without question, are Koner's merits, which he earned by his years-long commitment to humanitarian Freemasonry in Germany and for international Masonic relations. Beyond that, whether Koner in any way arranged things for himself with the Gestapo can only be speculated upon. It is clear that he was moved as soon as October 14 from Sonnenburg to the Berlin police prison, with its comparatively easier prison conditions; and on November 15 (nearly two weeks before the two others) he was released.[40] Incriminating material, which would suggest cooperation with the Gestapo or *Sicherheitsdienst*, however, in contrast to the case of Kurt Reichl alias Konrad Lerich, has so far not emerged. Possibly, Koner's gallstone problem[41] was the reason for his special treatment. However, Müffelmann's eroded state of health led to no early release. Instead, he spent a rather long time in the concentration camp military hospital and was finally allowed leave together with Bensch on November 26.

The dismissals of Müffelmann, Bensch, and Koner in November 1933 are, with great probability, to be attributed directly to the intervention of American Freemasons, through the German Embassy in Washington. John Henry Cowles, the Grand Commander of the Supreme Council (A.A.S.R.) Southern Jurisdiction, had a petition written, in which he demanded information on the whereabouts and treatment of the German brothers.[42] During an interview by the Gestapo after their release, Müffelmann, Bensch, and Koner were addressed about this. Later they were forced to sign a declaration according to which they would forbid themselves "any interference from Masonic circles," since they would regard Freemasonry as "antiquated," and in addition, that during protective custody, they had had no cause "for any complaints," but had been treated "accomodatingly."[43]

The seizure of the Symbolische Großloge archives, as well as the arrests of Koner, Müffelmann, and Bensch, were entered into a report of the Gestapa of April 1934.[44] It states that the seized lodge documents at Koner's home had already been prepared for dispatch, and confirmed the suspicion that "the lodges, disguised as associations," continued to exist.[45] Since there was no mention of exile of the Symbolische Großloge, this action of the Gestapo apparently was not discovered up to the time of the report. It does definitely mean, however, that the Symbolische Großloge, although it had "officially" dissolved on March 29, 1933, "continued working in secret, a phenomenon, that could be repeatedly observed in the case of other lodges."[46] The report further contains excerpts of the interrogation records of Koner and Müffelmann. Koner is quoted by the words: "I admit that the attitude of the Symbolische Großloge was based on the old humanity principle, that it had a pacifistic outlook, and therefore is no longer compatible with the today's state thought."[47] Müffelmann declared in his hearing: "I was formerly a member of the German-Democratic party, but resigned before the transformation of this party into the state party, because I had to be absolutely neutral politically as leader of an association. In the beginning of 1933, I joined the German National People's Party. I became a member of the Stahlhelm ('Steel Helmet') as well."[48] Müffelmann further admitted to his honorary memberships in foreign lodges. Beyond that, he stated, according to the report, that the Symbolische Großloge had dissolved, because "the Masonic concept of democracy and pacifism radically represented by it, is not compatible with the thought of the national state in Germany."[49]

5.2 THE OLD PRUSSIANS AS VICTIMS OF PERSECUTION AND AS SYMPATHIZERS OF NATIONAL SOCIALISM

5.2.1 THE FIGHT FOR SURVIVAL AND RECOGNITION

Regardless of the mobilization carried out by the (former) national grand lodges vis-à-vis the government since January 30, 1933, the ambiguity about the future of the Order persisted. In view of such a condition and the propagandistic as well as violent encroachments, massive insecurity spread in the Fraternity. In particular, the members of the Old Prussian lodges, who had always stressed their German-national, Prussian–Protestant conviction, were disturbed and insulted by the social disparagement as well as the public and private isolation they experienced. Even if the application of the "professional civil service law" generally did not lead to the dismissal of Freemasons, nevertheless, officials and members of the public service saw themselves exposed to substantial psychological pressure and various chicaneries. They had to realize that they were in fact stigmatized indiscriminately as "second class citizens" and barred from the National Socialist "community." It required no direct national interference to weaken the lodges quantitatively. The decrease in membership was dramatic. Owing to their personal and vocational situations, many Brothers did not see any alternative than to leave their lodges,[50] particularly since numerous municipal agencies, professional associations, and other organizations,[51] in the course of aligning themselves, accepted no more Freemasons into their ranks. Furthermore, in smaller cities and municipalities, there were boycotts of business owners known to be lodge members.

Many of those brothers, however, who withdrew in such situations, intended to return to their lodges in case of a political change. In the hope of that, the leadership of the Große Landesloge planned on not collecting "admission fees" and "letting the Masonic Brother concerned" into the degree immediately, "which he had previously held in the Order."[52] The other grand lodges presumably would have proceeded in exactly the same way. The shrinking number of lodges confronted them with substantial economic problems, not the least because of existing commitments into which they had entered in times when their lodges were prospering with more members. An example of this is the report of May 1933 from the subordinate lodges of the Große Landesloge in Jena to Landes Grand Master von Heeringen. According to the report, it would become impossible for them to meet their financial obligations if more members withdrew. In order to be able to pay for the maintenance of the building, the land and lodge building were encumbered with a mortgage.[53]

Meanwhile, some Freemasons felt that the process of "adjusting" their officers was unworthy, or in any case hardly promising, and pleaded, in view of an endless threatening fear, to shut down. Thus, the Master of Anna Amalia Lodge in Weimar, Dr. Siefert, wrote, "the three administrations of Freemasonry cannot let it come to that, that one lodge after the other succumbs, but by a common act of true manliness should prevent it at the right time."[54] In February 1934, Peters reported that the subordinate lodge of the Drei Weltkugeln ("Three World Globes") in Aachen had called off [Masonic] labor, because it was not ready to make the transformation into a German-Christian Order.[55] In contrast, the Master of St. John's Lodge, "The Royal Oak" in Hameln, to the astonishment of his Brothers, appeared in SS uniform and abruptly declared the Lodge dissolved.[56]Meanwhile, the Old-Prussian leadership did not leave a doubt about its expectations vis-à-vis the German National Socialist Workers' Party. In a letter to the party leaders, the National Christian Order Frederick the Great enumerated in detail, on April 12, 1933:

> "... 2. The great majority of our members counts itself by conviction and attitude as part of the National Socialist German Workers Party, and the administration of our Order is inspired by the same spirit.
>
> 3. The association of German Freemasons is dissolved, after we did not succeed in bringing it completely under the control of the subsequent Old-Prussian Grand Lodges.
>
> 4. Our Order always refused...the admission of Jews.
>
> 5. Our ritual (ceremonial) will be freed from the few still existing Old-Testament connections, which were applied in the medieval German stone-cutter symbolism ... On the other hand, we will work the ancient German Mystery cult—whose last guardians we are—even more emphatically into our practice, and thus make an indispensable contribution to the care of German nationality. Pave the way now for 20,000 patriotic men, who feel themselves called to cooperate in the development of the national socialistic republic!"[57]

The Party had no intention of doing that. Thus, the South Harz regional German National Socialist Workers' Party administration gave notice four months later that the assumption that the government and party positions would slowly become friendly with the Masonic idea was "completely wrong": "Only at the moment do more important tasks not allow these positions the necessary time for the disposal of the Masonry Question."[58] Answers from the government to the oft-repeated requests for carrying out the agreed-upon transformations remained absent at first. A petition of the Grand Masters Bordes and Feistkorn to Hitler in the early summer also was not answered. Instead of the hoped for "declaration of honor by the Führer," there was a wave of violent anti-Masonic actions in the following months.[59]

In view of this unsatisfactory situation for the German lodges, the German-Christian Order deplored publicly the "unfair" treatment, in its eyes, of the question of the "Christian non-Aryans." The Order's newspaper wrote about it in October 1933: "No officers' association, hardly a student corporation, no scientific society rejected non-Aryans who had converted to Christianity before the war. Among the millions of registered members of the German National Socialist Workers' Party there would have been very few who would have already devoted their attention to this question before the war. Why was there objection now to the previous admission of only Christian non-Aryans to the Order, which never accepted non-Christians as members and declared the regulations of the law for the re-establishment of the permanent civil service obligatory for its members?"[60] In the same way, the spirit of the Order and the thinking back to pre-Enlightenment traditions were strengthened: "the new usages already bring to bear the idea of the Order much more clearly on the two first stages (meaning the two first degrees [author's note]) than could be the case in the earlier ritual. The reason is that during the reorganization of the Order in the eighteenth century, the greatest value was put upon leading the Brothers to the goals of the Order by means of a long...course of instruction."[61] As of October 12, 1933, people concerned themselves in "confidential fundamentals" with the sought-after "supplementing" function of the German-Christian Order in the context of the *Weltanschauung* held in common with the German National Socialist Workers' Party. The Order teaches no worldview of one's own, but seeks to awaken the demand for religious depth in its members: "the attainment of this goal is possible only if the Order brothers think Teutonically, *völkisch*, and socially, and thus base their thinking firmly on the *Weltanschauung*, which with the elevation of the nation, is reaching general recognition in our Fatherland, and at the same time, is the basis of the teachings of the Order."[62]

Also in October, the National Christian Order Frederick the Great and the German-Christian Order "Friendship" published a circular that summarized the current situation from their perspective and evaluated its past development. Both organizations had moved close together in the last months and had coordinated their relations with respect to the state and the party. On the other hand, the Große Landesloge kept, as usual, a greater measure of self-sufficiency and considered very carefully from time to time whether common procedures with the two other Old-Prussian Orders appeared expedient for its purposes. The internal papers of von Heeringen, however, prove that the Große Landesloge differed little from other Old-Prussians in its fundamental course as well as in its assessment of the political situation. In their October circulars, it said, among other things, that they were pleased to be able to share that "now a prohibition or obligatory dissolution of our Order is not being considered." This results "from the fact that the Nat[ional] Soc[ialistic] Government dissolved all organizations and parties, about which it assumed that they strove against the opinions of the German National Socialist Workers' Party...from the government side, however, our Orders and groups of Orders have had no difficulties. If individual groups have been annoyed, or their Order houses were temporarily seized, it has always resulted from encroachments that subordinate party organs have made illegally."[63] In the same place, it was reported: "In negotiations with the government," a Ministry advisor (expert) guaranteed "us protection against any illegal encroachment." It would quickly turn out, however, that this announcement, if it had actually been made, was not put into practice. Meanwhile, the Grand Lodge officers labeled it their "main objective" to free "the way for our brothers in the Order to enter the German National Socialist Workers' Party or, first, to their sub- and auxiliary organizations. We approached the German National Socialist Workers' Party with the request to integrate our Orders into the overall organization."[64] At the conclusion, the report quoted, full of anticipation, a piece of information from the propaganda ministry—thanks to the input of a "Drei Weltkugeln" member—according to which a recognition of the Old-Prussian Orders allegedly would soon be forthcoming.[65]

Actually, however, the responsible government agencies were completely silent for months about how they meant finally to proceed with the converted national grand lodges, mostly because the lodges remaining in the form of an "Order" did not represent a danger for the consolidation of the National Socialistic rule. Also in matters of *Weltanschauung*, the Nazis concentrated first on the struggle against opponents, which they shared with the German national government parties: the Communists and the Social Democrats.

As of the end of June or the beginning of July 1933, not only were opposition parties and trade unions forbidden, but also the national forces including the "Stahlhelm"[66] were brought into line. After the Reichstag elections on 5 March, the Nazis had given up their tactically motivated, relative restraint, and had begun to take over total power with the help of unbridled terror. With this, Masonic establishments were repeatedly the targets of violent attacks by party associations and the Gestapo. Lodge meetings were monitored by the Gestapo, seizures took place, and individual subordinate lodges of different systems were dissolved after they had been declared enemies of the State. A definitively political or solely police-generated concept was not behind these actions. To the contrary: arbitrariness prevailed. As proven by Robert Gellately, the Gestapo remained, over the entire duration of its criminal workings, dependent on denunciation as "the most important resource of state-police action," and indeed with their increasing tasks, more—not less dependent on denunciation.[67] Heydrich, for his part, had the further intention of controlling the Gestapo's denunciation procedures. He imagined a "people's reporting service," with whose assistance undesirable denunciations—those which were motivated, by personal interests or by the informers' lust for revenge, not politically–ideologically—would be eliminated.[68] In the early phase, the measures of the Gestapo directed against lodges and/or their members depended on chance. Often, they were spontaneous and brought about by a local situation, or set off by denunciations, as for instance, the action against the Symbolische Großloge and their leading functionaries in the autumn of 1933.

Meanwhile, faithful to their purposeful optimism, the German-Christian Orders waited for positive indications of State authority, although the meeting with Goering in the spring and the uncompromising announcements of the NSDAP (German National Socialist Workers' "Nazi" Party) Reichs Administration had left no room for misunderstanding. In addition, the hope that Hugenberg (who had resigned from the cabinet in June 1933) and Seldte would be able to support the Old Prussians for the long term was dashed. The Freemasons belonging to the "Stahlhelm" felt this particularly painfully in the medium term. Before the "Stahlhelm" of the older soldiers was converted into the "National Socialist German Federation of Fighters on the Front," in April 1934, the "Stahlhelm" members up to 35 years of age had been integrated into the SA (Storm Troops) as the so-called "Military Stahlhelm," in July 1933. For the time being, it remained possible for members of Old-Prussian lodges according to the indication of the Order administrations of the "Drei Welt Kugeln" and Grand Lodge Zur Freundschaft ("Friendship") to join the "Military Stahlhelm" as new members.[69] The situation changed in an obvious way only in the course of the year 1934. In December 1933, the SA leadership had determined with respect to the "Stahlhelm" that opponents of the Nazi Party could not be accepted, which category expressly included Freemasons and "half-Jews." New acceptances of Freemasons—including those who belonged to the Old-Prussian lodges—were excluded by Röhm. It remained unclear how one was to proceed with those lodge members who had already been incorporated into the "Stahlhelm." According to Röhm's wishes, all those who still belonged to lodges should be given no alternative but to be excluded. Therefore, only those who had left their lodges before January 30, 1933, could remain in the SA or in the "Stahlhelm." Since, however, no consensus existed on this question, Freemasons were repeatedly requested by their local "Stahlhelm" leadership to leave either the lodge or the "Stahlhelm."[70] In a decree of February 22, 1934, Röhm affirmed his position, and stressed that "the national and *völkisch*" lodges also were affected. In this way, he tried to enforce that "Persons who do not have a completely unobjectionable likelihood of being accepted into the Nazi Party... would be kept out of the SA or excluded from it again."[71] On December 4, 1933, however, it was ordered by the highest SA administration that all former lodge members would have to sign a declaration, according to which it was assured "that I have withdrawn from the lodge and its successor organizations, such that in each regard I have dissolved the connections with such organizations and shall refrain from any activity on their behalf in the future."[72] The wording contradicts Röhm's order quoted above; it was indirectly implied that whoever resigned from the Lodge and broke off his contacts with Freemasonry could remain a member of the "Stahlhelm." The enforcement of this arrangement was handled differently from region to region. Meanwhile, the administration of the Große Landesloge tried to cause a reversal of this policy with the help of preformulated protest declarations as well as by petitions to Employment Minister Seldte. A personal conversation slated for February 27, 1934, was denied Landes Grand Master von Heeringen "due to Seldte's being completely extraordinarily overburdened."[73] Apparently, Röhm could thus claim, in the spring of 1934, for Seldte also, that only he who had terminated a possible lodge membership before the "seizure of power" was allowed to remain in the National Socialist German Front Fighter Federation. Despite this agreement, a clear line did not develop because of continuous disputes concerning authority and diversities of opinion within the SA administration, which only increased the anxiety in Masonic circles. After the murder of Röhm and the political dissolution of power of the SA at the end of June 1934, the situation continued to remain unclear. In any case, members of Freemasonry (the Grosse Landesloge) successfully opposed the unjustified demand of having to resign from their lodges or the National Socialist German Front Fighter Federation.[74] However, in November 1935, when the National Socialist German Front Fighter Federation (already operating the same way) was dissolved or absorbed into the SA, the gradual enforcement of the exclusion of former lodge members similar to the guidelines for the party and its arrangements was finally begun.[75]

Quite a considerable number of brothers were affected by the differences with the "Stahlhelm." As is evident from a letter of December 1933 from the Master of the Lodge "Zum Ölzweig" ('Olive Branch,' subordinate to the Große Landeslodge) in Bremen, approximately 75% of the lodge officers (lodge council) were members of the "Stahlhelm."[76] In light of the action of the highest SA Administration with respect to members "of patriotic lodges," an SA functionary saw himself obliged to report to his brigade leader on the personnel bottlenecks resulting from it: "seen purely organizationally, we lose a rather large number of the best leaders, personalities, who have fought in the front lines since the first days of our liberty movement," and whose views are above all doubt. At the same time, he urged that a way be found to take the edge off the guidelines of the SA Administration.[77] To prove the "complete loyalty and our joyful will to cooperative work,"[78] the Old Prussians, meanwhile, in December 1933 had taken Oscar Feistkorn's suggestion and offered the DAF ("Deutsche Arbeitsfront or German Work Front") free use of lodge buildings for holding events, although this group also closed itself to the membership of Freemasons.[79] In this connection, the Order tried to move its activity into the mindset of the "Strength through Joy" organization: It was announced that "Order meetings" were nothing other than "hours at the end of workdays, in which our members... find elevation and relaxation. Our Order buildings are nothing other than 'houses of work'," like those encouraged by the director of the DAF, Robert Ley, on the occasion of the introduction of "Strength through Joy." Therefore, the intention was stated of joining in the "end of workday work," started by the DAF, and a plan was drafted to open the lodge buildings for the "public end of workday hours."[80]

Up to this time—the end of 1933—the upper echelon of the Order essentially based its trust on a few official opinions, which it credited to their repeated interventions and personal conversations: A temporary relaxation brought information from the Prussian Ministry of the Interior of September 1933, according to which "the belonging of an official to a lodge ...[is] no cause for intervention against him based on Paragraph 4 of the law for there-establishment of the civil service with tenure of April 7, 1933."[81]

184

On August 9, the Grand Master of the Grosse Landesloge, von Heeringen, had met with Goering, according to his own statement, for a further consultation, this time "detailed," which remained at first without tangible results. Connections with the information about the application of the "civil service with tenure law" are rather improbable. If this problem had been discussed, von Heeringen would probably have mentioned it in the circular that he published following the interview with Goering. In it, von Heeringen communicated "that in agreement with the Reichs Ministry of the Interior, the Prussian Ministry of the Interior was declared the place responsible for all our affairs ... although at present still no formal declaration from the Prussian Prime Minister ... exists." Nevertheless, it could be concluded from the facts that the responsible minister had no reservations against the kind of activity of the Order.[82] In their striving to obtain a favorable basis for a decision, the Grand Lodge functionaries intensified not only their efforts to take in prominent Nazis for the good of the Order, but also their contacts with the ministerial bureaucracy on the consultant level.

A statement by Hans Heinrich Lammers, the Secretary of State in the Reichskanzlei, had a greater effect than Goering's obvious non-commitment. (Lammers had been Reichs Minister and chief of the Reichskanzlei since 1937). A circular of the Allgemeine Deutsche Waffenring ("General German Arms Group") of July 20, 1933, seized upon remarks that Lammers had made three weeks before during an exchange of letters. According to these, "members of military-student associations, who belong to the Old Prussian grand lodges, which had converted into Orders," could deliver a deposition that they did not belong to Freemasons' lodges. The report implied an important restriction at the same time: Since the Reichs Ministry of the Interior had indeed taken note of the transformation of the Old Prussian [lodges], but so far had taken no position, a changed situation could result if the Orders were considered "on the part of the Reichs Government or the Reichs Administration of the National Socialist Workers' Party as Freemasons' lodges or equivalent organizations."[83] From January to September 1935, Lammers also worked as "leader" of the GStV (Association of Student Federations, an umbrella organization that had been brought into being after the Students' Association in the Allgemeine Deutsche Waffenring, with its demand for the abolition "of the front fighter clause," could not prevail. Therefore, they had left and had started the short-lived "Völkisch Waffenring." Although at first an agreement between the "National Socialist German Student Federation" and the GStV had come into existence through Lammers, according to which the latter was considered as a "joint representation of the student corporation associations,"[84] it had "played for" only one episode: When parts of the Corps opposed the conversion of the "Aryan Paragraph" without reservation, Lammers withdrew, and the GStV dissolved. This, in turn, introduced the end of the corporations in the "Third Reich," which to a great extent either completely self-destructed or joined the Nazi Student Federation. How many Freemasons were forced to resign—and under which circumstances—or whether obligations made them refuse to has not yet been sufficiently investigated. In any case, it can be assumed that, as a result of Lammers' instructions of the summer of 1933 (which were entered into the guidelines of the Allgemeine Deutsche Waffenring), numerous old-Prussian Order Brothers managed to remain in corporations and to gain acceptance into the Nazi Party and the Nazi auxiliary organizations. This they did by answering the question about lodge affiliation in the negative on the spot. In the same vein, Witt-Höe had already expressed himself, in May 1933, by reaffirming the fact that "each Order Brother can sign today without pangs of conscience, that he is no longer a Freemason and does not belong to a secret society."[85] At approximately the same time, however, formulas were introduced by some Nazi Party local groups and subsidiary organizations, in which explicit questions about membership in an Order were asked.[86]

Finally, the German-Christian Orders bolstered their position with the so-called "Seldte Decree" of November 2, 1933. According to this, affiliation with the national-Christian Orders was not a reason to doubt the "national reliability" of those concerned.[87] Members who worked in an official capacity were requested by the executive committee of their

Order to refer to this decree in the case of discrimination. As much as the Reichs Employment Minister's omission of all still-existing (former) grand lodges was valued as an indication of sympathetic consideration on the part of the State, the fundamental and long-overdue reaction of the regime to the growth of the German-Christian Orders was still to come. In other words, the situation was open. The responsible Old-Prussian functionaries knew that, even if they formally took the view that a (new) recognition was not required, since grand lodges and subordinate lodges were still recognized as juridical personalities. Then, during January 1934, the Masonic question began to move in a way that at first sight appears contradictory. On January 4, Göring issued an order through the Secretary of State in the Prussian Ministry of the Interior, Wilhelm Grauert, with reference to the public status of the Old-Prussian bodies, as follows:

"without taking a position on the question as to whether the three Old-Prussian grand lodges and their subordinate lodges ... are to be regarded as alliances dangerous to the state, given the current unity of the German people created by the national movement, I can no longer discern any more need for the preservation of these lodges and for the special encouragement, which had been accorded them by the State. The effort to dissolve often put forth in local lodges, considering the whole political development in Germany must be taken into account. Special regulations in the statutes of the grand lodges mounting obstacles to or making more difficult the fulfillment of such desires I can no longer consider justified under these circumstances. Therefore I order the following as an alteration to existing lodge statutes:

1. The dissolution of a lodge takes place by resolution of the meeting of the members by a simple majority vote.

4. The resolutions...require my permission, no longer those of the Grand Lodge."[88]

Clearly, the decree aimed at driving Freemasons still more deeply into resignation. They had been worn down and demoralized anyway by police measures and social proscription.[89] That subordinate lodges in

Prussia were now moved by the state to bring about their own dissolution themselves, independently, meant a sensitive cutting off of the authority of the superordinate grand bodies. In this way, the regime promoted the erosive tendency and, at the same time, weakened the position of those grand lodge executive committees, which had decided to hold out. Despite the weight of this national interference, the state of suspension persisted, but the regulation precluded final decisions. In addition, the grand lodge administrations were concerned that as few as possible of their subordinate lodges follow the way indicated by the Ministry. Göring actually seems to have mis-estimated the effect, because a numerically significant break-up of the structure never happened. As von Heydrich stressed in November, altogether only 13 lodges had taken the January order as the reason to decide on their self-dissolution. This was, in his eyes, a proof of the stubbornness of the Old Prussians.[90]

On January 10, 1934, the state police had taken a position vis-à-vis the question in a kind of appraisal as to how the transformations from Masonic organizations were to be evaluated. With threadbare arguments and with reference to the allegedly "close meshing" between the systems, one came to the conclusion that "in sense and spirit" nothing had changed about the lodges. In addition, it appeared to be a given that Freemasonry was antipeople and antistate, and that it repudiated the facts of the "clandestine society" offence as well as disparaged nationally recognized religious communities.[91] The sleazy reference to the alleged revilement of religious communities further suggests that the open confrontation in the church struggle was indecisive from the beginning. At this time, the embracing tactics and the old Nazi formula of "positive Christianity" still dominated. The fact that some of the churches could be made allies, however, covered only temporarily the antithesis of Christianity and the Racial State.[92]

Likewise, at the beginning of 1934, the "Highest Party Court" of the Nazi Party repeatedly took a position vis-à-vis the "Freemasonry question" through its leader Walter Buch: the fundamental opposition to Freemasonry and the incompatibility between the Nazi Party and lodge membership were emphasized in a circular. Buch specified the handling of former Freemasons: According to it, only those who had withdrawn from their lodges before January 30, 1933, and had ensured that all connections with Freemasonry had been severed and dissolved, could be accepted into the Nazi Party. They would be restricted, however, remaining excluded from all party offices.[93] It was expressly confirmed in the circular that no differences between the different lodges would be made. Likewise, Buch maintained that humanitarian and Old-Prussian grand lodges as well would pursue the intention of camouflaging "their attitude of mind in relation to National Socialism by the formation of successor organizations."[94] A specification concerning a degree attained or possible lodge offices as a criterion for party membership had not yet been introduced in the circular of January 8.[95] That was "remedied" by August 1934: If it became known about someone that he had held "prominent positions," —for example, Master of the Lodge—or had achieved higher degrees, he would now not be accepted or would be expelled from the Party and its subordinate organizations.[96] On the other hand, it does not seem that having a simple membership in the National Socialist Public Welfare was dependent on the deadline of January 30, 1933. A condition for admission certainly was that the person concerned had left his lodge beforehand. [97]

Meanwhile, different local lodge establishments had increasingly become the target of violent actions by SA and SS units. In Bavaria, since the early summer of 1933, state organs in the form (of the SS-controlled) Bavarian political police had already taken action against Freemasons and invaded the lodges with a wave of searches and confiscations.[98] The severity of these anti-Masonic measures differed from region to region,[99] which can be considered as exemplary of the regional differences in the general penetration of the National Socialist rule.[100] The most violent actions, both qualitatively and quantitatively, had taken place in East Prussia and Silesia, whereas in Thuringia, for instance, the situation remained comparatively calm. The fact that since at the end of July 1933 the SA had increasingly taken action with outrages against Freemasons' lodges might be connected with the fact that by a so-called "leader instruction," Masonic affairs had been made subordinate to the SS.[101] The resulting competition between both organizations precipitated the actions against Freemasonry.

The second large wave of terror against the lodges began at the beginning of 1934. This was correctly attributed to the fact that the two orders of January that were hostile to Freemasonry—the "Göring decree" and the party judicial ruling—again directed the attention of executive bodies and paramilitary associations to the still existing lodges: "These groups seemed to interpret the new regulations as a declaration of war between the state and the party on Freemasonry and covered the Reich...with the heaviest wave of anti-Masonic excesses in the history of the National Socialism."[102]

An apparently new situation resulted from Hitler's so-called "opinion of will," which was conveyed in a radio speech on January 30, 1934, to the secret state police offices, and according to which it did not appear "opportune" to proceed "with measures against the lodges at the moment."[103] The corresponding order, dated February 21, 1934, issued by Hitler's deputy, Rudolf Hess, read: "In accordance with instructions of Der Führer, it is hereby forbidden that party agencies take measures against the existing lodges."[104] On April 3, 1934, the instruction of the Reichs Interior Minister instructed the Reichs governors and state governments that "for the present no further steps against the so-called Old-Prussian lodges '...were to be undertaken...' insofar as no special reasons in any particular case justify a procedure according to the regulation of February 28, 1933."[105] The Große Landesloge was at least informally instructed by the Ministry about this regulation, which was interpreted as "protective regulation."[106]

Consequently, new confidence temporarily accompanied the inexorable process of wearing out and wearing down. Immediately before Hitler's regulation, the Grand Master of the Große Landesloge, Balthasar-Wolfradt, had intended to recommend the dissolution of the Order at the forthcoming general meeting. Prompted by the apparent turn, the leadership now decided indeed to continue. Balthasar-Wolfradt, however, retired from his position at the helm of the Grand Lodge on February

11, 1934, because of his age and probably to some extent because he was resigned [to the state of Freemasonry—trans. note]. His successor in the office of the Grand Master was an architect, Friedrich Bolle.

While the German-Christian Orders construed the decree of the Reichs Chancellor as a breakthrough—now at least, tolerance by the state seemed possible—this apparent consideration was in truth only a momentary expression of deliberations on domestic affairs. Because of the tensions that had arisen in the "movement," the Nazi leadership wanted to avoid other burdens temporarily. In any case, the decree did not mean a change of mind concerning the "Masonic question," either for Hitler or in his circle. The apparently so promising "opinion of will" thus did not introduce the turn of events anticipated by the Old Prussians, but indeed represented a further delay. And even where the Gestapo ordered a halt to anti-Masonic lecture meetings (e.g. those of the lawyer Schneider), that was not in order to protect the lodges, but because it concerned "hidden propaganda of the Tannenberg Bund [Association]."[107]

Otherwise, outside of Prussia, the SA, independently of the Gestapa, continued its activities against Freemasons' lodges. Thus, for example, an "SA Music Campaign [Parade]" occupied the Zu den drei Kronen Lodge ("Three Crowns") in Königsberg during the first days of April. It is also to be understood as an expression of the pervasive controversy about authority that the ruling president of the Province of East Prussia, District Leader Koch, maintained that he had received "directly from Der Führer, immediate authority in the question of the treatment of the Freemasons' lodges."[108] This the Reichs Chancellery promptly rejected as unfounded. Rather, "only the guidelines set up by the Reichs Interior Ministry are valid."[109]

The so-called "opinion of will" did not lead to an end of actions aimed at Masonic establishments everywhere. Only in the course of the order of the Interior Ministry from April 3 was the course prescribed by the Central Office gradually enforced.[110] Even so on April 16, the three Old-Prussian Grand Masters saw themselves forced to protest, in a letter to the

Minister of Justice, against the encroachments to which the subordinate lodges found themselves exposed. With this form of self-assertion, the fact that the previous protestations of loyalty had remained unsuccessful also played a role, along with the immediate impetus caused by this situation. It may be very much doubted, however, whether the German-Christian Orders would have dispensed with the protests addressed to the Ministry of Justice if the department had been led by someone other than the former German nationalist Franz Gürtner, and whether a "change in the attitude might be derived vis-à-vis the new dictators" from these protests,[111] as Neuberger assumed.On the other hand, the note addressed to Gürtner is to be seen in the context of a common offensive of the Old-Prussian Orders, which were based on Hitler's order. Thus, the three Grand Masters had already turned in, a few days before (April 9, 1934), another letter from all of them to the main office of the German National Railroad company. The reason for this was the questionnaires circulated by the National Railroad, in which the personnel had to give information about possible affiliation to lodges or lodge-like organizations. What was actually criticized with reference to Hitler's order was that "even former members of the three Old-Prussian grand lodges were not promoted because they were formerly Freemasons." The letter goes on: "the opinion of the will of Der Führer" is based "obviously on the realization that a sharp line of separation is to be drawn between the humanitarian lodges and the three Old-Prussian grand lodges. We ask most submissively that one align himself corresponding according to the instruction of the Reich government, that nothing is brought about against officials who are members of our lodges, and that they also suffer no wrongdoing in matters of hiring and promotion."[112]

What is remarkable about the petition to the National Railroad, quoted here, is that while it is indirect, reference was made to the fact that the Old Prussians no longer construed themselves to be Freemasons. A direct reference in this regard, however, was lacking. Most of what is noticeable in the wording is that the grand masters completely avoided the use of the designations of the Orders added the previous year. The reluctance to use the Order names might be directly connected to the setback that the Old Prussians had already had to accept in the "name question" on March 10, 1934. In this regard, the NS regime had not changed its position of the late summer of 1933 at all. Rather, the Prussian Interior Ministry communicated to the GLL that "the use of the designation 'German-Christian Order' was approved only in connection with the name 'Grosse Landesloge der Freimaurer von Deutschland'; the use of the name 'German-Christian Order' without the main part of the name was thus inadmissible without express permission by the State."[113] An appropriate order was also issued to the Drei Weltkugeln Grand Lodge.[114] It is to be assumed that in the same way, the Grand Lodge Zur Freundschaft also received such a message as the third of the Old-Prussian Orders. The use of the new names in connection with the old lodge designations as permitted by the Ministry obviously did not appear opportune to the grand lodge functionaries—at least for their petition to the National Railroad.

Likewise, with reference to Hitler's order, the Old Prussian lodges turned in a petition to the Reichs president on June 1, 1934. For this, they could hark back to the visit of the three Grand Masters with Hindenburg on July 14, 1926. At that time he had expressed reserved good wishes.[115] Now, the main complaint was that the seizures of lodge buildings and lodge monies had not been stopped despite Hitler's instructions to undertake "nothing against the three Old-Prussian grand lodges." With express reference to Hindenburg's grandfathers, both of whom had been Freemasons, the Grand Masters asked for intervention and an order "furthermore, that all measures against the members of the three Old-Prussian grand lodges and their subordinate lodges cease immediately, and that measures already taken be retracted."[116] National Grand Master von Heeringen tried to make direct contact with the Reich president through Hindenburg's son Oskar. In addition, he had conversations with Secretary of State Otto Meissner and his representative[117] as well as with personnel in the Reich Interior Ministry. Apparently, these discussions did not lead to concrete results.

The Old Prussians clung to each sign, however small, that a different treatment of Old-Prussian and humanitarian lodges could be accomplished. Thus, there was no reaction when, at the beginning of 1934, Dr. Engelbert Huber, the Nazi Party's self-appointed "Advisor for Questions about Freemasons" published his book, *Freemasonry: The World Power behind the Scenes*.[118] The more than 300-page tome was the first of its kind after the wresting of power by the Nazis, and it gave the appearance of seriousness. The book had primarily an anti-Semitic direction of attack and concerned itself with "world Judaism" and "world Freemasonry" from the perspective of the Nazi world view. Huber opposed the Party line in regard to the Old Prussians, which soon got him into trouble. In the April issue of the "Ordensblatt" ("Order Newsletter") of the National Mother Lodge, there appeared a long-winded review in which Huber was praised for his "will beyond all doubt" that "the Masonic question be done justice." Above all, it was welcomed that Huber was the first "scientist" who differentiated sharply between world Freemasonry and Old-Prussian Freemasonry, "between the humanitarian lodges who went back to the Ancient Obligations and the Christian Freemasonry of the three Old Prussian lodges."[119] Indeed, Huber said that the Old-Prussian grand lodges stood "in sharp contrast to humanitarian Freemasonry in Germany and to nearly the entire world Freemasonry."[120] In the preface, Huber even expressly thanked the two Grand Masters Bordes and Feistkorn for the fact that they had unreservedly made available "the rich libraries and archives of their Order."[121] Even so, he held firmly to the idea that "the fundamental maintenance of the requirement of affiliation to the international Masonic 'world brother chain'" and "the emphasis on a strict national attitude" as well as "recognition of the 'Ancient Obligations,'" and "the demand of the Christian confession" by the Old Prussians "represented irreconcilable contradictions."[122] Whether knowingly or unknowingly, the facts that the Old Prussian lodges by no means construed themselves to be part of the "world brother chain," and that the tolerance postulate of the Ancient Obligations was generally just as little accepted, did not appear in Huber's work. In an open letter to

Huber, circulated in the June issue, which was apparently attached to the third edition by the publishing house (at least according to the copy in the German Masonic Museum), Ludwig Rohmann, author of the review and simultaneously editor of the "Order Newsletter," and member of the "Drei Welt Kugeln" Federal Board of Directors, deplored the fact that in Huber's numerous lectures on Judaism and Freemasonry a clear attitude in relation to the Old Prussian lodges could not be discerned.[123]

Meanwhile, the national grand lodges increasingly affirmed their conformity with the system in new statements to the outside world and internally. Thus, on the part of the administration of the Grand Lodge "Zur Freundschaft," in their Easter Message of 1934 "to the beloved Brothers," they never tired of declaring "that we stand on the ground of the National Socialistic idea." In addition, in the future, "the fully valid proof would be furnished, that it is true national socialism which the lodge has taught us to practice."[124] Meanwhile, individual Freemasons repeatedly turned to alleged or actual decision makers in the "Third Reich" as though to a monarch in the form of personal requests. Thus, for example, on January 30, 1934 (after the "Göring decree"), a brother from the Grand Landes Lodge of Freemasons of Germany addressed a request to Hindenburg for "protection for his and his comrades' honor." He complained that "slandering of fellow Germans" and the "inciting of the masses" had not diminished.[125] On September 9, 1934, a Freemason from Pirna wrote about the widespread "if Der Führer knew that" mentality,[126] "to the to be highly-revered Sir, the Chancellor of the Reich" on his petition, and expected from it "justice for German Freemasonry."[127] On the one hand, the same attitude was behind the persistent distinction made by the German-Christian Orders between the German National Socialist Workers' Party (or, more precisely, parts of the German National Socialist Workers' Party), to whose hostile position people had, in the meantime, obviously resigned themselves, and the government on the other hand, from which protection and assistance were expected. It would be too simple to attribute this concept solely to a loss of reality, because it corresponded to an understanding of the concept "state," which was deeply rooted in the conservative middle class. Aside from that, national positions repeatedly engendered a certain confidence in the eyes of the Old Prussians. Thus, for example, in March 1934, the Reichs Interior Ministry had communicated that the German-Christian Order should "better" take its complaints of encroachments to the Party administration: "Reichs Minister Dr. Frick has repeatedly specified in decrees that members of German lodges are not to be persecuted."[128] It is understandable that the Old Prussians would develop the expectation of permanent continuation from such a report, which belongs in the political context of Hitler's so-called "opinion of will." Actually, however, none of the Nazi centers of power had an interest in the continuance of Freemasons' lodges.

The Reichs Military Ministry increased its pressure on the lodges when, on May 26, 1934, it was ordered that membership in Freemasons' lodges or similar organizations was forbidden to every member of the armed forces, including workers and employees.[129] The Interior Ministry also immediately intensified the pace, to which Heydrich referred expressly in the already-quoted internal report to Goering of November 23, 1934. With reference to a petition addressed to the Gestapa by the Old Prussians, Heydrich announced that by a "decree" of June 11 "it was declared in no uncertain terms, that it was more than a strange interpretation if the Old Prussian lodges concluded from the fact that the Reichs Government had refrained so far from forcing dissolution, that Der Führer and the Reichs Government approved of the activity and the continuation of the lodges, as it were."[130] That the Old-Prussian grand masters in the course of the "discussion thereupon allowed" in the Interior Ministry had rejected the self-dissolution urged upon them corresponded to "their whole past conduct," in Heydrich's words.[131] The "decree" mentioned by Heydrich concerns itself with a message dated June 11, from the Secretary of State in the Reich Interior Ministry, Pfundtner, to the three Old-Prussian grand lodges. Beyond the remarks quoted by Heydrich, it was pointed out to the lodges that, by their behavior, they would force the Reich government "to effect a change in its past attitude."[132] At the same time, the grand masters were invited to a discussion, which was intended at first for June 15. Since the responsible Ministry Director, Dr. Nicolai, was prevented for a short time from coming, and the grand masters had to go without achieving their objectives, the conversation was postponed until June 28.[133] The outcome of the meeting seems not to have particularly discouraged the Old Prussians. In any case, von Heeringen turned to Nicolai on July 20 in the form of a private letter, in which the subject was a basis of trust established "by personal acquaintance—at least on my side."[134] The actual concern, however, consisted of expressing his solidarity with Hitler's "taking drastic steps" in connection with the Roehm affair and preventing the danger of possibly becoming entangled in the proceedings.

That never happened, but in September 1934, Party Judge Buch affirmed once more that he did not see a reason for the Nazi Party to change their attitude toward Freemasonry.[135] In the magazine "Arbeitertum," the organ of the "German work front," an article appeared in November 1934 in which it said among other things, if "the Freemasons state today, that they also look favorably upon the work of building, then this is, according to the sense of Masonic words, only one admission of its uncertainty; they mean, 'we must help, so as not to make our existence wholly impossible.' ... There are no national lodges ... Freemasonry is and remains international."[136]Meanwhile, a series of coercive measures, prohibitions, and confiscations was directed against individual local lodges. Some of these actions had probably been arranged directly by Himmler and were covered by papers of the secret state police. Thus, for example, lodge closings and seizings took place in July 1934 under the leadership of Maximilian Brand, the responsible SD (*Sicherheitsdienst*—Security Service) Head Battalion Commander for Freemasonry in Breslau and Weissenfels.[137] These measures were apparently introduced without the knowledge of Goering, who was the formal boss of the Gestapa. Only in reports to Goering after the fact did Heydrich explain that these actions had been taken because of Paragraph 1 of the regulation of the Reich president "for the protection of people and state" (February 28, 1933), which also formed the legal basis for all state-police measures directed against the lodges. The evaluation of the seized material suggested, according to Heydrich, that subversiveness could be determined by the Reichs Interior Minister. He explained in a summarizing statement to Göring, in July and August 1934: "Different Old Prussian subordinate lodges were seized and their libraries, archives, and ritual articles put into safekeeping."[138] Outside of Prussia, the measures were carried out, not by the Secret State Police Office, "but by SS Chief Battalion Officer Brand, [in] Munich, on behalf of the Political Police Commander" (i.e. Himmler [author's note]).[139] It goes on to say: "24 Old Prussian subordinate lodges have already taken legal action against these seizures in the district Administrative Court in Berlin. I took the view, however, that measures of the Political Police can be tested neither by the administrative nor the ordinary courts as to their lawfulness and appropriateness; rather, the only recourse against these measures is a complaint about supervision of service. In a similar circumstance, the District Administrative Court agreed with my view."[140]Likewise, with reference to the "Reichstag Fire Regulation," the Secret State Police Office in Berlin communicated to three St. John's lodges in Königsberg, in East Prussia, on September 25, that their properties were seized and that further activities were forbidden them. It was stated that the material which had been found and put into safekeeping was sufficient to give rise to a suspicion of anarchistic endeavors.[141] This was confirmed by Frick's decree of October 28, 1934. The lodges were declared anarchist in the sense of the law of July 14, 1933, and their assets frozen.[142] On November 1, complaints by 25 concerned lodges pending with the Berlin District Administrative Court were rejected in accordance with the legal concept expressed by Heydrich in opposition to Goering. In other words, the court decision was justified by the fact that "the course of law was inadmissible against measures of the Political Police,"[143] at which the Gestapo also obtained free rein legally. In February 1936, Gestapo affairs were finally exempted by law from judicial checking concerning previous practice. For the quasi-legal *modus operandi* of the National Socialist State, it had been said

in a directive from Heydrich (December 10, 1934) to one of the subordinate lodges of the Grosse Landesloge, "Zur gekrönten Unschuld"
("Crowned Innocence") in Nordhausen (Harz), that the sorting of the
material in safe-keeping had shown that the Freemasons' lodges "by
the admission of an exclusive class of persons who had an obligation
of secrecy, progressing from stage to stage; the absolute obedience to
unknown higher [personages]; its own Jurisdiction; and by application
of secret passwords, signs, and grips, represented a state within a state,
and thus assumed a hostile stance in the way of the goal of the National
Socialistic State: producing a true national community." Because of
this, all Masonic organizations were to be seen as anarchistic in the
sense of Paragraph 1 of the Regulation of February 28, 1933.[144] At
the turn of the year 1934/35, the consolidated "Order sheet" of the
Order of Frederick the Great and Friendship, also with reference to
the "Reichstag Fire Regulation," was finally forbidden.[145] Meanwhile,
some of the equally concerned Old-Prussian lodges exhausted the only
redress that formally remained against the seizures: they submitted
complaints against supervision of service, which were passed on to
Himmler for decision.[146] From this, one assumes that they also failed;
however, the amount of source material is very small. Nevertheless, it
seems possible that individual lodges later succeeded, in (partially?)
reversing the seizures in the course of the liquidation procedure of
Old-Prussian lodge assets.

At the same time as the intensified actions against the Old-Prussian
Orders in the autumn of 1934, there began the monitoring of "Drei Welt
Kugeln" Grand Master Dr. Otto Bordes. According to a report at a meeting of the Old-Prussian grand masters on January 5, 1934, Bordes had
been assigned to carry out negotiations with Reichs Administrator Buch
in the "Brown House" in Munich.[147] The fact that Bordes was unable to
accomplish anything is proven by the lack of success in his protest of
the devastation of the building in Mülheim an der Ruhr belonging to a
subordinate Lodge of the "Drei Welt Kugeln" in April 1934. There, Storm
Troopers had taken the pictures of emperors Wilhelm I and Friedrich

III from their frames and had left graffiti: "If you hang our Adolf Hitler between two Freemasons again, watch out!" German National Socialist Workers' Party Staff Chief Martin Bormann judged the objection of the National Grand Master unworthy of an answer. He forwarded the proceedings to Reich Administrator Buch with the remark that, in the opinion of the deputy of Der Führer, it was "an insolence to hang a picture of Der Führer between former princes dressed as Freemasons."[148]

More still: Apparently, Bordes made himself suspect in such a way that he came into the crosshairs of state terror. He was arrested twice and, at least during the month of October 1934, purposefully subjected to intelligence interrogation. From reports based on the findings of a "V-man" (detective) that concerned a sojourn of the Bordes family in Bad Kissingen in the autumn of 1934, it follows that the order for a "confidential monitoring" came down on October 3, 1934, via the Secret State Police Office. The identity of the V-man is unknown. Its information (mainly about the allegedly conspiratorial meetings of Bordes with other Freemasons, as well as about him and his family's other activities and opinions) was converted to reports and forwarded by police headquarters in Nürnberg-Fürth (Department II/2) to the Security Office of the Reichs Administration SS, Department V, at Wilhelmsstraße 102, Berlin.[149]Because of this, by the beginning of October 1934, the Main Office took action in parts of Berlin. In addition, questions about the organization of the SD which are of special interest in this connection—particularly since the business distribution or organization charts have not survived—can be reconstructed with little effort. The documents published by George C. Browder from records of the SD Main DivisionRhine give some reference points as to how the structure would have looked. According to them, the SD Office in Munich ca. 1933/34 consisted of seven departments, each subdivided, and two independent *Referaten* (subdivisions). Besides the so-called *Stabsabteilung* Staff Department and Department Z Headquarters were the Departments I Organization under the leadership of the notorious Dr. Werner Best, II Administration, III Information [domestic affairs], IV Counter-espionage and foreign questions, V Freemasons as well as the

Subdivisions for Press and Technical Assistance/Radio.[150] Department V covered six areas of responsibility:

1. Masonic card index (domestic and foreign);

2. Evaluation;

3. Lodge maps;

4. Library;

5. Archive; and

6. Museum.

The prominent position of Freemasonry is noticeable in the department structure. Browder assumed, probably rightfully, that the reason for this is not only to be sought in Himmler's and Heydrich's priority at that time. Rather, it might have been relevant that there were "coincidentally a sufficient number of 'experts'" for their own Masonic department.[151] Even in the structure of the early SD, the later office structure of the Security Headquarters was outlined. While the *Stabsabteilung*, Departments Z Headquarters, I Organization, and II Administration, as well as the two independent subdivisions, can be considered as germ cells of Office I, the Masonic Department V found its organizational–historical continuation both in the agency "J/I" Office Information—with which it existed in parallel for awhile—respectively in the Headquarters Departments I/1 and I/3—as well as in the Domestic Department II/111.[152]

In all probability, even before the transfer of the SD office from Munich to Berlin, the Masonic Department V had been led by Maximilian Brand, as named above. In addition to him, two other SS figures central to the "Masonic question" were already actively concerned: Gregor Schwartz Bostunitsch, of whom more will be said, and Erich Ehlers, who had worked full-time for the SD since November 1933 and who would remain by far the longest of all those in the SS apparatus concerned with Freemasonry.[153] The relevant person in the early phase, however, might have been Brand. He, a Nazi from the first hour and a farmer by occupation, came to the SD at the beginning of 1932. He had held the rank of Chief Storm Troops Battalion Commander since June15, 1934. His name is written, annoyingly, both in the sources and in the literature alternately as "Brandt" and "Brand," and by the same token, it is seen from the documents that the wrong service rank was used repeatedly in forms of address.[154] In February and March 1935, the Masonic Department appeared as "the Central Department V" in the Main Security Office, which covered several subdivisions according to a rotating plan and whose chief obviously had continued to be Brand.[155] As a consequence of the development of a three-part office structure, organizational tension arose, and a new balance of power developed within the SD Main Office. From this, it can be ascertained that the creation of the offices did not take place in one step. The Masonic Department V stood as a forerunner to the Domestic Service Office II/111, while the form of organization to be established in the future with the "Department of Information" as Office I, whose administration Brand temporarily took over,[156] was already "under construction." And even later, that is, at the end of June or beginning of July 1935—Department V was functioning.[157]

But back to Bordes: The material in his Berlin Document Center personnel file can be divided as follows: 1. Lodge and private correspondence; 2. exchanges of letters about his admission into the Nazi Party, as well as about his subsequent exclusion from the Party because of his lodge membership; 3. intelligence material about Bordes from observation, post office, and telephone monitoring; 4. reports about Bordes' political attitude, his private life, and fraternal circle based on the reports of the informant. In such a report dated October 11, 1934, one can read: "In his conversations with the V-man about lodges, church, and the German National Socialist Workers' Party, Dr. B. expressed again and again that he was personally connected to high positions. For example, he mentioned the personal discussions with Reichs Bishop Müller, conversations in the Cafe 'Hut,' (Potsdamer Straße, Berlin) with Reichs Commander of the Schutzstaffel Himmler and other high SS and SA leaders ... Dr. B. is of the opinion that Der Führer Adolf Hitler is not exactly informed about the struggle that is being carried on against Freemasonry in Germany;

otherwise, he would not permit it. He, Dr. B., regards the Chancellor of the Third Reich extremely highly; he knows, however, that the most important questions concerning the Reich often do not get directly to him."[158]

At the same time, with the siphoning off of information by the informer, the National Grand Master's mail and telephone calls were monitored and evaluated. From the exchange of letters with his wife and with acquaintances, it becomes evident that the family knew of the monitoring, or at least assumed it. In a letter to his wife of October 23, 1934, Bordes writes: "There is no more doubt for me that all our mail is examined."[159]

Bordes, who had temporarily become a member of the Nazi Party at the end of April or the beginning of May 1933 by concealing his lodge affiliation—although he obviously never received a membership card[160]—was arrested twice, together with his wife. The duration and circumstances of the arrests are uncertain. Peters determined that the first arrest was in 1933, and that a *Festschrift* of the National Mother Lodge was published the following year,[161] which is substantially more probable. The second arrest probably took place about the same time as the search and occupation of the "Drei Welt Kugeln" Grand Lodge building in the Splittgerbergasse in Berlin on March 4, 1935. Bordes was brought into the notorious concentration camp "Columbia House" in Berlin. There, he met Dr. Eduard Uterharck, the Past Master of the Hamburg lodge "Absalom zu den Drei Nesseln," who had been arrested on January 23, 1935, and brought to Berlin. Uterharck was taken back to Hamburg for one year's detention "because of offence against the perfidy law" before his condemnation, which took place on July 26, 1935. How long the National Grand Master remained imprisoned is unclear. Possibly he was freed after a relatively short time, since from several sources it becomes clear that Bordes took part in a conference in the Secret State Police Office in Berlin on March 22 on behalf of his Grand Lodge about the arrangements for its dissolution.[162] Either he was already free again and administered the official business of the Grand Lodge, or his detention was interrupted only for the duration of the discussion.[163] A last attempt to rescue the National

Grand Lodges was undertaken by Reichs bank president and economics minister, Hjalmar Schacht, the most prominent, but by no means only, former Freemason. He was quickly promoted in the "Third Reich."[164] Schacht, who served as Reich Economics Minister and Plenipotentiary for Military Economy until 1937 and as a Reichs bank president until 1939, seems never to have gotten into serious difficulties as a result of his earlier lodge membership, over the whole time up to his exit as Reichs Minister without Portfolio in 1943. From September 18, 1907, until February 11, 1933, Schacht had belonged to the Berlin lodge "Urania zur Unsterblichkeit,"a subordinate lodge of the Grand Lodge "Zur Freundschaft."[165] In the spring of 1935, Schacht went up to the Obersalzberg to see Hitler on a mediation mission on behalf of his former Grand Lodge. Hitler appeared to be convinced that there was "nothing to accuse" the Old Prussians of; he persisted in the demand for totality of the "movement" and thus for a dissolution, which, however, could take place while preserving the statutes and "customs."[166] Two years later, the liquidator of the Grand Landes Lodge of Germany, Paul Rosenthal, would expressly advise former lodge members against referring to the fact that Schacht was also a Freemason, trying to avoid discrimination, particularly since this would "in no case have any influence on changing [the treatment of former Freemasons"—author's note].[167]

On the other hand, one must assume that members of the Große Landesloge, with the help of their close connections there, tried to influence the government of Sweden to exert diplomatic pressure on their behalf. On the question of whether Stockholm actually used its influence in favor of the Große Landesloge, one can only speculate, because of the lack of source material. In any case, the archival material consulted for this study gave no indication of an alleged intervention by the Swedish King (and Grand Master) Gustav V.[168]

5.2.2 FORCED SELF-DISSOLUTIONS
AND LIQUIDATIONS

For the last months of the existence of the Masonic Orders, the amount of source material decreases considerably. This indicates that in the course of the progressive erosion, communication broke down to a great extent not only among grand lodges, but also between the subordinate lodges still working and their grand lodges. What actually happened just before the forced self-dissolutions in the summer of 1935 thus cannot be completely reconstructed.

It is clear that self-dissolution was unmistakably suggested to the Old Prussians in several meetings of the Reichs- and Prussian Interior Ministry. Upon the repetition of such a verbal report, a circular from the Old Prussians addressed to all subordinate lodges on April 10, 1935, made a connection, without however mentioning the conference on March 22 in the Secret State Police Office building.[169] The three Old-Prussian Grand Masters and the representatives of the responsible Nazi agencies participated in this no doubt decisive discussion. Those present were: for the Gestapa, the Administrator of the Review Board II 1 B 2 Dr. Haselbacherl; for the Reichs- and Prussian Interior Ministry, Ministerial Councillor Eickhoff; as well as, for the SD, Chief Storm Troops Battalion Commander Brand, who was responsible for Masonic affairs.[170] In the course of the conversation, the grand masters explained that they were ready, in order to forestall the employment of national instruments of power, "for their part, voluntarily to work toward the dissolution of their organizations." They wished, however, "to be absolved of the reproaches raised in public against them."[171] To this purpose, the grand masters wrote an explanation that they handed over to the Reichs and Prussian Interior Minister on May 28, 1935. In it, they wrote that it had always been "the highest principle" of the Old-Prussian grand lodges "that native country, state, and people were to stand in the forefront of all actions." Accordingly, they were ready, "as a consequence of the suggestion given them, to recommend dissolution to the grand lodges as well as their subordinate lodges."[172] The formal dissolution resolutions of the individual subordinate lodges followed the corresponding resolutions of the general meetings. The public "rehabilitation," which had been assured them, never took place, of course.[173] The closing ceremonies of the grand lodges took place in July 1935. Both Saxon (united) grand lodges, which had been transformed into Orders, went the way of the "voluntary" self-dissolutions in July or August "suggested" by the State.[174] Thus, the attempt at mobilization finally failed in the summer of 1935. Meanwhile, the anti-Masonic propaganda struggle and the argument about *Weltanschauung* were continued by the National Socialists. The traces thus left in the public consciousness continue to have an effect. The closing ceremonies mentioned above,[175] including memorials written because of them, show a unique mixture of stubborn persistence and melancholy farewell. This was because doubts of a National-Christian or *völkisch* sort were not yet voiced about Freemasonry or about content (re)orientation and outward adjustment. Contrariwise, in the written memorial, the Große Landesloge affirmed its *völkisch* understanding of Order, by stating that as "the third goal in the fight for German Christianity and Christian Germanness (Teutonicism)...the request for keeping the race pure" would be taken up. The dangers "of an unconsidered racial intermixture that threaten the roots of the population" had already been countered by the St. John's Festival Greeting of 1926, in a time, indeed, "in which one did not otherwise ascribe much meaning" to these questions. "Thus the Order—because it has called itself an Order since its establishment by the first Order Master Von Zinnendorf (1770)—has functioned in its nearly 165-year work in Germany, and in the course of this long time has filled many ten thousands of men with its spirit. It may well say of itself that in this way it brought quite a considerable number of Germans ... into effective contact with valuable patriotic and Christian ideals and silently accomplished much that is beneficial for people and native country."[176] Signs of self-doubt are not expressed here. However, next to all the pathos, a sincere despair does show itself over the loss of Freemasonry, which had been for many members an important component of their lives. During the last lodge meetings, members were introduced to the contents of the higher degrees, which they would never attain.[177]

At the beginning of August 1935, Interior Minister Wilhelm Frick declared that it was "high time that the Freemasons' lodges now also disappear from Germany as they had vanished from Italy." Frick added: "And if this realization does not gradually penetrate the circles of Free-masons, then I shall soon help in this direction."[178] In this connection, on August 17, 1935, he directed—based on §1 "of the Reichstag Fire Regulation,"—the immediate forced dissolution of Freemasons' lodges and "Freemason-like" associations (with the temporary exception of B'nai B'rith) that had not yet "voluntarily" dissolved. Their assets were declared hostile to the people and the State, and were frozen.[179] In April 1937, the tolerance for B'nai B'rith also ended: The German lodge buildings of B'nai B'rith were searched, and there were arrests as well as confiscations of the property of the organization.

With that, the lodges and organizations "similar to lodges" were formally forbidden in Germany, which did not cause the Nazi apparatus to lose sight of Freemasonry. Apart from material enrichment, Masonic politics in the "Third Reich" continued in a very complex way: on the level of police intelligence, on the political level (elimination of "Masonic influence" by restriction of former lodge members), on the level of ideo-logical training and mass propaganda, and on the level of fundamental discussions about *Weltanschauung.*In contrast to the forcibly-dissolved lodges, those Masonic organizations which had dissolved themselves were not declared as "anarchist" associations, and their assets were also not frozen on the basis of the "Reichstag Fire Regulation." Instead, for them, liquidation was introduced. This did not mean that their fortune was freely at their disposal. On the contrary, the liquidated assets were controlled by the Secret State Police—to which the national supervi-sion of lodges had been turned over—and used to cover the costs of the liquidation (including costs incurred during the "safekeeping" of lodge possessions). For real estate possessions—if they could be sold at all—usually only a symbolic price was obtained—never the real value. Each sale depended in principle on the permission of the Secret State Police Office. Often, this permission was denied, so that the possession finally went to, or was used by, the state, the German National Socialist Workers' Party, or a party division.[180] From the outset, the State Powers prescribed that the remaining lodge assets were not to be divided among the members, but should be applied to "charitable purposes."[181]

In the case of the Old Prussians, the liquidations, which can be treated here only briefly, were not uniformly carried out, and dragged on until 1941. The first and most important step in the procedure was to secure a liquidator from the Fraternity, who functioned from then on as the responsible contact person for state and party positions. He was allowed, of course, to represent the Grand Lodge and its subordinate lodges only in economic and financial questions in connection with the process of liquidation.[182] Now and then, however, his participation went beyond the monetary: Thus, Große Landesloge liquidator Paul Rosenthal led Nazi Party visitors' groups through the Masonic Hall on Eisenach Street several times between August and October 1935. These tours took place at the express desire of the Berlin Nazi Party local group Wittenbergplatz, and served "for training purposes." The tours seem to have been conducted, as seen from the correspondence, in a more or less friendly atmosphere. However, on October 19, such tours, were forbidden by the Gestapa.[183]

In the liquidation of real and property assets, three areas can be differentiated, which will be discussed briefly in succession. First, mobile inventory, archives, and library collections; second, house and estate property; third, financial assets, including the two areas mentioned above, which resulted in relatively small proceeds.

Concerning the archives, and libraries, the liquidators had been expressly forbidden to sell, give away, or destroy anything from the lodges without permission. After the initial ambiguity about the concrete procedure of the liquidations, the Report of the Department II 1 B 2 responsible for Freemasonry, dated April 6, 1936, in the Berlin Gestapa, formulated valid guidelines for the future. The circular was addressed to all state police offices in Prussia, and in addition was passed on to the political police offices outside Prussia. It summarized, under ideological as well as pragmatic criteria, how to proceed in order "to promote the liquidation of lodge assets," and "to eliminate unnecessary delays."[184] For the treatment of mobile property that was not needed by the central offices for ideological evaluation or exploitation—to which category all archival material belonged—it was most important to check the spreading of Masonic symbolism. Thus, confiscated gold and silver, as well as tableware, were "in principle to be turned over to the liquidator for silver plating (i.e. for selling, [author's note])." Exceptions, however, would be such pieces that had a completely Masonic character or Masonic symbols. Their release for silver plating was to depend on the guarantee of the liquidator to have the symbols removed beforehand at the expense of the remaining lodge assets. If that was impossible or disproportionately expensive or would reduce the value substantially, the articles concerned were to be sold to a goldsmith for melting down. The melting down was to be supervised by the Gestapo. Tableware of slight value was not to be melted "if possible, but in agreement with the liquidator, for a small recognition fee from the National Socialist People's Welfare, to be left to hospitals and such." In the same way, tableware that "because of symbols burned in and therefore not removable, could not be silverplated, was not to be smashed, but wherever possible to be given to these organizations."[185] As "Drei Welt Kugeln" liquidator Karl Manecke reported in the same month, after the Masonic emblems had been removed, the utensils could be sold. Artistically or culturally valuable neutral inventory from lodge possessions should be put at the disposal of museums and public libraries "according to agreements made in detail." On the other hand, lodge glasses, if Masonic symbols could not be removed, had to be destroyed. All "custom-made" articles with Masonic emblems were subject to the control of the Gestapo or the SD.[186] In isolated cases, private initiative succeeded in slipping past the confiscations, but usually those goods, just as with the archives, were spirited off to the Main Security Office, after some of it had been stored temporarily in the upper divisions of the SD. The resulting transportation costs, as decided by the Interior Ministry, had to be defrayed by the liquidation monies of the lodges.[187] The material was kept in Berlin (or now and again destroyed), evaluated, and re-used depending upon the need. The SD compiled a central Masonic card index from the membership registers, whereas ritual articles were used in anti-Masonic exhibits.[188] While those portions of lodge libraries that were not Masonic in content could be freely obtained, Masonica sometimes was incorporated (as duplicates) into the SD collection or public libraries.

As already briefly outlined, the decisions about buyers and prices during the disposal of lodge real estate depended on the political police in Prussia and all other allied countries. In February 1937, the report of the SD Freemasons Department II/111 stated that in the course of the liquidations, the real property of lodges was transferred (to a great extent) to state, local, or party possession. Otherwise, the "close connection of Freemasonry to the Protestant church" would become apparent by the fact that "some lodges convey their buildings to Protestant congregations by donation."[189] In some places, those National Socialist authorities, who concerned themselves with the struggle against Freemasonry, moved into former lodge buildings, just as members of the SD and Gestapo apparatus were housed in "arianized" Jewish possessions in Berlin—for instance, in the former Jewish fraternity building in the Kurfürstenstrasse—in the former Office for Palestine (Israel) in the Meinekestrasse, or in the former Jewish old-age home in the Berkaer Strasse. The Große Landes-loge building in the Eisenacher Strasse had to be left, free of charge, to a Gestapo agency by the name of "Lodge Legacy Administration" (probably concerned with the liquidations procedures) before it was conveyed to the Reich at a symbolically nominal price.[190] The SD settled itself into the building in the Emser Strasse, confiscated from the Hamburg Grand Lodge, and collected "secured" archives and library materials there. From the value of the "Drei Weltkugeln" real estate in the Splittgerbergasse, a "considerable" amount—otherwise not more precisely described—was added to the resources of a newly-created Masonic collection foundation,[191] which resulted from the use of the remainder of lodge assets. With the resolution of self-dissolution, the lodges dispensed for the time being with the execution of "every economic or financial transaction, that goes beyond the regular course of lodge business," in "agreement" with the Interior Ministry and Gestapa, in order to avoid "unpleasantnesses."[192] To all appearances, the settling between the authorities and the liquidators, of the financial liquidation assets that remained, went relatively agreeably. The money flowed in several directions: A part went to the "National Socialist War Victims Welfare Service"; some served as security for the pension requirements of former lodge employees; and a further part benefited three social agencies with a Masonic background: an old people's home for (former) Freemasons in Einbeck; an old people's home for female family members of (former) Freemasons in Dahme; and the Seitz-Reinke Forest Sanatorium in Kolberg, a care agency for children suspected of having tuberculosis, originally founded by lodge members. All previous donations of lodges were combined into the (non-legally responsible) collecting foundation already mentioned, and attached to the Seitz Reinke Forest Sanatorium as so-called "relief funds." According to the planning at that time, needy former Freemasons would be supported financially on request from these trust funds up to the year 1970. Afterward, the remaining funds were supposed to go into the Kolberger children's sanatorium.[193]

Chapter 6

CASE STUDY I: GROSSE LANDESLOGE DER FREIMAURER VON DEUTSCHLAND (GRAND LODGE OF FREEMASONS OF GERMANY OR GLL)

6.1 INTERNAL DEVELOPMENT

Despite the social upheavals and the multiplicity of political problems between 1918 and 1935, only a little pluralism showed itself in the ranks of the Grosse Landesloge. From the standpoint of structure and personnel, it was fixed in its fundamental theoretical and political principles. The increasing adoption of *völkisch* positions was not practiced only by the established leadership. Rarely was there any internal contradiction. Certainly, the appearance of the Order was shaped considerably by the narrow circle of the top men in the Grosse Landesloge. Changes in leadership, relatively late, did not lead to changes in trend—not when Kurt von Heeringen replaced Eugen Muellendorff in the office of Grand Master in 1931; nor as Friedrich Bolle succeeded William Augustin Balthasar-Wolfrath as the Order's Grand Master in 1934. As far as one can conclude from sources that have come down to us, there were no fundamental content controversies in the circle of leadership of the Grosse Landesloge.

In its social composition, the Grosse Landesloge did not differ substantially from the other established Jurisdictions. However, the reformed Freemasonry of the Freimaurerbund zur aufgehenden Sonne (Freemasons' Association of the Rising Sun "FaS") and the Symbolische Grossloge von Deutschland (Symbolic Grand Lodge of Germany "SGL") were more attractive to intellectual and artistic circles—although an actor and former theatrical director from Dresden did appear at the Grosse Landesloge— and were characterized by middle- and higher-level employees, officials, the independently wealthy members of the commercial, self-employed, and academic professions such as teachers, as well as—especially in the twentieth century—a fair number of Protestant clergymen. In other words, their members came from the new middle economic layers of a mainly urban environment. The lower middle class—petite bourgeoisie and tradesmen—in contrast, were fewer in number. The same applies to the profession of officer, although the "institution" of the reserve officer stood in high repute with the Old Prussians, as—not surprisingly—with all former officers, so it seems. They also, at least in terms of their effectiveness, played a larger role than in other Lodges. In the executive committee of the Grosse Landesloge—which became the German-Christian Order—however, the following picture manifests itself, relative to the composition by occupational groups for the year 1934: a career officer (retired lieutenant colonel Landes Grand Master von Heeringen), a dean and retired captain of the reserve, a physician, a manufacturer, a retired director, a count, a post office official, a bank clerk, a teacher, a director, a buyer, and a government or planning officer.[1]

The membership curve of the Grosse Landesloge during the Weimar years was similar to the membership development of the other established grand lodges. The number of lodges subordinate to the Grosse Landesloge rose from 168 (1924), past 171 (1926), 173 (1927), 176 (1928), to 177 (1929).[2] The following year, when the completely different development of regular German Freemasonry was constituted in the form of the

Symbolische Grossloge, the Grosse Landesloge numbered their members at 20,400 brothers. At the same time, it reached its highest number [of lodges][3] with 180 St. John's lodges. Thereafter, either no new lodges were founded or the number of new lodges was equal to the number of lodge closings. In any case, in 1932, there existed the same number of subordinate lodges.[4] However, since the middle of the 1920s, the *membership* numbers had generally declined. This "downward gap" hardly played a role in any [Masonic] system. The reason for this was less that the lodges opposed such a gap in principle, but rather that they made almost no effort to attract candidates from the working classes to the bourgeois institution of Freemasonry. In addition, the lodges traditionally mounted no membership recruitment "campaigns" and only rarely departed from that principle. As far as can be reconstructed from the sources, no great controversies arose because of the social origin of candidates—even with the Grosse Landesloge. To be sure, a social demarcation "downward" remained with the old Freemasonry as well as with the reforming wing in the case of contemplative work and by acceptance practice (sponsorship). However, the lodges became fundamentally more permeable, just like their "profane" [non-Masonic] environment. In the 20th and 21st centuries, one cannot speak of social exclusivity, as one could in the eighteenth century.

In contrast to the question of a social opening toward the working classes, the problem of obsolescence, which had become worse since the end of the 1920s, made for lively discussions in the lodges. The fact that, in the nationalistic environment under the influence of pervasive anti-Masonic agitation, the new generation was hardly interested in Freemasonry gave the Old Prussians—and not least the Grosse Landesloge—a lot to worry about. In 1929, therefore, Felix Witt-Hoë suggested to the Old-Prussian Grand Masters' Association that one should try to get university professors to strengthen their influence on academic youth for the cause of the Old Prussians.[5] From a completely opposite political perspective, the Symbolische Grossloge also concluded that youth kept completely away from Freemasonry. In the first issue of its magazine, *The*

Ancient Obligations, Leo Müffelmann therefore wrote that "something in the Masonic movement might not be in tune with the times." From this he derived the challenge of creating "the social program of Freemasonry." Furthermore, he announced that the "intellectual circles" should supply Freemasonry more than before.[6] In this way, he consciously distinguished himself from old German Freemasonry in terms of agenda.

The specific orientation of the Grosse Landesloge, in particular its appeal to the Order's tradition, was discussed in detail in the past chapters. The same applies to the consciously selected special role connected with it of the Grosse Landesloge within the Old-Prussian family. This course, which the administration of Order was anxious to carry out, however, encountered a lack of understanding and unwillingness in the subordinate lodges every now and then, particularly since it could be realized in local lodge life only with difficulty. Thus logically, Masonic polarization played itself out most violently on the personal level of the Grosse Landesloge functionaries.

Two examples are mentioned here: With the appearance of the *International Masonic Encyclopedia* at the end of 1931 and the beginning of 1932, Witt-Hoë warned his fraternity expressly about the work, pointing out that the authors belonged to grand lodges that were under the influence of the Grand Orient de France, and with which the Grosse Landesloge had broken off relations. This made clear that it would be "impossible to find explanations and orientation on Masonic questions" that would quote "objectively our opinions, teachings, ritual and historical development" in the book. Therefore, the work could serve "only such Brothers of the Order, who wanted to instruct themselves for comparative studies of the spirit of international Freemasonry, which was always opposing us, often inimically. In any case, it was foreign to our nature."[7] In the same way, the Grosse Landesloge leadership showed concern because of a possible exercise of influence by relevant SGL members on their (GLL) fraternal circle. At the beginning of of July 1932, Witt-Hoë wrote a lodge member that he had inferred "with fear" from a telephone conversation "that you were in the company of Mr. R. K.... (Raoul Koner [author's note]). I have already told you that one cannot be careful enough in relations with people from the Symbolic Grosse Landesloge, and in my opinion, must limit oneself to the purely personal."[8] Thereupon, the Brother concerned communicated that his contact with Koner had actually been limited to purely personal and business concerns. Nevertheless, this made "an extraordinarily good impression" on him.[9] Internally, the highest priority was given to the problem of defense of Freemasonry, whereby existing, unorthodox stances could not be applied. Thus, for example, in April 1929, the possibility suggested by the Mayor of Bremervörd and Grosse Landesloge member Dr. Erich Michaelis that he could broadcast lectures "about religious...and also patriotic thought in Freemasonry"[10] was rejected by Witt-Hoë with thanks. The negative vote of the Grosse Landesloge was borne out by "experience in this area here in Berlin," which had shown, "how much the opposition as well as the well-meaning profane public had taken umbrage at this kind of influence."[11] Indeed, the Grosse Landesloge gave up more and more the classical form of public enlightening lectures in favor of more purposeful defensive activity. Most often attempted, in social federations, was to influence the formation of opinions on Christian-Nationalistic Freemasonry from the inside outward, as well as, in a decentralized way, to correct the superficial picture of Freemasonry spread in newspapers. In Oldenburg around the turn of the year 1931-1932, when the Nazi Party agitated particularly militantly against the lodges, defense specialist Oswald Bielig gave a successful public lecture. It was decided, nevertheless, to have further lectures in Oldenburg and the vicinity only before invited guests.[12]

At the end of of 1929, Paul Buhlmann, a Masonic Brother from Rathenow, began to gather the names of the Grosse Landesloge members who had been killed or had died from war-related causes between 1914 and 1918, for the purpose of a defense (of Freemasonry). In 1932, the same year as a similar publication of the Reichs Federation of Jewish soldiers on the front, an honor roll was published in a brochure under the title "Honor Roll of those Brothers of the Grosse Landesloge of Freemasons of

Germany of the German-Christian Masonic Order who fell in the World War 1914–1918 or who succumbed to their wounds." On this occasion, Landes Grand Master von Heeringen stated that the work was "a spoken refutation of the statement made by those of ill-will" that "our Masonic Order and its members had not done their duty in the great fateful struggle of the German people."[13] In addition to the listing of 308 Masonic Order Brothers who had died—including birth and death dates, place of lodge membership, and the military rank—the brochure contained other statistics of interest: According to it, the Grosse Landesloge had 15,596 members at the outbreak of the war. The Brothers of the nine subordinate lodges in Berlin were, on the average, 51.3 years of age, which already pointed to an superannuation problem. It may be assumed, it went on to say, that "the same conditions are true of the remaining lodges."[14] Of the 3618 members of the Grosse Landesloge who took part in the war, 467 had fallen or had been permanently disabled. The statistics assumed that of the entire membership in Germany, approximately 32.75 percent of the lodge Brothers had been of military conscription age in 1914.[15] Besides its separation from other directions of Freemasonry and the emphasis on its own patriotic commitment, the Grosse Landesloge, in its arguments in its own defense, dissociated itself expressly from those politicians who were connected with Freemasonry by the *völkisch* or Nazi agitation. In November 1933, a paper by the Grosse Landesloge stated in this connection—"with all emphasis"—that "the following statesmen and politicians had never been members of a lodge of Freemasons, let alone our Masonic Brethren: Bethmann Hollweg, Prince Max von Baden, Rathenau, Scheidemann; also Ebert, General Groener, Hermann Mueller have never belonged to a Freemasons' lodge....We close...with the remark that the minister Dr. Ludwig Wessel, deceased father of the hero of liberty and champion of the Third Reich, Horst Wessel, was, until his death, our dear Masonic Brother...."[16] The resolution of the Grosse Landesloge of April 7, 1933, by which the transformation into the German-Christian Order was introduced, had not been issued gratuitously without a previous poll of the National Mother Lodge or the Grand Lodge "Zur Freundschaft."

Therefore, people were hardly pleased that other grand lodges—including the humanitarian lodges—followed this example. The Masonic Order (Grosse Landesloge) administration made clear to the subordinate lodges or "conventions" that they were to refrain from work in the first through fifth degrees, from May to September 1933, until the completion of the new rituals.[17] In practice, that meant little more than a brief extension of the usual lodge period of "darkness" (closing for holidays or vacation). On August 7, 1933, von Heeringen communicated to Goering that the departments of the Masonic Order would resume their activity again at the beginning of September, and that a part of the new ritual was finished.[18] Nothing indicates that Goering or other National Socialists concerned with lodge affairs would have attached any special significance to that. While internally the change in tradition manifested itself in the form of the new rituals, party and public authorities held firmly to the notion that the German-Christian Orders were nothing more than "camouflaged" lodges of Freemasons. It still remains to be shown that, in practice, there never was a fundamental distinction between national-Christian and internationalist-humanitarian Freemasonry in the "Third Reich," not even when the "essential" argument on the "Masonic question," pushed by the SD, had become the determining factor.

6.2 POLITICAL ORIENTATION

National conservative Freemasonry in the Germany of the Weimar years reached back to concepts that had developed persistently during the First World War, or as a direct consequence of it. Thinking and feeling were characterized by a deep hatred for each other on the part of enemies in war, whose intention it was—according to the St. John's Day greeting of the Grosse Landesloge Administration in 1919—"to wipe the German race off the face of the Earth with hunger and epidemics."[19]

What those drafts intended to do comes, for example, from an essay that a Freemason and upper-echelon medical officer in frontline service had written in 1916 on the question of "Freemasonry and the War."[20] According to it, Freemasonry's idea of the world citizen failed, and an abyss separated the German brothers from those of enemy states. Thus, a distinct historical parallel was drawn between the wars of liberation and the "the people's uprising of 1914."[21] It was deduced that because of the war, German Freemasons would have to assume a purely national point of view, in contrast to Romance (French) as well as English Freemasonry. A specifically German Freemasonry, including the attribution of a qualitatively higher value, was demanded. For this purpose, a "transformation of Germany's lodges into German (Teutonic) lodges was necessary," as also were "the complete turning away from much mental baggage of things survived and old-fashioned and, at the same time, a new construction, a rebirth of the entire German Freemasonry on a German basis and in a German spirit, free of all clichés and efforts toward a general world citizenry as well as a maudlin over-enthusiasm for humanity wallowing in the brotherhood of people."[22] In other words, out of the German fraternal circle a synthesis of political and Masonic categories was postulated, a *völkische* coordination or subordination among alleged national interests. The author of this essay, Dr. Max Volkenrath, lived off and on in Würzburg and belonged from approximately 1922 to 1926/1927 to the Nuremberg GLL subordinate lodge "Luginsland."[23]

Although the principles formulated in the text were not only found in the Grosse Landesloge, they *were* nevertheless, in the ensuing time, very consistently shifted to the Christian rubric among its ranks. In contrast to all other German Grand Lodges, one was strengthened by the concept of being able to build on an explicitly Christian-Germanic pre-Enlightenment tradition that derived from the characteristics determined by the kind of teaching. The "thought of the Order, based on Nordic Christianity[24]—closely linked with the mission of Templarism in the sense of a "mental legacy"[25]—and in the Weimar years played off against humanitarian Freemasonry—was brought into play as a basis for the transformation [into a Christian Order], after the Nazi "seizure of power." In 1934, that was formulated as follows: "Only the two 'source-streams,' Freemasonry as originated in the guild system and Christian orders of knighthood," would form the Order, "which is called Christian Freemasonry, and which caused those deep differences in mental attitude, that has gone so far that internationally-minded Freemasonry has for a long time disputed the right of this Christian-national species to call itself Freemasonry."[26]

From this perspective, the rituals and symbols "Aryanized" in 1933 were justified: "the spirit alive in the old custom," as it was carefully called by the Grosse Landesloge, was by no means "that of the religiously-indifferent eighteenth century," as was so often maintained by the opponents of Masonry. Rather, it had its sources "in the rich inner life of our ancestors from the time of German Mysticism."[27] "From year to year, the reservations about some words [for Hebrew/Jewish or Enlightenment concepts—translator's note] in our rituals, which were objectionable to contemporary people" had increased. „Because of the attitude of complete rejection of the opponents, who tried to make each self-evident and clear action of the Masonic Order contemptible by calling it 'camouflage'," one did not make a change "from the quite justifiable feeling of worth and good conscience." After the "victorious completion of the national revolution," however, the remaking had become a matter of course. With the organization of the new ritual, above all, the "purity of teachings of the Masonic Order" had to be protected, whereby now the idea of Masonic Order „became more valid already in the two first degrees."[28]

The implications and ramifications of politics play an important, probably even crucial, role for the understanding of Freemasonry as an intellectual and social-historical manifestation. The announcements of the established German lodges did not change anything in that regard, which usually meant the opposite and "sought to prove the apolitical" character of Freemasonry. The manifestations of political orientation of the lodges were subject to processes of change, which always stood in interdependence with the external world. During the Weimar years, they solidified themselves with the basic tendency of an increasing hardening and radicalization of political points of view.

The isolationism practiced by the Masonic Order was particularly challenged whenever events occurred that seemed to call it into question. Thus, for example, Grand Master Müllendorff saw himself compelled to make the following report in the Grosse Landesloge magazine in 1930: "the Chancellery of the 'Association Maçonnique Internationale' (A.M.I.) in Geneva had published a yearbook of World Freemasonry in 1930, in which the Grosse Landesloge and its subordinate lodges were cited. For clarification, let it be stressed that the Grosse Landesloge expressly rejected a request directed to it for corrections of the text and added: 'We would like to ask urgently that no statements concerning our Grand Lodge be included at all in this yearbook, as we do not belong to World Freemasonry, and do not want to.' The publisher tacitly disregarded this request, and we have no possibility of preventing it from being published. The fact that the data of this handbook under these circumstances, is sometimes incorrect, sometimes filled with gaps, cannot be surprising. There is no reason for us to go into this in detail here."[29]The new Grand Master, von Heeringen, defined Christian-national Freemasonry's understanding of itself in an exemplary way in a lecture held at a guest-speaking engagement in Nordhausen in 1931. He explained that it was not the task of Freemasonry, "to regulate the relationships of peoples to each other." Their work is "not outwardly, but inwardly oriented. It should turn to the individual and educate him. And if we talk about people, then it can concern only the German person. Individuality must be rooted in its own nationality."[30]

Domestic political developments, meanwhile, inevitably meant that the discussion of the widespread, anti-Masonic attitude in the *völkisch* environment was superimposed onto the concrete question about the relationship to the Nazi Party. With a view to this, Felix Witt-Höe wrote shortly after Hindenburg's reelection in April 1932 that the evaluation of the National Socialist movement was "completely different from our Masonic Order Brothers in the different parts of our Fatherland: Indeed, I may emphasize that we have large, important divisions of the Masonic

Order, whose fraternity is strongly pervaded by National Socialism." There was even a sitting Worshipful Master, "who had a respected position in the party." And further, "if the National Socialists still exclude the Freemason today, which seems to contradict what was just said, that is because of the necessities of outward agitation and propaganda. Even then, not everything is uniform; there are radical elements that are strongly anti-Masonic. Only Der Führer, even up to the present, is decidedly alone in this party!"[31] Witt-Höe set forth the completely untenable statement that even in *Mein Kampf* "nothing harsh, nothing fundamental" against Freemasonry is said. Rather, it was Rosenberg who was the anti-Masonic one in the party. "We are striving," opined Witt-Höe, "to capture the valuable goals of this neo-German romantic movement, to lessen and balance contradictions."[32] On another occasion, he explained that "members of the different Right-wing orientations up to the middle of the road" belonged to the Masonic Order,[33] quite an appropriate description of the (party) political spectrum within the Grosse Landesloge, which ran from national liberal to National Socialist.

With an unusually aggressive anti-Semitism even for his circumstances, the Masonic Order theoretician, Witt-Höe, said about the Grand Lodge of Vienna, which he hated: The Grosse Landesloge "was attacked for approximately forty years from no one more than by the organ of the Viennese Grand Lodge, *The Allegemeine Wiener Freimaurer Zeitung.*" It had, according to Witt-Höe, "regularly kept track of these infamous Jewish attacks on our Christian principles, against our tradition, our *völkisch* view, and our love for the Fatherland."[34] He, meanwhile, willfully ignored the limitation and disparagement that determined the attitude of his Jurisdiction in relation to the humanitarian systems, which he had helped to shape. Instead, he took the opportunity to point out the emnity of „this most dangerous Jewish Grand Lodge in expository writings."[35]

The men of the Grosse Landesloge thought similarly about the Symbolische Grossloge, after the latter had made its entrance onto the Masonic stage, not only because of its connections to Vienna. A letter from Müllendorff to his colleague Müffelmann dated November 1, 1930, will serve as an example of the behavior exhibited on the part of the Grosse Landesloge vis-à-vis the Symbolische Grossloge. Without using the fraternal form of address actually used between Freemasons, it referred to statements in the first issue of the SGL magazine, *The Ancient Obligations*. In it, the discussion was about the presence of Old Prussian Brothers at a "Bringing in the Light" ceremony during the meeting of a lodge subordinate to the Symbolische Grossloge, and of internationalist ideas, which were allegedly also present in the ranks of Old-Prussian Freemasons, but which "unfortunately did not come forward." Müllendorff explained: "Since we have forbidden our members all participation in any celebrations or meetings of those circles, we must dispute the allegations mentioned in your letter, as long as you do not furnish proof for the correctness of your statements by listing the names. We have no reason to enter into the rest of the contents of your letter, which shows the uncouth contrast to our Christian-patriotic conviction."[36]

While deviating views of the comparatively liberal Grosse Landesloge members were hardly expressed, the more strongly did such Brothers shape internal debate, for whom the conformity vis-à-vis the German national and *völkisch* forces practiced by the Grosse Landesloge administration did not go far enough. It did not concern only members of lodges that belonged to the *völkisch* "Ring Movement." Sometimes, individual Freemasons spoke up, who demanded results from "clarification work" because of experiences due to discrimination in the *völkisch* National Socialist environment, or who expected a more active position of the Grosse Landesloge in the Christian-national sense. For example, in October 1931, a Berlin town councillor and Grosse Landesloge Masonic Brother demanded that the added name "German-Christian Masonic Order" remain not only a word, but had to become deed. In the lodges, one now spoke a lot against the "Godless movement," and a struggle against godlessness was being called for. "I do not promise myself anything at all in the way of practical results of such speeches...," he wrote to his grand master. "Much more: the fact requires that the state imperiously allows the 'Godless Movement'... to smash this system (sic!). This is not just any policy, but a purely material German and Christian attitude." And further: "Also the Freemason, as a member of the Grosse Landesloge, must be educated actively in this sense; and I believe that an only an explanation of Grosse Landesloge to the public will really get attention and confidence in national circles. Today nothing more can be done with lukewarm restraint."[37]

Chapter 7

CASE STUDY II: SYMBOLISCHE GROSSLOGE VON DEUTSCHLAND (SYMBOLIC GRAND LODGE OF GERMANY OR SGL)

7.1 INTERNAL DEVELOPMENT

When the Supreme Council of Germany and the Symbolische Groß-loge (Symbolic Grand Lodge) were founded in quick succession in 1930, they drew considerable attention from both domestic and international Freemasonry. The results were correctly considered to be an indication of the political and domestic Masonic divergences that were coming to a head. Not only had the Higher-Degree (Ancient Accepted Scottish Rite, AASR), which was authoritative worldwide, also established itself as an institution in Germany, but in addition, an aggressive, internationalistic grand lodge had arisen, set up by this Scottish Rite, which put great value on its Masonic Regularity. In short, this describes the area of conflict because *both* organizations operated until the seizure of power by the Nazis.

The Symbolische Großloge competed in the two areas from which most of its membership came: it drew from liberal-minded members of established humanitarian grand lodges, and from those "Zur aufgehenden Sonne" Brethren who were trying to escape the stigma of being "irregular" Freemasons. The change was accomplished under the leadership of then Grand Master Peter H. Heinsen. Aside from that, the growing enmities of the Old Prussians clearly focused on the new grand lodge, which stood as the antithesis to the dogma of Christian-nationalistic Freemasonry. Those who rejected either the Symbolische Großloge or the Scottish Rite, or both, for various reasons, joined at the most sensitive point of the debate on Regularity: the question as to whether a higher-degree-rite organization was justified in bringing the "light of Freemasonry" into blue lodges.

The Supreme Council (of the Scottish Rite) for Germany was not founded until February 10, 1930 in Berlin. The Installation (Constitution) by the Supreme Council of the Netherlands followed on April 18. Dr. Johannes (real name: Edward Janos) Bing was elected Sovereign Grand Commander. There had been an AASR (Ancient Accepted Scottish Rite) Chapter in Stuttgart since August of 1929, which was subordinate to the Supreme Council of the Grande Loge de France. Chapters in Mannheim and Munich followed, which were also subordinate to the Supreme Council of the Grande Loge de France. The connection between the Symbolische Großloge and the Supreme Council reflected not only sympathies and personal relationships, but also concrete mutual interests. Because the established grand lodges vehemently objected to the spread of the AASR in Germany—and therefore put pressure on their Brethren— a new humanitarian grand lodge was the answer to their prayers. The Symbolische Großloge members, for their part, needed a regular Masonic body to "bring in the light" to their founding lodges. The Grande Loge de France had already indicated its readiness in this regard. However, in view of the anti-French feeling in the established Masonic circles in Germany, it was decided (in cooperation with the Supreme Council) to allow the Supreme Council to perform the Constitution ceremony. The Symbolische Großloge member-lodges preferred to bow in advance to the predictable opposition, rather than leave themselves open permanently to the reproach that they were dependent on France. When, in 1931, members of the Grand Lodges of Hamburg and Bayreuth were excluded because of their membership in the AASR, the new connection was kept; the affected Brethren were accepted by the Symbolische Großloge.[1]

The eleventh German jurisdiction (including the Grand Lodge "Zur aufgehenden Sonne") was founded on July 27, 1930. It was accomplished by 65 Freemasons in eight lodges,[2] two days after the aforementioned "bringing in the light" had been done by the Supreme Council. The Symbolische Großloge took its seat (meaning right of assembly) in Hamburg, while the administrative center was in Berlin, where two of the most influential leaders at the grand lodge level lived: Koner and Müffelmann.[3] The latter stepped down as acting chairman (Lieutenant Grand Commander) of the Supreme Council, after he, its spiritual father, was elected Grand Master of the Symbolische Großloge on July 28, 1930.[4] The Lodge "Labor" was founded in Berlin on November 14, 1930, with Grand Secretary Koner as its (Warrant) Master. Its very name expressed its connection with the Viennese lodge "Labor," which temporarily had been the Masonic home of several leading Symbolische Großloge members.

After an initial hesitation, the Grand Lodge of Vienna (under the influence of Eugen Lennhoff) looked favorably upon the Symbolische Großloge (SGL), although occasionally there were certain obvious disturbances in the personal relationship between Lennhoff and Müffelmann. Lennhoff was Grand Commander of the Supreme Council for Austria, and was included in the establishment of the Symbolische Großloge. On the other hand, Oskar Posner raised valid fundamental doubts about the German-speaking Czechoslovakian Grand Lodge "Lessing zu den Drei Ringen" (Lessing at the Three Rings). These doubts concerned Masonic Regularity as well as the role of the Higher Degrees, which Posner rejected. In addition, his Grand Lodge at first was not ready to take into consideration the forced schism with the established German humanitarian grand lodges. Furthermore, strategic considerations with respect to the political situation and the future of humanitarian Freemasonry in Germany played a role for Posner. He was afraid that an offensive internationalisticpacifistically oriented Freemasonry could strengthen the Nazis even more. He wrote to Müffelmann, "If the international aspect is emphasized too much, humanitarian Freemasonry will collapse, and the Old Prussians will know how to save themselves. And then it will have been your fault." Above all, Posner went on, "it looks very bleak for Germany." He therefore recommended that the Symbolische Großloge be merged "under sufferable conditions" into one of the humanitarian grand lodges.[5] As much as Posner's concern about the political development was justified, he was in error on the other point: The weakness of humanitarian Freemasonry in Germany lay substantially rooted in its defensive attitude and willingness to accommodate, completely aside from the fact that no established grand lodge—especially not at that time—would have been about to merge with the Symbolic lodges, at least not in combination with the integration of the Symbolic lodges' principles.

Indeed, the concentrated reaction of German Ancient Masonry against the Supreme Council and Symbolische Großloge was not long in coming. With the exception of the Große Landesloge, which had withdrawn itself from such a collective action, all the established jurisdictions—by resolution of their grand masters gathered in Weimar on October 25–26—departed from a position in which "solemn protest" was leveled against the "new organizations." These were designated "unGerman." They were to be rejected most vehemently—and, as expected, were denied Masonic recognition. [6] The Große Landesloge could correctly assume that no one would get the idea that it had any sympathy for either the Supreme Council or the Symbolische Großloge. However, the Große Landesloge saw itself constrained to justify its position because of many questions from its own Brethren as to why it had again separated itself from all other grand lodges. In an "official communication," Grand Master Müllendorff announced that again there had been no doubt "that we are not in a position either to participate in a general meeting of all German grand masters, or to sign any decisions concluded in such a meeting, since we are opposed to a revival, in any form, of the German Federation of Grand Lodges." [7] Even before the general resolution of the eight

German grand masters, a cautious attempt to contact with Drei Weltkugel (Three World Globes) Grand Master Habicht had failed. Habicht made it known that he was not permitted to receive Müffelman, "by the wish of the Federation Director's office."[8]

Additional fuel was added to the fire by disagreement within the ranks of the Supreme Council itself, which were played out before the whole Masonic public and of course exploited by their enemies. Thus, Grand Commander Bing, who was out of the country at the decisive moment, was either not sufficiently informed of the "Bringing in of Light," or was of a completely different understanding. In any case, he refused his consent, and declared the Symbolische Grossloge to be an "irregular organization." Two days later, however, he was forced to withdraw that declaration in the name of the Supreme Council.[9]

Bing (1894-1962) had been born in Budapest, and was a journalist even during his student days in Oxford. His international journalistic career led him to Berlin—as a correspondent for *The New York Herald Tribune*—and to the Greek–Turkish theatre of war for United Press International. In 1923, he was business manager of the United Press International department for continental Europe and Asia Minor. In this capacity, he built up a news service that first had its headquarters in Berlin. Because of political developments, the department administration was moved to Zürich in 1932. After that he lived—interrupted by many trips abroad—in Switzerland. In 1941, Bing, who was also an author, established a home in New York, and sought naturalization, which took place in 1947. At that time, he changed his name to Edward John Jefferson Byng.

Like Müffelmann and Koner, Bing was a member of the Viennese lodge "Labor." He also collaborated actively in the Allgemeine Freimaurerliga (General League of Freemasons) and kept in close touch with Lennhoff. After the affair about the establishment of the Symbolische Großloge, he resigned from the position of Grand Commander. His successor was Gottlieb Friederich Reber, a renowned art collector, who lived primarily in Lausanne. Reber belonged to the National Mother Lodge, but he also became a member of the Grande Loge de France and the Suprême Conseil de France. In spite of his supposedly good relationship with National Grand Master Habicht, Reber was forced to leave his Drei-Weltkugel lodge in Munich because of his involvement in the Scottish Rite. He went over to the Symbolische Großloge.[10] In 1941, Reber moved to Italy. There he was involved in spiriting artwork away to Hermann Göring's collection. Of course, he later disputed ever having met Göring, and denied any personal guilt.[11] In 1943, Reber and his relatives were stripped of their citizenship, and the family fortune—as much as could be grabbed—was confiscated. These measures were probably taken in connection with the Vichy Government's 1941 publication of the names of all ranking French Freemasons who were still living. Besides which, by his own account, Reber had criticized the procedures against the Jews as well as the Nazi education policies. [12] In the meantime, Fritz Bensch had been elected Deputy Grand Commander of the Supreme Council. Bensch's influence in German Freemasonry was enduring. It was he, not Reber, who actually led the Supreme Council until it went dormant. During the time it was forbidden, an opposition circle built itself around Bensch, who was Müffelmann's fellow prisoner in Sonnenburg.[13]

The fact that close connections to circles in the Grand Orient and Grand Loge de France could be quickly made or furthered is explained by the tradition of the Freimaurerbund zur aufgehenden Sonne (Association of Freemasons of the Rising Sun) and the many-faceted international connections of leading members of the Symbolische Großloge. Not only was a fundamentally francophilic outlook expressed, but so was a clear affinity for the politically active "romance" Freemasonry. On the other hand, recognition by the English was at first not even sought. Even with France, however, some obstacles had to be overcome at the institutional level. Particularly complicated was the relationship with the Grand Orient, which out of consideration for its old partner in Germany (the Aufge-hende Sonne), was hesitant vis-à-vis the new grand lodge. The Grand Orient did indeed grant recognition to the Symbolische Großloge in January 1932, and exchanged the obligatory tokens of fraternal friendship.

Meanwhile, a closer association existed with the Grande Loge de France. A real mark of success for the Symbolische Großloge with respect to its international reputation was—after initial difficulties—the recognitions by many foreign grand lodges, especially the official recognition of the Grand Lodge of Vienna on October 12, 1931. In connection with this, the Austrians expressed the hope that "the far-reaching agreement of interpretation in matters of the goals and purposes of Freemasonry, and especially of its mission of peace by the establishment of closer fraternal connections, would experience a further deepening." [14]

The long-sought full membership of the Symbolische Großloge in the Association Maçonnique Internationale (International Masonic Association - AMI), first by way of visitation rights, was proposed by the executive committee of the AMI in May 1932 for the next spring. This was formally possible only if it were decided at the same time that the statutes would be altered so that the usual waiting period would be reduced from ten to three years. [15] For internal development, it was also significant that on November 28, 1931, the Supreme Council of Germany and the Symbolische Großloge had concluded an agreement. In it, both sides reinforced their mutual recognition, their will to work together, and the limitation of jurisdiction as it concerned the work of the first three (Blue Lodge) and the higher degrees. [16] Indeed, the 16 chapters of the AASR existing in Germany until 1933 were also open to members of other jurisdictions.

There can be no doubt that the new German grand lodge got a good start: [17] Its inner structure had solidified itself quickly. On the international level, it was able to earn itself a reputation as well as to show its first recognitions. The number of its lodges had increased almost three-fold in only four months, and the membership much more than 10-fold. Of course, if one tries to quantify this exactly, discrepancies do appear. Müffelmann had reported in a letter to Lennhoff in November 1930 that there were 23 lodges, and the membership was already more than 1,000. [18] In his new year's 1930-31 circular letter, Müffelmann announced that there were 21 lodges and five more were being chartered.[19] According to Dalen's Freemasons-Calendar, 800 Brothers in 28 lodges belonged to the Symbolische Großloge; on the other hand, according to Müffelmann, the "luminaries" numbered the members at 1,173 in 25 lodges and a so-called "Masonic circle" (a preliminary step to the lodge; a group without charter). [20]

The monthly magazine of the Symbolische Großloge, *Die Alten Pflichten (The Ancient Obligations)*, edited by Müffelmann, served as a showpiece to the outside. [21] It was received with intense interest within and outside the country, and contributed greatly to the respect with which Symbolische Großloge members were regarded on all sides. The first issue of *Die Alten Pflichten* appeared in a publication run of only 1,000 copies and was quickly out of print. The next time, the print run was increased to 1,500 copies.

Müffelmann's dominant position in the history of the Symbolische Großloge justifies a look at his biography: [22] Leopold (Leo) Müffelmann was born on May 1, 1881 in Rostock. His father, the prominent Freemason, Dr. Ludwig Müffelmann, was a journalist by profession and until 1902 editor-in-chief of the liberal *Rostocker Zeitung (Rostock Newspaper)*. After that he was chief at the *Neue Zeit (New Time)* in Berlin. Leo Müffelmann was a Protestant. That he was Jewish is a widespread and occasionally purposely promulgated error. He studied law, political economics, and philosophy in Rostock, Munich, and Berlin. He earned his Ph.D. at the age of 20, and was employed in a variety of commercial positions, among them as assistant to Hjalmar Schacht at the Dresden Bank and finally as director of a chemical factory in Güstrov, of which he was chairman of the board of directors during the Weimar years. Between 1914 and 1918, Müffelmann was almost without interruption on the East and West Fronts. He ended the war, with many high honors, at the rank of captain. In 1919, Müffelmann belonged to the group of those who founded the employee union Vela, whose main office director he remained until April 1933.[23] Even before the dissolution and forbidding of unions, he was forced out of this position, for which—completely aside from the question of concrete evidence of Party membership[24]—his whole social- or liberal-democratic background may have played at least as great a role as his exposed position in the German "lodge scene." [25] In May 1933, with a Freemason of Jewish heritage with whom he was friendly, Müffelmann founded a pharmaceutical-cosmetics factory and distribution business, by the name of "Kosmasept GmbH." He became a partner and managing director. During his imprisonment in the Autumn of 1933, Müffelmann had his lawyer establish contact with Schacht, in the hope that the Reichsbank President would put in a good word for his former employee, with whom he had also had Masonic ties. Upon the inquiry of the lawyer as to whether Schacht would permit a "private discussion" in an affair concerning Müffelmann, Schacht basically said he was prepared to do so, but asked to be informed briefly in writing about the subject beforehand. [26] Whether the meeting actually took place is not clear. There is no evidence of any intervention by Schacht. Presumably he was not called into the case, as [Müffelmann] was released in the meantime. After his release from the Sonnenberg concentration camp, Müffelmann felt himself put out by his business partner. Whether Schacht had had to act under duress is unclear. In any case, Müffelmann had to have legal help to be paid for his share of the business.

In 1913, at the age of 32—rather late—Müffelmann was accepted into the "Humanitas" Lodge in Berlin, sponsored by Schacht. Müffelmann's father, who (as well as Schacht for a time) had been an active Deutsche Demokratische Partei (German Democratic Party) member, [27] had held the office of Worshipful Master of the Lodge. Together with his father, Müffelmann initiated the founding of the Lodge "Zu den alten Pflichten" (Ancient Obligations) in Berlin, which worked under the Grand Lodge of Hamburg. There followed, as already described, several system changes, which were like a Masonic odyssey, but were based on their straightforwardness upon the principles for which Müffelmann stood. He had to put up with constant denunciations from the established humanitarian camp. According to a flyer from the Große Landesloge von Sachsen (Grand

Lodge of Saxony) in 1932, Müffelmann had to quit German Freemasonry "because of his undisciplined behavior." Apparently he promptly founded an unrecognized (thus clandestine) grand lodge.[28] Müffelmann was supported in this by his brother Ronald, also a Freemason, who otherwise hardly ever appears. As can be seen in a message from "Labor" Lodge in Vienna of May 9, 1929, he had sought acceptance there. [29] Later, he belonged to a lodge of the same name under the Symbolische Großloge, and was secretary for awhile.[30]

On April 25, 1933, Leo Müffelmann applied for acceptance into the "Stahlhelm" [31] and presumably also in the Deutschnationale Volkspartei (German National People's Party). On June 6, 1933, after he had just lost his professional position, it was certified that his application had been forwarded to the office of the Deutschnationale Volkspartei in Berlin-Halensee [32] that was responsible for the area where he lived. Although one can only incompletely reconstruct the process because of the few sources available, one can say positively that the admissions were steps taken, not as expressions of political conviction, but instead only—and of prime importance—in hopes, on Müffelmann's part, of personal protection. Indeed, political developments caught up with him more quickly than expected: the "Stahlhelm" ceased to be an independent power, and by the end of June, the Deutschnationale Volkspartei had already been dissolved.

Concerning his earlier memberships in political parties, Müffelmann gave contradictory information. Not only does his possible short membership in the Sozialdemokratische Partei Deutschlands (German Social Democratic Party) [33] provide riddles, but so does the membership he said he held in the Deutsche Demokratische Partei. According to the Gestapo, in his application to the "Stahlhelm," Müffelmann declared that until then he had not belonged to any party, because as chief executive officer of the Vela, he had to remain neutral "on all sides." [34]

A problem to be taken seriously was that the Symbolische Großloge was significantly limited by financial concerns during its entire existence, because it could support itself on real and movable property even less

236

than the established grand lodges. Because of the general economic crisis, many Brothers had hardly enough money to afford their monthly lodge dues. In September 1932, the dues in arrears were up to a total of more than 5,000 Reichs Marks. [35] Thus, there were always controversies about obtaining travel expenses or permission for trips to allied grand lodges or to international Masonic events. There was even a dispute about the settling of accounts for Koner's work as Grand Secretary, which was aggravated by Koner's private financial troubles. This argument not only divided Koner from Grand Treasurer Adolf Bünger (who had held the same office with the "Aufegehende Sonne"), but also, in the interim, from Müffelmann.[36] The members of the Symbolische Großloge in Jerusalem complained about being unable to keep pace with their financial obligations to the Lodge. Thus Dr. Emmanuel Propper, the Worshipful Master of the subordinate lodge in Jerusalem "Zur Quelle Siloah" ("Well of Shiloh"), told Müffelmann that the lodges working in Palestine under other jurisdictions would assess lower membership dues, which would make the desired expansion of the Symbolische Großloge more difficult.[37] According to a statement on May 1932, the Symbolische Großloge administered three lodge buildings of its own—in Harburg, Mannheim, and Schwerin, a burial fund, and a bank account of about 15,000 Reichs Marks.[38]

The relationship between the Symbolische Großloge and the camp of the established humanitarian grand lodges remained conflicted, as always. Thus, the Großloge Zur Sonne (the Grand Lodge "Sun") felt itself challenged unjustly by the existence or competition of the Symbolische Großloge, which was additionally fueled by the outcome of the struggle over the "Heidelberg Theses"—as mentioned in Chapter 3. As can be seen in correspondence with Koner, Bernhard Beyer especially was irritated by the appearance of the Symbolische Großloge. He vehemently rejected the insistence that the re-establishment of contact with England was influenced by the Symbolische Großloge. Instead, it had been because of England that the re-establishment of contact could not take place until the beginning of 1932. Besides which, at the preliminary consultations between what was left of the German Association of Grand

Lodges and the English, "really not even one person had thought about the Symbolische Großloge." [39] Koner previously had sharply attacked the humanitarian grand lodges: the Symbolische Großloge members had brought life into the "calcified and degenerate Freemasonry" of the Ancient grand lodges, and the agreement with England was basically only a slap at the Symbolische Großloge. The Old Prussians, Koner went on, would wreak "denominational and political party terror," while the humanitarians would do the same, in that they would "convince the foreign grand lodges, in a letter-writing campaign, not to recognize the Symbolische Großloge." [40]

At the same time, the relationship with the "Aufegehende Sonne" was fraught with great tension, which is not surprising, because, aside from the fact that both organizations targeted more or less the same group, the transfer of many Brothers and whole lodges to the Symbolische Großloge must have necessarily given rise to unrest in the ranks of the old Reformed Grand Lodge. Nothing was changed by the fact that the separation was completed in the summer of 1930, after a "very dignified discussion" [41] at the convention of the "Aufgehende Sonne" in Halle. Nevertheless, the previous Grand Master of the "Aufgehende Sonne," Heinsen, officiated as Müffelmann's substitute.[42] Hans Lachmund, a Freemason from Schwerin, helped significantly with the split. Lachmund would then go on to get himself elected into the grand office council of the Symbolische Großloge, and play a pivotal role during the Third Reich in the liberal democratic resistance. [43] The connection between the two grand lodges was marked by reciprocal demarcation. The new Grand Master of the "Aufgehende Sonne," Dr. Max Seber, declared that according to his perception, a peaceful coexistence with the Symbolische Großloge members would be impossible. For its part, the Symbolische Großloge acted as though the "Aufgehende Sonne" did not exist, primarily because of the problems of Masonic Regularity. [44] In addition, the Grand Officers' Council of the Symbolische Großloge saw itself constrained to advise all Brothers by means of a circular letter "not to develop any promotion vis-à-vis members of the 'Aufgehende Sonne,' or to stimulate them in any way to join the

Symbolische Großloge. Only written questions from either circle could be answered, and that in a proper manner." [45]

Something unusual about the Symbolische Großloge, which certainly did not lack idiosyncrasies, was that it was the only German jurisdiction having subordinate lodges in Palestine, and that too even before the transfer of its seat into exile in Jerusalem. In the pre-history of these establishments, two personages played central roles: the physician (and later first Grand Commander of the Supreme Council for Israel) Dr. Emanuel Propper, and the philosophy professor Andor Fodor. Both at first belonged to "Pax" ("Peace") Lodge under the jurisdiction of the national Grand Lodge of Egypt. Like other Brothers who had been molded by European culture, they felt themselves mentally and linguistically as outsiders, and initiated a "Landesgruppe Palästina" ("Provinical group Palestine") of the General League of Freemasons, chaired by Propper. The idea of founding a German-speaking subordinate lodge of the Symbolische Großloge in Palestine originated from contacts within the activities of the League. This idea was supported by Eugen Lennhoff to the best of his ability. [46] The first inquiry directly pertaining to it was obviously addressed to Müffelmann by mail on November 30, 1930. It received immediate and enthusiastic support from him. [47] Müffelmann himself traveled to Jerusalem for the constitution of the new lodge named "Zur Quelle Siloah" ("Siloam Well") set for March 31, 1931, which consisted overwhelmingly of Jewish members. Propper was Warrant Master; Fodor was elected Deputy (Senior Warden). After his return, Müffelmann was unusually happy: "I am back again from Jerusalem, where I had fantastic success," he wrote to a friend. "Zur Quelle Siloah" Lodge was already playing "a big role in the public life of Palestine and Egypt." [48] On another occasion, he allowed as how his experiences in Palestine had been "perhaps the most meaningful in my whole life." [49]

In the spring of 1932, the National Grand Lodge of Palestine was created by the coming together of the four subordinate lodges of the Egyptian Jurisdiction in Jerusalem. The National Grand Lodge of Palestine seems to have been dominated by Arabs at this early date. From the beginning, the relationship with "Zur Quelle Siloah" was problematical. "Zur Quelle Shiloh's" position vis-à-vis the new Grand Lodge, by which it was not recognized at first, was strengthened, however, by the high social regard for, and influence of, its members.⁵⁰ That it could assert and firmly maintain itself in the face of some competition from the English and Scottish Grand Lodges, both of which maintained subordinate lodges in Palestine, can be attributed substantially to the personal influence of Propper and Fodor. It was even possible, in the form of the Hebrew-speaking lodge "Ari," to witness the founding of a provisional second subordinate lodge of the Symbolische Großloge in Palestine on January 3, 1933, even though it consisted of only seven Brothers.⁵¹ On Müffelmann's recommendation, or at least with his complete agreement, the founding of a so-called "Masters' Lodge" was planned, which came into fruition on June 4, 1934 in the form of "Zum Kubischen Stein" ("Perfect Ashlar") Lodge.⁵² The motive for this was—in consideration of the acceptance of the English even on the level of the special degree of Master in the English system—to spread humanitarian-Masonic principles in the spirit of the Symbolische Großloge. In the "house rule" of the Lodge from the time of its belonging to the Grand Lodge of the State of Israel, it says that one is to strive "to strengthen and spread pure humanitarian Freemasonry in the spirit of the Ancient Obligations, to guard and nurture true brotherhood without respect to social class, ethnic heritage, or religion, and to offer a nurturing home for spiritual life and liberty." ⁵³

The subordinate lodges were informed the next day by circular letter of the March 28, 1933 decision made by the executive committee that they were to cease work in the German Reich. According to the letter, the Grand Lodge would be "put to sleep," the association therein dissolved; the dissolution in the association books had already taken place and the treasurer had been authorized to dissolve all financial relationships.⁵⁴ There was a circular letter from Müffelmann dated the same day [March 29]. In it was a compulsory text "Concerning the struggle against news of atrocity," whose words were not only shared with several foreign grand lodges, but also broadcast by the last issue of *The Ancient Obligations*. It said that the Symbolische Großloge declared the "news of atrocity as shameless lies," and pleaded for "extremely energetic action in the interest of peoples' agreement against this agitation."[55] When the first edition of *The Ancient Obligations* appeared in exile in 1935, it was noted only cursorily that this declaration had proved "with each word and between all lines" that "behind the writer working against his will, clicked the cocked gun of a storm trooper."[56] Although Müffelmann and his cohorts had presumably already thought about an exiling of the Grand Lodge at the time of the "putting to sleep," the process was kept confidential for obvious reasons. On the eve of the decision to let activity in Germany "rest," the Symbolische Großloge stood united in "fraternal relations" with 44 grand lodges and had 26 subordinate lodges in the German Reich under it; in addition there was one in Saarbrücken and two in Jerusalem—an impressive statistic, considering that it had only existed for two years and eight months.

On June 30, 1933, Müffelmann wrote to Propper that the "putting to sleep" definitely did not affect the lodges in Saarbrücken and Jerusalem. He let it be known that he intended to set up an institution in exile.[57] When the decision to move to Palestine came in July, it could not be attacked even from the standpoint of Masonic regularity, because the Symbolische Großloge had the necessary three lodges outside of the territory of the German Reich. While Müffelmann was still in prison, the constitution of the Grand Lodge in Exile took place on November 17, 1933, after the appropriate permission from the British Mandate was received.[58] Müffelmann came to Palestine for the second time in April 1934. He used a Mediterranean cruise for the purpose, a cruise which he had originally scheduled for the spring of 1933, but because of political developments in Germany, had had to cancel on short notice. He traveled from Haifa to Jerusalem, where the constitution of the third subordinate lodge in Palestine took place on April 24 with him in attendance. It was the "Lebanon" Lodge, which moved to Haifa in 1938, and whose working language was Hungarian. In addition, during his visit, Müffelmann was elected Grand Master for life. Next to him, Propper held the office of "officiating" Grand Master. Physicians from the Fraternity in Jerusalem examined Leo Müffelmann and diagnosed heart problems and knee damage, as results of mistreatment during his imprisonment in the concentration camp. Despite that, he returned to Germany, where he died on August 29, 1934.[58a] In his memory the Lodge "Müffelmann Loyalty" was founded in Tel Aviv (its "Bringing in of Light", or constitution, was held on May 5, 1935).

In the meantime, the Symbolische Großloge managed to publish two issues of the *Ancient Obligations* as polyglot exile editions (English, French, German). [59] After that, the magazine had to cease publication—not the least because of the lack of funds. The growth of lodges sharpened the discord with the National Grand Lodge of Palestine. Finally, it was agreed that the development of additional subordinate lodges under the Symbolische Großloge would happen by mutual agreement, whereby the National Grand Lodge of Palestine, for its part, would accept that the right to this develop-ment would arise from further immigration of Freemasons from Europe. [60]

On September 4, 1939, one day after the declaration of war by Great Britain and France, Propper went to the Mandate Government in Jerusalem with a statement of loyalty. In it, he briefly explained the background of the existence of the Symbolische Großloge in Exile, as well as its fundamental principles, and expressed his gratitude for "the hospitality and physical and spiritual freedom in this land under British rule." Further he assured that each member was ready to put his service at the disposal of the royal government in the present struggle.[61] From the beginning, Propper wanted to forestall the danger that his Grand Lodge might be affected by the closing of German organizations in Palestine. The very friendly response from the District Commissioner of Jerusalem on September 16 expressed not only the gratitude and esteem of the high commissioner, but also stated that he might take them up on the offer of service, if necessary. [62]

The Grand Lodge (Symbolische Großloge) in Exile, which continued undisturbed during the war years, was a meeting place for those of Pales-tine's elite who had been shaped by western culture. This is shown by the list of professions of the grand officers during the period 1942-1945: there were eight physicians (among them Grand Master Propper), five lawyers, a pharmacist, three engineers, an architect, and a philosophy professor (Deputy Grand Master Fodor). There are no professions listed for two of the officers.[63]

After the "Light of Freemasonry" of the five lodges that had survived the "Third Reich" in exile returned to Germany in 1949, the subordinate lodges of the Symbolische Großloge in the former British Mandate, on November 19, 1949, became a district lodge within the Grand Lodge of Israel, which had arisen from the National Grand Lodge of Palestine in 1948. In this way, the members of the Symbolische Großloge built up Israeli Freemasonry from a small seed. These Isreali lodges, under their new Jurisdiction, were allowed to keep their freedom of language and ritual. This was important because differing Masonic currents were to be united under one roof. In 1954, four lodges that had belonged to the Grand Lodge of Scotland joined them. Recognition by the United Grand Lodge of England followed, and the name of the Israeli Grand Lodge was changed to the "Grand Lodge of the State of Israel." At the same time the former Symbolische "District Lodge No. 1" lost its special status, but that was compensated by a written document making their "minority rights" of language and ritual permanent. [64]

The spread of a humanitarian Freemasonry in Palestine/Israel obligated to a principle of tolerance is intimately connected with the history of German exile-Freemasonry, and strongly influenced by the effect of members of the Symbolische Großloge. Considering the acute problem of aging members in "Quelle Siloah" Lodge—especially because their working language remained German—the Hebrew-speaking lodge "Ari," which had become dormant at the end of the 1950s, was reactivated as its sister lodge. The Grand Lodge of the State of Israel has approximately 2,000 members of different religious persuasions. As was true with the Grand Lodge of Palestine, the emblem of the Grand Lodge of the State of Israel contains the symbols of the three monotheistic religions: the Star of Judaism, the Cross of Christianity, and the Crescent Moon of Islam "united in harmony." [65]

7.2 POLITICAL ORIENTATION

In February 1932, the Lodge "Isis zu den drei Sphinxen" (Isis of the three Sphinxes) in Schwerin, working under the Symbolische Großloge, with then-Lodge Orator Hans Lachmund in charge, concerned itself with questions of Freemasonry and politics. Lachmund informed Müffelmann of the results. According to Lachmund, there had been agreement that "true Freemasonry" could not dispense with "also making political questions a subject of its work." Although indeed the lodge should exclude "everyday and pure party-politics" from its work, it should admit politics insofar "as politics is an integral part of the world-view." Otherwise, the Lodge would run the risk of "drying up mentally." [66] In other words, the implication of politics was perceived as offensive, and because of its content, came under the opposite rubric as it did in the case of the Große Landesloge. In addition, one finds such judgments in source material, which, with the required depth of focus, came to the conclusion that behind the debate on Masonic Regularity in the foreground, political motives for the rejection of the Symbolische Großloge were influential. [67]

In its constitution, the Symbolische Großloge formulated as its guiding principle: "Standing for freedom of thought, belief, and conscience; against any kind of dogmatism in religion [profession of faith] and obstinate world-view; for love of mankind and general fraternity; against all sorts of hatred for any class, race, or group; for social justice and peaceful reconciliation," and that within Germany and the family of man. [68]

In the same vein, the Symbolische Großloge stated in its "General Masonic Rules," that every kind of coercion that threatened freedom of belief, conscience, or thought, or any persecution that was directed against those who believe or think otherwise, was to be repudiated. [69] The "Guiding Principles for Petitioners" (Seekers) therefore expressed that the main requirement (challenge!) of Freemasonry was that of tolerance. In addition, the Symbolische Großloge expressly professed that the "Ancient

Obligations" sacred to the Freemason were love of country and duties of a citizen. A Freemason saw "no conflict between love of country and love for all men." [70] Freemasonry, Müffelmann wrote in the first issue of the *Ancient Obligations*, wanted to bring all mankind together into a unified chain of brothers throughout the world. It was impossible to dismiss this fundamental idea of Masonic thinking and feeling by saying "that one considered the practical implementation of this idea impossible under the present economic and political conditions." It would further miss, "if, just because implementation is not possible, that one would replace the general chain of brothers with a specific chain of brothers in a certain country, or would demand, instead of the ethical and philosophical perfection of mankind, the ethical and philosophical perfection of the German man." Freemasonry had to be as precisely placed in the national-overarching international question as the Catholic Church was. The Catholic Church stood above all nations, it was a world-chain: "It has, however, not shut out the national interests and wishes of each individual country. It recognizes these from every direction. It is only that its sphere of work lies on another level." [71]

In his 1931 new year greetings to the members of the Grand Officers' Council, Müffelmann made it clear that it was necessary to establish firmly the position of the Symbolische Großloge vis-à-vis the most important problems of world Freemasonry: peace and the social question. [72] At another point, Müffelmann emphasized the necessity of taking a stand on all modern problems, because the time of pure contemplation was past. Freemasonry had to fight again for individualism and development of the personality; it had to turn to social problems and work for peace. [73] In the context of working for peace, for example, was the effort to further international youth exchanges. The Brethren were urged to stay active in this regard in a circular letter of July 1931 from the Grand Treasurer Bünger. There were two Masonic establishments at their disposal: "Fraternity-Reconciliation," established for the exchange between France and Germany, and the special group for youth exchange of the General League of Freemasons for exchanges with all countries. [74]

The orientation to Europe is further seen, for example, from the "Bundesthemen" (Federation themes) that were set up by the Administration of the Symbolische Großloge for the Masonic year 1932-33. These subjects were "Concept and Limits of Masonic Tolerance" and "The Creation of Europe." All subordinate lodges were obligated to treat at least one of the themes, whether in the form of a lecture or "drawing" with additional discussion, or a discussion of theses. The subject of Europe was worked on at the same time by the Grand Lodge of France, and included an evaluation of the status quo as well as "proposals for what should be done."[75] According to protocol, one heard it thus in the words of Müffelmann's substitute, the former Grand Master of the Grand Lodge "Aufgehende Sonne," Peter Heinsen: "The greatest, most beautiful, final goal of Freemasonry is eternal peace. Work for this eternal peace can be done only by him who believes unswervingly in it." Our opponents, Heinsen went on, would see eternal peace as an illusion. If war were to have been eliminated, it would have had to have been long ago. Freemasons, therefore, had "the sacred duty of proving to the world that we do not hang onto illusions, but that we show real ways to peace and want to increase them." [76]

In comparing the Old Prussians and the reform wing of German Freemasonry, one is struck by a difference in the social make-up. In the ranks of "Aufgehende Sonne" and the Symbolische Großloge, whose membership was oriented to world citizenship, and would be characterized as politically left-liberal to social-democratic, educated citizens were more numerous than was true of the Old Prussians. This was reflected in the higher intellectual level of the *Ancient Obligations* published by the Symbolische Großloge. Thus, at Müffelmann's urging, the beginnings of a Masonic social program were developed.[77] The concept of "national social policy" was a primary topic, seriously discussed. At the end of 1930, Gustav Slekow, who belonged to the subordinate lodge in Leipzig, "Zu den alten Pflichten" ("Ancient Obligations") and to the Supreme Council, wrote that the final purpose of this national social policy was "not economic or cultural emancipation, or even the higher development of the proletarian masses, but the binding of at least a part of these masses to the economic interests of the nation, and the ideology of the ruling classes." One of the characteristics of modern National Socialism was "the fundamentally inimical position against everything that did not belong to one's own nation, against anything foreign." Economic contrasts and rivalries had sharpened these "national inbreeding tendencies," and racial superiority and anti-Semitism were the "most luxuriant blooms" of just that modern National Socialism, through which "every fruitful social policy" had become decayed. The humanitarian Freemasonry of the Symbolische Großloge of Germany could not orient its social work by this kind of social policy: "the Christian, private charity, which corresponds to original-Christian communism" and "the charitable work as has been heretofore practiced in our lodges, which comes from individual social consciousness, the individualistic category of the member," could not accomplish the mission of social policy. Rather, "the emancipation of the proletariat would become a collective affair of human society and its socialistic responsibility for its higher development." In this whole thought complex, there was nothing, according to Slekow, that the humanitarian Freemason would have to reject. As such, he would test all requirements, and set up his social program according to the results of his test. "He would not do this as a party man, but he would obtain new elements for the thought edifice of the royal art (i.e., Freemasonry) from this test, and find the way to carry it out, ennobled by Masonic humanity and tolerance, into the living current of all social developments." [78]

In the next issue of the *Ancient Obligations*, the idea of the creation of a "social program of Freemasonry" was taken up by Friedrich Mart, a member of the Symbolische Großloge from Dresden. Freemasonry could not, in Mart's words, pass by the problem of material and spiritual existence, but it could always be concerned with "bringing the conditions of life into something approaching harmony." The precondition "to the avoidance of catastrophes, as they are shown in the extreme consequences of revolution or war" would determine the control of the question of material existence." And further, "In a world in which, besides need and most extreme parsimony, very visibly, widespread luxury lives, it must be possible to create equalizing fairness." [79]

A few more examples for the political implications of the activities of the Symbolische Großloge will suffice; already in the consolidation phase of the Symbolische Großloge, Adolf Bünger had pled for concentrating less on questions of [Masonic] recognition than on problems of content and purpose. In this connection, he advocated that the question of peace takes the foreground, and suggested strongly that grand lodges all over the world should institute peace committees, and insisted that a "peace campaign plan" had to be worked out. [80] In December 1931, Müffelmann told a confidante in Zürich that "everything tries to get into the National Socialistic shipping lane." He spoke for holding a "confidential meeting" with the Grand Lodge of France to state the political development: it seemed necessary "that Freemasonry...closes ranks for the struggle against Fascism and National Socialism." [81] Finally, in the last issue of the *Ancient Obligations*, the second of the two exile issues (December 1935), the duties of Freemasonry were mirrored against the background of the conflict between Jews and Arabs in the Holy Land. The tensions, according to Emanuel Propper rather optimistically, could be resolved only by means of Freemasonry: "Brothers of all races and nations are united under the different jurisdictions working in Palestine, and they can be made enthusiastic about the idea of peace! If we seek this internal peace, we believe we are acting in the interest not only of Palestine, but also of the concept of world peace." Propper opined further that Freemasonry was a power, despite its being suppressed: "Not a political power, as our enemies maintain, but a spiritual power, which wants to uphold the spirit of the world as created by it."[82]

There were thoroughly differing points of view concerning the relationship of humanitarian Freemasonry with Communism in the shaping of the Symbolische Großloge. Thus Max Zucker, Master of the Berlin Lodge "Kant zum ewigen Frieden" ([Emmanuel]Kant of eternal Peace), drawing on an article by Müffelmann in the *Ancient Obligations*, submitted his own essay (contribution) on "Freemasonry and National Socialism" [83] to the same journal. In it, he differed with the idea of National Socialism and Bolshevism being the same. While the thought "of even a temporary agreement" with National Socialism would have to be termed grotesque, there was no reason to condemn Bolshevism from a Masonic standpoint, in any case insofar as it represented the sequential carrying out and continuation of the Marxist doctrine of Socialism.[84] In a letter to the Grand Officers, Müffelmann expressed strong reservations about the publication of this essay. The pronouncements on Bolshevism were not acceptable, and would open the Grand Lodge (Symbolische Großloge) to difficulties. Koner agreed with Müffelmann's judgment, and added that the article would "give rise to consternation among our foreign friends." [85] Indeed, it must be maintained that Müffelmann's conception, according to which Bolshevism, Fascism, and National Socialism would stem from the same root, does not hold up—not only from an historical perspective—but also because there was no consensus within the Symbolische Großloge.

The Symbolische Großloge understood Freemasonry as an ethical movement in public society. It showed itself willing to reject anti-Masonic attacks, as well as to represent its own missions and goals with respect to the general public with the requisite clarity. In this spirit, the Symbolische Großloge pursued a modern public image in which it had regular press receptions that resounded in various ways in serious newspapers.

In the meantime, the activities of the international Masonic scene were affected adversely by the political situation in the last days of the Weimar Republic. In 1932, a convention of the General Masonic League organized in Berlin by the Symbolische Großloge had to be cancelled. General Masonic League state groups, like many countries (Austria, Czechoslovakia, France, the Netherlands, and Hungary) had spoken against Berlin as the convention city. The chairman of the General Masonic League, Fritz Uhlmann, who was based in Basel, wrote to Müffelmann in 1932 that since the fall of Reichs Chancellor Brüning, "on all sides, the confidence in order in Germany" had been lost: "the daily riots in Berlin…frighten the Brothers; they do not dare to come to Berlin." [86]

The political surroundings of the Symbolische Großloge would be only imperfectly sketched, if the situation in Palestine, or Israel as the case may be, were not looked at once more. As Jews of German origin, some of whom who had lived in the Mandate territory, had met in its circle before 1933, the Symbolische Großloge in Exile in Palestine developed into a gathering point for Jewish emigrants, because of the Nazi persecution of the Jews and the World War. Individual leading members of the Symbolische Großloge from Germany, such as the Past Master of the Berlin Lodge "Kant zum ewigen Frieden," Max Silberberg, found new Masonic purposes here. In 1935, he was elected Worshipful Master of "Quelle Siloah" Lodge. A plan that Müffelman had set up, took form upon the same background: the founding of a "settlement" of Freemasons in Palestine, which would serve as a landing place or new home for Brothers who had been force to emigrate. The settlement would be conceived as a combined town-farm (kibbutz-like) colony which would offer work and a place to live. In addition, the colony would be developed into a "World Center of Freemasonry." The members of the Symbolische Großloge threw themselves into this project. For this purpose, a few hundred dunam (one dunam = 1,000 square meters) of land had been bought by the end of 1935; altogether it amounted to about 500 hectares. A call went out "to the Freemasons of the whole world" to support the establishment of the Settlement.[87] Aside from the fact that financial problems soon cropped up, nothing is known of the further progress of the plan; in any case it could never be realized.

The struggle of the members of the Symbolische Großloge for a Freemasonry committed to the principle of tolerance, yet independent of nationality and religious beliefs, continued in Palestine or Israel, but under reversed conditions. Now, they found themselves under pressure from Jewish nationalists in their own ranks. In addition, even liberal Brothers had difficulty with the German heritage and the German language cherished in the work (of the lodge), especially as the extent and the details of the massacre of the Jewish people became known. Julius Fröhlich, alias Jon Aron, himself of German-Jewish background and

Master of the Tel Aviv Lodge "Barkai," in the 1920s, when it still belonged to the Grand Orient of France, in 1947 pressed for the secession of "Müffelmann zur Treue" ("Müffelmann Loyalty"), of which he was Master, from the Symbolische Großloge for Jewish-nationalistic reasons. A split occurred and a Hebrew-speaking lodge by the name of "Ner Tamid" under the Grand Lodge of Palestine was started. The remaining members of "Müffelmann zur Treue" moved their lodge to Jerusalem. Only 10 years later did they return to Tel Aviv, and continued working parallel to "Ner Tamid." In 1976, they reunited: "Ner Tamid" again became part of "Müffelmann zur Treue."

Chapter 8

NAZI STATE AND FREEMASONRY

8.1 ACTIVITIES OF THE GESTAPA AND THE SECURITY SERVICE (SD) OFFICES RESPONSIBLE FOR FREEMASONRY

After the forced self-dissolutions and the ban on those Masonic lodges and "Masonic-lodge-like organizations,"[1] which had not voluntarily dissolved themselves before August 17, 1935, Nazi Masonic politics pursued two main goals. The first was to eliminate the presumably destructive influence on State and society. That meant supervising the enforcement of the ban, meaning obtaining and monitoring the activities of former Freemasons, as well as enforcing the indeed very unsupervisable guidelines concerning dealing with former Freemasons with respect to their use in the service of the State and in the Party. The second goal was to continue the propagandistic exploitation of "Freemasonry—the Enemy" (lit: picture of Freemasonry as the enemy), especially in the form of the Jewish-Masonic conspiracy theory, which had become part of the State ideology.[2]

At the end of April 1934, when Himmler had been named to succeed Rudolf Diehl as Gestapo Inspector, and Gestapo Chief Göring's representative, it meant more than the disempowerment of the Head of Department I A. The event marked the end of the stepwise empowerment of the political police departments in the Reichs-provinces, which had been unified by the SS (Schutzstaffel). This process had begun with Himmler's activity as "political police commander" in Bavaria. The SS's broadening of power, which went on in the context of closely related jurisdictional competition among Himmler, Frick, and Göring, also affected German Freemasons. While the Masonic orders sent their petitions to various ministries, a shift in the balance of weight as of the "Führer's Order" of July 22, 1933, to the side of the offices of the Gestapa and SD in Berlin had placed Masonic business under the SS.[3] Especially with Heydrich, who functioned as both SD Chief and Head of the State Secret Police, the practical jurisdictions were unified. With the detachment of the Gestapo from the whole police apparatus, he had gained extensive independence early on. As "Chief of the Political Police Departments," Himmler determined the kinds of work each would do: the Gestapo fought enemies and the SD tracked down enemies. This led to an unavoidable, and probably purposeful, overlapping of jurisdictions. Himmler was then named "Reichsführer of the SS and Head of the German Police in the Reichs-Ministry of the Interior" in July 1936. This was connected with the establishment of the main office of the regulations police and that of the security police (composed of the Gestapo and criminal police).

After the SD office moved from Munich to Berlin in the Fall of 1934 and took up work in the building at Wilhelmstraße 102, not far from the Gestapa,[4] it was elevated to the rank of an SS main office at the end of January 1935. Before that, on October 1, 1934, Adolf Eichmann had begun working for the SD.[4a] Eichmann—later the leader of the so-called "Judenreferat" (Committee on the Jews) IV B 4 in the Reichs main security office—who was mainly responsible for the organization of the "end solution," was occupied in making a central Masonic card index and sorting out the Masonic materials stolen from the lodges.[5] In a hearing with the Israeli police in 1961, Eichmann maintained that he had been occupied, for his part, "in sorting and cataloguing hundreds of coins and seals."[6]

As expected, the organizational structure of the SD in this early phase cannot be fully reconstructed because it constantly changed. By the same token, an approximate picture can be drawn with the help of works by Browder, Wildt, and Hebert, as well as by using the documents that have turned up in Moscow. Despite some discrepancies, it corroborates Neuberger's depiction to a great extent. According to the description, Eichmann's office, at this point, was the so-called "Office Information" ("J/I"), which had already been formed in October 1934 and remained until at least March 1936. It functioned as a department of the Office I, being set up at the time under Staff chief Dr. Wilhelm Albert. It consisted of, above all, the registry. This phase of the existence of the Office "J/I" was an intermediate step, because relatively soon thereafter, the Central Department I/1, the so-called "Stabskanzlei" [Staff Chancellery], grew out of it, at which point the area "Press and Library" or "Press and Museum" became independent as "Central Department I/3.[7] The fundamental step toward organizational restructuring was taken probably about January 15, 1936.[8] It introduced the solidification of the three-part structure of the SD Main Office, which established itself in the form of the Offices I "Personnel and Administration," II "Interior," and III "Foreign Affairs"/"Defense."

Maximilian Brand, the Freemason-specialist, was head of the "Office Information" for a few months. Previously he was occupied, as already described, in the Freemason Department V, with things such as watching Three World Globes Grand Master Bordes. He took part in the meeting in the Gestapa for the self-dissolution of the Old Prussian Lodges on March 22, 1935. As of August 17, 1935, Brand was pulled out of the SD. Erich Ehlers provided continuity of personnel, however. He took over a "referat" in the Freemason Department of the Interior-SD;[9] more about this later. Meanwhile, Brand was given the leadership of the 60th, then the 70th SS regiment. After the German invasion of Austria, he was named Police-President of Graz at Himmler's direction; in 1944, he held the same post in occupied Gdingen.[10]

To the SS honorary professor Gregor Schwartz-Bostunitsch (actually Grigorij Bostunic), as "specialist-scholar leader," was given the "Office Information." Bostunitsch was a jurist from Russia who had become a German citizen in 1925. He belonged to the early group around Himmler and Heydrich, and appeared on the scene not only as "Masonic expert," but as author of sexual-anti-Semitic writings.[11] Bostunitsch, who had been, in the deprecatory words of Eichmann, "christened' the SS Battalion leader,"[12] mounted an anti-Masonic exhibition for the SD, that occupied several rooms in the Wilhelmstraße building before it was transferred in the beginning or middle of March 1936[12a] to the confiscated home of the Grand Lodge of Hamburg (Emserstraße12-13 in the Wilmersdorf section). The "Institute for Masonic Research," started by the notorious anti-Mason, Friedrich Hasselbacher, was also temporarily housed there.[13] In addition, one must deduce from this that all—or at least large portions of—the stolen lodge archives and libraries were stowed in the cellars of this building.[14]

Eichmann confirmed that a room in the SD Masonic "Museum" had been set up "as a real St. John's Degree Temple" and "another as a [St.] Andrew's Temple."[15] Bostunitsch used "certified" objects and furnishings from various grand lodges as well as items mostly confiscated from the Masonic Museum and lodge building in Bayreuth for his exhibition. The collection was already being built up during the initial phase of the Berlin SD Central, and finished in sections in the late summer of 1934.[16] This was the time when the national grand lodges, having metamorphosed into Orders, were fighting for their existence. The SD Masonic "Museum" was not open to the public, but was reserved for functionaries and groups of visitors from Nazi organizations. It was "Reinhard Heydrich's pride and joy," and he sometimes "would lead [these groups] through the exhibition himself."[17]

During this time, a great number of requests of all kinds came into the SD from various party and government offices. These concerned individual (former) Freemasons, interaction with local lodges, or fundamental world-view questions. Often, the SD wished to have a researcher/writer on the subject of Freemasonry placed at its disposal. On the other hand,

SD workers themselves, learning about Freemasonry on their own, tried to influence party functionaries for their own purposes. In the Interior Office, the SD formed its own department of Freemasonry in the process of building up the structure of the operation, which played an important role in this context. Office II was composed of two Central departments: II/1 "World-view Evaluation" or "Research on Enemies" and II/2 "Sphere of Life Evaluation" or "German Sphere of Life," which in turn consisted of main and subordinate departments.

Department II/111 concerned itself with Freemasonry. Ever since the move to Berlin, and at least until January 1937,[17a] Theodore Christensen had been at the office of Masonic service (Freimaurerdienststelle) of the Interior Security Service. Dr. Hellmuth Knochen took over at the beginning of 1937.[18] Department II/111 came under Department II/11 and as of February 1936 was led by Fritz Hartmann.[18a] It, in turn, was subdivided into four sections (Referate), which, having been further divided according to "partial areas," concerned themselves, independently of each other, with individual Masonic grand lodges or organizations. The first Referat was responsible for Christian-national Freemasonry in Germany, the second for the humanitarian grand lodges and the Supreme Council of Germany, the third for local lodges and appendant bodies, and the fourth for Freemasonry abroad.[19] According to a plan dated January 15, 1937,[19a] for dividing the department, Department II/111 had three reporting officers at its disposal: In addition to Erich Ehlers, they were Hans Harms (responsible for "Freemasonry abroad"), and Dieter Wisliceny. Wisliceny, who had concerned himself with "Winkellogen" ("corner, i.e., neighborhood lodges) and "Freemasonry abroad," took over the leadership of Department II/112 in April 1937 for about seven months until he was transferred to the Security Service in Danzig in November 1937.[19b] Since 1937, Dr. Alfred Franz Six, who had previously been in charge of the Central Department I/3, chaired Central Department II/1, which was above the Department of Freemasonry. With the establishment of the Main Security Office (RHSA), Six became chief of Office II (later VII). Before Six took over Central Department II/1, I had been co-administered by Dr. Hermann Behrends. The department plan of January 15, 1937, still lists him in this function.[19b] Behrends had most recently been the head of the "Information Office," and became the first chief of Office II in January 1936 during the overhaul of the Main Security Office. Otto Ohlendorf took over from him in 1937. While Behrends was in the Main Security Office, he continued his criminal career while a senior officer for Serbia and Montenegro. After the end of the war, he was handed over to Yugoslavia, condemned to death there, and executed in 1948.[20]

It would be misleading to imagine the *modus operandi* of the Main Security Office as being divided neatly into clearly defined areas. Rather, it should be understood that the structure described existed primarily only in theory. In practice, there were overlaps in personnel as well as in job descriptions. For example, the Registration Office moved into the "Information Office" or Central Department I/1. Most external operations came into contact with this office; thus, when necessary, its work was put into the hands of personnel from other departments.[21] The same sort of thing happened at the Gestapa, and later, at the Main Security Office. It must be emphasized that the value of any statement arising from the reconstruction of the formal structure of these offices is rather limited. Like every hierarchical flowchart, it depicts pseudo-reality to a certain extent. It is also necessary to consider that the Nazis' desired self-depiction of their police and propaganda system was mirrored in the formal structure of the offices. This veiled the danger that the desired Gestapo myth "from on high" would be reproduced. Actually, the Gestapo was "not a huge detective organization, but rather one limping behind a steady inflation of duties, undermanned, and overly bureaucratized, which needed the informing help of the citizenry for structural reasons."[22]

Within the Gestapa, in January 1934, the "Dezernat II F 2" ("Questions on Jews, Freemasons, and Emigrants") began its work. By June 1934 at the latest,[23] its corporate name was—under the "Referat" designation—II 1 B 2 (Jews, Freemasons, Emigrants, and Church Affairs"). Until 1939, it was led by Dr. Karl Haselbacher, a Gestapo officer, who also belonged to the SS; in his Gestapo role, he was assigned to the Security Service. In this way, "the unconditional loyalty of the Gestapo vis-à-vis the decisions by the Security Service affecting those holding the opposing world-view, was to be ensured." Haselbacher seems to have "recognized and accepted this priority of the Security Service."[24] Haselbacher was also the "Leader, responsible for all actions undertaken by the Gestapa against German Freemasonry since 1934."[25] His responsibilities also extended to church and sectarian affairs. In this connection, he was concerned with every kind of organization from the "German religious movement" to Jehovah's Witnesses.

In the Prussian Interior Ministry, Department I B, the senior civil servant, Eickhoff, was concerned with questions concerning Freemasonry. At the beginning of May 1934—shortly after Himmler was named Gestapo Inspector—Göring ordered (because "the handling of Freemasonry was of eminent political significance") that the previously separate spheres of the Prussian Interior Ministry and the Gestapa were to "unite in the State Secret Police Office as the sole responsible political authority."[26] It transferred "the work on all lodge affairs, that had been previously taken care of by the Prussian Interior Ministry to the State Secret Police Office."[27] One can assume that this order contributed to a strengthening of the Gestapa's position with respect to ministerial bureaucracy. It did not, in fact, happen that the Reichs and Prussian Interior Ministry, which resulted from this combination in 1934, stopped concerning itself with the "Freemasonry Question." Instead, it remained involved in Masonic politics (policies), in terms of both personnel and as an institution, until the self- and forced-dissolutions. The events show, however, that Göring, given the background of his competition with Frick and Himmler, was clearly intent on gathering to himself some weight in the Gestapa, with the help of work on the "Freemasonry Question." Presumably he still thought, at this time, that he would have control over the Gestapa, despite Himmler's functioning as Inspector. Neuberger comes to the conclusion that "practically all decreed administrative executive measures against Freemasonry"[28] were controlled (approved) by Haselbacher and his Gestapa office. Whether this actually went so far that the Security Service departments were subject de facto to his supervision[29] is questionable. Neuberger, despite his otherwise well-documented and detailed description of the Masonic department, lacks clear proof. The relevant documents of the Main Security Office illustrate, in any case, the great significance that was ascribed to the work on Masonic affairs, as well as its claim to the leadership position in ideological terms.

While Brand and Christensen did not belong to the narrower circle of intellectual strategists of the Nazi security apparatus, as did Dr. Werner Best or Dr. Alfred Franz Six, it seems as though Dr. Haselbacher and Dr. Knochen did belong. Best was the key figure on this functional level, on which ideological and technocratic thinking and action were inextricably bound together. At first with the Security Service in Munich, Best transferred to the Gestapa, becoming finally the head of the main office of the Security Police -- later the Main Security Office and acting as Heydrich's representative. Out of the concept of state and police, as defined in a *völkisch* manner, Best derived a pseudo-ethos of Nazi terror, by which "the people" ("das Volk") were made into a "concept of custom" and a plumb line for new areas and tasks of "state security."[30] Thus, Best justified the expansion of function of the Gestapo and the merciless fighting against those of opposing world-views. It is questionable, however, whether men like Christensen, Knochen, and Haselbacher really "determined essential parts" of Nazi Masonic policies.[31] One can discuss the idea that they stimulated, distorted, and executed these policies within the complex web of rival power centers, and in the context of the basic ideological consensus.

In the procedures against lodges, the "Stapo" units in Prussia and the political police on the same level in the provinces (*Länder*) worked with the upper echelons of the Security office. This often went on with more conflict than in the mostly smooth cooperation of the central Masonic Office in Berlin, where people worked assured of reciprocal checking and balancing.[32] Thus, the note of a Security Office worker meant for the central office in Berlin in February 1935 complained that the Bavarian political police had not attached the required priority to the confiscation of lodge material in Munich and Augsburg. Because of the delayed forwarding of a teletyped message from the Gestapa, the lodge in Augsburg was able to ensure that lodge possessions escaped confiscation. The "Oberkommissar" ("Supreme commissar") of the Bavarian political police had already said, "So what is the Security Service?" The impression exists, "that the Bavarian political police have absolutely no experience in dealing with Masonic affairs, because otherwise they would not treat such important matters so lightly." Or, as people in the Security Office in Bavaria asked, "should this give rise to other assumptions?"[33]

In August 1935, a memo went to all upper-level offices of the Security Office saying expressly that all regulations were to be carried out in concert with the local "Stapo" units. The "Stapo" units were similarly informed by the Gestapa.[34] After the confiscated inventory and material as well as membership lists had been transported to Berlin, the evaluation and—as already described—the survey of the lodge lists began—for the purpose of checking up on individual people. The Security Service also concerned itself with concepts relative to a world-view judgment of Freemasonry and propaganda use. It is not clear that the State Secret Police tried to contest these areas with the Security Office.

In 1933, the Masonic lodges often did not appear in Gestapa memoranda, though the German Communist Party was often mentioned.[35] The tendency being expressed there continued. Thus, in the log of the State Police station in Berlin for July 1934, it was merely reported that Masonic lodges "had given no cause for interference in this reporting month."[36] "Jews and Freemasons" were repeatedly mentioned in the same breath and dealt with rather cursorily. Of course, isolated transformations of Masonic lodges in Berlin (including some subordinate to the Grand Lodge of Hamburg) into neutral associations were registered. These transformations were obviously carried out under their own direction, mostly in the vain hope of forestalling the confiscation of the building on Emser Straße belonging to the Hamburg Provincial Grand Lodge.[37]

Also registered were attempts to rescue Masonic ritual items and valuables with Masonic symbols from seizure by the Gestapo.[38] In 1935, in the monthly logs of the "Stapo" unit in Berlin, the Freemason-Question was not mentioned at all save for a few exceptions, which is surprising, given that Berlin played a central role as the stage for the lodges fighting for survival and for the political arguments with them.

On the other hand, the Gestapa memoranda no. 5 of April 1934[39] dealt solely with Freemasonry and "Masonic-like" organizations, for which reason it is useful to take a careful look at this report. The individual grand lodges and associations listed with out-of-date figures, as well as the purposes and goals of the lodges, their "subversive activities," and their position in the State, were summarized from the point of view of the Gestapo. In connection with the political alignment of the Masonic lodges, it said:

"Even if members from several other organizations have gained entrance into the German National Socialist Workers' Party, for the most part they are former liberals or reactionaries, who because of their earlier views, are still to be regarded as subversive. The individual Masonic lodges and orders have tried to make manifest their alleged pro-state efforts toward the national socialistic revolution by changing their names, by conforming, and by introducing the principles of Aryanism and the 'Führer'. These superficialities have changed nothing in their inner positions. Also the voluntary dissolution of individual Masonic lodges and orders does not mean that these associations wish to manifest their positive position toward the national socialistic state. Rather, the dissolved associations themselves recognized, that after close examination they would have been forbidden, because they were not in accord with the interests of the State."[40]

Indeed, there was a certain difference between the Old Prussians and the humanitarian lodges.[41] By the same token, there would be no continuation of the national lodges. The Old Prussian lodges would not be reproached as having "a subversive attitude in the Marxist-Communistic sense. However, they are a collection basket of reactionary efforts." The report substantiated this by citing a letter from the subordinate lodge

"Irene" in Tilsit to the national Grand Lodge, according to which, "None of our Brothers wishes to become a member of the Party."[42]

In regard to the humanitarian lodges it said, irrelevantly (!), that seven grand lodges had voluntarily dissolved themselves; the last was in the process. The lodges had agreed that "their decidedly international outlook, the prominence of the principle of equality of the races, as well as their liberalistic and pacifistic attitude would necessarily and absolutely lead to being forbidden."[43] The Symbolische Großloge was then discussed in detail. Among other things, mention was made of the forced announcement, according to which the reports of atrocities were "shameless and fictitious," as well as the contradiction that followed in a secret meeting obviously held on the same day.[44]

In connection with the position in the State, the Secret Police Office wrote—as usual oversimplifying—"the ideal of all Masonic associations is the brotherhood of all men without regard to nationality or race." It was therefore "only logical, that one of the main points of their program would be the cultivation of international socialism. The most important duty of the members, to support each other ... is really only an obligation to their lodge brothers, and the thought of an all-encompassing socialism never became a fact. ...The lodges are composed almost entirely of wealthy people. ... The lodge members form a close-knit association in society by means of oaths, secret signs and passwords, a fact that stands in ... contradiction to the idea of unity of the people. Its [the lodge community's] existence can only be undesirable to the national State of the present, which has consciously replaced the fundamentals of liberalism with the heroic life-concept true to its characteristics."[45]

In sum, it has been determined that the Nazi State had not done anything against the lodges and the Order using force up to this time. The Old Prussian lodges had, for all practical purposes, made no use of the circular decree of January 8, 1934, from the Prussian Interior Minister, which had offered them an "easier way of dissolving themselves." The few lodges that had decided to dissolve were apprised of the "unconstitutionality" of their decisions, and informed that the Grand Lodge would have to reserve the "right to claims for damages," which in "lodge jargon" meant the same as an "invitation to passive resistance."[46] To all appearances, at this point, the Gestapa authors' imagination had gotten out of control. In any case, there is no mention in the lodge papers that the Grand authorities had tried to get around Göring's order using the threat of right to claims for damages. It is also not clear on what legal basis this could have occurred.

On the other hand, in spite of everything, it is to be noted that the lodges and the Order were as good as shut out "as a power factor in political life." The membership had fallen off sharply under the influence of the Nazi world of ideas. There would hardly be a succeeding generation. Yet this would not take care of the question of lodges and the Order once and for all. The "secret widespread influence" that these associations had practiced in the past was known. The Secret State Police would pay very close attention to lodge organizations.[47]

In 1936, responsibility for reporting on the situation was transferred from the Gestapo to the Security Service (SD). The situation reports of the Central Department II/1 followed a prescribed structure. They were divided into a general overview, followed by individual descriptions, which were in turn divided into Freemasonry, Jews, "political churches" (Marxism), Liberalism, and movement of justice. In evaluating the situation reports, one must not forget that the justification of one's own activity and the attempt to secure the relevant formulation plan played as much of a role as the regard for equipment, personnel needs, and position of the service area in question.

In February 1937, the continuation of the Three World Globes subordinate lodge "Eugenia zum gekrönten Löwen" ("Eugenia at the Crowned Lion") in the free city of Danzig was seen by the Freemasonry Department II/111 as an indication that the restraint of Freemasonry in reality was only a position of "wait-and-see." The people's interest in the "Freemasonry Question" was, however, very strong. A "healthy Enlightenment" would be damaged by "the many Anti-Masons," who "see in Freemasonry, not a world-view opponent of great proportions, but a world-conspiracy organization," which they would identify in part with Bolshevism.[48] This was a characteristic view for the SD, which will be discussed in more detail. Meanwhile in the next report, the springing up of Skat [a card game…trans.] and bowling clubs "all over, where there had been lodges" is judged to be "the expression of former Freemasons' efforts to preserve the spirit and ideas of Freemasonry under all circumstances."[49] It was noted in the situation evaluation report of August 3, 1937, that "gradually a firm organizational association" would develop out of such circles. In Koblenz, the police could have stepped in "because of illegal continuation of an Old Prussian lodge." A sentence against nine Freemasons was demanded.[50]

As a supplement to the report of February 17, Department Chief Knochen had pointed out vis-à-vis his division chief that up to now only the upper sections—West, Southwest, and Northeast—had turned in situation reports, "all of which were hardly usable, because they did not keep to the guidelines set forth in the report outline."[51] Indeed, the quality of most of the reports (also the later ones) showed that the SD had a considerable problem setting up a thorough, systematic situation evaluation when it had to do with Freemasonry. Occasionally, it was only reported that there had been no change in the situation. For the month of January 1938, it was merely noted that the intensity with which the Party and State rulings on Freemasonry were enforced caused "considerable nervousness" in former lodge circles. "A somewhat organized action of former Freemasons" could, however, not be ascertained.[52] Altogether, rather precise descriptions alternated with rather superficial ones, which increased the impression of a certain arbitrariness in reporting.

Nevertheless, a supposedly scholarly based form of interpretation became established in the security apparatus, the more the world-view or secret police concern with the lodges was institutionalized in the SD and Gestapo. This interpretation could indeed be characterized best by the concept "factualization."[53] The personnel in the higher positions who concerned themselves with Freemasonry for the intelligence service and in practice were often young, academically trained technocrats, thoroughly "marinated" in the National Socialistic world-view. They consciously opposed Party ideologues like Rosenberg, who clung to the most misguided allegations and accusations, similar to Wichtl's or Ludendorff's agitations. For example, they disavowed the idea that Freemasonry was founded purely to suit the purposes of the Jews. The process of "factualization" was introduced when the SD began to concern itself with confiscated lodge material. The phenomenon of "factualization" and the greater differentiation in the discussion of the "Freemason question" connected with it are intimately connected with the efforts of the SD to carry out their claim to sole political responsibility in affairs concerning Freemasonry. Thus, the necessity for the SD "to get the monopoly for itself" was noted in an internal memo of April 7, 1937, Department II/111 to the chief of Central Department II/1, Six. Examinations and evaluations had to be done by the SD, because other offices got their knowledge "almost without exception from known anti-Masonic tall-tale tellers."[54]

A "Freemason-Handbook" was a project carried out temporarily in connection with the efforts at "factualization." It was meant to be a kind of "Anti-Lennhoff-Poser," a reference work with systematically arranged articles, definitions, and an index—all from a Nazi point of view. Although the project had a very concrete outline around 1938, it obviously never got beyond the planning stages.[55] On the surface, the factualizing arguments by the SD did not result in a handbook, but rather were expressed in a series of writings, among which were the essays by Six, as well as theses and inaugural dissertations of the "scholarly" SS successors. These people were indeed ideologically colored in their own way and, under the scrutiny of general standards of research, were seen to have made no useful contribution. They have lost any validity formerly allowed them as the only ones with access to the "Masonic sources that were 'buried in the rubble' during the war."[56]

The SS magazine "Das Schwarze Korps" ("The Black Corps") presented a contrast to the SD's intention, although it was in the person of Dieter Schwarz who (of all people!) was one of the staff. He first formulated the "factualized" line already introduced (no less actively) primarily for the Party's publicity in his 1938 pamphlet "Die Freimaurerei: Weltanschauung, Organisation und Politik" (Freemasonry: World-view, Organization, and Politics").[57] In harmony with its style of publicity, the judgment of "Das Schwarze Korps" was that Freemasonry was within the spectrum of the current *völkisch* clichés of Jewish-Masonic world conspiracy theories.[58] "The Masonic lodges and their related organizations," which were also "under Jewish leadership," according to Heydrich at this point, had "as their purpose, pure and simple, to organize people into a seemingly benign societal form, and to influence them in a manner useful for the purposes of Judaism."[59] The primary direction of "Das Schwarze Korps" expressed in Heydrich's comments was the reason for the assumption that "there was no concrete cooperation between the SS's magazine and the SD."[60] However, that could not have been completely true. As can be deduced from previous correspondence between the editorial board and the main office of the SS in July–August 1935, an article slated for publication in "Das Schwarze Korps" was placed before the SD for approval. The SD did actually intervene, and insisted that the appearance of the article should "be stopped at all costs." The background of this was that one of the people mentioned in the text was clearly just about to be secured as an informant.[61] A new examination of the treatment of the subject of Freemasonry in "Das Schwarze Korps" resulted in the finding that over the years, in the (incidentally rather few) essays, no unified propaganda process could be identified; nor were there any beginnings of construction of a world-view theory. Otherwise, "Das Schwarze Korps" mostly followed Rosenberg's line with respect to lodges.[62]

In 1937, the year in which the initiative to forbid Freemasonry was voted upon in Switzerland, a remarkable essay appeared, allegedly in Bern and allegedly already in its second edition, entitled "Der Tempel Der Freimaurer" ("The Temple of the Freemasons"). It had been written, as one can see from the text, before the end of the lodges in Germany. The trial in Bern about the "Protokolle der Weisen von Zion" ("The Protocols of the Sages of Zion") is mentioned already in the second chapter.[63] The publication is different in two ways from other anti-Semitic and anti-Masonic writings of the *völkisch*-Nazi spectrum: first because of its author, Kurt Reichl, who, according to the publisher's blurb, was prompted to turn his back on the world organization because of "the serious "semiticization" of the mind and membership of the organization." The second difference was because of the specific manner of treating the subject.

Now, more on the author and his environment: Kurt Reichl, alias Konrad Lerich, was unquestionably a shadowy and contradictory figure, who would end up putting himself, and his knowledge of Freemasonry from the inside, at the disposal of the Nazi security apparatus. It is known that Reichl, a member of the Vienna lodge "Zukunft" ("Future"), the Supreme Council for Austria and the General Masonic League, went over to the camp of political Catholicism during Chancellor Englebert Dollfuss's term. Presumably, he already had connections with the Austro-fascistic milieu in 1933-34 when the liberal-humanitarian "Bluebooks" edited by him appeared. He may also have been working in the intelligence business for the Nazis. He went to Germany with a wave of refugees when Austrian justice readied itself for retaliation after Dollfuss was murdered during the Nazi Putsch in 1934.[65] This suggests that Reichl was a member of the circle of those people who were connected with the Putsch. Reichl had resigned his lodge membership in January 1934, but assured [everyone] that for him there would never be "a parting from the ideas and ways of thinking" of Freemasonry.[66]Reichl had already impressed Leo Müffelmann negatively when he was in Berlin in 1930. In a letter to Eugen Lennhoff, Müffelmann wrote that Reichl had "made a strange impression and made weird speeches," which were all "saturated with an inner enmity against the Symbolische Großloge of Germany."[67] Friedrich Hasselbacher, who presumably also worked for the obscure "World Service,"[68] invited Reichl to Berlin in 1935. It cannot be documented whether they worked together in the framework of Hasselbacher's "Institute." Finally, the chief of the Freemason Department II/111 in the SD main office, Dr. Hellmuth Knochen, was successful in getting Reichl attached to the SD, until December 1944.[69] The details of the cooperation with Reichl were set in 1937 at the latest. On August 19, 1937, Reichl met with Knochen and the Referent of the Foreign Service Office II/1114[70] in the Hotel Excelsior, Berlin. During the course of that meeting, Reichl declared himself ready to lecture on questions on Freemasonry and make contacts in foreign countries in order to provide the SD with material about Freemasonry. The connection with the SD had already been made some time before, at which time Reichl was clearly obligated from here on out to put his journalistic work exclusively at the service of the SS.[71] Thorough reports were worked out by Reichl for the SD date from the Spring of 1936.[71a] In August 1936, he drafted a report on the Aachen Conference of 1928.[71b] A letter of August 4, 1936, to Dr. Hans Harms—who later specialized in "Freemasonry abroad" for the SD—says that Reichl, who was staying in a residence for foreigners in Oberstdorf at the time, was paid for his work.[71c] An internal report of September 1937 clarified Reichl's sphere of action. According to it, he would work out of Switzerland. Under pretense of long-standing lodge membership, by using the modes of recognition of the AASR, as well as by using specific Masonic forms of writing, he would obtain Masonic source material from different countries.[72] In the meantime, the SD was becoming suspicious of the reliability of its informant. Reichl had, among other things, drawn suspicion because of his connections to Catholic circles, because of his "high living" and his constant "financial troubles," to the extent that he was temporarily taken into custody.[73] A detailed interrogation, presumably in July 1938, resulted in the SD's deciding to continue its conspiratorial work, possibly primarily to keep Reichl quiet or, as the case may be, under control.

The direction of the thrust that originated because of Ulrich Fleischhauer, the protagonist of "World Service," is unmistakable. Reichl dispensed with polemics on purpose, and showed himself to be concerned seemingly with objectivity. Some of the material mistakes were probably purposeful, others not. To a great extent, there are thoroughly relevant representations, connected with subliminal or open hostility. Generalizations, omissions, and falsifications mingle methodically subtly with a universally denunciatory undertone. The person and *modus operandi* of the author played most dangerously into the hand of German Masonic policies, because he explicitly or implicitly used the usual anti-Masonic terms. Thus, for example, it was said that mankind "should be ruled by the victory of Freemasonry," or that the Supreme Councils were "the real and most inside centers of action of 'world lodge-dom.'"[74] In the Afterword, the publisher and author assured the reader that the publisher "was, of course, equally well-instructed" and that there was "only one and the same Freemasonry in the whole world,"[75] a watering-down of the differentiation among the factions of German lodges that had been undertaken previously.

Worthy of notice from the standpoint of the history of the organization, meanwhile, is that Fleischhauer's "World Service" was assimilated into Alfred Rosenberg's so-called "Weltanschauungsamt" ("World-view office"). The rivalry with Goebbels Service offices and the "Reichsinstitut für Geschichte des neuen Deutschland" ("Reichs Institute for the History of the New Germany") under Walter Frank drove Fleischhauer into the protection of Rosenberg in 1937. Consequently, Fleischhauer was supplanted by August Schirmer, an aide to Rosenberg; and, according to internal terminology, the "World Service" was integrated in 1939 into the "Weltanschauungsamt" as the "Office for Jewish and Masonic Questions," although it continued to exist to the outside under the old name, but under Schirmer's editorship.[76] The "Office for Jewish and Masonic Questions," which "neither in public nor within Rosenberg's establishment garnered any significance,"[77] was combined with the "Office of World-view Information" into the new but equally ineffective "Main Office for International Powers" in the spring of 1942. The newspaper *World Service* was not transferred into the new department, but stayed independent with its own editor within Rosenberg's "world-view apparatus."[78]

In addition to the Berlin SD's Masonic "Museum", kept for the purposes of internal propaganda, the Nazi "powers-that-were" set up anti-Masonic museums in several other cities. They were open to the general public, and differed greatly from each other in terms of the way their exhibitions on the theme were prepared and mounted. So, for example, the "West German Masonic Museum" was set up in Düsseldorf. Former lodge halls in Erlangen, Nürnberg (Nuremberg), Hannover, and Hamburg were turned into "educational and research centers, and also used for anti-Masonic exhibitions."[79] Occasionally, ritual pieces confiscated from the lodge halls were even exhibited on the street to defame Freemasonry.[80]

A 1938 publication for the anti-Masonic "Museum" in Nürnberg maintains that many documents prove that Freemasonry is an "international power," which "slips subversively into each cultural group and dilutes all their concepts."[81] According to the old, well-known world-conspiracy theory, the publication presents Freemasonry—without differentiating among the individual grand lodges—as an international organization, whose aim is allegedly "to toss an international chain over and beyond peoples and nations, [an organization—trans.] which, according to international concepts, carries on with politics under the pretext of being merely an association of men, who are devoted to the idea of 'humanity,' that idea, which with its motto 'humanity' is of service to the Jews."[82] The text goes on, "The essence of Freemasonry has been declared the second destructive element [along with Jewry—author's note], as enemy number one of the German people by Der Führer himself. The equality of Jewry was possible only with the help of Freemasonry," which "became the pace-setter for Jewish politics and in practice brought forth this disintegration into middle class society, as Marxism did, as a Jewish weapon against workers."[83]

In a Nazi information flyer for the anti-Masonic exhibition in Düsseldorf, a differentiation was made: in no land in the world did Freemasonry have "so many forms" as in Germany. "Any racial thought" was foreign to the six humanitarian grand lodges. The Old Prussian grand lodges "possessed the so-called Christian principle in the higher degrees, and therefore accepted baptized Jews."[84] This flyer went on to say that after the national upheaval, the latter attempted "as a 'German-Christian Order' to be built into the structure of the National Socialistic state. They then saw the senselessness of their disguise, and dissolved themselves in 1935."[85] Aside from the statement that the German-Christian Orders were an expression of "disguise," and a few inaccuracies in the explanations of Christian Freemasonry, it is striking that now, after the destruction of the lodges, there are stronger distinctions made among the individual currents in Freemasonry, than was the case in 1935, at least in this text. In this publication, there is an indication that the Symbolische Großloge and the Zur Aufgehenden Sonne Grand Lodge were not recognized by the other grand lodges.[86]

The story of the dissolution of (all) the humanitarian grand lodges in 1933 is confusing.[87] For example, the truth is that the two grand lodges, in Dresden and Leipzig, which had transformed themselves into Orders, existed a little longer than the Old Prussians. Otherwise, the usual Jewish-Masonic world conspiracy and Freemasonry as an "instrument" of the Jews was trotted out in the text: "the Masonic teaching of equality and fraternity strengthened its (Jewry's—author's note) hope for equality with the host peoples and thus for solidification of its mastery of the world."[88]

The centralization of the police by the creation of the main offices of the Ordnungs (regulations, order) police and security police under the "Reichs-Führer SS und Chef der Deutschen Polizei im Reichsministerium des Innern" ("Reichs-Führer SS and Chief of German Police in the Reichs Ministry of the Interior") meant for Himmler the coupling of Party and State offices and encouraged the confusion of the police apparatuses with each other and with the SS. It was characteristic of the typical Nazi penchant for changing the purpose of existing bureaucracies. Even before this melding under the umbrella of the Reichssicherheitshauptamtes (Reichs Main Security Office [RSHA]), the Security Service (SD) sought a closer cooperation with the criminal police. So, for example, the Freemasonry Department noted, in May 1938, that lodge material still in private hands could be seized using "criminal police measures."[89]

At the end of September 1939, a central authority for conceiving and carrying out Nazi terrorism was created by the RHSA, the "fourth column in the *völkisch* State," along with the administration, Party and army.[90] Reinhard Heydrich assumed leadership of this authority, which was formed by combining the state Main Office of the Security Police and the SD as part of a Party organization. The administrative unification of the Security Police (SIPO) and the SD institutionalized the SS pervasion of state executive organs, and was simultaneously a manifestation of the power of Himmler and Heydrich. The tying of the SD into the state structure was finished. Nevertheless, the desired complete melding into a unified body of police, in the sense of a "*völkisch* theory of police," failed because of the internal rivalries in the security apparatus.[91]

In a style characteristic of the Nazi form of dominion—a mixture of "bureaucratism" and arbitrariness, "the orders…of the RSHA guided all the persecution and annihilation policies of the 'Third Reich.'"[92] The organizational pooling did not mean, however, the dissolution of the old offices.[93] Rather, the organizational structures of the Security Police and the SD were taken over to a large extent. Referat II B 2 in the Gestapa, which was previously concerned with lodge questions, was put into Office IV of the RSHA, which was identical with the Secret State Police. It was led by Heinrich Müller and made part of Group IV B, which was in turn divided into four Referats. Service office IV B 3 ("Other Churches, Freemasonry") was responsible for Freemasonry. Its chairmanship remained vacant until the end of 1942 according to the plans for dividing the offices.[94] One cannot deduce from the fact that there were vacant positions in the RSHA, that the Referats did not work. Rather, tasks that devolved on them could be taken care of by some existing group or office leaders. In the meantime, the catalogue of Freemasons originally begun by the SD was maintained by Office IV in Referat IV C 1, where the main catalogue and central "personal document administration" of the Gestapo had been placed.

Office I ("Personnel and Administration") of the SD's Main Office (without I/3) and the Office ("Administration and Law") of the Main Office of the Security Police were put together under the leadership of Best, in the new Office I of the RSHA. Both SD Central Department I/3 ("Press and Libraries") and II/1 ("Research into Opponents") were united in the new Office II under the leadership of Six.[95] With this, Office II of the RSHA, which was concerned with "world-view research and exploitation," took over the previous "Masonic Referat" of the SD, and that under the rubric II B 1.[96] The following year, in the course of restructuring, the previous Office II was turned into the new Office II, which in part was housed in the imposing former lodge building of the Große Landesloge, Eisenach-ertraße 11-13. At the same time, the "Freemason Referat" and the "Jews Referat" were combined into the new Office VII B 1 ("Freemasonry and Jews"). According to Rudolph, it seems that a division of labor in the form of "Auxiliary Referats" (a. Freemasonry b. Jews) continued to exist, although they do not appear in the office division plan. In addition, he assumes that the Referat did not remain unoccupied, but was covered by the leader of Group VII ("Archive, Museum, and Special scholarly projects") Paul Dietl, or as before by Erich Ehlers in a consolidation of personnel.[97]

In 1942, the two areas, "Freemasonry" and "Jews," were again sepa-rated into independent Referats in connection with an altered personnel structure. This can be taken as an indication that, in the meantime, an even greater significance was attached to the relevant world-view-pro-pagandistic discussion with respect to the progress of the War. Perhaps also, reasons relating purely to matters of personnel played a role. Heinz Ballensiefen assumed leadership of Referat VII B 2 (Jews), whose posi-tion in the Ministry of Propaganda had been eliminated, and for whom an appropriate position was sought. Erich Ehlers now officially served as chief of the Office VII B 1, which concerned itself with Freemasonry. Ehlers made himself known in this capacity in 1943 with a publication entitled "World Freemasonry," in which he summarized the ideological and political position of the SS with respect to Freemasonry.[98] When the RSHA was established, the SD's Masonic "Museum" in Berlin was at first also put under Office II. As of the restructuring of the groups in 1940, it was given to Office VII (Group VII C).

In the meantime, in the fall of 1934, the "Institute for Research into Freemasonry, Berlin, made its debut. It was housed in the above-mentioned previously confiscated lodge building of the Grand Lodge of Hamburg in Berlin. This institute was a project of the virulent anti-Mason Friedrich Hasselbacher, who at this time brought out the first of his five-volume complete works (up to 1941), *Entlarvte Freimaurerei (Freemasonry Unveiled)*.[99] An inflammatory pamphlet by the same author, "Das Todesurteil über die Freimaurerei in Deutschland" ("The Condemnation to Death of Freemasonry in Germany"),[100] was a direct reaction, from the völkisch-National Socialistic viewpoint, to the transformation of the Old Prussian grand lodges into German-Christian orders. In it, Hassel-bacher "uncovered" the members of the Order as "turncoats," declared the transformations to be a "fraud maneuver," and supported the "un-German essence of Freemasonry."[101] Hasselbacher also spread his kind of anti-Masonry in a magazine he founded, called "Blitz" ("Lightning").[102]

It must be emphasized that Hasselbacher's publication activity is not on the same plane as his so-called "Institute." This had already been closed in 1936, in connection with a ban against his speaking.[103] After Hasselbacher, whose conspiracy scenarios were mostly like those of Rosenberg, realized he was obliged to turn in his manuscripts in advance to the SD for censoring, and that he had to toe their ideological line, the ban on his speaking was lifted in 1938. Thereafter, he even received the (rather high) expense reimbursement of 150 Reichsmarks to finance his anti-Masonic agitation.[104] By this method of keeping him quiet, spread by his own news-service, Hasselbacher, who can certainly be regarded as one of the most dangerous "free-lance" opponents of Freemasonry, was tied to the SD.

Freemasonry in the politics and propaganda of the "Third Reich" was part of the sphere of tension between the competing Nazi centers of power under the umbrella of the "Führer"-State. The different interests of the state and party offices concerned with lodges are mirrored in the dif-fering assessments and treatment of the "Freemason Question." It seems that Himmler and Heydrich were led by the standard that more groups of victims meant more power. Indeed, the research controversy carried on between "Intentionalists" and "Structuralists" regarding the persecution of Jews cannot just be transferred to the Freemasons. However, not only because of the propagandistic coupling of Jews and Freemasons is it worthwhile to reflect again upon this and newer historiographic controversies in the context of the policy on Freemasonry. It can be seen that the intentionalist and structuralist arguments are not mutually exclusive. Rather, a synthesis of results of both strands of interpretation offers itself. Neither of the two models, however, can explain convincingly the history of the development of the "Third Reich."

Ideology and irrationality layered themselves with improvisation, pragmatism, and objectivity in connection with Freemasons and their institutions. Attempts to profile and implement played an important role, and the action against lodges in occupied Europe had characteristics of radicalization. In short, there was a mixture of apparently contradictory standards. What unified the operative personnel was a consensus on racist ideology, which was already rooted in the program of early Nazism. It included the decision to implement this racist ideology up to and including physical annihilation. Without doubt, it was a worthy contribution to research to consider the meaning of the technocratic levels, i.e., the role of "experts," the "advance thinkers of annihilation," and their rational calculation into the Nazi annihilation apparatus, which was radicalizing itself; as well as to point out the connections between economic rationalization and population policies in the occupied Polish and Soviet territories and the "final solution." This and similar attempts at interpretation, however, fall short when they confuse inherent and ideological motivations and legitimizations (rationalizations) of actions, and lose sight of the relevance of the radical-"bio-logistical" and anti-Semitic concept. This means, in other words: when the racist-state characteristic of the "Third Reich" is neglected.[105] In the same way, it must be emphasized that a "de-ideologizing" cannot be deduced from the practice and differentiation of Masonic policies by the SD. The constitutive *völkisch* and anti-Semitic ideological units were mixed with professional objectivity and striving for efficiency in the activity of the Security Police and SD apparatuses. This mixture also characterized the procedures against foreign lodges in the German sphere of influence and the intelligence treatment of (former) Freemasons in the central part of the Reich.

8.2 FORMER FREEMASONS IN THE "THIRD REICH"

The state measures directed against (former) Freemasons in the "Third Reich" can be classified into three phases, which partially overlap each other. The first phase was that of the destruction of lodge buildings in the German Reich. At the same time, getting hold of members, or lodge membership lists; the examination of officers and other people as to lodge membership; the inclusion and evaluation of confiscated lodge materials; as well as working out the guidelines for dealing with (former) Freemasons were all paramount. The second phase included more or less the execution of these guidelines and an ideological debate with Freemasonry making use of stolen archives and lodge materials, during which it can be observed that the Security Police followed a stricter procedure against Masonic circles as of 1937. The third phase began with the "Anschluß" [annexation] of Austria, and consisted of the transfer of Nazi Masonic policies onto the expanded German sphere of influence. The beginning of the War introduced, in addition, a new propaganda offensive for the masses going back to using the current world conspiracy theory.

After the dissolution of the lodges, many (former) Freemasons in Germany kept in contact with one another. They succeeded in organizing meetings in the form of Skat [the card game] clubs, neutral associations, or "Stammtische" [regular tables at local pubs]. Only some of these groups were fundamentally opposed [to the regime][106] Meetings of former members of Old Prussian lodges were sometimes even officially announced, according to the notices in a *Festschrift* of the national Mother Lodge, and sometimes permitted. Meetings of this kind sometimes "took place under the loose control of the Secret State Police."[107] In January 1937, the liquidator of the Große Landesloge, Paul Rosenthal, explained that a consultant in the office of the Secret State Police had assured him that "former members of our lodges are permitted to continue to meet in public places. They are only forbidden to meet in a closed room."[108] The decree is completely plausible, because it reflects the guidelines that Heydrich sent out in an order to all State Police offices on April 8, 1936. According to it, "meetings of former Freemasons in public inns and bars for evenings of Skat and other friendly entertainment, without any club or other organizational ties, and without demanding Masonic practices," were for the moment not to be objected to. However, such meetings were "to be monitored… unobtrusively according to the circumstances." Measures such as forbidding the use of the place were expressly to be used only in case of "grave reasons," because otherwise the groups would "gather in house communities," and thus "might completely slip out of (the over)sight of the Secret Police."[109] In contrast, "attempts to establish organizations that are successors to lodges in disguise" were to be thwarted. In Heydrich's eyes, these included the previously mentioned meetings in closed rooms, as well as associations, which, because of the composition of their membership, could be suspected of "encouraging Masonic tendencies." In accordance with this order, such organizations were to be dissolved and leading members were, if it was warranted, to be taken into "protective custody."[110]

At the beginning of 1937, SD-Referent for Freemasonry Erich Ehlers expressed his assessment in a report to his department head, Knochen, that former lodge members would try to use every means they could "to circumvent the dictates laid out by the Party, or to obtain an application of the exemptions for themselves." By means of the "nurture of social intercourse," they would strive to keep the "organizational cohesion" alive. Furthermore, it seemed that a "hope for the revival of Masonic organizations" existed. The execution of regulations on Freemasons ordered by the State and Party (which will be discussed in detail in this chapter) made considerable progress. For the "further treatment of this subject," it is desirable that on the regional level more "significance would be given to the opponent Freemasonry."[111] It seems that since 1937, Heydrich was putting a lot of effort into thwarting ever more the "nurturing of Masonic spirit." In July, the previously mentioned circular order against "Masonic lodge-like organizations" had been promulgated.[112] In addition, from now on, increased action by the police was ordered. For example, the anniversary publication of "Reinoldus zur Pflichttreue" (Reinhold of Loyalty to Duty), a subordinate lodge of the Große Landesloge in Dortmund, reported on an action by the Gestapo against a *Stammtisch* of former lodge members in November 1939. The participants were subjected to hearings that made clear that the offices of the SD and Gestapa had been well informed about the *Stammtisch* participants and their Masonic background.[113]

The situation reports of the SD describe how activities of former lodge members after 1935 are judged by State power, as well as how the "Freemason Question" in the Nazi government offices was assessed. As to the subordinate theme "Freemasonry," situation assessments concerned themselves with the affairs in the German Reich after the destruction of the lodges, with the momentary disposition of Freemasonry and its political alignment in various European countries and the United States, as well as with the question of reemployment of former Freemasons in the administration after the war began. Significant with respect to the structural solidity of the "Third Reich," to its *modus operandi*, and to its methods is the matter-of-fact—even honed—construction of these reports—in which the emotionless administrative execution of a criminal *Weltanschauung* is mirrored. From the situation evaluations, it is seen that meetings or other activities of former members of Masonic lodges and so-called "Masonic appendant organizations" were carefully registered (although, to a certain extent by chance). In addition, they indicate a different outlook on the lodges in which the scholarly demand made by the SS bureaucracy during the ideological debate with Freemasonry is expressed. Thus, for example, distinctions are made among the Old Prussian, Humanitarian, and Scottish Rite in the previously described "bringing to relevancy."[115] The concept of "higher degree Freemason," however, remained undifferentiated as it was used in various reports. The assessment according to which the "diffusion of the Masonic idea of humanity, tolerance, and, in its broader sense, liberalism … was common to all Freemasons,"[116] allows the conclusion that the Nazi creeds of the dissolved German-Christian Orders continued to be unwaveringly and falsely categorized as "disguise." By the same token, the socio-political differences in the merging of German Freemasonry were noted. At the same time, the SD Main Office came to the correct conclusion that "the opinions of these groups within German Freemasonry concerning individual important problems of domestic and foreign policy turn out differently."[117]

The situation report for the year 1938 took a position with respect to the previous results of Nazi Masonic policies. This meant "the fact that in Germany, the organization of regular Freemasonry and the main appendant bodies were destroyed" was not to disguise the fact "that the Masonic body of thought … still has effect on former Freemasons." Correspondingly, Freemasonry appeared in the Reich "almost solely in the individual members of the organizations."[118] The lecturing activities "of the well-known former 'higher-degree Mason,' Dr. Horneffer, who spoke on Greek philosophy, and thus represented Masonic ideas in a clever form," were especially mentioned.[119] In addition, a complaint was made that a large number of former Freemasons had gained entrance into the Party, and that a "complete exclusion of even the leading former Freemasons had not succeeded perfectly," and consequently the "measures had not been carried out with the desired severity."[120] Concerning the political position of former lodge members with respect to the Nazi regime, it was to be taken into consideration that, "as with other former opponent groups, some of the former Freemasons doubtless had also transformed themselves inwardly." Certainly "characteristically" in all aspects of Freemasonry, "a nearly unanimous rejection … of the actions directed against Jews" had been ascertained.[121]

Those remarks in which the results of the strategy of the SD for "bringing to relevancy" were reflected are enlightening. According to this, it appeared that an "irrelevant Enlightenment" basing itself "more on sensations" was shoved aside. This "Enlightenment" often had Freemasonry appear as a harmless organization. In contrast, a strengthened "relevance indoctrination made itself noticeable." In this respect, the "Lodge museum" in Nürnberg was especially successful, where "in a complete and relevant way, Freemasonry was shown to be the organization for the methodical carrying out of Jewish ideals and aims."[122]

The comments of the SD on the situation of Freemasonry outside Germany for 1938 or 1939 cannot be explained in detail in the framework of this examination. The collective attention was turned to the participation and anti-fascist positions of the Supreme Councils of the AASR and thus to "higher-degree Freemasonry," which was especially hated by the regime.[123]

The remarks in the situation reports should be considered in detail in terms of the treatment of former Freemasons in general and in terms of the rehiring of former Freemasons into the administration after the war began, because they are relevant to an obscure and progressive regimentation and regulation of former lodge members in the State and Party.

For the Party after the "seizure of power," only those former Freemasons who had resigned from their lodges before January 30, 1933, and declared that they had broken all connections to Freemasonry were accepted into the Party. However, they still could not hold Party offices. There was no distinction among the grand lodges.[124] As early as 1934, the limitations were increased. Now, "those former Freemasons who had shown special Masonic activity by holding positions of leadership during their membership, or belonging to higher degrees, were to be expelled from the Party and its branches."[125]

As concerns the State, it was decreed by the Reichs- and Prussian Interior Minister that every official under service oath had to declare on a written form whether and how long he had "belonged to a lodge, lodge-like organization, or a substitute organization of such." Further, information was required about which position, offices, and degree, if any, were held, and under what circumstances the man had left the organization.

A corresponding declaration had to be given by the official in charge, before the person could be hired.[126]

On November 2, 1935, Frick ordered that, except in cases whose decisions were not by definition reserved for the Minister, reports about officials who had belonged to a lodge or "lodge-like organization" had to be filed with him before they could be hired or promoted.[127] In a circular decree of February 18, 1936, it was made clear—probably for reasons of overburdening—that this did not apply to officials of communities, community associations, or other such bodies under public law.[128]

On September 2, 1936, measures were decreed by which people tried to regulate in detail new hirings and promotions of former Freemasons. It was aimed, politically speaking, at former lodge members, especially to keep them from holding leading positions in the personnel and education fields. Like the practice of the Nazi Party with respect to petitions for acceptance, the date of the "seizure of power" was the deadline: any official who resigned from his lodge after January 30, 1933, was "completely excluded from hiring and promotion." Exceptions were possible, "only with the consent of a representative of der Führer."[129] For former Freemasons who had resigned from their lodges before January 30, 1933, distinctions were made: Those people who had become Party members before the "seizure of power" or who had "distinguished themselves in the national socialistic movement," were not to suffer disadvantage." But the decree said that for those to whom that did not apply, decisions would be made on a case-by-case basis. Criteria would be, among others, whether "leadership positions," lodge offices, or higher degrees had been held. For all former Freemasons—except those who had left their lodges and become Party members before the "seizure of power"—including those who had held no leadership position, office, or higher degree—the rule was that they could be employed in personnel affairs "only with the permission of a representative of der Führer."[130] There was also the circumstance that the Deutsche Beamtengesetz (German Officials'

Law) of January 26-27, 1937, did not contain anything pertaining to the treatment of former Freemasons. This gave rise to speculation that the decree of September 1936 had perhaps been cancelled, which, however, was not the case.[131]

On April 27, 1938, Hitler loosened the Party regulations a little with a so-called "Amnesty Enactment," to allow access to Party offices (with exceptions) for those former Freemasons who had held no degree higher than the third and no leadership position. In addition, whomever this concerned could stay or be reinstated in the Nazi Party if he had "previously been in possession of the red membership card."[132] In practice, this odd-sounding specification applied to several groups: first, Freemasons, who, despite their membership in the lodge, had been temporarily admitted against Party guidelines.[133] Final admission would occur only with the delivery of the Party membership book, which could take several months. The decision on final acceptance was therefore predicated on the "conferral" of that "red membership card." Second, those who either had kept their lodge membership totally secret, or backdated their resignation to the time before the "seizure of power," and thus had become (temporary) members of the Nazi Party.

The determination made on May 2, 1938, in a decree of execution on the part of the Party Supreme Court, that those who held a higher degree than the third, or an "essential" office, did not fall under the Amnesty was later clarified. According to this clarification, "essential" meant [the function] of Master of a lodge, and related offices (i.e., deputy or warden) as well as orator or secretary.[134] In addition, the Party Supreme Court hastened to make clear that former lodge members were not suited for such offices, "which presuppose a special reliability as to world-view, as they had the assignment of education and judgment of Party members— for example, bearers of high rank, indoctrinators, personnel office heads and Party judges." In addition, it was emphasized that "nothing in the fundamental attitude of the Nazi party toward the Freemason Question would be touched by the Amnesty."[135]

After the promulgation of the Amnesty, the general cessation of acceptance that had been decreed on April 20, 1937, remained unchanged. The relevant ruling said that from now on, former Freemasons would not be newly accepted into the Party, regardless of the date of resignation, degree, or possible offices held. Of course, for "the recompense for hardship cases", the possibility of a "demonstration of grace" was created, about which the "representative of der Führer" was to decide.[136] The annual report of the SD for 1938 says this about the so-called "Amnesty decree:" although the loosening was at first only for the Nazi party, and included only those who belonged to the lowest three degrees and held no offices, in practice one could often perceive "a fundamental deviation of understanding of Party and State with respect of Freemasonry per se," and further, one could count on "a matching of the State to the Party Amnesty."[137]

Although such an "equalization" was carried out later, there was no fundamentally new judgment on the "Freemason Question." The governance was more or less transferred to the State sector by the circular decree from the Reichs Interior Ministry of June 6, 1939, the most detailed of its kind. This regulation was to take place "with consideration of the decree of April 27, 1938, from der Führer and the Reichs Chancellor concerning amnesty for the jurisdiction of the Party." The decisive ruling said that persons who had not reached a higher degree than the third, and who had held neither a position of leadership nor an office, should "not suffer any disadvantage because of their lodge membership." As usual, there were limitations: If they had not left the lodge before January 30, 1933, or entered the Nazi Party previously, they could "be called neither as chiefs of public authorities, nor employed as case-workers (or officials in charge) in personnel affairs."[138] That means that the idea still existed that former Freemasons would have a destructive influence, and favor other former lodge members in their professional careers and with respect to influential posts.

Concerning the hiring and promotion of people who had held a degree higher than the third, a leading position, or an office in the lodges, but had resigned from the lodge before the "seizure of power," the decree

284

said that decisions had to be made on a case-by-case basis. Those who had resigned after January 30 were to be flatly denied hiring and promotion. The decision about the admission of exceptions, with respect to officials of the higher service [ranks], again lay with the "representative of der Führer," while for all others the relevant area commander of the Nazi Party would decide.[139]

All officers who were born before August 1, 1917, were to declare, under oath, about the length of time and the kind of possible lodge membership from about 1935.[140] In addition, the decree made clear that all rulings were to apply to public service workers who were not officials,[141] a ruling that was watered down, so that from then on, this would only happen if it seemed necessary, "considering their position in service (supervisory, leadership position)."[142] To summarize, an individualization in the treatment of former lodge members can be seen, especially in light of the possibility of exceptions and "special dispensations." In addition, there was a shift in emphasis, which at first was laid on the moment of resignation from the lodge, and then on degrees and offices held.

Although there had never been a unified system of higher degrees—as explained in Chapter 1, with the declaration of June 6, 1939, the regime continued to hold onto the distinction between former Freemasons of St. John's [like American Blue Lodge—trans. note] degrees and the so-called "higher-degree Freemasons." Also, the number of the degree achieved was used in combination with the function held as the most important criterion of distinction. Those humanitarian Freemasons whom the State machinery knew had worked in the AASR higher degrees were also affected by this procedure. The ruling meant that many members of Old Prussian lodges were excluded from the Amnesty. That working in the Party and for the national socialistic state was made more difficult for or refused them caused the Old Prussians to complain, as follows from the situation evaluations. "In these circles, to which the so-called Old Prussian 'national' lodges belonged, it was often declared, and to a certain extent rightly so, that the Amnesty showed a preference for the members of humanitarian lodges who worked only in three degrees, who were often more dangerous to the State, than for those [who worked in] the middling higher degrees of the Old Prussians." In spite of this, the measures directed by the SD against the former lodge members were justified thus: "A special treatment of the humanitarian Freemasons," the rationale said, "would not have been possible in the interest of the creation of clear Masonic determinations."[143]

The question of the use of former lodge members in the service of the State was generally given attention once again after the war began, in connection with the reemployment of officials who had retired. A day after the German invasion of Poland, the Nazi regime started the reactivation of retired officials. This measure, which served the purpose of making up for the lack of personnel because of the war, obviously made for the employment of former Freemasons "of the third and higher degrees."[144] The report of the SD complained in this context that the rules in the circular decree of June 6, 1939, were insufficiently adhered to, and that the officials in question had been "assigned against the existing rules, even sometimes to positions of leadership," which had "led to estrangement" among the officials.[145] This state of affairs could have been the result of non-uniform treatment because of the obscure handicaps given and the room for play in the decisions connected with them. It seems that a circular decree from the Interior Ministry of August 21, 1940, did not contribute to the clarification. It said that there were no reservations against the reemployment of retired officials, "in so far as the responsible area commanders" or, in the case of officials of the higher service [ranks], the "representative of der Führer" agreed. In case of doubt, the decision was to be made by the highest service- or supervisory authority, which would be valid especially "if the retired official had belonged to the third degree or higher in a Masonic lodge or similar organization, or other political reasons had played a role in the retirement."[146]

Concerning the area of the Reichswehr (the armed services), an order of May 26, 1934 said that every member of the armed services, meaning also [blue and white-collar] workers and officials, was fundamentally forbidden to be a member of a Masonic lodge or similar organization.[147] For officers, at first the rule was that former Freemasons who had reached a degree higher than the second, and had not resigned from their lodges before October 1, 1932, were not allowed to assume their officer's commissions. Later the treatment of former lodge members of the officers' corps, as well as the use of former Freemasons as officials and employees of the armed services was, for the most part, made similar to the practice resulting from the stipulations of the Interior Ministry for the rest of the State sector.[148]

On April 23, 1938, an order signed by Himmler went out that regulated the jurisdiction and procedural methods for the issuance of so-called "political proofs of un-dubiousness of character" (good-character attestations) for former lodge members. In general, the rules for the treatment of former lodge members that were laid down by the Supreme Court of the Party were to be used. The issuance of good-character attestations, which served as a model in Party and State positions (obviously mostly with the armed forces) devolved on Heydrich as Chief of the SD Main Office. Insofar as this applied to SS members, the decision was "to be applied" in addition "with the consent of the chief of the SD Main Office." Absolutely no good-character attestations would be received by former Freemasons who had been excluded from Party membership by any existing criteria. For those whose membership had limitations, this circumstance had to be specifically noted in the attestation.[149]

At the same time it was made clear that the responsibility for permitting an exemption from the guidelines of the Supreme Court of the Party, on the grounds of a so-called "petition for clemency," would lie with the "Führer's Chancellery." The prerequisite would be "only a short membership in a lodge in the lower degrees, as well as the existence of evidence of considerable service in the building up of the National Socialistic movement before the 'seizure of power.'"[150] Even though Himmler had formally considerably limited the room for exceptions, it was actually larger in practice.

The Nazis' political goal of keeping former Freemasons out of more or less influential positions in the State, Party, and their subdivisions, was fueled by the conviction that those bearers of the so-called "Masonic spirit" still remained, even though they had long since left the lodge. Indeed, exceptions to this limitation were made repeatedly, which, as a rule, the individual had to fight for by way of the "petition for clemency." Insofar as the concerned person was already in a leading position or had good connections at his disposal, pragmatism ruled. The most prominent example was without question Hjalmar Schacht. Not only did he still belong to his lodge at the "seizure of power," but, as previously described, he could even afford to intervene with Hitler on behalf of the Old Prussians.

Other former lodge brothers did well as Nazis: the notorious Wilhelm Kube, ultimately "General Commissar for White Ruthenia," was a member of the "United St. John's Lodge" in Breslau for awhile.[151] He listed his membership as lasting from the summer of 1919 to November 1920; in reality it was longer: September 29, 1919 to April 24, 1924.[152] In May 1934, Kube informed Walter Buch about his sometime lodge membership.[153] How Buch reacted to that and whether Kube got into difficulties has not come down to us. In any case, it is clear that he did not lose his high Party office as area commander in the Kurmark in the light of the existing guidelines.[154]

Presumably Dr. Alfred Meyer, the later Secretary of State in Rosenberg's "Ministry for the Occupied Eastern Territories," was also a lodge member for a time. Meyer's "Sturmabteilung-Führer Fragebogen" (questionnaire) of 1936 forms a point of reference. He did not answer "yes" in the column, "I affirm that I have never belonged or still belong to a lodge or other secret associations," but made reference to an enclosure which was neither identified nor remaining in the file.[155] That did not seem to have harmed his career.

In addition, Otto Bernhard and Dr. Richard Markert were regionally prominent persons, both of whom had a "lodge past," and held high offices in Bremen during the "Third Reich." Otto Bernhard, an industrialist and honorary consul of Thailand, had already joined the Nazi Party in 1930, and enjoyed an especially cordial relationship with Hitler since then. Also a member of the Bremen Citizens, he was their president for a short time in 1931. In 1932 he was County Commissioner and took over the Nazi Party chairmanship. After the "seizure of power," he became the first commissarial member of the Senate, and then on October 1, 1933, he was put in as Senator for Economics. Bernhard stayed in this position until 1945, when the British put him out and imprisoned him for nearly two years, after he had vainly hoped to be named their deputy. Allegedly, since 1940, he was supposed to have been connected with the national conservative resistance around Carl Friedrich Goerdeler by way of the "International Tobacco Science Society," which was very possible. He was also supposedly being considered for chief of the civil administration of Bremen.[156] According to his own changing allegations, Bernhard had belonged to the lodge "Zur Treue" (Loyalty), a subordinate lodge of the Three World Globes [Grand Lodge] in Berlin from November 1911 to March 1928, or even November 1930. When he got into difficulties because of his earlier lodge membership, and the SA (Storm Troops) stripped him of his rank as "Sturmbannführer" ("storm battalion leader") as well as his function as "political leader," his wife, Helene Bernhard, turned to Hitler's Adjutant Wilhelm Brückner on April 10, 1934.[157] He passed the facts on to Bormann, with the note that "der Führer and also I have often been guests" at Bernhard's home.[158] Bormann engaged Party legal leader Buch. Even in such a case, the process stretched out over more than two years, including a negative vote of the "Office of Information" on December 2, 1935.[159] On July 1, 1936, the Staff of the "representative of der Führer" of the Supreme SA Administration announced that "der Führer" had decided that Bernhard was to suffer no disadvantage because of his earlier lodge membership. "Der Führer" has ordered this in recognition of Party member Bernhard's services, because he has been a member of the Party since 1930 and "der Führer" was often a guest in his home during his stay in Bremen."[160]

On the other hand, Richard Markert's Nazi career was comparatively short. Upon Bernhards proposal, he had been installed in Bremen after the Reichstag elections as Reichs Commissar for Police Affairs in March

1933. Markert, who had belonged to the Three World Globes subordinate lodge "Esiko—Flaming Light" in Dessau from November 1923 to April 1931, and became a member of the Nazi Party three months later, was named mayor of Bremen on March 18, 1933. From the beginning Markert found himself in a fierce rivalry with Reichs Federal Representative and Area Commander of Oldenburg-Bremen Carl Röver, who repeatedly used Markert's lodge membership against him. The discussions, which also emphasized economic questions, were primarily of a personal nature. The conflict escalated when Markert tried to get the Reich to take Bremen from Röver's sphere of responsibility. Röver finally succeeded in forcing Markert to resign. Consequently, Markert not only lost his second function in the State as "trustee of work" for Lower Saxony, but in spite of his "appeal for mercy," he lost his Party office as "Gauredner (area speaker)."[161]

The preparation of the "Petition for Clemency" clearly remained with the "Führer's Chancellery," headed by Philipp Bouhler, even after the Chancellery lost influence with the Party Chancellery under Martin Bormann. Nevertheless, Bormann was included because, according to the relevant decrees of "the representative of the Führer," he was responsible for the admittance of exceptions, and the corresponding proposals as a rule landed in the Party Chancellery office. There seems never to have been a clear delineation of jurisdiction in this area.[162] "Consultants'" points of view were part of the set procedure for the testing of "petitions for clemency" of former Freemasons, which were prepared by "Office Information" or Department II/111. It was these "petitions for clemency," in which the petitioners were judged and recommendations for decisions were given.

As has already been described, it was mostly the top leaders of the Old Prussians who tried to effect a change in attitude relative to the "German" lodges by using the Nazi politicians' Masonic relationships. From the perspective of the lodges, this method was plausible, but it did not lead to permanent results. Instead, Masonic functionaries had to look on helplessly as their (former) members were exposed to professional and private discrimination, before as well as after the forced self-dissolutions. For example, a former Große Landesloge Brother, who for several years had been head of the post office in Solingen, was transferred to another city as punishment for his lodge membership in 1937, and forced to move his family out of the house that came with the position.[163] The director of a secondary (higher) school in Hannover, who had also belonged to the Fraternity (Große Landesloge), was told in December 1936 that he could no longer head the school, and would be demoted to assistant master, whereupon he retired.[164]

Although the majority of these "petitions for clemency" for acceptance into the Nazi Party remained unsuccessful, the cases of two Freemasons should be presented. These two survived their "lodge past" in the "Third Reich" nearly "undamaged," and after the war reconnected to their membership without interruption. They were the professor of medicine Karl Hoede and the conductor Erich Böhlke.

Karl Hoede had belonged to the Three World Globes subordinate lodge in Zerbst or Würzburg from the beginning of his medical studies in 1920 until July 1933, and held the office of orator. After the end of World War I, in which he had participated as a volunteer, Hoede became a volunteer corps fighter and member of the "Stahlhelm" (Steel Helmet). Rumor had it that he was actively involved in the Kapp "Putsch" in Frankfurt am Main.[165] Hoede received his medical degree and qualified as a university lecturer in 1931. As a dermatologist and specialist in sexually transmitted diseases, Hoede worked after the "seizure of power" at the University Dermatology Clinic in Würzburg and was a member of the medical faculty. Being associate professor since the end of 1938, he was called to be full professor in 1939–40. In 1935, because of his earlier lodge membership, Hoede had to leave the Sturmabteilung to which he had belonged—as "Sturmbann-physician" and platoon leader—after the "Stahlhelm" was incorporated into it. At the beginning of the war, for the same reason, he was categorized as "unworthy to bear arms." At first his application (obviously not the first one) on July 14, 1939 for acceptance into the Nazi Party was also rejected. In the "petition for clemency" that he initiated, the Supreme Court of the Party, the Area Command, and the Regional Court spoke out in Hoede's favor. On August 4, 1942, the "Führer's Chancellery" announced that Hitler had decided that Hoede was to be accepted into the Nazi Party effective immediately with no limitations.[166] Hoede was let go in 1946, and lived from then on in Würzburg as an established specialist. His Nazi past did not stand in the way of his further Masonic career. Hoede returned to his lodge in Würzburg, which now came under the umbrella of the new humanitarian United Grand Lodge. At the side of its first Grand Master, Theodor Vogel, whose daughter married Hoede's son, he was very involved in the building up of post-war German Freemasonry, among other things, as Grand Orator and chief of the United Grand Lodge magazine *Die Bruderschaft* (*The Brotherhood* or *Fraternity*).[167] By action of the Bavarian Ministry of State, Hoede was given the status of an emeritus full professor. He died in 1973.

The conductor and composer Erich Böhlke had become the general music director in Magdeburg in the year of the "seizure of power." He stayed in this position throughout the whole time of the "Third Reich." In addition, he served for awhile as manager. Böhlke, unlike most of such cases, did not wait for a rejection of a formal petition, but immediately attached a "petition for clemency" to his declaration of intent and desire to enter the Nazi Party.[168] According to the investigation of the SD, he had belonged to "The Three Golden Anchors-Love and Loyalty" Lodge in Stettin (under the Grand Lodge of Friendship) from June 10, 1926 to April 9, 1933. According to his own declaration, he had already resigned in September 1932.[169] In the supporting opinion of the Supreme Court of the Party, which based itself on a similar opinion of the area command, it said, among other things, that Böhlke had placed himself and his orchestra "unselfishly at the service of the Party." As of 1939, he was "artistic advisor" to the Hitler Youth. In addition, his "successful activity" and his "good cooperation with the Party" were praised.[170] Hitler's decision to accept him without limitations into the Party was announced by the chief of the "Führer's Chancellery" on March 13, 1941.[171] Although

Böhlke was not further employed in Würzburg after the war, he was able to continue his professional career in West Germany unmolested. He accepted the position of general music director in Oldenburg, and worked with top orchestras such as the Berlin and Munich Philharmonics. Böhlke also enjoyed international success. He joined the Oldenburg subordinate lodge of the Große Landesloge. In addition, he became an honorary member of several other lodges. The Fraternity (Große Landesloge) also awarded him its "Grand Emblem of Honor."[172] He died in 1979.

Some (former) lodge members more or less successfully carried out their mobilizations; innumerable others were discriminated against in their social milieu and in their professional advancement, and suffered financially. There were brutal attacks, arrests, and mishandlings—also ending in death. The quantification of all of these remains problematic. Dependable and detailed numbers of human victims and economic losses among the members of the German lodges or their families are difficult to obtain and nearly impossible to specify with respect to locality. Steffens, who made a study of the losses suffered by 91 lodges with 4,800 members (about 6.5 percent of the Freemasons before the "seizure of power"), concluded that 62 former lodge members had been murdered, 238 had been driven out, and 254 suffered (severe) financial losses. 377 Brothers from those lodges had lost their office or profession, and 53 were put in concentration camps[173] in which politically or "racially" motivated persecution is difficult to distinguish from the Masonic background. Therefore, it remains at least questionable to what extent lodge membership defined who suffered.

In the Masonic Museum of Bayreuth, there are individual sources that testify very poignantly to the personal fates of German Freemasons. For instance, a lodge member from Heidelberg-Neuheim (first a member of FzaS—the Grand Lodge of the Rising Sun—then of the Symbolische Großloge) was driven to commit suicide because of being fired from the State (civil) service and losing his pension rights. With his suicide, he hoped to secure a widow's pension for his wife.[174] Bernhard Beyer reported on the persecution of another Freemason in 1951 in the context of a lecture on the occasion of the "Bringing in of Light" in the research lodge Quatuor Coronati. The case under discussion was that of Rudolf Ramges, a teacher and social democrat, who lived near Düsseldorf, and was sometimes town councillor for his party. His Masonic career is reminiscent of Müffelmann. Ramge had first become a member of the National Mother Lodge, but after the end of World War I, he changed to the subordinate lodge of the Grand Lodge "Sun" in Essen. When he was put under pressure because of his membership in the Bayreuth AASR, he joined the lodge "Schiller" (subordinate to the Grand Lodge of Vienna). After Ramge had been temporarily arrested, he was apparently rather casually arrested again in 1944, and brought to the concentration camp in Sachsenhausen. Presumably, he died at the end of January or beginning of February 1945, during a transport to Bergen-Belsen, which somehow got redirected for no known reasons toward the Baltic Sea. Nothing is known about the background of this transport.[175]

8.3 TERRITORIAL EXTENSION OF ANTI-MASONIC MEASURES AND THE FUNCTION OF ANTI-MASONIC PROPAGANDA DURING THE WAR.

It has already been briefly mentioned that in the framework of the preoccupation with Freemasonry institutionalized in the Main Office of the Security Service that foreign grand lodges also provided a subject for (ideologically colored) political analyses, which were regularly recorded in situation reports. At the end of 1937, the foreign report of the SD Department II/111 concerned the obtaining, evaluating and utilizing of membership lists of foreign lodges.[176] In the same way, the patterns of argumentation of later anti-Masonic war propaganda were prepared long before and had only to be turned into the concrete requirements. For example, in November 1937, in a report by SD Expert Harms, who was responsible for foreign Freemasonry, the subject was "the struggle of the bearers of the liberalistic world-view of racial equality and tolerance against National Socialism and

Fascism." It went on to say, "the binding element of the 'democratic' states against the 'dictatorships' is in essence the organization of world Freemasonry of the 33rd degree." It was no coincidence that "'Higher-Degree Freemasonry' has put its most influential men at the top [leadership] of these countries all over, who are going in the same direction." The top place in this context was occupied by the name 'Roosevelt.'[177] A year later, the so-called "Guidelines for the Field of Knowledge II/111 made clear that the development of Freemasonry in "bordering countries," its presumed influence on politics, society, and private life, its connections to lodges of other countries; as well as "the Masonic influences on international policy/politics" were to be observed.[178]

Significantly, the Nazi Party directive "Against Freemasonry" appeared in 1939, in which Heydrich took a position on the "Topicality of the Freemason Question" (or "Freemasonry: Question of the Moment").[179] "The spiritual power that Freemasonry manifests," Heydrich announced, had to be taken into consideration and conquered again and again.[180] Using proven methods, the message for the purpose of mass propaganda latched onto the current slogans from the repertoire of the world conspiracy theory ("Freemasonry's World-plan") and advocated the "Struggle against those powers…which were working in the service of international Jewry using clever disguises."[181] A rather long piece written by Six was dedicated to his special theme: "Freemasonry and Emancipation of Jews." According to it, the lodges would try to deny their "characteristic as an international platform for the political work of Jews," by calling it "political, scholarly, unprovable slander."[182] That the group of authors of the directive was composed mostly of workers from the SD[183] led to the fact that it was—at least in the text—not marked by the cliché-filled polemics in the style of Wichtl, Ludendorff or Rosenberg.

Very clearly mirrored in the anti-Enlightenment anti-Masonry of this propaganda pamphlet is that the ideology and policies of the National Socialists, likewise, were aimed at canceling out the results of the French Revolution. The struggle of the National-Socialistic state, so it said, directed itself against the "Masonic, liberalistic idea of humanity and tolerance, the ... comprehension of God, humanity, and state set free from racial and *völkisch* restrictions."[184] As was already discussed in the second chapter, the Race-State model was set as irreconcilably in opposition to the western, democratic, pluralistic model—exemplified by Freemasonry. Such argumentation brought with it that—whether reasonable or not—the existence of opposing forces within the German lodges was to a great extent obliterated.

With respect to the effect of the directive about the German Work Front dispersed in an edition of nearly five million copies, the understanding was that, despite the otherwise mostly indifferent audience, the directive may have led to a "certain consolidation of anti-Masonic thought."[185] More probable, however, is that ignorance and the very probably existing reservations in the public consciousness were strengthened. In any case, the "Masonic Directive" reintroduced an offensive use of the conspiracy theory, which from now on was adapted to the specific restrictions of the war propaganda.

After the death of Heydrich, who had also played an important role in Nazi Masonic policies, a further essay entitled "World Freemasonry" appeared in 1943. This often-cited publication,[186] devoted to lodges, was tailored to the worldview education of members of the security apparatus. Written by Erich Ehlers, Chief of the Freemasonry Department (Referat) VII B 1 of the Main Office of the Reichs Security and under the direction of Heydrichs successor as Chief of the Security Police and SD (Security Service), Ernst Kaltenbrunner, the essay demonstrates that even at this relatively late date, and despite the military turn of events in the war, the SD still bet on a specially- tailored line of argumentation. The lack of "really unimpeachable, well-founded, anti-Masonic literature" as there used to be, was bemoaned, and a distinction was made between that and "certain anti-Masonic Enlightenment literature." Its "service in the stimulation of the struggle against Freemasonry" was not to be diminished in any way. The writings had, however, overshot the mark.

They had attributed an essence and a sort of activity to Freemasonry that would not be true of the "real character" of Freemasonry. In addition, Freemasons had been given the means "to defend themselves from these attacks, and to expose the attackers, in part, to ridicule."[187]

The essay also implied that despite the divergent interests of power politics, and in spite of distinctly different emphases on the "Freemason Question" by Rosenberg, there was an ideological consensus of national Socialists. Four fundamental schemes can be distinguished, all unfounded. First, although there were differences among grand lodges of different states, and a "certain 'national' attitude"[188] could not be denied in the case of the Old Prussian grand lodges, Freemasonry did have unified mental/spiritual foundations and objectives. Second, in terms of organization and agenda, Freemasonry was uniformly directed by the ideal of equality and the principle of tolerance, and thus enlightened-emancipatory, internationalistic and humanistic. Third, there was a tight connection between Jews and Freemasonry, in the sense of Freemasonry as a helper for the carrying out of Jewish interests and in the form of Old Testament elements in the ritual and in the symbolism of Masonic Work. Fourth, when the Old Prussian grand lodges changed into German-Christian Orders, that was camouflage.

From this interpretation, an "unbridgeable chasm" between National Socialism and Freemasonry was derived or deduced: Lodge members were estranged from their "nationhood," and were "in the service of 'anti-*Volk*,' Masonic ideology." Aside from that, the "claim of National Socialism on the total inclusion of the German people would exclude the simultaneous existence of a society like Freemasonry anyway."[189]

The closing chapter of the publication is reserved for the putative "necessity of a further struggle against Freemasonry and further training." The self-justification of his position in the Main Office of the Reichs Security Service should not be seen as the least of Referat-Chief Ehlers' motives as he composed this. As support for his position, Ehlers not only referred to the fundamental necessity of "spreading the knowledge of essence and activity of Freemasonry," he also asserted that "Freemasonry cooperated today as a factor in the front against the National Socialistic Germany, Italy and Japan."[190]

Anti-Masonry was accorded the same significance as the struggle against the Jews in the publications of the "House of Ludendorff."[191] Although from the beginning, it took a definite back seat to the persecution of the Jews in the National Socialistic State, it was never given up or taken out of the ideological context of anti-Semitism. Rather the relevance of the "Freemason Question" was firmly grasped from the viewpoints of world-view debate (discussions of *Weltanschauung*) as well as mass propaganda. Already before the Second World War, the topos of "international Freemasonry" was brought into play with various goals. Thus, the declarations of loyalty deposed by the Grand Orient of Spain and the grand lodges of other countries in favor of the republican government during the Spanish Civil War were presented as proof of the existence of the Jewish-Masonic World Conspiracy. In the *Bremer Zeitung (Bremen Newspaper)* of August 20, 1936, it said in this context: "international Freemasonry had dropped its mask." In "the battle for the 'sovietization' of Spain" obviously the last reserves had to be deployed in order to reinforce the "collapsing people's front." The Masonic lodges, which had previously encouraged the "Bolshevik Revolution only from behind the scenes," were now forced "to confess their true colors."[192]

In the process of German expansion, anti-Masonic measures were extended to the occupied parts of Europe and considerably intensified. The first to be affected by this was Austrian Freemasonry, after the invasion and "*Anschluss*" (annexation) by the *Wehrmacht* (army) in March 1938. Some of the Masonic institutions in the Nazi sphere of influence resisted the forced closings. Above all, the German attitudes in their dealings with Freemasonry were more practiced and logical.[193] They operated on the same pattern: lodges were closed. Their possessions and archives were confiscated and Freemasons were excluded from public life. Crackdowns, police-raids, and arrests followed evaluation of the membership lists. In Paris, material from the archives of the Grand Orient fell into the hands of the Germans, which, after Franco's victory in the Spanish Civil War, was given to Freemasons in France for safe-keeping. As had been done previously in Germany, anti-Masonic exhibitions in occupied Europe were mounted in converted lodge halls. In occupied countries, merely belonging to a lodge could mean an immediate threat to life and limb. The Grand Commander of the Supreme Council of Slovenia, Veljko Varicak reported in a letter dated March 21, 2001 to the Grand Commander of the Supreme Council of the Southern Jurisdiction of the Scottish Rite in the United States that his father and uncle, members of a Masonic lodge in Zagreb, were arrested and put in a concentration camp. Almost all Masons in Zagreb were imprisoned right after the German occupation began. Varicak enclosed a copy of the membership list of the Zagreb lodges that had been sent by the local office to the Reichs Security Main Office—Office VI D—on January 8, 1941. The original list, in which are the names of his father and uncle, is in the Archive of the Slovenian Interior Ministry.[193a] There was extensive theft of Jewish and Masonic cultural material, libraries, and archives. These were to form the foundation of the so-called "high school," a "central institution for National Socialist research, teaching, and education," planned for after the war. In 1942, Alfred Rosenberg, who was assigned by Hitler to be responsible for "the intellectual struggle against Jews and Freemasons," succeeded in providing himself with far-reaching powers. His "operations staff" received by "Decree of the Führer," a free hand to comb "libraries, archives, lodges and other 'worldview' ('philosophical') and cultural institutions of all kinds for relevant materials, and to confiscate them for the 'worldview' ('philosophical') purposes of the Nazi Party and later research work of the 'high school'." It stated expressly that the "intellectual battle planned against" Jews and Freemasons was "a necessary effort for the war," whose execution was Rosenberg's obligation, "in agreement with the Chief of the High Command of the *Wehrmacht*."[194] Completely, aside from the fact that there had been no lodges at all in Poland and the Soviet Union before the Germans attacked, the whole process is to be understood only against the background of the friction that had come to exist in Western Europe among the *Wehrmacht*, the SS Apparatus and the "operations staff." In any case, Rosenberg clung temporarily to his plan of setting up "institutes" of the "high school" in various cities, for the examination of special racist-ideological questions, among them one for "Questions on Jews and Masons" in Frankfurt on the Main.[195]

The repressive policy against Freemasonry in the territories under German control after the beginning of the war can only be touched upon here. Their main concerns can be described relatively clearly, despite the rivalries among the participating agencies. In addition to the motive of material enrichment, and of confiscating ideologically relevant goods for the purpose of later evaluation or utilization, the policy aimed at destroying Masonic organizational structures, stealing their assets, as well as taking lodge members out of influential positions. "Operations staff Reichs-Chairman" Rosenberg, the secret field police, as well as the military administration and even diplomatic representatives took part in the transformation of these concerns borne by a fundamental ideological consensus. The Security Police and the SD, even outside the borders of the Reich succeeded in putting themselves forward as the controlling powers. At least in France, Hellmuth Knochen, who now worked for the "foreign division" of the SD played an important role in the police or intelligence measures directed by the Reichs Security Main Office against Jews, Freemasons, as well as other "philosophical (world view) opponents.[196] Already on August 13, 1940, the Vichy government had begun action against lodge members. It promulgated a decree, according to which Freemasons in the unoccupied part of France were to be completely excluded from public functions and placed under surveillance as "enemies of the Fatherland."[197] In addition, the slogan, "the Jews and the Freemasons," served the French collaborators as a propaganda weapon in their attempt to establish the National Socialist ideology.[198]

In 1941 a "satchel-letter" from the supreme command of the *Wehrmacht* dealt with the "Freemasons' war against Germany."[199] The myth of the Jewish-Masonic world conspiracy was used in Nazi war agitation both within and without. In terms of content and method, one harked back to the time after the First World War: the "Protocols of the Sages of Zion" again came to the fore as a propaganda instrument.[200] According to the course of action (lit: agitation) as dictated by the course of the war, Freemasons would stir up a "fear of bombs" against Germany. U.S. President Roosevelt was the main target of the campaign directed against Jews and Freemasons: for instance it said in the July 22, 1941 *Tagesparole* (*Daily Words*) of the Reichs Press Chief, "A pictorial document that shows Roosevelt in Masonic regalia among Jews and famous public figures as members of a New York lodge," provided faultless and undeniable documentary proof of the "previous determinations of the Jewish-Masonic bondage of the warmonger Roosevelt."[201] While the deportation trains rolled into the concentration camps, "Jews, Freemasons and the philosophical (weltanschaulich) opponents of National Socialism connected with them" were labeled as "the originators of the present war directed against the Reich" in the "Führer's Decree" of March 1, 1942, cited above.[202]

8.4 RESISTANCE AND THE MASONIC MILIEU

Concerning the connection between Freemasonry and resistance, it is important to make a clear distinction between concept and content. For the Nazi agencies, for matters ideology as well as the intelligence-police, the persecution of individual lodge brothers was not paramount, but the destruction of the Masonic organizational structure, the opposition to the so-called "Masonic spirit (intellect)" and the closing-off of the alleged Masonic influence on State and society was.

As already described, it was mostly in the beginning phase that repeated defamations and violent attacks on lodge members took place. Yet as a rule, the (former) characteristic of being a Freemason in the "Old Reich" was not the sole reason for specific personal persecution—at least not as long as the individual behaved otherwise in conformity with the

301

system. In many cases, however, for victims who for political or "racial" reasons came to the attention of the state terror machinery, a lodge membership made it worse.

If (former Freemasons) suffered personal and professional disadvantage in the "Third Reich" it did not mean that they were necessarily opposed to National Socialism—not by a long shot. In contrast it must also be emphasized that opposition to National Socialism often fed off the Masonic spirit. An example of the "locking" at this point of intersection of political disfavor and one's (additional) character as an open, internationally-oriented Freemason would be the persecution of Leo Müffelmann, even though, according to Müffelmann's own statements, the hearing by the Gestapo extended only to his personal Masonic involvement and the operations of his grand lodge. Of course, this cannot be proven, because, as already explained, the report was clearly written in expectation of censorship by the State Police. In any case, the accusations piled up in the words of the reporting official (Müffelmann called him a "partner in crime"), according to whom, Freemasonry was, in contrast to the State, inimical to the Fatherland, Jewish, and dependent on Jews.[203]

Freemasons from different former St. John's lodges, like members of the "dormant" AASR, were more or less organized and met regularly during the time they were forbidden. Even if the meetings were not for ritual purposes, they contributed to maintaining the superstructure of the lodge. Naturally they discussed the question of whether and when Masonic work would again be possible. Not all such groups, by far, had the character of political resistance cells—but some did.[204] In those cases, Masonic contacts and organizations proved themselves extraordinarily helpful for covert activities.

It seems to be a good idea, at this point, to discuss critically and to summarize the term "resistance" against the background of the most important research trends in the Federal Republic of Germany: The problem is the extent of the concept. After the excessive emphasis on the national-conservative, military, and ecclesiastical resistance, in the 1960s there was a change of paradigm, which at first led to the consideration of resistance by left-wing workers. Since the beginning of the 1970s, one observes that the initial areas of research into the Resistance have been extended. On the one hand, resistance groups and forms of resistance that were previously neglected by scholars or purposely disregarded for political reasons, have been examined, such as Jehovah's Witnesses, the Deserters, the Jewish Resistance,[205] the so-called "Red Orchestra," or people who protected victims of persecution. On the other hand, the broadened perspective contributed to confusion of concepts and the lack of distinction between opposing positions and activities. The attempts of researchers on the Resistance to work out ideal, typical relationship patterns and name them led to the differentiation among different forms of passive and active resistance, which worked directly toward the overthrow of the regime[206] or toward the internal differentiation of the Resistance among "conscious political opposition," "societal refusal" (of an "institutional" and "individual" kind) as well as "worldview (philosophical) dissidence."[207] With the necessary distinction of kinds of action, it should be clearly understood—as already proposed by Hans Rothfels in 1969—that the use of the term "Resistance" or "Opposition" is only justifiable, when, over and above "partial dissidence," a general political opposition has been articulated, meaning when the rejection extends "to the whole criminal regime, with all its principles."[208] Not the least with respect to questioning about Resistance and the Masonic milieu, there is an important distinction: lack of understanding, disappointment and fury about Nazi policies vis-à-vis the lodges did not constitute resistance.

Martin Broszat differentiated among three main types of Resistance and placed them into three phases: the communist-socialist Resistance in 1933-34; the partial Resistance and "Peoples' Opposition" of levels mostly bound ecclesiastically religiously in 1935-40/41; and the fundamental opposition of the conservative elite since 1938.[209] Despite the implied, important distinction between "the Resistance" and resistance (opposition), Broszat's attempt at interpretation is unable to encompass the complexity of the historical event. The forms of Resistance and opposition within the overwhelming acceptance of the system by the Germans were multi-faceted, and overlapped to a great extent. Besides that, in building criteria, one has to take into consideration by way of limitation that the lines between partial and fundamental opposition, like the lines between the Resistance and the opposition were in a state of flux. Like human thought and action, the relevant attitudinal and action patterns were not fixed. Rather, they were dynamic as a result of the interplay among a multitude of external and internal factors. Against this background—apart from the political implications—it is not surprising that the debates on the research problem "Resistance" and especially the controversies about the meaning and extent of the concept have not ended.

It has already been mentioned in another context that Freemasons were among the leading representatives of the Resistance, which was shaped by the social-democratic-union influence. The question of the connections with Masonic circles that were supported most probably by Julius Leber and Wilhelm Leuschner even during the time they were forbidden can be recognized here as an especially desirable subject of research. In any case, in the trials against them in the Land-courts and for high treason, or in this later phase, Freemasonry was not necessary as a reason for increased criminality, because it was clear anyway that political blood-justice of the People's Court (*Volksgerichtshof*) would decide on the death sentence. Thus considered, it is not surprising, that in the indictment of the *Oberreichsanwalt* (a high ranking Reichs attorney) in the People's Court against Leber,[210] as well as in the indictment and judgment in Leuschner's case,[211] their lodge membership was not mentioned. Otherwise their (former) character as Freemasons would have been exploited to their credit in the Resistance fighters' demagogic propaganda that they were betrayers of the people. Therefore, the question arises as to whether possibly the aspect of Freemasonry did not come up, only because no one thought of checking to see if the accused had been lodge members.

Horst Sassin has earned himself commendation, by contributing to the first clarification of the correlation between the Resistance cooperating with the Social Democrats and the Masonic hierarchy in his dissertation, which was published in 1993.[212] This question was not even the main point of his study. Several members of the previously largely unknown Robinsohn-Strassmann Circle were Freemasons, and that mostly in lodges subordinate to the "Zur Aufgehenden Sonne" and Symbolische Großloge. This means that the milieu was social-democratic to bourgeois-left-wing liberal, which because of the Masonic spirit, was marked by a sustained tolerant, internationalistic character.

The group, named after Hans Robinsohn and Ernst Karl Otto Strassmann—neither man a Freemason—arose in 1934. The Jewish, Deutsche Demokratische Partei (DDP, German Democratic party) functionary, jurist, and merchant Robinsohn fled to Denmark in 1938 (then finally to Sweden in October 1943), and continued his work against Nazi Germany from exile. Strassmann, also a DDP activist, jurist and personal friend of Robinsohn's was arrested in 1942, and remained in custody until 1945. He managed to maintain his connection to the group from prison.[213] Sassin comes to the conclusion that the Circle had no members who fit the main types of people in the Resistance, as outlined by Broszat. Sassin criticizes, and rightly so, the concept of "conservative elite." If the concept were broad enough that it included the liberal spectrum and thus the political center, Sassin adds that the Robinsohn-Strassmann Circle would fall within it. Indeed, they understood themselves as bourgeois-left, and in contrast to the conservatives, stood in "liberal-democratic fundamental opposition to the Nazi Regime from the beginning. Sassin characterizes the group as a "singular appearance in the Resistance, and not only because there were so many Freemasons in its ranks. Here Liberals and Social Democrats, Jews, Christians and atheists worked together; in addition, the group sometimes had the effect of a hinge joint in the German Resistance. The political conception for the time after the subduing of the Nazi Regime stemmed from a "realistic, modern, urban-industrial picture of society."[214] A philosophical closeness and personal overlapping existed with the "Kreisau Circle:" Strassmann worked with Leuschner; however, there were also contacts with Goerdeler and the military Resistance.[215] Strassmann's liaison to Goerdler was the former Mayor of Berlin, Dr. Fritz Elsas. After the failed assassination attempt on Hitler of July 20, 1944, Elsas was arrested and murdered in the Sachsenhausen concentration camp on January 4, 1945.

In addition to the aid for those persecuted, the group's activity consisted largely of building an opposition network by collecting information or establishing contacts abroad as well as with other Resistance groups in Germany. They succeeded in getting in contact with British government offices.[216] In this area, Masonic connections played an important role for the inner network of the Resistance work as well as for the establishment of contacts abroad. Thus Dr. Hans Lachmund, who stumbled upon the Robinsohn-Strassmann Circle in 1934, met several times with French and Danish Freemasons in Paris and Copenhagen. The jurist Lachmund had held the post of (Oberjustizrat) Chief Counsel in the Mecklenburg-Schwerin Provincial (Landes) Ministry of Justice from 1929 until his dismissal because of the "Professional Officials Law" in 1933.[217] He had joined the DDP in 1919; in 1930 he joined the German State Party (DStP) for a short time; and as of 1931, he was a member of the German Social-Democratic Party (SPD). As a member of "Zur Aufgehenden Sonne," Lachmund had been one of the founding members of the Symbolische Großloge. He had been Master of "Isis zu den Drei Sphinxen" (Isis of the Three Sphinxes) Lodge in Schwerin (which changed from being subordinate to "Zur Aufgehenden Sonne" to being subordinate to the Symbolische Großloge). He had also been a grand officer (Grand Orator) of the Symbolische Großloge, and a member of the General Freemasons League.[218] The international level connections that grew out of these affiliations could now be put to use profitably for the purposes of opposition. At the same time Lachmund showed up as a V-Man. According to the activity report of Department II/111 of March 2, 1939, covering the second half of the year 1938, the use of V-Man Lachmund was expanded: he was called upon "to procure authentic lodge material from France as well as Scandinavia. More recent magazine and book materials were successfully obtained this way."[218a] Lachmund's case was qualitatively quite different from that of Kurt Reichl: in contrast to

Reichl, his cooperation was not actively pushed. Lachmund, after being contacted by the SD, most likely reported to it in a modest way, telling of his trips and handing over certain Masonic material. In this way, he assured himself freedom of movement and escaped the threat of arrest. According to Horst R. Sassin's reports, Lachmund also informed his associates that he had been "skimmed off" by the SD.[218b] Thus, Lachmund specialized in funneling into Germany Masonic literature as well as material from the Grand Orient and the Grand Lodge of France that he had obtained during his journeys abroad (about which he reported in detail to Strassmann). Presumably much of that literature was primarily documentation of the relationship of Freemasonry to Catholicism and the Treaty of Versailles, with which he—as Sassin rather optimistically says—could refute, or try to refute: "propaganda concerning the guilt of Freemasons in the First World War."[219] Obviously, the lodge hierarchy of "Isis zu den Drei Sphinxen" was also maintained. As can be determined from a lodge trestleboard (agenda), members of the "dormant" lodge had met presumably since 1934 in a conspiratorial lodge society, that called itself "Isis zur verborgenen Freiheit" ("Isis of Hidden Freedom").[220] Lachmund's wife, Margarethe, who also worked actively in the Robinsohn-Strassmann Circle, and who was representative of Grüber's Office for Pomerania, used connections stemming from her membership in the Quaker organization for resistance work. Lachmund had supported the Republicans in the Spanish Civil War with help from French Quakers.[221]

That Lachmund's activity was not only incidentally inspired by Freemasonry, can be seen in a diary entry made in 1939. The task of a Freemason in National Socialism is "to have a humanitarian conscience, to be effective without working perfunctorily, and to be an ideal in opposition to a completely different kind of reality."[222] In this spirit, other Brothers of the Schwerin Lodge worked in the sphere of the Robinsohn-Strassmann Circle. Communication between Mecklenburg and the group's administration in Berlin functioned not only via Masonic contacts. Trusted people in Hamburg, Kiel and Rostock had been members of "Zur Aufgehenden Sonne," or of the Symbolische Großloge. Thomas Dehler, a member of the group since about 1935, and its conduit for Bavaria, had however, belonged to "Zur Verbrüderung an der Regnitz" ("Brotherhood on the Regnitz" in Bamberg) a subordinate of the "Sun" Grand Lodge.[223] The cooperation on such good terms between the groups of "Zur Aufgehenden Sonne," and the Symbolische Großloge led Sassin back to the "respectful form of distinction"[224] of parts of the Reform Masonic Association, although the cooperation was in truth not really so smooth. Of course, the problems between the grand lodges, which held a lesser position on the personal level anyway, retreated completely into the background under the exigencies of Resistance work.

The fact that the bourgeois-conservative, military, and ecclesiastical Resistance was given prominence in the Federal Republic of Germany into the 1960s just as the communist Resistance was in the German Democratic Republic throughout its existence, bears witness to the extent to which, in each narrow perspective, the Resistance against Nazism in each part of Germany helped forge its identity. In a comparable way, that is true for Freemasonry in the post-war history of Freemasonry and its historiography. By means of delusion and abridgement, a self-styling arose in the sense of "Freemasons provided resistance," which is as distorted and untrue as the "legend" of camouflage or disguise. In this gross imprecision, it is as invalid as the idea of a Freemasonry with more or less unified intellectual and spiritual foundations.

The connection between the Resistance and the Masonic milieu, which could only be drawn in rough outline in this description, presents an important subject for research. Future individual studies, which this is intended to stimulate, should yield enlightening results.

Epilogue

NEW BEGINNING AND "OVERCOMING THE PAST"

While Freemasonry remained forbidden in the Soviet-occupied zone and later in the German Democratic Republic, in the territory for which the Allies were responsible, the reorganization of lodge life was begun soon after the liberation. Among the first to reassemble, already in the summer of 1945, were "Absalom zu den Drei Nesseln" (Absalom—Three Nettles) in Hamburg, "Anschar zum Friedenshaven" ("Group at Peace Harbor") in Cuxhaven, "Zum Füllhorn" ("Cornucopia") in Lübeck, and "Zu den Drei Ankern" ("Three Anchors") in Bremerhaven.[1] The first grand lodge to be revived was clearly that of the jurisdiction of Hamburg —in the fall of 1945.[2] Of course, the Brothers had to do without Ritual Work for awhile, because the permits to constitute themselves as Masonic organizations were only later given out by the military authorities. In contrast to the Soviet zone, where only scattered, unofficial Masonic meetings were tolerated, in the second half of 1946, lodge life began again in West Berlin. Until the Berlin Wall was built, Freemasons from the Eastern zone could participate in the Work in the Western sectors. Even before the Allied administration split [itself into the three Zones—trans. note] and the Soviets left the control council

311

and garrison headquarters, the representative of the latter protested in the beginning of February 1948 against allowing the Grosse Landesloge into the American Sector, —which was of no avail.[3]

At first, organizational contacts among lodges in different Allied occupation zones were not permitted. Later, the old grand lodges were revived and new organizational structures were developed as well. The Grosse Landesloge and the National Mother Lodge were reactivated. The solemn Constitution of a new humanitarian United Grand Lodge, the "United Grand Lodge of the Ancient Free and Accepted Masons (A.F. & A.M.) of Germany," took place in St. Paul's Church, Frankfurt [am Main] on July 19, 1949.[4] In addition the "Masonic Light" returned to Germany from exile in Jerusalem, and even earlier opponents, such as Bernhard Beyer, were concerned with the integration of the formerly hostile Brothers.[5] Various lodges formerly belonging to the Old Prussian systems joined the movement to gather together subordinate lodges of the old humanitarian jurisdictions and some newly founded ones (since 1945). On May 17, 1958, the United Grand Lodge and the Grosse Landesloge, in connection with the German Federation of Grand Lodges (Deutsche Grosslogenbund), formed the "Vereinigten Grosslogen von Deutschland" ("United Grand Lodges of Germany"—UGL) as a general umbrella organization. In this connection, the humanitarian member grand lodge renamed itself the "Grosse Landesloge der A.F. und A.M." and then finally "Grossloge der A.F. und A.M. von Deutschland" ("The Grand Lodge of Ancient Free and Accepted Masons of Germany"). The National Mother Lodge has been a member of the UGL since 1963. Even though the Grand Lodge (Royal York) "Friendship" was also newly constituted in the Federal Republic of Germany, it did not continue its work as an independent jurisdiction. It exists today [as of 1999, at least—trans. note] as a lodge association in the sense of a ritual community of four subordinate lodges, which also belong to the Grand Lodge of Ancient Free and Accepted Masons of Germany. It has its own grand master as always. In addition, two English-speaking grand lodges work under the UGL: the American-Canadian Grand Lodge of Ancient Free and Accepted Masons and the Grand Lodge of British Freemasons in Germany. Of course these are establishments which go back to the association of military and civilians of the Western Allies, but even before the unification of the Federal Republic of Germany and the German Democratic Republic, Germans were accepted. In addition to the "mother institutions"—the "Blue" lodges, the Ancient Accepted Scottish Rite has been represented in Germany with a Supreme Council since 1947.

As soon as post-war Freemasonry appeared, it found itself on the horns of a fundamental dilemma: to what extent should connections be made after the end of Nazism and after decades that were characterized by deep internal divisions, external hostility, and prohibition?

The functionary echelon concerned with unity quite clearly decided to ignore the Fraternity's divergent outlooks. They preserved continuity, while at the same time postulating a break in it, and thereby instantly brought together currents that could hardly have been more at odds. This proved to be an almost impossible task, at which they promptly failed. Yet, in order to achieve the squaring of the circle, and instead of having a clear mental pause, the new beginning was made under purely functional premises. The conflicts were artificially marginalized, and the historical objections were obliterated to a great extent. It became very clear because of a declaration that the UGL published in January 1949, even before the "Bringing in of the Light." On one hand, it was assured that one knew that he had to become "a member of the Brotherhood of the world"[6] On the other, however, the historical self-description was "transfiguring" and deceptive in essential details: "National Socialism, which swept away the German Masonic lodges in 1933," it said, oriented to the declarations of the churches (in Stuttgart and Fulda), "has wounded humanity's culture terribly. Even though there is no one in our circles who participated in these crimes, no one, who felt either inwardly or outwardly connected to the deadly force of the Third Reich, and even though many of us were opponents and victims of this Reich, we remain, as Germans, conscious of our obligation to aid in the healing of these wounds to the best of our ability."[7] Furthermore, equally undifferentiated, it was lamented "from the depths of our hearts" that, already in the First World War, the bonds with the Brotherhood of all nations "in contrast to that of the peoples" (sic!) had been torn apart, and German Freemasonry succeeded only in part "in reconnecting these bonds by entanglement and error in the time between the two great wars."[8] The delegation of guilt and the projection of political responsibility onto a loosely described group "of criminal people" in whose hands "our people and State" had landed[9] is to be perceived an example of the way German society as a whole often dealt with, or "overcame" the past.

During the "Third Reich" the national grand lodges immediately made their *modus operandi* subservient to a specific "re-interpretation." Thus in 1955, the Grosse Landesloge asked "the Fraternity of the world for understanding of the errors of 1932–1935." The kind of errors was explained immediately: "We were subject to the error of the times that one could escape the fate intended for German Freemasonry by camouflage."[10] In this way, the legend of "camouflage" got started, and the topos circulated with its one-sided self-styling as a victim.

For continuity of *dramatis personae*, the following will serve to give just a few examples:

The former chairman of the Bielefeld Ring, Erich Awe, distinguished himself from the narrower group of *völkisch* Freemasons. Awe had a part in the "Frankfurt Convention" of 1947 which preceded the formation of the United Grand Lodge. In the same year, he was a member of the AASR, soon thereafter also a member of the Supreme Council of Germany. It was Awe who tried, in the beginning of the 1960s, to justify the agreement made at the "Convention" to let silence reign, by way of historical complicity, for the sake of simplicity. "Recognizing that just the report of conflict has an unfavorable influence on the human psyche," Awe wrote, the participants promised each other that "all conflicts of our ancestors [and also one's own!—author's note] before 1935 would be consigned to oblivion." This "dragon's seed of constant turmoil," so he hoped, should, if at all, lurk in archives, and be accessible at most only for scholarly purposes." Awe stubbornly insisted that no one had demanded that the historical antecedents of public Freemasonry be "forced open." "The old Freemasons did not, because they were happy not to hear about these conflicts for decades, and those who have joined more recently also did not because of the terrible events of their youth, they did not want to know anything about the conflicts of their predecessors."[11] A commotion caused by Walther Hörstmann's candidacy for the position of AASR Chairman formed the background of these explanations. Hörstmann was supposed to become the new Grand Commander as proposed by Theodor Vogel. The plan failed after a letter from Hörstmann dated May 4, 1933 became known. In it, he had announced his resignation from Freemasonry and confirmed his intention of becoming a member of the Nazi Party. The possibility of gaining recognition, so Hörstmann said at the time, did not seem to be given, although "it removed not only the name 'Freemason', but also the form and the connection to past epochs, and thus created the prerequisite for a completely new construction." He continued, opining that "we may no longer stand aside waiting to see what will happen, but it is just we, who are even obligated because of our decades-long education in the association, to carry on and enlarge the national revolution that began on January 30."[12] The constitutional judge Dr. Erich Schalscha was elected instead of Hörstmann, although previously in a conversation "of a rather small number of members of... the choice of Brother Schalscha for the German Supreme Council was described as unfavorable for the German Supreme Council, because of his Jewish heritage (sic!) and for other personal reasons."[13]

Erich Awe, on the other hand, seems not to have gotten into difficulties because of his past. In 1963, he experienced a testimony of appreciation on the occasion of his 80th birthday in *Eleusis*, the journal of the German Supreme Council. He was acknowledged as being able to rejoice in the great respect accorded him "because of his many-faceted effectiveness in German Freemasonry." There was not one critical word concerning his German-*völkisch* activity. The Bielefeld Ring, "whose origin and effectiveness was due above all to Awe's initiative," was mentioned, but without making a problem of its [political] alignment. Instead, it said that Awe had been able to utilize his knowledge "in the best way for his efforts, begun in the 1920s, to intensify the speculative work in the German lodges."[14] Awe died four years later, and the *in memoriam*, also published in *Eleusis*, was no different. Without critical reflection, Awe's own justification was reprinted, in which, concerning the Bielefeld Ring, there was nothing about "a caustic remark from the national side against the universality of Freemasonry," but about a basis for intensifying Masonic work "within the lodges and in contact among the lodges."[15] At the same time, however, a claim was raised by the Supreme Council that "only politically clean, unencumbered Freemasons would be accepted."[16] Since the role that Awe had played in the Bielefeld Ring, and the outlooks and opinions represented there must have been generally known, the conclusion is obvious that his biography was not seen as 'encumbered.' It was probably enough from the point of view of "Overcoming the Past" that he did not belong to the Nazi Party, or only did for a short time, which, of course was not to Awe's credit, but only attributable to the Nazi guidelines.

Publicly, post-war German Freemasonry distanced itself from *völkisch* positions, for the most part, as these were discredited after the collapse of the "Third Reich." The inner break was not completed, let alone self-critical reflection on the political implications and historical responsibility in view of the unique German crimes. In other words, the *Völkisch* Freemasonry was not discussed critically, but silently integrated. Erich Awe was by no means a unique case. In just the same way, Oskar and Christian Zetzsche, surfaced as active Freemasons again (in, among others, the AASR), and, unhindered, even re-established connections with positions that had developed in Herman Wirth's circle. In his memoirs, mentioned in Chapter 4,[17] Christian Zetzsche, self-righteous and unteachable, promulgated *völkisch* thinking later in 1975. Apparently Masonic circles were not upset by that.

All the while, a man with an SS past, in the person of Georg C. Frommholtz, led the destiny of the Grosse Landesloge; he was Grand Master in

1973–1981. Frommholtz joined the lodge "Zum schwarzen Adler" ("Black Eagle"), a subordinate of the Three World Globes Grand Lodge in Berlin, at age 28 in 1931.[18] After his acceptance without a hitch into the Nazi Party in the spring of 1933, he attained the rank of "Truppführer" ("troop leader") or "Haupttruppführer" ("Chief troop leader") in the Nazi hierarchy in April 1934.[19] His further career in the "Third Reich" is unclear.

An order, presumably for dismissal, dated May 25, 1937, from the SS-Oberabschnitt-Ost (Main Section—East) because of his alleged formal resignation request on November 29, 1934 seems to be a forgery undertaken with great probability by Frommholtz as an afterthought.[20] Although this fact was uncovered already in 1973, in lodge circles, i.e., at the time of his becoming Grand Master of the Grosse Landesloge, neither Frommholtz nor the Grosse Landesloge felt compelled to make anything of it. In other cases, however, the revealing of the former SS membership did force the Freemasons concerned to resign from their lodges.[21]

Looking back, Theodor Vogel thought that the enemies of Freemasonry in the Weimar Republic and the "Third Reich" were attacking an already divided Fraternity, a Fraternity in which "Brothers opposed Brothers, teachings opposed teachings." They could not pull themselves together and unite "for true resistance,"[22] from which he drew the consequence of a questionable unification strategy, personified by himself. Vogel continued: the hour in which German Freemasonry had been called to struggle against inhumanity and tyranny became instead "the hour of breakdown."[23] This is doubtlessly true for by far the majority of lodges, —though not all. "German Freemasonry" as a power in society with a common spiritual (mental) foundation, which might have been in the position for "true resistance," did not exist.

Summary

reemasonry in National Socialism: One might ask, "Is that a chapter of forgotten persecution or a legend of a persecution?" The answer would have to be differentiated: "Neither, nor; yet some of both." The history of the German lodges and their members in the Weimar Republic and the "Third Reich" is a history of conflict *and* conformity. The question would be falsely put, if it were based on the fundamental assumption of a more or less unified Freemasonry. There was, however, never any such thing, especially not in Germany, and definitely not in the first half of the twentieth century. Heterogeneous currents had developed long since in lodges all over the world. With the radicalization of society in the first Republic, the polarization of Freemasonry became increasingly sharp. The path that the small number of groups of "internationalistic" Freemasons defended against hostilities from many sides, led them into opposition to Nazism and finally exile. The path that especially the Old Prussians chose, led, in the Weimar years, to the establishment of *völkisch* Freemasonry, and ended with the racist German-Christian Orders in the "Third Reich"—including the forfeiting of Masonic identity. However, that did not enable them to continue. However, it did not hinder them from remembering their Masonic tradition again after the fall of Nazism, and reconnecting to it; in other words, to begin a renewed change in tradition.

When the tradition was changed in 1933, there was a radical shifting of weight, which could happen without an ideological distortion. The

Old Prussians went back to the rejection of "world Freemasonry" that they had always espoused, and to their special role under the protection of the Hohenzollerns. Now they really played the "Spirit of the Order" off against the "Spirit of the Lodge," and they substituted the national Christian orders for their Masonic tradition, calling up Templar and allegedly "Aryan" tradition as they did so. Freemasonry was really only an outer shell that was used for a time. The advance work done by the extreme right wing proved helpful during this reorientation. It allowed them to grab onto the pseudo-scholarly derivation of Freemasonry from "ancient Germanic customs" and the "Nordic culture of light." The grand lodge administration took over the radical positions of the "ring lodges" in a limited way, in their official announcements, even after the seizure of power. They definitely did make use of ideas developed there, in order to legitimize ideologically their continuation, and to recommend themselves as "the last keepers" of the "ancient German mystery cult."[1]

There were greater or lesser differences in essence [basic character] among the German jurisdictions. Only the group of established humanitarian grand lodges was heterogeneous in and of itself. The relationship between the two poles—between the Christian-national or *völkisch* Freemasons and the liberal Freemasons obligated to the principle of tolerance [who belonged to] the (Grand Lodge) Aufgehende Sonne and the Symbolische Grossloge—was characterized by deep, unbridgeable differences. In all, the spectrum of German lodges was so differentiated that it would be more correct to speak of Freemasonries.

The sharp contours of the lodge landscape in Germany showed more clearly than in other countries that the development of Freemasonry since its origin in the early eighteenth century had been influenced by a progressive and a reactionary line of tradition. Cross-connections and reciprocal influences existed with the Enlightenment, emancipation proposals, and liberalism, but also just as much with the thought of Christian-*völkisch* orders and anti-Enlightenment, conservative-authoritarian planning. Categories determined both by politics and the kind of teaching (Masonic-esoteric) overlapped each other, and entered an indissoluble connection on both sides, which also put the claim of "apolitical" into question. Free-masonry's consciously assumed abstinence from party-political arguments and its traditional definition as an ethical alliance of political organizations are plausible. On the other hand, the established German lodges' continued to understand themselves as "apolitical," per se, while the effects of this understanding were highly political. Most Freemasons, especially the Old Prussians, identified themselves with an uncritical "National interest," and demanded that all individual interests were to be made subordinate to the dominant interest. They felt that the Weimar Republic was opposed to this "national interest," and therefore rejected it. Because of Masonic reticence and a politically passive fundamental position, its picture of the State was turned more backward than forward in the sense of a "conservative Revolution" aimed at a new *völkisch* humanity, in which nevertheless, there were commonalities with respect to the world-view.

In the context of the *völkisch* movement of the nineteenth century, a tendency began to manifest itself in the German lodges that consolidated itself into a concept of Christian-"Aryan" Freemasonry after World War I, in which religious and *völkisch* paradigms were mixed. The development of this line of thought, the endeavors of which would go far beyond the national-conservative, was fostered by a framework of conditions. Thus, German nationalism finally lost its, at first, democratic-emancipatory function. After that the esoteric character of Freemasonry moved into the foreground in the circles of the regular grand lodges in general, and, in connection with the supposedly "apolitical" inwardness, completed a turn to conservatism.

The self-elimination of opposition or coordination of different grand lodges in 1933 marked the endpoint of a continuous developmental process in the Weimar years. The division, which crystallized around the so-called "Jewish Question" and the political post-war problems, was made outwardly visible by the break-up of the German Federation of Grand Lodges, and it became ever more lasting. That which separated the wings of German Free-masonry finally became so great that by the end of Weimar (i.e. the Weimar

Republic), there was hardly anything remaining in common. The personal comprehensions of being a Freemason of, for example, Leo Müffelmann or Felix Witt-Hoë were in total opposition, although each was completely and deeply convinced of the validity of his own version.

Indeed for that reason there could be no antagonism between Freemasonry and so-called totalitarianism. Aside from the fact that the hostile position of Bolshevism vis-à-vis the lodges did not change the structural differences between Nazism and the Soviet system, many former lodge members later held leading positions in the "Third Reich," while others belonged to the Resistance. By far most Old Prussians, and even some members of humanitarian lodges, felt that the central ideological elements of Nazism were not fundamentally contradictory, but actually complementary to their understanding of Freemasonry. In this vein, the chairman of the Association of German Freemasons, Diedrich Bischoff, recommended to the "Third Reich"—before the "seizure of power"—that it should seek inspiration from Masonic idealism.[2] After the "seizure of power" by the Nazis, that which was *"völkisch"* became the normative main line of Old Prussian grand lodge policy.

Parts of German Freemasonry were in complicity with the "Third Reich." In the ranks of the Fraternity, and especially among the responsible functionaries, people succumbed to the self-delusion that the Nazis would possibly be amenable to the continuance of the new Orders. For this reason, they were ready and willing to be mobilized. The term "complicity" is justified, first, because racist categories—and therefore the constitutive elements of National Socialism[3]—were taken over from the *völkisch* opponents of Freemasonry, shown externally and applied internally. For this reason, the inclination still found today in lodge circles, to speak vaguely of the "dark time," or to transfigure all German Freemasons into resistance fighters is not justified by the actual situation.

It is significant that neither the well-thought-out *völkisch* manifestations during the Weimar years nor the development of the Old Prussian Order in 1933 were expressions of camouflage. In the sources, there is

322

not one hint—not even an indirect one—that would support the "camouflage thesis." Quite the opposite was confirmed, for example, by Kurt von Heeringen, the "Chancellor of the Order" in the Grosse Landesloge on May 12, 1933: "It has already been emphasized that our Order is not really in a position to keep its own spiritual content, without making use of a "camouflaged" Freemasonry."[4] If one interprets the many internal Masonic self-witnesses in connection with the deep, far-reaching contrasts among the lodge systems against the background of historical development, in no way do they prove to be pretended. The conflict, in which the members of the right-leaning lodges found themselves with their own, the national milieu, resulted from the fact that their picture of themselves and the outside's picture of them did not agree. The self-picture can be clearly derived, and must thus be taken seriously.[5] The position that the right-leaning Freemasons very consciously adopted had a component strongly influenced by tradition and desirous of conformity. In certain respects, a fundamental misunderstanding was expressed in the focusing on the creation of the German-Christian Order and on the question connected with it as to whether it was a change in mentality or indeed a camouflaged one. The transformations were not a camouflage just for this reason: the body of thought expressed was previously already the authority; thus, one could have dispensed with outward transformation. After the liberation, the maintaining of the idea of "camouflage," originally a weapon of the Nazis, was taken over by the Freemasons, and handed out as a reason for their actions, by way of self-justification.

In the case of *völkisch* Freemasonry, there was a phenomenon that infringed upon the grand lodges. It was, however, rooted and spread out differently in the individual systems, on the whole, clearly more among the Old Prussians than the humanitarians. Nevertheless, if one can ever speak of a convergence in the context of German lodge history up to 1935, it was in the sense of a nationalization of established Freemasonry. Particularly, the attitude of resistance of the less extreme systems was increasingly influenced by the strategy of the right wing of the German lodges. The fear of ending up in the rear guard, in case the most important and decisive delimitation strategy would fail, encouraged the general public contest for the favor of the nationalistic powers.

When the humanitarian Orders originated in 1933, there was no comparable expression of political opinions conforming to the system among them.[6] The primary reason was to gain time to save financial and tangible goods. Of course, that could not happen in the case of the Old Prussians. Despite the political pressure and only very small space for action, the grand lodge functionaries sought an active role for their organizations in the National Socialistic state. All attempts to secure an officially-sanctioned special status, for example, to fit into the structure of the "Third Reich" while maintaining a certain independence remained futile.

Freemasons—even the Christian-National ones—were persecuted under the Nazi terror-rule; lodge members collectively were exposed to sharp defamation; many had to put up with professional and social discrimination; some were—mainly for political or "racist" reasons— persecuted and imprisoned. Masonic organizations sometimes lost considerable financial assets. They were driven to self-dissolution, in case they had not already fled Germany or were forbidden by decree of the Reichstag. Lodge inventories and Masonic archives were confiscated. In no small amounts was this material then misused for exhibits denouncing Freemasonry, or for other propaganda purposes. Not the least, individual Freemasons participated in significant ways in the Resistance and paid for that with their lives.

The immediate connection with the Jews on the levels of ideology and action lent the "Freemason Question" a central meaning in the Nazi racist state. Anti-Semitic, anti-enlightenment, anti-liberal, anti-democratic, and anti-intellectual elements all united within the opposition to the lodges stigmatized as "übervölkisch" (above the proper, conforming, pro-Teutonic, pro-Nazi ordinary people). Already in the Weimar years, the connection between anti-Semitism and anti-Masonry was established as a topos of a Jewish-Masonic conspiracy, which suggested that the reasons for visible societal conditions or crisis situations were to be sought in the effects of hidden powers. The "ideologized" conspiracy thought implied and reproduced a disposition of thought that closed itself to cognitive reason. Therefore all resistance strategies failed, whether they were rational, argumentative discussions with the same absurd accusations, or statistics on men who fell or were wounded in the First World War, or assurances that one was as nationalistic as the attacker.

No different from the *völkisch* groupings with respect to their propaganda struggle were the Nazis in power after January 30, 1933 neither willing nor in a position to distinguish between Freemasons and Freemasons. In contrast, the Old Prussians misinterpreted the fact that they were not immediately forbidden, and allowed nothing to be untried, over more than two years, trying to convince the Party and the government of their world-view (philosophical) dependability. Familiarity and self-subjugation, however, did not help; the decision makers were not about to tolerate Freemasonry—even *völkisch* Freemasonry—or integrate it into the Party structure. Other esoteric buildings and, of course, their forms of organization into lodges stood diametrically opposed to the Nazi model of a racistically organized people's community, and its own adaptation of the ideology of an order. It did not matter that the German-Christian Order understood its activity as a complementary element in the "Third Reich."

The attempt of the Masonic orders to continue to exist failed not only because of the purposefulness of firm images of an enemy among propagandistic viewpoints, but also because of the methodical way that those in power enforced their world-view concept. As little as the mobilization of the Old Prussian lodges was "camouflage," just as little were Party and Government inclined, after years of struggle, to accept a correction to their rejection of any kind of Freemasonry. The Orders were generally put down as "camouflage," and a mostly undifferentiated anti-Masonry belonged to the "common sense" of the national milieu beyond the Nazi Party. The differences in interest and opinion that existed among Hitler, Himmler, Heydrich, Rosenberg, Buch, and the no less ideologized technocrats in the security apparatus were after all secondary. The corners of the political and propagandistic treatment of the "Freemason Question" were defined by a fundamental consensus shared by the Nazi power centers. According to it (despite certain differences), all lodges were led by common internationalistic goals, carried by the ideals of equality and tolerance, and a tool of the Jews. For this reason, the thesis according to which Hitler and his Party people "in another historical situation..." would have "just as well sought an alliance with Freemasonry,"[7] remains completely abstract. Although pragmatism did characterize Nazi Masonic policy, it would have been neither good to aid the formation of such an alliance, nor would it have fit into the accomplishment of their political and world-view realities, except with great difficulty.

Heinrich August Winkler made a note that contemporaries would have answered the question in another way—according to the demands of the Weimar democracy—than the historians from the distance of many decades would have been inclined to: "For most Germans who consciously experienced the time between 1918 and 1933, the fourteen years of the first Republic were not under the shadow of the Empire, but that of Versailles."[8] One must of course add that the nationalistic powers successfully set everything in motion to gain political capital out of the widespread mental rejection of the Treaty of Versailles and to mobilize latent resentment. *Völkisch* ideologues had understood that the fairy tale of the world conspiracy suited their purposes perfectly. The Jews were more often made scapegoats, but then, they were more widely supplemented by the Freemasons who were allegedly allied with them. In such a societal climate, the attempts supported by individual Masonic organizations to seek a political–economic equalization of interests and an equitable peace arrangement according to practical solutions had, from the outset, a very slim chance of succeeding.

Although collectively atypical because of its double role as persecuted and sympathizer of the Nazi regime, the example of the members of the right wing lodges shows very clearly the continuities of anti-democratic-*völkisch* thinking. This led to the fact that the end of Weimar was cheered in many sectors of the population. In the case of national Freemasonry, apprehensive anticipation mixed itself with the fundamental political agreement with respect to the "seizure of power." It was clear to the Fraternity as well as the leadership of grand lodges, despite a show of optimism that their own future under the new circumstances was anything but assured.

It was not possible to treat exhaustively all aspects of the complex of questions raised here. Some answers are outstanding and must be reserved for future works. For example, a thorough, detailed examination of the activities of individual St. John's lodges of the Wetzlar and Bielefeld Rings between 1933 and 1935 is necessary. The same is true for the clarification of the discrepancies already mentioned, as to whether and to what extent subordinate lodges of the Grosse Landesloge and the grand Lodge "Friendship" were affiliated with the Wetzlar Ring. An exact quantification of Ring lodges and their members, i.e. a statistical inclusion of Ring adherents between 1925 and 1935, is desirable. In addition, it is necessary to illuminate the *völkisch* leanings in humanitarian lodges in more detail, especially with those which existed as Christian orders for a rather long time after the "seizure of power." Aside from the attempts already mentioned at a more extensive study of the historiographic problems of Freemasonry in the narrower sense, there is need for a special discussion of how the treatment of the German-Christian Orders fits into early Nazi church policy. Not to be omitted is an indication of the desirability of discussing the Masonic background of leading representatives of the German Resistance in the context of their personal and political lives. There are still gaps in the research on the connections between Freemasonry and other organizational forms in society. An example of this is the well-known Masonic influence on corporations. In addition, it has not been sufficiently studied how anti-Masonry has affected the internal workings of student connection even to the question of how in detail the incompatibility determinations shifted between 1933 and 1935.

Although the German-*völkisch* body of thought was not completely undisputed in any system, there was a constitutive character for a quantitatively strong, independent strength in the lodge spectrum. Just as anti-Semitism and ethnically derived nationalism could win a base in the masses in Germany, so *völkisch* Freemasonry succeeded in building a lasting influence within the Fraternity. Generally, political-social tendencies found their image in the world-view discussions among Freemasons. Aside from the questionable postulate of the "apolitical," the lodges were, as always, interdependent with the "profanes" on the outside.

It has become clear how misleading it would be to cling to the image of Freemasonry as a unified entity with common mental-spiritual foundations. The characteristics of German Freemasonry differ so profoundly, and the membership belonged to other political milieus. Therefore, it is not surprising, that in the face of the *völkisch* body of thought and finally of the "seizure of power," German Freemasons took differing positions. The reactions ranged from consistent opposition to consistent self-elimination and consolidation. In other words: they ranged between conflict and conformity towards the "Third Reich." These contrasting forms of action were the result of patterns of approach or divergence of attitudes, in which collective mental and social dispositions of middle-class Germany in the first half of the twentieth century are mirrored.

Illustrations and Documents

Document 1: Photograph of Dr. Leo(pold) Müffelmann taken in 1931 (private collection)

הלשכה הגדולה למדינת ישראל
של בונים חופשים קדמונים ומקובלים
The Grand Lodge of the State of Israel
of Ancient Free and Accepted Masons

I.: B.: V.: D.: A.: B.: A.: W.:
לשכת מיפלמן אומן מספר 29
FM.: L.: MUEFFELMANN Z.: TR.:
תחת חסותה של הלשכה הגדולה למדינת ישראל
OR.: TEL-AVIV   מור: תל-אביב
5, Weizmann St. 5 רחוב ויצמן
Tel Aviv   64239 תל אביב

Document 2: Freemasonry Seal (logo-letterhead) of the Grand Lodge of the State of Israel with the "united in harmony" symbols of Judaism, Christianity, and Islam. Also the seal of the Lodge "Müffelmann zur Treue" in Tel Aviv (private collection)

FACING PAGE, TOP >

Document 3: Anti-Masonry-Conspiracy Myth: the fan chart of the "Jewish secret government." (From: Anonymous. *"The Hangmen and Arsonists of the World", Revealed and Their 2000-year-old Conspiracy System: The Key to World History and World Politics* (Munich: 1928) p. 105. Bundesarchiv ZSg 2.126 [8]).

Fan chart: hub labeled Jewish Secret Government: Left to right each spoke/rib having a label: Freemasonry–Communism; Freemasonry–Social Democracy; Freemasonry–Roman Church–Jesuitism–Center; Freemasonry–Protestant Church–Capitalist World–German Folks Party; Freemasonry–Protestant Church–Large Land holdings–German National Party; no spoke/rib but a label: Völkisch Groups.

FACING PAGE, BOTTOM >

Document 4: Anti-Masonry-Conspiracy Myth: Manuscript (postcard) of Wilhelm II written in Doorn on August 23, 1928. GLL Archives.

"Enclosed is a copy from secret documents of Freemasonry, with the copyist's notes. How can officers participate in such work! And Knights of St. John! Wilhelm."

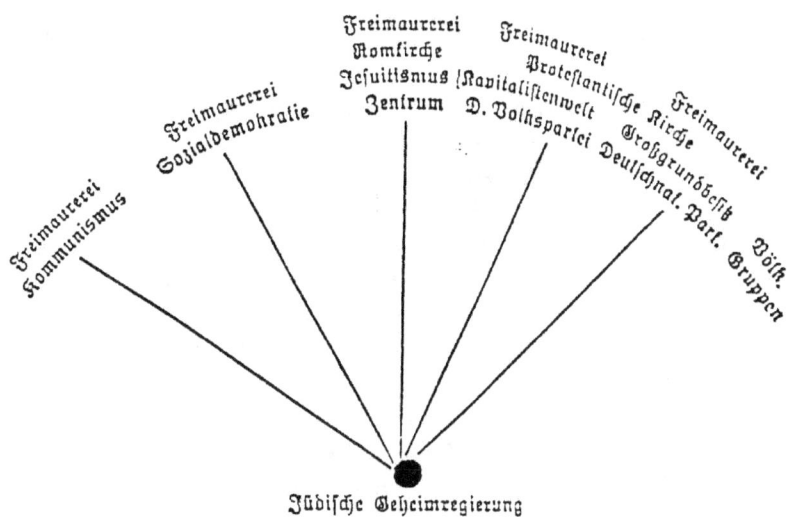

Freimaurerei Kommunismus · Freimaurerei Sozialdemohratie · Freimaurerei Romkirche Jesuitismus Zentrum · Freimaurerei Protestantische Kirche Kapitalistenwelt D. Volkspartei Großgrundbesitz Deutschnat. Part. Völk. Gruppen

Jüdische Geheimregierung

Doorn 23. VIII. 28

Anbei Abschrift eines Geheimaktstückes der
Freimaurerei mit Anmerkungen des
Abschreibers. Wie können Offiziere an
solchem Werk sich beteiligen!
Auch Johanniterritter.

Wilhelm I. R.

333

LUDENDORFF ODER DER VERFOLGUNGSWAHN

Hast du Angst, Erich? Bist du bange, Erich?
Klopft dein Herz, Erich? Läufst du weg?
Wolln die Maurer, Erich – und die Jesuiten, Erich,
dich erdolchen, Erich – welch ein Schreck!
    Diese Juden werden immer rüder.
    Alles Unheil ist das Werk der ∴ ∴ Brüder.

Denn die Jesuiten, Erich – und die Maurer, Erich –
und die Radfahrer – die sind schuld
an der Marne, Erich – und am Dolchstoß, Erich –
ohne die gäbs keinen Welttumult.
    Jeden Freitag abend spielt ein Kapuziner
    mit dem Papste Skat – dazu ein Feldrabbiner;
    auf dem Tische liegt ein Grand mit Vieren –
    dabei tun sie gegen Deutschland konspirieren ...
    Hindenburg wird älter und auch müder ...
    Alles Unheil ist das Werk der ∴ ∴ Brüder.

Fährst du aus dem Schlaf? Die blaue Brille
liegt auf deinem Nachttisch wohl bereit?
Hörst du Stimmen?
                Das ist Gottes Wille,
Ludendorff, und weißt du, wer da schreit –?
    Hunderttausende, die jung und edel
    sterben mußten, weil dein dicker Schädel
    sie von Grabenstück zu Grabenstück gehetzt
                bis zuletzt.

Ackerkrume sind, die Deutschlands Kraft gewesen.
Pack die Koffer! Geh zu den Chinesen!
Führ auch die bei ihren Kriegen!
Ohne Juden wirst du gleichfalls unterliegen.
    Geh nach China! Und komm nie mehr wieder –!
    Alles Unheil ist das Werk der Heeresbrüder.

< FACING PAGE

Document 5: "All Mischief is the Work of the Brethren": satirical poem by Kurt Tucholsky about Ludendorff from 1927. Mary Gerold-Tucholsky, ed. *Gedichte* (Reinbek: Rowohlt Verlag GmbH ©1960, 1983): 621f. The poem is called "Ludendorff or the Persecution Complex."

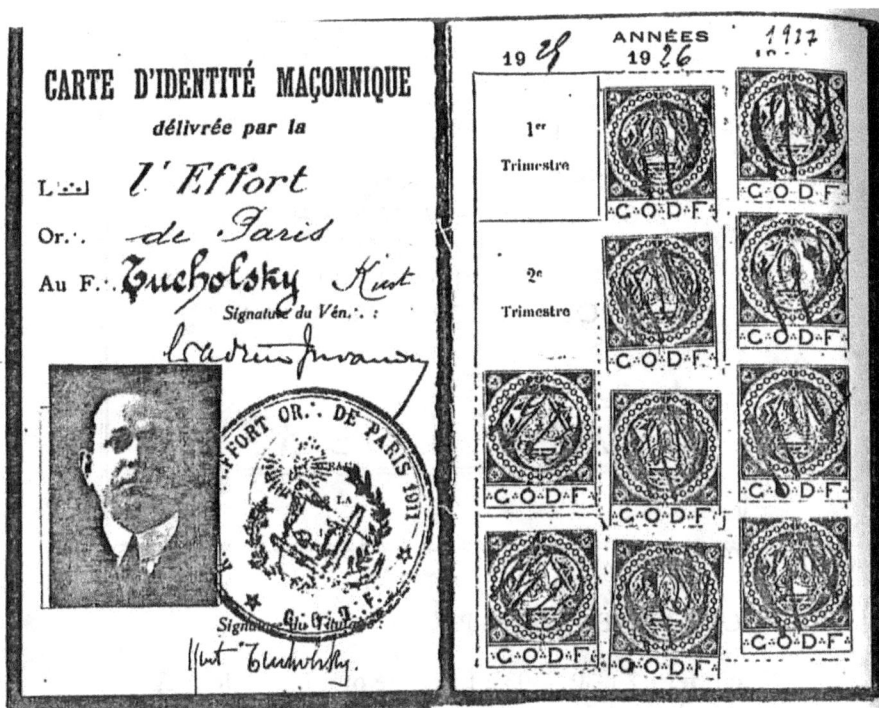

Document 6: Kurt Tulcholsky's membership card in the Lodge "L'Effort" in Paris (Grand Orient de France) in 1926–1929 (private collection).

SYMBOLISCHE GROSSLOGE VON DEUTSCHLAND

ARBEITSPLAN

DER

JOHANNIS-LOGEN

„MOZART"
„KANT ZUM EWIGEN FRIEDEN"
„LABOR"
„SETTEGAST ZUR TREUEN HAND"
„POST NUBILA PHOEBUS"

OR. BERLIN

APRIL 1932

ABOVE ^ AND FACING PAGE>

Document 7 (301-303): Example of a Masonic lodge notice (including the trestleboard: the "work plan" or agenda) of the four subordinate lodges of the Symbolische Grossloge (Symbolic Grand Lodge of Germany) in Berlin. April 1932 (private collection).

Zeit	Arbeit
Freitag 1. April	**Kant z. ewigen Frieden** — Arbeit in I. Leitung M.·. v.·. St.·. Br.·. Zucker. Affiliation von Brrn.·. u.Vortrag des Ehrw.·. Brs.·. Zucker über die Bundesthemen.
Dienstag 5. April	Reserviert für **A.·.F.·.L.·.**
Freitag 8. April	**Labor** — Arbeit in I. Leitung M.·. v.·. St.·. Br.·. Koner. "Bundesthemen". Anschließend Diskussion an der weißen Tafel.
Dienstag 12. April	Reserviert für **A.·.u.·.A.·.S.·.R.·.**
Freitag 15. April	**Vereinigte Bundeslogen** Instruktion für Brr.·. aller Grade. Leitung M.·. v.·. St.·. Br.·. Bensch. Vortrag des Ehrw.·. Brs.·. Koner: "Mr.·. Verkehrsformen in Wort und Schrift". Anschließend Aussprache.
Sonntag 17. April ³/₄9 Uhr vm.	**Vereinigte Bundeslogen** Führung durch das **Pergamon-Museum** und Vortrag d. Kunsthistorikers Dr. Fritz Schiff (Dozent an der Humboldt-Hochschule) über: "Tron des Satans" (Off.Joh.Kap.2,13) **Treffpunkt:** ³/₄9 Uhr vorm. vor der Nationalgalerie am Amazonen-Denkmal. Teilnahme pro Person RM 1.30. Schw. und Gäste sehr erwünscht. **Anmeldungen** mit Angabe der Personenzahl **b. spätestens** 12.April an Br. Ernst Borchardt, Berlin SO 16, Köpenickerstr. 109
Dienstag 19. April	**Kant z. ewigen Frieden** Leitung M.·. v.·. St.·. Br.·. Zucker. Vortrag von Dr. Wolf Zucker über: "Kann Goethe heute noch Vorbild sein?" für Brr.·. Schw.·. und Gäste.

Zeit	Arbeit
Freitag 22. April	**Mozart** — Mitgliederversammlung. **Labor** — Mitgliederversammlung. **Post nubila Phoebus** — Mitgliederversammlung. Anschließend **Stuhlmeister-Konferenz**
Dienstag 26. April	**Settegast z. tr. Hand** — Arbeit in III. Leitung M.·. v.·. St.·. Br.·. Liebermann. Erhebung der Brr.·. Ges.·. Schrayer und Andres in den Meistergrad.
Freitag 29. April	**Mozart** — Arbeit in I. Leitung M.·. v.·. St.·. Br.·. Loewe. Instruktion. Anschließend Diskussion an der weißen Tafel.

Zur Beachtung!

Die Arbeiten und Veranstaltungen finden, soweit nichts anderes angegeben ist, im Logenheim in Berlin, Kurfürstendamm 48/49 statt und beginnen **pünktlich 8 Uhr abends.**

Bei **Tempelarbeiten,** die im Arbeitsplan als **"Arbeiten"** kenntlich gemacht sind, ist Frack oder Smoking (evtl. dunkler Anzug) und mr. Bekleidung erforderlich.

Die gemeinsamen Arbeiten oder Veranstaltungen der in Berlin arbeitenden Bundeslogen der Symbolischen Großloge von Deutschland werden im Arbeitsplan künftig unter der Bezeichnung **"Vereinigte Bundeslogen"** angekündigt werden.

Berlin, den 29. März 1933

An die
    Logen der Symbolischen Grossloge von Deutschland !

Gel. Br. !

        Grossmeister und Grossbeamtenrat der Symbolischen Grossloge
von Deutschland haben unter dem 27./28. März 1933 den nachfolgenden Beschluss
gefasst:

        " Die Symbolische Grossloge von Deutschland wird eingeschläfert.
        Der eingetragene Verein Symbolische Grossloge von Deutschland wird
        aufgelöst. Die Löschung im Vereinsregister in Hamburg ist unter dem
        28. März 1933 bereits erfolgt. Der bisherige Br. Schatzmeister ist zu
        der Abwicklung der finanziellen Verhältnisse (Sterbekasse) bevoll-
        mächtigt. "

        Begründung:

        Die Symbolische Grossloge von Deutschland hat seit dem Tage
ihrer Gründung mit allen Kräften daran gearbeitet, das Programm der Alten
Pflichten durchzuführen. Sie hat auf den Alten Pflichten aufgebaut und diese
Grundlage niemals verlassen. Neben der Arbeit an dem einzelnen Menschen, der
sittlichen Erziehung des Einzelnen, hat sie sich eingesetzt für die Verstän-
digung der Völker, für die Schaffung der Menschheitskette.
        Diese ihre Arbeit läuft nun aber Gefahr, in ein falsches
Licht zu geraten. Es wird schwer, ja geradezu unmöglich, die Aufgaben und
Ziele der Freimaurerei, wie sie sich auf den Alten Pflichten gründen, klar
und rein zu vertreten. Es werden Gegensätze konstruiert, die ganz sicher
nicht vorhanden sind, die aber als vorhanden angenommen werden. Heisst doch
Satz II der Alten Pflichten:

        " Der Maurer ist ein friedfertiger Untertan der bürger-
        lichen Gewalt, wo er auch wohnet und arbeitet und muss sich nie in
        Meuterei und Verschwörung gegen den Frieden und die Wohlfahrt der
        Nation einlassen, noch sich pflichtwidrig gegen die Unterobrigkei-
        ten betragen ".

        Und in den allgemeinen maurerischen Grundsätzen der Symbo-
lischen Grossloge von Deutschland ist festgelegt:

        " Der Freimaurerbund ist ein sittlicher, kein politischer
        Verein. Er beteiligt sich nicht an politischen oder kirchlichen Par-
        teikämpfen und vermeidet in den Logen alles, was zu politischen oder
        konfessionellen Auseinandersetzungen führen kann.

ABOVE ^ AND FACING PAGE>

Document 8: (304-306): Two circular letters from the
Symbolische Großloge dated March 29, 1933.

338

Dem Freimaurer sind Vaterlandsliebe und Pflichten des Staatsbürgers heilig. Er sieht aber keinen Gegensatz zwischen Vaterlandsliebe und Liebe zu allen Menschen. "

Grossmeister und Grossbeamtenrat glauben aber, dass es heute nicht zweckmässig und wünschenswert ist, das Problem der Freimaurerei zur Diskussion zu stellen und die Bedeutung der Alten Pflichten zu erörtern.

Aus diesem Grunde haben Grossmeister und Grossbeamtenrat beschlossen, die Symbolische Grossloge von Deutschland einzuschläfern und gleichzeitig die vereinsrechtlichen Konsequenzen aus diesem Beschluss zu ziehen.

Mit brdl. Grüssen
i.d.u.h.Z.

Berlin, den 29. März 1933

An die
Logen der Symbolischen Grossloge von Deutschland !

Gel. Br. !

Betr. Kampf gegen Greuelnachrichten.

Die Symbolische Grossloge von Deutschland hat an die Grosslogen des Auslandes, darunter auch an die Grossloge von New York, Grossloge von England, Grande Loge de France, Tschechoslowakische Grossloge und die Grossloge " Alpina " das nachstehende Telegramm gesandt:

" Symbolische Grossloge von Deutschland erklärt Greuelnachrichten für schamlos erlogen und erbittet dringend energisches Eingreifen im Interesse der Völkerverständigung gegen diese Hetze ".

Mit brdl. Grüssen
i.d.u.h.Z.

Deutsch-Chriftlicher Orden
St. Johannis-Konvent Berlin
gen.: „Friedrich Wilhelm zur Morgenröte"
Deutsch=Chriftlicher Orden
St. Johannis-Konvent
genannt

Berlin, den 7ten September 1933

Lieber Ordensbruder!

Unter Bezugnahme auf nachstehende auszugsweise wiedergegebene Verordnung bitte ich Sie, beifolgenden Fragebogen mir bis spätestens 1. November d. J. genau ausgefüllt zurückzusenden.

„Deutsch-Chriftlicher Orden   Berlin, den 6. September 1933.
Der Ordens * Meister   Tgb.-Nr. 961.

Die mit dem Siege der nationalen Revolution zur allgemeinen Anerkennung gelangte, für unser Volk schicksalhafte Bedeutung der Raffenfragen gibt mir Veranlaffung zu der nachstehenden, auf Grund des Ermächtigungsgesetzes vom 23. April 1933 erlaffenen

Verordnung.

1. Ordensbrüder, die nicht arischer Abstammung sind, sind aus dem Orden mit sofortiger Wirkung ehrenvoll entlaffen.
2. Diese Bestimmung gilt nicht für Ordensbrüder, die bereits vor dem 1. August 1914 in den Orden eingetreten sind oder im Weltkriege in der Front für das Deutsche Reich oder für seine Verbündeten gekämpft haben oder deren Söhne und Väter im Weltkriege gefallen sind.
3. Personen arischer Abstammung im Sinne dieser Verordnung sind solche, deren Eltern und Großeltern Arier gewesen sind.
4. Für Ordensbrüder, deren Ehefrauen Jüdinnen sind, gilt das in Punkt 1 Verordnete.
5. Bestehen im Einzelfalle Zweifel, ob die Vorausfetzungen der Punkte 1 bis 4 gegeben sind, so ist die Entscheidung der Ordensleitung einzuholen, deren Beschluß endgültig ist.

Der Ordens * Meister
J. V.:
Volle
Ordens-Statthalter."

Mit ordensbrüderlichem Gruß!

Berman

ABOVE ^ AND FACING PAGE>

Document 9: (307-308) *Völkisch* Freemasonry: Order (Decree) about the introduction of the "Aryan Paragraph" and questionnaire of the Große Landeloge/German-Christian Order, September 1933 (GLL Archives).

340

Vordruck,

1. Zuname

   Vornamen
   (Rufname zu unterstreichen)

   Geburtsort

     Kreis

     Staat

   Geburtstag

   Religion

   Beruf
   (Genaue Angabe der Stellung in diesem)

2. Welche Persönlichkeiten können
   Auskunft über Sie erteilen?

3. Jetziger Wohnort

     seit

     Wohnung

   Früherer Wohnort

     von   bis

4. Tag und Jahr der Verehelichung

   Ruf- und Geburtsname der Frau

   Religion der Frau

   Ledig oder Witwer?

5. Zu- und Vorname des Vaters

   Religion des Vaters

   Stand des Vaters

6. Sind oder waren Ihre Eltern
   und Großeltern Arier?

   Sind oder waren die Eltern und
   Großeltern Ihrer Frau
   Arier?

7. Was bestimmt Sie, die Auf-
   nahme in den Orden zu suchen?

---

*) Die Stellung weiterer Fragen bleibt den einzelnen Konventen überlassen.

An den Führer!

Gehöre, Führer, meine Klage,
Die mir des Herzens bitt'rer Gram,
Das Leid erpresst, das ich ertrage,
Nachdem man mir die Ehre nahm.
Als Vaterlandsverräter soll ich gelten;
So dürfen Deutsche mich verblendet schelten!

Von deutschen Eltern streng erzogen,
Hab' über alles ich geliebt
Die Heimat und sie nie betrogen,
So wahr es einen Höchsten gibt,
Der über Alles einst gerecht wird richten,
Was ich versäumt, was ich erfüllt an Pflichten.

Die Sonne deutschen Geistesgutes
Hat wärmend mir die Brust durchglüht,
Wenn ich im Ringen meines Blutes
Nach Freiheit strebend mich bemüht,
Durch deutschen Geist hab' ich den Weg gefunden
Zu meiner Seele Werden und Gesunden.

Nur deutscher Geist hat mich geleitet
Zu dem Erkennen höchster Pflicht,
So tret' ich denn, wohl vorbereitet,
Dereinst vor Gottes Angesicht;
Denn nichts kann mir den hohen Christenglauben
An Gott und an Unsterblichkeit mehr rauben.

Jetzt fühlen Millionen Seelen
Durch Deutschland Frühlingslüfte weh'n.
Und ich, ich soll beim Aufbau fehlen;
Ich soll verfehmt bei Seite steh'n?
„Für welche Schuld," so muss voll Stolz ich fragen,
„Bin ich verdammt, die Schande zu ertragen?"

Man sagt, der Bund, dem ich verschworen,
Durch dessen hohe Geisteszucht
Der Seele Freiheit nur geboren,
Sei falsch, — im innern Kern verrucht?
Ich bin ein frommer deutscher Christ geworden
Durch meinen reinen christlich deutschen Orden,

Und schmerzvoll schrei' ich's in die Lüfte:
„Ihr, die Ihr richtet, seid betört!"
Es mögen öffnen sich die Grüfte;
Der „Grossen" Stimme sei gehört,
Die einst mit uns in uns'rem Bund gewandelt,
Ob jemals wir in fremdem Dienst gehandelt.

Mit mir erheben ihre Hände
Viel tausend Brüder an der Zahl
Zu Dir, mein Führer, sprich und wende
Erkennend uns're Qual!
Streck' uns, die wir im Geist auf Deinen Wegen,
Vertrauend Deine Führerhand entgegen.

Und schenke Deiner Führung Segen
Auch uns, dass wir im Vaterland
Die höchsten Güter können pflegen
Mit Dir vereint, an Deiner Hand.
Als deutsche Christen woll'n wir treu sie halten,
Um uns're Kraft, Dir folgend, zu entfalten.

H. E. Hug. Meyer

Verf. Meister des St. Johannis-Krenerts „Zum Pelikan"
der Großen Landesloge der Freimaurer von Deutschland
Deutsch-Christlicher Orden,
im Verbande der drei Altpreußischen Großlogen.

Mit Zustimmung des Verfassers gezeichnet von Theodor Rougemont, Hamburg.

Document 10: *Völkisch* Freemasonry: "To 'Der Führer.'"
Undated (1933 or later) poem by the Sitting Master of the Lodge
"Zum Pelikan," a subordinate lodge of the Große Landeloge
(Deutsches Freimaurer-Museum Bayreuth [German Masonic
Museum Bayreuth], No. 80 III AB)

342

Document 11: *Völkisch* Freemasonry: Emblem of the office of the Worshipful Master—a stylized left-facing swastika, formed of compasses. Used by the National Christian Order Fredick the Great and the German-Christian Order "Friendship"—1933 or later. (from *Treue-Information*, No. 122/1/86, 64)

Erklärung

Die drei altpreußischen Großlogen geben hiermit dem Herrn Reichs- und Preußischen Minister des Innern, nachdem er ihnen unter Hinweis auf die Einheit des deutschen Volkes und die Ausschließlichkeit des in der NSDAP verkörperten Staatsgedankens die Auflösung nahe gelegt hat, folgende Erklärung ab:

Es ist stets der oberste Grundsatz der altpreußischen Großlogen und ihrer Tochterlogen gewesen, daß Vaterland, Staat und Volk bei sämtlichen Handlungen voran zu stehen haben. Demgemäß sind die drei Großmeister bereit, der ihnen erteilten Anregung Folge zu geben und den Großlogen sowie ihren Tochterlogen die Auflösung zu empfehlen.

Wenn bis heute die Großmeister sich zu diesem Schritt noch nicht entschließen konnten, so beruht dies darauf, daß sie angesichts der schwerwiegenden Angriffe gegen die Ehre der Altpreußischen Großlogen, der in ihnen zusammengeschlossenen Logen und deren Mitglieder nicht glaubten, um der Ehre willen die Verantwortung vor ihren Mitgliedern übernehmen zu können, solange auf ihnen der Vorwurf der feindlichen Einstellung zum Staate haftete. Dieser Vorwurf mußte von den in den Logen zusammengeschlossenen Mitgliedern um so schwerer empfunden werden, als sie stets eingedenk waren ihrer großen geschichtlichen Tradition, die von Friedrich dem Großen, dem größten Preußischen König, über die Helden der Freiheitskriege, wie den Fürsten Blücher, Scharnhorst und den Freiherrn vom Stein, über Kaiser Wilhelm I., den Gründer des Deutschen Reiches, zu den Helden des Weltkrieges führte. Die große Zahl der aus den Logen hervorgegangenen, um Volk und Staat hochverdienten Männer zeigt, daß der oberste Grundsatz der Logen auch stets von den Mitgliedern befolgt worden ist. Sie wissen sich frei von aller Schuld gegenüber den Angriffen, die gegen ihre Ehre erhoben worden sind.

Nachdem der Reichs- und Preußische Minister des Innern nunmehr an diesen unseren Grundsatz erinnert und von uns das schwerste Opfer der freiwilligen Auflösung erwartet, bringen wir es dar und fordern die Großlogen und ihre Tochterlogen auf, ihre Auflösung zu beschließen. Wir geben den Mitgliedern gemäß der Erklärung der Regierung als letzte Anordnung mit, daß sie getreu der bei uns immerbar gepflegten Gesinnung durch rastlose Arbeit an dem Neuaufbau des Staates und des deutschen Vaterlandes mitschaffen.

Document 12: *Völkisch* Freemasonry: Declaration of the Old Prussian grand lodges of their readiness for voluntary self-dissolution, May 1935 (GLL Archives)

344

Document 13: Anti-Masonry/Naziism: Poster or placard by Richard Schwarzkopf from the West German Masonic Museum, Düsseldorf (Düsseldorf 1935) From Düreigel & Winkler, eds. *Freimaurer: Solange die Welt Besteht* (Catalogue, Second Edition, Vienna: 1992/1993): p. 358.

Berlin, VI. Jahrgang
7. Folge 1939

Der Schulungsbrief

Das zentrale Monatsblatt der NSDAP und DAF (Hauptschulungsamt der NSDAP und Schulungsamt der DAF) Herausgeber-Der Reichsorganisationsleiter

Zur Stärkung seiner politischen Stellung versucht der Jude, die rassischen und staatsbürgerlichen Schranken einzureißen, die ihn zunächst noch auf Schritt und Tritt beengen. Er kämpft zu diesem Zwecke mit aller ihm eigenen Zähigkeit für die religiöse Toleranz und hat in der ihm vollständig verfallenen Freimaurerei ein vorzügliches Instrument zur Verfechtung wie aber auch zur Durchschiebung seiner Ziele. Die Kreise der Regierenden sowie die höheren Schichten des politischen und wirtschaftlichen Bürgertums gelangen durch maurerische Fäden in seine Schlingen, ohne daß sie es auch nur zu ahnen brauchen. Adolf Hitler: „Mein Kampf", Seite 345

Document 14: (313-314) Excerpt from the "Party Directive against the Freemasons" of the Nazi Party from 1939 (with a quote from *Mein Kampf*—GLL Archives)

BERLIN, VI. JAHRGANG   7. FOLGE, 1939

Der Schulungsbrief

Gegen die Freimaurerei

NORDEN

WESTEN   OSTEN

SÜDEN

Herausgeber: Der Reichsorganisationsleiter der NSDAP.

𝕹otes

INTRODUCTION

(1)   Hartmut Mehringer/Werner Röder. "Gegner, Widerstand, Emigration," in: Martin Broszat/Norbert Frei (Hrsg.), *Das Dritte Reich im Überblick. Chronik, Ereignisse, Zusammenhänge*, München, 2nd ed., 1990, p. 109.

(2)   Eberhard Aleff (Hrsg.). *Das Dritte Reich*, Hannover, 4th ed., 1970, p. 74.

(3)   Quoted from Friedrich John Böttner. *Zersplitterung und Einigung. 225 Jahre Geschichte der deutschen Freimaurer. An Hand von Dokumenten dargestellt*, Hamburg, 1962, p. 198.

(4)   Adolf Hitler. *Mein Kampf*, vol. 1: *Eine Abrechnung;* vol. 2: *Die nationalsozialistische Bewegung.* 2 vol. in 1, unabridged ed., München, 29th ed., 1933, p. 45.

(5)   Compare Helmut Reinalter, "Zur Aufgabenstellung der gegenwärtigen Freimaurer- forschung," in: Reinalter (ed.), *Freimaurer und Geheimbünde im 18. Jahrhundert in Mitteleuropa*, Frankfurt/M, 3rd ed., 1989, p. 9ff. and especially p. 20 (note 1).

Reinalter emphasizes "that modern complete depictions of the development of Freemasonry in individual European countries must be written." Historical-systematic examinations for the assessment of Freemasonry from the National Socialist viewpoint. Compare his essay, "Geheimgesellschaften und Revolution. Freimaurerei und Nationalsozialismus am Beispiel Alfred Rosenbergs," in: *Q.C.-Jahrbuch* no. 21/1984, Bayreuth, 1984, p. 55ff. The extensive catalogue of the international Masonic exhibit 1992-1993 (Katalog der Internationalen

Freimaurerausstellung) in Vienna affords a first look into the state of research into the history of Freemasonry, the tradition of anti-Masonry (including the anti-Masonry of the Nazis) as well as into individual problems: Günter Düriegl/Susanne Winkler (Hrsg.), *Freimaurer. Solange die Welt besteht,* Wien, 2nd ed., 1992/1993.

(6)   Compare the findings of Ralf Melzer, "Völkische Freimaurerei" 1922-1935 [M.A. thesis, Free University of Berlin], Berlin, 1994 as well as his "Die deutschen Logen und die völkische Herausforderung," in: *Q.C. Jahrbuch* no. 31/1994, Bayreuth, 1994, p. 151ff. In many ways noteworthy in this connection is the substantial material in the International Masonic Lexicon that appeared in 1932: Eugen Lennhoff/Oskar Posner, *Internationales Freimaurer-Lexikon,* Zürich/Leipzig/Wien, 1932 [or the unchanged reprint Wien/München, 1975]. From the contemporary perspective, the Lexicon takes different positions on political and Masonic problems in the Weimar Republic. The stature of this standard work, which is much more than a lexicon, is undiminished even today! It also contains a compilation of anti-Masonic publications after the World War I. The writer and journalist Lennhoff functioned in leading positions in the Grand Lodge of Vienna, the Supreme Council, and the general Masonic league (see Chapters 3.3 and 7.1). For "professional reasons" Lennhoff left his Lodge "Zukunft" ("Future") in November 1933. Shortly thereafter he left his post as editor-in-chief of the "Wiener Freimaurer-Zeitung." The circumstances of and motives for this surprising step remain unclear. Lennhoff himself said the reason was that his actvities as a journalist and writer required of necessity "internal and external freedom," but this is not completely convincing. Compare Lennhoff's explanation in the *Wiener Freimaurer-Zeitung,* no. 9/12, 1933, p. 91f. Possibly also, Lennhoffs disappointment at not becoming grand master was the reason for his resignation. Posner was a physician by profession, and among other things co-founder of the German-speaking Czech Grand Lodge "Lessing zu den drei Ringen." ("Lessing of the Three Rings"). In 1924 he took over the editorship of its journal, "Die drei Ringe."

(7)   Norman Cohn. *Die Protokolle der Weisen von Zion. Der Mythos von der jüdischen Weltverschwörung,* Köln/Berlin, 1969; Jacob Katz. *Jews and Freemasons in Europe, 1723-1939,* Cambridge/MA, 1970; Johannes Rogalla von Bieberstein,"Die These von der freimaurerischen Verschwörung," in: Helmut Reinalter (ed.), *Freimaurer und Geheimbünde im 18. Jahrhundert in Mitteleuropa,* Frankfurt/M. 3rd ed. 1989, p. 85ff.

(8)   Armin Pfahl-Traughber. *Der antisemitisch-antifreimaurerische Verschwörungsmythos in der Weimarer Republik und im NS-Staat*, Wien, 1993. Compare also the condensed description by François Morvan, *Aspects du mythe conspirationniste antimaçonnique en Allemagne*, Paris, 1994. Unfortunately the author does not free himself from the category of totalitarianism. He calls a comparative analysis of the conspiracy theory-myth in Europe desirable. Helmut Reinalter offers a short and pertinent description of the subject (with a certain emphasis on its history in Austria) in his "Auf der Suche nach Sündenböcken. Freimaurer im Mittelpunkt einer Verschwörungstheorie," in: *Q.C.-Berichte*, Heft 15/1995, Wien, 1995, p. 112ff.

(9)   Helmut Neuberger. *Freimaurerei und Nationalsozialismus*, first his dissertation: München, 1977, then: vol. 2., Hamburg, 1980. vol. 1: *Der völkische Propagandakampf und die deutsche Freimaurerei bis 1933*; vol. 2: *Das Ende der deutschen Freimaurei*.

(10)   Neuberger, *Freimaurerei und Nationalsozialismus*, vol. 2, p. 232.

(11)   Ibid.

(12)   Ibid., vol. 1, p. 257ff.

(13)   Compare in detail: Ralf Melzer "Völkische Freimaurerei im Spiegel der Historiographie," in: Helmut Reinalter (Hrsg.), *2. International Conference in Innsbruck 19./21. Mai 1995. Freimaurerische Historiographie im 19. and 20. Jahrhundert.Forschungsbilanz -Aspekte – Problemschwerpunkte*, Bayreuth, 1996, p. 27ff.

(14)   Compare Reinalter, "Geheimgesellschaften und Revolution: Freimaurerei und Nationalsozialismus am Beispiel Alfred Rosenbergs" (see note 5); Werner Freudenschuß, "DerWetzlarer Ring—Völkische Tendenzen in der deutschen Freimaurerei nach dem 1. Weltkrieg," in: *Q.C.-Jahrbuch* no. 25/1988, Bayreuth, 1988, p. 9ff.; Wolfgang Fenner/Joachim Schmitt-Sasse, "Die Freimaurer als 'nationale Kraft' vor 1933, in: Thomas Koebner (ed.). *Weimars Ende. Prognosen und Diagnosen in der deutschen Literatur und politischen Publizistik 1930–1933*, Frankfurt/M., 1982, p. 223ff. With limitations, compare also Bruno Peters. *Die Geschichte der Freimaurerei im Deutschen Reich. 1870-1933*, Berlin, 1986. The work by Rick de Jong, *Freimaurer an Rhein und Ruhr im Dritten Reich*, Düsseldorf, 1986, stands out from other Masonic self-descriptions because of its critical and regional-historical stance. Henri Pauvrert [d.i. Thomas Richert] offers a good summary of the state of research shortly after Neuberger's

study, in "Die deutschen Großlogen, 1933-1935," in: *Eleusis*, 36. Jg., No. 6, November/Dezember 1981, p. 443ff. A paper for the state examination by Frank Neumann, "Die Involvierung der, altpreußischen' Freimaurerei in die Politik am Beispiel der Großen Loge von Preußen im Spiegel ihrer Zeitschrift *Am rauhen Stein* 1914-1933/35," Köln, 1995. Another state examination paper is concerned with the journal of the Grand Lodge "Zur Freundschaft:" Apart from the evaluation of the organ of the grand lodge, this study is limited mostly to reviews of the literature and takes much material without critique from Neuberger.

(15)   Jörg Rudolph. *Überlieferung des Reichssicherheitshauptamtes Amt VII "Weltanschauliche Forschung und Auswertung:" Anmerkungen zur Bestands- und Institutionsgeschichte eines nachrichtendienstlichen Archivs* [Thesis, Humboldt University, Berlin], Berlin, 1996. This study is being expanded into a dissertation.

(16)   Thus, for example, in the essay by Theodor Sand, "Der Beginn der dunklen Zeit und die Große Landesloge, o.O./o.J., p. 1:" While so-called humanitarian grand lodges suspended work in 1933, the Old Prussian gand lodges put up resistance...in order to save Freemasonry and the idea of an Order, without sacrificing masonic fundamental principles, they changed the name to 'Deutsch-christlicher Orden der Tempelherren' ("German-Christian Order of the Knights Templar") on April 10, 1933. Almost everything is factually irrelevant and untenable. Compare in the same connection the somewhat different description by Dietmar Schulte, "Der Deutsch-Christliche Orden. Eine Betrachtung seiner Vorgeschichte, seines Existenzkampfes und seines Scheiterns," in: Z.K., vol. 123, November 1995, p. 398ff. This essay, originally a lecture before the research association of the Große Landesloge "Frederik," also contains errors, and is extensively apologetic. Typical of this is Manfred Obermann's depiction in "Zur Geschichte der Freimaurerei in Berlin," in: Berlin Museum (Hrsg.), *Freimaurer in Berlin. Gemälde, Plastik, Graphik, Kleinkunst* (Catalog) Berlin, 1973, p. 8: "It goes without saying that neither National Socialism nor any other 20th-century dictatorships tolerated Masonic ideas such as tolerance and brotherhood above and beyond nationality and race."

(17)   Compare in this regard the calendar by Götz Aly/Susanne Heim, *Das zentrale Staatsarchiv in Moskau ("Sonderarchiv"). Rekonstruktion und Bestandsverzeichnis ver-schollen geglaubten Schriftguts aus der NS-Zeit,* Düsseldorf, 1992. The documents surrendered to the German Democratic Republic

after 1957 appear in this survey-like list of contents. Compare also Horst Romeyk, "Das ehemals sowjetische Sonderarchiv in Moskau," in: *Der Archivar*, 45 (1992), no. 1, column 118 and Kai von Jena/Wilhelm Lenz, "Die deutschen Bestände im Sonderarchiv in Moskau," in: *Der Archivar*, 45 (1992), no. 3, column 457ff.

(18)   Renate Endler/Elisabeth Schwarze. *Die Freimaurerbestände im Geheimen Staats-archiv Preussischer Kulturbesitz*, Helmut Reinalter, ed. vol. 1: *Großlogen und Protektor. Freimaurerische Stiftungen und Vereinigungen*, Frankfurt/M. 1994/ vol. 2: *Tochterlogen*, Frankfurt/M., 1996/ vol. 3: *Freimaurerische Stiftungen und Vereinigungen* (in preparation). The summaries give points of reference, especially the introduction of the first volume. Compare also the paper by Renate Endler, "Die Freimaurerbestände im Geheimen Staatsarchiv Preussischer Kulturbesitz, Abt. Merseburg," in: Helmut Reinalter (ed.) *International Conference in Innsbruck 22./23.5.1992. Aufklärung und Geheimgesellschaften: Freimaurer, Illuminaten und Rosenkreuzer: Ideologie, Struktur und Wirkungen*, Bayreuth, 1992, p. 103ff.

(19)   Compare Endler/Schwarze, *Die Freimaurerbestände*, vol. 1, p. 48.

(20)   For archival and source condition questions in general, see Ibid., vol. 1, p. 47f.; Aly/Heim, "Das zentrale Staatsarchiv," p. 7, 56f. (note 2) as well as especially p. 47; also Jena/Lenz, "*Die deutschen Bestände im Sonderarchiv in Moskau*," *loc.cit.*, column 458; Reinhard Rürup (ed.), *Topographie des Terrors: Gestapo, SS, Reichssicherheitshauptamt auf dem Prinz-Albrecht-Gelände. Eine Dokumentation*, Berlin, 1989, p. 80. The castle, "Fürstenstein" in Lower Silesia is presumably identical with the place others call "(Castle) Althorn."

(21)   The relevant documents belong to the Bestand 500 (RSHA=ReichsSecurity Office).

(22)   *Die Geschichte der Symbolischen Großloge von Deutschland 1930–1949*, compiled by Heinz Klasen, paperback (with an introduction by the editor), Hamburg, 1984 (unpublished): Deutsches Freimaurer-Museum Bayreuth, No. 9398.

(23)   Bernhard Beyer, *Der Übertritt der Altpreußischen Großlogen ins Völkisch-Nationalsozialistische Lager. Akten zur Freimaurerei in Deutschland 1920–1946*, paperback edition (with commentary by the editor), Bayreuth, 1955 (unpublished), Deutsches Freimaurer-Museum Bayreuth, No.10115. Beyer's internal knowledge of Masonic relationships in Germany and his involvement in the historical events

contribute decisively to the value of this collection of source material. Of course they are subjective. Beyer, also Associate Grand Master of the Grand Lodge Zur Sonne in the Weimar years, was in office from 1913 to1933 and then was Director of the Masonic Museum in Bayreuth, 1949-1955. He died in 1966. The material was probably left unpublished in order not to burden the already difficult process of unification of German lodges reactivated after liberation within the parameters (lit: perimeter) of the establishment of a Masonic umbrella organization in the Federal Republic (see more on this problem in the Epilogue). Furthermore, questions of protection of personalities may have played a role.

(24)   Compare the bibliography by Herbert Schneider, *Deutsche Freimaurer Bibliothek*; Part 1: *Katalog* (and typed supplement: *Stand* August 1996), Part 2: *Register*, Fankfurt/M. 1993 (Deutsches Freimaurer-Museum Bayreuth, No. 10735). For the organization of subordinate lodges, and for the comprehension of the changes in the systems, the reference work by Ernst-Günther Geppert/Karl Heinz Francke, *Die Freimaurer-Logen Deutschlands und deren Großlogen 1737-1985*, Bayreuth 1988 is useful.

(25)   According to oral information from Barbara Bettacs to the author, there is also source material that had been fetched back to Germany from Sweden in 1976 by a delegation from the Große Landesloge. These documents had been shipped to Stockholm to the friendly Swedish Grand Lodge in two batches, in 1932 and 1934, by the then archivist Felix Witt-Hoë. In 1976, they came first to Kiel. Later, they went by way of Hamburg und Braunschweig back to Berlin. By far, most of the material has to do with ritual and teaching methods, as well as documents on the early history of the Order and its connections to Sweden (compare Otto Schwartz. *Bericht über die Rückführung der im Jahre 1932 nach Schweden ausgelagerten Teile des deutschen Ordens-Archivs im März 1976* [paper], Kiel, 1976, Archiv GLL. (The report, which concerns the material shipped out in 1934, contains the inventory of part of the documents and records that had been brought back.)

(26)   The resignation of the Old Prussians was driven forward especially by the Große Landesloge (compare, for example Beyer, "Der Übertritt," p. 45). Additional grand lodges resigned later.

CHAPTER 1

(1)   Cited in Lennhoff/Posner, *Int. Freimaurer-Lexikon*, column 532.

(2)   Compare re: the duties of the Fraternity in general, the very good summary in: *Wegweiser zur Freimaurerei*, ed. by The German Supreme Council AASR, Frankfurt/M. 1980, especially p. 11.

(3)   Ibid., p. 12.

(4)   Compare Endler/Schwarze, *Die Freimaurerbestände*, vol. 2, p. 18. This second part of the overview of the former Merseburger Masonic documents makes it easier to get a grip on the archival material of individual subordinate lodges. It contains information on the kind and extent of the material, the length of time the lodges worked, and the Masonic systems to which they belonged.

(5)   Compare. Düriegl/Winkler (Eds.), *Freimaurer*, Foreword.

(6)   Ibid.

(7)   Compare. Düriegl, "Bauhütten," in: ibid., p. 83.

(8)   Compare. Reinalter, "Zur Aufgabenstellung," in: his (as ed.), *Freimaurer und Geheimbünde*, p. 13.

(9)   Of course the spiritual experience of Freemasonry evades scholarly or purposefully rational forms of explanation and interpretation to a certain extent. Compare ibid., p. 20. On p. 31 (note 56) there are bibliographic references to the question of the essence of Freemasonry.

(10)   Here is cited: *Des verbesserten Konstitutionenbuch der alten ehrwürdigen Bru-derschaft der Freymaurer erster Theil. Geschichte des Ordens, auf Befehl der Großen Loge aus ihren Urkunden, Traditionen und Logenbüchern zum Gebrauch der Logen*. By Jakob Anderson. Aus dem Englischen übersetzt, vierte vermehrte Auflage, Frankfurt/M. 1783. Compare Reinalter. *Freimaurerei und Nationalsozialismus am Beispiel Alfred Rosenbergs*, pp. 58, 77 (Anm.22). "Die Alten Pflichten"/Konstitutionsbuch Andersons also in: Lennhoff/Posner, *Int. Freimaurer-Lexikon*, Einleitender Teil, p. 13ff. According to the "Allgemeinen maurerischen Grundsätzen" ("General Masonic Principles" of the Grand Masters' Conference in Hamburg on June 7, 1870, the purpose of Freemasonry is the "Moral ennoblement of man and the encouragement of human

blessedness in general .... Love God above all and your neighbor as yourself." (cited in: *Neue Leipziger Zeitung*, 26.1.1928).

(11) Lennhoff/Posner, *Int. Freimaurer-Lexikon*, column 791.

(12) Compare in this connection Düriegl, "Vorwort," in: Düriegl/ Winkler (ed.), *Freimaurer*; G.Schenkel, in: Kurt Galling et al. (eds.), *Die Religion in Geschichte und Gegenwart, Handwörterbuch für Theologie und Religionswissenschaft*, vol. 1-7, Tübingen. 3rd ed. 1986, vol. 2, column 1114; Irmgard Schweikle, in: Günther und Irmgard Schweikle (eds.), *Metzler Literatur Lexikon*, Stuttgart, 1984, p. 29ff. As well as Jürgen Mittelstraß (ed.), *Enzyklopädie Philosophie und Wissenschaftstheorie*, vol. 2, Mannheim/Wien/Zürich, 1984, p. 976.

(13) Compare Lennhoff/Posner, *Int. Freimaurer-Lexikon*, column 327ff.

(14) Compare in regard to this question Reinalter, „Freimaurerei und Nationalsozialismus am Beispiel Alfred Rosenbergs ", *loc. cit.*, p. 71.

(15) Reinalter. „Zur Aufgabenstellung ", *loc. cit.*, p. 14.

(16) Lennhoff/Posner. *Int. Freimaurer-Lexikon*, column 1720. In the second half of the 18th century, Rosicrucian influences found entry into Masonic lodges especially in Berlin: "This led to confusion and unrest because the Golden- and Rosicrucians declared that Freemasonry had been invented by the Order's leaders, and only they understood the true and secret meaning of Masonic symbolism." (Susanne Winkler, in: Düriegl/Winkler [Eds.], *Freimaurer*, p. 309). The mystic association "Orden des Gülden und Rosen-Creutz" ("Order of the Golden and Rosy-Cross") established itself at the beginning of the 18th century in the tradition of the earlier Rosicrucian movements founded by Johann Valentin Andreae (1586-1654). In his two Rosicrucian "manifestos," the "Fama Fraternitatis oder Bruderschaft des Hochlöblichen Ordens des R.C." (1614) and "Die Chymische Hochzeit des Christiani Rosencreutz" (1616), the life of Christian Rosenkreutz (1378-1484) and his ancient Christian-spiritualist teaching were narrated. Whether such a person as Rosenkreutz and his alleged fraternity had ever actally existed, or whether these "manifestos" were really a satire on the alchemical-theosophical Zeitgeist, has never been clear.

(17) On Weishaupt and the Illuminati, compare among others Paul Naudon. *Geschichte der Freimaurerei*, Frankfurt/M./Berlin/Wien, 1982, p. 123; Lennhoff/Posner, *Int. FreimaurerLexikon*, column 729ff., 1678ff.; Susanne Winkler, in: Düriegl/Winkler (eds.), *Freimaurer*, p. 313.

(18)   Thus also Garry Allen, "Die Insider," reprinted in: *Christusstaat International, Extrablatt* No. 9, November 1991, the organ of the "Ancient Christian" Association of the New Jerusalem in the Universal Life. The texts have pathological characteristics. They concern themselves, for example, with the "world domination of the Illuminati, the secret cooperation of Freemasonry and the Vatican, as well as with the latest status of „the general plan for a world dictatorship" based on the *Protocols of the Sages of Zion*.

(19)   Compare Reinalter., „Freimaurerei und Nationalsozialismus am Beispiel Alfred Rosenbergs", *loc.cit.*, p. 72. In this conection, Reinalter refers to, among others, the works of Johannes Rogalla v. Bieberstein as well as to the essays in his (self-published) collection *Freimaurer und Geheimbünde im 18. Jahrhundert in Mitteleuropa* (see note Introduction/5).

(20)   Concerning the function of Freemasonry for the emancipation of the Jews, see Chapter 2.

(21)   Compare Lennhoff/Posner, *Int. Freimaurer-Lexikon*, column 1308. On Danton, who was a member of a lodge in Paris, compare ibid., column 321. Robespierre was not a Freemason (Compare ibid., column 1325).

(22)   Reinalter. „Freimaurerei und Nationalsozialismus am Beispiel Alfred Rosenbergs", *loc.cit.*, p. 71. Compare also his „Zur Aufgabenstellung", *loc.cit.*, p. 14.

(23)   Compare Lennhoff/Posner, *Int. Freimaurer-Lexikon*, column 1308.

(24)   Reinalter. "Auf der Suche nach Sündenböcken," *loc.cit.*, p. 113.

(25)   Compare ibid., p. 123. On the conspiracy theory, see more in Chapter 2.   Reinalter, who defines Freemasonry as a broad spectrum of systems, directions (orientations), and jursidictions, emphasizes in the same place, that some of these directions played an important part in the emancipation of Judaism (the Jews), and that there were intensive cross-connections and influences between Freemasonry and Enlightenment or Liberalism. Beyond that, the lodges were much more political than is usually assumed: "Freemasonry condemned huge, forceful changes in the existing state and societal order, but it also did not accept every extant politcal system, especially if it stood in contradiction to the (of course, very different – author's note) aims and efforts of Freemasonry." (Ibid..). Reinalter criticizes, and very rightly so, the widely used Masonic claim of being "unpolitical" and demands a modification.

(26)   This concerns the Lodge "Absalom zu den 3 Nesseln," which still exists.

(27)   Concerning the function of lodges in Prussia in the 18th century, and Frederick II's relationship to Freemasonry, compare now the excellent description by Rüdiger Hachtmann, "Friedrich II. von Preußen und die Freimaurerei," in: *Historische Zeitschrift*, vol. 264/1997, p. 21ff. At the same time, the work presents the most recent state of research into this problem.

(28)   On the spread and development of Freemasonry up to the Convention of Wilhelmsbad in 1782, compare Endler/Schwarze, *Die Freimaurerbestände*, vol. 1, p. 13ff. Details concerning the acceptance (initiation) of Frederick and the lodges he established are also in: *250 Jahre Große National-Mutterloge "Zu den drei Weltkugeln" 1740-1990*, ed. by the 3 WK-Großloge, Berlin, 1990, p. 11ff.

(29)   Endler/Schwarze, *Die Freimaurerbestände*, vol. 1, p. 15.

(30)   Hachtmann, "Friedrich II.," *loc.cit.*, p. 34. As examples, Hachtmann names the principles from the "Ancient Obligations," initiation fees, and the mentoring (guide, lit: godfather) system for seekers.

(31)   Wolfgang Hardtwig, "Eliteanspruch und Geheimnis in den Geheimgesellschaften des 18. Jahrhunderts," in: Helmut Reinalter (Ed.), *Aufklärung und Geheimgesellschaften. Zur politischen Funktion und Sozialstruktur der Freimaurerlogen im 18. Jahrhundert*, München, 1989, p. 66, here citing Hachtmann, "Friedrich II.," *loc.cit.*, p. 34.

(32)   Hachtmann, "Friedrich II.," p. 35.

(33)   Compare Ferdinand Zörrer, "Hochgrade," in: Düriegl/Winkler (Eds.), *Freimaurer*, p. 285ff. Beyond that, the higher degrees (Knights' Degrees) of various systems derive from the alleged flight of members of the forbidden Templars to Scotland in 1312.

(34)   The designation "Strict Observance" is understood from the commandment of unconditional obedience, as opposed to the "Laten[t] Observance" of humanitarian Freemasonry of English origin. (Compare. Endler/Schwarze, *Die Freimaurerbestände*, vol. 1, p. 17 [note 5]). For different systems of higher degrees and the tradition of Knight Templary, see Chapter 1.2.

(35)   Lennhoff/Posner, *Int. Freimaurer Lexikon*, column 1524. Compare also Endler/Schwarze, *Die Freimaurerbestände*, vol. 1, p. 13.

(36)   From: "Zur Erinnerung:" Closing exercises of the St. John's lodges working under the Grand Lodge of Prussia "Friendship" in Berlin and Vicinity, Berlin, July 16, 1935, p. 14.

(37)   Compare Karl Nies. *Der Freimaurerbund zur Eintracht. Festschrift zur fünfzigjährigen Jubelfeier seines Bestehens*, Mainz, 1896, p. 16ff. Later tolerant tendencies were accepted by the Darmstadt lodges. Because of the anti-Semitic movement of 1880-1881, the Conference of Grand Lodges adopted a protest resolution, which said, among other things, that because "of the regrettable events, unheard of for our time, that remind one of centuries long-gone ... the Grand Lodge considers it a duty to urge all associated lodges to protest the so-called anti-Semitic outrage in a united, decided, and energetic manner" (cited ibid., p. 93).

(38)   Neuberger, *Nationalsozialismus und Freimaurerei*, vol. 1, p. 191.

(39)   Lennhoff/Posner, *Int. Freimaurer-Lexikon*, column 70.

(40)   Ibid.., column 1294.

(41)   Compare ibid., column 70f. (keyword "Anerkennung").

(42)   Neuberger, *Freimaurerei und Nationalsozialismus*, vol. 1, p. 204.

(43)   Compare Lennhoff/Posner, *Int. Freimaurer-Lexikon*, column 344.

(44)   After a text on teaching methods of the Große Landesloge, undated (Archives of the Großen Landesloge).

(45)   Werner Brägger. "Die öffentlich-rechtliche Sonderstellung der drei altpreußischen   Grosslogen. Begründung, Wandlungen, Ende." Diss., Leipzig, 1931, p. 8. The patronages for the Große Landesloge and Three World Globes were renewed and confirmed by Friedrich Wilhelm II. in 1796.

(46)   Cited ibid., p. 12ff.

(47)   Ibid.

(48)   Instructions about some prinicples of the future constitution, § 4 I-III, 6.4.1848. The basic rule of freedom of the association formulated here was included and expanded on in Articles 29 and 30 of the Constitution document of January 31, 1850.

(49)   Compare Lennhoff/Posner, *Int. Freimaurer-Lexikon*, column 1453ff. For background on the Settegast struggle, see also Chapter 1.2.

(50)   Compare. Urs Lüthi. *Der Mythos von der Weltverschwörung: Die Hetze der Schweizer Frontisten gegen Juden und Freimaurer am Beispiel des Berner*

Prozesses um die "Protokolle der Weisen von Zion," Zürich, 1992, p. 15; also Neuberger, *Freimaurerei und Nationalsozialismus*, vol. 1, p. 180.

(51)   Neuberger, *Freimaurerei und Nationalsozialismus*, vol. 1, p. 181.

(52)   Ibid.

(53)   Compare the important socio-historical essay by Stefan Ludwig Hoffmann, "Sakraler Monumentalismus um 1900. Das Leipziger Völkerschlachtdenkmal," in: Reinhart Koselleck/Michael Jeismann (eds.). *Der politische Totenkult: Kriegerdenkmäler in der Moderne*, München, 1994, p. 249ff.

(54)   Cited ibid., p. 277.

(55)   The question of the development of *völkisch* Freemasonry remains almost untouched in Fenner/Schmitt-Sasse, *Die Freimaurer als "nationale Kraft."* See for this problem and the preconditions in detail Chapters 1.2, 1.3, 3.1 and 4.1.

(56)   According to C. van Dalens *Kalender für Freimaurer*, 1901, p. 175ff. Under grouping of the five independent Saxon lodges (later the Grand Lodge "Deutsche Bruderkette" ["German Brothers' Chain"]).

(57)   According to Peters, *Die Geschichte der Freimaurerei*, p. 273; There are no listings for the grand lodge in Darmstadt and the five independent Saxon lodges.

(58)   Of all the systems, the Große Landesloge is the most strongly oriented to Christianity. More detail in Chapter 1.2. The number of clergy varied in 1900 in each grand lodge only between ca. 0.1% (also, the Große Landesloge) and 0.3% (per-cent according to Peters' numbers, p. 273).

(59)   In this connection, Reinalter refers to the study by Ludwig Hammermayer (Compare Reinalter, „Zur Aufgabenstellung," *loc. cit.*, p. 20, note 1). Studies on the social structure of the lodges in the Austrian Netherlands and in the Principality of Liège come to the conclusion that, "noblesse" as well as "bourgeois mean" were more strongly represented than the "grande bourgeoisie," while the "petite bourgeoisie" can hardly–and the "popular classes" cannot be–documented at all (cited ibid., p. 15). More differentiation must be made. For Prussia, compare Karlheiz Gerlach, "Zur Sozialstruktur der Großen National-Mutterloge, Zu den drei Weltkugeln' 1775-1805 in Berlin," in: *Q.C.-Jahrbuch* no. 28/1991, p. 105ff.; See also his "Die Große Landesloge der Freimaurer von Deutschland 1769-1807: Zur

Sozialgeschichte der deutschen Freimaurerei im 18. Jahrhundert," in: *Q.C.-Jahrbuch* no. 30/1993, p. 79ff.; and his "Royale York zur Freundschaft in Berlin, 1762-1806: Ein Beitrag zur Sozialgeschichte der Freimaurerei in Brandenburg-Preußen," in: *Q.C.-Jahrbuch* no. 31/1994, p. 51ff. As already explained at the beginning, special analyses with respect to the social structure of the Masonic lodges for the 19th and 20th centuries, briefly, can also be found in Chapters 6.1 and 7.1.

(60) Compare Johannes Drechsle. *Die Brüder vom FZAP: Ein Streifzug durch die Geschichte des Freimaurerbundes Zur Aufgehenden Sonne*, Hamburg, 1971, p. 11. On the influence of monism on the Freimaurerbundes Zur Aufgehenden Sonne, see Chapter 3.3.

(61) Compare ibid., p. 12.

(62) Hachtmann, „Friedrich II.," *loc.cit.*, p. 49.

(63) Ibid., p. 50.

(63a) The exact date is unknown, as is true for the Grand Lodge of Ireland (written information from Alain Bernheim to the author).

(64) The Ancient and Accepted Scottish Rite (AASR) has a 33-step system of higher degrees, according to Lennhoff/Posner ein "really universal world rite."

(65) The higher degrees of the Grand Orient and Supreme Council are the same. Since the Paris Convention of Supreme Councils in 1929, the separation of St. John's (Blue or Symbolic) lodge and higher degrees exists in general. The first three degrees are administered by a regular grand lodge. The Supreme Council of the AASR directs the 4th-33rd Degrees in each country. In Germany, this division exists today between A.F. &.A.M. and Supreme Council. The grand lodge system of the Three World Globes and the Große Landesloge have their integrated higher degrees. Also "Royal York" worked out its own higher degrees (see Chapter 1.2; there and in Chapter 7.1 also concerning an attempt of almost all German grand lodges to hinder the establishment of the AASR in Germany after the First World War).

(66) This incorrect description is also in Neuberger, *Freimaurerei und Nationalsozialismus*, vol. 1, p. 337 (note 205). Compare, on the other hand, the original text of the Constitution of the Grand Orient with its modifications since1849 in Alain Bernheim, "1877 et le Grand Orient de France," in: *Travaux de la Loge nationale de recherches*, Villard de Honnecourt, ed. of the Grande Loge Nationale Française, Série 2,

no. 19/1989, Neuilly-sur-Seine, 1989, p. 113ff., Appendix 2. On the "Weißbuch" see also Chapter 1.2.

(67) Lennhoff/Posner, *Int. Freimaurer-Lexikon*, column 765.

(68) Written communication from Alain Bernheim to the author. Compare also *Humanität: Das deutsche Freimaurer Magazin* no. 5/1992, p. 14.

(69) Susanne Winkler, in: Düriegl/Winkler, *Freimaurer*, p. 27.

(70) Also, English masonry has further steps in Masonic activity, which are not defined as ritual higher degrees, and futhermore are not based on a hierarchy [lit hierarchical principle]. Whoever has been a Master Mason in an English lodge for four weeks, can, without further ado be raised into the status of the "Royal Arch." This is not another degree, but rather a kind of order. In addition, there are other steps taking one farther, whose characteristics are like those of the higher degrees. Only Christians may enter some. Therefore the principle of tolerance is somewhat compromised in English Masonry. Compare in this respect, John M. Hamill, "Die Freimaurerei in England," in: Düriegl/Winkler (Ed.), *Freimaurer*, p. 159ff., especially p. 166ff.

(71) A positive example for practices of different religions being observed with each other in one lodge is shown by the current Israeli Grand Lodge. In its seal are, as symbols of the three monotheisitc religions, the Jewish Star of David, the Christian Cross, and the Islamic Crescent "united in harmony." (see the documents appendix). The Grand Lodge is keeping the tradition set by the National Grand Lodge of Palestine, which was established during the time of the British Mandate. See also Chapter 7.1.

(72) Compare Lennhoff/Posner, *Int. Freimaurer-Lexikon*, column 231f.

(73) Ignaz Aurelius Feßler (1756-1839) is considered the founder of the teaching method of "Royal York." He himself stated that he had wanted to do away with the higher degrees in this grand lodge system, but had been thwarted by existing resistance. Actually he was interested in reforming the higher degrees, which he thought were important in themselves. Compare Florian Maurice. "Ignaz Aurelius Feßler und die Reform der Großloge Royal York in Berlin: Kultur- und Geistesgeschichte um 1800 im Spiegel der Freimaurerei," Diss., München, 1995. For a differing opinion, see Lennhoff/Posner, *Int. Freimaurer-Lexikon*, column 469ff.

(74) Compare ibid., column 1248.

(75)   The designation "Freimaurerorden (F.O.)" [Masonic order] is
also used for the Große Landesloge.

(76)   The Berlin publicist and Freemason Bruno Peters, himself a
member of a lodge of the Humanitarian A.F. and A.M., vehemently
represented the view that the designation „Christian Freemasonry" in
Germany was only to be used for the Große Landesloge.

(77)   Compare the Festschrift, *Zum 50. Stiftungsfest der Loge 'Die vereinigten
Freunde an der Nahe" ("United Friends on the Nahe")* im Orient Kreuznach,
Bad Kreuznach, 1908, p. 19: According to this, the National Mother
Lodge had decided, on May 8, 1868, that subordinate lodges should
be justified in allowing non-Christian Brothers, who were still active
members of recognized lodges, to be admitted as permanent visitors.
"Thereupon two Jewish Brothers were immediately accepted as
permanent visitors." Friedrich Wilhelm also put pressure on the Große
Landesloge in this connection (see below).

(78)   Lennhoff/Posner, *Int. Freimaurer-Lexikon*, column 1453.

(79)   The concept "Sprengelrecht" (lit. "Sprinkle Right," i.e. the right
to sprinkle holy water) is to be understood as the right of a Masonic
authority to be the only one allowed to constitute subordinate
lodges and make Masons in a given territory or state. While the
Old Prussians set up lodges outside Prussia, they did not allow the
Humanitarians this right in Prussian territory.

(80)   Concerning "red" or "Scottish" Masonry, compare. Zörrer,
Hochgrade, loc.cit., p. 286ff., as well as Böttner, *Zersplitterung und Einigung*,
especially p. 36f., 134. The year numbers are from written information
from Alain Bernheim to the author. Compare also Bernhard Beyer,
"Die sogenannte Symbolische Großloge von Deutschland," Offprint
from essays in various issues of the "Mitteilungen der GL Zur Sonne,"
Bayreuth, 1931 (Deutsches Freimaurer-Museum Bayreuth, No. 2368).
The higher degrees had always been special targets of anti-Masonic
attacks. Alfred Rosenberg, for example, was firmly convinced that
many Jews were active in the higher degrees. (Compare Reinalter,
"Freimaurerei und Nationalsozialismus am Beispiel Alfred Rosenbergs,"
loc.cit., p. 69). The next chapters concern themselves in detail with this
complex of problems.

(80a)   These numbers are based on information in an e-mail of
December 10, 2001 to the author from the Supreme Council of the
AASR, Southern Jurisdiction, USA

(81)   Concerning the form of organization and content of AASR, compare in condensed form, Herbert Keßler, "Der Schottische Ritus-Ein Gang durch seine Grade," in: *Q.C. Jahrbuch* no. 23/1986, Bayreuth, 1986, p. 179ff. The author, born in 1918, served from 1984 to 1993 as Grand Commander of the AASR in the Federal Republic of Germany Bundesrepublik. In 1941 he became a member of the Nazi Party; previously he had been a "file leader" and "training leader" in the Hitler Youth. Compare Bundesarchiv, Zwischenarchiv Dahlwitz-Hoppegarten, Z/A VI 379, A. 10).

(82)   Compare August Pauls, "Der Deutsche Alte und Angenommene Schottische Ritus," in: Amtliche Mitteilungen des Deutschen Obersten Rates des AASR [concerning the name, see note I/85] vol. 4, 15.6.1949, no. 1, p. 1ff. und Lennhoff/Posner, *Int. Freimaurer-Lexikon*, column 19f. August Pauls was chosen Grand Commander of the German Supremem Council in 1947.

(83)   Beyer, *Die sogenannte Symbolische Großloge*, p. 4f.

(84)   Compare Pauls, "Der Deutsche Alte und Angenommene...," *loc.cit.*, p. 3. Beyer seems to have played down his own part in the conflict with the Scottish Rite or with the Supreme Council at the end of the 1920s to beginning of the 1930s, including its political implications.

(85)   The Supreme Council of Germany played an important role in the founding of the Symbolic Grand Lodge. (For the detailed circumstances, see Chapter 7.1.) When the AASR could be "resurrected" in West Germany in 1947, the Board, taking the political situation in post-war Germany into consideration , assumed the designation "German Suprem Council" and, at the same time, moved its headquarters from Berlin to Frankfurt am Main. In 1995, the name was changed back to Supreme Council for Germany.

(86)   Concerning the problem of the special position of Sonderstellung, compare also Lennhoff/Posner, *Int. Freimaurer-Lexikon*, column 1249.

(87)   On the Edict of 1798, compare, as cited previously: Brägger, "Die öffentlich-rechtliche Sonderstellung," p. 12ff. Compare also Peters, *Die Geschichte der Freimaurerei*, p. 246.

(88)   See Chapters 4.2 and 5.2.1 for a detailed discussion.

(89)   The position that Freemasonry is "unpolitical," is held rather inconsistently.

(90)   Neuberger, *Freimaurerei und Nationalsozialismus*, vol.1, p. 183.

(91)   The position of the Grand Master is the highest office in the Große Landesloge, responsible, among others, for ritual and usage. In addition, all the Order officers are under him. The Grand Master is the highest authority for internal affairs; the Landes (Provincial) Grand Master is that for external affairs.

(92)   Friedrich Wilhelm, Crown Prince (as Kaiser Friedrich III.). *Ansprachen des Ordens-Meisters 1870-1874*, Berlin, 1874. Darin: "Ansprache bei der Feier der Niederlegung der Würde als Ordens-Meister am 7. März 1874" (p. 22ff.). Concerning background, compare also Posner/Lennhoff, *Int. Freimaurer-Lexikon*, column 709ff.

(93)   Friedrich Wilhelm, Kronprinz, "Ansprache bei der Feier der Niederlegung der Würde als Ordens-Meister," *loc.cit.*, p. 24ff.

(94)   Ibid., p. 28.

(95)   Ibid., p. 23.

(96)   Information can be had from a letter dated May 15, 1934 from the Old Prussian grand lodges to Reichs-Bank President Schacht (Archives of the Große Landesloge). According to it, under pressure from the Protector, Prince Friedrich Wilhelm, in the 1860s, Jews were granted the right of visitation—i.e. the right to participate in the Work—by the Three World Globes and the Große Landesloge. The source also says that "Men of the Jewish faith were never accepted," [as members – author's note] in either of these grand lodges. Royal York accepted Jewish Brothers since 1872 (see also note. I/77).

(97)   Compare Zörrer, „Hochgrade", *loc.cit.*, p. 287.

(98)   On the "Strict Observance" and the Swedish System of the Große Landesloge, compare Endler/Schwarze. *Die Freimaurerbestände*, vol. 1, p. 95ff.; Böttner, *Zersplitterung und Einigung*, p. 77ff.; Lennhoff/Posner, *Int. Freimaurer-Lexikon*, column 719ff., 1434ff. 1520ff.; Susanne Winkler,"Die Templer," in: Düriegl/Winkler (Ed.), *Freimaurer*, p. 43ff; Archives of the Große Landesloge, passim.

(99)   On Ramsay see note I/33.

(100)   According to Henry Corbin, *Temple et contemplation*, Paris, 1980, p 373, "the 'Traditio Templi' postulates *per se* the Tradition of a templar chivalry, a spiritual and initiatic knighthood."

(101)   Endler/Schwarze, *Die Freimaurerbestände*, vol. 1, p. 95.

(102) Ibid., p. 96.

(103) The Andrew Degrees four and five are earned at the same time. The Grand Lodge "Friendship" worked according to the "Fessler System" in eight degrees (see also note I/73).

(104) Compare Böttner, *Zersplitterung und Einigung*, p. 36.

(105) Lennhoff/Posner, *Int. Freimaurer-Lexikon*, column 435.

(106) According to a lecture by Prof. Claus Ritters on "Christliche Freimaurerei" ("Christian Freemasonry") on January 18, 1993 in the Große Landesloge in Berlin.

(107) Compare also Beyer, *Der Übertritt*, p. 53.

(108) According to information passed on by the Große Landesloge, de Molay died on March 11, 1314, not March 18, 1314. The changing date of the Großen Ordensfestes (the Grand Order Festival)=Annual Grand Communication??? at the end of March has nothing to do with the question of the exact date of death.

(109) Gisela Jaacks, "Der Tempel in Jerusalem in jüdischer und christlicher Überlieferung: Rekonstruktion und Ideal, " p. 26, in: A. Bekemaier (ed.), *Reisen nach Jerusalem. Das heilige Land in Karten und Ansichten aus fünf Jahrhunderten (Katalog Berlin Museum)*, Wiesbaden, 1993, p. 25ff.

(110) Ibid.

(111) Compare ibid., p. 34.

(112) Neuberger, *Freimaurerei und Nationalsozialismus*, vol. 1, p. 183.

(113) It was Cäsar Wolf, the Master of the Hamburg lodge "Absalom zu den 3 Nesseln," ("Absalom of the 3 Nettles")who spurred his lodge Brothers on to "the greatest charitable contributions in the service of the Fatherland" and even organized a complete hospital train (Ibid., p. 184). Cäsar Wolf committed suicide in 1933 when his own Grand Lodge of Hamburg decided to introduce the "Aryan Paragraph."

(114) Ibid., p. 185f.

(115) Compare ibid. Concerning "military lodges" and the objection repeatedly leveled at them, that they were in a treasonous conspiracy, see Chapter 4.1.

(116) Compare. Jacob Katz, *Jews and Freemasons in Europe: 1723-1939*, Cambridge, Massachusetts, 1970, p. 175.

(117)   Compare Ellic Howe, "The Collapse of Freemasonry in Nazi-Germany," at first a manuscript, London, 1973, then in: *Ars Quatuor Coronatorum*, vol. 95/1982, London, 1982, p. 21ff., here p. 25. Editor-in-Chief of the gutter press, "Auf Vorposten" was Ludwig Müller zu Hausen, alias Gottfried zur Beek, a personal friend of Ludendorff, who was the publisher of the *Protokolle der Weisen von Zion* (*The Proceedings of the Sages of Zion*). For more see Chapter 2.2.

(118)   Compare Beyer; *Der Übertritt*, p. iv.

(119)   The name is in connection with the Swiss constitutional lawyer and Freemason Johann Kaspar Bluntschli (1808-1881), who was the Grand Master of the Grand Lodge Zur Sonne ("Sun") between 1872 and 1878. The Lodge "Bluntschli zur reinen Erkenntnis" ("Bluntschli of Pure Recognition") named for him, worked under the Grand Lodge Zur Sonne in Berlin.

(120)   Cited in Manfred Steffens [d.i. Stefan Zickler], *Freimaurer in Deutschland. Bilanz eines Vierteljahrtausends*, Flensburg, 1964, p. 357.

(121)   *Announcements no. 5* of the Secret Police Office of April 18, 1934: "Die Freimaurerlogen, Logen, Orden und ähnliche Verbindungen in Deutschland," p. 5, GStA PK (Secret State Archives of the Prussian Cultural Possession), I, 90 p. 129.

(122)   Beyer, *Der Übertritt*, p. ii. According to the words of Grand Master of the Große Landesloge Müllendorff from 1922, "Our Lodge Work exhausts itself completely with the illustration of the ritual and symbolism for building the characters and hearts of the Brothers " (cited ibid., p. 35).

(123)   Compare Ellic Howe, "The collapse...," p. 22f. For Howe it was the Jewish Question above all, that split German Freemasonry (compare p. 21). He calls the Old Prussians "ultra-conservative, " and the Humanitarians "more liberal," in which he refers to the fact that, with the Humanitarians, the rejection of Jewish candidates by means of the "black ball" was not unknown (compare ibid.).

(124)   Compare ibid., p. 22.

(125)   Conceptually the Old Prussians in the present work, to the extent that it is concerned with their societal-political alignment, are designated as national, national-Christian, national-conservative, or right wing conservative grand lodges.

(126) From the founding document (letter) of the Old Prussians on the occasion of their resignation from the German Asociation of Grand Lodges (1922). Cited in Beyer, *Der Übertritt*, p. 43.

(127) On the Assocciation of German Freemasons, compare among others, Neuberger. *Freimaurerei und Nationalsozialismus*, vol. 1, p. 204f. The Association was the forerunner of today's Masonic Research Society, Quatuor Coronati, in Bayreuth.

(128) Ibid., p. 205.

(129) Compare Beyer, *Der Übertritt*, p. 31.

(130) Compare ibid.., p. 33. In the same place the Master of a subordinate lodge of the Grand Lodge Zur Freundschaft was citied in the following words: The national disposition of the members of the board of directors was, "in Masonic as well as in profane life, above all reproach (doubt)... Brother Bischoff is also of a good national, honest German disposition, as is the whole board of directors."

(131) Compare ibid., p. 11ff. Theodor Fritsch was one of the signers of a letter cited by Beyer having to do with this. Fritsch was the publisher of the anti-Semitic journal, „The Hammer". On Fritsch see Chapters 2.2 und 4.1.

(132) Ibid., p. 23.

(133) Cited ibid., p. 27f.

(134) Cited in Lennhoff/Posner, *Int. Freimaurer-Lexikon*, column 347. Representatives of the Old Prussian Grand Lodges continued to meet in the context of the Old Prussian Association of Grand Masters. The board, to which leading representatives of the Old Prussian Grand Lodges belonged, served for the exchange of information and a procedure they adapted to each other in such affairs where this seemed sensible to the participants.

(135) Figures according to C. van Dalen's *Kalender für Freimaurer*, vol. 1923/24, including the five independent Saxon lodges attached to the Grand Lodge "Deutsche Bruderkette" ("German Brothers' Chain") but without the Aufgehende Sonne (Rising Sun) in 1924. For comparison, the Dalen Freemasons' Calendar for 1919 shows the number of members at only about 58,500 altogether, based on the reports of the grand lodges for 1917. The Old Prussians, with almost 39,300 made up a little more than 67%. Thegreatest numerically among the Old Prussians until 1935 was usually the Three World

Globes, followed by the Große Landesloge. For the progress of memberships until the turn of the [20th] century, compare Peters, *Die Geschichte der Freimaurerei*, p. 270. Concerning the development of membership in the Weimar Republic, and the number of members in the individual grand lodges, see more in Chapter 3.1.

(136)   Compare Ferdinand Runkel. *Geschichte der Freimaurerei in Deutschland*, vol. 3, Berlin, 1932, p. 430 (Runkel was a member of the Große Landesloge); Alain Bernheim, *Research on the History of the AASR in Germany* (2d. ed., paperback), Büsingen, 1983, p. 3; Endler/ Schwarze, *Die Freimaurerbestände*, vol. 1, p. 38. This circumstance is even more significant, as the five independent Saxon lodges, with the Association of Grand Lodges, had entered into association as the Free Union in 1917.

(137)   And indeed already since August 1932 (Compare Endler/ Schwarze, *Die Freimaurerbestände*, vol. 1, p. 257). As of publication deadline for the *Int. Freimaurer-Lexikon*, which appeared in 1932, the Grand Lodge of Darmstadt was still a member of the Association of Grand Lodges (Compare column 347).

CHAPTER 2

(1)   Reinalter, „Auf der Suche nach Sündenböcken," *loc.cit.*, p. 121.

(2)   Neuberger, *Freimaurerei und Nationalsozialismus*, vol. 1, p. 19.

(3)   Rainer Hubert, "Antimasonismus," in: Düriegl/Winkler (Ed.), *Freimaurer*, p. 353.

(4)   Compare ibid.

(5)   Compare u.a. Lennhoff/Posner, *Int. Freimaurer-Lexikon*, Introduction, p. 46. The Codex Iuris Canonici includes Freemasons in the "societates ab ecclesia damnatae" (Compare G.Schenkel, in: Galling et al. (Eds.) *Die Religion in Geschichte und Gegenwart*, vol. 2, column 1117). Articles 1399 and 2335f. decree the excommunication of any Freemason from whichever system or lodge. Even in 1950, the Vatican officially rejected lodges, and strengthened the impossibility of acceptance of Freemasonry by Catholicism.

(6)   1751 by Benedict XIV, 1775 by Pius VI, 1821 by Pius VII, 1825 by Leo XII, 1829 by Pius VIII, 1832 by Gregor XVI. Pope Pius IX alone promulgated six encyclicals against Freemasonry between 1846 and 1873 [add 1884 Leo XIII?].

(7)   Regarding the "Taxil-Fraud," compare Neuberger, *Freimaurerei und Nationalsozialismus*, vol.1, p. 28 und Urs Lüthi, *Der Mythos von der Weltverschwörung: Die Hetze der Schweizer Frontisten gegen Juden und Freimaurer am Beispiel des Berner Prozesses um die Protokolle der Weisen von Zion*, Zürich, 1992, p. 18f.

(8)   Neuberger, *Freimaurerei und Nationalsozialismus*, vol. 1, p. 28.

(9)   Cited in Johannes Rogalla von Bieberstein, "Die These von der freimaurerischen Verschwörung," in: Reinalter (Ed.), *Freimaurer und Geheimbünde*, p. 85 after Fritz Valjavec, *Die Entstehung der politischen Strömungen in Deutschland*, München, 1951, p. 515.

(10)   Compare Hubert, "Antimasonismus," in: Düriegl/Winkler (Ed.), *Freimaurer*, p. 354.

(11)   Compare Rogalla von Bieberstein, "Die These von der freimaurerischen Verschwörung," *loc.cit.*, p. 85.

(12)   Susanne Winkler, in: Düriegl/Winkler (Ed.), *Freimaurer*, p. 303.
(13)   Compare. Reinalter, Freimaurerei und Nationalsozialismus am Beispiel Alfred Rosenbergs, *loc.cit.*, p. 70. More detail on Barruel's three-step model of a Masonic world conspiracy can be found there.

(14)   Neuberger, *Freimaurerei und Nationalsozialismus*, vol. 1, p. 21.

(15)   Ibid., p. 26.

(16)   Compare Lüthi, *Der Mythos von der Verschwörung*, p. 11 f.

(17)   Compare on this whole complex, Yehuda Bauer, "Vom christlichen Judenhaß zum modernen Antisemitismus: Ein Erklärungsversuch," in: Wolfgang Benz (Ed.), *Jahrbuch für Antisemitismusforschung 1*, Frankfurt/M./New York, 1992, p. 77ff. As well as the collection by Julius H. Schoeps/Joachim Schlör (Ed.), *Antisemitismus: Vorurteile und Mythen*, München, 1995.

(18)   Compare Norman Cohn, *Die Protokolle der Weisen von Zion. Der Mythos von der jüdischen Weltverschwörung*, Köln/Berlin, 1969, p. 34ff.

(19)   Compare Ibid., p. 42ff.

(20)   Reinalter, „Auf der Suche nach Sündenböcken," *loc.cit.*, p. 112.

(21)   Compare, for a summary of this as well as various models for explanation of modern anti-Semitism, Herbert A. Strauss, "Deutsch-Jüdische Geschichtswissenschaft und Antisemitismusforschung heute. Festvortrag aus Anlaß der 22. Jahrestagung der Historischen Kommission zu Berlin, 28.11.1980," in: *Hiko-Beilage zu Informationen, Neue Folge*, Heft 5, vol. 1981, p. 30ff.

(22)   Arndt wrote thus in 1814: "The Jews as Jews do not fit into this world...and therefore I do not want them to multiply unduly in Germany. But I also do not want it because they are a thoroughly foreign people, and because I wish to keep the Germanic pedigree as pure as possible from outside strains ... seriously, every mixing of peoples with foreign material is its downfall ... because the Jews are a depraved and degenerate people" (Ernst Moritz Arndt, *Blick aus der Zeit auf die Zeit*, Frankfurt/M. 1814, p. 188ff.). On Arndt, Fichte and other advocates of earlier *"völkisch* Utopias," compare i.a. Jost Hermand, *Der alte Traum vom neuen Reich: Völkische Utopien und Nationalsozialismus*, Frankfurt/M. 1988, especially p. 32ff. Hermand is interested in a very different picture of this early nationalistic propagandist. He (Hermand) emphasizes indeed its "germanophilic" and "Christian-Germanic" viewpoint as well as the increasing ideological narrowing into the German-Nationalistic, underscored however, by its "idealististic" initial stance, and he disputes that there are already "tendencies toward the pre- and protofascistic."

(23)   Compare Ibid., p. 34 and Karl Dietrich Bracher, *Die deutsche Diktatur: Entstehung, Struktur, Folgen des Nationalsozialismus*, Köln 4th ed. 1972, p. 23f.

(24)   On Fichte as a Freemason, compare. Lennhoff/Posner, *Int. Freimaurer-Lexikon*, column 474ff.

(25)   Fenner/Schmitt-Sasse, „Die Freimaurer als ‚nationale Kraft'," *loc.cit.*, p. 225.

(26)   Kurt Schmidt, *Die Freimaurerei im Dienste deutscher Nationalbildung*, Wetzlar, 1927, p. 28.

(27)   Joseph Arthur de Gobineau, *Essai sur L'inégalité des races humaines (1st ed. 1853-1855)*, German edition: *Versuch über die Ungleichheit der Menschenrassen*, vol. 1-4, Stuttgart, 1900-1904. Gobineau's ideas can be reduced to a few theses, that include a definition of racism. According to it, races or species of human beings (which do not exist) differ in their physical and mental characteristics as well as their

efficiency, and are of differing value. Furthermore, "miscegenation" (in the long run) would mean the degeneration of mankind. Anti-Semitism did not yet play a role in the "Essai sur L'inégalité des races humaines," but appeared only in Gobineau's later works.

(28)   Richard Wagner. "Was ist deutsch?" *Bayreuther Blätter* 1, 1878, p. 29ff., reproduced in: Karl Heinrich Rengstorf/Siegfried von Kortzfleisch (Ed.). *Kirche und Synagoge: Handbuch zur Geschichte von Christen und Juden*, vol. 2, Stuttgart, 1968ff. (New ed. München, 1988), p. 293f.

(29)   Houston Stewart Chamberlain. *Die Grundlagen des neunzehnten Jahrhunderts*, 2 v. München, 29th ed., 1944 (Orig.ed.,1899). Chamberlain and the circle around Wagner apply Gobineau's scepticism, as at this time they expected "positive" results from the transformation of the concept of race.

(30)   Cited in Vaclav Chysky. "Antijudaismus, Antisemitismus," in: *Humanität* Nr.7/1992, p. 15. Compare summarizing concerning Stoecker, Marr und zum "Berliner Antisemitismus-Streit," Willi Jasper, *Enzyklopädie der Judenfeindschaften*, p. 712-714. in: Andreas Nachama/Gereon Sievernich (Eds.), *Jüdische Lebenswelten* (Katalog), Berlin, 1991, p. 712ff. As well as the *Handbuch zur "Völkischen Bewegung" 1871-1918*, ed. by Uwe Puschner et al., München/New Providence/London/Paris, 1996, passim. Concerning the conceptual characteristics and popularization of the expression "Anti-Semitism according to Marr, compare Shulamit Volkov, *Jüdisches Leben und Antisemitismus im 19. und 20. Jahrhundert*, München, 1990, p. 26ff.

(31)   Compare Reinhard Rürup, "Die 'Judenfrage' der bürgerlichen Gesellschaft und die Entstehung des modernen Antisemitismus," in: his *Emanzipation und Antisemitismus. Studien zur 'Judenfrage' der bürgerlichen Gesellschaft*, Göttingen, 1975, p. 74ff. For the characterization as "Weltanschauung," compare p. 91.

(32)   Compare Volkov: *Jüdisches Leben und Antisemitismus*, especially p. 13ff. The relevant controversies of research, in whose center is the question of continuity and discontinuity, cannot be treated in detail here. Basically, two partially overlapping discussions of continuity must be differentiated: First the question as to whether and how much "modern" anti-Semitism represents a break, or whether the continuity of anti-Semitism since ancient times and the Middle Ages predominate. Second, the debate as to whether there is a more or less direct line of connection "from Stoecker to Hitler," i.e. whether the

origin of the Nazis' persecution of the Jews can be seen in the *völkisch* anti-Semitism of the Empire.

(33)   Strauss, Deutsch-Jüdische Geschichtswissenschaft, *loc.cit.*, p. 31.

(34)   A certain Abbé Chabauty put forth this statement in 1881/82. Compare Lüthi. *Der Mythos von der Weltverschwörung*, p. 21.

(35)   Reinalter. „Auf der Suche nach Sündenböcken ", *loc.cit.*, p. 119.

(36)   The preoccupation with "international powers" was a specialty of Luden-   dorff's. From time to time, the concept was used by the Nazis, as, for example by Heydrich in the Nazi Party's directive "Gegen die Freimaurerei" ("Against Freemasonry") of 1939 or in the framework of Rosenbergs "Weltanschauungsamt" ("World View Office;" see Chapters 8.1 and 8.3).

(37)   Armin Pfahl-Traughber. *Der antisemitisch-antifreimaurerische Verschwörungsmythos*, p. 45. The page numbers refer to the version in the dissertation manuscript, which Armin Pfahl-Traughber graciously put at the author's disposal.

(38)   Friedrich Wichtl. *Weltfreimaurerei - Weltrevolution - Weltrepublik. Eine Untersuchung über Ursprung und Endziele des Weltkrieges*, München, 1919.

(39)   Compare concerning the whole subject in general: Neuberger. *Freimaurerei und Nationalsozialismus*, vol. 1, p. 40ff. and Armin Pfahl-Traughber. "Der Mythos vom Freimaurer-Mord in Sarajewo," in: *Humanität*, no. 2/1992, p. 17ff.

(40)   Albert Mousset. *L'attentat de Sarajewo. Documents inédits et Texte intégral des Sténogrammes du Procès*, Paris, 1930.

(41)   Letter from Witt-Hoë of 12/1/1928 to the Master of the subordinate lodge in Flensburg, GStA PK (Secret State Archives of the Prussian Cultural Possession, Berlin), Logen, 5.1.3, 4355. In the meantime, at the State Archives, instead of the designation "Logen" ("Lodges"), the term "Freimaurer" ("Freemasons") is now used in the relevant main section!

(42)   Wichtl, *Weltfreimaurerei - Weltrevolution - Weltrepublik*, here the 11th ed. 1928, p. 62 is cited.

(43)   Compare Neuberger. *Freimaurerei und Nationalsozialismus*, vol. 1, p. 46. The "Alldeutsche Verband" ("Pan-Germanic Union"), founded in 1891 for the furthering of German colonial interests, was doubtless one of the most influential *völkisch* groups. From the beginning, the colonial-political-imperial motive was involved with *völkisch* and anti-

Semitic agendas. In February 1919, the Pan-Germans had defined central positions of the anti-democratic camp such as clinging to "Imperial thought" or demanding the return of the "stolen overseas territories," in the co-called "Bamberg Declaration." (Compare Michael Peters, "Der ,Alldeutsche Verband'," in: *Handbuch zur* "*Völkischen Bewegung*," p. 302ff., here p. 313).

(44)   Cited in Josef Ackermann. *Heinrich Himmler als Ideologe*, Göttingen/Zürich/Frankfurt/M. 1970, p. 25.

(45)   Compare Neuberger. *Freimaurerei und Nationalsozialismus*, vol. 1, p. 45.

(46)   Concerning Schneider, compare a notice from the Große Landesloge of November 11, 1931, or the elaboration (January 15, 1932) correcting some points. (GStA PK, Logen, 5.1.3., 4434 or Osobyi Archives, Moscow, 1412-1-4933. Compare also Archiv GLL (Archives of the Große Landesloge), passim. Schneider's father, "whose memory this slanderer profanes (according to Witt-Hoë), had been a good Freemason" (Letter of Witt-Hoë of December 10, 1930, GStA PK, Logen, 5.1.3., 4329). On December 19, 1935 a notice from the Office of the Secret Police in Darmstadt to State police, county, and police offices Staatspolizeistellen, Kreis- und Polizeiämter, said that Schneider "should receive no special support or preference in the future. The meetings at which he speaks are to be watched very carefully. Detailed reports on the proceedings are to be turned in within 24 hours." (BA [Federal Archives] Schumacher Collection, vol. 221 [complete text in Neuberger, vol. 2, Appendix, p. 320]). The background of the order was that Schneider, although he had been installed by Nazi offices as a speechmaker, had remained allied with Ludendorff and further allied himself with the "Tannenbergbund," which had been forbidden. After his new edition of Wichtls "Weltfreimaurerei" appeared in 1938, Schneider never appeared in public again.

(47)   For more detail on the origin and effect of the *Protokolle*" in Czarist Russia, compare Pfahl-Traughber, "Der antisemitisch-antifreimaurerische Verschwörungsythos," p. 15ff. and Cohn. *Die Protokolle der Weisen von Zion*, p. 75ff. A short summary can be found in Eberhard Jäckel et al. (Eds.), *Enzyklopädie des Holocaust, Die Verfolgung und Ermordung der europäischen Juden*, vol. 1-3, Berlin, 1993, vol. 2, p. 1169ff. For the history of the origin and reception of the *Protokolle* in various contries, compare Katz, *Jews and Freemasons*, p. 193ff. In France, the *Protokolle* were translated twice. The first version was published by the "Action française," the other by the

Catholic publicist Ernest Jouin, the editor of the anti-Semitic "Revue Internationale des Sociétés Secrètes," who introduced the new concept "Judeo-Masonry."

(48)   Ernst Piper, "Die jüdische Weltverschwörung," p. 130, in: Schoeps/Schlör (Ed.), *Antisemitismus*, p. 127 ff.

(49)   *Die Geheimnisse der Weisen von Zion*. Published in German by Gottfried zur Beek (= Ludwig Müller von Hausen = Ludwig Müller), Berlin, 1920. Concerning financing of the publication by members of the House of Hohenzollern, compare Pfahl-Traughber. *Der antisemitisch-antifreimaurerische Verschwörungsmythos*,   p. 60.

(50)   Compare Neuberger, *Freimaurerei und Nationalsozialismus*, vol. 1, p. 47.

(51)   Here sketch after Cohn, *Die Protokolle*, p. 76 ff.

(52)   Beek (Ed.), *Die Geheimnisse der Weisen von Zion*, (*Protokolle*, 9), p. 47. For this work, the 8th edition (Berlin, 1923) was consulted. Here the 24 chapters are called "Richtlinien der Weisen von Zion" ("Guidelines of the Sages of Zion"). In the "Introduction to the 8th Edition," the editor also takes on the attacks against the pamphlet, in that he assumes that their authenticity would be only bolstered by them. However, "the Jewish press in Germany carefully avoided discussing their own guidelines" (p. 19).

(53)   Compare Katz. *Jews and Freemasons*, p. 181.

(54)   Beek (Ed.). *Die Geheimnisse der Weisen von Zion*, (*Protokolle*, 5), p. 40f.

(55)   Alfred Rosenberg. *Die Protokolle der Weisen von Zion und die jüdische Weltpolitik*, München, 1923; Theodor Fritsch (Ed.), *Die Zionistischen Protokolle. Das Programm der internationalen Geheimregierung*, Leipzig, 1924. Concerning the early years of Fritsch's activity in the 1880s, compare Katz. *Jews and Freemasons*, p. 185, 277 (note 66); more on Fritsch in chapter 4.1.

(56)   Theodor Fritsch, "Wesen und Geheimnis der Freimaurerei," in: Hammer. *Blätter für deutschen Sinn*, vol. 26, No. 605, September 9, 1927, p. 433 ff., hier p. 438.

(57)   Ibid.

(58)   Compare, Cohn. *Die Protokolle*, p. 181 ff.; Piper, „Die jüdische Weltverschwörung," *loc. cit.*, p. 132.

(59)   Compare in theis context in detail, Lüthi. *Der Mythos von der Weltverschwörung*;

Cohn. *Die Protokolle*, p. 278 ff., there also on the Bern Trial, p. 281 ff.

(60) Konrad Lerich [d.i. Kurt Reichl], *Der Tempel der Freimaurer. Der 1. bis 33.Grad. Vom Suchenden zum Wissenden*, Bern [supposedly the 2nd. ed.] 1937. The reprint can still be obtained easily and quickly by appropriate methods! For more detail on this work, see Chapter 8.1.

(61) On Fleischhauer, the "Welt-Dienst" ("World Service"), compare Reinhard Bollmus, *Das Amt Rosenberg und seine Gegner. Studien zum Machtkampf im nationalsozialistischen Herrschaftssystem*, Stuttgart, 1970, P. 121f.; Neuberger. *Freimaurerei und Nationalsozialismus*, vol. 2, pp. 38, 56f.; Cohn, *Die Protokolle*, p. 276ff. Der "Welt-Dienst" dissolved into Rosenberg's "Weltanschauungsamt" ("World-view Office") in 1939 (see Chapter 8.1).

(62) Compare Fleischhauer's Forward, in: Lerich, *Der Tempel der Freimaurer*, p. 3.

(63) Ibid., p. 4.

(64) The initiative for the fobidding of Freemasonry in Switzerland, driven by the head of the "Fédération Faschiste Suisse," Colonel Arthur Fonjallaz, and substantially financed by Italy, was set up on October 31, 1934. On November 28, 1937 a vote of the people was taken. The Swiss rejected it by 64.5% (513,553 to 232,466). Compare Lüthi, *Der Mythos von der Weltverschwörung*, p. 107ff.; Liberté, 1871, Anon., ed. by the Lodge Liberté in Lausanne, Lausanne (no year), p. 13ff. Yet Swiss Freemasonry, influenced by the Nazis, recorded a considerable loss of membership. The number of Brothers in the Grand Lodge Alpina sank from 5022 to 2684, between 1932 and 1945 (written note from Jean Bénédicts to the author).

(65) According to Lennhoff/Posner, *Int. Freimaurer-Lexikon*, column 1295, the "non-binding discussion" with Gruber saying that on the Catholic, more precisely, Jesuit side, "the struggle against Freemasonry was to be carried on only on the level of philosophical and scholarly debate, and that there was to be an end to the lying- and accusatory literature." Ludendorff capitalized on the "Aachen Conference" as a reinforcement of his theory of a Masonic-Jewish conspiracy (compare ibid., column 645). Gruber died in 1930.

(66) Compare Pfahl-Traughber, *Der antisemitisch-antifreimaurerische Verschwörungsmythos*, p. 44; also Archives of the Große Landesloge, passim.

(67) Friedrich's efforts at reform were already discussed in chapter 1.2.

(68) Otto von Bismarck. *Gedanken und Erinnerungen*, vol. 1-3, Stuttgart/(Berlin) 1898-1921. In all the three volumes, the subject of

Freemasonry is only very peripherally mentioned: In vol. 1, p. 204, an officer is mentioned, considered by Bismarck to be incompetent, but who, because he was a Freemason, enjoyed the support of Wilhelm I. Wilhelm, complained Bismarck, fulfilled his "obligations to his Brothers with an almost religious loyalty." In another place (vol. 3, p. 62) Bismarck criticized the "feminine and masonic influences," and (ibid., p. 130) "masonic effects" on Wilhelm, because of which he found himself in opposition [to Wilhelm]: "I have been neither courtier nor Mason," thus Bismarck, insulted in his "personal feelings of honor."

(69)   Compare Robert Ebeling, "Den Freimaurern zum neuen Jahr," in: *Volk unterm Hakenkreuz*, no. 1/1934, p. 3.

(70)   Hitler. *Mein Kampf*, München 29th. ed. 1933, p. 337.

(71)   Hermann Rauschning. *Gespräche mit Hitler*, Zürich/New York 5th ed. 1938 (New ed. Zürich, 1973). Concerning Hitler's views pursuant to Rauschning's representation, see below. As is well known, there are no authentic sources for these "conversations;" indeed some of Hitler's statements are invented. The use of Rauschning is, of course, therefore done very cautiously and with the required critical reservation. Concerning this whole complex of questions, also compare Katz. *Jews and Freemasons*, p. 187.

(72)   Hitler. *Mein Kampf*, München 29th ed. 1933, p. 345. This excerpt is also in the Nazi Party directive of 1939 (see Document appendix).

(73)   *Hitlers Zweites Buch. Ein Dokument aus dem Jahre 1928, eingeleitet und kommentiert von Gerhard L. Weinberg* (Accompanying word by Hans Rothfels). Stuttgart, 1961, p. 222. In another place, Hitler expresses himself on the "Protest of all the States directed by World Freemasons" vis-à-vis Mussolini and Italian Facism (p. 182).

(74)   Compare Hitler. *Sämtliche Aufzeichnungen 1905-1924*, ed. by Eberhard Jäckel and Axel Kuhn, Stuttgart, 1980, p. 137 (Speech of May 31, 1920), p. 199 (Speech of August 8, 1920),   p. 221 (Speech of August 8, 1920), pp. 235, 237 (Speech of September 22, 1920), p. 642f. (Speech of May 29, 1922), p. 691 (Speech of September 18, 1922), p. 885f., 891 (Speech of April 13, 1923), p. 955 (Speech of August 1, 1923). The sources named here do not belong to the writings of this publication, which are proven to be forgeries. (Compare Jäckel/Kuhn, "Neue Erkenntnisse zur Fälschung von Hitler-Dokumenten," in: VfZ, vol. 32., no. 1/1984, p. 163f.

(75)   Compare Rogalla von Bieberstein. "Vom Antimasonismus zum (Vernichtungs-) Antisemitismus," in: Helmut Reinalter (Ed.), *2. Internationale Tagung in Innsbruck*, p. 99ff. Peripherally it might be noted that Bieberstein is moving into the vicinity of the theses propounded by Ernst Nolte in "Historikerstreit."

(76)   Ibid., p. 108.

(77)   Detail concerning this is in Neuberger. *Freimaurerei und Nationalsozialismus*, vol. 1, p. 104ff., and in the notes, vol. 1, p. 305ff. Also there is material on Mathilde Ludendorff's position in the circle of the *völkisch* movement, which latter was determined by men.

(78)   From a speech by Mathilde Ludendorffs in Rendsburg on September 16, 1928, GStA PK, Logen, 5.1.3., 4409.

(79)   Eugen Lennhoff, "Ludendorff marschiert an der Spitze," in: Reichl (Ed.), *Blaubuch*, vol. 1933, p. 39ff., here p. 39.

(80)   Compare Neuberger. *Nationalsozialismus und Freimaurerei*, vol. 1, p. 306.

(81)   Compare Pfahl-Traughber. *Der antisemitisch-antifreimaurerische Verschwörungsmyhos*, p. 47.

(82)   Erich Ludendorff. *Vernichtung der Freimaurerei durch Enthüllung ihrer Geheimnisse*, München, 1927. The edition numbers according to Neuberger in *Freimaurerei und Nationalsozialismus*, vol. 1, p. 115.

(83)   Cited after Neuberger. *Freimaurerei und Nationalsozialismus*, vol. 1, p. 115f. Compare auch Steffens. *Freimaurer*, p. 344. Also Archiv GLL, passim.

(84)   Compare, for example a letter of October 25, 1927, in this vein from the main administration of the Pan-Germanic Union to a member of the Große Landesloge (GStA PK, Logen, 5.1.3, 4398). It states that "we... have defended the national-monarchist and Christian Lodges in Germany against unjustified attacks." Aside from Ludendorff's attacks, the Old Prussians found themselves temporarily under pressure because of a lettter entitled "Aus der Werkstatt der Freimaurer und Juden im Österreich der Nachkriegszeit" ("From the workshop of Freemasons and Jews in post-war Austria"). The author, the Austrian Nazi Dr. Paul Heigl, used the pseudonym Dr. Friedrich Hergeth. He initiated a debate whose main thrust was the relationship of the German lodges to the Grand Lodge of Vienna (compare GStA PK, Logen, 5.1.3., 4398, passim). Certainly Heigl's letter, consisting primarily of a listing of Austrian Jews and Freemasons, as well as their more or less influential positions, remained in

both distribution and effect, far behind Ludendorff's pamphlets. However, its resonance was not so small as Neuberger described it. Compare vol. 1, p. 130f. Heigl was later employed by the SD (Security Service). More detail concerning Heigl in Neuberger. *Freimaurerei und Nationalsozialismus*, vol. 2, p. 155f.

(85)   Compare concerning this, the report of a discussion between the Grand Archivist of the Große Landesloge, Felix Witt-Hoë, and the board of the Pan-Germanic Union on December 21, 1927, GStA PK, Logen, 4398.

(86)   Cited after Lennhoff/Posner, *Int. Freimaurer-Lexikon*, column 1519f. Stresemann was accepted into the Three World Globes subordinate lodge, "Friedrich der Große" in 1923. Compare Peters. *Berliner Freimaurer*, p. 62). That he affiliated with Old Prussian Freemasonry is not surprising because Stresemann's political heritage was monarchistic-national, and he belonged to the Pan-Germanic Union. Concerning Stresemann, compare Hagen Schulze. *Weimar: Deutschland 1917-1933*, Berlin, 1982, p. 256f. Schulze refers to Stresemann's also later abiding "deep veneration of the Hohenzollern monarchy." Everything speaks for the idea that he "remained who he was, yet he had the capability to learn from his mistakes, and to carry on politics without much rancor." (Ibid., p. 257). In the medium term, after the creation of public room for action on the revision of the Treaty of Versailles, this aimed at winning back an equal postion for Germany in the European sphere of influence (lit: field of power).

(86a)   Letter from Stresemann to Habicht, January 23, 1927, USHMM.

(86b)   Letter from Alpina (Grand Lodge) to Stresemann, January 4, 1927, *loc. cit.*

(86c)   Letter from Habicht to Stresemann, January 24, 1927, *loc. cit.*

(87)   Compare on this "Hermann der Deutsche" [i.e. Hermann Hesse]. *Die Weltrevolution des Roten Propheten: Die Verschwörung der Freimaurer und Finanzmagnaten*, Berlin, 1928 (GStA PK, I. HA, Rep. 84a, no. 15 085). Walther Rathenau is called the "Red Prophet" in this publication, which was confiscated shortly after it appeared, by action of the the police presidium and State Attorney's Office in Stettin, or Stagard, because it was against the Law for the Protection of the Republic. Behind the author hid a Berlin jurist, an author named Dr. Hermann Hesse, who is not the same as the author and Nobel Prizewinner. Hesse was sentenced to four months in

prison because it was in violation of the Law for the Protection of the Republic. The judgment of the extended lay assessors' court in Berlin-Lichterfelde was at first confirmed by the Landgerichts II in Berlin, and lastly by the Reichsgericht (Imperial Court) on October 16, 1930. Compare "Schriftverkehr und Urteile" in: *GStA PK*, I. HA, Rep. 84a, No. 15 085.

(88)   Thus Wolfram Sievers, who had held significant positions with the "Ahnenerbe" ("Ancestors" heritage/inheritance) since 1935. Cited in Michael H. Kater. *Das "Ahnenerbe" der SS 1935-1945: Ein Beitrag zur Kulturpolitik des Dritten Reiches*, Stuttgart, 1974, p. 176. According to Kater, Sievers had become the real key figure of the "Ahnenerbe" already in the summer of 1935. He was the one who "gave the association the stamp of the SS." (p. 28). For more on the "Ahnenerbe" and its first chairman, Herman Wirth (for whom Sievers had worked as private secretary for awhile) see Chapter 4.1.

(89)   Neuberger. *Freimaurerei und Nationalsozialismus*, vol. 1, p. 167. Neuberger maintains that the Nazi leaders Heydrich, Wessel, and probably even Göring, came from Masonic families "houses," and he pointedly makes a connection between the politcal social milieu of the Old Prussian lodges and the German-*völkisch* circles. (Compare vol. 1, p. 166f.). This context-connection is not so odd as Neuberger assumed. In terms of the history of ideas, it can be convincingly shown. Horst Wessel's father can be documented as a member of a lodge (under the Große Landesloge), because the Fremasons make repeated reference to it. For example, a Masonic Brother referred to it as late as 1936; a district commander forbade him acceptance into the Officer Corps because of his earlier lodge membership (compare the correspondence on this of April/May 1936, in: GstA PK, Logen, 5.1.3., 4337). In the case of Göring's father, the information on his membership in Freemasonry rests on an oral statement of the journalist and writer, Harry Wilde to Neuberger (compare vol. 1, p. 318, note 41). In many sources, it is shown that a half-brother of Göring's was a member of the subordinate lodge of the Große Landesloge "Nassau-Oranien zu den beständigen Quellen" in Wiesbaden, and had intervened in the contact made by his grand lodge with Hermann Göring before the "Seizure of Power." (Compare GStA PK, Logen, 5.1.3., 4443, passim). See also Chapter 3.1. Furthermore, Goebbels' father-in-law, Oscar Ritschel was a Freemason. He belonged to the the subordinate lodge of the Große Landesloge "Eos" in Krefeld. For a short time the Große Landesloge

tried to build up contact with Goebbels through him. (Compare GStA PK, Logen, 5.1.3., 4461, passim; see also Chapter 3.1). In the case of Heydrich's father, Neuberger depends on Aronson (compare p. 32). There it says only that Bruno Heydrich had been a co-founder of the "Schlaraffia" in Halle, and–as founder of otherwise not further-named "lodges"–had figured in business conversations. From this information, at least, one cannot be sure that he was a Freemason. The friendship association, "Schlaraffia," founded in Prague in 1859 for the furthering of art and humor, in any case, has nothing to do with Freemasonry, but was falsely connected with it. For more on the problem (question) of the treatment of former lodge members in the "Third Reich," see more detail in Chapter 8.2.

(90)   See Chapter 8.1.

(91)   Cited after Rogalla von Bieberstein, "Vom Antimasonismus zum (Vernichtungs-) Antisemitismus," *loc.cit.*, p. 108.

(92)   Compare Henry Picker. *Hitlers Tischgespräche im Führerhauptquartier*, Frankfurt/M./Berlin, 1989, pp. 77, 234, 208. The basic tone of the elaborating commentary is intolerably flattering to Hitler and Nazi politics, rendering [atrocities–trans.note] insignificant, pro-Germanic, and militaristic. The position vis-à-vis Freemasonry is brought in, to undertake a politically motivated identification between Hitler and Stalin, which levels the singularity (uniqueness) of the "Third Reich" (compare p. 77). In addition, "Hitler's spectacular closing of the Masonic lodges in Germany on August 17, 1935" is discussed is a transfiguring manner. The truth is that on this date all the still-existing lodges and lodge-like associations (at first, except B'nai B'rith) wereforcibly dissolved (see Chapter 5.2.2). Most of the Masonic organizations in the Reich territory were already gone by this time.There was absolutely nothing "spectacular" about the order.

(93)   Rauschning. *Gespräche mit Hitler*, p. 227. oncerning the problem of the use of Rauschning, see note II/71.

(94)   Ibid., p. 226.

(95)   Ibid.

(96)   Concerning Rosenberg see also Chapter 8.1. Compare in this context Neuberger. *Freimaurerei und Nationalsozialismus*, vol. 1, p. 58ff. and Reinalter, „Freimaurerei und Nationalsozialismus am Beispiel Alfred Rosenbergs," *loc.cit.*, p. 55ff. See there (pp. 55, 63f.)

also concerning the meaning of Houston Stewart Chamberlain for Rosenberg and the Nazi world-view (Weltanschauung).

(97) Compare Reinalter. „Freimaurerei und Nationalsozialismus am Beispiel Alfred Rosenbergs,"*loc.cit.*, p. 65f. In 1934 Rosenberg took over the function of chief of Nazi Party training ("Reichsschulungsleiter").

(98)   Compare *Völkischer Beobachter*, Nos. 54-57, March 6, 1930-October 10, 1930. The pocedure also had a juducial epilogue. Compare Bundesarchives, NS 8/120, folio 27ff.

(99)   It is important to emphasize that B'nai B'rith was an independent organization. More than in German Freemasonry, B'nai B'rith – besides the strengthening of Judaism – had social and charitable functions. Despite external similarities and Masonic content, there is no organizational connection to Freemasonry. Although members of B'nai B'rith sometimes belong to masonic lodges, Freemasons, if they are not Jewish, cannot become members of B'nai B'rith. A history of B'nai B'rith in Germany would be an excellent research subject. The only inportant work is that by Karin Voelker, "The B'Nai B'rith Order (U.O.B.B.) in the Third Reich (1933-1937," in *Leon Baeck Institute Yearbook*,Vol. 32. P. 269ff., which was written without access to the Archives in Eastern Europe and Russia. For an overview, but with difficult access, compare E.M. Seeligsohn, *Vorträge, Zeichnungen, Gedanken [s.l.]*, 2.Aufl. 1986.

(100)   Cited according to a legal deposition [anwaltlichen Stellungnahme] in the context of a [legal] proceeding on February 13, 1935, because of slander and calumny. GStA PK, Logen, 5.1.3., 4336.

(101)   Compare the circular ordinance from April 10, 1937 of the "Reichsführers SS" and Chief of the German Police reproduced in *Versuch einer Darstellung der Verfolgung der deutschen Großlogen und deren Tochterlogen und freimaurerähnlichen Organisationen. Dargestellt nach amtlichen Verlautbarungen des 3.Reiches, der NSDAP, der gleichgeschalteten Presse und sonstiger führender Freimaurer ehemaliger deutscher Großlogen aller Systeme*, compiled by Karl Günther, paperback (with compiler's commentary), Köln, 1954, p. 133.

(102)   Alfred Rosenberg, *Das Verbrechen der Freimaurerei. Judentum, Jesuitismus, Deutsches Christentum*, München 2nd. Aufl. 1922. cited after Reinalter. „Freimaurerei und Nationalsozialismus am Beispiel Alfred Rosenbergs, *loc.cit.*, P. 57. An explanation of the question of the

Freemasons and Jesuits in t"he context of Nationalsocialism will not be undertaken in the framework of this study.

(103)   Alfred Rosenberg. *Der Mythus des 20. Jahrhunderts: Eine Wertung der seelisch-geistigen Gestaltungskämpfe unserer Zeit*, first published in München, 1930. For this work, the Munich 31-32 edition (1934) was used.

(104)   Neuberger. *Freimaurerei und Nationalsozialismus*, vol. 1, p. 157.

(105)   Compare concerning this the fundamental essay by Johannes Rogalla von Bieberstein, "Aufklärung, Freimaurerei, Menschenrechte und Judenemanzipation in der Sicht des Nationalsozialismus," in: *Jahrbuch des Instituts für Deutsche Geschichte an der Universität Tel Aviv*, 7/1978, p. 339ff., here especially p. 350. Already ten years before, a Jewish-Marxist conspiracy had been suggested by *völkisch* circles because of a reference to Lenin und Trotzky (Compare Katz. *Jews and Freemasons*, p. 177).

(106)   Neuberger. *Freimaurerei und Nationalsozialismus*, vol. 1, p. 160.

(107)   Rosenberg. *Der Mythus des 20. Jahrhunderts*, p. 699.

(108)   Katz. *Jews and Freemasons*, p. 174. The social-democratic *Vorwärts* reported an example of the application and effect of the conspiracy theory in the Weimar time: A member of the Nazi Party had to answer a charge of insulting the labor office before a lay assessor's court in Altona. At the beginning of the proceedings, the defendant asked the question "'whether Jesuits, Jews, or Freemasons were among the judges.' Instead of rejecting this effrontery out of hand," continued the *Vorwärts*, "the court withdrew to consult among themselves, and announced in a small voice, that one of the judges, although not belonging to the Jewish faith himself, had a Jewish father." Thereupon the defendant rejected the judge because of prejudice,and actually had his way in court. The *Vorwärts* asked sarcastically whether one would, in the future, perhaps call upon race-snooper Günther, who had been called to the University of Jena by Mr. Frick, as an expert to [testify in] every case against Nazis. (*Vorwärts*, 6.8.1930 [GStA PK, Logen, 5.1.3., 4330]).

(109)   Cited in Steffens. *Freimaurer*, P. 354.

(110)   Rogalla von Bieberstein. „Die These von der freimaurerischen Verschwörung," *loc. cit.*, p. 87.

(111)   Compare ibid. und Morvan. "Aspects du mythe conspirationniste," p. 3.

(112)   Compare for example Ernst Nolte. *Der Faschismus in seiner Epoche. Die Action française. Der italienische Faschismus. Der Nationalsozialismus,* München, 1963, p. 488.

(113)   Compare ibid.

(114)   Hitler. *Mein Kampf,* München 29th ed. 1933, p. 351.

(115)   Hjalmar Kutzleb. *Mord an der Zukunft.* Mit Zeichnungen von A. Paul Weber, Berlin, 1929, pp. 16, 24. Cited after Christiane Hoss et al. (eds.), *100 Jahre deutscher Rassismus,* ed. by the Kölnische Gesellschaft für Christlich-Jüdische Zusammen   arbeit, Köln, 1988. p. 198. Consistent with the text are the especially disgusting, defamatory and dehumanizing drawings.

(116)   Artur Moeller van den Bruck. *Das dritte Reich,* 1st ed. 1923. For this study the 3rd (Hamburg, 1931) edition was used. According to Kurt Sontheimer this is without doubt the most effective book of the "conservative Revolution" (compare Sontheimer, *Antidemokratisches Denken in der Weimarer Republik,* München 4th ed. 1962, p. 303 [note169]). Moeller died by his own hand in 1925.

(117)   Sontheimer. *Antidemokratisches Denken,* p. 301.

(118)   Compare ibid., p. 72f.

(119)   On the Wetzlar Ring, see Chapter 4.1.

(120)   Schmidt. *Die Freimaurerei im Dienste deutscher Nationalbildung,* p. 36.

(121)   Moeller van den Bruck. *Das dritte Reich,* pp. 32, 74. In Freemasonry, says Moeller elsewhere, one is concerned with the attempt "to find a substitute for the world 'un-deified' by it, which substitue Freemasonry found in a fraternal world." (ibid., p. 78).

(121a)   Saul Friedländer. *Das Dritte Reich und die Juden, Bd. 1: Die Jahre der Verfolgung 1933-1939.* 2d. ed. (Munich, 1998), p. 99.

(122)   Compare in this connection Rürup. *"Die 'Judenfrage' der bürgerlichen Gesellschaft," loc.cit.,* p. 74ff.; Monika Richarz (Ed.), *Bürger auf Widerruf: Lebenszeugnisse deutscher Juden 1780-1945,* München, 1989; Rainer Erb/ Werner Bergmann, *Die Nachtseite der Judenemanzipation: Der Widerstand gegen die Integration der Juden in Deutschland 1780-1860,* Berlin, 1989.

(123)   Engelbert Huber. *Freimaurerei: Die Weltmacht hinter den Kulissen,* Stuttgart, 1934, here is cited the 3rd ed., no year., p. 296. On Huber and this letter, see also chapter 5.2.1. More information on Huber and this work in Chapter 5.2.1.

(124) Compare ibid., especially p. 143ff.

(125) Alfred Franz Six. *Das Reich und der Westen*, Berlin, 1940, p. 27, cited after Rogalla von Bieberstein. *Aufklärung, Freimaurerei...*, loc.cit., p. 340. Concerning Six,compare among others Rürup. Topographie des Terrors, pp. 77, 80; Pfahl-Traughber. *Der antisemitisch-antifreimaurerische Verschwörungsmythos*, p. 172; Ulrich Herbert, *Best.Biographische Studien über Radikalismus, Weltanschauung und Vernunft 1903-1989*, Bonn, 1996, passim. See also chapter 8.1. Six was moved [lit: kicked] to the SD in 1935 and in the following year, by machinations of the SS, was made Professor of Foreign Studies at theUniversity of Berlin without any scholarly accomplishment on his part. In Six' "put-up job" of 1938 called "Freimaurerei und Judenemanzipation" ("Freemasonry and Emancipation of the Jews") it says in typical fashion, "the religious tolerance of Freemasonry opened the lodge doors to Jewishness (i.e. the Jews), from which, by way of the salons of the bourgeoisie, one was to continue the journey into political life." (cited after Rogalla von Bieberstein. *Aufklärung, Freimaurerei...*, p. 347, note 39).

(126) Cited after Hermann Gilbhard. *Die Thule-Gesellschaft. Vom okkulten Mummenschanz zum Hakenkreuz*, München, 1994, p. 50.

(127) Rogalla von Bieberstein. „Die These von der freimaurerischen Verschwörung," *loc.cit.*, p. 85.

(128) Compare Katz. *Jews and Freemasons*, p. 174f.

(129) Compare ibid., p. 177.

(130) Reinalter. "Auf der Suche nach Sündenböcken," *loc.cit.*, p. 120.

(131) Rogalla von Bieberstein. *Aufklärung, Freimaurerei...*, *loc.cit.*, p. 347.

(132) *Bericht der Abteilung II/111*, undated, ca. 1936, Osobyi Archives, Moscow, 500-3-411.

(133) Cited after Rogalla von Bieberstein, „Aufklärung, Freimaurerei...," *loc. cit.*, p. 348.

(134) Ernst Graf zu Reventlow. *Judas Kampf und Niederlage in Deutschland*, Berlin, 1937, p. 8, cited ibid., p. 347. Felix Witt-Hoë, one of the major funtionaries of the Große Landesloge corresponded with Reventlow in 1928. Much more will be said about Witt-Hoë, who reacted with a rather long letter to being sent Reventlow's Traktate "Für Christen, Nichtchristen, Antichristen" ("For Christians, non-Christians, anti-Christians") by the author, together with the suggestion that the piece be reviewed "in theMasonic press." (Letter from Reventlow to Witt-Hoë

of May 29, 1928, GStA PK, Logen, 5.1.3., 4378).Witt-Hoë explained at the beginning of his letter, that if he answered now, he did it "because of an old feeling of gratitude and respect for the man, who, in the long years of time before our people's turn of fate, as a loyal warning voice (admonishment) on lonely watch posts, had been even for us younger officers a beacon and advisor of rare clarity." Then Witt-Hoë assured him, that the Große Landesloge did not have any influence on "the Masonic press." It would be difficult "to sketch in a few sentences even approximately the variety of the many concepts contained in this concept." The outsider forgets too easily, "that these different concepts have struggled with each other most vehemently since their conception." The Große Landesloge, continued Witt-Hoë, was "no Masonic grand lodge in the ordinary sense, but a Christian order, and therefore something fundamentally different from that which outsiders and adherents of other kinds of teachings than ours understand under 'Freemasonry'" (Witt-Hoë's letter of June 2, 1928 to Reventlow, ibid.).

(135) Rudolf Kommoss. *Juden machen Weltpolitik*, Berlin (no year), p. 11, cited by Piper. "Die jüdische Weltverschwörung," *loc.cit.*, p. 132.

(136) Rosenberg. *Der Mythus des 20. Jahrhunderts*, p. 200f.

(137) Wilhelm Stuckart/Hans Globke, *Kommentare zur deutschen Rassengesetzgebung*, vol. 1 [Reichsbürgergesetz [Reichs citizenship law] of September 15, 935; Gesetz zum Schutze des deutschen Blutes und der deutschen Ehre [Law for the protection of German blood and German honor] of September 15, 1935; Gesetz zum Schutze der Erbgesundheit des deutschen Volkes (Ehegesundheitsgesetz) [Law for the protection of hereditary health – Marriage health law] of October 18, 1935 together with all the implementation manuals and the relevant laws and ordinances, München/Berlin, 1936.

(138) Ibid., p. 13.

(139) Ibid., p. 3.

(140) Compare ibid., pp. 12, 20.

(141) "Der Ewige Jude: 265 Bilddokumente gesammelt von Hans Diebow," München; Berlin, 1937, p. 2, cited after Rogalla von Bieberstein, *Aufklärung, Freimaurerei...*, *loc.cit.*, p. 344.

(142) Compare E.H. Schulz/R. Frerks (Eds.), *Warum Arierparagraph? Ein Beitrag zur Judenfrage*, Berlin 6th expanded ed. 1937, p. 16, cited ibid., p. 345.

(143)   Reventlow. *"Judas Kampf und Niederlage in Deutschland,"* p. 386, cited ibid.

(144)   Hitler. *Mein Kampf,* München 29th ed. 1933, p. 70.

(145)   Joseph Goebbels. *Der Faschismus und seine praktischen Ergebnisse,* Berlin, 1934, p. 13, cited after Rogalla von Bieberstein, *Aufklärung, Freimaurerei...*, *loc. cit.*, p. 350 (note 51).

CHAPTER 3

(1)   Compare Endler/Schwarze, *Die Freimaurerbestände,* vol. 1, p. 37.

(2)   Compare in this connection, the correspondence of Felix Witt-Hoë, the first delegated Grand Master of the Große Landesloge, with opponents and representatives of subordinate lodges (GStA PK, Logen 5.1.3., 4331f., passim). Compare also circular letters of the Landes Grand Master Müllendorff of June 9, 1929 and August 1, 1930 (Osobyi Archives, Moscow, 1412-1-4933), in which all Brothers, in accordance with a decision of the grand communication, were invited to increase the defense fund with a one-time contribution of .5 Reichsmark. Additional costs could be settled by motion of subordinate lodges. In individual cases, honoraria for lectures or their written versions were financed thus. In this connection, for example, Friedrich Schiffermüller, a former theater director and Große Landesloge Brother from Dresden, wrote in September 1932: "I, who am almost broke, would be eternally grateful if I could begin a new occupation, even if only of a temporary sort with the help of the defense fund, so that I would not have to anticipate the coming winter with such depressing concern" (GStA PK, Logen, 5.1.3., 4332).

(3)   Letters of the Loge "Nordstern" vom 16.6.1920, GStA PK, Logen, 5.1.3., 4342. There is also to be found the summons of the Landes Grand Master and the reactions of the other lodges.

(4)   The letter of October 19, 1926 said: "I most cordially thank the Große Landesloge of the Freemasons of Germany for the friendly invitation to the dedication of the the Memorial Tablet of the Brethren who have fallen for the Fatherland. I regret that because of the number of similar requests, and in consideration of my official duties, I am unable to take part personally in your memorial service.

I assure you, however, that I will be there in spirit unted with you in grateful remembrance of the dead comrades, and with mourning thoughts of our fallen ones. Most respectfully and sincerely yours, signed von Hindenburg." (Original in: GStA PK, Logen, 5.1.3., 4342).

(5)   Report of the "solemn unveiling of a Memorial Tablet to the memory of the Brethren who have fallen for the Fatherland" in the Hall of the Große Landesloge of the Freemasons of Germany in Berlin on October 31, 1926, ed. by the Große Landesloge *ZK-Sonderdruck*, Berlin, 1926, no page number (GStA PK, Logen, 5.1.3., 4343).

(6)   Compare Neuberger, *Freimaurerei und Nationalsozialismus*, vol. 1, p. 211. The indication of the average age from Steffens, *Freimaurer*, p. 326.

(7)   See in the example of the Große Landesloge, Chapter 6.1. The compilation appeared in 1932, that is, the same year as the memorial book of the Reichs Association of Jewish Soldiers on the Front.

(8)   Endler/Schwarze, *Die Freimaurerbestände*, vol. 1, p. 39.

(9)   See more on that in this chapter.

(10)   Hartwig Lohmann (Grand Master of the Große Landesloge). Speech on the Bringing in of the Light into the St. John's Lodge, Friedrich zur Standhaftigkeit" ("Frederick and Steadfastedness") in Halle/Saale on March 20, 1993, in: Z.K. 121. Vol., May issue 1993, p. 164. An altogether gratifying, self-critical speech. The citation refers to the Große Landesloge, but applies in exactly the same way to the other Old Prussians.

(11)   Ibid., p. 165. After the seizure of power by the Nazis, the Old Prussians were supposed to indicate that they had not sought state protection during the years of the Republic.

(12)   Compare Heinrich August Winkler, Weimar 1918–1933. *Die Geschichte der ersten deutschen Demokratie*, München, 1993, p. 601.

(13)   Schulze, *Weimar*, p. 421.

(14)   Cited after Raoul Koner, *Ein Freimaurerleben: Erlebnisse und Betrachtungen*, Bielefeld, 1976, p. 63.

(15)   Cited after Ibid. On the 4th World Congress of the Comintern compare *Sowjetsystem und Demokratische Gesellschaft*, ed. von C.D. Kernig, vol. 3, Freiburg/Basel/Wien, 1969, column 777f.

(16)   Herbert, *Best.*, p. 12.

(17)   Compare ibid., passim. The excellent trail-blazing study by Ulrich Herberts may long remain the standard work in this connection.

(18)   See below. Best seems actually to have been surprised by the differences within Freemasonry as presented by him.

(19)   Cited after Hans Buchheim. "Befehl und Gehorsam" in: Hans Buchheim/Martin Broszat/Hans-Adolf Jacobsen/Helmut Krausnick (Ed.), *Anatomie des SS-Staates*, München 5th. Aufl. 1989, vol. 1, p. 235. From this "realistic" affirmation of "reality" and against the background of Jüngers main idea, which says it is not the essential for which one fights, but how, Best arrived at the concept of "an heroic morality," which was not defined by content, but by form (compare ibid., p. 236).

(20)   Compare Strauss on this in: *Deutsch-Jüdische Geschichtswissenschaft und Antisemitismusforschung heute*, loc.cit., p. 31.

(21)   According to G. Pösche. *25 Jahre Freimaurerei 1906-1931*, Berlin, 1931, p. 61, cited in Katz, *Jews and Freemasons*, p. 189 (note78).

(22)   The broad penetration of the German educated middle class with with *völkisch*-anti-Semitic Ideas paired with the weakness of political liberalism led to the Jews' being more and more homeless in terms of society and party politics (compare Strauss. *Deutsch-Jüdische Geschichtswissenschaft und Antisemitismusforschung heute*, loc.cit., p. 33). Before 1918 the "rhetorical-revolutionary form" scared [people off from] the SPD (Social Democratic Party of Germany). In addition, the social composition of the German Jews stood in contrast to a broad spreading of social democracy.

(23)   With the issue no. 12/1930 the addition of "Deutsch-Christlicher Orden" to the letterhead of circular correspondence came into use.

(24)   Compare the lodge newsletter (notice?) of the Grand Lodge of Hamburg, no. 1/1931, cited in Peters, *Die Geschichte der Freimaurerei*, p. 222.

(25)   Bolle's opinion from the year 1940 (Archives of the Große Landsloge).

(26)   A Brother from Hanau, of the administration of the Große Landsloge, circulated relevant proposals in October 1930.

(27)   Compare Neuberger, *Freimaurerei und Nationalsozialismus*, vol. 2, p. 80.

(28)   Compare ibid., vol. 1, p. 258f. and How, "The Collapse," p. 27. In addition, as rightly noted by Neuberger, the passive-anti-Semitic basic position expressed here, was a phenomenon that did not remain limited to the Old Prussian lodges (compare vol. 1, p. 259). More details on this are in Chapters 3.3 and 5.1. Graf Waldersee, who promulgated a sharp anti-Semitism, and believed in the Jewish world conspiracy, was considered as a sort of foster father of Wilhelm II.

(29)   Witt-Hoë's response of July 27, 1925, p. 2 (GStA PK, Logen, 5.1.3., 4390). It is unclear whether the reponse in this detailed version was actually sent.

(30)   Ibid., p. 3. See also chapter 4.1 on this. For more details on the National Association of German Officers see chapter 3.3.

(31)   Compare Endler/Schwarze, *Die Freimaurerbestände*, vol. 1, p. 37.

(32)   The listing of the figures of 1925 is from C. van Dalens *Kalender für Freimaurer*, vol. 1926, p. 94. Most of the growth until 1925 was registered by the Große Landsloge, the National Mother Lodge, and the Provincial Grand Lodge of Saxony. According to its annual report for 1924, the Freemasons' Association of the Rising Sun ("Aufgehende Sonne") had 2,664 members in 61 Lodges and 17 "Kränzchen" ("Circles"). The numbers are according to Endler/ Schwarze in *Die Freimaurerbestände*, vol. 1, p. 291.

(33)   Listings for 1932 are according to C. van Dalens *Kalender für Freimaurer*, vol. 1933/34, p. 184. This volume appeared in 1933, and was supposed to remain the last edition. The considerable decline in membership because of the Nazi "seizure of power" was also not included. Noteworthy is that the Dalen calendar as of the volume for 1931, included the new Symbolic Grand Lodge and "Aufgehende Sonne" in the listing. For 1932, 800 members of the Symbolic Grand Lodge (in 28 lodges) and 1,250 of "Aufgehende Sonne" (in 50 lodges) were recorded. Ibid. Meanwhile, Dr. Leo Müffelmann, Grand Master of the Symbolic Grand Lodge, was dissatisfied with the treatment in the Dalen calendar: In a letter to Grand Treasurer Adolf Bünger on December 16, 1931, he complained that the journal *Die Alten Pflichten*, did not mention the lodges in Berlin or the "Exile" Lodge in Palestine (GStA PK, Logen, 5.1.11., 17). See in this connection also chapters 3.3 and 7.1. The Dalen Calendar years 1931 and 1932 contain pages oddly having completely identical figures with those of 1930. It seems that either a new edition did not succeed, or something was overlooked in the production stage. In the Forward to

the volume for 1933-1934, the publisher and editor found that it had not been possible for many Grand Lodges to set up proper statistics, because in principle, statistical prerequisites were not used (applied): for example, honorary members were counted twice. Presumably that is the reason, as Neuberger opines, that "after 1931" (vol. 2, p. 250) one could not obtain exact figures any more. There exist only estimates of the dramatic drop between 1933 and 1935. Also the Gestapa came up with figures in its internal "Mitteilungen No. 5" (GStA PK, I, 90 P, 129) in April 1934 that varied only slightly from those in the "Größenordnung" of 1932. On what these listings were based, was not given. One thing is certain: they do not reflect the actual membership in 1934. On membership development in general, compare also Neuberger, *Freimaurerei und Nationalsozialismus*, vol. 1, p. 213f. Also, with caution, Peters' *Die Geschichte der Freimaurerei*, pp. 207, 270. In Peters it says, irrelevantly, that the high point of the rise in membership was reached in 1928. A statistic from the Verein Deutscher Freimaurer (V.d.F., Association of German Freemasons) shows the number of Old Prussian members as 57,000; that of the Humanitarian grand lodges at 24,000. Cited in Katz' *Jews and Freemasons*, p. 189. In the case of the Old Prussians, these figures are a little above, in that of the Humaniarians somewhat above, those that the 1929 Dalen calendar lists for 1927, and very little (even less) different from those for 1928.

(34)   Endler/Schwarze, *Die Freimaurerbestände*, vol. 1, p. 37.

(35)   Cited in: Renate Endler, "Zu Entstehung und Inhalt der Freimaurerei, ihrer Entwicklung in Deutschland und zur Geschichte der Loge ‚Amalia' in Weimar. " Vortrag, Weimar, November 3, 1990. Compare in this regard Beyer. *Der Übertritt*, p. 74. In the course of the change in system, two lodges in Nürnberg left the Eclectic Association and joined the Grand Lodge "Zur Freundschaft." They made sure, in a contract, that their Jewish brothers would be permitted to retain membership for a while (compare Beyer, *Der Übertritt*, p. 74). Beyer showed definitely with this case, how deep the ethical sensibilities in one part of German Freemasonry had sunk "under the pounding fire of *völkisch* and Nazi slogans." Obviously, there was comprehension of the "unmasonic," deep humiliation of the Jewish Brethren. (Ibid.)

(36)   Neuberger, *Freimaurerei und Nationalsozialismus*, vol. 1, p. 244.

(37)   Ibid., p. 252.

(38)   Ibid., vol. 2, p. 69.

(39)   Lennhoff/Posner, *Int. Freimaurer-Lexikon*, column 1072.

(40)   Cited in Beyer, *Der Übertritt*, p. 119. Beyer summarizes sufficiently: "Really a very meager result for a Masonic evening of enlightenment." (Ibid.).

(41)   Mss. of Wilhelm II of August 23, 1928. The original postcard is in the Archives of the Große Landesloge. See also the appendix of documents.

(42)   From: "Jehovah. Der Herr der Freimaurerei" (Jehovah: the Lord of Freemasonry in the Archives of the Große Landesloge).

(43)   The exact process of the procedures can be only partially reconstructed from the data in the collection of the Große Landesloge in the GStA PK. When Seldte—who, according to Groche—came from a Masonic family, was part of the government after the Nazis' "seizure of power," the Große Landesloge hoped for support from his side. The old contacts proved, however, to be useless. The "Stahlhelm" was absorbed into the SA ("Storm Department"). See Chapter 5.1.

(44)   The decision of May 10, 1927 was given in confidential circular letter no. 273 of May 12, 1931 (GStA PK, Logen, 5.1.3., 4392). The corresponding instructions of the Deutschen Adelsgenossenschaft (German Society of Nobility) of December 3-4, 1926, had left it to the indivdual's own conscience to decide whether membership in the German Society of Nobility and in an Old Prussian lodge were compatible (compare GStA PK, Logen, 5.1.3., 4428, passim).

(45)   Reproduced ibid.

(46)   Führer-Nachrichten-Blatt der Bundesleitung des "Stahlhelm, Bund der Frontsoldaten" (Führer's Newsletter of the Federal Administration of the Stahlhelm, the Association of the Soldiers on the Front), no. 31, July 13. 1926, p. 3 (GStA PK, Logen, 5.1.3., 4392).

(47)   Concerning this problem see Chapter 3.3. Possibly their pertinent experience with the National Association of German Officers led to the fact that the Old Prussians fought more stubbornly for remaining in and restraining the "Stahlhelm."

(48)   From a letter of Groche to the Bundesrat (Federal Adminstration) "Stahlhelm" of February 12, 1928, Archives of the Große Landesloge.

(49)   Ibid.

(50)   Witt-Hoë's letter to Groche of February 18, 1928, GStA PK, Logen, 5.1.3., 4392.

(51)   Compare Witt-Hoë's letter to Feistkorn of June 5, 1930, ibid. Feistkorn, a retired postal official had served since June 1930 as the last Grand Master of the Grand Lodge "Zur Freundschaft" before Freemasonry was forbidden.

(52)   Compare GStA PK, Logen, ibid., passim. For the Große Landesloge, surprisingly, the National Mother Lodge also decided, in May 1925, not to work any longer with the "Stahlhelm"-Commission (according to a letter from Korsch to Witt-Hoë of May 27, 1929, ibid.). In the same letter it says that the St. John's Order had made a decision, according to which, in the future, only Freemasons who were members of the Große Landesloge could belong to it.

(53)   Compare Korsch's letter of April 25, 1929 to Witt-Hoë, ibid. In a draft of a response to a question of the Commitee concerning foreign lodges, Korsch wrote on May 22, 1929, that to him "every foreigner, without exception, was an abomination." He assumed, in the depths of his heart, that every German was a decent man, until he would prove otherwise, "I consider every foreigner a scoundrel, until he has convinced me of his decency. A German Jew I consider just like a foreigner." (ibid.). August Wilhelm left the "Stahlhelm" in 1930 and joined the Nazi Party.

(54)   Korsch's letter to Witt-Hoë, December 23, 1930, ibid.

(55)   Circular letter of December 5, 1931. See note. III, 44.

(56)   *Alldeutsche Blätter*, no. 4, February 18, 1928 (GStA PK, Logen, 5.1.3., 4398).

(57)   Ibid.

(58)   Ibid.

(59)   Compare ibid.

(60)   Compare *Deutsches Adelsblatt*, no. 2, January 10, 1931, p. 22 (GStA PK, Logen, 5.1.3, 4429). After the "seizure of power," the corresponding passage of the statute was changed to read, "Members of Masonic lodges and such organizations as are to be considered like Masonic lodges," could not be members of the German Society of Nobility (cited after a letter from Grand Master of the Große

Landesloge Kurt von Heeringen of October 21, 1933) (GStA PK, Logen, 5.1.3, 4429).

(61)   Circular letter of January 4, 1927 (GStA PK, Logen, 5.1.3., 4419).

(62)   List of the members of the Students' Associations who belonged to the Große Landesloge, ibid. It cannot be assumed that this list is complete.

(63)   Letter of Witt-Hoë of July 13, 1928, ibid.

(64)   Compare a letter of Grand Master von Heeringen of July 24, 1933, which contains information concerning this (GStA PK, Logen, 5.1.3., 4445). The procedure resulted from instructions of the State-Secretary in the Reichs Chancellery, Hans Heinrich Lammers, of June 29, 1933 to the ADW (General German Armaments Ring), according to which "Members of student groups who bear arms, who belong to the Old Prussian grand lodges, which had been transformed into Orders" could make a deposition that they did not belong to a Masonic lodge (see Chapter 5.2.1).

(65)   The journal "Zur Aufklärung: Mitteilungen über die Angriffe gegen die Große Landesloge der Freimaurer von Deutschland und über ihre Abwehr" appeared as a supplement to the Zirkelkorrespondenz ("Circle Correspondence"). It was begun in order to reinforce the position of the GroßeLandesloge in the press ("journalistically") The only issue in this form was to confront "humanitarian Freemasonry with the simultaneous assertion of its own patriotic conviction by means of polemic agitation." (Neuberger, vol. 1, p. 254). Neuberger does not make it sufficiently clear that this real polemic agitation was an expression of the deep-seated antagonism between liberal and *völkisch* Fremasonry.

(66)   Felix Witt-Hoë on May 9, 1930 (Archiv GLL).

(67)   Groche's corresponence with Witt-Hoë (Archiv GLL, passim).

(68)   Undated, presumably1932/33, Archiv GLL. Politically the national-Christian lodges were indeed best included with the forces of the "Harzburg Front."

(69)   From a letter of von Heeringen of August 6, 1929 (Archiv GLL).

(70)   Compare concerning this and the following: Lennhoff/Posner, *Int. Freimaurer-Lexikon*, column 764ff.

(71)   Quoted according to the Announcement no. 5 of the Gestapa of April 18, 1934, p. 12 (GStA PK, I, 90 P, 129).

(72)   The law contained a provision forcing the turning in of membership lists and forbidding officials to be members of "secret societies."

(73)   Compare a call of the Grande Oriente D'Italia published in exile in London onDecember 18, 1932 (GStA PK, Logen, 5.1.11., 53), with which it emphasized the fact that it was still in existence and demanded freedom and justice for Italy.

(74)   *Zirkelkorrespondenz*, vol. 59, 2d June issue, 1930, p. 267ff.

(75)   Compare, for example, Endler/Schwarze, *Die Freimaurerbestände*, vol. 1, p. 235.

(76)   Published as a supplement to the journal *Am rauhen Stein*, no. 6/1932, p. 136.

(77)   Beyer, *Der Übertritt*, p. 139f.

(78)   Quoted after ibid., p. 143f. The flyer here quoted remarks from 1926. It is also in the Archives of the Große Landesloge. The responsible party was Col. Oswald Bielig from Erfurt, who had made himself known also in lectures as an exponent of the specific understanding of resistance espoused by the Große Landesloge.

(79)   Beyer, *Der Übertritt*, p. 145.

(80)   See note no. 14 in the Introduction.

(81)   In May 1933, after the transformation of the Grand Lodge Zur Freundschaft into a German-Christian order, the name of its journal was changed to *Der rauhe Stein (the Rough Ashlar)*. Its publication was temporarily stopped with the issue for October/November. Between September 1934 and January 1935 the (successor) journal appeared under the Name *Ordensblatt (Page* or *Newsletter of the Order)*, to which name the *Bundesblatt* had already been changed. This journal was published by both grand lodges together, and forbidden by the chief of police in Berlin.

(82)   Fenner/Schmitt-Sasse, „Die Freimaurer als 'nationale Kraft," *loc.cit.*, p. 227.

(83)   Quoted from ibid., p. 238 (Note 18).

(84)   Compare ibid., p. 226.

(85)   Compare ibid.

(86)   Sontheimer, *Antidemokratisches Denken*, p. 154.

(87)   Compare ibid., pp. 149, 152.

(88)   Quoted from ibid., pp. 150, p. 153. Edgar Jung, sometime advisor to Franz von Papen, was killed during the murders in connection with the Rohm Affair in 1934 .

(89)   For example, in the Essays of Karl Lüdemann im *3 WK-Bundesblatt*. Compare ibid., p. 226ff., 239f.

(90)   Quoted ibid., p. 240 Note 34). Horneffer confessed in his Memoirs, criticizing his own weakness for the concept *völkisch* Konzept (Compare Katz, *Jews and Freemasons*, p. 191). Concerning the activities of the brothers Ernst und August Horneffer, see also Chapter 8.2).

(91)   Compare Neumann, *Die Involvierung der "altpreußischen" Freimaurerei in die Politik*, p. 57f. Conditioned by his limited examination perspective, Neumann's study could not encompass completely the complexity of Freemasonry in the Weimar Republic and the "Third Reich." Therefore it falls short in its conclusions. In addition to some generalizations, for example, the question of anti-Semitism in German lodges is glossed over. It is questionable whether the analysis of a lone grand lodge journal constitutes a methodologically sensible beginning (or contribution?).

(92)   Compare *Am rauhen Stein (ArSt.)*, no. 4/1923, no. 5/1923, here cited ibid., p. 18 (note 77).

(93)   Horneffer's article appeared under the title "Was erwarten wir vom Nationalsozialismus?" in *ArSt.* no. 8-9/1932, here cited ibid., p. 82.

(94)   A member of the Große Landesloge obviously seems to have managed to establish a personal connection with Hitler, which, however in this connection, turned out to be of no help. The fact was accepted hesitantly by Witt-Hoë. The brother in question clearly did not toe the line given by Witt-Hoë regarding the "Body of the Order" in his presentation. (Compare a letter of Witt-Hoë's of December 10, 1930, GStA PK, Logen, 5.1.3, 4443).

(95)   Compare Neuberger, *Freimaurerei und Nationalsozialismus*, vol. 1, p. 261. The wording of the letter is cited in Steffens, *Freimaurer*, p. 367f. Bröse offered the immediate dissolution of the Großloge in case the examination should result in inferences concerning the "sacrificing of theinterests of the Fatherland."

(96)   Cited in Neuberger, *Freimaurerei und Nationalsozialismus*, vol. 1, p. 262.

(97)   Compare a letter from the lodge to Grand Master von Heeringen of October 14, 1931, and two handwritten letters from

Friedrich Wilhelm Göring of November 11 and November 13, 1931 (GStA, PK, Logen, 5.1.3, 4443). In the last letter it says that his brother [Hermann] was ready to facilitate a meeting with Hitler. Such a meeting, in all probability, never took place. (Compare a letter of the Grand Master of April 12, 1932, GStA PK, Logen, 5.1.3., 4443). Friedrich Wilhelm Göring can be proven to have held the office of lodge secretary already in 1927. As a rule this position requires the Master Mason's degree and a membership of at least two years. If and even when he left his lodge is not known.

(98)   Letter of Witt-Hoë of November 27, 1931 (GStA PK, Logen, 5.1.3., 4443). Neu-berger also mentions this "half-private contact." (compare vol. 2, p. 85 and ibid., note XIII/56).

(99)   Letter of Friedrich Wilhelm Göring, January 25, 1932 (GStA PK, Logen, 5.1.3., 4443. There is no evidence for possible concrete results of the intervention of Friedrich Wilhelm Görings or for a continuance of the personal conversation between the Große Landesloge leadership and Hermann Göring before the "Seizure of Power."

(100)   Compare the letter of von Heeringen to Hermann Göring of January 18, 1932 (Bundesarchiv [BA]NS 8/258, Bl.3). In this letter one learns positively that the appointment date for the conference with Göring was November 19, 1931.

(101)   Compare the procedure in: BA, NS 8/258, p. 1ff.

(102)   Compare the correpondence in GStA PK, Logen, 5.1.3., 4461. Haasen carried on the correspondenc chiefly from his home, Düsseldorf. The seat of the Lodge "Eos" was, however, Krefeld.

(103)   Letter from Rosenthal to Haasen of June 7, 1933 (GStA PK, Logen, 5.1.3., 4461).

(104)   Compare the handwritten letter from Haasens to Rosenthal of September 15, 1933, ibid.

(105)   Letter of Dr. Carl Happich, who was obviously Master of the Lodge, to Witt-Hoë, January 29, 1932 (GStA PK, Logen, 5.1.3., 4443).

(106)   Compare for example, Beyer, *Der Übertritt*, pp. 146, 148.

(106a)   USHMM, RG-11.001 M.07, Reel 78, passim.

(107)   Compare a letter from Happich to Witt-Hoë on November 15, 1931 (GStA PK, Logen, 5.1.3., 4443).

(108) Compare as an example, the correspondence of the Reichs Chief of Organization, Gregor Strasser, with a member of the Große Landesloge in Berlin, ibid.

(109) Lette of Grand Master von Heeringen of April 12, 1932, ibid.

(110) Compare GStA PK, Logen, 5.1.3, 4369, passim. Concerning the Evangelischen Bund (Evangelical Association), which had been founded in 1886, compare K.Nitzschke, in: Galling et al. (Ed.), *Die Religion in Geschichte und Gegenwart*, vol. 2, Tübingen, 1958, column 789ff. According to this, there were more than 500.000 members in 1914. Still today, his work is dedicated to the "battlefield" between church and state and the relationship to Catholicism.

(111) Information from the Evangelische Oberkirchenamt (E.O. = Evangelical Chief Council) I 6381/32 of March 31, 1932, EZA (Evangelisches Zentral Archiv), 7/3627.

(112) Letter of the "Deutsch-Völkischen Offiziersbundes" to the E.O. December 19, 1927, ibid.

(113) Cited after the draft by Witt-Hoë, undated, presumably. 1926 (or later), GStA PK, Logen, 5.1.3., 4369.

(114) Letter of General Superintendent Dibelius to Habicht October 29, 1926, ibid.

(115) Letter from Paulsen to Witt-Hoë February 27, 1929, GStA PK (Logen, 5.1.3., 4355).

(116) Compare the decision announcement from the meeting of October 25, 1929, EZA, 7/3627.

(117) According to the announcement of the Provincial Church Council of the Mark Brandenburg to the Evangelical Consistory of the Mark Brandenburg on November 8, 1929, EZA, 14/1478.

(118) Sasse's letter to the Berlin General Superintendent Karow on January 21, 1933, EZA, 7/3628.

(119) Compare ibid, passim.

(120) Compare for example the issue of "Sonntagsgruß" ("Sunday greeting") of April 26, 1931, p. 4, in which Probst advocated the position "that Freemaonry stands as a direct antithesis to positive Christianity," under the title "Freimaurerei und Christentum" („Freemasonry and Christianity"). Compare also the correspondence between Fahrenhorst and the Großloge concerning Probst in June

1931 (GStA PK, Logen, 5.1.3., 4369). In a letter of June 6, 1931, Witt-Hoë declared that one should "always keep an eye on this man, with his opposition to Freemasonry, which doubtless comes from inner conviction." It should also be considered "whether influence by means of enlightenment" might be possible. Just because of "his passionate national spirit" such a winning-over might be valuable (ibid.).

(121)   Reproduced in the circular letter 295/28 of the President of the Evangelical Chuch Committee on February 14, 1928, EZA, 14/1478.

(122)   Compare H-N. Burkert/K.Matußek/W.Wippermann, "Machtergreifung" Berlin, 1933, Berlin 2nd ed. 1982, p. 132.

(123)   Goesch's letter to Witt-Hoë on July 4, 1932, GStA PK, Logen, 5.1.3., 4369.

(124)   Witt-Hoë's letter to Kiesow on October 11, 1932, ibid.

(125)   Essay by Behm on the production of January 16, 1928, in: "Das Evangelische Deutschland: Kirchliche Rundschau für das Gesamtgebiet des Deutschen Evangelischen Kirchenbundes," February 5, 1928, p. 43f. (GStA PK, Logen, 5.1.3., 4370).

(126)   Quoted from the *Frankfurter Zeitung,* January 22, 1928 (GStA PK, Logen, 5.1.3., 4378). Even the Große Landesloge dropped the plans to "change Behm's tune" after the sole pastor in Mecklenburg who belonged to the Order (Große Landesloge) showed himself to be convinced of the futility of such an undertaking (Compare a letter from Dr. Gustav Bruger, Master of a subordinate lodge of the Große Landesloge in Rostock to Müllendorff on January 10, 1928, GStA PK, Logen, 5.1.3., 4378). Behm died in 1930.

(127)   Cited after the copy of an opinion (no more details) of Ludendorff, undated, (January 1928), GStA PK, Logen, 5.1.3., 4370.

(128)   Report on the statements of the highest church governing body of May 31,   1928, EZA, 1/A2/489.

(129)   Compare ibid.

(130)   Excerpt of the *Protokoll* (Minutes) of the committee meeting of June 8-9, 1928, EZA, 7/3627.

(131)   Ibid.

(132)   Ibid.

(133)   Hartwig Lohmann (Grand Master of the Große Landesloge), Lecture upon the "Bringing in of Light," March 20, 1993, *loc.cit.,* p. 165.

(134)   Neuberger, *Freimaurerei und Nationalsozialismus*, vol. 1, p. 262.

(135)   Ibid. The Old Prussians saw—to some extent correctly—the primary danger of the attacks was that they would be cut off permanently from their successors in the national milieu. (Compare in this vein also a report on the occasion of the spring communication of the Große Landesloge on April 1, 1931, Osobyi Archives, Moscow, 1412-1-8714).

(136)   Ibid., p. 263.

(137)   Thus in Groche's letter of October 31, 1929 (Archiv GLL), in which it talks about Brothers "who have no time for associations like the Stahlhelm, the Nazi Party (...) [and the DNVP (German National Folk's Party)." Groche regretted their democratic position: Circles "of local Brothers" stood on other political ground, which did not stay him from his "work of enlightenment," whose goal was to awaken "understanding for our Order's views" among national-*völkisch* groups. From this one may conclude that the ideological line of the Große Landesloge functionaries did not always coincide with those positions promulgated in the inividual subordinate lodges.

(138)   In both categories of journalism, which cannot always be sharply distinguished from each other, the affinity with the National-Socialistic thought process (body of thought) is expressed. Compare in this connection the criticism of Fenner/Schmitt-Sasse (loc. cit., p. 238, note10) of Neuberger, according to which the latter concentrated too much on the security letters. One of the few examples of a discussion without *völkisch* rhetoric and without a denunciation of humanitarian Freemasonry should not go unmentioned: In a radio speech by Rudolf Hartnack, the deputy master of the Hamburg Lodge "Zum Gral," completely atypical for the the Große Landesloge Freimaurerei, the "Bulwark of Peace" was called the ideal picture of Germany. The lecture concluded with the words, "It (the secret of Freemasonry, here sketched as the "love of mankind"—author's note) shines like gold from prehistoric times, and will shine its life- and fruit-yielding beams into the farthest future as long as the earth has human beings who are filled with the spirit of the of the great trinitarian Master Builder of all worlds, who was, is, and shall be" (Speech of November or the beginning of December 1931, quoted from GStA PK, Logen, 5.1.3., 4331).

(139)   Katz, *Jews and Freemasons*, p. 90.

(140)   Peters, *Die Geschichte der Freimaurerei*, p. 228. It is revealing that von Stradonitz, who had been the grand archivist of his grand lodge, did not hesitate to discuss a letter from the *völkisch* Wetzlar Ring in mostly positive terms, in the Tree World Globes' "Bundesblatt". Compare Freudenschuß, "Der Wetzlarer Ring," *loc.cit.*, p. 19. Along the same line as Stradonitz was Heinrich Junker, with his letter published also by the Association of German Freemasons (V.d.F.) "Der nationalsozialistische Gedankenkreis: Eine Aufklärung für Freimaurer," Leipzig, 1931: In it an equation was made among a community of people, a community of God, and cathedral-building by Masons, in which the conclusionwas that the concept of community is understood the same way in both National Socialism and in Freemasonry.

(141)   Diedrich Bischoff, *Nationalsozialismus und Freimaurerei*, o.O. 1931, quoted from Fenner/Schmitt-Sasse, „Die Freimaurer als ‚nationale Kraft'," *loc. cit.*, p. 242 (Note 61). According to Bischoff, Freemasonry was also in a position to correct over-strained racist positions of Naziism (compare ibid., p. 242f.).

(142)   Lennhoff/Posner, *Int. Freimaurerlexikon*, column 185. Bischoff's assertion and its characterization by Lennhoff/Posner brings up, at the same time, the problem of the definitions as to what (and what *not*) one is really to understand by the term "humanitarian Freemasonry."

(143)   This explanation is cited (among other places) in Neuberger, *Freimaurerei und Nationalsozialismus*, vol. 1, p. 114. Compare also Lennhoff/Posner, *Int. Freimaurer-Lexikon*, under the term 'Ludendorff' (column 962ff.), and Steffens, *Freimaurer*, p. 347. It is noteworthy that the Ludendorff letter pertaining to this specifically attacks the Große Landesloge. Presumably that was also a reason why the Order did not forbid cooperative action. In addition, some steps against Ludendorff were discusssed (compare Archiv GLL, passim).

(144)   Letter of the Order Grand Master to Landes Grand Master Müllendorff of July 28, 1927, GStA PK, Logen, 5.1.3., 4388.

(145)   Müllendorff's response of July 29, 1927, ibid.

(146)   Guidelines for the defense against *völkisch* attacks, February 1929, ibid.

(147)   Compare Witt-Hoë's letter to the lodge masters in Königsberg on December 16,

1930, Osobyi Archives, Moscow, 500-1-192.

(148)   Such a list (compare Archiv GLL) was sent by Witt-Hoë for example, to Adolf Groche, his representative in Chemnitz.

(149)   From a lecture from the Old Prussian point of view, delivered at a student association evening in Hannover on May 17, 1922, p. 4 (Archiv GLL). It says, ibid., „I have not the faintest notion whether the Grand Lodge of Vienna has been ,be-jewed' (Trans. own term=infiltrated by Jews) in connection with Wichtl's anti-Semitic outbursts. Indeed he was characterized as an "ugly, illogical, Party man." The text calls the Große Landesloge "hierarchical," the Grand Lodge Zur Freundschaft and Humanitarians as "democratic" (p. 9).

(150)   This picture results from the abundance of material in the GLL archives, which cannot be discussed in more detail here.

(151)   From a memorandum for the governance communication of the Große Landesloge April 11, 1927, p. 2 (Archiv GLL). In the same it was strongly suggested that one dispense with the traditional Masonic symbols such as the Compasses, Square, and six-pointed Star (Seal of Solomon).

(152)   Letter of March 1, 1929 (Archiv GLL).

(153)   Compare Endler/Schwarze, *Die Freimaurerbestände*, vol. 1, p. 234.

(154)   Quoted from GStA PK, Logen, 5.1.3., 4332. Compare, in this vein, Witt-Hoe's letter to the master of a lodge in Königsberg on June 28, 1930, Osobyi Archives, Moscow, 500-1-192. Compare, in contrast,a Masonic work honoring the life and work of Stresemann from the Symbolische Großloge (Symbolic Grand Lodge of Germany) in: Osobyi Archives, Moscow, 1412-1-4904.

(155)   Müllendorffs letter of June 17, 1922, GStA PK, Logen, 5.1.3., 4385.

(156)   Dr. Carl Happich's letter to Witt-Hoë on January 14, 1932, GStA PK, Logen, 5.1.3., 4443. In addition, Happich expressed, in the same letter, his position that "the humanitarian lodges have really lost their right to exist."

(157)   Circular letter of the subordinate lodge in Heidelberg "Ruprecht zu den fünf Rosen" of May 8, 1931, reproduced in: Bauhüttennot, *Bonner Blaubuch—Eine Sammlung von Akten und Aufsätzen*, Bonn, 1931, p. 23f. The most important essays on the controversy are collected in this publication.

(158) Paul Selter's letter of July 12, 1931 to the Grand Master of the Großloge Zur Sonne, Hermann Koelblin, in: ibid., p. 29ff, here p. 33.

(159) This originates in an essay by Selter entitled "Politik und Ethik," which he presumably wrote in August 1940 and published the next year (his own printing?) (Private archives of Alain Bernheim). Before Selter came to the Bayreuth Grand Lodge, he had belonged to the Große Landesloge

(160) Letter of the Chairman of the National Association of German Officers, Graf Waldersee to Müllendorff February 28, 1925, GStA PK, Logen, 5.1.3., 4387.

(161) Compare Witt-Hoë's confidential message of December 6, 1926, ibid. However, it would be, according to Witt-Hoë, "completely wrong if this news became known in larger circles. The common enemy, the leftist parties, the Jews, and others would profit by it." (ibid.). Retired Generalmajor Heinrich von Ledebur, was the chairman in northwestern Germany, who was friendly with the Old Prussians, but was not a Freemason himself. Later, in August 1934, a reunification occurred under the name "Reichsverband Deutscher Offiziere (R.D.O. Reichs Association of German Officers)" in which no limits were imposed by the leadership of the Association on the members of Old Prussian lodges, but "international Masonic lodges" remained barred (compare GStA PK, Logen, 5.1.3., 4450, passim).

(162) Compare the joint declaration of the Old Prussian grand lodges of March 11, 1925 (GstA PK, Logen, 5.1.3., 4387).

(163) Cited in "An den Hauptvorstand des Nationalverbandes Deutscher Offiziere," no author, signed by Martin Anger, Heinrich Herrling and others, Erfurt (9. September) 1925, p. 1f. (Private archives of Bruno Peters, Berlin).

(164) Ibid., p. 1ff. Compare also Katz, *Jews and Freemasons*, p. 192. Felix Witt-Hoë had already been excluded as of June 10, 1925, from the National Association of German Officers under protest against "the insulting remarks about the Old Prussian grand lodges and their members" (GStA PK, Logen 5.1.3., 4386). Even earlier, on March 3, 1924, the lawyer and Große Landesloge brother, Martin Korsch, had resigned from the National Association of German Officers, after he had learned that it was planned to exclude Freemasons (compare his letter of March 1, 1924 to the Landesverband Groß-Berlin (Greater Berlin Chapter) of the National Association of German Officers,

GStA PK, Logen, 5.1.3., 4387). It is striking how fast Korsch came to his conclusion and acted with respect to the National Association of German Officers. It was clearly not an isolated case. According to a letter of Landes Grand Master Müllendorff, the attempts of the National Association of German Officers in Berlin "to move members, who belonged to our Order, toward resignation ... were answered by their resignations from the National Association of German Officers." (Müllendorff' letter of September 23, 1924, GStA PK, Logen, 5.1.3., 4387).

(165)   Joint declaration of the three Old Prussian grand masters of February 16, 1924, GstA PK, Logen, 5.1.3., 4387.

(166)   Declaration of the five independent Saxon lodges. Addition to the letter to the Große Landesloge of April 27, 1924, ibid.

(167)   Announcement of the National Association of German Officers, December 12, 1925, ibid.

(168)   Habicht's letter to Müllendorff February 3, 1926, ibid.

(169)   Compare the minutes of the meeting of February 24, 1926, ibid.

(170)   Compare Graf von Waldersee's essay "Zehn Jahre N.D.O. Ein Rückblick und ein Ausblick," in: *Gedenkschrift des N.D.O. zum 10jährigen Bestehen vom 16.12.1928* (ibid.).

(171)   Obviously this was "tried here and there by individual units of the National Association of German Officers, anyway" (von Heeringen's letter of April 23, 1929 to Groche, GStA PK, Logen, 5.1.3., 4392).

(172)   According to a letter by Beyer on April 23, 1934, Deutsches Freimaurer-Museum Bayreuth, No. 80 III A,B.

(173)   Ernst Haeckel (1834-1919), a professor of zoology in Jena, starting with Darwin, formulated the "biogenetic fundamental law," according to which the embryonic development of an animal repeats the evolutionary history of the species in shortened form.

(174)   G. Höft, "Bedeutung und Aufgaben unseres Bundes." *Aufklärungsschriften des FZAS*, no. 5, Nürnberg, 1917, p. 5.

(175)   Ibid.

(176)   Ibid., p. 15.

(177)   Ibid., p. 16.

(178)   Quoted from Frank Simon-Ritz, "Die freigeistige Bewegung im Kaiserreich," in: *Handbuch zur "Völkischen Bewegung*," p. 208ff., hier p. 216.

(179)   Compare ibid., p. 217.

(180)   Quoted from Edler/Schwarze, *Die Freimaurerbestände*, vol. 1, p. 290. Concerning the national-Christian understanding of Old Prussian Freemasonry, Kurt Tucholsky stated, rather amused: "A rather odd sort of Freemasons, and their idea of humankind reaches only to Saarbrücken" (quoted after de Jong, *Freimaurer an Rhein und Ruhr*, p. 4). Tucholsky was accepted into the Grand Lodge of the Association of Freemasons of the Rising Sun (FzaS) lodge, "Zur Morgenröte," ("Dawn") in Berlin on March 24, 1924. During the time he worked as a correspondent in Paris für *Weltbühne und Vossische Zeitung,* he was a visiting member of the Lodge "L'Effort" of the Grand Orient de France (see also the documents appendix). On Tucholskys as a Freemason, which has scarcely been taken up by literary and historical scholarship, compare Hans-Detlef Mebes, "Kurt Tucholsky, 1924-1935. Ein zweites Leben im Geheimen?" In: *Humanität* no. 7/1985, p. 8ff. A detailed study of this reform-minded Grand Lodge by the same author, a specialist in the Grand Lodge of the Association of Freemasons of the Rising Sun (FzaS), is in preparation. Carl von Ossietzky had already become a member of "Menschentum," the Hamburg lodge subordinate to the "Rising Sun" in April 1919.

(181)   Compare Johannes Drechsler, *Die Brüder vom FZAS*, p. 18. Penzig no longer ran for the office of Grand master, after a proposal to have the board pursue regularization more vigorously was accepted at the annual convocation. He died in 1931.

(182)   Quoted from Edler/Schwarze, *Die Freimaurerbestände*, vol. 1, p. 290f. On the "Rising Sun," Compare also Koner, *Freimaurerleben*, p. 19f. Koner had been Grand Secretary and Grand Expert of the Supreme Council of the AASR for Germany since its establishment in July 1930, and in addition Grand Secretary of the Symbolische Großloge. Because of problems with the source, one is asked to be very cautious in using Koner's Memoirs, and not only because of the author's motives. The writings originated mostly out of his memory without use of sources, so that inaccuracies and mistakes could slip in. Raoul Koner died on March 29, 1977.

(183)   Compare Lennhoff/Posner, *Int. Freimaurerlexikon*, column 57ff. Compare also Helmut Traulsen, "75 Jahre Universelle Freimaurerliga 1905–1980," Dortmund, 1982, p. 21f.

(184) The concepts "Universelle Freimaurerliga" ("Universal League of Freemasons") and "Allgemeine Freimaurerliga" ("General League of Freemasons") which are used interchangeably in the literature, denote the same organization. In this work, the name "Allgemeine Freimaurerliga" ("General League of Freemasons") is used.

(185) Compare concerning this and the following, Lennhoff/Posner, *Int. Freimaurer-Lexikon*, passim, and Thomas Richert, "Die deutsche Landesgruppe der Allgemeinen Freimaurer-Liga von 1927 bis 1933," in: *QC-Jahrbuch* no. 23/1986, Bayreuth, 1986, p. 141ff, especially p. 141-148.

(186)   Compare. Endler/Schwarze, *Die Freimaurerbestände*, vol. 1, p. 234.

(187)   Concerning this incident compare Richert, "*Die deutsche Landesgruppe*," loc.cit., p. 147. At the meeting of their association of grand masters on February 14, 1928, the Old Prussian attendees agreed to warn people about the League. According to the Minutes (p. 4), Three World Globes Grand Master Habicht read a declaration with the same content (GStA PK, Logen, 5.1.3, 4378).

(188)   Exhortation to join the "Reichsdeutschen Landesgruppe" of the "General League of Freemasons" in April 1928, reproduced in full in Richert, "Die deutsche Landesgruppe," p. 145ff.

(189)   Ernst Klein, in: *Vossische Zeitung*, evening edition December 30, 1929 (*GStA, PK*, Logen, 5.1.3., 4375).

(190)   Compare in this connection, a letter by the chairman of the "Gruppe für aktive Friedensarbeit" (Group for Active Work for Peace), Henry La Fontaine, to Leo Müffelmann January 22, 1932, GStA PK,Logen, 5.1.11., 20 and one from the Grand Lodge of Vienna to Müffelmann April 27, 1932, GStA PK, Logen, 5.1.11., 53. In contrast to that, the Grand Lodge "Deutsche Bruderkette" ("German Chain of Brothers") made known its "indignation" that its members were expected "to sign a petition to the Völkerbund (Peoples' Association), which offended the German sensibility most deeply." (quoted from the *Wiener Freimaurer-Zeitung*, No. 6/7, 1932, p. 78).

(191)   After Peters, *Die Geschichte der Freimaurerei*, p. 214. Neither source nor reference is named, to which exact point in time this number refers.

(192) Compare for example, the essays in the very extensive, liberal-humanitarian "Blaubüchern" ("Blue Books"). The Große Landesloge was called a "sect" in that work (vol. 1933, p. 63): Kurt Reichl, (Ed.) on assignment of the "General League of Freemasons"), *Das Blaubuch der Weltfreimaurerei*, vol. 1933–1934, Wien 1933–1934. The publisher, Kurt Reichl alias Konrad Lerich, was one of the leading Austrian Freemasons before he went over to the enemy camp, and at the end, worked for the Sicherheits Dienst (see Chapters 2.2 and 8.1). The run of the "Blaubücher" was continued in 1935: Paul Nettl (Ed.), *Das Jahrbuch der Weltfreimaurerei 1935*, Wien, 1935.

(193) Heinrich Kraft at the conference in Basel in August 1925, cited in Lennhoff/Posner, *Int. Freimaurer-Lexikon*, column 537. Prof. Kraft was a radiologist. At first he belonged to the Lodge "An Erwins Dom" [Eklectic Association] in Strassburg. The Lodge was reactivated in Frankfurt after Alsace belonged to France. Later Kraft lived in Dresden and was an active member of the Supreme Council.

(194) Compare. Richert, *Die deutsche Landesgruppe, loc. cit.*, p. 142.

(195) Concerning the name "Bluntschli" and the "Bluntschli-Ausschuß," (Bluntschli Committee), see Chapter 1.3 and Note I/119. Müffelmann was accepted first into the Lodge "Humanitas" in 1913, under the sponsorship of Hjalmar Schacht. Later, he founded the Lodge "Zu den Alten Pflichten" ("Ancient Obligations"), with his father, in Berlin. He also belonged to the Grand Lodge of Hamburg. There will be much more, and in detail on Schacht and Müffelmann in the next chapters.

(196) Neuberger, *Freimaurerei und Nationalsozialismus*, vol. 1, p. 249, among others reports on this incident.

(197) Compare Leo Müffelmann, "Zur deutsch-französischen freimaurerischen Annäherung," in: *Wiener Freimaurer-Zeitung*, No. 5, 1928, p. 1ff.

(198) Various documents concerning these proceedings are in the private archives of   Bruno Peters (Berlin).

(199) A description of these proceedings–confusing, and sometimes even irrelevant—probably distorted by age and memory problems is found in Koner, *Freimaurerleben*, p. 20. A compilation of subordinate lodges of the Symbolischen Großloge with their dates of founding can be found in: *Die Geschichte der Symbolischen Großloge von Deutschland 1930-1949* compiled by Heinz Klasen, paperback

(with an introduction by the editor/compiler), Hamburg, 1984 (Deut sches Freimaurer Museum Bayreuth No. 9398).

(200) According to Koner in a letter of May 26, 1932 (GStA PK, Logen, 5.1.11., 14) this applied to *about 500 to 600* Brothers from the Rising Sun Grand Lodge.

(201) As opposed to a corresponding communication, (Compare the declaration of *January 6, 1931, reproduced in the proceedings of the Großloge Zur* Sonne, 2/1931, p. 275f., in: Dokumente, Veröffentlichungen, Briefe zur Entstehung der Symbolischen Großloge von Deutschland und des Deutschen Obersten Rates des Alten und Angenommenen Schottischen Ritus 1930/31, Bad Kissingen, 1961, p. 41). It appears that there was no formal decision of the German Landesgruppe not to accept members of the Symbolische Großloge (compare GStA PK, Logen, 5.1.11., 17, passim). A grotesque argument, considering the majority rejection of the General League of Freemasons in the established humanitarian camp in contrast to the broad agreement of positions of the League and the Symbolische Großloge.

(202) Compare Eugen Lennhoff, in: Reichl (Ed.), *Blaubuch,* vol. 1933, p. 60.

(203) Quoted in Peters, *Die Geschichte der Freimaurerei,* p. 225.

(204) Ibid.

(205) Ibid.

(206) Leo Müffelmann, "Die Symbolische Großloge," in: Reichl (Ed.), *Blaubuch,* vol. 1933, p. 54.

CHAPTER 4

(1) Compare Lennhoff/Posner, *Int. Freimaurer-Lexikon,* column 359f., 765 and Neuberger, *Freimaurerei und Nationalsozialismus,* vol. 1, p. 244f. Only in 1932 could the Grand Lodges of Bayreuth, Hamburg and Frankfurt make the decision to reestablish "fraternal contact" with the Grand Lodge of England. More in this chapter.

(2) Compare Neumann, *Die Involvierung der "altpreußischen" Freimaurerei in die Politik,* p. 73.

(3) Circular letter of the Große Landesloge of February 4, 1927, *GStA PK,* Logen, 5.1.3, 4434.

(4)	Ibid.

(5)	Decision of the grand communication (main meeting) of the Order (Große Landesloge) from 1932, Archiv GLL. In 1928 the Grand Lodge of England had rescinded the rules of exclusion, which had been passed against the Lodges of the Central Powers during the war. In doing this, The Grand Lodge of England had met the prerequisites for a normalization. The objections raised to this step taken by the Große Landesloge were rejected by the Grand Lodge of Hamburg in a declaration by its Grand Master Bröse: The Große Landesloge had seen the welcome opportunity to complete the break with the humanitarian lodges, which had been considered before the year was out. Bröse justified the reestablishment of relations with the Freemasons "of a people related to us by race and essence" not least with "national motives" (Reprint [of] Hamburger Logenblatt, no. 44/Mai 1932, GStA PK, Logen, 5.1.11, 14).

(6)	Declaration of the Grande Loge de France, undated [1932], GStA PK, Logen, 5.1.11., 21.

(7)	Neuberger, *Freimaurerei und Nationalsozialismus*, vol. 1, p. 244.

(8)	Compare ibid. Neuberger does not provide documentation for the statement that the *völkisch* tendencies were "fought against sharply" at their inception. I disagree with Neuberger's interpretation, according to which the effects of the nationalistic position developed in the whole of German Freemasonry, had been limited to specifically masonic questions (compare ibid.). The meaning of Freemasonry in the entire sociological discussion is opposite to that. Also, just this very postion determined its relationship to the State and to other intsitutions.

(9)	The German Grand Lodge Convention sent out an announcement on May 29, 1915 vis-à vis Wilhelm II. It said among other things: "In this world war with which predatory neighbors have overrun us, the German Freemasons honor with deepest gratitude the visionary ruler and defender of the Fatherland, in Your Majesty crowned with victory, but also at the same time the leader desired by God for the elevation of the honor and the wellbeing of civilized humanity, and for the guarding of their holiest qualities" (cited in Drechsler, *Die Brüder vom FZAS*, p. 9f.). The communication of German Freemasons refused to allow the enemy states to belong to "civilized humanity." The military lodges dissolved themselves after the end of the war. Neuberger reports that only the military lodge,

"Frisia zur Nordwacht" ("Frisia–Guard of the North") founded on Sylt in 1917, became a peacetime lodge (vol. 1, p. 189).

(10) Compare Endler/Schwarze, *Freimaurerbestände*, vol. 2, p.14f.

(11) The former German military lodge "Stern von Brabant" ("Star of Brabant"), founded on December 8, 1915 in Brussels, and originally based there, was reactivated in Berlin on September 8, 1923. It was a bastion of *völkische* Anti-Semitism. Its Master was the later National Grand Master Dr. Otto Bordes. More details in this chapter.

(12) Cited after Steffens, *Freimaurer*, p. 323.

(13) The same among others also from Friedrich Hasselbacher, an anti-Masonic political commentator, who came from the circle around Ludendorff, and who was able to continue his activities (with a forced pause) in the "Third Reich" (see Chapter 8.1).

(14) "Das Freimaurerlogen-Museum in Nürnberg." Off-print from the journal *Das Bayerland*, ed. by Ludwig Deubner, München, 1938, p. 46 (Library of Congress Washington, ms. 394.F 73 / 53-48835).

(15) Ibid.

(16) Compare Neuberger, *Freimaurerei und Nationalsozialismus*, vol. 1, p. 264f. and Chysky, „Antijudaismus, Antisemitismus", *loc.cit.*, p. 14.

(17) Eskau's circular letter, undated [ca. 1924], Deutsches Freimaurer-Museum Bayreuth, no. 964. Complete text also in Neuberger, *Freimaurerei und Nationalsozialismus*, vol. 2, Appendix, p. 291f.

(18) Ibid.

(19) Compare Neuberger, *Freimaurerei und Nationalsozialismus*, vol. 1, p. 79.

(20) Compare Sontheimer, *Antidemokratisches Denken*, p. 166.

(21) The "Werkbund deutscher Freimaurer" ("Work Association of German Freemasons") demanded, among other things in an "open letter" to the Reichs government that the "confession of war guilt" be revised. (Compare the "Open Letter" of March 6, 1924. Deutsches Freimaurer-Museum Bayreuth, no. 621. Complete text also in Neuberger, vol. 2, Appendix, p. 293).

(22) Compare, Neuberger, *Freimaurerei und Nationalsozialismus*, vol. 1, p. 268ff.

(23) "Völkische Freimaurerei" ("*Völkische* Freemasonry." Comments on the entries of the St. John's Lodge Freundschaft im Hochland in Munich to the Grand Lodge of Prussia, "Freundschaft" in Berlin,

1924 (Spring Communication) written by Dr. Johannes Bühler, Deutsches Freimaurer-Museum Bayreuth, no. 2477, p. 1.

(24) Ibid., p. 3.

(25) Ibid., p. 5.

(26) Ibid., p. 10f.

(27) Cited in Neuberger, *Freimaurerei und Nationalsozialismus*, vol. 1, p. 333 (Note 135), after C. van Dalens *Kalender für Freimaurer*, vol. 1931, p. 82.

(28) Minutes of a meeting on March 6, 1928 among the grand masters of the Old Prussian grand lodges and the leadership of the Alldeutschen Verbandes (Pan-German Association), GStA PK, Lodges, 5.1.3., 4398.

(29) Compare ibid.

(30) Cited after Lennhoff/Posner, *Int. Freimaurer-Lexikon*, column 1315.

(31) Freudenschuß reports this (see below), p. 13f. There (p. 14f.) also information on the social levels of the members of the Wetzlar Ring-Lodge. The largest group by far were the 35 Brothers who were directors and "leading" (white-collar) workers. There was only one Brother each in the groups [designated] artists and farmers. Astonishingly, in 1927, not one officer in the garrison city Wetzlar belonged to the local Three World Globes subordinate lodge.

(32) Although Neuberger says that as time went on, both organizations experienced an influx of members from other Old Prussian grand lodges. Compare vol. 1, p. 266, also p. 332 [note.131], according to Freudenschuß (see below) the Wetzlar Ring, in contrast to its subsidiary in Bielefeld, remained a union of subordinate lodges of the National Mother Lodge from western Germany, Hesse and Thuringia (compare p. 13). At this point, this study must be limited to mentioning the exact composition of the Ring movements as a desirable subject for Masonic historiography. It should be emphasized, however, that there were efforts in subordinate lodges of all three Old Prussian jurisdictions to anchor Freemasonry in German customs.

(33) Compare de Jong, *Freimaurer an Rhein und Ruhr*, p. 4. The author describes the Masonic scene in Berlin as "radical-nationalistic."

(34) Minutes of the meeting of the Association of Old Prussian Grand Masters on March 3, 1928, p. 3 (GStA PK, Logen, 5.1.3., 4378).

(35)   Compare the Minutes of the meeting of the Grand Masters of November 11, 1932, p. 9, GStA PK, Logen, 5.1.3., 4459.

(36)   Compare the acknowledgement of receipt of the chairman of the Bielefeld Ring of Old Prussian Lodges of February 22, 1926, GStA PK, Logen, 5.1.3., 4387.

(37)   Bundesarchiv formerly BDC (Berlin Document Center), personnel record of Erich Awe. The member number 2463991 was temporarily assigned to him. The record consists only of Awe's file card.

(38)   More detail on this problem in the Epilogue.

(39)   This comes from Awe's correspondence with Grosse Landesloge Grand Master Müllendorff in April 1926 (GStA, PK, Logen, 5.1.3., 4387).

(40)   Compare Witt-Hoës manuscript draft of a letter to Awe, dated June 15, 1926, ibid. Content and context can only be incompletely pieced together. Literally it says: "I must however, tell you that the expression 'You could advance this sum' and the payment might be 'reimbursed' to you, is not really right. Your work is voluntary, of course received with gratitude, but not offically demanded or led (administered). Therefore I must tell you also on behalf of the three grand masters, that the three grand lodges (...) want to grant you the amount for which you asked– 860 Marks – but that they wish to declare that therewith the monetary support for your work is completed."

(41)   Compare the minutes of the "Kirchenführertagung" (church leaders' convention) of December 4, 1934, EZA, 1/A4/182. Compare also Schneider, *Reichsbischof Ludwig Müller*, p. 214. There there is no indication that Heep was a Freemason. The concept "Reichskirchenkabinett" (Reich Church Cabinet) or "Reichskirchenregierung" (Reich Church Government) refers to a special term of Müller's authority which is not to be confused with the Reichs Church Ministry, which was created in July 1935.

(42)   Compare the important essay by Werner Freudenschuß, "Der Wetzlarer Ring Völkische Tendenzen in der deutschen Freimaurerei nach dem 1.Weltkrieg," in: *Quatuor Coronati Yearbook* no. 25/1988, Bayreuth, 1988, p. 9ff., hier p. 11.

(43)   Heep's remarks from 1927. Cited ibid., p. 15.

(44)   Cited ibid.

(45)   Cited ibid.

(46)   Cited according to the minutes of the convention of April 20/21, 1928, GStA PK, Logen, 5.1.3., 4419.

(47)   Cited after Freundenschuß, Der Wetzlarer Ring, *loc.cit.*, p. 19. A secondary school principal from Coburg by the name of August Reukauf expressed himself in a similar vein during an evening with guests at his Three World Globes subordinate lodge in 1932: "Just as according to good Christian conviction, Christianity, as the highest religion, is called to be victorious over other religions, thus according to our conviction the most noble form of humanity is contained in Christian Freemasonry." In these times, Christian Freemasonry, with its firm alliance, can be a means of closer unification to form in the Geman people a source of strength for a will to live. (printed in: *Allgemeine Logen-Zeitung (General Lodge Newspaper)*, vol. V, no. 1, April 1932, p. 6 [GStA PK, Logen, 5.1.3. 4330]). The magazine was published by the National Mother Lodge, and appeared at first in Berlin, later, until its demise, in Würzburg.

(48)   Report about the first indoctrination convention of the Bielefeld Ring of Old Prussian lodges on October 8/9, 1927 in Bielefeld, p. 4 (GStA PK, Logen, 5.1.3., 4378).

(49)   Wirth's omissions were printed afterward in the association news of the Three World Globes (Issue for February 1933, p. 23), cited in Freudenschuß, *Der Wetzlarer Ring*, loc.cit., p. 21, among others.

(50)   Compare Ingo Wiwjorra, "Herman Wirth: Ein gescheiterter Ideologe zwischen 'Ahnenerbe' und Atlantis," in: Barbara Danckwortt et al. (Ed.), *Historische Rassismusforschung:Ideologen—Täter—Opfer*, Hamburg/Berlin, 1995, p. 91ff., here p. 104f.

(51)   Compare ibid., p. 106f. As Wiwjorra reports in the same place based upon Wirth's BDC (Berlin Document Center) document, in 1938 he was stripped of his professorial positions. However, he maintained regular contact with Himmler until at least 1943. In addition he received 500 RM every month as a "research aide" from the Reichs Education Ministry and an equal amount from the German Research Society. Concerning Wirth's activity in the German Federal Republic until his death in 1981, compare ibid., p. 107ff. On Wirth and the "Ahnenerbe" in general, compare again Kater, Das "Ahnenerbe."

(52)   Ibid., p. 96.

(53)   Cited after ibid., p. 98.

(54)   Cited in Freudenschuß, „Der Wetzlarer Ring", *loc. cit.*, p. 21.

(55)   Kurt Schmidt, *Völkische Weltanschauung und Freimaurerei*, Gotha (?) 1932.

(56)   Ibid., p. 5.

(57)   Ibid., p. 16, 20. Schmidt opined that he recognized that "indeed Hitler, who was in the building trades, loved to formulate his illustrations by using the symbolism of building." (Afterword, p. 25).

(58)   Compare Freudenschuß, „Der Wetzlarer Ring", *loc. cit.*, p. 22. A report on the convention was published in the Three World Globe's *Bundesblatt*t (the issue for January 1933, p. 27f.).

(59)   Rudolf John-Gorsleben, *"Hoch-Zeit" der Menschheit*, Leipzig, 1931, p. 86. Cited in Freudenschuß, „Der Wetzlarer Ring", *loc.cit.*, p. 22. Following is a selection of writings that promulgate *völkisch* Freemasonry from the area of the Wetzlarer Ring: Both previously-mentioned works by Kurt Schmidt: *Die Freimaurerei im Dienste deutscher Nationalbildung*, Wetzlar, 1927; *Völkische Weltanschauung und Freimaurerei*, Gotha (?) 1932. In addition: Jakob Heep, *Deutsches Ringen um die Seele der K.K.—Wege zur Besinnung und Gestaltung*, Wetzlar, 1926; August Pfannkuch, *Freimaurerei und völkische Frage*, Berlin, 1928; Rudolf Baumbach, *Die religiöse Zukunftsaufgabe der deutschen Freimaurerei*, Gotha [no year]. Compare in this connection also Oswald Bielig, "Kampf gegen die deutsche Freimaurerei und unsere Abwehrbestrebungen,"unpublished lecture (Lodge Masters Conference, Erfurt, May 3, 1932 [Archiv GLL]).

(60)   *Wiener Freimaurer-Zeitung* no. 4/5, 1933, p. 64.

(61)   Compare ibid. p. 63.

(62)   The lecture is printed in: Christian Zetzsche, *200 Jahre Freimaurerei in*Pyrmont. *Geschichte und Selbsterlebtes*, Bad Pyrmont, 1975, p. 44ff. More on the the history of the Pyrmont Lodge before 1928 is also here. The explanatory part, not at all thought through, is intellectually wanting, and is an example showing that Old Prussian Freemasonry for decades was neither willing nor able even to attempt to grapple critically with National Socialism, let alone with its own idelogical complexities. Instead, this essay presents an avowal of *völkisch* Freemasonry. Wirth's anti-Semitic thoughts are reproduced without commentary, and the convention of Apirl 2, 1933 is proclaimed irredeemably a great success (Compare 57ff.). The Zetzsches continued their Masonic careers without interruption after 1948. The Lodge "Friedrich zu den drei Quellen" today belongs to the Grand Lodge A.F.&A.M. In this conection, see also the Epilogue.

(63)   Oskar Zetzsche, "Was sagen uns Freimaurern die Externsteine?" *loc.cit.*, p. 44.

(64)   Ibid., p. 45.

(65)   Compare ibid., p. 55.

(66)   Ibid.

(67)   Compare Neuberger, *Freimaurerei und Nationalsozialismus*, vol. 1, p. 266.

(68)   Ibid. It is also incorrect that the work of the *völkisch* Ring movements "threatened" German Freemasonry. Rather, they wer a part of German Freemasonry.

(69)   Lennhoff/Posner, *Int. Freimaurer-Lexikon*, column 1216 reinforces the exercise of influence in the conflict with Vienna. The background is that the Austrians had made connections with the lodges of the victorious powers and had recognized the Symbolische Großloge. The Grosse Landesloge had already broken with the liberal Grand Lodge of Vienna in 1926. The other established German grand lodges affiliated with the National Mother Lodge (compare Freudenschuß, p. 10).

(70)   Schmidt, *Die Freimaurerei im Dienste deutscher Nationalbildung*, p. 44.

(71)   Fenner/Schmitt-Sasse, "Die Freimaurer als 'nationale Kraft'," *loc.cit.*, p. 229.

(72)   Ibid.

(73)   "Johannis-Gruß" of the Order Administration of 1932, Archiv GLL. See also Chapter 3.1.

(74)   Bielig in the previously-mentioned lecture (see note IV/59).

(75)   Freudenschuß, "Der Wetzlarer Ring," *loc. cit.*, p. 20.

(76)   Letter of Witt-Hoë of November 12, 1927, GStA PK, Logen, 5.1.3, 4398.

(77)   Compare Freudenschuß, "Der Wetzlarer Ring," *loc. cit.*, p. 16.

(78)   Relevant indications from the minute book of the Wetzlar Lodge could be "considered thoroughly representative of German Freemasonry," according to   Freudenschuß (ibid., p. 10).

(79)   Compare Neuberger. *Freimaurerei und Nationalsozialismus*, vol. 1, p. 249.

(80)   Compare Endler/Schwarze, *Die Freimaurerbestände*, vol. 1, p. 256.

(81)   Letter from Witt-Hoë to Groche May 6, 1932, Archiv GLL.

(82)   Neuberger, *Freimaurerei und Nationalsozialismus*, vol. 1, p. 253.

(83)   From a position paper of the Grosse Landesloge, Januar 1930, p. 2f. (Archiv GLL).

(84)   From Witt-Hoë's reply to the National Association of German Officers of July 27, 1925, cited in Chapter 3.1, p. 3, GStA PK, Logen, 5.1.3., 4390.

(85)   Newsletter of the German-Christian Order (Deutsch-Christlich Orden) [formerly Circle Correspondence], notebook for Mai 1933, p. 135. The pages cited literally or paraphrased from the Circle Correspondence or Newsletter are numbered according to those of the cumulative volume for the year.

(86)   From a letter of a deputy lodge master from April 27, 1933, Archiv GLL.

(87)   Compare Wippermann, *Der konsequente Wahn*, P. 66.

(88)   Klaus Hornung, "Der jungdeutsche Orden." *Beiträge zur Geschichte des Parlamentarismus und der politischen Parteien*. Vol. 14, Düsseldorf, 1958, p. 24. Compare in connection with this problem, see also Wolfgang Wippermann, *Der Ordensstaat als Ideologie. Das Bild des Deutschen Ordens in der deutschen Geschichtsschreibung und Publizistik*, Berlin, 1979, p. 242ff. Wieshaupt's Order of Illuminati and other associations of Illminati are otherwise indicated (see Chapter 1.1). In another context, the oft-mentioned Jewish organization, B'nai B'rith, which, modeled on Freemasonry, is also divided into lodges. Here the label "Order" in the narrower sense, is correct only in a very limited way. The "United Ancient Order of Druids" founded in 1781 in London refers to the Celtic priesthood of England and Ireland. It has similarities to Freemasonry in its basic ethical views, organizational structure and ritual (three degrees); its charitable orientation reminds one of B'nai B'rith.

(89)   On the Empire (*Kaiserreich*) compare the essays in: *Handbuch zur "Völkischen Bewegung" 1871-1918*, ed. von Uwe Puschner et al., München/New Providence/London/Paris, 1996.

(90)   '*Volk*' was stylized in time to a "moral-religious, socio-political, and historical final authority" and came to be a "central factor in reflexive consciousness training." In addition, the specifically German concepts "*Heimat*" (native place) and "*Reich*" (Empire), served to give the '*Volk*' as German *Volk* genuine space. (Otto Brunner, Werner Conze, Reinhart Koselleck (Ed.), *Geschichtliche Grundbegriffe. Historisches Lexikon zur politisch-sozialen Sprache in Deutschland*, vol. 7, Stuttgart, 1992, pp. 389, 391). The *völkisch* topos integrated all of this in that

nationalism, racism and anti-Semitism were bound up in it (Compare Günter Hartung, "Völkische Ideologie," in: *Handbuch zur "Völkischen Bewegung*," p .22ff., hier p. 22).

(91)   Compare René Freund, *Braune Magie? Okkultismus, New Age und Nationalsozialismus,* Vienna, 1995, p. 29ff., 35f. On Lanz, compare also Ekkehard Hieronymus, Jörg Lanz von Liebenfels, in: *Handbuch zur "Völkischen Bewegung*," p. 131ff.; Wolfgang Wippermann, *Der konsequente Wahn: Ideologie und Politik Adolf Hitlers*, Gütersloh/ München, 1989, especially p. 66ff.; as usual, within limits, also Wilfried Daim, *Der Mann,der Hitler die Ideen gab. Von den religiösen Verirrungen eines Sektierers zum Rassenwahn des Diktators*, München, 1958. Hieronymus and Freund do not agree with Daim, according to whom Lanz had a very direct influence on the development of Hitler's *Weltanschauung.*

(92)   Freund, Braune *Magie*, p. 34.

(93)   Daim, *Der Mann, der Hitler die Ideen gab*, p. 20.

(94)   Cited after ibid., p. 36. Lanz published the "Ostara" issues as of 1905, which was named after the Germanic goddess of Spring, and glorified "Urgermanentum" ("Original-Germanic-ness"). It appeared for a time in a run of 100,000 (Compare Freund, *Braune Magie*, p. 30).

(95)   Reinalter, "Freimaurerei und Nationalsozialismus am Beispiels Alfred Rosenbergs," *loc. cit.*, p. 56. The second edition of Sebottendorffs book, *Bevor Hitler kam*, was forbidden after the "Seizure of power," and the Thule-Gesellschaft (Thule Society) was dissolved in 1933. Sebottendorff, who worked as an agent in Turkey for the German Resistance died in 1945 under mysterious circumstances. His corpse was found in the Bosporus (compare Freund, *Braune Magie*, p. 45f.).

(96)   Gilbhard, *Die Thule-Gesellschaft*, p. 12. Orignally it was the task of the Thule-Gesellschaft, "to help with the selection of members for the Munich Group of the "Germanen," and to protect the activities of this secret society, which had its headquarters in Berlin, from the outside world." (ibid., p. 11f.).

(97)   Compare Joachim C. Fest, *Hitler: Eine Biographie*, Frankfurt/M./ Berlin/Wien, 1973, p. 168f. Wippermann points to the "not unimportant political and above all financial influence (of the Thule-Gesellschaft [author's note]) on the German Workers' Party and even on theNazi Party." (*Der konsequente Wahn*, p. 67).

(98)   Compare Wippermann, *Der konsequente Wahn*, p. 67f. Himmler conceived of the Wewelsburg near Paderborn as a kind of "Grail Castle" of the SS in allusion to the King Arthur legend, and analogous to the Marienburg of the medieval German Order. Here is where the urns of the highest SS leaders were to be displayed. (Compare. Wippermann, *Der Ordensstaat*, p. 260; Bradley F. Smith/Agnes F. Peterson (eds.), *Heinrich Himmler. Geheimreden 1933 bis 1945 und andere Ansprachen*, Frankfurt/M., Berlin, Wien, 1974 [Illustrations, p. 128ff.]).

(99)   Hitler, *Mein Kampf*, cited here after *Wippermann, Der konsequente Wahn*, p. 64.

(100)   Compare Wippermann, *Der Ordensstaat*, p. 258. The influence of rapturous mysticism and the thought-processs of the Order on Nationalsozialism is an important, however often neglected, aspect: "The National Socialist Party did not tolerate secret societies, because it was itself a secret society complete with its own grand master, racist gnosis, rites, and initiations" (René Alleau, *Hitler et les sociétés secrètep. Enquete sur les sources occultes du nazisme*, Paris, 1969, p. 214). In the same vein, see also Rauschning, *Gespräche mit Hitler*, P. 226f. On the problem of using Rauschning, see Note II/71. On the whole quite informative, even though only cursory: Freund, *Braune Magie*, passim. In the whole book, Freemasonry is unfortunately treated only very superficially.

(101)   Rauschning, *Gespräche mit Hitler*, p. 227. Again, on the problem of using Rauschning, see Anm. II/71.

(102)   Compare Wippermann, *Der konsequente Wahn*, p. 67.

(103)   Cited ibid.

(104)   Himmler on November 8, 1937. Cited after Bradley F. Smith/ Agnes F.Peterson (Ed.), Heinrich Himmler. *Geheimreden 1933 bis 1945 und andere Ansprachen*, Frankfurt/M., Berlin, Wien, 1974, p. 61.

(105)   Cited after Ackermann, *Heinrich Himmler als Ideologe*, p. 201. On understanding the Orders of the SS altogether, compare. Heinz Höhne, *Der Orden unter dem Totenkopf. Die Geschichte der SS*, Gütersloh, 1967, especially p. 125ff.

(106)   Martin Broszat, "Das weltanschauliche und gesellschaftliche Kräftefeld," in: Martin Broszat/Norbert Frei, *Das Dritte Reich im Überblick. Chronik, Ereignisse, Zusammenhänge*, München 2nd ed. 1990, p. 107.

(107)   Ibid.

(108)   Ibid.

(109)   For example Treitschke praised the German Order (Deutschen Orden)for its "merciless race struggle" against the "barbaric" and "half-barbaric" Pruzzen, Lithuanians, and against the "deadly enemy," Poland. Cited after nach Wippermann, *Der konsequente Wahn*, p. 65.

(110)   Compare, Hans Schwarz, "Foreword," in: Moeller van den Bruck, *Das dritte Reich*, p. 13. Besides which, Moeller connected anti-Marxism and anti-Semitism in a cynical way, and created prototypes of later Nazi clichés: Karl Marx had been a stranger in Europe "as a Jew" and had, moreover, gotten himself involved "in the affairs of the European peoples," as though he wanted to "gain a belated right to hospitality among them" (Moeller van den Bruck, *Das dritte Reich*, p. 38).

(111)   Compare Wippermann, *Der konsequente Wahn*, p. 70.

(112)   Cited after Ackermann, *Heinrich Himmler als Ideologe*, p. 205. For a summary of the meaning and function of the picture of an "Order-State" in National Socialism, compare Wippermann, *Der Ordensstaat*, p. 253ff.

(113)   Wippermann, *Der konsequente Wahn*, p. 70.

(114)   Minutes of a meeting with representatives of the German Association of Nobility on February 20, 1928, GStA PK, Logen, 5.1.3., 4428.

(115)   Ibid.

(116)   Newsletter of the German-Christian Order, issue for May 1933, p. 135ff.

(117)   This concerned Three World Globes Grand Orator Rosbach, who caused an uproar with his appearance at the St. John's celebration on June 25, 1924. The comparatively liberal Grand Master, Habicht, shared the indignation of his lodge Brother Stresemann (compare Neuberger, vol. 1, p. 266, 332 [Note 128af.]).

(118)   Cited among other places in: Reichl (Ed.), *Blaubuch*, vol. 1934, p. 77f. In May of 1933, the "Newsletter" of the German-Christian Order published the response from the Reichs Chancellery: "The Reichs Chancellor. Berlin, March 1933. For good wishes sent to me in the most friendly manner on the occasion of the solemn, ceremonial opening of the Reichstag in Potsdam, and the loyal memory, I express my most heartfelt thanks. A. Hitler" (*Ordensblatt*, 5/1933, p. 157).

(119)   Compare Habicht's message to the Evangelical High Consistory of April 28, 1933 (Evangelical Central Archive [EZA], 7/3628.

Compare also Beyer, *Der Übertritt*, p. 128. Habicht died on May 17, 1937 at the age of 70.

(120) According to Neuberger, *Freimaurerei und Nationalsozialismus*, vol. 2, p. 83. For personal information on the Three World Globes Grand Master, see details in Chapter 5.2.1.)

(121) Situation report of March 30, 1933, Archiv GLL.

(122) On April 11, 1933, Göring was named by Hitler as Deputy Federal Representative and Prime Minister of Prussia.

(123) Compare Peters, *Geschichte der Freimaurerei*, p. 242.

(124) Circular letter of the Three World Globes Grand Lodge of April 11, 1933 (Private collection).In a lecture on the German-Christian Order by Dietmar Schultes published in the Circle Correspondence of the Grosse Landesloge (Z.K.), no. 11/1995, p. 398ff., it is maintained that Göring had declared in the relevant conversation that "the Grosse Landesloge could resume its work if it would decide to give up its old, oft-attacked usages, and would undertake a new version of the ritual, in which it omitted the parts based on the Od Testament." (p. 403). On p. 405, it says that it came to "Görings pledge about the continuation of the Große Landesloge." Schulte still owes documentation for this. That Göring actually expressed himself so explicitly appears very questionable. Rather one is suspicious that this was the hopeful interpretation of the leadership of theGroße Landesloge, and is thus wishful thinking.

(125) Witt-Hoë's handwritten letter of April 1933, Archiv GLL.

(126) Circular letter of April 7, 1933, ibid. Worthy of note is that the author has a circular letter of the Three World Globes' Federal Director's Office (Bundesdirektorium) that literally reports it right away—indeed on April 7—thus on the day of the meeting with Göring and expressly connecting it with conversation between Göring and the Landes Grand Master of the Grosse Landesloge. Obviously, the Three World Globes' leadership of the Grosse Landesloge is *at first* only about that, not about Göring's doubtless more important information. According to this, one was informed that there was no place in a national socialist state for Freemasons, and for the steps introduced at the Grosse Landesloge.

(127) Decree of the Highest Order Department of April 7, 1933 about the new structure of the Order, Archiv GLL. The handwritten additions "Grail" and "of the Templars" are already on the

document, also struck through by hand. The idea of a relationship "German-Christian Order Grail of the Templars" was clearly not pursued farther. It is unclear who brought it up. By the same token, in a letter of April 11, the Grand Lodge of the State of New York—the only jurisdiction except for Christian Freemasonry in Scandinavia—with which contact was maintained, was informed that the [Order's] Grosse Landesloge had laid aside its characteristic as a Masonic body, and for this reason "Masonic relationship" was no longer possible (compare the letter of April 11, 1933, GStA PK, Logen, 5.1.3., 4459).

(128)   Thus it is incorrect, as it says in the *Blaubuch (Blue Book)*, that the National Mother Lodge was the first to make the transformation into a Christian order (vol. 1934, p. 83). In Neuberger there is only a rather cursory description of the transformations (compare vol. 2, p. 85f.).

(129)   Expert opinion of 15.4.1933, Archiv GLL.

(130)   Circular letter of the German-Christian Order of June 15, 1933, GStA PK, Logen, 5.1.3., 4472.

(131)   Minutes of the meeting of the Committee on Grand Lodges (Großlogen-Ausschuss) of April 23, 1933, in: *Ordensblatt*, Heft Mai, 1933,vol. 62, p. 140. Finally, the Old Prussians remained with the following designations: Grosse Landesloge: German Christian Order (Deutsch-Christlicher Orden); Three World Globes: National-Christian Order of Frederick the Great (National-Christlicher Orden Friedrich der Große); Grand Lodge of Prussia "Friendship" (Große Loge von Preußen gen. Zur Freundschaft): German Christian Order "Friendship" (Deutsch-Christlicher Orden Zur Freundschaft).

(132)   Ibid., p. 148f.

(133)   From the "Rules of the Order" of the German Christian Order given on April 23, 1933 of the Constitutional Assembly of the German Christian Order in: Ibid. p. 153.

(134)   Letter of the National-Christian Order of Frederick the Great to the Nazi Party Administration April 12, 1933 (Private collection).

(135)   Letter of the National-Christian Order of Frederick the Great to Reichs Minister Goebbels April 12, 1933 (Private collection).

(136)   This comes from a letter from von Heeringen of May 19, 1933 (GStA PK, Logen, 5.1.3., 4445).

(137)   From a circular letter of the National-Christian Order of Frederick the Great of April 12, 1933, cited in Neuberger, *Freimaurerei*

und Nationalsozialismus, vol. 2, (Appendix), p. 309. With respect to the laying aside of Masonic identity, compare also Reichl (Ed.), *Blaubuch*, vol. 1934, p. 86 and Archiv GLL, passim.

(138)   Compare Freudenschuß, *Der Wetzlarer Ring*, loc.cit., p. 22.

(139)   Concerning such efforts by the Humanitarian grand lodges, Howe writes in *The Collapse*, p. 28, „In 1931 the Hamburg, Frankfurt am Main (Eclectic Union) and Bayreuth Grand Lodges revised their Craft rituals so that everything which had an Old Testament connotation was eradicated." In this sense, taken from Neuberger, *Freimaurerei und Nationalsozialismus*, vol. 1, p. 260. As can be determined with the help of the hand-corrected manuscript, Howe refers to an essay by Gustav Slekow in the *Alten Pflichten*, no. 1, 4.vol. [1935], p. 6ff., in which he complains briefly and rather generally , that the Grand Lodges of Hamburg, Frankfurt und Bayreuth as well as the two Saxon grand lodges "jumped into the shipping lanes of the Old Prussians" (p. 6): Already in 1931 they gathered around a Germanicized ritual that expurgated anything relating to (smacking of) the Old Testament (ibid.). Slekow, a journalist from Leipzig and founding member of the Supreme Council, discharged the function of the Grand Chancellor of the Grand Lodge in Exile when he wrote the relevant article in Palestine. Concerning Slekow see also Chapter 7.2. Aside from Howe's description, which as said before, is based on Slekow, nothing was made known about *völkisch*ly motivated changes in the Humanitarian ritual before 1933. That they were actually realized at this stage as von Howe maintains, is questionable.

(140)   Compare Freudenschuß, *Der Wetzlarer Ring*, loc.cit., p. 23 (note 11) und Neuberger, *Freimaurerei und Nationalsozialismus*, vol. 2, p. 87f. On the legend of Hiram, the master builder of Solomon's Temple, compare Düriegl/Winkler (Ed.), *Freimaurer*, p. 107ff. Concerning changes in ritual, in detail, compare Jürgen Luckas, "Nicht alles war Selbstschutzmaßnahme. Ritualänderungen der altpreußischen Großlogen von 1933–1935,"in Q.C.-Berichte, Heft 15/1995, Wien, 1995, p. 72ff.

(141)   Compare Jürgen Luckas, "Freimaurerabzeichen mit Hakenkreuz," *Quatuor Coronati Informationsblatt des Arbeitszirkels Nordrhein-Westfalen*, Sonderdruck [s.l.], 1995, p. 6. Luckas assumes , because of the similarity in names, that this is about a splitting of the "Drei Schlüssel zum aufgehenden Licht" Lodge in Regensburg, which might have happened because of political differences among the Brethren.

(142)   Cited ibid., p. 7, merely with the note that the dissolution took place a few months after the "seizure of power," without giving a concrete date.

(143)   Cited ibid., p. 8.

(144)   Cited ibid., p. 10. Luckas is on the right track with his assumption that the Brethren in Mainz had contributed to the tendencies toward nationalization of German Freemasonry. Thus they set up a "freedom celebration" on the 13th and 14th of July 1930, on the occasion of the Allied troops' pulling out of the Rhineland, and expressed in the invitation that the celebration had to be "a public confession of our true German sentiment" at which no German Masonic lodge could fail to show up (cited ibid.).

(145)   Circular letter of the National Christian Order Frederick the Great no. 157 of January 26, 1934 (Private collection).

(146)   Compare *Treue-Information*, Issue 122, no. 1/1985 "Die dunkle Zeit," ed. Three World Globes Grand Lodge, Berlin, 1985, pp. 13, 64, as well as "Freimaurerlogen in Berlin und Freimaurerisches Kunsthandwerk" (Berliner Freimaurermuseum im Logenhaus Berlin), no. 1, Oktober, 1976 [s.n.]., p. 5ff. Compare also Luckas, "Freimaurerabzeichen mit Hakenkreuz," p. 3ff. See also the documentation appendix.

(147)   Cited in Beyer, *Der Übertritt*, p. 168f.

(148)   *Verordnungsblatt der Reichsleitung der NSDAP*, Series 47, vol. 2. München, 1933. Cited i.a. in: Reichl (Ed.), *Blaubuch*, vol. 1934, p. 91. According to Peters, *Geschichte der Freimaurerei*, p. 244, the Berlin Nazi paper, "Angriff" ("Attack") of May 22, 1933 indicated the view of the Party under the title "Order of Frederick the Great Not Recognized." According to this, "the gathering together of German men in smaller groups" is to be rejected (not approved).

(149)   Letter of June 27, 1933, cited after ibid., p. 87ff. Also cited in Beyer, *Der Übertritt*, p. 170f. There with the date June 21, 1933. On the question of the "camouflage," the three former Grosse Landeslodge Brothers took a stand in a letter of May 25, 1933, to the Reichs Chancellery. They gave as a reason for their resignation from the Grosse Landesloge Order that it was "as always a Masonic lodge" and thus stood in opposition to the new government [Reproduced in full in Neuberger, *Freimaurerei und Nationalsozialismus* (appendix), vol. 2, p. 313]. Whether this denunciatory letter had any effect on the development of leading Nazis' opinions on the "Freemasonry

Question" may be seriously doubted. Everything points to the authors' completely false estimation of their administration's attitude.

(150) Member's Petition to the Three World Globes Lodge "Empor" in Munich of June 4, 1933, Archiv GLL.

(151) Decree of the Order Master of September 6, 1933, ibid. See also the documentation appendix. Deciding factors, that the decree was rejected by the Brethren (except by those to whom it applied), or that individual lodges refused the transformation, are not to be found.

(152) Ibid.

(153) Cited according to Reichl (Ed.), *Blaubuch*, vol. 1934, p. 86.

(154) Cited according Beyer, *Der Übertritt*, p. 162.

(155) The corresponding decisions on exceptions (§ 3 [part 2]) in the *Law on the Restoration of the Professional Official* of April 7, 1933 (*Reichsgesetzblatt* 1933 I, p. 175), especially the "Clause on the Soldiers on the Front" were based mostly on Hindenburg's intervention the "Frontkämpferklausel." Of course, they remained in effect for just two and one-half years. More anti-Semitic rules and decrees are in: Joseph Walk (Ed.), *Das Sonderrecht für die Juden im NS-Staat. Eine Sammlung der gesetzlichen Maßnahmen und Richtlinien—Inhalt und Bedeutung*, Heidelberg, Karlsruhe, 1981. There is also (p. 3ff.) information on the "Aryan Paragraph" by registry representatives, application by student corporations. Compare the monograph by Rosco G.P. Weber, *The German Student Corps in the Third Reich*, London, 1986 (German edition being printed). More critically vis-à-vis the Corps in Michael Grüttner, *Studenten im Dritten Reich*, Paderborn, 1995.

(156) Compare the circular letter no. 12 of the Supreme Party Court of January 8, 1934 (GstAPK, Logen, 5.1.3., 4424). The making equal of spouses was taken over into the rules of the "Reichs Citizens Law" in 1935. Compare the first decree of the "Reichs Citizens Law" of November 14, 1935, § 5 (part 2 [b]), in: *Reichsgesetzblatt* 1935 I, p. 1333f. Ironically, the "closely related persons" and Freemasons were excluded in the same context by the Nazi Party: persons with "connections, which come from a marriage with carriers of Jewish or 'Colored' blood," and from such connections "that were made with societies or associations, which the Nazi Party has rejected or fought against from its inception," namely "all Masonic lodges," were contrary to the efforts of the Nazi Party (Circular Letter no. 12 of the Supreme Party Court of January 8, 1934, loc.cit).

(157)   Rules for fulfillment (execution) of November 6, 1933, GStA PK, Logen, 5.1.3., 4472.

(158)   Reproduced in *Ordensblatt des Deutsch-Christlichen Ordens*, Issue November 1933, 62nd vol., p. 320.

(159)   Cited in Beyer, *Der Übertritt*, p.175.

(160)   Circular letter of the German Christian Order of August 7, 1933, Archiv GLL.

(161)   Minutes of the conference in the Prussian Interior Ministry of September 12, 1933, ibid.

(162)   Compare Thomas Martin Schneider, *Reichsbischof Ludwig Müller: Eine Untersuchung zu Leben, Werk und Persönlichkeit*, Göttingen, 1993, p. 147ff. Unfortunately this otherwise detailed study by Müller leaves out the relationship between the Evangelical (Protestant) Church and Freemasonry completely.

(163)   Compare Neuberger, *Freimaurerei und Nationalsozialismus*, vol. 2, p. 96f. According to this work, this initiative was traced to a lodge brother, in whose house Müller grew up as the son of a housekeeper.

(164)   Göring's then chief highlands forester, Jäger, maintained this in a later conversation with Prof. Adolf Schmitt (oral information from Prof. Schmitt to the author).

(165)   Compare Archiv GLL, passim.

(166)   Compare the letter of retired Rector Perrey to von Heeringen of May 11, 1933 and von Heeringen's letter of May 18, 1933, GStA PK, Logen, 5.1.3., 4444.

(167)   Letter of the later GLL-Liquidator Paul Rosenthal to a colonel in East Prussia on October 17, 1933, GStA PK, Logen, 5.1.3, 4446.

(168)   Compare the letter of November 3, 1933, GStA PK, Logen, 5.1.3., 4448.

(169)   Responding letter of the "Reichs Church Government" on November 18, 1933, ibid.

(170)   Compare Joachim Hossenfelder's letter to his father on November 4, 1933, GStA PK, Logen, 5.1.3., 4374 and ibid., passim.

(171)   Compare ibid. The sometimes handwritten correspondence.

(172)   The Order administration expressed this in a letter of July 3, 1933 (ibid.) as opposed to Müller. Among other things, it said that one was

completely of the conviction that it was a "thing of impossiblility" to have such an odd entity closed in unto itself in the face of "a large movement that was taking the whole German people with it."

(173) Compare Kurt Hossenfelder's letter to Paulsen on November 6, 1933, ibid.

(174) Compare in this connection the situation report of the State Police office in Berlin for the month of April dated May 5, 1934, BA R 58/2631, p. 309ff.

(175) Reichl (Ed.), *Blaubuch*, vol. 1934, p. 94.

(176) Fenner/Schmitt-Sasse, "Die Freimaurer als 'nationale Kraft'," *loc.cit.*, p. 236.

CHAPTER 5

(1) Müffelmann's membership in the SPD [German Socialist Party], according to- Neuberger, *Freimaurerei und Nationalsozialismus*, vol. 2, p. 17, 68 is without notation as to the length. Based on the information available to the author, a membership in the SPD cannot be denied, or shown to be impossible but neither can it be proven. In the same manner, research undertaken at the request of the author was without results. It is also unclear that Müffelmann at some time joined the DDP [German Democratic Party]. For more on the problem of Müffelmann's party membership(s), see also note V/48 and Chapter 7.1.

(2) Bruno Peters permits an understanding with respect to people even though it is limited in *Berliner Freimaurer: Ein Beitrag zur Kulturgeschichte Berlins* 2d. ed. Berlin, 1994. Wilhelm Leuschner was a member of the lodge "Johannis der Evangelist," which belonged to the Grand Lodge of Darmstadt. It differs from from Peters, in *Berliner Freimaurer*, p. 39, in that it is not about a lodge in Berlin. Rather its home was in Darmstadt and still works there today as a subordinate lodge of the Grand Lodge A.F. and A.M. of Germany. Julius Leber belonged to the Rising Sun Grand Lodge.

(3) Cited after Lennhoff/Posner, *Int. Freimaurer-Lexikon*, Introduction, p. 15.

(4)   In connection with its dissolution in Germany, the "Light of Freemasonry" of the Rising Sun Grand Lodge was given to the subordinate lodges working in Czechoslovakia (oral information from Dr. Hans-Detlef Mebes to the author). The liquidation of the Rising Sun's secretariat devolved upon Johannes Drechsler. He could not stop the confiscation of the majority of the Archive in 1933. Despite this, even at the end of 1934, the Gestapa clearly knew almost nothing about the Rising Sun Grand Lodge. Thus a circular letter went out to all State Police stations on November 30, 1934, from the Gestapa-Referat II 1 B 2 which was responsible for Freemasonry. It said, "Concerning the Masonic Association 'Rising Sun', not much material exists. Especially true is that the members cannot all be gathered yet into a card file. Thus I wish to notify the subordinate authorities that they should immediately obtain the membership rolls of the lodges in their area belonging to the Rising Sun Grand Lodge, and send them to me. At the same time, I request a report on whatever is known or can be found out about the Association 'Rising Sun'. A list of the lodges...is in the enclosure for our information." (reproduced in *Versuch einer Darstellung*, p. 105). The circular letter was signed by the chief of the Masonic Section (Referat), Dr. Karl Haselbacher. For more on Haselbacher, see Chapter 8.1. Some of the "Rising Sun's" papers not confiscated were lost in bomb attacks on Hamburg in 1943. (Compare Drechsler, *Die Brüder vom FZAS*, p. 25ff.). The archivists at Merseburg combined the "Rising Sun" papers with those of the Symbolische Großloge (5.1.11.) which is with the other former Merseburg Lodge papers in the Secret State Archives in Berlin. In 1952, the "Rising Sun" Grand Lodge joined the United Grand Lodges of Germany after accepting both the laying of the Bible [on the altar – trans. note] as the symbol of ethical efforts (i.e. not signifying a tie to a specific religious denomination) and the inclusion of the Grand Architect of the Universe (A.B.A.W./ G.A.O.T.U., again not signifying a personal concept of God) in its ritual (compare ibid., p. 43f).

(5)   On the process of "Causing the lodges to go dormant," compare Lennhoff/Posner, *Int. Freimaurer-Lexikon*, column 409. Neuberger also sees a "clever move" in the procedure, because it avoided a "formal capitulation" to the political opponent (vol. 2, p. 69f.). In the meantime, Müffelmann, had stood up for active work in the ritual as late as March 21, but could not get his motion through the Supreme Council. However, he tried to maintain his position in

spite of political pressure and close personal danger. He possibly considered the "going dark" that took place ten days later as being too soon (compare Müffelmann's letter of March 22, 1933 to a member of the Supreme Council in the private archives of Alain Bernheim). Hans Lachmund expressed himself in a similar vein on March 30, 1933 in connection with the Symbolische Großloge's "going dark" (Compare concerning this a letter to Müffelmann of the same date, GStA PK, Logen, 5.1.11., 25). On Lachmund see Chaper7.1 and 8.4. Concerning more detailed circumstances surrounding the decisions of the Supreme Council and the Symbolische Großloge to "go dormant," see also Chapter 7.1. In the same way the German leadership of the Odd-Fellows, one of the so-called "lodge-like" organizations traditionally with many Jewish members, also clearly came to the conclusion that continuing in the "Third Reich" would be untenable. On April 2, 1933, therefore, one day after the anti-Semitic boycott, they decided to dissolve themselves. The Odd-Fellows numbered about 8,000 members at the end.

(6)   While August Pauls, *Der Deutsche Alte und Angenommene*, loc.cit., p. 2, still speaks of the existence of a Supreme Council of Germany in Exile, Alain Bernheim calls it a legend (compare "Für Leo Müffelmann. Fünfzig Jahre nach seinem Tod," in: *Eleusis*, vol. 39, no. 3, Mai/Juni/Juli 1984, p. 170ff.). A contemporary witness reported, "The work of the Supreme Council of Germany was carried on in exile in the Orient of Jerusalem," said Benno Grünfelder, in "Die Entwicklung der Symbolischen Großloge von Deutschland im Exil, " (typed lecture) Jerusalem January 31, 1948, p. 10. One thing is sure: out of the circle of German Grand Lodges in exile, advances in the Scottish Rite were undertaken. There had already been AASR-lodges (workshops) under the authority of the Supreme Council of Egypt, which led to tension with the British Mandate. Müffelmann, the oldest one possessing the 33d Degree, was named "Commissary Grand Commander" of the dormant Supreme Council for Germany, after the authorities had forbidden the last regular Grand Commander, Gottlieb Friedrich Reber, to travel.

(7)   Substantiated by Neuberger (compare vol. 2, p. 16f.). Also not verifiable is Neubergers assessment, according to which there was no doubt of a "fundamental rejection of Nationalsozialism" (ibid., p. 71) on the part of the established humanitarian Grand Lodges. An imprecise representation of what happened to the humanitarian

and the Old Prussian grand lodges is given by Pfahl-Traughber, *Der antisemitisch-antifreimaurerische Verschwörungsmythos*, p. 143.

(8)   Compare *Die drei Ringe*, no. 5, 1933, p. 124 and the *Wiener Freimaurer-Zeitung* no. 4/5, 1933, p. 59.

(9)   Beyer's Circular letter of April 12, 1933, Osobyi Archives, Moscow, 500-1-192.

(10)   Compare Beyer's Circular letter of April 18, 1933, ibid. On the events with the Grand Lodge "Sun," compare also *Die Drei Lichter*, ni. 27/28, (Hannover) 1948, p. 204f.

(11)   According to oral information to the author from Herbert Schneider, the former Director of the Masonic Museum in Bayreuth (Bayreuther Freimaurer-Museums) and his succesor, Hans-Georg Lesser van Waveren. Neuberger also reports the event (vol. 2, p. 75). Compare in addition a letter from the Main Security Office to the Security Service, Main District – South (SD-Oberabschnitt Süd) on July 7, 1936, *Osobyi Archives, Moscow*, 500-3-334.

(12)   Compare Böttner, "Gab es eine 'Große Loge von Hamburg im Exil' in Chile?" in: *TAU*, I/1989, p. 50ff., here p. 50.

(13)   Endler/Schwarze, *Die Freimaurerbestände*, vol. 1, p. 236.

(14)   Compare Pauvrert, „Die deutschen Großlogen 1933 bis 1935", *loc.cit.*, p. 443ff.

(15)   Endler/Schwarze depict the further development sketchily, presumably because of lacking sources. According to them, the Gestapo and other Party organs clearly acted equally rigorously against the Grand Lodge in Frankfurt as they had in Hamburg. The treasury of the Eklektischen Bundes (Eclectic Association) was confiscated. When this happened was not noted. The Archive of the Frankfurt Grand Lodge had been taken away in 1935. The "Wolfstieg-Gesellschaft" is not mentioned (compare vol. 1, p. 236).

(16)   Compare Neuberger. *Freimaurerei und Nationalsozialismus*, vol. 2, p. 74.

(17)   Compare Jürgen Luckas. "Freimaurerei im Nationalsozialismus," in: *TAU*, II/1993, p. 132ff.

(18)   Letter of April 24, 1933 (Archiv GLL). According to Luckas, the transformation was mandated on April 17, to take effect immediately (compare „Freimaurerei im Nationalsozialismus," *loc.cit.*, p. 136).

(19)   Compare Endler/Schwarze, *Die Freimaurerbestände*, vol. 1, p. 197.

(20)   Compare Friedrich John Böttner, "Gab es eine ‚Grosse Loge von Hamburg im Exil' in Chile?," *loc. cit.*, p. 51; Endler/Schwarze, *Die Freimaurerbestände*, vol. 1, p. 257f. The subordinate lodges were instructed about these proceedings rather generally, with the announcement of more news to come in a circular letter on April 15, 1933, and asked "to remain in connection with the the same loyalty and friendship as previously" with the transformed mother institution "under a new name and statement of goals." It seems that the new name was decided upon later. In any case, Bröse proposed the name "Confederation of Brothers of the German House" in another circular letter on April 18, 1933. Both Circular letters are reprinted in: *Wiener Freimaurer Zeitung*, no. 4/5, 1933, p. 58f.

(21)   *Satzung des Deutschen Ordens* (Rechtsfähiger Verein) Hamburg [1933], p. 2.

(22)   Letter of October 29, 1933 from a Brother of a subordinate lodge of the Grosse Landesloge in Darmstadt to the later Master of the Order Friedrich Bolle (Archiv GLL). Cäsar Wolf's suicide out of despair because of the introduction of the "Aryan Paragraph" was already being discussed.

(23)   Compare Peters, *Die Geschichte der Freimaurerei*, p. 241. No year is noted at the appropriate place, but from the context it would seem that the year would be 1933. Possibly there is only a mix-up, since the actual closing speech took place on a July 30, but in 1935.

(24)   Bröse's speech on July 30, 1935, reprinted in: *Versuch einer Darstellung*, p. 301ff.

(25)   The assumption of the existence of a Grand Lodge in exile in Chile is based to a great extent on Steffens. In the same vein also, Edgar von Borries' *Loge "Drei Ringe": Der Weg von der Großen Loge von Hamburg zur Gran Logia de Chile*, (Private printing), Santiago de Chile 1994. On the other hand, among others: Friedrich John Böttner, "Gab es eine ‚Grosse Loge von Hamburg im Exil' in Chile?," *loc.cit.*, p. 50ff. and the authors of the Festschrift for the 60th Anniversary of the founding of the Lodge "Zur Quelle Siloah" in Jerusalem (see note V/33) came to the conclusion that the idea of a Hamburg Grand Lodge in exile was a legend. Details also in Neuberger, *Freimaurerei und Nationalsozialismus*, vol. 2, p. 73f. Compare also Peters, *Die Geschichte der Freimaurerei*, p. 241.

(26)   Compare Endler/Schwarze, *Die Freimaurerbestände*, vol. 1, p. 258.

(27)   Cited according to Drechsler, *Die Brüder vom FZAS*, p. 32. Compare also Reichl (Ed.), *Blaubuch*, vol. 1934, p. 78.

(28)   Cited according to the *Wiener Freimaurer-Zeitung*, no. 4/5, 1933, p. 60.

(29)   Compare Fischer's letter of June 15, 1933, to von Heeringen, Archiv GLL.

(30)   Compare a circular letter from Beyer on May 5, 1933 and one from Dresden Grand Master Fischer of May 8, 1933, Osobyi Archives, Moscow, 500-2-95.

(31)   Compare the corresponding letters from Leipzig (April 25, 1933) and Dresden (June 15, 1933) as well as the replies from von Heeringens of May 6, 1933 and June 19, 1933. In the latter one, von Heeringen opined to the Saxon Order: "I am of the opinion that it is impossible to transform an organization which has practiced humanitarian Freemasonry suddenly into one that is an ‚Order‘ as we understand it." (all letters Archiv GLL).

(32)   The consolidation (union) arises from an announcement directed to Goebbels on November 3, 1933 (Archiv GLL). Exactly when and how the union took place is not explained. In June 1935, people complied with the "voluntary" self-dissolution (compare Endler/Schwarze, *Die Freimaurerbestände*, vol. 1, p. 212).

(33)   Heinz D. Bar-Levi, Nathan Fischer, Efraim F. Wagner (Ed.), *Zur Quelle Siloah no. 26 im Orient Jerusalem*, Jerusalem, 1991, p. 10. In this connection, see a detailed explanation in Chapters 7.1 and 7.2.

(34)   Werner Ansorge, a member of the Lodge "Müffelmann zur Treue" in Tel Aviv, and Representative of the United Grand Lodges of Germany in Israel, suggested this completely correct assessment to the author.

(35)   This is in reference to Müffelmann's depiction, from his papers, which were kindly put at the author's disposal by Henning Wolter (Delmenhorst). The unfinished report, under the heading "Three months of protective custody, September-November 1933, because of Masonic membership," divided into five chapters, was written presumably after the end of February 1934, based on arrest notices and memories. In addition to the description of the time in prison, and later hearings, it includes general biographical notes and some concerning war operations and his Masonic vitae. The manner of the (re)presentation leads one to conclude that Müffelmann figured that his notes would be censored sooner or later. The apparent naiveté concerning conditions in concentration camps, the noticeable reserve about politics, the silence

about the activities in Palestine, or even an explicit note to that effect, indicated that his father was an "Aryan." Furthermore, Müffelmann gives the impression that he was completely surprised by his arrest, which is highly improbable. Instead he should have been well aware of his personal danger. Despite Müffelmann's fears, his notes did not fall into the hands of the Gestapo. They belong to the small part of his estate of which his brother Ronald managed to get custody (compare Ronald Müffelmann's letter of August 30, 1947 to Emanuel Propper (Archiv Henning Wolter, Delmenhorst). On Ronald Müffelmann see Chapter 7.1. In Neuberger, *Freimaurerei und Nationalsozialismus*, vol. 2, passim, the concentration camp Sonnenburg was mistakenly called "Sonneburg."

(36)   Compare ibid., p. 8f. See also Chapter 8.4. It may have played a role in the hearing that Müffelmann as a person and his "passionately championed internationalism" were mentioned in the *Internationales Freimaurer-Lexikon* by Lennhoff und Posner (column 1071), which was at the disposal of the Gestapo.

(37)   On Bensch see Chapters 7.1, 7.2 and 8.4.

(38)   Bensch, the Lieutenant Grand Commander of the Supreme Council for Germany was obviously arrested in place of the Grand Commander Gottlieb Friedrich Reber, who lived in Lausanne, and thus evaded the clutches of the Gestapo.

(39)   Legacy of Müffelmann's estate, *Drei Monate Schutzhaft*, P. 40 (Archiv Henning Wolter, Delmenhorst). After their release, Bensch, Koner, and Müffelmann had to sign a statement saying that they had "voluntarily put at disposal" their confiscated books and lodge furnishings (ibid., p. 45).

(40)   According to Koners arrest warrant (Compare Neuberger, *Freimaurerei und Nationalsozialismus*, vol. 2, p. 237 [note 41]). That Bensch and Müffelmann were released "at about the same time" as Koner, can therefore not be stated," as Neuberger" (vol. 2, p. 18).

(41)   Legacy of Müffelmann's estate, *Drei Monate Schutzhaft*, p. 24 (Archiv Henning Wolter, Delmenhorst).

(42)   Compare *The New Age* (now the *Scottish Rite Journal* [trans. note], the Journal of the Supreme Council of the AASR, Southern Jurisdiction of the US) 1935, p. 108f. The journal has nothing to do with the so-called "New-Age Movement." Endler/Schwarze (*Die Freimaurerbestände*, p. 301), express themselves in a similar way, although indeed without giving concrete sources. According to

them, even [F.D.] Roosevelt had personally intervened. The author was also assured by Henning Wolter who had learned in personal conversations with American Freemasons, that a note from the Supreme Council, AASR, SJ and the Grand Lodge of the District of Columbia came to the German representative in Washington. One month before the seizure of power, John Henry Cowles, while on a trip to Germany, learned that "Hitler has announced his opposition toFreemasonry, and I think has even claimed that Freemasonry and the Jesuits are in league to hurt the country—a most absurd proposition; and yet (...) quite a number of Masons voted for him ..." (William L. Fox, *Two Centuries of Scottish Rite Freemasonry in America's Southern Jurisdiction*, Arkansas, 1997, p. 234).

(43)   Compare the Legacy of Müffelmann's estate, Müffelmann, *Drei Monate Schutzhaft*, p. 42ff. (Archiv Henning Wolter, Delmenhorst). Portions of Koner's correspondence from the years 1928–1930 are in Osobyi Archives, Moscow (500-2-111). These documents fell into the hands of the Gestapo during his arrest in 1933. Also, aside from the questionable circumstances of his arrest and release in 1933, there is a different judgment of Koner. According to his own allegations, he was repeatedly the object of persecution by the Security Police, but no political opposition in the "Third Reich" can be deduced from his own representation. (Compare *Freimaurerleben*, p. 49ff.).

(44)   Gestapa Messages, no. 5 of April 18, 1934: Masonic lodges, lodges, orders, and similar associations in Germany (GStA PK, I, 90 p. 129). See also Chapter 8:1

(45)   Ibid., p. 9.

(46)   Ibid., p. 10.

(47)   Ibid., p. 9.

(48)   Ibid. Other than this copy of this announcement by Müffelmann, there is nothing more known about a sometime membership in the German Democratic Party. Given his political philosophy, it seems completely possible. The evident contradiction of why German Democratic Party membership had not already "collided" with the claim of political neutrality is still unsolved. Müffelmann had led the "Vela" (Society of executive workers) since 1919. Presumably there was no relationship. Müffelmann had quit, when the change in direction, connected with the creation of the German State Party (Deutschen Staatspartei [DStP])

began to distinguish itself from the formerly left-liberal German Democratic Party. Müffelmann would naturally have concealed any such connection with the Gestapo. Concerning the circumstances of his entrance into the DNVP (German National Folk Party) and "Stahlhelm" (Steel Helmet) in 1933, see Chapter 7.1. He probably did not enter the German National Folk Party at the beginning of 1933, but only in the Spring, at the same time as he sought admittance into the "Stahlhelm." Members of the Große Landesloge belonged to the "Jungdeutschen Orden" ("Young German Order"), which united with the German Democratic Party in 1930 (compare Witt-Hoë's letter of June 6, 1929 to Adolf Groche (GStA PK, Logen 5.1.3., 4392). The Young German Order stood in opposition to the German National Folk Party as well as the Nazi Party. He did not notice any clear political contours.

(49)   Ibid. The nearly identical wording of Koner's and Müffelmann's announcements is striking.

(50)   Altogether an estimated 30-90% of the Brethren left the organization. There are reliable figures only in isolated cases. For example 170 of the 284 members (as of 1931) left the Breslau Lodge (Grosse Landesloge) "because of Naziism" until the dissolution (Archiv GLL, undated). Many sources report on the distress of the Fraternity: Compare for example GStA PK, Logen, 5.1.3., 4444f., passim. The situation was much the same for the membershp of other grand lodges; for the Humanitarian grand lodges it was even worse.

(51)   During the development of the situation, the German Red Cross announced in the beginning of October 1934 that membership in Masonic lodges and similar organizations would preclude belonging to any branches of the German Red Cross. Former lodge members who had resigned before January 30, 1933, had to sign a declaration that they had dissolved all connections to Freemasonry. Those who had left their lodges after that, could hold office in the German Red Cross in special cases, and only then when there were no political reservations concerning them. (Cf. Circular Letter no. 347 Main Administration of the German Red Cross dated October 1, 1934, GStA PK, Logen, 5.1.3., 4433). The Old Prussians promptly sent a petition to the President of the German Red Cross, Duke Carl Eduard von Sachsen-Coburg and Gotha, in which they indicated Hitler's so-called "Willensmeinung" ("Opinion of My Will") of January 1934, according to which nothing would be done against the Old Prussians (see below) and because of this, they sought an

exception for their members (Letter of October 27, 1934, ibid.). Carl Eduard had renewed the "Confirmation patent" and the ducal protection of the Gotha Lodge in 1906 when he over his government as Duke of Gotha. He did not, however, belong to the lodge. The petition was rejected Janaury 15, 1935 (Compare ibid.). One can assume that most (former) Freemasons were forced to leave the German Red Cross.

(52)   Letter dated June 7, 1933, of the later liquidator of the Grosse Landesloge, Paul Rosenthal, to a Brother in Flensburger, GStA PK, Logen, 5.1.3., 4445.

(53)   Compare the letter of May 18, 1933, ibid. Compare in this connection Neuberger, *Freimaurerei und Nationalsozialismus*, vol. 2, p. 99.

(54)   From a letter (December 20, 1933) to the Bundesdirektorium Nationalen Christlichen Ordens (National Director's Office of the National Christian Order) "Friedrich der Große," cited in: Endler, "Zur Entstehung und Inhalt der Frei-maurerei, ihrer Entwicklung in Deutschland und zur Geschichte der Loge *'Amalia' in Weimar.*" Lecture, Weimar November 3, 1990, Manuscript p. 26f. Siefert had been suspended as Headmaster of a gymnasium in Weimar in 1930 by the former Thüringian Minister of [People's!] Education and later Reichs Interior Minister Frick vom Dienst. Siefert had again refused to allow the *völkisch*-National Socialistic youth organization "Adler und Falken" in his school (Compare ibid.).

(55)   Compare Peters, *Geschichte der Freimaurerei*, p. 248. Neuberger dispensed with any discussion as to whether and to what extent any contradiction came from the subordinate lodges, citing the very sketchy source material. (Compare vol. 2, p. 82). The Archives of the Grosse Landesloge show that there was not much. Beyer did opine, that a greater part of the Old Prussian membership stayed on "general Masonic ground," more than the grand lodge administrations wanted to admit. (Compare. *Der Übertritt*, p. 158). This supposed "general Masonic ground," frankly, did not exist.

(56)   Neuberger, among others, reports on this incident in *Freimaurerei und Nationalsozialismus*, vol. 2, p. 98.

(57)   From the letter of April 12, 1933, signed by Grand Master Bordes to the Nazi Party leadership (Private collection).

(58)   Letter of October 21, 1933 from the Nazi Party administration for the Südharz, Archiv GLL. The point of view was expressed

in connection with the case of a Grosse Landeslodge Brother
and official physician, who as a Freemason, finally lost this state
position. At first, the Pussian Interior Ministry confirmed that
lodge membership was no reason for proceedings because of
the "Berufsbeamten-tumgesetzes" ("law concerning professional
officialdom"). See below.

(59)   Compare Neuberger, *Freimaurerei und Nationalsozialismus*, vol.
2., p. 91. The Masonic Order (Grosse Landesloge) did not agree
to the petition, because according to Provincial Grand Master von
Heeringen, such a thing "could cause only damage" (Appendix to the
Circular Letter of June 13, 1933, GStA PK, Logen, 5.1.3., 4445).

(60)   *Ordensblatt des Deutsch-Christlichen Ordens*, October 1933 issue, p. 290.

(61)   Ibid., p. 291.

(62)   "Vertrauliche Leitgedanken," ("Confidential leading thought"
October 12, 1933, Archiv GLL.

(63)   Circular letter from the National Christian Order Friedrich
der Große and the German-Christian Orders Zur Freundschaft of
October 16, 1933, ibid. Also in: "Versuch einer Darstellung," p. 224ff.

(64)   Ibid.

(65)   Compare ibid.

(66)   For details on the "Stahlhelm" see below.

(67)   Gerhard Paul/Klaus-Michael Mallmann, "Auf dem Wege zu
einer Sozial-geschichte des Terrors: Eine Zwischenbilanz," in: Dies.
(Ed.), *Die Gestapo—Mythos und Realität*, Darmstadt, 1995, p. 3ff.,
here p. 9. Compare in addition Robert Gellately, "Allwissend und
allgegenwärtig? Entstehung, Funktion und Wandel des Gestapo-
Mythos," in: ibid., p. 47ff., here p. 56. Gellately shows that the
Gestapo was anchored in German society in many ways. He
describes the phenomenon as a myth whose social reception
manifested itself in different variants. These changed over time
and were influednced by subjective psychological factors within the
populace. In addition, he comes to the conclusion that his myth was
promulgated on purpose "from above" on the one hand, but was
nourished "from below" on the other. Nazi Germany, according
to Gellately, became a society that policed itself. (Compare ibid.,
especially p. 49, 65ff.). Compare also Paul/Mallmann, *Auf dem Wege
zu einer Sozialgeschichte des Terrors*, loc.cit., p. 10.

(68)   Compare Gellately, "Allwissend und allgegenwärtig?," *loc. cit.*, p. 63.

(69)   Situation in Oktober 1933. Compare Archiv GLL, passim.

(70)   Compare concerning the procedures GStA PK, Logen, 5.1.3., 4393, passim.

(71)   Order no. 3383 of February 22, 1934, ibid.

(72)   According to an enclosure with a letter of January 16, 1934 from a Brother (Grosse Landesloge) to von Heeringen, ibid.

(73)   Message of February 27, 1934, ibid.

(74)   Compare GStA PK, Logen, 5.1.3, 4393, passim. On November 16, 1934 a Three World Globes subordinate lodge instigated the formation of a United Front of Freemasons, who belonged to Nazi organizations (compare a letter of November 16, 1934 to Dr. Bordes at the "Bundesdirektorium"; Federal Directory), (ibid.).

(75)   Compare in this connection, i.a., Adolf Groche's remarks on Freemasonry and "Stahlhelm" ("Steel Helmet"); undated, Archiv GLL. Bundesführer ("Federal leader") Seldte "played a traitorous role in this." On the supervision (regulation) of (former) Freemasons in the Party and State, see Chapter 8.2.

(76)   Compare a letter of December 14 to the Großloge, GStA PK, Logen, 5.1.3.,4448.

(77)   Letter of March 22, 1934, in the Bundesarchiv, formerly BDC (Berlin Document Center), Ordner 880, Bl.30f. In the same place, are examples of appeal or "mercy" proceedings (answered overwhelmingly negatively) arranged alphabetically by name. More detail in Chapter 8.2.

(78)   Letter from the later Grand Master of the Grosse Landesloge Friedrich Bolle to Feistkorn dated December 6, 1933, GStA PK, Logen, 5.1.3., 4455.

(79)   Compare ibid., passim. Feistkorn hinted to Bolle (December 1, 1933) that "we feed 35 people daily in our place for free. These people were sent to us by the National Socialistic Welfare Office, although we are not allowed access to it." (ibid.). On May 24, 1934 the organization Office of the "deutsche Arbeitsfront" ("German Work Front") announced the decision that former lodge members who delivered a written statement in lieu of an oath that they belonged to no Masonic successor organization, could be accepted, but could not assume "leadership positions" (GStA PK, Logen, 5.1.3., 4477).

(80)   Undated draft, by the German-Christian Order "Friendship" of a circular letter to the Order Groups of the German-Christian Orders, GStA PK, Logen, 5.1.3., 4455. With minor changes, the draft, which in the meantime had clearly been approved by Bordes, was sent on to Bolle. It is questionable whether the circular letter was sent out that way, and whether these ideas were ever delivered to Ley.

(81)   According to the Grosse Landesloge Archives (September 1933). Such a practice is not surprising, because from the standpoint of the the Nazis, the opposition to the organization "lodge" always took precedence over the persecution of the the individual Freemason. On the other hand, in October 1933, the State Ministry of Oldenburg announced that the membership of officals in Masonic lodges and "substitute orgnizations" was not consistent with the duties of an offical in the National Socialistic State, and actions in violation of this would be subject to discipliary action in the future. (Compare the corresponding announcement in: Amtliche Nachrichten/Oldenburger Anzeiger, no. 202 of 17.10.1933, GStA PK, Logen, 5.1.3., 4446).

(82)   Circular letter from von Heeringen August 9, 1933, Archiv GLL.

(83)   Circular letter no. 5/1933 of the Allgemeiner Deutscher Waffenring (General German Weapons Ring) of July 20, 1933, BA, R 43, 4232, p.15f., here p. 15 verso. Compare also the insert in a circular letter of the German-Christian Order September 16, 1933, GStA PK, Logen, 5.1.3., 4446 as well as Archiv GLL, passim. Lammers' letter dated June 29, 1933 to the ADW is printed in: Deutsche Corpszeitung, vol. 52., no. 5, August/September 1935, p. 151f. In contrast, the Nazi government leadership maintained that there was no distinction made between the Order and other lodges (see Chapter 4.2). Even before this from Lammers, acceptances into the Nazi combat groups were managed repeatedly, if the petitioners declared that they were of "Aryan descent" and belonged "only" to a German-Christian Order. All this according to Felix Witt-Hoë in a letter to a Brother of the Order in Nürnberg (March 29, 1933; i.e., before the formal transformation! GStA PK, Logen, 5.1.3., 4444).

(84)   Compare concerning the whole affair, Grüttner, *Studenten im Dritten Reich*, p. 302.

(85)   Witt-Hoë's letter to a Brother of the Order in Neustettin, May 5, 1933, GStA PK, Logen, 5.1.3., 4444.

(86)   Compare GStA PK, Logen, 5.1.3., 4445, passim.

(87)   Ordinance of the Reichsarbeitsministers (Minister of the Ministry of Work), dated November 2, 1933, Archiv GLL.

(88)   Circular Ordinance of the Prussian Interior Minister January 8, 1934 (MBlPiV., no. 3, 1934, column 70f.) according to the corresponding order of January 4, 1934 to the Old Prussians. Several newspapers ran stories of lodges' self-dissolutions during the following months. The desired wave of self-dissolutions, however, did not come to pass (see below).

(89)   Compare Neuberger, *Freimaurerei und Nationalsozialismus*, vol. 2, p. 23.

(90)   According to Heydrich's to Göring (November 23, 1934 no. 61463/1731), GStA PK, I, 90 P. 74, Heft 2, pp.102ff. [incomplete] Heydrich relies on the Circular Ordinance of the Prussian Interior Minister of September 14, 1934. One learns that, up to this point, the decisions to dissolve 13 lodges in various governmental districts within Prussia were approved on the basis of the Ordinanc of January 8, 1934 (MBlPiV., no. 38, 1934, column 1168b). The Circular Ordinance des Reichs and Prussian Interior Ministry of December 15, 1934 (MBlPiV., no. 51, 1934, column 1543f.) listed ten additional approvals of dissolution as well as two registered dissolutions; the one of May 22, 1935 (MBlPiV., No. 22, 1935, column 693f.) showed nine more approved dissolutions and one registered.

(91)   Compare the position of the State Police in Hamburg (Tgb.-no. 41209/33. St. p. 2) of January 10, 1934, GStA PK, I, 90 P. 74, issue 2, p.143f. Already before that, people in the Gestapo in Bremen formed the opinion that an there would be an announcement forbidding "all lodges, orders, and 'substitute' organizations." This according to a note of October 29, 1933 (Archiv Henning Wolter, Delmenhorst).

(92)   Nazi church politics cannot be discussed in more detail here. It is known that Hitler (at least publically) at first upheld the significance of both Christian religions ("confessions," i.e. Catholic and Protestant (Evangelical) as factors for "the maintenance of Nationhood." In the campaign of 1933, he declared that Nationalsozialism "wished to protect Christianity as the basis of our whole Morality" (cited after Burkert/Matußek/Wippermann, "Machtergreifung," p. 132). In fact, however, Christianity and the principle of race were incompatible in his eyes.

(93)   Compare Circular Letter no. 12 of the Supreme Party Court January 8, 1934 (GStA PK, Logen, 5.1.3., 4424).

(94)   Ibid.

(95)   Incorrect in Neuberger, *Freimaurerei und Nationalsozialismus*, vol. 2, p. 23f.

(96) Compare: a summary of the measures taken against (former) Freemasons in: *Die Weltfreimaurerei*, ed. by the Chief of the Security Police and Security Service prepared by [SS-Sturmbannführer] Erich Ehlers, *Schriftenreihe für politische und weltanschauliche Erziehung der Sicherheitspolizei und des SD*, no. 3, Leipzig, 1943, p. 47. See also Chapter 8.2.

(97)   Compare in this vein a letter to a Grosse Landesloge Brother in Bonn from the National Socialist Welfare Reichs Adminstration of April 5, 1934, GStA PK, Logen, 5.1.3., 4479. In contrast, the chairman of the Nazi Party District Court Westfalen-Süd was of the opinion that although the National Socialist Welfare indeed decided whom it accepted, the same criteria should be applied "as in political organizations and other sections of the Party" (Letter from the District Adminstration Westfalen-Süd to an Order Brother, dated May 11, 1935, GStA PK, Logen, 5.1.3., 4481).

(98)   On the situation in Bavaria compare Pfahl-Traughber, *Der antisemitisch-antifreimaurerische Verschwörungsmythos*, p. 141.

(99)   This picture results from theperusal of the GLL-Archives. Compare also Endler/Schwarze, *Die Freimaurerbestände*, vol. 1, p. 41.

(100)   Compare. in this connection the individual very revealing essays on regional history in: Gerhard Paul/Klaus-Michael Mallmann (Ed.), *Die Gestapo—Mythos und Realität* (Darmstadt, 1995).

(101)   This conclusive assessment in Neuberger, *Freimaurerei und Nationalsozialismus*,vol. 2, p. 13. On the "Führerbefehl" („Führer's Order") of July 22, 1933 see (IfZ, MA 398, SS (II), 9866 and PS 2202). Compare ibid. At least formally, The SS was still in association with and under the leadership of the Sturmabteilung. Only at the end of June-beginning of July 1934, after the "Röhm-Affäir" did the SS become independent (20. July).

(102)   Neuberger, *Freimaurerei und Nationalsozialismus*, vol. 2, p. 24.

(103)   Hitler's "Willensmeinung" („Views of Purpose") promulgated January 30, 1934 cited after the Archiv GLL.

(104)   Order of the "Stellvertreters des Führers" („Deputy Führer") of February 21, 1934, GSTA., MA 106 561 (reprinted in its entirety in Neuberger, vol. 2, Appendix, p. 315).

(105) Order of the Interior Minister of April 3, 1934, GSTA., Reichsstatthalter   638 (reprinted in its entirety in Neuberger, vol. 2, Appendix, p. 315).

(106) Compare in this connection a letter from von Heeringen to a captain dated March 24, 1934, GStA PK, Logen, 5.1.3., 4449.

(107) Compare the note of a lawyer for the Grosse Landesloge on October 10, 1934, GStA PK, Logen, 5.1.3., 4336. The reason was an Erfurt Gestapo decision made in concert with the Gestapa, to take action against such activities.

(108) According to a letter from the Gestapo Inspektor to the Prussian Prime Minister, dated April 6, 1934, GStA PK, I, 90 P, 74, Heft 1, Bl.44.

(109) Letter from the Secretary of State of the Reichs Chancellory to the Secretary of State of the Prussian Ministry of State, April 21, 1934, GStA PK, I, 90 P, 74, Heft 1, Bl.46. As soon as February 16, 1934, Perrey, the Master of the Grosse Landesloge subordinate lodge in Königsberg, "Zum Todten-kopfe und Phönix" ("Skull and Phoenix"), Perrey, had been temporarily taken into "protective custody." According to an announcement of the Gestapa on June 11, 1934, he was arrested because he had declared that the area command had stolen the Lodge's silverware (GStA PK, I, 90 P, 74, Heft 1, Bl.51). For more on the Lodge "Zum Todtenkopfe und Phönix" see below (note V/142).

(110) Compare Neuberger, *Freimaurerei und Nationalsozialismus*, vol. 2, p. 25ff.

(111) Ibid., p. 92.

(112) Letter from the Old Prussian Grand Lodges to the main administrative office of the German Reichs Railroad Company on April 9, 1934, GStA PK, Logen, 5.1.3., 4432.

(113) Announcement no. 147 of the Referats I B 7 in the Prussian Interior Ministry, dated March 10, 1934, Archiv GLL. In this connection, see also Chapter 4.2.

(114) The administration of the Grosse Landesloge informed its readers about this in Circular Letter no. 168 of March 26, 1934, put at the author's disposal, as follows: "The Prussian Minister of the Interior has made us aware that the Grand National Mother Lodge of the Three World Globes must keep its former name in interaction with the authorities and their subordinate lodges until a change is

mandated according to protocol, and allowed by him. " In obvious misjudgement of the situation it said further that this "suggestion" (!) by the Minister would be followed. No instruction for the naming of the subordinate lodges is in the letter. According to the circular letter, the new ritual (lodge procedures) and the term "Ordensbruder" should stay as they were.

(115)   To the Grand Master's lecture on the attacks "that German Freemasonry has so recently experienced from such circles, with whom it should have been called to work hand in hand, given its position on belief in God and with respect to the Fatherland," the Reichspräsident had responded that „he himself had always regarded these attacks objectively, and that it would not have been necessary on the part of the representatives of the Old Prussian grand lodges to assure the loyal German and Fatherland-loving view of the Representative of the Old Prussian grand lodges, because he himself had never had any other opinions. Both of his grandfathers had been Freemasons at the time of the Wars of Liberation, and he did not doubt that the spirit of the Fatherland, which at that time fired the souls of Freemasons, still existed in their circles." (undated remark of the Grosse Landesloge, noted July 1926, GStA PK, Logen, 5.1.3., 4336).

(116)   Letter from the Old Prussian grand lodges to the Reichs President of June 1, 1934,   GStA PK, Logen, 5.1.3., 4350.

(117)   On the efforts re Hindenburg, compare von Heeringen's letter to Hindenburg's son on June 6, 1934 and the letter of the Adjutant of the Reichs President to the Grand Master, dated June 19, 1934 (both ibid.).

(118)   Engelbert Huber, *Freimaurerei: Die Weltmacht hinter den Kulissen*, Stuttgart, 1934. For this work, the 3d. edition (without year --Deutsches Freimaurer-Museum Bayreuth, No. 3093) was used. Huber was chief of the so-called "Forschungsstelle über Freimaurerei" ("Research Office on Freemasonry") of the "Antikomintern," which was a part of the Ministry of Propaganda. He was considered the "Expert" in the Party on Masonic concerns (compare Neuberger, *Freimaurerei und Nationalsozialismus*, vol. 2, p. 37). During the year 1934, he fell out of favor. To all appearances, Friedrich Hasselbacher and Gregor Schwartz-Bostunitsch cut him out. Cf. a report by Hasselbacher dated June 29, 1934 [USHMM, RG-11.001 M, Reel 292] and an "expert opinion" by Schwartz-Bostunitsch of September 26, 1934 [USHMM, RG-15.007 M, Reel 43]. There will be more on both men. According to a note by

Schwartz-Bostunitsch of September 13, 1934, Huber's book was forbidden and the author arrested [USHMM, RG-15.007 M, Reel 43]. From an undated note of the Gestapa-Referat II 1 B 2, which was responsible for Freemasonry, one learns that Huber was expelled from the Party [USHMM, RG-11.001 M, Reel 291]. Allegedly, he „was even paid to prepare exposés of the Old Prussian lodges for presentation at central offices of the Reich." (*ibid.*) Clearly Huber had given himself the title of "Referent für Freimaurerfragen" (Referent for Masonic Questions").

(119) Discussion by Ludwig Rohmann, in: *Ordensblatt* (formerly *Bundesblatt*), Heft April, 1934, p. 4ff., here p. 5.

(120) Huber, *Freimaurerei*, p. 127. Huber undertook, foolishly, to make a distinction in connection with Germany, between "symbolic" and "humanitarian" lodges.

(121) Ibid., Foreword, p.vi.

(122) Ibid., p. 127f.

(123) Compare Ludwig Rohmann, Open letter to Dr. E. Huber, in: *Ordensblatt*, Heft Juni 1934, p. 80ff., here p. 80f. Emphasized also in Huber, *Freimaurerei* (see Note. V/118). Rohmann writes further: "You are fighting world Jewry, or really the world- and money power that it represents. All right. Our sympathy (good wishes) accompanies you in so far as we also reject the Jews and have always rejected them (...) It is possible that now, in the corrupt French lodge life, which, deeply diseased because of Jewish and Marxist elements, has gone completely to the dogs, catastophes will occur. The world won't lose anything, but the struggle against the German lodges also can't help it." (p. 91). Different from Huber's case, Rohmann wrote an extremely sharp rebuttal when the first volume of Friedrich Hasselbacher's *Entlarvte Freimaurerei* (*Freemasonry Exposed*) appeared in the autumn of 1934. At the end, Rohmann wrote: "After I worked my way through the book, and got over the feeling of deep disgust, I lay it down with a feeling almost of sympathy." (Ludwig Rohmann, in: *Ordensblatt* [formerly *Bundesblatt* and *Am rauhen Stein/ Der rauhe Stein*], Heft Oktober/1934, p. 57ff., here p. 70). On Hasselbacher, whose insane hatred of Freemasonry went along the lines of Ludendorff's argumentation, see Chapter 8.1.

(124) "Announcement to the beloved Brothers" ed. by the Grand Lodge of Prussia, called "Zur Freundschaft," Berlin, 1934, p. 7f.

(125) "Bitte" des Majos d.R. (retired) Heinrich Fischer (Presiding Master ot eh St. John's "Convent" of the German-Christian Order in Oldenburg) of January 30, 1934, BA.R 43 II/821 (Reichskanzlei), p. 67f. (reproduced in its entirety in Neuberger, vol. 2, Appendix, p. 314). The designation "Convent" or "Konvent" was used in the German-Christian Order after the transformation of the Grosse Landesloge, instead of the loaded concept "Lodge."

(126) Compare, for example, Neuberger, *Freimaurerei und Nationalsozialismus*, vol. 2, p. 80. Also, the Grosse Landesloge Groche described as "moderate" „ (Archiv GLL, undated). The Chairman of the Verein Deutscher Freimaurer (Association of German Freemasons), Diedrich Bischoff, held similar views (Compare Neuberger, vol. 2, p. 79). In this connection, see also Chapter 3.3.

(127) Petition of the assistant master (Studienrat), Freemason, and clergyman Plotz from Pirna (Große Landesloge von Sachsen/ Christlicher Orden Deutscher Dom) of September 9, 1934. BA. R 43 II/821, p. 87f. (reproduced in its entirety in Neuberger, vol. 2, Appendix, p. 316f.). Plotz wrote a second, similar letter to Hitler on November 5, 1934 (GStA PK, Logen, 5.1.3., 4481).

(128) From a letter from the personal Referent of the Reichs Minister of the Interior, March 17, 1934 (Archiv GLL).

(129) Instruction of the Reichs Defense Ministry 1p90J (Ia) no. 2066 34 dated May 26, 1934, Archiv GLL. See also Chapter 8.2.

(130) Heydrichs message to Göring of November 23, 1934 (No. 61463/1731), GStA PK, I, 90 p. 74, Heft 2, Bl.102ff. [incomplete]. In the relevant petition, the grand masters, referring to the Instruction of April 3, expressed their expectation that the Gestapo would intervene in favor of the Old Prussians, and would end the attacks, to which the Orders felt themselves exposed.

(131) Ibid.

(132) Letter from the Reichs Ministry of the Interior of June 11, 1934, GStA PK, Logen, 5.1.3., 4477.

(133) In his letter of June 23, 1934 Ministerial Director Nicolai emphasized to the Old Prussians that Frick's order of April 3 was often so falsely misinterpreted by the lodges that it was "as if the Reichs government had given specific recognition to the lodges and expressed approval of their activities" (ibid.).

(134) Von Heeringen's letter to Nicolai July 20, 1934, ibid.

(135) Compare Beyer, *Der Übertritt*, p. 185f.

(136) Herbert Reith, "Eine Abrechnung mit den letzten Saboteuren nationalsozialistischer Aufbauarbeit. Freimaurerei und was der schaffende Deutsche von ihr wissen muß," in: *Arbeitertum* (Organ of the German Work Front [Deutsche Arbeitsfront DAF]), Folge 16, November 1934, P. 12f. (*GStA PK*, Logen, 5.1.3., 4379).

(137) Cocerning these procedures, compare GStA PK, I, 90 P, 74, Heft 1, passim.

(138) Letter from Heydrich to Göring September 19, 1934, ibid., p. 80.

(139) Ibid.

(140) Ibid.

(141) Compare the instructions from the Gestapa to the Lodge "Zu den drei Kronen" of September 25, 1934, BA, ehem. BDC (Berlin Document Center), Personalakte Dr. Otto Bordes. The same sort of messages went to both of the other Königsberg Lodges (see the next note).

(142) Compare Endler/Schwarze, *Die Freimaurerbestände*, vol. 1, p. 140. This concerns the lodges "Zum Todtenkopfe und Phönix" (subordinate to the Grosse Landesloge), "Immanuel" (under the Grand Lodge "Zur Freundschaft") and "Zu den drei Kronen" (under theThree World Globes), which had been searched and temporarily closed in the Fall of 1933. The relevant law of July 14, 1933 about collection of "property hostile to the people and state," had served to legalize the dispossession of the German Social Democratic Party after the fact.

(143) Cited after the oft-mentioned announcement by Heydrich to Göring of November 23, 1934.

(144) Heydrich's signed instruction of December 10, 1934, Archiv GLL. Instructions with the same or similar wording may have been received by the rest of the lodges that had raised objections.

(145) The "Ordensblatt" of the Grosse Landeloge suspended publication only with the end of lodge activity in July 1935.

(146) Compare *GStA PK*, I, 90 P, 74, Heft 2, p.115.

(147) Compare Endler/Schwarze, *Die Freimaurerbestände*, vol. 1, p. 140.

(148) BA, formerly BDC (Berlin Document Center), Personalakte Dr. Otto Bordes.

(149)   Compare ibid.

(150)   Compare George C. Browder, "Die Anfänge des SD. Dokumente aus der Organisationsgeschichte des Sicherheitsdienstes des Reichsführers SS," in: VfZ, 27.V., Heft 2/1979, P. 299ff., especially p. 306f., 309ff. Compare also in this regard also Michael Wildt (Ed.), *Die Judenpolitik des SD 1935-1938. Eine Dokumentation*, München, 1995, p. 14.

(151)   Ibid., p. 307. Browder adds that, in Security Service Headquarters and regional offices, "the availability of usable personnel was a prime factor for the determination of the initial tendency in development." (ibid.).

(152)   Concerning this, see Chapter 8.1.

(153)   On Ehlers, compare Rudolph, *Überlieferung des Reichssicherheitshauptamtes Amt VII, p.* 36ff. For more details on Brand, Schwartz-Bostunitsch und Ehlers see Chapter 8.1. In his curriculum vitae, Ehlers allowed that since the beginning of his activity in the Munich Security Office on November 12, 1933 (in department V) he had worked on the card index of Freemasons (Compare Browder, *Die Anfänge des SD*, loc.cit., p. 306). This was perhaps the earliest indication of the existence of the Security Service Department of Freemasonry.

(154)   Compare BA, formerly BDC (Berlin Document Center), Personalakte Dr. Otto Bordes, passim; Osobyi Archives, Moscow, passim; Shlomo Aronson, *Heydrich und die Anfänge des SD und der Gestapo (1931-1935)*, Diss., Berlin, 1967, p. 423 (note 39); correctly in Neuberger, *Freimaurerei und National-sozialismus*, passim. On the spelling of the name and curriculum vitae, compare Brand's personnel in BA, formerly. BDC (Berlin Document Center).

(155)   Compare a letter to the Security Service Oberabschnitt Süd (South District Office) dated March 13, 1935, Osobyi Archives, Moscow 500-3-334. See also note VIII/33.

(156)   For more details, see Chapter 8.1.

(157)   Compare the correspondence of June 26.6 and July 8, 1935 with respect to the planned filming of lodge rituals for the purposes of propaganda (Osobyi Archives, Moscow, 500-3-337). This had been a proposal of the well-known lawyer, Robert Schneider to the Security Service (compare a letter of the Security Service Oberabschnitt Süd-West [Southwest District Office] to the Main Office, Department

V, of February 14, 1935, Osobyi Archives, Moscow, 500-3-338).
Whether the project came to fruition, is not known.

(158)   BA, formerly BDC (Berlin Document Center), Personalakte Dr.
Otto Bordes.

(159)   Ibid. On the basis of this, the family exchanged certain messages
in encrypted form. One found out about the most recent status of a
development in terms of an inquiry as to how "the weather" was at
the moment.

(160)   Ibid. A party disqualification procedure was carried out
against Bordes after which is was known that he had "made untrue
statements about his lodge membership" (ibid.).

(161)   Compare Peters, *Geschichte der Freimaurerei*, p. 245 and "250 Jahre
Große National-Mutterloge 'Zu den drei Weltkugeln'," (Festschrift),
Berlin, 1990, p. 465. The latter assumes the year 1934 for both arrests.

(162)   Compare the minutes of the conference of March 22, 1935
(Archiv GLL), see note V/170. Compare also Neuberger, *Freimaurerei
und Nationalsozialismus*, vol. 2, p. 96. Concerning Uterharck, compare
Endler/Schwarze, *Die Freimaurerbestände*, vol. 1, p. 258. There are
several competing versions of Bordes' further fate (Compare
Neuberger, vol. 2, p. 250 (notes 101-102a). He probably died in
1943. Rumors, according to which Bordes and his predecessor
in office, Habicht, were murdered in a concentration camp could
not be substantiated (compare ibid., p. 83, 247 [note51] and p.
250 [note101]). Nothing is known about the possible arrests and
imprisonments of the other two Old Prussian Grand Masters, von
Heeringen und Feistkorn. It seems improbable that such did happen.
Kurt von Heeringen died on January 6, 1937 as the result of a stroke
(compare a letter of Grosse Landesloge liquidator Paul Rosenthal of
February 15, 1937, GStAPK, Logen, 5.1.3., 4337). Felix Witt-Hoës
further life is unknown. The last Grosse Landesloge Grand Master
(Ordens-Meister) before Masonry was forbidden, Friedrich Bolle, was
arrested by the Soviets after the end of the war, and died in 1951 in a
work camp in Siberia (Compare Ernst Glaser-Gerhard, *Zur Geschichte
der Großen Landesloge der Freimaurer von Deutschland zu Berlin 1920-1970.
Aus den Beiträgen der Ordensgliederungen und Logen*, Berlin, 1970, p. 5).
The background is unclear.

(163)   The latter possibility according to the statement of accounts
of the liquidator of the National Mother Lodge, Dr. Karl Manecke,

dated October 22, 1945, in: *Versuch einer Darstellung*, p. 371ff., here p. 373, according to which Bordes was released from custody.

(164) See Chapter 8.2. Neuberger means in this connection that Schacht was the only former Freemason who was (en)trusted with a high state office by the Nazi regime. Schacht's position was such a bone of contention in the early years, that his former lodge membership was ignored (compare vol. 2, p. 97). In 1932, Schacht was one of the signers of a declaration of economic representatives who announced support for Hitler (compare Schulze, *Weimar*, p. 388f.).

(165) This follows from a letter from Grosse Landesloge liquidator Paul Rosenthal—of Februarry 15, 1937 (GStA PK, Logen, 5.1.3., 4337). Compare also Peters, *Berliner Freimaurer*, p. 54. Schacht remained in custody from July 1944 until the end of the War, because of his loose contacts with conservative Resistance groups.

(166) Compare Neuberger, *Freimaurerei und Nationalsozialismus*, vol. 2, p. 97. Cited there after the corresponding reproduction by (among others) Zetzsche, *200 Jahre Freimaurerei in Pyrmont*, p. 80f.

(167) Compare Rosenthal's letter of February 15, 1937, GStA PK, Logen, 5.1.3., 4337.

(168) The possibility of an intervention by Gustaf Adolf seemed rather improbable to Neuberger, as such an unreasonable demand would have been certainly exploited by Nazi powers for propaganda purposes as obvious proof for international ties on the part of the Grosse Landesloge (compare Neuberger, vol. 2, p. 95). As already noted in the Introduction, presumably with the help of the Swedish Embassy in Berlin, portions of the Archives of the Grossloge could be rescued from the Gestapo and taken to Stockholm.

(169) Compare the collective Circular Letter of April10, 1935, GStA PK, Logen, 5.1.3., 4459. It says that the grand lodges were in negotiations about the "encouragement toward voluntary dissolution" or the "presuppositions under which this could happen."

(170) Minutes of the meeting of March 22, 1935 in the Secret State Police Office, drawn up by the Gestapa-Referat II 1 B 2 (Archiv GLL). On Haselbacher, Eickhoff and Brand see also Chapters 5.2.1 and 8.1.

(171) Ibid.

(172) Excerpted from the declaration of the three Old Prussian grand masters concerning the voluntary self-dissolution; ibid. See the complete text in the document appendix.

(173) Thus the "Honor Declaration," of the three Old Prussian grand lodges in connection with the "voluntary" self-dissolution, of which the Reichs and Prussian Interior Minister took note, was supposed to have been published this way, according to an assurance by von Herringen. However, it did not happen. (compare a letter from the liquidator of the Grosse Landesloge, Paul Rosenthal of August 27, 1937, GStA PK, Logen, 5.1.3., 4337).

(174) Compare Neuberger. *Freimaurerei und Nationalsozialismus*, vol. 2, p. 100ff. According to this, both organizations reappeared separately.

(175) The author has access to the the memoirs of the Grosse Landesloge and the Grand Lodge "Zur Freundschaft: " "In the Headquarters Building of the Große Landesloge of Freemasons of Germany German-Christian Order," Berlin 2nd ed. 1935; "Zur Erinnerung. Schlußfeier der unter der Großloge von Preußen, gen. Zur Freundschaft in Berlin und Umgebung arbeitenden St.-Johannis-Logen," (In Remembrance: Closing Ceremonies of the St. John's Lodges working under the Grand Lodge of Prussia 'Zur Freundschaft' in Berlin and Vicinity). Berlin (July 16) 1935.

(176) Im Ordensstammhause der Großen Landsloge (In the Headquarters Building of the Große Landesloge), p. 8, 11.

(177) Oral information from Bruno Peters to the author.

(178) *Badische Zeitung,* August 5, 1935 (GStA PK, Logen, 5.1.3., 4379).

(179) The wording of the decree of August 17, 1935, which at first was distributed only in the press, was reproduced in an order from the Bavarian Political Police of September 6, 1935 (compare Neuberger, vol. 2, p. 105, 252 and Appendix, p. 319). Already on September 3, 1935, it was specifically confirmed by the Interior Ministry to the liquidator of the Große Landesloge, that the decisions of the decree of August 17 would not be applied to the Große Landesloge (Mitteilung III P Log. B. Gr. 1 IV. [Archiv GLL]). The same could have been said to the the other grand lodges, which had "voluntarily" dissolved themselves (upon request). To be sure, the decree applied to those subordinate lodges which had not as yet obeyed their mother institutions' decisions to dissolve themselves.

(180)   As stated in a note from the Security Service (Sicherheitsdienst) of March 1936, for example, the lodge building of the subordinate lodge in Husum was bought (certainly not at market price), and used by the National Socialistic Peoples' (*Volks*) Welfare, the Hitler Youth, and the National Socialistic Womens' Group (compare the note with the abbreviation "Office Information" [J/I] of March 12, 1936, Osobyi Archives, Moscow, 500-3-336).

(181)   Compare the already-mentioned statement of accounts by the liquidator of the the Three World Globes, Karl Manecke, October 22, 1945, *loc. cit.*, p. 375.

(182)   This was decided by the Reichs Court in context of a suit brought by the Große Landesloge against the well-enough-known lawyer, Schneider, because of his insistence that the founding father of the Masonic Order's Große Landesloge was a Jew (sic!). Because of the decision, according to the words of the first liquidator of the Große Landesloge, Rosenthal, there was no effective legitimation, to bring suits against slanderers (sic!), unless a (former) member of the Order was personally attacked, and could, for that reason, raise a personal complaint. The dissolution of the Großloge fell in the early phases of the appeal of this case. The Landes (District) Court Berlin obviously took this as the incentive to deny the complaint. Nevertheless, Rosenthal inserted the appeal to the Reichs Court. Compare a letter from Rosenthal on the proceedings August 26, 1936, GStA PK, Logen, 5.1.3., 4337, and a newspaper article, with neither date nor any further identification from the same year, ibid. Alfred Burzlaff suceeded Rosenthal in office for the period 1938–1941.

(183)   Compare concerning the proceedings, GStA PK, Logen, 5.1.3., 4481, passim. For general information on the liquidation of the Große Landesloge, compare Alfred Burzlaff (Liquidator 1938-1941), *Erinnerungen und Dokumente*. 1935-1945, Berlin 1958.

(184)   A circular letter of April 6, 1936 signed by Werner Best as representative, BA, R 58/405, p. 67f. On Dienststelle II 1 B 2 and Best, see Chapter 8.1.

(185)   Ibid.

(186)   Compare Manecke's announcement of April 23, 1936, in: *Versuch einer Darstellung*, p. 359ff.

(187)   Compare a letter of the Reichs- and Prussian Interior Ministry to Manecke dated May 22, 1936, in: *Versuch einer Darstellung*, p. 364.

(188) See Chapter 8.1.

(189) Situation report of February 17, 1937, Osobyi Archives, Moscow, 500-3-413.

(190) Compare Maneckes statement of accounts of October 22, 1945, *loc.cit.*, p. 377, as well as Neuberger, *Freimaurerei und Nationalsozialismus*, vol. 2, p. 111 in conection with Steffens, *Freimaurer*, p. 395.

(191) Compare Maneckes statement of accounts of October 22, 1945, *loc.cit.*, p. 378.

(192) Circular letter of the National Mother Lodge of June 17, 1935, in: ibid., p. 312 f.

(193) For the financial liquidation, compare Maneckes statement of accounts of October 22, 1945, *loc.cit.*, p. 377ff. as well as a closing report about the liquidation of April 4, 1941, in: ibid., p. 367ff.

CHAPTER 6

(1) According to a notarized copy of a certificate from the Prussian Interior Ministry, I B 7/131. IV, Stand August 1934, GStA PK, Logen, 5.1.3., 4336. It is obvious that Witt-Hoë no longer belonged to the leadership of the Grand Lodge at this time.

(2) Figures according to C. van Dalens *Kalender für Freimaurer*, vol. 1925, p. 104; vol. 1927, p. 247; vol. 1928, p. 71; vol 1929, p. 254 and vol. 1930, p. 311.

(3) Compare ibid., vol. 1931, p. 239.

(4) Compare ibid., vol. 1933/34, p. 184.

(5) According to the minutes of the meeting of February 14, 1929, p. 2, GStA PK, Logen, 5.1.3, 4378.

(6) Compare Leo Müffelmann, "Unsere Aufgabe," in: *Die Alten Pflichten* no. 1, Oktober 1930, p. 1ff., hier p. 3. The problem of younger people in the lodges was discussed intensively and controversially during the plenary meetings of the Symbolische Grossloge in 1931 and 1932. Compare the minutes of the deliberations of May 31, 1931 (GStA PK, Logen, 5.1.11., 32) and September 25, 1932 (GStA PK, Logen, 5.1.11., 50). Hans Lachmund

was assigned to develop "Guidelines for the inclusion of youth" ("Richtlinien für die Erfassung der Jugend"). For more on Lachmund, see Chapters 7.1 and 8.4.

(7)   Postscript to a Circular letter of November 10, 1931, GStA PK, Logen, 5.1.3., 4434. For the personal backgrounds of Lennhoff and Posner, see Chapter 7.1 and notes [on the] Introduction, no. 6.

(8)   Witt-Hoë's letter of July 5, 1932, GStA PK, Logen, 5.1.3., 4431.

(9)   Compare the response of July 7, 1932, ibid.

(10)   Compare Michaelis' letter to Witt-Hoë April 4, 1929, GStA, PK, Logen, 5.1.3., 4378.

(11)   Witt-Hoë's response of April 12, 1929, ibid.

(12)   Compare Witt-Hoë's correspondence with Bielig, in: GStA PK, Logen, 5.1.3., 4331.

(13)   Von Heeringe's Circular Letter of January 5, 1932, GStA PK, Logen, 5.1.3., 4339.

(14)   *Honor Roll for those Brothers of the Grosse Landesloge (of the Freemasons of Germany-Christian Order who fell or died of their wounds in the World War 1914-1918,* ed. by der Wissenschaftlichen Abteilung der Großen Landesloge der Freimaurer von Deutschland Deutsch-Christlichen Ordens, Berlin, 1932, p. 29 (ibid.).

(15)   Compare ibid., p. 30.

(16)   "Zur Abwehr!" ("to the Defense!" writing of November 1933), GStA PK, Logen, 5.1.3., 4334.

(17)   Compare Ernst Glaser-Gerhard, "Zur Geschichte der Großen Landesloge der Freimaurer von Deutschland zu Berlin, 1920–1970." From the *Beiträge der Ordensgliederungen und Logen*, Berlin, 1970, s. 213.

(18)   Compare von Heeringens letter of August 7, 1933, GStA PK, Logen, 5.1.3., 4472.

(19)   Greeting for St. John's Day to the subordinate lodges from May 14, 1919, Osobyi Archives, Moscow, 1412-1-4933.

(20)   Max Volkenrath, *Deutsche Freimaurerei als Ergebnis des Weltkrieges: Kriegsbetrachtungen eines deutschen Freimaurers im Felde*, Leipzig, 1916.

(21)   Compare ibid., p. 6.

(22)   Ibid., p. 11.

(23)   Compare in this regard, the membership list (records) of the lodge for 1926, now located in the Deutsche Freimaurer-Museum. According to that, he became a Freemason in 1906. The list for 1928 noted his departure due to his moving away. Previously (presumably also at the time of the appearance of the cited writing) Volkenrath had belonged to the jurisdiction of Bayreuth Zuvor as noted by Jürgen Luckas in "Aspekte vom Weg der deutschen Freimaurerei in die 'Dunkle Zeit'," in: *TAU*, I/1996, p. 49ff., hier p. 50. According to it, he was Worshipful Master of "Zu den zwei Säulen am Stein" Lodge in Würzburg. This designation cannot, however, be proven by the documentation in the Freimaurer-Museums. In 1931/32, a (Dr.) Max Volkenrath appeared as a member of the Würzburger Three World Globes subordinate lodge "Zur festen Burg am Main," and as author of essays in the *Bundesblatt* (Issues March/1931, p. 89 and April/1932, p. 98). It is unclear whether these are the same person. If so, Volkenrath managed another change of system affiliation, this time to the National Mother Lodge.

(24)   Walther Lührs, *Zur gegenwärtigen Lage des deutsch-christlichen Ordensgedankens*, Berlin, 1934, p. 3.

(25)   Ibid., p. 16.

(26)   Ibid., p. 12.

(27)   Cited after the *Wiener Freimaurer-Zeitung*, no. 6/8, 1933, p. 75.

(28)   Ibid., p. 75f. The term "Step" replaced the expression "Degree," which had been discredited by the Nazis.

(29)   Circle correspondence *Ordensblatt der GLL*, 2.May-issue 59, vol. 1930, p. 217.

(30)   Lecture of October 2, 1931, GStA PK, Logen, 5.1.3., 4331. The comments elsewhere testify impressively to the inner sincerity of the search for God by individual Freemasons: Von Heeringen spoke of the significance that the ring with the three red crosses and the inscription "In deo spes" ("In God is my hope") that he wore on his right hand middle finger had for him personally in connection with the image of the son he lost. He asked "Does not each person ... often have feelings, that he cannot master life by his own abilities? Has not the hour come for each of us...where he said, 'I cannot do it!' That he had a feeling of inner emptiness? That he, like Jesus on the Cross wanted to cry out, 'My God, my God, why have you forsaken me?' And he is the one who has forsaken God. In such a situation, the memory of the lost

son should give him a moral incentive ...: I want to set out and go to my Father. Then the happy certainty that his Father is hurrying toward him will come over him, and, as it says in the metaphor, puts a ring on his [finger]. It is this ring that gives him his ‚son's rights' again ... I believe that the guests who do not agree with us on all points, will grant us that we are honest seekers of God."

(31)   Witt-Hoë's letter to a captain on April 15, 1932, GStA PK, Logen, 5.1.3., 4331.

(32)   Ibid.

(33)   Witt-Hoë's letter to the GrosseLandesloge "defense speaker" Oswald Bielig of April 16, 1932, ibid.

(34)   Witt-Hoë's letter of November 12, 1927, GStA PK, Logen, 5.1.3., 4398.

(35)   Ibid.

(36)   Müllendorff's letter to Müffelmann on November 1, 1930, GStA PK, Logen, 5.1.11., 15. The two other Old Prussians reacted similarly, and in the same form, sending letters with the same wording to the Symbolische Grossloge (compare GStA PK, Logen, 5.1.11., 53).

(37)   Stadtrat Dr. Graff's letter to the Landes Grand Master of October 29, 1931, GStA PK, Logen, 5.1.3., 4373.

CHAPTER 7

(1)   On the addition of these Brothers to the Symbolic Grand Lodge, compare Pauls, *Der Deutsche Alte und Angenommene*, loc.cit., p. 2. Aside from the Symbolische Grossloge, also the Scottish Rite was disavowed by the German grand lodges. This was the reason that the Supreme Council of the Southern Jurusdiction USA refused to recognize the Scottish Rite. Grand Commander John Henry Cowles set as a prerequisite for the usual exchange of letters of friendship, that at least one of the established German grand lodges had to allow its brothers to work with the AASR. Cf. Cowle's correspondence of the years 1930-1931 in: *Archives of the SupremeCouncil, AASR, SJ* (Washington, D.C.). Especially after 1930, the political developments

in Germany and the tensions within German Masonry were regular subjects of reports in the magazine *The New Age*.

(2)   Compare Franz Carl Endres, "Zum Problem der Symbolischen Großloge von Deutschland," in: *Die Leuchte*, no. 5/1932, p. 73ff., here p. 74. The independent magazine *Die Leuchte* (*The Beacon*), was an important publicity support for the members of the Symbolische Grossloge. The founding lodges were: 1. "Erkenntnis zur Sonne" (Harburg); 2. "J.G. Fichte" (Hamburg); 3. "Pythagoras zu den 5 Rosen" (Mannheim); 4. "Lessing zu den 3 Ringen" (Stuttgart); 5. Isis zu den 3 Sphinxen" (Schwerin); 6. "Mozart" (Berlin); 7. "Wieland" (München); 8. "Weltkette" (Dresden). Eugen Lennhoff was named honorary member of the Symbolische Grossloge on the day of its founding.

(3)   Müffelmann wound down the activity of the Symbolische Grossloge mostly from his Vela (Federation of Leading Workers) office at Berliner Straße 160 in the Charlottenburg district. His home adress was Seesenerstraße 54 in Halensee. Koner lived at Augsburger Straße 24 in Schöneberg, where he carried out the duties of the Grand Secretary.

(4)   Compare Müffelmanns request to retire of July 28, 1930, GStA PK, Logen, 5.1.11., 10. Compare concerning this whole issue, also *Die Geschichte der Symbolischen Großloge* (*History of the Symbolische Grossloge*), Introduction. Müffelmann, however, continued to work actively with the Supreme Council.

(5)   Posner's letter to Müffelmann October 2, 1930, GStA PK, Logen, 5.1.11., 15. Later the Grand Lodge "Lessing zu den drei Ringen" [the German-speaking Czechoslovak Grand Lodge – trans. note] recognized the Symbolische Grossloge, after it had recognized the Czechoslovak National Grand Lodge [the Czech-speaking - trans. note]. Posner resigned as deputy Grand Master for external (and business?) affairs, obviously in this connection. He died only a short time later. The "Alpina" [the Swiss Grand Lodge] held back conspicuously with respect to the Symbolische Grossloge, out of consideration for the established humanitarian grand lodges in Germany. In October 1931, the leadership of the Symbolische Grossloge could announce that its regularity was recognized by the Swiss, and that "fraternal relations" had been recommended to its subordinate lodges, but without the otherwise usual exchange of vouchers of friendship. On the recognition question, especially the position of the lodges of the United States of America vis-à-vis the

Symbolische Grossloge, compare also Osobyi Archives, Moscow, 1412-1-4900f., passim.

(6)   Declaration of the Grand Master October 25, 1930, reproduced in: *Dokumente, Veröffentlichungen, Briefe*, p. 42f., here p. 43.

(7)   Official announcement (i.e.from the office) no. 19 of July 11, 1930, GStA PK, Logen, 5.1.3., 4411.

(8)   According to a letter from Müffelmann October 3, 1930, GStA PK, Logen, 5.1.11., 15. Before the election of the Bundes Direktorate, Habicht had made known that he was basically in favor of a meeting on September 9, because of Müffelmann's request of September 1. He did not leave any doubt whatsoever that there would be no recognition of the Symbolische Grossloge by the National Mother Lodge. Compare the correspondence in: Archiv Henning Wolter, Delmenhorst).

(9)   Possibly Bing was of the opinion that the founding of the Supreme Council per se had made enough waves. Müffelmann hat apparently not reckoned at all with such a reaction from Bing. Compare, on Bing and the early phase of the Supreme Council, Thomas Richert, "E.J. Bing (Byng) 1894–1962," in: *Der Schottische Ritus in Geschichte und Gegenwart*, ed. at the behest of the Supreme Council of Germany, Issue II, Frankfurt/M., 1986, p. 90ff. Also there, the public declarations verbatim.

(10)   According to report, Reber still identified himself while in the USA in 1931 by a paper [travelling commission] from the Three World Globes. Compare, on this issue, a letter from Müffelmann to Reber of August 19, 1931, GStA PK, Logen, 5.1.11., 12.

(11)   Compare a preliminary memorandum of June 25, 1945 from the US-Office of Strategic Services (Research and Analysis Branch) made available for the suit against Göring. Private archives Alain Bernheim, Gottmadingen.

(12)   According to ibid; compare on Reber also Henning Wolter, "Wer war Bruder Gottlieb Friedrich Reber?" in: *Der Schottische Ritus in Geschichte und Gegenwart*, ed. for the Supreme Council of Germany no. II, Frankfurt/M. 1986, p. 111ff., here p. 118.

(13)   See Chapter 8.4. Compare also Pauls, "Der Deutsche Alte und Angenommene," *loc.cit.*, p. 2. Bensch was Worshipful Master of the Symbolische Grossloge subordinate lodge "Post nubila Phoebus," founded January 11, 1931 in Berlin. Former members of the

Grand Lodge of Hamburg met there. After liberation, Bensch was arrested by the Soviets, and died August 28, 1945 in Berlin. From the beginning, Reber seems to have been only casually concerned with the leadership of the Supreme Council. In any case, there were repeated complaints about that. At first he did not react to the decision of March 31, 1933 to go dormant, which had been made in his absence. Then on April 9, he refused his assent, but did finally give it by telegraph on April 23 (compare a letter, probably written by Koner to a member of the Supreme Council on August 1, 1933. GStA PK, Logen, 5.1.11., 49). Apparently, communication with the Brethren in Germany was nearly cut off since Reber's last sojourn in Berlin in the beginning of December 1932.

(14)   Letter of the Grand Lodge of Vienna to the Symbolische Grossloge October 12, 1931, GStA PK, Logen, 5.1.11., 12. The first international recognitions came from the Grand Loge de France, the Symbolic Grand Lodge of Hungary, and the Grand Orient of Greece in 1930.

(15)   Compare the report signed by Koner on the results of the conversation in the A.M.I. Executive Committee on May 4 & 5, 1932, GStA PK, Logen, 5.1.11., 54.

(16)   Compare the Concordat in the original, GStA PK, Logen, 5.1.11., 6. Compare in this connection also Pauls, "Der Deutsche Alte und Angenommene," *loc.cit.*, p. 2. Neubergers description concerning the Supreme Council and the Symbolischen Grossloge in contrast, contains many mistakes or inaccuracies.

(17)   The freedom of ritual practice permitted them at first presented certain difficulties for the subordinate lodges. There were differences of opinion, for example, with the lodge in Schwerin, "Isis zu den 3 Sphinxen," which had belonged to the "Rising Sun" Grand Lodge, demanded a greater amount of freedom than the Mother Lodge wanted to allow. According to the Müffelmann's Circular letter of February 6, 1932 (GStA PK, Logen, 5.1.11., 32) the Grand Officers' Council (Großbeamtenrat) made the decision to dispense with freedom in the ritual until further notice on January 23, 1932. Compare also the correspondence between the Schwerin Masons and Grand Secretary Koner (GStA PK, Logen,   5.1.11., 13, passim).

(18)   Müffelmann's letter to Lennhoff November 26, 1930, GStA PK, Logen, 5.1.11., 15. The number of former "Rising Sun" Grand Lodge Brothers is usually put at approximately 600 in the source materials.

(Compare for example Endres, "Zum Problem der Symbolischen Großloge," in: *Die Leuchte*, no. 10/1930, p. 143ff., hier p. 144).

(19)   New Year's Circular letter of December 30, 1930, GStA PK, Logen, 5.1.11., 11, 16.

(20)   Compare C. van Dalens *Kalender für Freimaurer*, vol. 1933/34, p. 184. According to the same source, the "Rising Sun" Grand Lodge still numbered 1,250 Brothers in 50 lodges. Compare in contrast, Endres, "Zum Problem der Symbolischen Großloge von Deutschland," in: *Die Leuchte*, no. 5/1932, p. 74. As one can see from a letter from Müffelmann (September 27, 1932) to the Schwerin Worshipful Master Alfred Dierke (GStA PK, Logen, 5.1.11., 21) the actual membership numbers were rounded up only slightly for public consumption. In any case, the real number of members was probably closer to the figure 800 as shown in Dalen.

(21)   In Peters, *Die Geschichte der Freimaurerei*, p. 217, it says, irrelevantly, that Koner was responsible for this task.

(22)   This is described in a biographical sketch by Müffelmann himself: NL Müffelmann, "Drei Monate Schutzhaft," p. 1ff. (Archiv Henning Wolter, Delmenhorst).

(23)   The exact time of Müffelmann's expulsion is unknown. As is known from a letter of April 13, 1933 to Lennhoff vom 13.4.1933, he had, at this point, had to take his former office superior "as a representative of the Nazi Party" into the business administration.

(24)   See below.

(25)   Already in the beginning of 1931, Müffelmann had shown himself to be worried in the face of attacks against Freemasonry and explicitly against him in the "Völkischer Beobachter," that he could get an "awful row" from the Vela office. Compare a letter of January 16, 1931 to the Grand Treasurer of the Symbolische Grossloge. einen Adolf Bünger, GStA PK, Logen, 5.1.11., 17).

(26   Compare NL Müffelmann, "Drei Monate Schutzhaft," p. 32f. (Archiv Henning Wolter, Delmenhorst. On the circumstances and background of Müffelmann's arrest, see Chapter 3.3.

(27)   Ludwig Müffelmann belonged for a time to the City Representatives' Assembly for the Berlin District of Wilmersdorf as a representative of the German Democratic Party.

(28) Cited from a letter from Koner to Ferdinand Runkel Febuary 18, 1932, GStA PK, Logen, 5.1.11., 13.

(29) Compare Osobyi Archives, Moscow (Center of Documentary-Historical Collections, Moscow, 500-2-111, p. 88.

(30) This emerges from the correspondence of "Labor" in 1931 (GStA PK, Logen, 5.1.11., 18) as well as from a letter from his brother, December 4, 1930 (GStA PK, Logen, 5.1.11., 16). After the War, he lived in West Berlin and joined a Masonic lodge there. In a letter from Ronald Müffelmann to Emanuel Propper on August 30, 1947, (Archiv Henning Wolter, Delmenhorst) he talks about "both" his brothers, who were buried in the family grave, which is in the "Wilmersdorfer Friedhof" in Stahnsdorf near Berlin, after it was transferred from the Berlin-Schöneberg Cemetery. Nothing is known of the third brother. Perhaps this was a step- or adopted brother, since Ronald Müffelmann speaks specifically of his "biological brother", Leo, at the beginning of the letter.

(31) Compare the membership petition of April 25, 1933, GStA PK, Logen, 5.1.11., 30. Müffelmann wrote on Vela stationery, a sign that he was still its chairman.

(32) Compare the letter of the DNVP (German National Folk Party) or "Deutschnationalen Front" (German national Front) of June 6, 1933, GStA PK, Logen, 5.1.11., 30.

(33) Compare Announcement no. 5 of the Gestapa of April 18, 1934: Die Freimaurerlogen, Logen, Orden und ähnliche Verbindungen in Deutschland, Masonic Lodges, Lodges, Orders and similar Associations in Germany) GStA PK, I, 90 P, 129, p. 9.

(34) Membership letter of April 25, 1933. In the same way, there are no indications of party memberships in a curriculum vitae from about May 1933 (GStA PK, Logen, 5.1.11., 30).

(35) Compare a letter from Grand Treasurer Bünger to Müffelmann September 9, 1932, GStAPK, Logen, 5.1.11., 21.

(36) Compare GStA PK, Logen, 5.1.11., 21, passim.

(37) Compare the Propper-Müffelmann correspondence of April/May 1932, GStA PK, Logen, 5.1.11., 22. Concerning Propper himself and the situation in Palastine, see below.

(38) Undated statement with deadline May 1, 1932, GStA PK, Logen, 5.1.11., 34.

(39)   Beyer's letter to Koner, July 26, 1932, GStA PK, Logen, 5.1.11., 14.

(40)   Koner's letter to Beyer, July 21, 1932, ibid.

(41)   Lennhoff/Posner, *Int. Freimaurer-Lexikon*, column 530.

(42)   Heinsen died in 1938. (Compare a letter from Adolf Bünger to the physician and Grand Secretary of the Symbolische Grossloge in Exile, Dr. Joseph Treu, written August 24, 1946, in: *Die Geschichte der Symbolischen Großloge von Deutschland 1930-1949*, compiled by Heinz Klasen (paperback, with an introduction by the editor. Hamburg, 1984). The details of his death are unknown.

(43)   See Chapter 8.4. November 2, 1930, GStA PK, Logen, 5.1.11., 15.

(45)   Circular Letter of the Grand Officers' council, undated, November 1930, ibid.

(46)   Oral information from Nathan Fischer (Israel) to the author. Only later did Propper and Lennhoff get to know each other personally.

(47)   Compare Propper's letter to Müffelmann November 12, 1930, GStA PK, Logen, 5.1.11., 15. The members of the Symbolische Grossloge connected the founding of a subordinate lodge in Palestine, which was conceived of as the germ cell for a new grand lodge there, with the expectation of strengthening their position vis-à-vis the Grand Lodge of England (compare the Minutes of the meeting of the Council of Grand Officers, February 28 and March 1, 1931, p. 2).

(48)   Letter of April 25, 1931, GStA PK, Logen, 5.1.11., 17.

(49)   Müffelmann's letter to Propper May 8, 1932, GStA PK, Logen, 5.1.11.,19.

(50)   Oral information from Nathan Fischer to the author. From the beginning, there was a good relationship with the Jaffa Lodge "Barkai," a subordinate of the Grand Orient de France. (Compare *Die Alten*, No. 12, 1.V., September 1931, p. 120). At first, Propper looked down slightly on the National Grand Lodge of Palestine. (Compare for example his essay "Zur Lage der Freimaurerei in Palästina," in: *Die Alten Pflichten*, no. 3, 3.V., Dezember 1932, p. 32f.).

(51)   Compare a letter from Propper to Müffelmann of January 4, 1933, GStA PK, Logen, 5.1.11., 25.

(52)   Compare *Die Alten Pflichten*, no.1, 4.V. [1935], p. 10. According to other sources the lodge had worked only since 1935.

(53)   By-laws of the Hausgesetz der Stuhlmeister-Loge [past-masters' lodge] "Zum Kubischen Stein." Orient of Jerusalem No.25 der Grand Lodge of the State of Israel [s.l., s.d.1953 or later], p. 1.

(54)   Compare the Circular letter of March 29, 1933, GStA PK, Logen, 5.1.11., 8, also printed in: *Die Alten Pflichten*, no. 6, 3rd. volume., March 1933, p. 66, in full in the Dokuments appendix. A board of trustees was formed for the purpose of dissolving the survivors' aid by means of reimbursement of money paid in. Among others, Müffelmann, Lachmund and Bünger were on this board. Bünger was, according to his own testimony, relieved of his position as a city official and watched by the police. He was subjected to several house searches until 1944. (compare Bünger's letter of August 24, 1946 to Treu, *loc.cit.*). In 1949 Bünger undertook the staging of a ceremony in St. Paul's Church, Frankfurt, in which the "Light of Freemasonry" was brought back to Germany from exile in Jerusalem (see Epilogue).

(55)   Circular Letter of March 29, 1933, GStA PK, Logen, 5.1.11., 8, also printed in: *Die Alten Pflichten*, vol. 3, no. 6, March 1933, p. 65, in full in the Dokuments appendix.

(56)   *Die Alten Pflichten*, vol. 4, no.1 1935, p. 1.

(57)   Compare Müffelmanns letter to Propper June 30, 1933. Nathan Fischer was so kind as to put a copy of this letter at the author's disposal.

(58)   The number of sources on the the Exile of the Symbolische Grossloge is relatively small, primarily because the Symbolische Grossloge destroyed its archives as Rommel marched into Egypt in 1942, for fear of what would happen in the case of a victory over the English in the North-Africa-Midde-East Theatre of war.

(58a)   In a letter from Ronald Müffelmann to Propper of August 30, 1947 (Archiv Henning Wolter, Delmenhorst) it says that his brother had been taken to the hospital because of a medical diagnosis of pleurisy, and had died the following night. In the Federal Republic of Germany, he has been remembered since 1996 with the founding of the the Münster A.F.u.A.M. subordinate lodge "Müffelmann zur Treue."

(59)   No. 1, 4th volume [1935]; vol. 4, no. 2-4, dated December 1, 1935.

(60)   Compare in this connection Andor Fodor, *Die Symbolische Großloge von Deutschland im Exil*, Tel Aviv, 1943, p. 25f.

(61)   Compare Propper's letter to the Britischen High Commissar of September 4, 1939 (Archiv Henning Wolter, Delmenhorst).

(62)   Letter from the Government of Palestine No. J:D: 1/347 to Propper September 16, 1933 (Archiv Henning Wolter, Delmenhorst).

(63)   Compare Andor Fodor, *Die Symbolische Großloge von Deutschland im Exil*, Tel Aviv, 1943, p. 31. Concerning the pre-history and story, compare also Benno Grünfelder, *Die Entwicklung der Symbolischen Großloge von Deutschland im Exil*, especially p. 5ff.

(64)   Oral information from Nathan Fischer to the author.

(65)   See the Dokuments appendix. It is little known that Yitzak Rabin, the Israeli Prime Minister, assassinated in 1995, was a Freemason.

(66)   Lachmund's letter to Müffelmann February 16, 1932, GStA PK, Logen, 5.1.11., 20. on Lachmund see Chapter 8.4.

(67)   Compare, for example, Endres, "Zum Problem der Symbolischen Großloge," in: *Die Leuchte*, No. 10/1930, p. 143.

(68)   Constitution of the Symbolische Grossloge from the year 1930, GStA PK, Logen, 5.1.11., 3.

(69)   Compare the Rules and Regulations und Satzung of Germany (1930), GStA,PK, Logen, 5.1.11., 4.

(70)   "Leitsätze für Suchende" ed. by the Symbolische Grossloge of Germany, o.Verf., [s.l., s.d. (probably 1930)], pages unnumbered (Archiv Henning Wolter, Delmenhorst).

(71)   Leo Müffelmann, "Unsere Aufgabe," in: *Die Alten Pflichten*, vol. 1, no.1, October 1930, p. 1ff.

(72)   Compare the New Year's Circular Letter of December 30, 1930, GStA PK, Logen, 5.1.11., 11 or 16.

(73)   Reproduced in: *Wiener Freimaurer-Zeitung*, No. 1, 1932, p. 2f., here p. 3, according to a lecture by Müffelmann in the same year.

(74)   Compare Bünger's Circular letter of July 29, 1931, GStA PK, Logen, 5.1.11., 32.

(75)   Compare a Circular letter by Lachmund of October 24, 1932, in his capacity as Grand Orator of the Symbolische Grossloge, GStA PK, Logen, 5.1.11., 52. Cf. *Die Alten Pflichten* vol. 3 no. 1 October 1932, p. 12.

(76)   Peter H. Heinsen, "Arbeit am Frieden," in: *Die Alten Pflichten*, No. 3, Volume 1, December 1930, p. 17f.

(77)   In contrast the socio-political debate in the journal of the Grand Lodge "Zur

Freundschaft" was carried on from the viewpoint of misuse of social acomplishments (compare Neumann, *Die Involvierung der "altpreußischen" Freimaurerei in die Politik*, p. 76f).

(78)   Gustav Slekow, "Schafft ein soziales Programm der Freimaurerei," in: *Die Alten Pflichten*, vol. 1, no. 3, Dezember 1930, p. 19f. Slekow, the editor of the "Leipziger Volkszeitung", later emigrated to Palestine.

(79)   Friedrich Mart, "Materielles und geistiges Sein. Zur Frage eines sozialen Programms der Freimaurerei," in: *Die Alten Pflichten*, vol.1, no. 4, January 1931, p. 28f.

(80)   Compare a Circular letter of Bünger of September 21, 1931, GStA PK, Logen, 5.1.11., 12.

(81)   Müffelmann's letter of December 8, 1931, GStA PK, Logen, 5.1.11., 18.

(82)   *Die Alten Pflichten*, vol. 4, no. 2/4, 4.V., December 1935, p. 30.

(83)   Compare Leo Müffelmann, "Freimaurerei und Nationalsozialismus," in: *Die Alten Pflichten*, vol. 2, no. 3, December 1931, p. 21ff.

(84)   Max Zucker, "Kampfgegner und Kampfgenossen" (Manuscript), *GStA PK*, Logen, 5.1.11.,13. Müffelmann had previously encouraged the struggle of "true Freemasonry (...) against Bolshevism, Fascism, and National Socialism" on the basis of individualism and a plan for a free state. He represented the opinion—disputed in his circle of Brothers—that they "stood side by side with the Roman Church, despite all opposing positions" (*loc. cit.* p. 25).

(85)   Compare Müffelmann's letter of February 9, 1932 and that of Koner of February 10, 1932, both ibid.

(86)   Uhlmann's letter to Müffelmann of July 4, 1932, *GStA PK*, Logen, 5.1.11., 23.

(87)   Compare *Die Alten Pflichten*, vol. 4, no. 2/4, December 1935, p. 43ff.

(88)   After the German occupation of France it transferred to the Grand Lodge of Palestine. Compare Andor Fodor, *Die Symbolische Großloge von Deutschland im Exil*, Tel Aviv, 1943, p. 10.

CHAPTER 8

(1)   In the Circular Edict (Rund-Erlaß) of the Reichs and Prussian Interior Minister of December 7, 1936 (MBlRuPrMdI. no. 53, 1936, column 1628f.) in connection with the former lodge membership of officers and in the supplement to the Circular Edict of September 2, 1936 with the eleven German grand lodges, were listed 33 Masonic-lodge-like organizations, among them, for example the Odd Fellows, the Orders of Druids, Illuminati, the International Workers Masonic Lodge, the Workers Masonic Association, the Theosophical Society, and the Anthroposophical Society. On July 20, 1937, a decree from the "Reichsführers SS und Chefs der deutschen Polizei" ["the SS of the Reichs Führer and Chief of the German Police"] went out under the aegis of and in connection with the "Reichstagsbrandverordnung" ["Order to burn the Reichstag"] for the dissolution of additional Masonic-lodge-like organizations (GSTA. Reichsstatthalter 638 [reproduced in toto in Neuberger, vol. 2, Appendix, p. 329ff.]).

(2)   On the conspiracy myth as part of the Nazi State ideology, compare in summary, Pfahl-Traughber, *Der antisemitisch-antifreimaurerische Verschwörungsmythos*,   p. 131ff.

(3)   On the "conquest" of the political police forces in the German states by Himmler and the SS, compare Aronson, Heydrich, p. 229ff. After the end of Freemasonry in Germany, Himmler continued to remain responsible for lodge affairs. Compare in this connection, the correspondence between the Main Office of the Security Service (SD) and the Prussian Secret State Archives between the SD-Hauptamt and the Preußischen Geheimen Staatsarchiv in 1936 (Osobyi Archives, Moscow, 500-3-381).

(4)   Neuberger, in *Freimaurerei und Nationalsozialismus*, vol. 2, p. 45, says irrelevantly that the move was undertaken at the same time as the elevation of the Security Service (SD) to Main Office, in January 1935.

(4a)   Information from Bettina Stangneth (Hamburg) in an e-mail of May 16, 2008 to the author

(5)   According to oral information from Rick de Jong, the central file on Freemasons files as well as locally gathered data, remained incomplete. This assessment is based on the evaluation of documents from the Gestapo army post office in Düsseldorf, which are in the

Main State Archives of Nordrhein-Westfalen. The results of the evaluation are to be included in a study-in-progress, in which the effect of the Freemasons of Düsseldorf and the social composition of their lodges over two hunderd years are being examined.

(6)   "Joachim Kannicht, Adolf Eichmann und die Freimaurer," in: *Die Bruderschaft*, (the journal of the United Grand Lodges of Germany), Issue 1, 1962, Frankfurt/M. 1962, p. 19ff., here, p. 20. The report is based on Eichmann's testimony during a hearing on December 11, 1961 in Jerusalem. All in all, Eichmann's depiction indicated that neither he nor others in his office had a sense of the connection of their activities with the whole situation. Thus from the beginning, for example, they had no idea that they belonged to "Amt I" (compare p. 19). Once can assume that Eichmann purposefully wanted to arouse an unnecessary impression with this testimony. This goes along with the fact that during his trial in Jerusalem, he expressly said that he had landed in the Security Service (SD) by chance. (compare Aronson, Heydrich, p. 268). According to Bettina Stangneth in an e-mail to the author on May 16, 2008, Eichmann was occupied with this work until July 1935 at the latest.

(7)   Compare on this position the diagram in: Herbert, Best, p. 578 and Document 4, in: Wildt, *Die Judenpolitik des SD*, p. 73ff. (Heydrich's order of January 15, 1936 for the construction of the Security Service with its effect, Osobyi Archives, Moscow 500-1-907). Indeed the terminology and numbers of the departments in the headquarters (Zentral) vary, probably because they changed over time. In addition, in Heydrich's order there is nothing (yet) about an "Amt I," but only something about the "Stabskanzlei I" and the headquarters departments I 2-I 4 (Zentralabteilungen I 2-I 4). The Security Service Abroad's Department of Freemasons was not yet incorporated in this early organizational structure. Although it had hardly appeared, as Neuberger briefly notes (compare vol. 2, p. 51f.), and the domestic area had its own section (Referat) for lodges abroad, clearly offices of the Amt III had also concerned themselves with Freemasonry–for example, in the form of procurement of supplies. In any case, as a letter of February 18, 1938 from the Department of Freemasonry of Amt II to the appointed headquarters department makes plain, the proposals for reciprocal voting and avoidance of overlapping were presented (Osobyi Archives, Moscow, 500-3-382). At the same time, it was made clear that it would hold the jurisdiction even on lodge

questions. The structure and responsibilities in this office, Amt II, will be discussed more fully below.

(8)   According to the named plan of organization per January 15, 1936. Based on an announcement with the date stamp March 12, 1936, in which the abbreviation "J/I" (Osobyi Archives, Moscow, 500-3-336), it is to be surmised that the "Information Office" remained during a time of transition, also after the last chief Dr. Hermann Behrends became head of the new "Amte II" in January 1936 (see below).

(9)   Compare Neuberger, *Freimaurerei und Nationalsozialismus*, vol. 2, p. 64.

(10)   Bundesarchiv, formerly BDC (Berlin Document Center), personal papers Maximilian Brand.

(11)   Bostunitsch wrote among other works: *Die Freimaurerei: Ihr Ursprung, ihre Geheimnisse, ihr Wirken*, Weimar, 1928; *Jude und Weib: Theorie und Praxis des jüdischen Vampyrismus, der Ausbeutung und Verseuchung der Wirtsvölker*, Berlin, 1939.

(12)   Kannicht, "Adolf Eichmann und die Freimaurer," p. 20. Eichmann announced that Schwartz-Bostunitsch seemed "strange, not to say odd" to him (ibid.).

(12a)   Detemination by Bettina Stangneth in an e-mail to the author on May 16, 2008.

(13)   At the beginning of 1937 Schwartz-Bostunitsch left active service in the Security Service (SD-Dienst) and was retired. Abteilung II/111, which was an interested party in the "Versachlichung" had pressed decisively for his removal (on the "versachlichten" line of the SD, see below). A note in the records of Abteilung II/111 complains as late as October 31, 1936, that Bostunitsch was still preparing decisions for the literature office ("Schrifttumsstelle") that could "in no way be accounted for." (Note of October 31, 1936, Osobyi Archives, Moscow, 500-3-382). The "Reichs-Orator" was forbidden to wear the SS-Uniform at subsequent appearances; his texts were censored by the Reichs Security Office. Compare on all of this complex of events, for example, Reinalter, „Freimaurerei und Nationalsozialismus am Beispiel Alfred Rosenbergs", p. 79f. (note 74) and Neuberger, *Freimaurerei und Nationalsozialismus*, vol. 2, p. 46f., 161, 203. Bostunitschs influence on early Nazi Masonic policies was considerable. On Hasselbacher and his "Institute" see below.

(14)   Compare, within limits, H.D. Heilmann, "Die Bibliothek in Zeit und Räumen," in: *Bibliotheksinformationen* (FU Berlin), no. 18, Dezember 1988, p. 2ff., especially p. 4–6. The essay has a few imprecise or irrelevant descriptions and is, in general, somewhat confusing.

(15)   Kannicht, „Adolf Eichmann und die Freimaurer", *loc. cit.*, p. 20.

(16)   Compare Neuberger, *Freimaurerei und Nationalsozialismus*, vol. 2, p. 46.

(17)   Ibid. Neuberger refers here to Aronson, *Heydrich*, p. 423 (note 38). Aronson in turn, uses the incorrect name "Schwarz-Postaniz" for Schwarz-Bostunitsch.

(17a)   Cf. the Geschäftsverteilungsplan (Plan for the Distribution of Business) of Security Service Main Office, "Stabsbefehl" N0. 3/37 dated January15, 1937 [USHMM, RG-11.001 M.01, Reel 14].

(18)   On the development of Christensen und Knochen, compare Neuberger, *Freimaurerei und Nationalsozialismus*, vol. 2, p. 47ff.

(18a)   Cf. Browder. *Hitler's Enforcers*, p. 189.

(19)   Division of labor of the department II/111 in the SD-Main Office, undated, BA, R 58/792, leaf 52.

(19a)   USHMM, RG-11.001 M.01, Reel 14.

(19b)   Cf. Wildt, p. 27f. Here is more on Wisliceny's biography.

(19c)   USHMM, RG-11.001 M.01, Reel 14.

(20)   On the development of Six and Behrends, compare Wildt, *Die Judenpolitik des SD*, pp. 19, 26. Especially for Six, cf. Lutz Hachmeister, *Der Gegnerforscher: Die Karriere des SS-Führers Franz Alfred Six*, München, 1998.

(21)   Thus for example, a telegram on September 3, 1935 from the Office of Information ("Amt Information" to the SD-Oberabschnitt ("Upper Sector") South (Osobyi Archives, Moscow 500-3-334) carries the signature of the (later) department head of II/111, Theodor Christensen, who already at this time belonged to the SD-Interior department, and in the (previous) department V had been concerned with questions on Freemasonry.

(22)   Paul/Mallmann, „Auf dem Wege zu einer Sozialgeschichte des Terrors", *loc.cit.*, p. 11. Compare also Gellately, „Allwissend und allgegenwärtig", *loc.cit.*, p. 48ff.

(23)   This is seen from a letter from the des Gestapa of June 11, 1934 (GStA PK, I, 90, p.   74, Heft 1, p. 51). Incorrectly dated in Neuberger, *Freimaurerei und Nationalsozialismus*, vol. 2, p. 56.

(24)   Neuberger, *Freimaurerei und Nationalsozialismus*, vol. 2, p. 55.

(25)   Ibid. Haselbacher, at the rank of SS-Obersturmbannführers was Chief of the Stapo-Leitstelle (State Police Headquarters) in Düsseldorf at the end of his career, and was killed in an automobile accident in 1940. He is not to be confused with the anti-Masonic journalist Friedrich Hasselbacher, who in Felix Witt-Hoë's estimation (May 6, 1932) was an "Agent of the Tannenbergbund" (Archiv GLL). After the dissolution of the German lodges, Hasselbacher continued his anti-Masonic agitation, which had temporarily been forbidden him by decree of the Secret State Police Office (see below). Hasselbacher, who at least for a time held the rank of an SS-Standartenführers (regiment leader) was an employee of the Nazi journal *Volkswart*, and also its interim publisher. While Neuberger writes that they had no relationship to each other (compare vol. 2, p. 243 [note 50]), according to Rudolph, they were cousins. In any case, Dr. Karl Haselbacher stayed away from Friedrich Hasselbacher, avoided contact, and made an effort to shut him out of Nazi Masonic politics as much as possible, in which both personal as well as business differences probablyplayed a role. It is not clear—given the kinship connection—what the origin of the difference in the spelling of their names was. In Aronson, *Heydrich*, p. 236, one finds the incorrect spelling "Hasselbacher" for Karl Haselbacher.

(26)   Göring's remark of 2.5.1934, GStA PK, I, 90 P, 74, Heft 1, Bl.70.

(27)   Göring's letter to the Prussian Interior Minister (to the attention of. Secretary of State Grauert), ibid.

(28)   Neuberger, *Freimaurerei und Nationalsozialismus*, vol. 2, p. 56.

(29)   Ibid. Exactly as in other situations, there was no clearly demarcated division of jurisdiction between Security Service and the Gestapa with respect to policy on Freemasonry. Pfahl-Traughber (*Der antisemitisch-antifreimaurerische Verschwörungsmythos*, p. 169), comes to the same conclusion. Since Neuberger, as mentioned before, has concerned himself quite extensively with the development and interaction (working together) as well as with the personnel of the Freemasonry "Referate" of the Security Service and the Gestapa, one can dispense with a repetition of the explanation, except for the

critical discussion of some of his evaluations. For the background and socialization of SD and Gestapo personnel, as well as recruiting practices, cf. Jens Banach, *Heydrichs Elite. Das Führerkorps der Sicherheitspolizei und des SD 1936–1945*, Paderborn/München/Wien/ Zürich, 1998. In Rosenberg's office and in the German Work Front (DAF)there were also "Referats" that concerned themselves with Freemasonry (compare Neuberger, vol. 2, p. 57ff.). On the business of the DAF in this context, compare also BA, R 58/1066f., passim. Concerning (previous) lodge memberships, the Office of Information of the DAF made determinations, or turned its requests over to the Main Office of the Security Service. Compare, concering the entirety and its restrictions, Pfahl-Traughber, *Der antisemitisch-antifreimaurerische Verschwörungsmythos*, p. 162ff., 167ff.; Fundamentally opposed to that, the work by Ulrich Herbert; for the early phases of Security Services and Gestapo, as always, the study by Aronson.

(30)   Compare Gellately, "Allwissend und allgegenwärtig," *loc.cit.*, p. 60f.

(31)   Neuberger, *Freimaurerei und Nationalsozialismus*, vol. 2, p. 56.

(32)   Neuberger already indicated that (compare ibid., p. 55). In addition, in connection with the RSHA (Main Office of Reichs Security)—Offices IV und VII, according to Rudolph, there was a very agreeable relationship within the leadership levels (oral information to the author).

(33)   Letter of February 4, 1935, Osobyi Archives, Moscow 500-3-334. Brand was the recipient of this letter (pursuant to the order by telephone). He was in Department V, which was responsible for Freemasonry. On the good personal relationship among Brand, Christensen and Haselbacher, compare Neuberger, *Freimaurerei und Nationalsozialismus*, vol. 2, p. 55.

(34)   Circular letter of August 23, 1935, Osobyi Archives, Moscow 500-1-231a.

(35)   Compare St A Bremen, 4.65, 1693. This is about the existence of the archives of the Nachrichtenstelle der Polizeidirektion, vol. 17 (Polizeipräsidium Landes-kriminalamt I A Berlin-Mitteilungen).

(36)   Situation report of the Stapostelle Berlin of August 6, 1934, GStA PK, I, 90 P, 76, Heft 2, Bl. 219. In similar words also in the reports for the months of August and September 1934. The regular situation reportage was initiated by Rudolf Diels.

(37)   Thus many former subordinte lodges in Hamburg which had become clubs formed themselves into a real estate company, which was the owner of the Emser Straße lodge building, until it was confiscated. The rest of the property of the clubs (lodges) which had been forced to disband was also confiscated. Compare in this connection the situation report of the Stapostelle Berlin for May 1934 (June 2, 1934 BA, R 58/2026, Bl.216), for September 1934 (October 10, 1934 BA, R 58/2657, Bl.14f.), for October 1934 (November 5, 1934 GStA PK, 90 P, 79, Heft 1, Bl.156) and for November/Dezember 1934 (January 18, 1935 (BA, R 58/2657, Bl.88).

(38)   Compare the situation report of the Stapostelle Berlin for April 1935, undated GStA PK, I, 90 P, 80, Heft 2, Bl.65.

(39)   Bulletins no. 5 of April 18 1934: "Die Freimaurerlogen, Logen, Orden und ähnliche Verbindungen in Deutschland" ("The Masonic Lodges, Orders and Similar Associations in Germany" GStA PK, I, 90 P, 129).

(40)   Ibid., p. 7.

(41)   Already in Bulletin no. 4 March 1934 (BA, formerly BDC (Berlin Document Center, Ordner 880, Bl. 57f.) a distinction was made between the Old Prussian and the Humanitarian grand lodges: While the documents confiscated from the Symbolische Großloge showed "an outlook decidedly inimical to the State" on the part of the Humanitarians, that was not provable in the case of the Old Prussians.

(42)   Bulletins no. 5 vom 18.4.1934, p. 7f.

(43)   Ibid., p. 8

(44)   Compare ibid., p. 9f.

(45)   Ibid., p. 12.

(46)   Ibid., p. 13.

(47)   Compare ibid.

(48)   Situation report of the Department II/111 of February 17, 1937, Osobyi Archives, Moscow, 500-3-413. At least sometimes the Freemasonry Department composed reports at two-week intervals.

(49)   Situation report of the Department II/111 of March 2, 1937, ibid.

(50)   Situation report of the Department II/111 August 3, 1937 (Berichtszeitraum 16.-31.7.1937), ibid.

(51)   Enclosure with the Situation Report of February 17, 1937, ibid.

(52)   Situation Report for Januar 1938, p. 1, BA, R 58/999.

(53)   This expression was proposed by Neuberger (Compare vol. 2, p. 184ff.).

(54)   Letter of April 7, 1937, Osobyi Archives, Moscow 500-3-382.

(55)   Compare an undated "Instruction for the Freemasons-Handbook" note 1938, Osobyi Archives, Moscow, 500-2-103.

(56)   Neuberger, *Freimaurerei und Nationalsozialismus*, vol. 2, p. 189.

(57)   Compare ibid., vol. 2, p. 190f.; 185ff. After Neuberger had already determined that there was nothing known about Dieter Schwarz personally (compare vol. 2, p. 186), Rudolph told the author of his assumption that Schwarz might have used a pseudonym.

(58)   Compare as an example Heydrich's early essay "Wandlungen unseres Kampfes," in: *Das Schwarze Korps*, Folge (Sections) 9–13, Mai 1935.

(59)   Ibid., Folge 11 of May 15, 1935, p. 3.

(60)   Neuberger, *Freimaurerei und Nationalsozialismus*, vol. 2, p. 191.

(61)   Compare the process in: Osobyi Archives, Moscow, 500-1-231a.

(62)   Compare Thomas Michatsch, "Das 'Schwarze Korps' und die Freimaurerei [Master's thesis FU Berlin] Berlin, 1996, especially p. 164ff.

(63)   Konrad Lerich [i.e. Kurt Reichl], *Der Tempel der Freimaurer. Der 1. bis 33. Grad. Vom Suchenden zum Wissenden*, Bern [supposedly 2.ed.] 1937. See Chapter 2.2.

(64)   Ibid., p. 4.

(65)   Oral information to the author from Rudolphs. Compare in this connection his "Überlieferung des Reichssicherheitshauptamtes Amt VII," p. 57ff.

(66)   Reichl's letter of resignation to the Worshipful Master of the Lodge "Zukunft," Dr. Hans Schlesinger, January 17, 1934, Osobyi Archives, Moscow, 500-2-104.

(67)   Müffelmann's letter to Lennhoff of November 24, 1930, GStA PK, Logen, 5.1.11., 15.

(68)   On "World Service" see chapter 2.2.

(69)   According to Rudolph, "Überlieferung des Reichssicherheitshauptamtes Amt VII," p. 58, he takes the opposite view from Neuberger, who had assumed that the Security Service had

dispensed with Reichl's services before the war (compare vol. 2, p. 156). It is questionable however, how long he remained active as an informant or responsible for the area of Freemasonry.

(70)   This was concerned with the SS- "Untersturmführer" Harms.

(71)   Compare a note in a document of the Security Service Department of Freemasonry (SD-Freimaurerabteilung II/111) of August 19.8.1937, Osobyi Archives, Moscow, 500-3-419.

(71a)   Cf. USHMM, RG-15.007 M, Reel 47f., passim.

(71b)   Cf. the correspondence with Harms und Christensen, USHMM, RG-15.007 M, Reel 44. Oddly enough, Reichl addressed his letter to the private addresses of both SD officials. For the Aachen Conference, see chapter 2.2 and note 2/65.

(71c)   Cf. the letter from Reichl to Harms dated August 4, 1936, USHMM, RG-15.007 M, Reel 44.

(72)   Report of the Referat II/1114 vom 13.9.1937, ibid.

(73)   Compare the documents gathered by Reichl for the upcoming examination of July 6, 1938, Osobyi Archives, Moscow, 500-2-104.

(74)   Lerich, *Der Tempel der Freimaurer*, pp. 36, 50.

(75)   Ibid., p. 55.

(76)   Compare Bollmus, *Das Amt Rosenberg*, p. 121f. In this connection,Cohn has clearly confused the "Außenpolitische Amt" (Foreign Policy Office) and the so-called "Weltanschauungsamt" (World View Office), which were both led by Rosenberg. (Compare Cohn, *Die Protokolle*, p. 277).

(77)   Bollmus, *Das Amt Rosenberg*, p. 122.

(78)   Compare ibid., p. 122f.

(79)   Compare Peters, *Geschichte der Freimaurerei*, p. 250. In the framework of anti-Masonic exhibitions, there is shown, first of all, a portrait of Wilhelm I in a Masonic apron. After an objection by the Reichs Defense Ministry (Reichswehrministerium) the paiting was removed again (compare Steffens, *Freimaurer*, p. 347).

(80)   On March 18, 1936 Ritual objects were paraded by masked men through the streets of Tilsit. A letter written on the same day by an officer of the Große Landesloge reports about this event (*GStA PK*, Logen, 5.1.1.3, 4337).

(81)   The Masonic Lodge Museum in Nürnberg, offprint of the journal *Das. Bayerland*, ed. by Ludwig Deubner, München, 1938, p. 1 (Library of Congress Washington, HS 394.F 73 / 53-48835).

(82)   Ibid., p. 2.

(83)   Ibid.

(84)   A. Fuchs, *Westdeutsches Freimaurer-Museum*, Düsseldorf 2. Aufl. s.d., p. 4. The Düsseldorf exhibition poster reproduced in the documents appendix is from the year 1935.

(85)   Ibid.

(86)   Ibid.

(87)   Ibid.

(88)   Ibid., p. 5.

(89)   Compare the letter of Department II/111 to Chief Six of the Central Department (Zentralabteilung) II/1, May 3, 1938, Osobyi Archives, Moscow, 500-3-419.

(90)   Herbert, *Best*, p. 13.

(91)   Compare Paul/Mallmann, "Auf dem Wege zu einer Sozialgeschichte des Terrors," *loc.cit.*, p. 17. Zur "*völkisch* theory for the police," compare Gellately, "Allwissend und allgegenwärtig," *loc.cit.*, p. 58.

(92)   Rürup, *Topographie des Terrors*, p. 70.

(93)   Compare ibid.

(94)   Compare Neuberger, *Freimaurerei und Nationalsozialismus*, vol. 2, p. 66.

(95)   On the structure of the offices of the RSHA (Reichs Main Security Office), compare Hans Buchheim, "Die SS - das Herrschaftsinstrument," in: Buchheim, Hans/Broszat, Martin/ Jacobsen, Hans-Adolf/Krausnick, Helmut (Ed.), *Anatomie des SS-Staates*, München 5th ed. 1989, vol. 1, p. 66ff. The structure of the Main Security Office shows the simultaneous splintering and fusion of responsibilities typical of the Nazi power apparatus.

(96)   According to Rudolph, *Überlieferung des Reichssicherheitshauptamtes Amt VII*, p. 36ff., Erich Ehlers continued his activity at this point.

(97)   Oral information from Rudolph to the author. After Six was recalled from the Main Security Office, Dietl was entrusted with the leadership of Office VII as his successor.   Compare ibid., the company plan of job distribution (flow chart) in the second enclosure

(plan) or that situation of March 1, 1941 in Rürup, *Topographie des Terrors*, p. 76ff., which shows the Referat VII B 1 vacant.

(98)   See Chapter 8.3.

(99)   Friedrich Hasselbacher, *Entlarvte Freimaurerei*, vol. 1-5, Berlin, 1934-1941. Compare also Peters, *Geschichte der Freimaurerei*, p. 250.

(100)   Hasselbacher, *Das Todesurteil über die Freimaurerei in Deutschland* [s.l., s.d. about 1935]. In a later work by Hasselbacher: *Frankreichs Totentanz um die Men- Schenrechte*, Berlin 3.Aufl. 1941, p. 82 it says: "The sentence 'People are born free and equal in their rights and should remain so;' the thought that Mr. Ebert repeated in the Revolt of 1918, remains the basic tenet of human rights." (cited from Rogalla von Bieberstein, *Aufklärung, Freimaurerei...*, p. 345.

(101)   Hasselbacher, *Das Todesurteil*, p. 3f.

(102)   Compare a letter of the liquidator of the Große Landesloge, Paul Rosenthal, of January 12, 1937, GStA, Logen, 5.1.3., 4337.

(103)   Compare Rudolph, *Überlieferung des Reichssicherheitshauptamtes Amt VII*, p. 54ff.

(104)   Compare ibid., p. 55. In the interim, Hasselbacher sought contact with the Security Service. For example, in September 1937, he offered to provide, with the help of a facilitator, the materials from Parisian Masonic lodges if the shipping charges would be paid for him. Of course, he had to know "how he might operate with the Gestapa or the Security Service" (Note on a document, dated September 14, 1937 of the Security Service Referat II/1114 – responsible for Freemasonry abroad, Osobyi Archives, Moscow, 500-3-419).

(105)   Also in Götz Aly/Susanne Heim, *Vordenker der Vernichtung. Auschwitz und die Pläne für eine neue europäische Ordnung*, Hamburg, 1991. Compare also the criticism in Herbert, *Best*, p. 541. Not so marked in Aly, *"Endlösung," Völkerverschiebung und der Mord an den europäschen Juden*, Frankf./M. 1995, esp. p. 374ff. The significance of the racial anti-Semitic and "biologistic" ideology is more strongly incorporated (including its acceptance by the people) for forming decisions and transformation of the "final solution." I disagree with Goldhagen, because he removes the "elimination aspect of anti-Semitism" too much from the context of racial politics. (Compare Daniel J. Goldhagen, *Hitlers willige Vollstrecker. Ganz gewöhnliche Deutsche und der Holocaust*, Berlin, 1996). Compare in this connection the convincing interpretation of the "Third Reich" as a singular (and single!) racial state

474

in: Michael Burleigh/Wolfgang Wippermann, *The Racial State: Germany 1933–1945*, Cambridge, 1991. Compare also Wippermann, *Europäischer Faschismus im Vergleich (1922–1982)*, Frankfurt/M. 1983, p. 55ff.

(106)   See Chapter 8.4.

(107)   *250 Jahre National-Mutterloge "Zu den drei Weltkugeln*," Festschrift, Berlin. 1990, P. 67. The fact that the Freemasons were succesful in keeping in contact with one another during ther Nazi dictatorship, made it easier to re-found lodges in the Federal Republic after liberation.

(108)   Paul Rosenthal's letter of January 12, 1937, Gesta, Logen, 5.1.3., 4337.

(109)   Gestapa instruction signed by Heydrich April 8, 1936, BA, R 58/266. Informative with respect to the limited personnel and logistical capacities of the Gestapo: The concern here is to "pull out entirely," not that the supervision (controls) should otherwise be made more difficult!

(110)   Ibid.

(111)   Bericht Ehlers' letter to Knochen November 1, 1937, Osobyi Archives, Moscow, 500-3-413.

(112)   See Note VIII/1. Compare also Pfahl-Traughber, *Der antisemitisch-antifreimaurerische Verschwörungsmythos*, p. 144.

(113)   *75 Jahre Ordensloge in Dortmund. "Johannisloge Reinoldus zur Pflichttreue" 1910–1985*, p. 22 (Archiv GLL).

(114)   Compare *Meldungen aus dem Reich: Die geheimen Lageberichte des Sicherheitsdienstes der SS aus dem RSHA*. 1938–1944, ed. by Heinz Boberach, Herrsching, 1984.

(115)   Compare ibid., vol. 2, P. 8f. (Yearly situation Report for 1938); auch BA, R 58/1094.

(116)   Ibid., p. 8.

(117)   Ibid.

(118)   Ibid. In addition there are elaborations on the group of so-called "Masonic Ancillary Organizations." This is not the place for detailed discussions of such groups: Rotarians, Theosophists, Anthroposophists, etc.

(119)   Ibid., p. 9. Presumably this meant Dr. August Horneffer, previously mentioned, one of the most prominent German Freemasons, who as administrator of the Caritas Fund since 1935, "officiated" at the liquidation of the Grand Lodge "Zur

Freundschaft." Of course, it cannot be ignored that his brother Ernst might have been the one being referred to. Ernst was a philosophy professor in Gießen and also a Mason, who had appeared before the "Seizure of Power" giving lectures for the Association of German Freemasons. Concerning August and Ernst Horneffer, compare Lennhoff/Posner, *Int. Freimaurerlexikon*, column 714f.

(120)   *Meldungen aus dem Reich*, vol. 2, p. 10.

(121)   Ibid., p. 11.

(122)   Ibid., p. 12.

(123)   Compare ibid., p. 216ff. (1. *Vierteljahresbericht* 1939). On the situation of European Freemasonry as a whole, it says among other things, "Slovakia's being made independent, the inclusion of Bohemia and Moravia as well as the Memel Territory (Klaipèda Region), and the end of the Spanish Civil War pushed Freemasonry more intensly into a desperately defensive situation" (p. 216). In the situation report of February 1937, the Freimaurer-Dienststelle II/111 was quite concerned with respect to the Spanish Civil War, with the entrance of the Spanish Grand Orient on the side of the Republic or with the alleged "work of Freemasonry for the Spanish Bolshevists" (Compare the Situation Report of February 17, 1937, Osobyi Archives, Moscow, 500-3-413).

(124)   Compare the Circular Letter no. 12 of the Supreme Party Court dated January 8, 1934, GStA PK, Logen, 5.1.3., 4424.

(125)   *Die Weltfreimaurerei*, p. 47; referring to an essay by Reichs leader Buchs of August/September 1934.

(126)   Compare RdErl (Circular Letter) of the RuPrMdI (Reichs and Prussian Interior Ministry) of July 10, 1935 (MBlPiV., no. 29, 1935, column 888a f.).

(127)   Compare RdErl. des RuPrMdI. November 2, 1935 (MBlPiV., no. 46, 1935, column 1367).

(128)   Compare RdErl. des RuPrMdI of February 18, 1936 (MBlRuPrMdI., No. 9, 1936, column 252).

(129)   Compare RdErl. des RuPrMdI. Of September 2, 1936 (MBlRuPrMdI., No. 39, 936, column 1186).

(130)   Compare ibid., column 1186f. Compare also the guidelines of the Reichs Interior Minister of Spetember 26, 1936, BA, R 58/1066.

(131)   Compare a letter of the Grosse Landeslodge Liquidators Paul
Rosenthal dated February 15, 1937, GStA PK, Logen, 5.1.3., 4337.
Rosenthal rightly took as his point of departure that "the attitude
against us" would also remain.

(132)   *Die Weltfreimaurerei*, p. 48.

(133)   For example, the Worshipful Master of the Neubrandenburg
Lodge (subordinate to the Grosse Landesloge) reported (May
1933) about such cases, which were usually based on decisions of
subordinate Party offices. According to the report, a group-captain
and assistant master at the local gymnasium (high school) was
accepted into the Nazi Party, presumably, "because he enjoyed general
respect here, partly because he had been the longtime chairman,
and partly because as a member of the boards of all sorts of
military clubs, no one could doubt his national(istic) point of view."
Generally speaking, so the "Conventmeister" reported, up to this
time, there had arisen "no real differences with the local group of the
Nazi Party. A whole cadre of Brothers of the Order" were members
of the Party. (Letter to von Heeringen of May 25, 1933, GStA PK,
Logen, 5.1.3., 4445). Compare also the correspondence between a
group-captain in Kiel (to whom was given "the Red Membership
Card" despite his membership in the Grosse Landesloge—though
subsequently it was taken away again—and the Grosse Landesloge
adminstration of August 1934 (GStA PK, Logen, 5.1.3., 4450). From
this we also learn that there were several cases of this sort of thing.

(134)   Compare undated, BA, R 58/998.

(135)   Circular letter of the Supreme Party Court of May 25, 1938, BA,
R 58/998.

(136)   Compare *Die Weltfreimaurerei*, p. 48.

(137)   *Meldungen aus dem Reich*, vol. 2, p. 10.

(138)   RdErl. (Circular Letter) des RMdI (Reichs and Prussian
Interior Ministry) of June 6, 1939 (MBlRuPrMdI., No. 24, 1939,
column 1258ff., hier column 1259); alsoBA, R 58/998. Exceptions
were tolerated according to the letter, that is the so- called"mercy
procedure" ("Gnadenverfahren") had to be exerted.

(139)   Compare ibid.

(140)   Compare ibid., column 1258, 1264. A circular letter from
Himmler of September 3, 1941 made clear that reserve officers of

the "Ordnungs" Police, just like the acive officers, had to turn in a "Declaration on Lodge Membership" according to the Circular Letter of June 6, 1939 (MBlRuPrMdI.,no. 37, 1941, column 1588).

(141)   Compare ibid., column 1263.

(142)   RdErl. (Circular Letter) des RMdI of July 27, 1940 (MBlRuPrMdI., no. 32, 1940, column 1573).

(143)   *Meldungen aus dem Reich*, vol. 2, P. 11. Since this concerns the reporting time of 1938, the previously mentioned protests of the (former) Old Prussians are to be seen relative to Party amnesty. When these determinations were applied to the the Staatsdienst the following year, the reactions would surely have been the same.

(144)   Compare ibid., vol. 5, p. 1706 (no. 134 of October 21, 1940).

(145)   Ibid., p. 1706f.

(146)   RdErl. des RMdI. "with consent of the representative of der Führer" August 21, 1940 (MBlRuPrMdI., no. 35, 1940, column 1690ff.).

(147)   Compare the Order of the Reichs Armed Forces Ministry (1p90J (Ia) no. 2066 34 of May 26, 1934, Archiv GLL). In a petition to the Reichs Armed Forces Ministry (June 11, 1934), the Old Prussians expressed their assumption that this decree would not apply to them. In a letter of July 31, 1934 to the German-Christian Order, the Reichs Armed Forces Ministry said that the prohibition of membership was not based on §37 of the Wehrgesetz (defense, armed forces law) but on political reasons. No exceptions could be made to this prohibition, which caused the lodges to write another letter, in which they declared that the political reasons were "completely incomprehensible." They enclosed a report "about the views of the late Reichs President" ("über die Auffassung des Verewigten Herrn Reichspräsidenten"), and asked for a meeting in person. The Reichs Armed Forces Ministry declared (dated August 29, 1934)that they could give no more information, and therefore wanted to forego such meeting. The complete correspondence is in: GStA PK, Logen. 5.1.3., 4350.

(148)   Compare the order of Reichs War Minister von Blomberg of January 8, 1937, BA, R 58/998 as well as a summary in *Die Weltfreimaurerei*, p. 48f.

(149)   Compare Himmler's decree of April 23, 1938, BA R 58/266.

(150)   Ibid.

(151)   This concerns a subordinate lodge of the Grosse Landesloge
that originated from the consolidation of the Lodges "Zu den drei
Totengerippen," "Zur Säule" and "Zur Glocke" in 1844.

(152)   Compare a letter (January 19, 1932) from a former Worshipful
Master in Düsseldorf to Landes Grand Master von Heeringen (GStA
PK, Logen, 5.1.3., 4443). The allegations in it could be verified from
membership lists in the Masonic Museum. Kube reached only the
Second Degree.

(153)   Compare Neuberger, vol. 1, p. 166, 318 (Note 38). Kube's letter
to Walter Buch dates from May 23, 1934 (BA, R 18/5563). Kube
explained that he had "never made a secret" of the fact of his former
lodge membership, and had repeatedly spoken about it to Ludendorff.

(154)   In August 1935, he told Interior Minister Frick that he, "as the
Führer knows," had belonged to a lodge in 1919; he enclosed his
correspondence with Buch in his letter (letter of August 7, 1935, BA,
R 18/5563). In neither this document nor in Kube's personnel file
could any more information be found (Compare BA, formerly BDC
[Berlin Document Center], Personalakte Wilhelm Kube).

(155)   Compare BA, former. BDC (Berlin Document Center),
Personalakte Dr. Alfred Meyer.

(156)   Compare BA, former. BDC (Berlin Document Center),
Personalakte Otto Bernhard. Compare also the *Bremische Biographie*
1912–1962, ed. von der Historischen Gesellschaft zu Bremen und
dem Staatsarchiv Bremen, ed. Wilhelm Lührs et al., Bremen, 1969, p.
35ff. There is found more on Bernhards "Hilfsbereitschaft gegenüber
Juden" (no more specifics), which was the cause for "several instances
of friction with Party Offices (Parteistellen)" The disputes were,
however, "repeatedly reconciled" (p. 37).

(157)   Compare BA, former BDC (Berlin Document Center),
Personalakte Otto Bernhard.

(158)   Brückner's letter to Bormann May 17, 1934, ibid. A first, similar-
sounding letter from Brückner to Bormann concerning this, dates
from April 30, 1934.

(159)   Compare the letter signed by the then chief of the Information
Office ("Amt Information"), Hermann Behrends, December 2, 1935, ibid.

(160)   Letter of July 1, 1936, ibid.

(161)   Compare BA, former BDC (Berlin Document Center), Personalakte Dr. Richard Markert. Compare also *Bremische Biographie*, p. 329ff. Markert left Bremen after his removal from power and first went to Braunschweig for three years as member of the board of the "Mühlenbau- und Industrie AG." After that he lives as an independent exporter in Berlin.

(162)   As described, for example in Bernhard's case, there followed the announcement from the staff of the "Representative of the Führer" about Hitler's decision.

(163)   Compare the letter about this from a friend and former colonel to the Liquidator of the Grosse Landesloge Paul Rosenthal March 18, 1937 with the request for advice (GStA PK, Logen, 5.1.3., 4337) as well as the letter with detailed description of the situation from former member Georg Jäkisch, subject of the lecture (ibid.). In his response (April 2, 1934 – ibid.), Rosenthal elaborated on the viewpoint of the Nazi party, according to which a former lodge member could not hold any position, "that had anything to do with questions of personnel." With the help of an attorney he repeatedly sought "to bring about a change, thus far, unfortunately, without success." As Liquidator, he was not authorized to engage himself actively, therefore was unable to help, and could only advise sending a detailed report to the responsible office (in this case, the Reichs Post Office Ministry in Berlin). The Ministry would ask the Gestapa in such cases (to be correct, it should have been the Security Service—SD). This way the applications would have had the possibility of success.

(164)   Compare a letter of June 27, 1937 to Grosse Landesloge Liquidator Paul Rosenthal, GStA PK, Logen, 5.1.3., 4337. Rosenthal answered on June 28, 1937 (ibid.), that it would not be about a single case, but that headmasters "everywhere, " who had formerly been Freemasons would be relieved of their offices, or their pensions would be taken away if they did not declare themselves ready to take over the position of a senior assistant master. So far as he knew no exceptions had been made. Legal attempts to avoid this procedure remained unsuccessful.

(165)   Compare a letter (March 24, 1937) from the Nazi area administration for Main-Franconia to the district administration in Würzburg (BA, former BDC (Berlin Document Center), Personalakte Dr. Karl Hoede.

(166)   Compare the letter from the Chief of the "Kanzlei des Führers" (Führer's Chancellry) to the area administration for Main-

Franconia (August 4, 1942, ibid.). For Hoede's biography, compare ibid., passim., as well as Theodor Vogel, *Der Großmeister und seine Werkleute. Von der Frankfurter Paulskirche zum Berliner Konvent* [s.l., s.d.], p. 53. An unfortunately completely uncritical article devoted to Hoede's memory totally omits his *völkisch*-Nationalsocialistic Engagement: *Karl Hoede 1897–1973*, ed. from the Forschungsloge Q.C., Bamberg, 1974, especially p. 6ff.

(167)   Henning Wolter's oral information to the author.

(168)   Compare BA, formerly BDC (Berlin Document Center), Personalakte Erich Böhlke.

(169)   Compare a letter of July 15, 1940 from the area court for Magdeburg-Anhalt to the Supreme Party Court as well as its acceptance form filled out *after* the "Gnadenerlaß" ("Mercy Decree") on April 8, 1941 (Both BA, formerly BDC (Berlin Document Center), Personalakte Erich Böhlke.

(170)   Vote of the Supreme Party Court (November 5, 1940, BA, formerly BDC (Berlin Document Center), Personalakte Erich Böhlke.

(171)   Compare the letter from the Chief of the "Kanzlei des Führers" (Führer's Chancellry) to the area administration Magdeburg-An halt (March 13, 1941, BA, formerly BDC (Berlin Document Center), Personalakte Erich Böhlke.

(172)   Henning Wolter's oral information to the author.

(173)   Compare Steffens, *Freimaurer*, p. 389. According to the information sheet of the Communist Party, Landes District Administration Bavaria no. 3/4 of April 15, 1947, the concentration camps office in Hamburg recognized 7,563 people as "political" victims in their territory at this point. Of them, 1,265 were Freemasons. Reasons for the criteria for this recognition could not be found in the source.

(174)   Compare concerning this process Deutsches Freimaurer-Museum Bayreuth,no. 80 III A,B.

(175)   Compare Bernhard Beyer, Rudolf Ramge. "Ein Angehöriger des AASR als Märtyrer der national-sozialistischen Terrorzeit," in: *Amtliche Mitteilungen des Deutschen Obersten Rates des AASR*, vol. 6 (December 15, 1951), no. 5, p. 8ff.

(176)   Compare Osobyi Archives, Moscow, 500-3-419, passim.

(177)   Letter from the Referats II/1114 to the appointed department head Knochen dated November 1, 1937, Osobyi Archives, Moscow, 500-3-413.

(178)   Guidelines for the Department II/111 of November 1, 1938, Osobyi Archives, Moscow, 500-3-419.

(179)   Nazi Party directive "Gegen die Freimaurerei" ("Against Freemasonry"), vol. 4, 7/1939, Berlin, 1939.

(180)   Ibid., p. 2

(181)   Ibid.

(182)   Ibid., p. 35. This essay by Six is an excerpt from his previous work by the same name. (see note II/125).

(183)   Compare Neuberger, *Freimaurerei und Nationalsozialismus*, vol. 2, 187.

(184)   Party Directive, p. 3.

(185)   Neuberger, *Freimaurerei und Nationalsozialismus*, vol. 2, Epilogue, p. 233.

(186)   *Die Weltfreimaurerei*, ed. by the Chief of the Security Police and the Secirity Service (SD), revised by [SS-Sturmbannführer] Erich Ehlers, *Schriftenreihe für politische und weltanschauliche Erziehung der Sicherheitspolizei und des SD*, Issue 3, Leipzig, 1943.

(187)   Ibid., p. 50, 29.

(188)   Ibid., p. 22.

(189)   Ibid., p. 30, 43.

(190)   Ibid., p. 50.

(191)   Compare Neuberger, *Freimaurerei und Nationalsozialismus*, vol. 2, Epilogue, p. 233.

(192)   *Bremer Zeitung,*August 20, 1936, GStA PK, Logen, 5.1.3., 4337.

(193)   Compare Pfahl-Traughber, *Der antisemitisch-antifreimaurerische Verschwörungs-mythos*, p. 144f.

(193a) Documents in the Archives of the Supreme Council AASR S.J. (Washington D.C.).

(194)   "Führererlaß" ("Führer's Decree") of March 1, 1942, IfZ. NG 5142 Nürnberger Akten. Compare Lammers' Circular Letter of July 5, 1942, which distributed the contents of this decree, ibid. (both reproduced in full in Neuberger, vol. 2, Appendix, p. 341f.).

(195)   Compare Kater, Das "Ahnenerbe," p. 278. On the robbing of Masonic cultural assets, compare also Helmut K. H. Keiler, "Freimaurerische Bibliotheksbestände in Deutschland und die Bibliotheca Klossiana in Den Haag," in: Reinalter (Ed.), *Internationale Tagung in Innsbruck*, p. 109ff., especially p. 112f.

(196)   On the the struggle against the lodges in occupied France, compare Osobyi Archives, Moscow, 500-4-235, passim. Cf. André Combes. *La franc-maçonnerie sous l'occupation. Persécution et Résistance 1939–1945*, Monaco, 2001. Concerning the role of the Secret Field Police (GFP) and the "Einsatzstab Reichsleiter Rosenberg" (Action Staff Reichs Chief Rosenberg), as well as the cooperation of other authorities, compare Neuberger, *Freimaurerei und Nationalsozialismus*, vol. 2, p. 209ff. There also (p. 213ff.) more detail on Kochen's activities.

(197)   Cited after Neuberger, *Freimaurerei und Nationalsozialismus*, vol. 2, p. 219.

(198)   Compare Katz, *Jews and Freemasons*, p. 195.

(199)   Compare Bieberstein, „*Aufklärung, Freimaurerei...* ", *loc.cit.*, p. 350.

(200)   Compare Pfahl-Traughber, *Der antisemitisch-antifreimaurerische Verschwörungsmythos*, p. 191, 193. Details on the function of the conspiracy myth in Nazi war propaganda, compare ibid., p. 191ff. as well as Neuberger, *Freimaurerei und Nationalsozialismus*, vol. 2, p. 195ff. on the propaganda activitiesistischen Betätigung Rosenbergs "Weltanschauung Office," compare. Reinalter, „Freimaurerei und Nationalsozialismus am Beispiel Alfred Rosenbergs ", *loc.cit.*, p. 73f.

(201)   "Tagesparole des Reichspressechefs" of July 22, 1941, IfZ. NG 4506 Nürnberger Akten (reproduced in full in Neuberger, vol. 2, Appendix, p. 340). Less known, therefore less a subject of propaganda exploitation, is that British Prime Minister Winston Churchill was also a Mason. Churchill was accepted into a lodge in London in 1901(cf. Martin Gilbert, *Winston S. Churchill, Vol. VI: Finest Hour 1939-1941*, Boston, 1983, p. 27, note.4). Roosevelt had been made a Mason in 1911 in a lodge in New York City (vgl. http://www.bessel.org/presfmy.htm).

(202)   "Führererlaß" March 1, 1942 (see Note. VIII/194).

(203)   Compare NL Müffelmann, "Drei Monate Schutzhaft," p. 8 (Archive Henning Wolter, Delmenhorst).

(204)   On the solidarity among AASR members, compare Pauls, *Der Deutsche Alte und Angenommene*, loc.cit., p. 2. One takes as a point of

departure, that this group which gathered around Fritz Bensch, had an opposing view – in the sense of Rothfels' definition (see below). The same is true of the meetings of the Brethren from the Grand Lodge "Rising Sun" (Compare Drechsler, *Die Brüder vom FZAS*, p. 30f.).

(205) On the Jewish Resistance, compare Wolfgang Wippermann, *Die Berliner Gruppe Baum und der jüdische Widerstand*, Berlin 2nd ed. 1982. Especially in the case of the Jewish Resistance, one could often find overlapping with other areas of the Resistance, as for example, the Youth Resistance or that of the Socialists and Communists.

(206) Compare, Ger van Roon, *Widerstand im Dritten Reich. Ein Überblick*, München 6th revised ed. 1994, p. 18ff., 26ff.

(207) Compare Richard Löwenthal, "Widerstand im totalen Staat," in: Richard Löwenthal/Patrick von zur Mühlen (Ed.), *Widerstand und Verweigerung in Deutschland 1933-1945*, Berlin/Bonn, 1982, p. 11ff., especially, p. 13ff. In contrast, Löwenthal's stamp on the whole discussion of totalitarianism remains questionable.

(208) Thus Hans Rothfels, who himself emigrated from Germany, in the Foreword to the enlarged edition (1969) of his study on the German Opposition to Hitler, which first appeared in 1949 in German. An appreciation is cited here after the Edition of Frankfurt/M. 1986, p. 18.

(209) Compare Martin Broszat, "Zur Sozialgeschichte des deutschen Widerstands," in: VfZ, 34.Vol., Heft 3/1986, p. 293ff., especially p. 295.

(210) Compare the indictment of August 9, 1944, BA, NJ/1583. Julius Leber was arrested on July 5, after a meeting on June 22 in the apartment of the Berlin physician Dr. Rudolf Schmid, of representatives of the Social Democratic and Communist Resistance concerning the perspectives of cooperation. The meeting, in which Leber, Adolf Reichwein, Franz Jacob, Anton Saefkow, Ferdinand Thomas, as well as a certain "Hermann" took part, was betrayed by a Gestapo informer (probably the same "Hermann"), who had infiltrated the communist Saefkow-Jacob-Bästlein-Group. Many arrests and executions were the result. After the failed assassination atempt of July 20, Leber, who had been in close contact with the Kreisau Circlenden, and was supposed to have been Interior Minister in Goerdeler's Cabinet, was brought before a hearing on the preparations for the attempted overthrow and mercilessly tortured. In September, the Oberreichsanwalt ("Supreme Reichs attorney")

accused him of High and Country treason in a second indictment. In October 1944, the People's Court (Volksgerichtshof) condemned him to death. (Compare, in this connection, also Martin Schumacher (Ed.), *M.d.R. Die Reichstagsabgeordneten der Weimarer Republik in der Zeit des Nationalsozialismus. Politische Verfolgung, Emigration und Ausbürgerung 1933-1945: Eine biographische Dokumentation*, Düsseldorf, 3.erw. und überarb. Aufl. 1994, p. 278ff.). The second indictment and the text of the verdict did not come down to us, but one should surmise that his lodge membership was also not discussed there. After more torture, Julius Leber was executed in Plötzensee Prison on January 5, 1945. At first, Adolf Reichwein, Rudolf Schmid and Ferdinand Thomas were indicted with Leber. Thomas had made the contact with the German Communist Party group. Reichwein, who was a member of the Kreisau Circle, and Thomas were also condemned to death and executed. Schmid was acquitted, because, according to the verdict, it was not sufficiently proven that he had knowingly put his home at the disposal of a "meeting inimical to the Reich" (BA, NJ/1583). Saefkow, Jacob, and Bernhard Bästlein were condemned to death on September 5, 1944 by the Volks Court, and executed on September 18, 1944.

(211)   Indictment of the Oberreichsanwaltes ("Supreme Reichs attorney") in the Volks Court September 3, 1944; Verdict of September 8, 1944 (Both in BA, NJ/17548, vol. 1). Carl Friedrich Goerdeler, Josef Wirmer, Ulrich von Hassell and Paul Lejeune-Jung stood with Leuschner, who was supposed to have been Vice Chancellor of a new government before the Court, in connection with the 20th of July. The death judgment against Leuschner was carried out on September 29, 1944, against Goerdeler not until February 2, 1945. Wirmer, von Hassell, and Lejeune-Jung sind were executed right away on September 8, 1944 (compare ibid., vol. 1-2).

(212)   Horst R. Sassin, *Liberale im Widerstand. Die Robinsohn- Strassmann-Gruppe 1934-1942*, [at first as a dissertation], Hamburg, 1993.

(213)   Compare ibid., p. 384, 386. After liberation, Strassmann went over to the SPD (German Socialist Party), Robinsohn remained without party affiliation.

(214)   Compare ibid., p. 248ff.

(215)   Compare ibid., p. 497 (note 17), 251.

(216)   Compare condensed in Sassin "Strassmann-Gruppe," in: Wolfgang Benz/Walter H. Pehle (Ed.), *Lexikon des deutschen Widerstandes*, Frankfurt/M. 1994, p. 306ff.

(217)   Compare Sassin, *Liberale im Widerstand*, p. 139, 380.

(218)   His successor in the office of Worshipful Master, Alfred Dierke, committted suicide in the lodge building in 1933, after it was vandalized by the Nazis, and he had lost his job. (Compare Bünger's letter of August 24, 1946, to Joseph Treu, cited in Chapter 7.1).

(218a) Activity report of the Department II/111 of March 2, 1939, USHMM, RG-11.001 M, Reel 292.

(218b) Oral information from Horst R. Sassins to the author.

(219)   Sassin, *Liberale im Widerstand*, p. 139f.

(220)   Written information from Dr. Hans-Detlef Mebes to the author.

(221)   Compare Sassin, *Liberale im Widerstand*, p. 139f., 381.

(222)   Note of January 13.1.1939, cited after ibid., p. 100.

(223)   Compare in this connection, ibid., p. 95ff., 373, 497 (note 17). Dehler became the first Minister of Justice of the Federal Republic of Germany in 1949.

(224)   Ibid., p. 102. Sassin gives only short sketches of the histories of the historical events in the Grand Lodge "Rising Sun" and the Symbolische Grossloge.

EPILOGUE

(1)   Compare Henning Wolter,"Der Wiederaufbau der deutschen Freimaurerei nach 1945," unpublished lecture (1995), p. 3 (Archive Henning Wolter, Delmenhorst). Eduard Uterharck, who had been imprisoned for a time during the "Third Reich," was re-elected Master of the Lodge "Absalom zu den 3 Nesseln."

(2)   Compare ibid., p. 12. Compare also Bünger's letter an Propper of July 27, 1949. A copy of this letter was generously put at the disposal of the author by Nathan Fischer (Jerusalem). In 1949, the Grand Lodge of Hamburg merged with the new humanitarian United Grand Lodge (see below).

(3)   Compare Wolter, "Der Wiederaufbau der deutschen Freimaurerei nach 1945," p. 11. On the division of Berlin, compare Ralf Melzer, "Ausgewählte Dokumente zur Geschichte der Alliierten in Berlin 1944–1994," in: *Berlin und die Alliierten*, ed. vom Berliner Institut für Lehrerfort-und-weiterbildung, vol. 2, Berlin, 1995, p. 123ff., here, especially p. 153ff.

(4)   The complex pre-history of the founding cannot be treated in a detailed manner here.

(5)   Compare a letter from Beyer to Bünger January 15, 1946, in: *Die Geschichte der Symbolischen Großloge*.

(6)   Declaration of the United Grand Lodge of the Freemasons of Germany (Archive Henning Wolter, Delmenhorst).

(7)   Ibid.

(8)   Ibid.

(9)   Ibid.

(10)   From the confidential "Frankfurt Protokols" between the United Grand Lodge A.F.u.A.M.and the Grosse Landesloge (II.d. / 8.1.1955) at the beginning of the planned creation of a Masonic umbrella organization. Cited here after Beyer, *Der Übertritt*, Appendix, p.7a.

(11)   Erich Awe, *Was ist richtig und brüderlich?* (Printed by the author?) [s.l., s.d. probably July 1961), p. 24.

(12)   Hörstmann's letter of May 4, 1933 (Private archives Alain Bernheim, Gottmadingen).

(13)   *Das Verhältnis der Großen Landesloge der Alten Freien und Angenommenen Maurer von Deutschland zum Deutschen Obersten Rat des Alten und Angenommenen Schottischen Ritus*, ed. by the Deutschen Obersten Rat, Frankfurt/M. 1961, p. 9.

(14)   Carl Kühne, "Erich Awe - 80 Jahre alt," in: *Eleusis*, vol. 18, no. 4, Juli/August 1963, p. 243.

(15)   Herbert Buchwald, "In Memoriam Br. Erich Awe," in: *Eleusis*, vol. 22, no. 3, Mai/Juni 1967, p. 141.

(16)   Pauls, *Der Deutsche Alte und Angenomme*, loc.cit., p. 3.

(17)   Christian Zetzsche, *200 Jahre Freimaurerei in Pyrmont. Geschichte und Selbsterlebtes*, Bad Pyrmont 1975. Concerning the activities of the Zetzsche brothers in the AASR, compare ibid., p. 148ff. In the St John's Lodge "Friedrich zu den drei Quellen" in Pyrmont, they

assumed their old functions: Oskar Zetzsche the office of orator, and Christian Zetzsche the Worshipful Master (until 1968), after which he was Past and Honorary Master.

(18)   Compare Z.K., vol. 121, issue March 1993, p. 97ff.

(19)   Compare BA, formerly BDC (Berlin Document Center), Personalakte Georg C. Frommholz. While April 20, 1934, was noted as the the Day of the Promotion to "Truppführer" in the so-called "Excerpt of the Nominal Roll of the SS" ("S-Stammrollen-Auszug,") it says in a "document of duty performed" ("Dienstleistungszeugnis"), that already on April 1, 1934, Frommholz had been named "Haupttruppführer." It appears in a (on the whole positive) judgment, that he was assigned the "care of the duties of the Haupttruppführers." All three documents carry the date May 20, 1934.

(20)   Compare the copy of an (alleged) instruction of the SS-Oberabschnitts Ost (Eastern Main Section of the SS) of May 25, 1937. (Archive Henning Wolter, Delmenhorst). In the BDC (Berlin Document Center)-Akte. No basis for this proceeding can be found.

(21)   Thus for example in the case of Hans Titschack, he resigned from his lodge in Delmenhorst in 1978 (oral information to the author from Henning Wolters). In the SS, which he had joined in 1941 he had the rank of a "Rottenführers" since April 1944. Compare BA, formerly BDC (Berlin Document Center), Personalakte Hans Titschack).

(22)   Cited after Böttner, *Zersplitterung und Einigung*, p. 198.

(23)   Ibid.

SUMMARY

(1)   Compare the letter from the National Christian Order Friedrich der Große to the Nazi Party Administration of April 12, 1933 (Private collection).

(2)   Compare Diedrich Bischoff, *Nationalsozialismus und Freimaurerei*, p. 10f. Compare also Fenner/Schmitt-Sasse, „Die Freimaurer als ‚nationale Kraft‛," *loc.cit.*, p. 232.

(3)   The grand concept of racial ideology formed not only the basis for the expansionist striving for "Lebensraum" and for the wiping out of whole peoples, but also determined all political segments including "social politics" ("Sozialpolitik"). As opposed to what is maintained by revisionist historians, racial boundaries regulated life in a much greater measure because [the usual] social boundaries may have lost significance.

(4)   Circular letter of May 12, 1933, Archives of the Grosse Landesloge.

(5)   In expressing an opinion concerning a publication in the *völkisch* magazine "Campana Mundi" (no. 3/1933), Witt-Hoë determined (March 9, 1933): "There are more kinds of Freemasonry than there are nations, and the most different, even opposite, *Weltanschauungen* are not even touched by this guarded catchword." Within German Freemasonry there existed "completely different currents and contrasts" (GStA PK, Logen, 5.1.3., 4379).

(6)   For future studies, it would be worth making a start here at separately examining the basic motivations for the relevant differentiation procedures over a long period of time–grand lodge by grand lodge.

(7)   Steffens, *Freimaurer*, p. 350.

(8)   Winkler, *Weimar 1918–1933*, p. 602. Winkler also emphasizes that Versailles was "no 'Punic peace':" ("kein 'Karthagofriede'"): "The Reich had been amputated, but it continued to exist, and after some time would have had good prospects for taking its place among the European big powers." (ibid.).

Sources and Literature

I. SOURCES

A) UNPUBLISHED SOURCES/ARCHIVES

Archiv der Großen Landesloge der Freimaurer von Deutschland, Berlin (ohne Signaturen).

Archives Supreme Council AASR S.J., Washington D.C. (ohne Signaturen).

Bayerisches Geheimes Staatsarchiv, München:
MA 106 561.
Reichsstatthalter 638.

Bundesarchiv, Koblenz:
ZSg 2/126 (8).

Bundesarchiv, Berlin-Lichterfelde:
R 58/266 (RSHA).
R 58/405 (RSHA).
R 58/792 (RSHA).

R 58/998f. (RSHA).

R 58/1066f. (RSHA).

R 58/1094 (RSHA).

R 58/2026 (RSHA).

R 58/2657 (RSHA).

R 58/2631 (RSHA).

R 43, II/821 (Reichskanzlei).

R 43, 4232 (Reichskanzlei).

R 18/5563 (Reichsinnenministerium).

Sammlung Schumacher, Bd. 221.

NS 8/120 (Dienststelle Rosenberg).

NS 8/258 (Dienststelle Rosenberg).

NJ/1583.

NJ/17548, Bd. 1-2.

Bundesarchiv, Berlin-Lichterfelde (former Berlin Document Center [BDC]):

Personalakte Erich Awe.

Personalakte Otto Bernhard.

Personalakte Erich Böhlke.

Personalakte Dr. Otto Bordes.

Personalakte Maximilian Brand.

Personalakte Georg C. Frommholz.

Personalakte Dr. Karl Hoede.

Personalakte Wilhelm Kube.

Personalakte Dr. Richard Markert.

Personalakte Dr. Alfred Meyer.

Personalakte Hans Titschack.

Ordner 880 (Freimaurer).

Bundesarchiv, Zwischenarchiv Dahlwitz-Hoppegarten (Berlin):

Z / A VI 379, A.10.

Deutsches Freimaurer-Museum, Bayreuth:

Nr.80 III A, B.

Nr.91.

Nr.621.

Nr.964.

Nr.10115: Der Übertritt der Altpreußischen Großlogen ins Völkisch-Nationalsozialistische Lager. Akten zur Freimaurerei in Deutschland 1920-1946, zusammengestellt von Bernhard Beyer, broschiert, (mit Kommentaren des Bearb.), Bayreuth 1955.

Nr. 9398: Die Geschichte der Symbolischen Großloge von Deutschland 1930-1949, zusammengestellt von Heinz Klasen, broschiert, (mit einer Einleitung des Bearb.), Hamburg, 1984.

Evangelisches Zentralarchiv in Berlin:

1/A2/489.

1/A4/182.

7/3627f.

14/1478.

Geheimes Staatsarchiv Preußischer Kulturbesitz, Berlin:

N.B.: Since this work was begun, in the GStA PK, instead of the term "Logen" the term "Freimaurer" has been adopted for the relevant main division!

HA Logen, Rep. 5.1.3. (GLL),   Nr.4325 ff.

HA Logen, Rep. 5.1.3. (GLL),   Nr.4338 ff.

HA Logen, Rep. 5.1.3. (GLL),   Nr. 4350.

HA Logen, Rep. 5.1.3. (GLL),   Nr.4355 ff.

HA Logen, Rep. 5.1.3. (GLL),   Nr.4369 ff.

HA Logen, Rep. 5.1.3. (GLL),   Nr.4375.

HA Logen, Rep. 5.1.3. (GLL),   Nr.4378 ff.

HA Logen, Rep. 5.1.3. (GLL),   Nr.4419 ff.

HA Logen, Rep. 5.1.3. (GLL),   Nr.4428 ff.

HA Logen, Rep. 5.1.3. (GLL),   Nr.4434.

HA Logen, Rep. 5.1.3. (GLL),   Nr.4443 ff.

HA Logen, Rep. 5.1.11. (SGL),   Nr.3 ff

HA Logen, Rep. 5.1.11. (SGL),   Nr.9 ff.

HA Logen, Rep. 5.1.11. (SGL),   Nr.30.

HA Logen, Rep. 5.1.11. (SGL),   Nr.32 ff.

HA Logen, Rep. 5.1.11. (SGL),   Nr.46 ff.

HA Logen, Rep. 5.1.11. (SGL),   Nr.50 ff.

HA Logen, Rep. 5.1.11. (SGL),   Nr.53 ff.

I. HA, Rep. 84a, Nr.15 085.

I. HA, Rep. 90 P, Nr.74, Heft 1 f.

I. HA, Rep. 90 P, Nr.76, Heft 2.

I. HA, Rep. 90 P, Nr.79, Heft 1.

I. HA, Rep. 90 P, Nr.80, Heft 2.

I. HA, Rep. 90 P, Nr.129.

Institut für Zeitgeschichte, München:
MA 398, SS (II), 9866 and PS-2202.

NG 5142 Nürnberger Akten.

NG 4506 Nürnberger Akten.

Privatarchiv Alain Bernheim, Gottmadingen
(ohne Signaturen).

Privatarchiv Bruno Peters, Berlin
(ohne Signaturen).

Archiv Henning Wolter, Delmenhorst
(ohne Signaturen).

Circular letter der Großen National-Mutterloge Zu den drei Weltkugeln/ Nationaler Christlicher Orden Friedrich der Große, 7. April 1933, 11. April 1933, 26. Januar 1934, 26. März 1934 (Private).

Schreiben des Nationalen Christlichen Ordens Friedrich der Große an die NSDAP-Parteileitung, 12. April 1933 (Private).

Schreiben des Nationalen Christlichen Ordens Friedrich der Große an Reichsminister Goebbels, 12. April 1933 (Private).

Staatsarchiv Bremen:
4.65, 1693.

United States Holocaust Memorial Museum Archives, Washington D.C.
RG-11.001 M.01 (RSHA [Osobyi fond #500, Moscow]) Reel 4ff.

RG-11.001 M.01(RSHA [Osobyi fond #500, Moscow]) Reel 288ff.

RG-11.001 M.07 (NSDAP [Osobyi fond #519, Moscow]) Reel 78

RG-11.001 M.15 (Deutsche Polizeieinrichtungen in den okkupierten Gebieten [Osobyi fond #1323, Moscow]) Reel 80

RG-11.001 M.19 (Propagandaministerium [Osobyi fond#1363, Moscow]) Reel 93

RG-11.001 M.21 (Einsatzstab Rosenberg [Osobyi fond #1401, Moscow]) Reel 131f.

RG-15.007 M (RSHA [Institute of National Memory fond #362, Warsaw]) Reel 5ff.

RG-18.002 M (Sipo and SD Latvia [Central State Historical Archives fond # R-1026, Riga])Reel 16

RG-37.001 *01 [Main State Archives Nordrhein-Westfalen, Düsseldorf]
Microfiche

Osobyi Archives, Moscow (former German Special Archives):
Bibliothek des Obersten Rates für Deutschland des AASR, Frankfurt am Main
Nr. 807: *Versuch einer Darstellung der Verfolgung der deutschen Großlogen und deren Tochterlogen und freimaurerähnlichen Organisationen. Dargestellt nach amtlichen Verlautbarungen des 3. Reiches, der NSDAP, der gleichgeschalteten Presse und sonstiger führender Freimaurer ehemaliger deutscher Großlogen aller Systeme,* Karl Günther, compiler (with his commentary), Köln, 1954.

Zentrum der dokumentar-historischen Sammlungen, Moskau (ehem. Zentrales Staatsarchiv/ "Sonderarchiv"):

1412-1-4900ff. (Symbolische GL).

1412-1-4732ff (GLL).

1412-1-8714 (GLL-Tocherlogen).

500-1-154ff (RSHA).

500-2-95ff. (RSHA).

500-3-325ff. (RSHA).

500-4-235 (RSHA).

B) PRINTED SOURCES

Allocution of the Sovereign Grand Commander of the Supreme Council of the Thirty-Third Degree of the Ancient and Accepted Scottish Rite of Freemasonry of the Southern Jurisdiction of the United States of America, Washington D.C. (October) 1935, (October) 1937, (October) 1939, (October) 1943.

Am rauhen Stein/Der rauhe Stein [später *Ordensblatt*], (Zeitschrift der Großloge Zur Freundschaft), Nr. 6/1932.

An den Hauptvorstand des Nationalverbandes Deutscher Offiziere, o.Verf., unterzeichnet von Martin Anger, Heinrich Herrling et al. [broschiert]., Erfurt (9. September) 1925. (Privatarchiv Bruno Peters, Berlin).

Anderson, Jakob. *Des verbesserten Konstitutionenbuch der alten ehrwürdigen Bruderschaft der Freymaurer erster Theil. Geschichte des Ordens, auf Befehl der großen Loge aus ihren Urkunden, Traditionen und Logenbüchern zum Gebrauch der Logen verfasset*, Frankfurt am Main, vierte vermehrte Aufl. 1783.

Arndt, Ernst Moritz. *Blick aus der Zeit auf die Zeit*, Frankfurt am Main, 1814.

Awe, Erich, *Was ist richtig und brüderlich?* (self-print?) [s.l., s.d] (presumed Juli 1961).

Bauhüttennot. Bonner Blaubuch—Eine Sammlung von Akten und Aufsätzen, Bonn, 1931. (Deutsches Freimaurer-Museum Bayreuth, Nr. 3506).

Baumbach, Rudolf, *Die religiöse Zukunftsaufgabe der deutschen Freimaurerei*, Gotha o.J.

Beyer, Bernhard (Bearb.), *Die sogenannte Symbolische Großloge von Deutschland*. Sonderdruck von Ausführungen verschiedener Nummern der "Mitteilungen der GL Zur Sonne," Bayreuth, 1931. (Deutsches Freimaurer-Museum Bayreuth, Nr. 2368).

Beyer, Bernhard. "Rudolf Ramge: Ein Angehöriger des AASR als Märtyrer der nationalsoziali-stischen Terrorzeit," in: *Amtliche Mitteilungen des Deutschen Obersten Rates des AASR*, 6 Jahrgang., 15.12.1951, Nr. 5, S. 8ff.

Bischoff, Diedrich, Nationalsozialismus und Freimaurerei, o.O. 1931.

Bischoff, Diedrich. *Freimaurerei und Deutschtum. Eine Auseinandersetzung zwischen Freimaurerei und Antisemitismus*, Leipzig, 1920 (Library Supreme Council AASR S.J., Washington D.C.).

Bismarck, Otto von. *Gedanken und Erinnerungen*, 3 Bd. Stuttgart/(Berlin) 1898-1921.

Brägger, Werner. *Die öffentlich-rechtliche Sonderstellung der drei altpreußischen Grosslogen. Begründung, Wandlungen, Ende, Disp.*, Leipzig, 1931.

Bundesblatt [später *Ordensblatt*], (Zeitschrift der 3 WK-Großloge),

Heft März/1931.
Heft April/1932.
Heft Februar/1933.
Heft April/1934.
Heft Juni/1934.

Chamberlain, Houston Stewart, *Die Grundlagen des neunzehnten Jahrhunderts*, 2 Bd., München 29th Aufl. 1944 (erstmals 1899).

Christusstaat International, ed. von der "urchristlichen Bundgemeinde Neues Jerusalem im Universellen Leben," Extrablatt Nr. 9, November 1991.

Das Freimaurerlogen-Museum in Nürnberg. Sonderdruck aus der Zeitschrift "Das Bayerland," ed. von Ludwig Deubner, München, 1938. (Library of Congress Washington, HS 394.F 73/53-48835).

Deutsche Corpszeitung, 52.Bd., Nr. 5, August/September 1935.

Die Alten Pflichten (Zeitschrift der Symbolischen Großloge von Deutschland [im Exil]),

Nr. 2, 1.Bd., November 1930.
Nr.12, 1.Bd., September 1931.
Nr. 1, 3. Jahrgang, Oktober 1932.
Nr. 2, 3. Jahrgang, November 1932.
Nr. 4, 3. Jahrgang, Januar 1933.
Nr. 6, 3. Jahrgang, März 1933.
Nr. 1, 4.Jahrgang, [1935].
Nr. 2/4, 4.Bd., Dezember 1935.

Diebow, Hans (Bearb.), *Der Ewige Jude.* 265 Bilddokumente, München/ Berlin, 1937.

Die Drei Lichter, Nr. 27/28, (Hannover) 1948, S.204 f.

Die drei Ringe (Zeitschrift der tschechoslowakischen Großloge), Nr. 5, 1933.

Anon. *Die entdeckten 'Henker und Brandstifter der Welt' und ihr 2000jähriges Verschwörungssystem. Der Schlüssel zur Weltgeschichte und Weltpolitik,* München, 1928.

Die Weltfreimaurerei, ed. vom Chef der Sicherheitspolizei und des SD, bearb. von [SS-Sturmbannführer] Erich Ehlers, Schriftenreihe für politische und welt-anschauliche Erziehung der Sicherheitspolizei und des SD, Heft 3, Leipzig, 1943. (Bundesarchiv, Berlin-Licherfelde, R 58/RD 19/9-3).

Dokumente, Veröffentlichungen, Briefe zur Entstehung der Symbolischen Großloge von Deutschland und des Deutschen Obersten Rates des Alten und Angenommenen Schottischen Ritus 1930/31, (Bayreuther Reihe Nr. 6) Bad Kissingen, 1961.

Ebeling, Robert, "Den Freimaurern zum neuen Jahr," in: *Volk unterm Hakenkreuz,* Heft 1/1934.

Ehrentafel für die im Weltkriege 1914-1918 gefallenen und die ihren Wunden erlegenen Ordensbrüder der Großen Landesloge der Freimaurer von Deutschland Deutsch-Christlichen Ordens, ed.

von der wissenschaftlichen Abteilung der Großen Landesloge der Freimaurer von Deutschland Deutsch-Christlichen Ordens, Berlin, 1932. (GStA PK, Logen, 5.1.3., 4339).

Endres, Franz Carl, "Zum Problem der Symbolischen Großloge (von Deutschland)," in: *Die Leuchte*, Nr. 10/1930, S. 143ff.; *Die Leuchte*, Nr. 5/1932, S. 73ff.

Endres. "Wenn die Lichter erlöschen," in: *Die Leuchte*, Nr. 5/1933, S. 65ff.

"Enthüllte Welt-Freimaurerei," Sonderdruck aus der *Der Aufbau* (Alleiniges amtliches Organ für Handwerk und Handel der NSDAP und der DAF für die Reichsbetriebsgemeinschaften 17 und 18) Berlin 6. Aufl. S.d. (Library Supreme Council AASR S.J., Washington D.C.).

Anon. *Festschrift zum 50.Stiftungsfest der Loge Die vereinigten Freunde an der Nahe im Orient Kreuz*nach, Bad Kreuznach, 1908.

Fodor, Andor, *Die Symbolische Großloge von Deutschland im Exil*, Tel Aviv, 1943.

Friedrich Wilhelm, Kronprinz (als Kaiser Friedrich III.), *Ansprachen des Ordens-Meisters 1870-1874*, Berlin, 1874.

Fritsch, Theodor, "Wesen und Geheimnis der Freimaurerei," in: *Hammer. Blätter für deutschen Sinn*, 26.Bd., Nr. 605, 1. September 1927, S. 433ff.

Fuchs, A., *Westdeutsches Freimaurer-Museum, Düsseldorf* 2.Aufl. s.d. (Deutsches Freimaurer-Museum Bayreuth, Nr. 142).

Gobineau, Joseph Arthur de, *Versuch über die Ungleichheit der Menschenrassen*, 4 Bd., Stuttgart, 1900-1904 (frz. erstm. 1853-1855).

Goebbels, Joseph, *Der Faschismus und seine praktischen Ergebnisse*, Berlin, 1934.

Grünfelder, Benno, "Die Entwicklung der Symbolischen Großloge von Deutschland im Exil," Lecture (typescript), Jerusalem (31. Januar) 1948 (Deutsches Freimaurer-Museum Bayreuth, Nr. 9938).

Hasselbacher, Friedrich. *Entlarvte Freimaurerei*, Bd. 1-5, Berlin, 1934-1941.

Hasselbacher. *Das Todesurteil über die Freimaurerei in Deutschland*, s.l., s.d. (etwa 1935).

Hasselbacher. Frankreichs Totentanz um die "Menschenrechte," Berlin 3.Aufl. 1941.

Anon. Hausgesetz der Stuhlmeister-Loge Zum Kubischen Stein. Or. Jerusalem Nr. 25 der Großloge des Staates Israel, Jerusalem [s.d. 1953 oder später].

Heep, Jakob, *Deutsches Ringen um die Seele der K.K. - Wege zur Besinnung und Gestaltung*, Wetzlar, 1926.

Heinsen, Peter H., "Arbeit am Frieden," in: *Die Alten Pflichten*, Nr. 3, 1.Bd., Dezember 1930, S. 17f.

Hergeth, Friedrich [d.i. Paul Heigl], *Aus der Werkstatt der Freimaurer und Juden im Österreich der Nachkriegszeit*, Graz, 1927.

Hermann der Deutsche [d.i. Hermann Hesse], *Die Weltrevolution des Roten Propheten. Die Verschwörung der Freimaurer und Finanzmagnaten*, Berlin, 1928. (GStA PK, I. HA, Rep. 84a, Nr. 15 085).

Heydrich, Reinhard, "Wandlungen unseres Kampfes," in: *Das Schwarze Korps*, Folge 9-13, Mai 1935.

Himmler, Heinrich. *Geheimreden 1933 bis 1945 und andere Ansprachen*, ed. von Bradley F. Smith und Agnes F. Peterson, Frankfurt am Main/Berlin/Wien, 1974.

Hitler, Adolf, *Mein Kampf*, Bd. 1: Eine Abrechnung; Bd. 2: Die nationalsozialistische Bewegung. Zwei Bände in einem Band, ungekürzte Ausg., München 29th. Aufl. 1933.

Hitlers Zweites Buch. Ein Dokument aus dem Jahre 1928, eingeleitet und kommentiert von Gerhard L. Weinberg (Geleitwort von Hans Rothfels), Stuttgart, 1961.

Hitler. *Sämtliche Aufzeichnungen 1905-1924*, ed. von Eberhard Jäckel und Axel Kuhn, Stuttgart, 1980.

Höft, G., "Bedeutung und Aufgaben unseres Bundep." *Aufklärungsschriften des FZAS*, Nr. 5, Nürnberg, 1917.

Huber, Engelbert, *Freimaurerei. Die Weltmacht hinter den Kulissen*, Stuttgart 3. Aufl. o.J. (Erstaufl. 1934). (Deutsches Freimaurer-Museum Bayreuth, Nr. 3093).

Anon. *Im Ordensstammhause der Großen Landesloge der Freimaurer von Deutschland Deutsch-Christlichen Ordens*, Berlin 2.Aufl. 1935.

Informationsblatt der Kommunistischen Partei, Landesbezirksleitung Bayern, Nr. 3/4, 15.4.1947.

John-Gorsleben, Rudolf, *"Hoch-Zeit" der Menschheit*, Leipzig, 1931.

Junker, Heinrich, *Der nationalsozialistische Gedankenkreis—Eine Aufklärung für Freimaurer*, ed. vom Verein deutscher Freimaurer, Leipzig, 1931.

Kommoss, Rudolf, *Juden machen Weltpolitik*, Berlin s.d.

Koner, Raoul, *Ein Freimaurerleben. Erlebnisse und Betrachtungen*, Bielefeld, 1976.

Kutzleb, Hjalmar, *Mord an der Zukunft.* Mit Zeichnungen von A. Paul Weber, Berlin, 1929.

"Leitsätze für Suchende," ed. von der Symbolischen Großloge von Deutschland, o.Verf., o.O./o.J. (verm.1930). (Archiv Henning Wolter, Delmenhorst).

Lennhoff, Eugen, "Ludendorff marschiert an der Spitze," in: Kurt Reichl (Ed.), *Das Blaubuch der Weltfreimaurerei,* Bd. 1933, S. 39ff.

Lerich, Konrad [d.i. Kurt Reichl], *Der Tempel der Freimaurer. Der 1. bis 33.Grad. Vom Suchenden zum Wissenden,* Bern [angebl. 2.Aufl.] 1937.

Logenblatt der Großloge von Hamburg, Heft 1/1931.

Ludendorff, Erich, *Vernichtung der Freimaurerei durch Enthüllung ihrer Geheimnisse,* München, 1927.

Lührs, Walther, *Zur gegenwärtigen Lage des deutsch-christlichen Ordensgedankens,* Berlin, 1934. (Deutsches Freimaurer-Museum Bayreuth, Nr. 7615).

Mart, Friedrich, "Materielles und geistiges Sein. Zur Frage eines sozialen Programms der Freimaurerei," in: *Die Alten Pflichten,* Heft 4, 1.Bd., Januar 1931, S. 28ff.

Meldungen aus dem Reich: Die geheimen Lageberichte des Sicherheitsdienstes der SS aus dem RSHA. 1938–1944, ed. von Heinz Boberach, Herrsching, 1984.

Ministerial-Blatt des Reichs- und Preußischen Ministeriums des Innern; vor 1936: Ministerialblatt für die Preußische innere Verwaltung.

Rund-Erlasse des Reichs- und Preußischen Ministeriums des Innern bzw. des Preußischen Ministeriums des Innern,
Nr. 3, 1934, column 69ff. (Rund-Erlaß des PMdI. vom 8.1.1934).
Nr. 38, 1934, column1168 b (Rund-Erlaß des PMdI. vom 14.9.1934).
Nr. 51, 1934, column 1543f. (Rund-Erlaß des RuPrMdI. vom 15.12.1934).
Nr. 22, 1935, column 693f. (Rund-Erlaß des RuPrMdI. vom 22.5.1935).
Nr. 29, 1935, column 888 a f. (Rund-Erlaß des RuPrMdI. vom 10.7.1935).
Nr. 46, 1935, column 1367f. (Rund-Erlaß des RuPrMdI. vom 2.11.1935).
Nr. 9, 1936, column 252 (Rund-Erlaß des RuPrMdI. vom 18.2.1936).
Nr. 39, 1936, column 1186ff. (Rund-Erlaß des RuPrMdI. vom 2.9.1936).
Nr. 53, 1936, column 1628ff. (Rund-Erlaß des RuPrMdI. vom 7.12.1936).
Nr. 24, 1939, column 1258ff. (Rund-Erlaß des RMdI. vom 6.6.1939).
Nr. 32, 1940, column 1571ff. (Rund-Erlaß des RMdI vom 27.7.1940).
Nr. 35, 1940, column 1689ff (Rund-Erlaß des RMdI. i. Einv. m. d. StdF. vom 21.8.1940).
Nr. 37, 1941, column 1588 (Rund-Erlaß des RFSS im RMdI.vom 3.9.1941).

Mitteilung an die geliebten Brüder, ed. von der Großen Loge von Preußen, gen. Zur Freundschaft, Berlin, 1934. (Deutsches Freimaurer-Museum Bayreuth, Nr. 4733).

Moeller van den Bruck, Artur, Das dritte Reich, (erstm. 1923), Vor- und Nachwort von Hans Schwarz, Hamburg 3.Aufl. 1931.

Mousset, Albert, *L'attentat de Sarajewo. Documents inédits et Texte intégral des Sténogrammes du Procès*, Paris, 1930.

Müffelmann, Leo, "Zur deutsch-französischen freimaurerischen Annäherung," in: *Wiener Freimaurer-Zeitung*, Nr. 5, 1928, S. 1ff.

Müffelmann., "Unsere Aufgabe," in: *Die Alten Pflichten*, Nr. 1, 1.Bd., Oktober, 1930, S. 1ff.

Müffelmann, "Freimaurerei und Nationalsozialismus," in: *ibid.*, Nr. 3, 2.Bd., Dezember, 1931, S. 21ff.

Müffelmann., "Die Symbolische Großloge" in: Reichl (Ed.), *Das Blaubuch der Weltfreimaurerei*, Bd. 1933, S. 54.

Nettl, Paul (Ed.), *Das Jahrbuch der Weltfreimaurerei 1935*, Wien, 1935 [Auszüge].(Archiv Henning Wolter, Delmenhorst).

Neue Leipziger Zeitung, 26.1.1928.

Nies, Karl, *Der Freimaurerbund zur Eintracht. Festschrift zur fünfzigjährigen Jubelfeier seines Bestehens*, Mainz, 1896.

NSDAP-Schulungsbrief "Gegen die Freimaurerei," 4. Jahrgang., 7/1939, Berlin, 1939. (Deutsches Freimaurer-Museum Bayreuth, Nr. 91).

Nuremberg Trial Proceedings Bd. 13, 120th Day, Friday, 3 May 1946, quoted from The Avalon Project at the Yale Law School (http://www.yale.edu/lawweb/avalon/imt/proc/05-03-46.htm).

Ordensblatt [aus Bundesblatt und Am rauhen Stein/Der rauhe Stein], (Zeitschrift der 3 WK-Großloge und der Großloge Zur Freundschaft),

Heft Oktober/1934.

Pfannkuche, August, *Freimaurerei und völkische Frage*, Berlin, 1928.

Pharos, Prof. [d.i. Puntigam, Pater SJ], *Der Prozeß gegen die Attentäter von Sarajewo, aktenmäßig dargestellt*, Berlin, 1918.

Picker, Henry, *Hitlers Tischgespräche im Führerhauptquartier*, Frankfurt am Main/Berlin, 1989.

Pösche, G., *25 Jahre Freimaurerei 1906-1931*, Berlin, 1931.

Propper, Emanuel, "Zur Lage der Freimaurerei in Palästina," in: *Die Alten Pflichten*,Nr. 3, 3. Jahrgang., Dezember 1932, S. 32f.

"Protokolle der Weisen von Zion": *Die Geheimnisse der Weisen von Zion. In deutscher Sprache herausgegeben von Gottfried zur Beek* (= Ludwig Müller von Hausen [d.i. Ludwig Müller]), Berlin 8.Aufl. 1923. Die Zionistischen Protokolle. Das Programm der internationalen Geheimregierung. Ed. von Theodor Fritsch, Leipzig, 1924.

Rauschning, Hermann, *Gespräche mit Hitler*, Zürich/New York 5.Aufl. 1938, (unver. Neuaufl. Zürich, 1973).

Reichl, Kurt (Ed.) im Auftrag der Universellen Freimaurerliga [= Allgemeine Freimaurerliga]), *Das Blaubuch der Weltfreimaurerei*, Jahrgang 1933-1934, Wien 1933/1934.

Reichsgesetzblatt
1933 I, S. 175.
1935 I, S. 1333f.

Reith, Herbert, "Eine Abrechnung mit den letzten Saboteuren nationalsozialistischer Aufbauarbeit. Freimaurerei und was der schaffende Deutsche von ihr wissen muß," in: *Arbeitertum* (Organ der DAF), Folge 16, November 1934. (GStA PK, Logen, 5.1.3., 4379).

Reventlow, Ernst Graf zu, *Judas Kampf und Niederlage in Deutschland*, Berlin, 1937.

Rosenberg, Alfred, *Der Mythus des 20. Jahrhundertp. Eine Wertung der seelisch-geistigen Gestaltungskämpfe unserer Zeit*, München 31-32. Aufl. 1934.

Rosenberg. *Das Verbrechen der Freimaurerei. Judentum, Jesuitismus, Deutsches Christentum*, München 2. Aufl. 1922.

Rosenberg. *Die Protokolle der Weisen von Zion und die jüdische Weltpolitik*, München, 1923.

Runkel, Ferdinand, *Geschichte der Freimaurerei in Deutschland*, Bd. 3, Berlin, 1932.

Satzung des Deutschen Ordens (r.V.) Hamburg [1933]. (Deutsches Freimaurer-Museum Bayreuth, Nr. 9980).

Schmidt, Kurt, Völkische Weltanschauung und Freimaurerei, Gotha (?) 1932. (Deutsches Freimaurer-Museum Bayreuth,Nr. 51).

Schmidt. *Die Freimaurerei im Dienste deutscher Nationalbildung*, Wetzlar, 1927.

Schulz, E.H./Frerks, R. (Bearb.), *Warum Arierparagraph? Ein Beitrag zur Judenfrage*, 6. erw. Aufl. Berlin, 1937.

Schwartz-Bostunitsch, Gregor [d.i. Gregorij Bostunic], *Die Freimaurerei. Ihr Ursprung, ihre Geheimnisse, ihr Wirken*, Weimar, 1928.

Schwartz-Bostunitsch. *Jude und Weib. Theorie und Praxis des jüdischen Vampyrismus, der Ausbeutung und Verseuchung der Wirtsvölker*, Berlin, 1939.

Six, Alfred Franz, *Das Reich und der Westen*, Berlin, 1940.

Slekow, Gustav, "Schafft ein soziales Programm der Freimaurerei?" in: Die Alten Pflichten, Nr. 3, 1. Jahrgang., Dezember 1930, S. 19f.

Stradonitz, Stephan Kékulé von, *Der Mord von Sarajewo. Eine Aufklärung*, Leipzig, 1931.

Stuckart, Wilhelm/Globke, Hans, *Kommentare zur deutschen Rassengesetzgebung*, Bd. 1 [Reichsbürgergesetz vom 15.9.1935; Gesetz zum Schutze des deutschen Blutes und der deutschen Ehre vom 15.9.1935; Gesetz zum Schutze der Erbgesundheit des deutschen Volkes (Ehegesundheitsgesetz) vom 18.10.1935 nebst allen Ausführungs-vorschriften und den einschlägigen Gesetzen und Verordnungen], München/Berlin, 1936.

The New Age (Journal of the Supreme Council AASR, SJ, USA). 1930ff.

Treue-Information (Zeitschrift der 3 WK-Großloge), Nr. 122, 1/1986.

Verordnung über einige Grundlagen der künftigen Verfassung. § I-III, 6.4.1848 und Verfassungs-Urkunde, 31.1.1850, Artikel 29f.

Verordnungen, Grundsätze und Satzungen der Symbolischen Großloge von Deutschland im Exil, Anon., Jerusalem, 1945.

Verordnungsblatt der Reichsleitung der NSDAP, Folge 47, 2. Jahrgang., München, 1933.

Völkischer Beobachter, Nr. 54-57, 6.3.1930-1939./10.3.1930.

Völkische Freimaurerei. Ausführungen zu den Anträgen der Johannis-Loge Freundschaft im Hochland in München an die Große Loge von Preußen, gen. zur Freundschaft in Berlin, (verm. verfaßt von Johannes Bühler) München, 1924. (Deutsches Freimaurer-Museum Bayreuth, Nr. 2477).

Volkenrath, Max, *Deutsche Freimaurerei als Ergebnis des Weltkriegep. Kriegs-betrachtungen eines deutschen Freimaurers im Felde*, Leipzig, 1916. (Deutsches Freimaurer-Museum Bayreuth,Nr. 191).

Wagner, Richard, "Was ist deutsch?" *Bayreuther Blätter* 1, 1878, S. 29ff., wiedergeben in: Karl Heinrich Rengstorf/Siegfried von Kortzfleisch (Ed.), *Kirche und Synagoge. Handbuch zur Geschichte von Christen und Juden*, Bd. 2, Stuttgart, 1968ff. (Neuaufl. München, 1988), S. 293f.

Walk, Joseph (Ed.), *Das Sonderrecht für die Juden im NS-Staat. Eine Sammlung der gesetzlichen Maßnahmen und Richtlinien—Inhalt und Bedeutung*, Heidelberg, Karlsruhe, 1981.

Wichtl, Friedrich, *Weltfreimaurerei—Weltrevolution—Weltrepublik. Eine Untersuchung über Ursprung und Endziele des Weltkrieges*, München, 1919 (und folgende Auflagen).

Wiener Freimaurer-Zeitung (Zeitschrift der Großloge von Wien),
Nr.1, 1932.
Nr.6/7, 1932.
Nr.4/5, 1933.
Nr.6/8, 1933.
Nr.9/12, 1933.

Zetzsche, Oskar, "Was sagen uns Freimaurern die Externsteine?" Vortag vom 2. April 1933, in: Christian Zetzsche, *200 Jahre Freimaurerei in Pyrmont. Geschichte und Selbsterlebtes*, Bad Pyrmont, 1975, S. 44ff. (Deutsches Freimaurer-Museum Bayreuth, Nr. 6852).

Zirkelkorrespondenz [später *Ordensblatt*], (Zeitschrift der GLL),
2.Mai-Heft / 59. Jahrgang. 1930.
2.Juni-Heft / 59. Jahrgang 1930.
Mai-Heft / 62. Jahrgang 1933.
Oktober-Heft / 62. Jahrgang 1933.
November-Heft / 62. Jahrgang 1933.

Zur Erinnerung. Schlußfeier der unter der Großen Loge von Preußen, genannt Zur Freundschaft in Berlin und Umgebung arbeitenden St.Johannis-Logen, o.Verf., Berlin (16. Juli) 1935.

II. RESEARCH

Ackermann, Josef, Heinrich Himmler als Ideologe, Göttingen/Zürich/ Frankfurt am Main, 1970.

"After Fifteen Years. Freemasonry in Germany." Report of the Special Mission sent by The Masonic Service Association of the United States to investigate Masonic conditions in Germany, Washington D.C. 1949.

Aleff, Eberhard (Ed.), *Das Dritte Reich*, Hannover 4. überarb. Aufl. 1970.

Alleau, René, *Hitler et les sociétés secrètes. Enquete sur les sources occultes du nazisme*, Paris, 1969.

Aly, Götz/Heim, Susanne, *Vordenker der Vernichtung. Auschwitz und die Pläne für eine neue europäische Ordnung*, Hamburg, 1991.

Aly, Götz, *"Endlösung". Völkerverschiebung und der Mord an den europäschen Juden*, Frankfurt am Main, 1995.

Aronson, Shlomo, *Heydrich und die Anfänge des SD und der Gestapo (1931-1935)* [Diss.], Berlin, 1967.

Banach, Jens, Heydrichs Elite. *Das Führerkorps der Sicherheitspolizei und des SD 1936-1945*, Paderborn/München/Wien/Zürich, 1998.

Bar-Levi, Heinz/Fischer, Nathan/Wagner, Efraim F. (Ed.), *Zur Quelle Siloah Nr. 26 im Orient Jerusalem*, Jerusalem, 1991.

Bauer, Yehuda, Vom christlichen Judenhaß zum modernen Antisemitismus. Ein Er-klärungsversuch, in: Wolfgang Benz (Ed.), *Jahrbuch für Antisemitismusforschung Nr. 1*, Frankfurt am Main/New York, 1992, S. 77ff.

Bernheim, Alain. *Nachforschungen über die Geschichte des Alten und Angenommenen Schottischen Ritus in Deutschland* (2. Fassung), broschiert, Büsingen, 1983.

Bernheim. "1877 et le Grand Orient de France," in: *Travaux de la Loge nationale de recherches*. Villard de Honnecourt, ed. von der Grande Loge Nationale Française, Série 2, Nr. 19/1989, Neuilly-sur-Seine, 1989, S. 113ff.

Bernheim. "Für Leo Müffelmann. Fünfzig Jahre nach seinem Tod," in: Eleusis (Organ des Deutschen Obersten Rates), 39. Jahrgang, Nr. 3, Mai/Juni/Juli, 1984, S. 170ff.

Bieberstein, Johannes Rogalla von, "Aufklärung, Freimaurerei, Menschenrechte und Judenemanzipation in der Sicht des Nationalsozialismus," in: *Jahrbuch des Instituts für Deutsche Geschichte an der Universität Tel Aviv*, Nr. 7/1978, S. 339ff.

Bieberstein. "Die These von der freimaurerischen Verschwörung," in: Reinalter (Ed.), *Freimaurer und Geheimbünde im 18. Jahrhundert in Mitteleuropa*, S. 85ff.

Bieberstein. "Vom Antimasonismus zum (Vernichtungs-) Antisemitismus," in: Helmut Reinalter (Ed.), 2. *Internationale Tagung in Innsbruck*, S. 99ff.

Böttner, Friedrich John, *Zersplitterung und Einigung. 225 Jahre Geschichte der deutschen Freimaurer. An Hand von Dokumenten dargestellt*, Hamburg, 1962.

Böttner. Gab es eine "Große Loge von Hamburg im Exil" in Chile? in: TAU (Halbjahresschrift der Forschungsloge Q.C.), I/1989, S. 50ff.

Bollmus, Reinhard, *Das Amt Rosenberg und seine Gegner. Studien zum Machtkampf im nationalsozialistischen Herrschaftssystem*, Stuttgart, 1970.

Borries, Edgar von, *Loge "Drei Ringe" 1894-1994. Der Weg von der Großen Loge von Hamburg zur Gran Logia de Chile*, (Privatdruck), Santiago de Chile, 1994. (Deutsches Freimaurer-Museum Bayreuth, Nr. 11270).

Bracher, Karl Dietrich, *Die deutsche Diktatur. Entstehung, Stuktur, Folgen des Nationalsozialismus*, Köln 4.Aufl. 1972.

Broszat, Martin/Frei, Norbert (Ed.), *Das Dritte Reich im Überblick. Chronik, Ereignisse, Zusammenhänge*, München 2. Aufl. 1990.

Broszat, Martin, "Das weltanschauliche und gesellschaftliche Kräftefeld," in: *ibid.*, S. 94ff.

Broszat. "Zur Sozialgeschichte des deutschen Widerstands," in: VfZ, 34. Jahrgang., Heft 3/1986, S. 293ff.

Browder, George C., "Die Anfänge des SD. Dokumente aus der Organisations-geschichte des Sicherheitsdienstes des Reichsführers SS," in: VfZ, 27. Jahrgang., Heft 2/1979, S. 299ff.

Browder. *Hitler's Enforcers. The Gestapo and SS Security Service in the Nazi Revolution*, New York/Oxford, 1996.

Buchheim, Hans/Broszat, Martin/Jacobsen, Hans-Adolf/Krausnick, Helmut (Ed.), *Anatomie des SS-Staates*, 2. Jahrgang, München 5. Aufl. 1989.

Buchheim, Hans, "Die SS - das Herrschaftsinstrument," in: *ibid.*, Bd. 1, S. 15ff.

Buchheim. Befehl und Gehorsam, in: *ibid.*, Bd. 1, S. 215ff.

Buchwald, Herbert, "In Memoriam Br. Erich Awe," in: *Eleusis* (Organ des Deutschen Obersten Rates), 22. Jahrgang., Nr. 3, Mai/Juni 1967, S. 140f.

Burkert, Hans-Norbert/Matußek, Klaus/Wippermann, Wolfgang, "Machter-greifung" Berlin, 1933, Berlin 2.Aufl.: 1982.

Burleigh, Michael, *The Third Reich. A New History*, New York: 2000.

Burleigh, Michael/Wippermann, Wolfgang. *The Racial State: Germany 1933-1945*, Cambridge, 1991.

Burzlaff, Alfred, *Erinnerungen und Dokumente, 1935-1945*, Berlin, 1958.

Chysky, Vaclav, "Antijudaismus, Antisemitismus," in: Humanität. Das deutsche Frei-maurermagazin, Nr. 7/1992, S. 14ff.

Cohn, Norman, Die Protokolle der Weisen von Zion. Der Mythos von der jüdischen Weltverschwörung, Köln/Berlin, 1969.

Combes, André, *La franc-maçonnerie sous l'occupation. Persécution et Résistance 1939-1945*, Monaco, 2001.

Corbin, Henry, *Temple et contemplation*, Paris, 1980.

Daim, Wilfried, *Der Mann, der Hitler die Ideen gab. Von den religiösen Verirrungen eines Sektieres zum Rassenwahn des Diktators*, München, 1958.

Das Verhältnis der Großen Landesloge der Alten Freien und Angenommenen Maurer von Deutschland zum Deutschen Obersten Rat des Alten und Angenommenen Schottischen Ritus, ed. vom Deutschen Obersten Rat, Frankfurt am Main, 1961. (Deutsches Freimaurer-Museum Bayreuth, Nr. 7357).

Drechsler, Johannes, *Die Brüder vom FZAP. Ein Streifzug durch die Geschichte des Freimaurerbundes Zur Aufgehenden Sonne*, Hamburg, 1971.

Düriegl, Günter/Winkler, Susanne (Ed.), *Freimaurer. Solange die Welt besteht (Katalog der Internationalen Freimaurerausstellung in Wien 1992/1993)*, Wien 2.Aufl. 1992/1993.

Düriegl, Günter, "Bauhütten," in: *ibid.*, S. 83f.

Endler, Renate, "Die Freimaurerbestände im Geheimen Staatsarchiv Preußischer Kulturbesitz, Abt. Merseburg," in: Helmut Reinalter (Ed.), *Internationale Tagung in Innsbruck 22./23.5.1992. "Aufklärung und Geheimgesellschaften: Freimaurer, Illuminaten und Rosenkreuzer: Ideologie, Struktur und Wirkungen,"* Bayreuth, 1992, S. 103ff.

508

Endler. "Zu Entstehung und Inhalt der Freimaurerei, ihrer Entwicklung in Deutschland und zur Geschichte der Loge 'Amalia' in Weimar" (unveröffentlichter Vortrag), Weimar, 3.11.1990.

Erb, Rainer/Bergmann, Werner, Die Nachtseite der Judenemanzipation. Der Widerstand gegen die Integration der Juden in Deutschland 1780-1860, Berlin, 1989.

Fenner, Wolfgang/Schmitt-Sasse, Joachim, "Die Freimaurer als 'nationale Kraft' vor 1933," in: Thomas Koebner (Ed.), *Weimars Ende. Prognosen und Diagnosen in der deutschen Literatur und politischen Publizistik 1930-1933*, Frankfurt am Main, 1982, S. 223ff.

Fest, Joachim C., *Hitler. Eine Biographie*, Frankfurt am Main/Berlin/ Wien, 1973.

Fox, William L., *Two Centuries of Scottish Rite Freemasonry in America's Southern Jurisdiction*, Arkansas, 1997.

Freemasonry and The Nurnberg Trials. A study in Nazi Persecution, Missouri, 1959.

Freudenschuß, Werner, "Der Wetzlarer Ring—Völkische Tendenzen in der deutschen Freimaurerei nach dem 1. Weltkrieg," in: *Quatuor Coronati Jahrbuch* Nr. 25/1988, Bayreuth, 1988, S. 9ff.

Freund, René, *Braune Magie? Okkultismus, New Age und Nationalsozialismus*, Wien, 1995.

Friedländer, Saul, *Das Dritte Reich und die Juden. Erster Band: Die Jahre der Verfolgung* 1933-1939, München 2. Aufl. 1998.

Gellately, Robert, "Allwissend und allgegenwärtig? Entstehung, Funktion und Wandel des Gestapo-Mythos," in: Gerhard Paul/Klaus-Michael Mallmann (Ed.), *Die Gestapo—Mythos und Realität*, S. 47ff.

Gerlach, Karlheinz, "Zur Sozialstruktur der Großen National-Mutterloge 'Zu den drei Weltkugeln' 1775-1805 in Berlin," in: *Quatuor Coronati Jahrbuch* Nr. 28/1991, S. 105ff.

Gerlach. "Die Große Landesloge der Freimaurer von Deutschland, 1769–1807. Zur Sozialgeschichte der deutschen Freimaurerei im 18. Jahrhundert," in: *Quatuor Coronati Jahrbuch* Nr. 30/1993, S. 79ff.

Gerlach. "Royale York zur Freundschaft in Berlin 1762-1806. Ein Beitrag zur Sozialgeschichte der Freimaurerei in Brandenburg-Preußen," in: *Quatuor Coronati Jahrbuch* Nr. 31/1994, S. 51ff.

Gilbert, Martin. *Winston S. Churchill, Bd. VI: Finest Hour 1939-1941*, Boston, 1983.

Gilbhard, Hermann. *Die Thule-Gesellschaft. Vom okkulten Mummenschanz zum Hakenkreuz*, München, 1994.

Glaser-Gerhard, Ernst. "Zur Geschichte der Großen Landesloge der Freimaurer von Deutschland zu Berlin 1920-1970." Aus den *Beiträgen der Ordensgliederungen und Logen*, Berlin, 1970.

Goldhagen, Daniel Jonah. *Hitlers willige Vollstrecker. Ganz gewöhnliche Deutsche und der Holocaust*, Berlin, 1996.

Grüttner, Michael. *Studenten im Dritten Reich*, Paderborn, 1995.

Hachmeister, Lutz. *Der Gegnerforscher: Die Karriere des SS-Führers Franz Alfred Six*, München, 1998.

Hachtmann, Rüdiger "Friedrich II. von Preußen und die Freimaurerei," in: HZ, Bd. 264/1997, S. 21ff.

Hamill, John M. "Die Freimaurerei in England," in: Günter Düriegl/ Susanne Winkler (Ed.), *Freimaurer*, S. 159ff.

Handbuch zur "Völkischen Bewegung" 1871-1918, ed. von Uwe Puschner et al., München/New Providence/London/Paris, 1996.

Hardtwig, Wolfgang. "Eliteanspruch und Geheimnis in den Geheimgesellschaften des 18. Jahrhunderts," in: Helmut Reinalter (Ed.), *Aufklärung und Geheimgesellschaften. Zur politischen Funktion und Sozialstruktur der Freimaurerlogen im 18. Jahrhundert*, München, 1989, S. 63ff.

Hartung, Günter. "Völkische Ideologie," in: *Handbuch zur "Völkischen Bewegung,"* S.22ff.

Heilmann, H.D. "Die Bibliothek in Zeit und Räumen," in: *Bibliotheksinformationen* (FU Berlin), Nr. 18, Dezember 1988, S. 2ff.

Herbert, Ulrich. *Best. Biographische Studien über Radikalismus, Weltanschauung und Vernunft, 1903-1989*, Bonn, 1996.

Hermand, Jost. *Der alte Traum vom neuen Reich. Völkische Utopien und Nationalsozialismus*, Frankfurt am Main, 1988.

Hieronymus, Ekkehard. "Jörg Lanz von Liebenfels," in: Handbuch zur "Völkischen Bewegung," S. 131ff.

Höhne, Heinz. *Der Orden unter dem Totenkopf. Die Geschichte der SS*, Gütersloh, 1967.

Hoffmann, Stefan Ludwig. "Sakraler Monumentalismus um 1900. Das Leipziger Völkerschlachtdenkmal," in: Reinhart Koselleck/Michael Jeismann (Ed.), *Der politische Totenkult. Kriegerdenkmäler in der Moderne*, München, 1994, S. 249ff.

Hornung, Klaus. *Der jungdeutsche Orden*, Düsseldorf, 1958.

Hoss, Christiane (Bearb./et al.). *100 Jahre deutscher Rassismus*, (Katalog), ed. von der Kölnischen Gesellschaft für Christlich-Jüdische Zusammenarbeit), Köln, 1988.

Howe, Ellic. "The Collapse of Freemasonry in Nazi-Germany," in: *Ars Quatuor Coronatorum* (Zeitschrift der Forschungsloge der Großloge von England), Bd. 95/1982, London, 1983, S. 21ff.

Hubert, Rainer. "Antimasonismus," in: Günter Düriegl / Susanne Winkler (Ed.), *Freimaurer*, S. 353ff.

Jaacks, Gisela. "Der Tempel in Jerusalem in jüdischer und christlicher Überlieferung. Rekonstruktion und Ideal," in: A. Bekemaier (Bearb.), *Reisen nach Jerusalem. Das heilige Land in Karten und Ansichten aus fünf Jahrhunderten* (Katalog Berlin Museum), Wiesbaden, 1993, S. 25ff.

Jäckel, Eberhard/Kuhn, Axel. "Neue Erkenntnisse zur Fälschung von Hitler-Dokumenten," in: VfZ, 32.Bd., Heft 1/1984, S. 163f.

Jong, Rick de. *Freimaurer an Rhein und Ruhr im Dritten Reich*, (Selbstverlag des Autors), Düsseldorf, 1986.

Kannicht, Joachim. "Adolf Eichmann und die Freimaurer," in: *Die Bruderschaft* (Zeitschrift der Vereinigten Großlogen von Deutschland), Nr. 1/1962, Berlin, 1962, S. 19ff.

Karl Hoede 1897-1973, ed. von der Forschungsloge Quatuor Coronati, Bamberg, 1974.

Kater, Michael H. *Das "Ahnenerbe" der SS 1935-1945. Ein Beitrag zur Kulturpolitik des Dritten Reiches*, Stuttgart, 1974.

Katz, Jacob. *Jews and Freemasons in Europe. 1723-1939*, Cambridge/ Massachusetts, 1970.

Keiler, Helmut K.H. "Freimaurerische Bibliotheksbestände in Deutschland und die Bibliotheca Klossiana in Den Haag," in: Helmut Reinalter (Ed.), *Internationale Tagung in Innsbruck*, S. 109ff.

Keßler, Herbert. "Der Schottische Ritus—Ein Gang durch seine Grade,"in: *Quatuor Coronati Jahrbuch* Nr. 23/1986, Bayreuth, 1986, S. 179ff.

Kornblum, Aaron T. "Freemasonry and the United States Holocaust Memorial Museum," in: *Scottish Rite Journal*, Bd. 10/1998, S. 54ff.

Kuéss, Gustav R./Scheichelbauer, Bernhard. *200 Jahre Freimaurerei in Österreich*, Wien, 1959.

Kühne, Carl. "Erich Awe - 80 Jahre alt," in: *Eleusis* (Organ des Deutschen Obersten Rates, 18. Jahrgang, Nr. 4, Juli/August 1963, S. 243f.

Liberté 1871, Anon., ed. von der Loge Liberté in Lausanne, Lausanne s.d.

Löwenthal, Richard. "Widerstand im totalen Staat," in: Richard Löwenthal/Patrick von zur Mühlen (Ed.), *Widerstand und Verweigerung in Deutschland 1933-1945*, Berlin/Bonn, 1982, S. 11ff.

Lohmann, Hartwig. "Ansprache zur Lichteinbringung in die Johannis-Loge "Friedrich zur Standhaftigkeit" in Halle/Saale," (20.3.1993), in: Z.K., 121. Jahrgang, Heft Mai 1993, S. 163ff.

Luckas, Jürgen, "Freimaurerabzeichen mit Hakenkreuz, Quatuor Coronati Informationsblatt des Arbeitszirkels Nordrhein-Westfalen," Sonderdruck, s.l. 1995.

Luckas. "Nicht alles war Selbstschutzmaßnahme. Ritualänderungen der altpreußischen Großlogen von 1933-1935," in: Q.C.-Berichte, Heft 15/1995, Wien, 1995, S. 72ff.

Luckas. "Freimaurerei im Nationalsozialismus," in: *TAU* (Halbjahresschrift der Forschungsloge Q.C.), II/1993, S. 132ff.

Luckas. "Aspekte vom Weg der deutschen Freimaurerei in die 'Dunkle Zeit'," in: *TAU* (Halbjahresschrift der Forschungsloge Q.C.), I/1996, S. 49ff.

Lüthi, Urs. *Der Mythos von der Weltverschwörung: Die Hetze der Schweizer Frontisten gegen Juden und Freimaurer—am Beispiel des Berner Prozesses um die "Protokolle der Weisen von Zion,"* Zürich, 1992.

Maurice, Florian. *Ignaz Aurelius Feßler und die Reform der Großloge Royal York in Berlin. Kultur- und Geistesgeschichte um 1800 im Spiegel der Freimaurerei* [Diss.], München, 1995.

Mebes, Hans-Detlef. "Kurt Tucholsky 1924-1935. Ein zweites Leben im Geheimen?" In: *Humanität. Das deutsche Freimaurermagazin*, Nr. 7/1985, S. 8ff.

Mehringer, Hartmut / Röder, Werner. "Gegner, Widerstand, Emigration," in: Martin Broszat/Norbert Frei (Ed.), *Das Dritte Reich im Überblick*, S. 108ff.

Melzer, Ralf. "Völkische Freimaurerei" 1922-1935 [Magisterarbeit FU Berlin], Berlin, 1994.

Melzer. "Die deutschen Logen und die völkische Herausforderung," in: *Quatuor Coronati Jahrbuch* Nr. 31/1994, Bayreuth, 1994, S. 151ff.

Melzer. "Völkische Freimaurerei im Spiegel der Historiographie," in: Helmut Reinalter (Ed.), *2. Internationale Tagung in Innsbruck*, S. 27 ff.

Melzer. "Ausgewählte Dokumente zur Geschichte der Alliierten in Berlin 1944-1994," in: *Berlin und die Alliierten, ed. vom Berliner Institut für Lehrerfort- und -weiterbildung*, Bd. 2, Berlin, 1995, S. 123 ff.

Michatsch, Thomas. *"Das 'Schwarze Korps' und die Freimaurerei"* [Magisterarbeit FU Berlin] Berlin, 1996.

Morvan, François. *Aspects du mythe conspirationniste antimaçonnique en Allemagne*, (Politica Hermetica - Paris), Paris, 1994.

Naudon, Paul. *Geschichte der Freimaurerei*, Frankfurt am Main/Berlin/Wien, 1982.

Neuberger, Helmut. *Freimaurerei und Nationalsozialismus* [zunächst Diss.], Bd. 1: *Der völkische Propagandakampf und die deutsche Freimaurerei bis 1933*; Bd. 2: *Das Ende der deutschen Freimaurerei*, Hamburg, 1980.

Neumann, Frank. "Die Involvierung der 'altpreußischen' Freimaurerei in die Politik am Beispiel der 'Großen Loge von Preußen' im Spiegel ihrer Zeitschrift 'Am rauhen Stein' 1914-1933/35," [Staatsexamensarbeit Universität Köln], Köln, 1995.

Nolte, Ernst. *Der Faschismus in seiner Epoche. Die Action française. Der italienische Faschismus. Der Nationalsozialismus*, München, 1963.

Obermann, Manfred. "Zur Geschichte der Freimaurerei in Berlin," in: Berlin Museum (Hrsg.), *Freimaurer in Berlin. Gemälde, Plastik, Graphik, Kleinkunst* (Katalog) Berlin, 1973.

Paul, Gerhard/Mallmann, Klaus-Michael, *Die Gestapo-Mythos und Realität*, Darmstadt, 1995.

Paul, *et al.* "Auf dem Wege zu einer Sozialgeschichte des Terrors. Eine Zwischenbilanz," in: *ibid.*, S. 3 ff.

Pauls, August. "Der Deutsche Alte und Angenommene Schottische Ritus," in: *Amtliche Mitteilungen des Deutschen Obersten Rates des AASR*, 4. Jahrgang, 15.6.1949, Nr. 1, S. 1 ff.

Pauvrert, Henri [d.i. Thomas Richert], "Die deutschen Großlogen 1933–1935," in: *Eleusis* (Organ des Deutschen Obersten Rates) 36. Jahrgang, Nr. 6, November/Dezember 1981, S. 443 ff.

Peters, Bruno. *Die Geschichte der Freimarerei im Deutschen Reich. 1870-1933*, Berlin, 1986.

Peters, Michael, "Der 'Alldeutsche Verband'," in: *Handbuch zur* "*Völkischen Bewegung,*" S. 302ff.

Pfahl-Traughber, Armin. *Der antisemitisch-antifreimaurerische Verschwörungs-mythos in der Weimarer Republik und im NS-Staat* [zunächst Diss.], Wien, 1993.

Pfahl-Traughber. "Der Mythos vom Freimaurer-Mord in Sarajewo," in: *Humanität. Das deutsche Freimaurermagazin*, Nr. 2/1992, S. 17ff.

Piper, Ernst. "Die jüdische Weltverschwörung," in: Julius H. Schoeps/ Joachim Schlör (Ed.), *Antisemitismus*. Vorurteile und Mythen, S. 127ff.

Reinalter, Helmut (Ed.), *Freimaurer und Geheimbünde im 18. Jahrhundert in Mitteleuropa*, Frankfurt am Main 3.Aufl. 1989.

Reinalter. "Zur Aufgabenstellung der gegenwärtigen Freimaurer-forschung," in: *ibid.*, S. 9ff.

Reinalter. "Geheimgesellschaften und Revolution. Freimaurerei und Nationalsozialismus am Beispiel Alfred Rosenbergs," in: *Quatuor Coronati Jahrbuch* Nr. 21/1984, Bayreuth, 1984, S. 55ff.

Reinalter. "Auf der Suche nach Sündenböcken. Freimaurer im Mittelpunkt einer Ver-schwörungstheorie," in: *Q.C.-Berichte*, Heft 15/1995, Wien, 1995, S. 112ff.

Reinalter. (Ed.) *Internationale Tagung in Innsbruck 22./23.5.1992.* "Aufklärung und Geheimgesellschaften: Freimaurer, Illuminaten und Rosenkreuzer: Ideologie, Struktur und Wirkungen," Bayreuth, 1992.

Reinalter. (Ed.), *2. Internationale Tagung in Innsbruck 19./21.Mai 1995.* "Freimau-rerische Historiographie im 19. und 20. Jahrhundert. Forschungsbilanz—Aspekte—Problemschwerpunkte," Bayreuth, 1996.

Reinalter. (Ed.), *Aufklärung und Geheimgesellschaften. Zur politischen Funktion und Sozialstruktur der Freimaurerlogen im 18. Jahrhundert*, München, 1989.

Richarz, Monika (Ed.). *Bürger auf Widerruf. Lebenszeugnisse deutscher Juden 1780-1945*, München, 1989.

Richert, Thomas. "Die deutsche Landesgruppe der Allgemeinen Freimaurer-Liga von 1927 bis 1933," in: *Quatuor Coronati Jahrbuch* Nr. 23/1986, Bayreuth, 1986, S. 141ff.

Richert. "E.J. Bing (Byng) 1894-1962," in: *Der Schottische Ritus in Geschichte und Gegenwart*, ed. im Auftrag des Deutschen Obersten Rates, Heft II, Frankfurt am Main, 1986, S. 90ff.

Ritters, Claus. "Christliche Freimaurerei" (unveröffentlichter Vortrag), Berlin, 1993.

Roon, Ger van. *Widerstand im Dritten Reich. Ein Überblick*, München 6. überarb. Aufl. 1994.

Rothfels, Hans. *Deutsche Opposition gegen Hitler. Eine Würdigung*, neue, erw. Ausg. Frankfurt am Main, 1986.

Rudolph, Jörg. *Überlieferung des Reichssicherheitshauptamtes Amt VII "Weltanschauliche Forschung und Auswertung." Anmerkungen zur Bestands- und Institutionsgeschichte eines nachrichtendienstlichen Archivs* [Diplomarbeit HU Berlin], Berlin, 1996.

Rürus, Reinhard (Ed.). *Topographie des Terrors: Gestapo, SS, Reichssicherheitshauptamt auf dem Prinz-Albrecht-Gelände. Eine Dokumentation*, Berlin, 1989.

Rürus. "Die 'Judenfrage' der bürgerlichen Gesellschaft und die Entstehung des modernen Antisemitismus," in: Ders., *Emanzipation und Antisemitismup. Studien zur 'Judenfrage' der bürgerlichen Gesellschaft*, Göttingen, 1975, S. 74ff.

Sand, Theodor, *Der Beginn der dunklen Zeit und die Große Landesloge*, s.l., s.d.

Sassin, Horst R.. *Liberale im Widerstand. Die Robinsohn-Strassmann-Gruppe 1934-1942*, [zunächst Diss.], Hamburg, 1993.

Sassin. "Strassmann-Gruppe," in: Wolfgang Benz/Walter H. Pehle (Ed.), *Lexikon des deutschen Widerstandes*, Frankfurt am Main, 1994, S. 306ff.

Schmid, Hans-Dieter. "Völkerschlachtdenkmal, Völkerschlachtgedenken und deutsche Freimaurerei im Jubiläumsjahr 1913," in: *Nationalsozialismus und Region. Festschrift für Herbert Obenaus zum 65. Geburtstag*, hrsg. von Malis Buchholz, Claus Füllberg-Stolberg und Hans-Dieter Schmid, Hannover'sche Schriften zur Regional- und Lokalgeschichte, Bd.11, Bielfeld, 1996, S. 355ff.

Schneider, Thomas Martin. *Reichsbischof Ludwig Müller. Eine Untersuchung zu Leben, Werk und Persönlichkeit*, Göttingen, 1993.

Schoeps, Julius H./Schlör, Joachim (Ed.); *Antisemitismus. Vorurteile und Mythen*, München, 1995.

Schulte, Dietmar. "Der Deutsch-Christliche Orden. Eine Betrachtung seiner Vor-geschichte, seines Existenzkampfes und seines Scheiterns," in: Z.K., 123. Jahrgang., Heft November 1995, S. 398ff.

Schulze, Hagen. *Weimar: Deutschland 1917-1933*, Berlin, 1982.

Seeligsohn, E.M.. *Vorträge, Zeichnungen, Gedanken* [broschiert]. S.l. 2. Aufl. 1986. (Archiv Henning Wolter, Delmenhorst).

Simon-Ritz, Frank. "Die freigeistige Bewegung im Kaiserreich," in: *Handbuch zur "Völkischen Bewegung,"* S. 208ff.

Sontheimer, Kurt. *Antidemokratisches Denken in der Weimarer Republik. Die politischen Ideen des deutschen Nationalismus zwischen 1918 und 1933,* Müchen 4. Aufl. 1962.

Steffens, Manfred [d.i. Stefan Zickler]. *Freimaurer in Deutschland. Bilanz eines Vierteljahrtausends,* Flensburg, 1964.

Strauss, Herbert A. "Deutsch-Jüdische Geschichtswissenschaft und Antisemitismus-forschung heute. (Festvortrag) 22.Jahrestagung der Historischen Kommission zu Berlin, 28.11.1980," in: *Hiko-Beilage zu Informationen,* Neue Folge, Heft 5, Bd. 1981, S. 30ff.

Traulsen, Helmut. *75 Jahre Universelle Freimaurerliga 1905–1980,* Dortmund, 1982.

Valjavec, Fritz. *Die Entstehung der politischen Strömungen in Deutschland,* München, 1951.

Voelker, Karin. "The B'nai B'rith Order (U.O.B.B.) in the Third Reich (1933–1937)," in: *Leo Baeck Institute Yearbook* Bd. 32, 1987, S. 269ff.

Volkov, Shulamit. *Jüdisches Leben und Antisemitismus im 19. und 20. Jahrhundert,* München, 1990.

Weber, Rosco G.P. *The German Student Corps in the Third Reich,* London *1986.* (deutsche Ausgabe im Druck).

Wildt, Michael (Ed.). *Die Judenpolitik des SD 1935–1938. Eine Dokumentation,* München, 1995.

Winkler, Heinrich August. *Weimar 1918-1933. Die Geschichte der ersten deutschen Demokratie,* München, 1993.

Winkler, Susanne. "Die Templer," in: Günter Düriegl/Susanne Winkler (Ed.), *Freimaurer,* S. 43ff.

Wippermann, Wolfgang. *Europäischer Faschismus im Vergleich (1922-1982),* Frankfurt am Main, 1983.

Wippermann. *Der konsequente Wahn. Ideologie und Politik Adolf Hitlers,* Gütersloh/München, 1989.

Wippermann. *Der Ordensstaat als Ideologie. Das Bild des deutschen Ordens in der deutschen Geschichtsschreibung und Publizistik* [zunächst Diss.], Berlin, 1979.

Wippermann. *Die Berliner Gruppe Baum und der jüdische Widerstand,* Berlin 2. Aufl, 1982.

Wiwjorra, Ingo. "Herman Wirth—Ein gescheiterter Ideologe zwischen "Ahnenerbe" und Antlantis," in: Barbara Danckwortt et al. (Ed.), *Historische Rassismusforschung. Ideologen—Täter—Opfer*, Hamburg/Berlin, 1995, S. 91ff.

Wolter, Henning. "Wer war Bruder Gottlieb Friedrich Reber?" in: *Der Schottische Ritus in Geschichte und Gegenwart*, ed. im Auftrag des Deutschen Obersten Rates, Heft II, Frankfurt am Main, 1986, S. 111ff.

Zetzsche, Christian. *200 Jahre Freimaurerei in Pyrmont. Geschichte und Selbsterlebtes*, Bad Pyrmont, 1975. (Deutsches Freimaurer-Museum Bayreuth, Nr. 6852).

Zirkelkorrespondenz (Zeitschrift der GLL), 121. Jahrgang, Heft März 1993, S. 97ff.

Zörrer, Ferdinand. "Hochgrade," in: Günter Düriegl/Susanne Winkler (Ed.), *Freimaurer*, S. 285ff.

250 Jahre Große National-Mutterloge "Zu den drei Weltkugeln" 1740-1990, Festschrift, Anon., ed. von der 3 WK-Großloge, Berlin, 1990.

III. SECONDARY LITERATURE/ PERIODICALS/ENCYCLOPAEDIAS

Aly, Götz/Heim, Susanne. *Das zentrale Staatsarchiv in Moskau ("Sonderarchiv")*. *Rekonstruktion und Bestandsverzeichnis verschollen geglaubten Schriftguts aus der NS-Zeit*, Düsseldorf, 1992.

Bremische Biographie 1912-1962, ed. von der Historischen Gesellschaft zu Bremen und dem Staatsarchiv Bremen, bearb. von Wilhelm Lührs et al., Bremen, 1969.

Brunner, Otto/Conze, Werner/Koselleck, Reinhart (Eds.). *Geschichtliche Grund-begriffe*. *Historisches Lexikon zur politisch-sozialen Sprache in Deutschland*, Bd.7, Stuttgart, 1992.

Dalens, C(arl) van *Kalender für Freimaurer*. *Statistisches Jahrbuch*, Leipzig. Jahrgänge, 1901, 1919, 1925, 1926, 1927, 1928, 1929, 1930, 1931, 1933/34.

Endler, Renate/Schwarze, Elisabeth. *Die Freimaurerbestände im Geheimen Staatsarchiv Preußischer Kulturbesitz*, ed. von Helmut Reinalter. Bd. 1: *Großlogen und Protektor. Freimaurerische Stiftungen und Vereinigungen*, Frankfurt am Main, 1994. Bd. 2: *Tochterlogen, Frankfurt am Main* 1996; Bd. 3: *Freimaurerische Stiftungen und Vereinigungen* [in Vorbereitung].

Freimaurerlogen in Berlin und Freimaurerisches Kunsthandwerk (Berliner Freimaurer-Museum im Logenhaus Berlin), Anon., Nr. 1, Oktober, 1976.

Galling, Kurt et al. (Ed.). *Die Religion in Geschichte und Gegenwart, Hand-wörterbuch für Theologie und Religionswissenschaft*, 7 vols., Tübingen 3. Aufl. 1986.

Geppert, Ernst-Günther/Francke, Karl Heinz. *Die Freimaurer-Logen Deutschlands und deren Großlogen 1737-1985* Bayreuth, 1988.

Jasper, Willi, "Enzyklopädie der Judenfeindschaften," in: Andreas Nachama / Gereon Sievernich (Ed.), *Jüdische Lebenswelten*, Berlin, 1991, S. 712ff.

Jäckel, E./Longerich, S./ Schoeps, J.H. (Ed.). *Enzyklopädie des Holocaust. Die Verfolgung und Ermordung der europäischen Juden*, 3 vols., Berlin, 1993.

Jahrbuch der Vereinigten Großlogen von Deutschland, Berlin, 1992 (und folgende Jahrgänge).

Jena, Kai von/Lenz, Wilhelm. "Die deutschen Bestände im Sonderarchiv in Moskau," in: *Der Archivar*, Bd. 45, 1992, Heft 3, column 457ff.

Kernig, C.D. (Ed.). *Sowjetsystem und Demokratische Gesellschaft. Eine vergleichende Enzyklopädie*, Bd. 3, Freiburg/Basel/Wien, 1969.

Lennhoff, Eugen / Posner, Oskar. *Internationales Freimaurer-Lexikon*, Zürich/Leipzig/Wien, 1932.

Mittelstraß, Jürgen (Ed.), *Enzyklopädie Philosophie und Wissenschaftstheorie*, Bd. 2, Mannheim/Wien/Zürich, 1984.

Peters, Bruno. *Berliner Freimaurer. Ein Beitrag zur Kulturgeschichte Berlins*, Berlin 2. Aufl., 1994.

Schumacher, Martin (Ed.) *M.d.R. Die Reichstagsabgeordneten der Weimarer Republik in der Zeit des Nationalsozialismus. Politische Verfolgung, Emigration und Ausbürgerung 1933-1945. Eine biographische Dokumentation*, Düsseldorf, 3. erw. und überarb. Aufl. 1994.

Schwartz, Otto. *Bericht über die Rückführung der im Jahre 1932 nach Schweden ausgelagerten Teile des deutschen Ordens-Archivs im März 1976*, (broschiert), Kiel, 1976. (Archiv GLL).

Romeyk, Horst. "Das ehemals sowjetische Sonderarchiv in Moskau, " in: *Der Archivar* Bd. 45, 1992, Heft 1, column 118.

Schneider, Herbert, *Deutsche Freimaurer-Biblio*thek. Teil 1: Katalog (und Suppl. [maschinenschriftl. Stand August 1996]); Teil 2: Register, Frankfurt am Main, 1993. (Deutsches Freimaurer-Museum Bayreuth, Nr. 10735).

Schweikle, Günter und Irmgard (Ed.) *Metzler Literatur Lexikon*, Stuttgart, 1984.

Vogel, Theodor. *Der Großmeister und seine Werkleute. Von der Frankfurter Paulskirche zum Berliner Konvent*, s.l., s.d

Wegweiser zur Freimaurerei, ed. vom Deutschen Obersten Rat des Alten und Angenommenen Schottischen Ritus, Frankfurt am Main, 1980.

ABBREVIATIONS

3 WK:	Große Nationalmutterloge "Zu den drei Weltkugeln"
AASR:	Alter und Angenommener Schottischer Ritus
AASR, S.J.:	Ancient and Accepted Scottish Rite, Southern Jurisdiction
A.B.A.W.:	Allmächtiger Baumeister aller Welten; freimaurerische Bezeichnung für eine bekenntnisübergreifende göttliche Instanz
ADW:	Allgemeiner Deutscher Waffenring
AFL:	Allgemeine Freimaurerliga
A.F.u.A.M.	Alte Freie und Angenommene Maurer (Großloge der A.F.u.A.M. von Deutschland)
A.M.I.:	Association Maconnique Internationale
ArSt.:	Am Rauhen Stein, Zeitschrift der Großloge zur Freundschaft
BA:	Bundesarchiv
BDC	Berlin Document Center
Br.:	Bruder, Mitglied einer Freimaurerloge (pl.: Brr.)
DAF:	Deutsche Arbeitsfront
DAG:	Deutsche Adelsgenossenschaft
DAP:	Deutsche Arbeiterpartei
DDP:	Deutsche Demokratische Partei
DNVP:	Deutschnationale Volkspartei
DOR:	Deutscher Oberster Rat (des AASR)
DRK:	Deutsches Rotes Kreuz
DStP:	Deutsche Staatspartei
E.O.:	Evangelischer Oberkirchenrat
EZA:	Evangelisches Zentralarchiv in Berlin
F.O.:	Freimaurerorden = Große Landesloge der Freimaurer von Deutschland
FzaS/FZAS:	Freimaurerbund zur aufgehenden Sonne
FU:	Freie Universität Berlin
Gestapa:	Geheimes Staatspolizeiamt

Gestapo:	Geheime Staatspolizei
GFP:	Geheime Feldpolizei
GL:	Großloge
GLL:	Große Landesloge der Freimaurer von Deutschland, auch F.O.
GSTA.:	Bayerisches Geheimes Staatsarchiv, München
GStA PK:	Geheimes Staatsarchiv Preußischer Kulturbesitz, Berlin
GStV:	Gemeinschaft studentischer Verbände
Hiko:	Historische Kommission zu Berlin
HJ:	Hitlerjugend
HUB:	Humboldt Universität Berlin
HZ:	Historische Zeitschrift
i.d.u.h.Z.:	In der uns heiligen Zahl: freimaurerische Grußformel
IfZ:	Institut für Zeitgeschichte, München
K.K.:	"Königliche Kunst" = Freimaurerei
KPD:	Kommunistische Partei Deutschlands
KZ:	Konzentrationslager
LGM:	Landesgroßmeister
MBlPiV.:	Ministerial-Blatt für die Preußische innere Verwaltung [MBliV.]
MBlRuPrMdI.:	Ministerial-Blatt des Reichs- und Preußischen Ministe-riums des Innern [RMBliV.]
N.D.O.:	Nationalverband Deutscher Offiziere
NL:	Nachlaß
NS:	Nationalsozialismus, nationalsozialistisch
NSDAP:	Nationalsozialistische Deutsche Arbeiterpartei
NSV:	Nationalsozialistische Volkswohlfahrt
Obr.:	Ordensbruder, Mitglied der Großen Landesloge, nach den Umwandlungen z.T. auch für die anderen altpreußischen Freimaurer gebraucht
Or.:	Orient
OR:	Oberster Rat des AASR
PMdI.:	Preußischer Minister des Innern/Preußisches Ministerium des Innern

521

Q.C.:	Quatuor Coronati (freimaurerische Forschungseinrich-tungen in Österreich und Deutschland; Herausgeber der gleichnamigen Jahrbücher)
RdErl.:	Rund-Erlaß
RFSS:	Reichsführer SS
RjF:	Reichsbund jüdischer Frontsoldaten
RMdI.:	Reichsminister(ium) des Innern
RSHA:	Reichssicherheitshauptamt
RuPrMdI.:	Reichs- und Preußischer Minister des Innern/Reichs- und Preußisches Ministerium des Innern
r.V.:	Rechtsfähiger Verein
SA:	Sturmabteilung
SD:	Sicherheitsdienst der SS
P.Gr.L.v.D/ SGL:	Symbolische Großloge von Deutschland
Sipo:	Sicherheitspolizei
SJ:	Societatis Jesu = Jesuit
SPD:	Sozialdemokratische Partei Deutschlands
SS:	Schutzstaffel
St A Bremen:	Staatsarchiv Bremen
Stapo:	Staatspolizei
StdF.:	Stellvertreter des Führers
TL:	Tochterloge
USHMM:	United States Holocaust Memorial Museum
V.d.F.:	Verein deutscher Freimaurer
Vela:	Vereinigung der Leitenden Angestellten
VfZ:	Vierteljahreshefte für Zeitgeschichte
VGL:	Vereinigte Großlogen von Deutschland (Dachorganisation der Freimaurergroßlogen in der Bundesrepublik)
ZdhS:	Zentrum der dokumentar-historischen Sammlungen, Moskau (ehemals Zentrales Staatsarchiv/"Sonderarchiv")= Osobyi Archives, Moscow
Z.K.:	Zirkelkorrespondenz, Zeitschrift der Großen Landesloge

About the Author:

Ralf Melzer, born 1967, worked as a freelance journalist until 2003, primarily for German print media. Since then he has assumed a variety of responsibilities as a staff member of the Friedrich Ebert Stiftung, a non-profit German political foundation committed to the advancement of public policy issues in the spirit of social democracy. From 2009 to 2011 he served as the foundation's resident director in Tunisia. He holds Master's Degree in History, German philology, and Journalism and a Ph.D. in Modern History, both from the Freie Universität Berlin.

About the Translator:

Glenys A. Waldman holds the doctorate in Germanic Languages (University of Pennsylvania 1975), and the Master of Library Science (Drexel Uiversity, 1978). She has taught both German and French, and had more than thirty years experience in the library field. Since 1987, she has been Librarian at The Masonic Library and Museum of Pennsylvania of the Grand Lodge of Free and Accepted Masons of Pennsylvania.